Walk-Behind Lawn Mower

SERVICE MANUAL ■ *5TH EDITION*

Intertec Publishing
P.O. Box 12901 ■ Overland Park, KS 66282-2901

Cover photograph courtesy of: Deere & Company, 4401 Bland Road, Raleigh, NC 27609

Walk-Behind Lawn Mower

SERICE MANUAL ■ 5TH EDITION

Walk-Behind Lawn Mower Manufacturers:

- Ace
- Aircap
- Allis-Chalmers
- Ariens
- Atlas
- Bolens
- Bunton/Goodall
- Craftsman
- Cub Cadet
- John Deere
- Deutz-Allis
- Dynamark
- Ford
- Gilson
- Homelite
- Honda
- Husqvarna
- International Harvester
- Jacobsen
- King O'Lawn
- Kubota
- Lawn-Boy
- Lawn Chief
- Mastercut
- Mono
- MTD
- Murray
- Parmi
- J.C. Penney
- Roper
- Sensation
- Simplicity
- Snapper
- Southland
- Toro
- Wards
- White
- Yard-Man

Engine Manufacturers:

- Briggs & Stratton
- Clinton
- Craftsman
- Honda
- Jacobsen
- Kawasaki
- Kubota
- Lawn-Boy
- Sachs
- Tecumseh
- Toro

INTERTEC BOOKS

President and CEO Raymond E. Maloney

Vice President, Book Group Ted Marcus

The following books and guides are published by Intertec Publishing.

CLYMER SHOP MANUALS
Boat Motors and Drives
Motorcycles and ATVs
Snowmobiles
Personal Watercraft

ABOS/INTERTEC/CLYMER BLUE BOOKS AND TRADE-IN GUIDES
Recreational Vehicles
Outdoor Power Equipment
Agricultural Tractors
Lawn and Garden Tractors
Motorcycles and ATVs
Snowmobiles and Personal Watercraft
Boats and Motors

AIRCRAFT BLUEBOOK-PRICE DIGEST
Airplanes
Helicopters

AC-U-KWIK DIRECTORIES
The Corporate Pilot's Airport/FBO Directory
International Manager's Edition
Jet Book

I&T SHOP SERVICE MANUALS
Tractors

INTERTEC SERVICE MANUALS
Snowmobiles
Outdoor Power Equipment
Personal Watercraft
Gasoline and Diesel Engines
Recreational Vehicles
Boat Motors and Drives
Motorcycles
Lawn and Garden Tractors

CONTENTS

Page

INTRODUCTION
Tools 9
Threaded Fasteners 9

ENGINE OPERATING PRINCIPLES
Otto Cycle 11
Two-Stroke Cycle 11
Four-Stroke Cycle 12

MOWER FAMILIARIZATION
Rotary Mowers 12
Reel Mowers 14

ENGINE AND MOWER IDENTIFICATION
Ace 15
Aircap. 15
Allis-Chalmers. 15
Ariens. 15
Atlas. 15
Bolens 15
Bunton/Goodall 15
Cub Cadet 15
John Deere 15
Deutz-Allis. 16
Dynamark 16
Ford 16
Gilson. 16
Homelite 16
Honda 16
Husqvarna. 16
International Harvester 16
Jacobsen 16
King O-Lawn 17
Kubota 17
Lawn-Boy. 17
Lawn Chief 18
Mastercut 18
Mono 18
MTD. 18
Murray. 18
Parmi 18
J.C. Penney 18
Roper 18
Sears-Craftsman 18
Sensation. 19
Simplicity. 19
Snapper 19
Southland 19
Toro 19
Wards 19
White 19
Yard-Man 19

STARTING AND OPERATION 19

PROBLEMS AND REMEDIES 23
Troubleshooting. 24
Noises. 25
Engine Will Not Start. 25
Engine Hard To Start 27
Engine Performance Is Rough and/or Power is Low . 27

Page

PROBLEMS AND REMEDIES (CONT.)
Engine Surges 29
Engine Starts Then Stops. 29
Engine Uses Too Much Oil 29

TROUBLESHOOTING CHART. 31

SAFETY TIPS 33

ROUTINE MAINTENANCE
Engine 34
Rotary Mowers 35
Reel Mowers 39

CARBURETOR SERVICE
General Carburetor Service 40
Troubleshooting. 40
Pressure Testing 42
Adjustment 43

ENGINE SERVICE
Disassembly And Assembly 43
Repairing Damaged Threads 43
Valve Service Fundamentals 43
Installing Oversize Piston And Rings . . . 45
Two-Stroke Engine Crankcase Pressure Test 45

ENGINE
Briggs & Stratton
Identification 46
Two-Stroke Models. 48
Four-Stroke Models
Except Europa, Quantum And Vanguard 53
Quantum. 73
Vanguard OHV 81
Europa 88
Special Tools 95
Central Parts Distributors 96
Clinton
Identification 97
Two-Stroke Models. 98
Four-Stroke Models 107
Accessories 116
Craftsman
Cross Reference 123
Four-Stroke Differences 136
Honda
Valve-In-Block Models 138
Overhead Valve Models 145
Jacobsen
Two-Stroke Models. 153
Accessories 161
Kawasaki
Two-Stroke Models. 162
Overhead Valve Models 165
Kubota 170
Lawn-Boy
C- and D- Models 174
F- Series 188
M25 Models 195

CONTENTS (CONT.)

Page

ENGINE SERVICE (Cont.)
Sachs 204
Tecumseh
  Two-Stroke Models 210, 219
  Four-Stroke Models
    Except Vector And Overhead Valve Engines 226
    Vector Models. 244
    OHV Models. 253
Toro
  Two-Stroke Models 260
  Four-Stroke VM Models 264
  Four-Stroke GTS Models 269

SELF-PROPELLED DRIVE SYSTEMS
Ariens Disc Drive 277
Chain Drive Systems 277
Craftsman Gearbox. 278
Foote Gearbox 280
Homelite/Jacobsen 281
Honda 283
Husqvarna. 292
John Deere Self-Drive 294
John Deere 299
Kubota 302

Page

SELF-PROPELLED DRIVE SYSTEMS (Cont.)
Lawn-Boy Self-Drive
  Series C, D And F 303
  Series M 308
  Silver Series 309
  Gold Series 311
MTD 313
Murray 319
Snapper Disc Drive 321
Toro Gearbox 322
Yard-Man 326

BLADE BRAKE CLUTCHES
Ariens. 327
Comet 327
Honda. 328
Kubota 330
Lawn-Boy 331
MTD 332
Ogura 332
Toro. 333
Worthington. 336

STORAGE 337

DUAL DIMENSIONS

This service manual provides specifications in both the U.S. Customary and Metric (SI) systems of measurement. The first specification is given in the measuring system perceived by us to be the preferred system when servicing a particular component, while the second specification (given in parenthesis) is the converted measurement. For instance, a specification of "0.011 (0.28 mm)" would indicate that we feel the preferred measurement, in this instance, is the U.S. system of measurement and the metric equivalent of 0.011 inch is 0.28 mm.

SAFETY

The operator is directly responsible for the safe and practical use of the equipment; however, it is important that the operator know how to use and control the equipment. Manufacturers provide detailed instructions for operating their equipment. New operators should be taught correct procedures, then tested to determine their level of understanding. Observe equipment use to assure that operators are continuing to follow safe practices.

High speed movement, sharp cutting surfaces and very strong forces characterize the normal actions of many types of lawn and garden power equipment. Cautious operation by personnel who know and exercise approved, safe procedures can minimize the risk of injury. Safe operation of damaged equipment may not be possible. It is important that the equipment be maintained correctly in the interest of safety as well as ease of operation.

Operators should be alert, constantly monitoring equipment performance. Any change could indicate equipment problems, but prompt action may prevent injury or damage.

All mowers are designed to cut and they operate with absolutely no regard for what is being cut. The cutting blade will try just as hard to cut fingers, hands and feet, as it does roots, grass, weeds and children's toys. Observing the following warnings will reduce the possibility of injury.

Always observe the following check list of STANDARD SAFETY PRACTICES.
1. Do not operate equipment if under the influence of alcohol or drugs.
2. Do not allow irresponsible people or people not trained in proper use (regardless of age) to operate powered equipment.
3. Know how to immediately disengage the power and stop the engine before starting engine.
4. Be especially cautious when operating equipment in area where children usually play. A child may suddenly enter the area causing a hazard.
5. Keep people and animals away from the working area.
6. Use only approved grip locations and always control unit as intended by the manufacturer.
7. Make sure that all guards are installed and all safety devices operate properly. NEVER by-pass any safety device provided by the manufacturer.
8. Know how to correctly operate all controls.
9. Do not smoke while servicing gasoline or diesel powered equipment in any way. Smoking should also be discouraged while operating equipment.
10. Be careful of fire hazards.
11. Don't run any gasoline or diesel engine in an enclosed area.
12. NEVER permit any part of your body or clothing near a cutting blade or any other moving parts. If clothing wraps around a rotating part, your body can be pulled in and injured. Always keep all protective shields in place.
13. NEVER compromise safety of operating equipment in a way that you or the equipment could accidentally move and cause injury. This includes pulling instead of pushing and mowing extreme grades.
14. Stop engine and properly ground the spark plug wire before cleaning, inspecting, adjusting or repairing anything driven by the engine.
15. Always stop the engine when equipment is left unattended. Allow engine to cool completely before covering or storing in any enclosure.
16. NEVER store gasoline or diesel powered equipment or extra fuel in an area where fuel or fuel vapor may accumulate or may travel to an open flame or spark.
17. Practice routine maintenance.

Observe the following check list in addition to STANDARD SAFETY PRACTICES.
1. NEVER insert any part of your body into or even near the cutting blade. This includes reaching into the discharge chute to dislodge whatever is clogging it, sliding your feet under the mower deck and lifting mower while it is running. All similar actions are far too dangerous to even consider.
2. NEVER compromise safety by operating the mower in a way that you or the mower could accidentally move and cause injury. This includes pulling instead of pushing and mowing extreme grades.
3. Mow ONLY with good daylight or artificial light. Be sure of what you are mowing.
4. NEVER run the operating mower over any loose objects.
5. Stop engine and ground spark plug whenever inspecting or adjusting anything near the cutting blade.
6. Stop mower and inspect carefully after striking any object or if it begins to vibrate. Repair damage before restarting.
7. Do not operate in wet grass or anywhere that traction for mower or operator is unsure.
8. Mow terrace or slope only in lengthwise direction. NEVER up or down the incline. Some inclines are too steep for safe mowing.
9. Be especialy cautious when mowing in area where children usually play. A child may suddenly enter the area causing a hazard and toys are probably scattered in the grass.
10. Wear appropriate close fitting clothing, shoes and eye protection. Consider appropriate breathing filter for operator, especially in dusty conditions.
11. Check parts regularly for looseness, wear, cracks or other damage and make sure mower is properly adjusted before starting engine.
12. Keep cutter properly adjusted and sharp.
13. Use only approved grip locations and always control unit as intended by the manufacturer.
14. Operate mower only over grass or firm clean surface. Never operate mower over loose rock or area covered with sand.
15. Keep people and animals away from working area. Never aim discharge toward people that could be injured or property which could be damaged by an object being thrown.
16. Keep feet and hands in safe locations as indicated by manufacturer while starting engine. NEVER by-pass any safety device provided by the manufacturer.
17. Stop engine and properly ground the spark plug wire before cleaning, removing an object or performing any maintenance to the mower.

⚠ DANGER

Always disconnect spark plug and ground detached wire to the engine before doing anything under the mower, even inspecting.

Fuel may drain from tank when mower is tipped for examination of blade. Be careful of fire hazard. Fuel spilled on ground can also damage or kill grass.

SAFETY HINT

NEVER fill the fuel tank inside any enclosed building. Gasoline near an open flame water heater or an electrical switch, light or an appliance which is NOT Explosion Proof is a major cause of fires.

SAFETY HINT

If the lawn mower vibrates noticeably, something is probably very wrong. A bent blade or shaft on rotary mowers can cause so much violent vibration that it's hard to control where it's going to jump next. Stop the mower and repair the cause of vibration. The vibration is dangerous, but it will also shake parts loose adding to the danger.

SAFETY HINT

Mowers manufactured after June 30, 1982, must be able to stop the blade within 3 seconds by killing the engine or by stopping the blade with a clutch sytem. Earlier mowers must be considered more dangerous to use. NEVER remove or modify this or any other safety device.

HELPFUL HINT

If you hit something with a rotary mower and the engine stops, you may have used a safety device. Briggs & Stratton and some other manufacturers of vertical shaft engines designed for rotary mowers use a soft metal drive key between the engine crankshaft and the flywheel. The soft key is used to prevent damage (and injury) if the blade is stopped suddenly. If this drive key is sheared, the engine will not start or will be very hard to start. It will be necessary to remove the flywheel and install a new key, but the blade or other parts may have also been damaged. Be sure to inspect for damage and repair if necessary.

INTRODUCTION

Repairing a lawn mower can be an interesting and rewarding experience. Ability will increase as you gain experience. Your selection of tools can limit your ability to perform certain repairs, but only a few are necessary for most service and other tools can be acquired as they are needed. This book explains commonly used procedures and will help you to develop your knowledge of how to fix lawn mowers. Easy to read fundamental theory, basic service procedures and troubleshooting hints are combined with professional service data, specifications and recommendations.

Lawn mowers equipped with gasoline engines have been manufactured for a long time by many different companies. All of the known lawn mower designs and all of the known forms of repair are not included in this book. The procedures that are included are based on sound practices and many can be used when repairing other lawn mowers, engines or even unrelated equipment not specifically included in this book. Many repair procedures should be thought out individually. The cost of repair, the tools required and other factors should be considered before deciding upon a method of repair.

On mowers equipped with safety equipment, MAKE SURE all equipment is connected and in good working condition at all times. The equipment was installed on the mower for a purpose, SAFETY; bypassing or disconnecting safety equipment is not recommended.

TOOLS

The specific tools required to service lawn mowers will depend upon the extent to which you want to service the mower and the origin of the mower manufacturer. Special tools that save time can be a valuable aid but may be too expensive, if used only once.

Standard or metric hand tools are required for most service. Refer to Fig. 2.

Wrenches (standard sizes ¼ to ¾ in., metric sizes 8 to 19 mm), screwdrivers, hammer, thickness (feeler) gauge, file and ruler will be all that is required for

most basic service. An inexpensive puller is recommended for removing some flywheels. The puller may be fabricated, purchased or rented.

Wrench sizes are determined by measuring across the flats of the hex as shown in Fig. 3. Be careful when measuring and be sure the correct wrench is used. The size of the head determines the size of the wrench used and is related to the size of the screw, but is not the screw size. The procedure to determine the correct screw size is outlined in the following section.

THREADED FASTENERS

Screws and bolts are the two common types of threaded fasteners. The primary difference between a screw and a

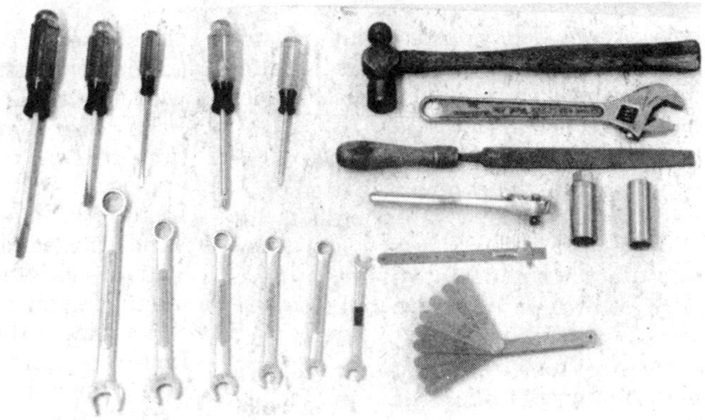

Fig. 2—Most service can be performed using only the tools shown.

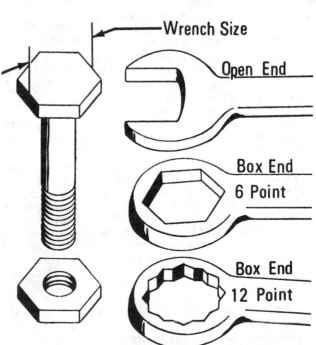

Fig. 1—Don't go in over your head when servicing lawn mowers.

Fig. 3—Wrench size is determined by measuring across the flats of a screw head. This is not the size of the screw.

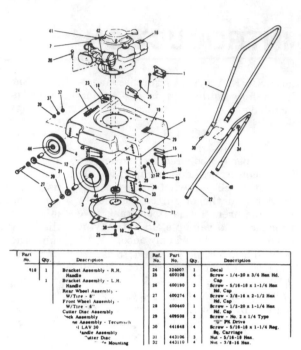

Fig. 4—A parts catalog for a typical lawn mower. The screw size is sometimes listed as shown at 25,26,27,28,29 and 30.

Part No.	Qty.	Description	Ref. No.	Part No.	Qty.	Description
918	1	Bracket Assembly - R.H. Handle	24	324007	1	Decal
	1	Bracket Assembly - L.H. Handle	25	400108	4	Screw - 1/4-20 x 3/4 Hex Hd. Cap
		Rear Wheel Assembly - W/Tire - 8"	26	400190	3	Screw - 5/16-18 x 1-1/4 Hex Hd. Cap
		Front Wheel Assembly - W/Tire - 6"	27	400274	4	Screw - 3/8-16 x 2-1/2 Hex Hd. Cap
		Cutter Disc Assembly	28	400440	1	Screw - 1/2-20 x 1-1/4 Hex Hd. Cap
		...ch Assembly	29	409508	2	Screw - No. 2 x 1/4 Type "U" PK Drive
		...ne Assembly - Tecumseh	30	441648	4	Screw - 5/16-18 x 1-1/4 Reg. Sq. Carriage
		...l LAV 30	31	443106	3	Nut - 5/16-18 Hex.
		...andle Assembly	32	443110	4	Nut - 3/8-16 Hex.
		...utter Disc				
		...e Mounting				

bolt is that a bolt requires a nut to fasten something together. A screw is installed directly into a piece that has a threaded hole to receive the threads.

There are many types of screws and bolts but the type which was used originally is the type which should be installed if renewal is necessary. Some manufacturers indicate in their parts books the type of screw or bolt to be used. Refer to Fig. 4.

Be sure to select a fastener which is manufactured under the same measurement system as the piece of equipment it is to be used on. Also make certain it has the same diameter, thread pitch and length as the original fastener. The fastener must be long enough to engage the correct number of threads, but should not be so long that it contacts or obstructs another part. Check all questionable threaded parts carefully. Threaded parts should be easily joined by hand without looseness. Looseness or tight fitting threaded parts usually indicate incorrectly matched or damaged threads. Occasionally threaded parts are tight-fitting (self-locking) to prevent accidental loosening. These self-locking threaded parts may be threaded completely together smoothly using proper wrenches. Self-locking threaded parts are not often used, and the most common method to prevent loosening is through the use of lock washers or a chemical thread locking compound. The service section for the various components will call attention to these locking devices.

Most threaded fasteners described as having "right-hand" threads are installed by turning the fastener in a clockwise direction and removed by turning the fastener in a counterclockwise direction.

Fasteners for some special applications are cut with "left-hand" threads and are usually marked with an "L". Install threaded fasteners with "left-hand" threads by turning the fastener counter-clockwise and remove by turning the fastener in a clockwise direction.

The size of threaded fasteners manufactured using the "inch" system of measurement is given according to the ISO (International Organization for Standardization) inch system. This system was established in 1964 and is equivalent to the old Unified Thread system.

The size of threaded fasteners manufactured using the "metric" system of measurement is given according to the Optimum Metric Fastener System established in the 1970's.

ISO INCH SYSTEM. The ISO inch system identifies threaded fastener size using three dimensions: length, diameter and thread pitch.

Length is measured from the underside of the bolt head to the end of the threads. Refer to L—Fig 5.

Diameter is the actual outside diameter of the threads. Refer to D—Fig 5.

Thread pitch is measured by counting the number of threads in one inch. Refer to TI—Fig. 5. The ISO inch system retains the Unified National Fine (UNF) thread pitch designations to provide two different thread pitch possibilities for the same diameter threaded fastener.

Threaded ISO inch system fastener sizes are written as follows: 1/4-20

(UNC) × 1, which indicates a 1/4 inch diameter fastener with 20 threads per inch with a length of 1 inch. The same fastener with UNF threads would be written as follow: 1/4-24 (UNF) × 1, which indicates a 1/4 inch diameter fastener with 24 threads per inch with a length of 1 inch.

Threaded fastener strength is indicated by the number of marks on the fastener head. Refer to Fig. 5. No markings on fastener head indicate a grade 1 or 2 fastener. Two marks indicate a grade 4, three marks indicate a grade 5, five marks indicate a grade 7 and six marks indicate a grade 8 fastener. The fastener strength increases as the number of marks increase. There are many critical fastener applications where fastener strength and hardness have been carefully calculated and under no circumstances should a fastener with a different rating be substituted.

OPTIMUM METRIC FASTENER SYSTEM. The Optimum Metric Fastener System identifies threaded fastener size using three dimensions: length, diameter and thread pitch.

Length and diameter for Optimum Metric Fastener System fasteners are measured in the same manner as an ISO inch system fastener. Refer to L and D—Fig. 5.

Thread pitch for Optimum Metric Fastener System fasteners are measured from one thread peak to another thread peak. Refer to TM—Fig. 5. Most metric fasteners have one standard thread pitch matched to fastener diameter, however, fine or coarse thread pitch may be used in specialized applications.

Threaded fastener strength is indicated by a number stamped on the fastener head. Refer to Fig. 5. The larger the number stamped on fastener head, the greater the strength of the fastener. There are many critical fastener applications where fastener strength and hardness have been carefully calculated and under no circumstances should a fastener with a different rating be substituted.

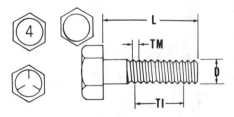

Fig. 5—Screw size is not determined by size of head. Size of fasteners manufactured under the ISO Inch System is determined by length (L), diameter (D) and number of threads per inch (T). Size of fasteners manufactured under the Optimum Metric Fastener System is determined by length (L), diameter (D) and distance between threads (TM). Refer to text.

ENGINE OPERATING PRINCIPLES

The small gasoline engines used on lawn mowers are technically known as "Internal Combustion Engines." The source of power is heat caused by burning a combustible mixture of petroleum products and air. In a reciprocating engine, this burning takes place in a closed cylinder containing a piston. Expansion of the fuel-air mixture causes the piston to move which in turn causes a shaft (crankshaft) to rotate. A complete series of timed events (or cycle) must take place for the engine to run. These events will all occur once during one complete revolution of the crankshaft for engines called two-stroke engines or during two revolutions of the crankshaft for four-stroke engines. The term strokes refers to the movement of the piston from one extreme to the other (Top to Bottom or Bottom to Top) in the cylinder.

OTTO CYCLE

In a spark ignited engine, a series of five events is required in order for the engine to provide power. This series of events is called the "OTTO CYCLE" (or "Work Cycle") and is repeated as long as work is being done. This series of events which comprises the "Cycle" is as follows:

1. A combustible mixture of fuel and air is pushed into the cylinder.

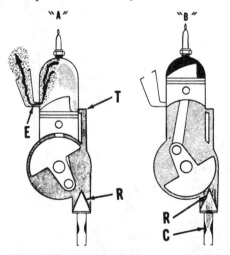

Fig. 6—Schematic diagram of a two-stroke cycle engine operating on the Otto Cycle (spark ignition). View "B" shows piston near top of upward stroke and atmospheric pressure is forcing air through carburetor (C), where fuel is mixed with the air, and the fuel-air mixture enters crankcase through open reed valve (R). In view "A", piston is near bottom of downward stroke and has opened the cylinder exhaust port (E) and transfer (intake) port (T); fuel-air mixture in crankcase has been compressed by downward stroke of engine and flows into cylinder through open port. Incoming mixture helps clean burned exhaust gases from cylinder.

2. The mixture of fuel and air is compressed by the piston moving upward in the cylinder.

3. The compressed fuel-air mixture is ignited by a timed electric spark.

4. The burning air-fuel mixture expands, forcing the piston downward in the cylinder thus converting the chemical energy generated by combustion into mechanical power.

5. The gaseous products formed by the burned fuel-air mixture are exhausted from the cylinder so a new "Cycle" can begin.

The above described five events which comprise the work cycle of an engine are (1), INTAKE; (2), COMPRESSION; (3), IGNITION; (4), EXPANSION (POWER); AND (5), EXHAUST.

The events necessary to complete a cycle must occur at specific times in order to continue repeating these events or "Run."

TWO-STROKE CYCLE

In two-stroke cycle engines, the piston is used as a sliding valve for the cylinder intake and exhaust ports. The intake and exhaust ports are both open when the piston is at the bottom of its downward stroke (bottom dead center or BDC). The exhaust port is open to atmospheric pressure; therefore, the fuel-air mixture must be elevated to a higher than atmospheric pressure in order for the mixture to enter the cylinder.

As the crankshaft is turned from BDC and the piston starts on its upward stroke, the intake and exhaust ports are closed and the fuel-air mixture in the cylinder is compressed. When the piston is at or near the top of its upward stroke (top dead center or TDC), an electric spark across the electrode gap of the spark plug ignites the fuel-air mixture. As the crankshaft turns past TDC and the piston starts on its downward stroke, the rapidly burning fuel-air mixture expands and forces the piston downward.

As the piston nears bottom of its downward stroke, the cylinder exhaust port is opened and the burned gaseous products from combustion of the fuel-air mixture flows out the open port. Slightly further downward travel of the piston opens the cylinder intake (or transfer) port and a fresh charge of fuel-air mixture is forced into the cylinder. Since the exhaust port remains open, the incoming flow of fuel-air mixture helps clean (scavenge) any remaining burned gaseous products from the cylin-

der. As the crankshaft turns past BDC and the piston starts on its upward stroke, the cylinder intake and exhaust ports are closed and a new cycle begins.

Since the fuel-air mixture must be elevated to a higher than atmospheric pressure to enter the cylinder of a two stroke cycle engine, a compressor pump must be used. Coincidentally, downward movement of the piston decreases the volume of the engine crankcase. Thus, a compressor pump is made available by sealing the engine crankcase and connecting the carburetor to a port in the crankcase. When the piston moves upward, volume of the crankcase is increased which lowers pressure within the crankcase to below atmospheric. Air will then be forced through the carburetor, where fuel is mixed with the air, and on into the engine crankcase.

In order for downward movement of the piston to compress the fuel-air mixture in the crankcase, a valve must be provided to close the carburetor to crankcase port. In Fig. 6, a reed type inlet valve is shown. Spring steel reeds (R) are forced open by atmospheric pressure as shown in view "B" when the piston is on its upward stroke and pressure in the crankcase is below atmospheric. When the piston reaches TDC, the reeds close as shown in view "A" and fuel-air mixture is trapped in the crankcase to be compressed by downward movement of the piston. The cylinder intake (or transfer) port (T) connects the crankcase compression chamber to the cylinder; the transfer port is the cylinder intake port through which the compressed fuel-air mixture in the crankcase is transferred to the cylinder when the piston is at bottom of stroke as shown in view "A".

Due to rapid movement of the fuel-air mixture through the crankcase, the crankcase cannot be used as a lubricating oil sump because the oil would be carried into the cylinder. Lubrication is accomplished by mixing a small amount of oil with fuel; thus, lubrication oil for the engine moving parts is carried into the crankcase with the fuel-air mixture.

Normal lubrication oil to fuel mixture ratios vary from one part of oil mixed with 16 to 50 parts of fuel by volume. In all instances, manufacturer's recommendations for oil type and fuel-oil mixture ratio should be observed.

Two-stroke engines are characterized by their light weight. Some Ariens, Clinton, Jacobsen, Lawn-Boy and Sensation mowers are equipped with two-stroke

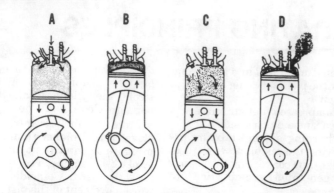

Fig. 7—Schematic diagram of four-stroke cycle engine operating on the Otto (spark ignition) cycle. In view "A", piston is on first downward stroke and atmospheric pressure is forcing fuel-air mixture from carburetor into cylinder through open intake valve. In view "B", both valves are closed and piston is on its first upward stroke compressing the fuel-air mixture in cylinder. In view "C", spark across electrodes of spark plug has ignited fuel-air mixture and heat of combustion rapidly expands the burning gaseous mixture forcing the piston on its second downward (expansion or power) stroke. In view "D", exhaust valve is open and piston on its second upward (exhaust) stroke forces the burned mixture from cylinder. A new cycle then starts as in view "A".

As the piston starts on its first upward stroke, the mechanically operated intake valve closes and, since the exhaust valve is closed, the fuel-air mixture is compresses as in view "B".

Just before the piston reaches the top of its first upward stork, a spark at the spark plug electrodes ignites the compressed fuel-air mixture.

As the engine crankshaft turns past top center, the burning fuel-air mixture expands rapidly and forces the piston downward on its power stroke as shown in view "C". As the piston reaches the bottom of the power stroke, the mechanically operated exhaust valve starts to open and as the pressure of the burned fuel-air mixture is higher than atmospheric pressure, it starts to flow out the open exhaust port.

As the engine crankshaft turns past bottom center, the exhaust valve is almost completely open and remains open during the upward stroke of the piston as shown in view "D". Upward movement of the piston pushes the remaining burned fuel-air mixture out of the exhaust port. Just before the piston reaches the top of its second upward or exhaust stroke, the intake valve opens and the exhaust valve closes. The cycle is completed as the crankshaft turns past top center and a new cycle begins as the piston starts downward as shown in view "A."

engines and some other mower companies use Tecumseh two-stroke engines.

FOUR-STROKE CYCLE

The five events of the Otto cycle take place in four strokes of the piston (two revolutions of the crankshaft) in four-stoke engines. Therefore, a power stroke occurs on alternate downward strokes of the piston.

In view "A" of Fig. 7, the piston is on the first downward stroke of the cycle.

The mechanically operated intake valve has opened the intake port and, as the downward movement of the piston has reduced the air pressure in the cylinder to below atmospheric pressure, air is forced through the carburetor, where fuel is mixed with the air, and into the cylinder through the open intake port. The intake valve remains open and the fuel-air mixture continues to flow into the cylinder until the piston reaches bottom of its downward stroke.

MOWER FAMILIARIZATION

Learn the correct names for common parts. Notice that different manufacturers may call similar parts or parts that serve the same function by different names. Refer to Fig. 8.

The name of the manufacturer of the mower and engine is sometimes displayed on a decal or plate, but sometimes identification must be accomplished by noticing small details of construction peculiar to one manufacturer. To order parts and for some service, the complete model and serial numbers must be known.

ROTARY MOWERS

GENERAL. The engine of a rotary mower is used to turn a cutting blade. The blade may be constructed in several different ways, but most are solid, one piece steel. The blade may be straight or curved to conform to deck configuration. Refer to view of blade in Fig. 9.

Blades are not all constructed the same and will have mounting holes to fit a particular engine. Be sure the correct blade is being used on the mower.

Fig. 8—Drawing of typical mower showing most of the typical parts.

1. Handlebar
2. Handlebar attaching brackets
3. Engine
4. Mower deck
5. Wheel support plates
6. Key
7. Blade drive clutch
8. Friction washers
9. Blade
10. Clamp washer
11. Lockwasher
12. Cap screw
13. Wheel
14. Bushing
15. Washer

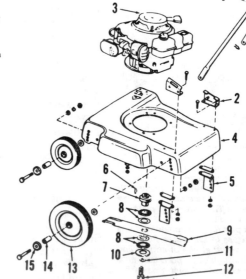

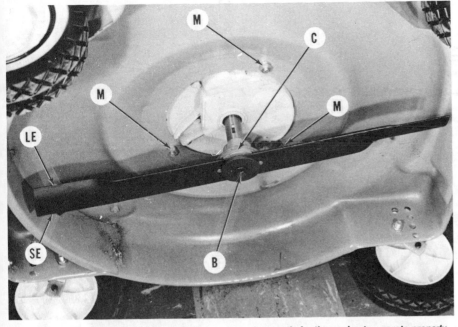

Fig. 9—The cutting blade must be installed securely and correctly for the engine to operate properly.

B. Blade attaching
    screw
C. Blade clutch

LE. Lift edge of blade
    (up)

M. Engine mounting
    bolts

SE. Sharp cutting edge
    (down)

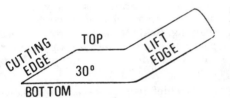

Fig. 10—Drawing of typical blade cross-section identifying parts of blade. The cutting edge should form approximately a 30° angle with bottom.

Most rotary mower blades have a bent edge on the rear of the blade. This is the "lift" portion of the blade and it creates a suction as the blade is moving to lift the grass for cutting and to discharge cut grass. Blades with a lot of lift are designed for cutting thick grasses such as Bermuda and Zoysia and when using a grass catcher. Low lift blades are for use with the thinner grasses such as Blue grass and Fescue.

Several methods may be used to drive a rotary mower blade. The simplest method is to attach the blade to the end of the engine's crankshaft. When the rotary blade is mounted remotely, a V-belt is generally used to transfer power from the engine to the blade.

Regardless of the type of blade drive used, the blade must be mounted correctly to cut properly. Lift edge on blades so equipped must be pointing up. On all blades the blade must be installed with the sloping portion of the cutting edge up and the flat side of the cutting edge down. Refer to Fig. 10.

On models so equipped, slip clutches are designed to allow the blade to turn when sufficient force is exerted against the blade.

Two types of clutches are generally used. Clutch shown at (A and C—Fig. 11) have two lugs (1) which engage holes in the blade. The lugs will shear off when the blade is forced to turn in a direction different than the clutch body.

Clutch lugs should be inspected periodically as vibration and wear will cause lugs to fail during normal use of mower. Clutch shown at (B) consists of a clutch body and washers (2) which fit on both sides of blade. Blade can slip

Fig. 11—Views of typical blade clutches. Lugs (1) engage holes in blade and friction washers (2) clamp blade tightly.

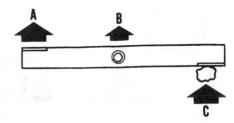

Fig. 12—The inertia of blade (A) when other end hits a solid object (C) results in a side force (B) against the crankshaft.

between washers when force is exerted on blade.

Washers may be made of rubber, fiber or steel. If washers become loose, blade may move during normal operation and create enough heat to deform washers. Be sure blade is secured tightly.

Slip clutches will allow the blade to turn around the crankshaft end but they may not prevent the crankshaft from bending if the end of the blade strikes an immovable object. The inertia of the free end of the blade keeps the free end of the blade moving until the crankshaft stops it. Note in Fig. 12 that the force generated by the inertia of the free end of the blade is against the crankshaft and not around it. The slip clutch protects the crankshaft from damaging forces rotating around it but not against it.

If a slip clutch is not used to attach the blade to the crankshaft, the blade may be mounted rigidly to the crankshaft. A single screw may hold blade between ridges of the adapter (E—Fig. 13) or screws and nuts may be used to secure blade to the adapter as shown at (D). The blade is mounted rigidly and is not permitted to slip at all.

Some late model mowers may be equipped with a blade brake/clutch, re-

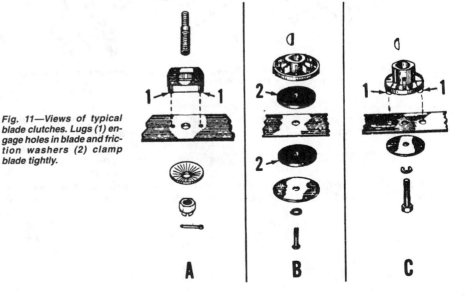

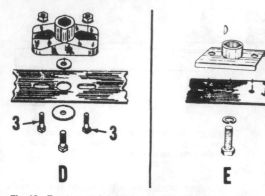

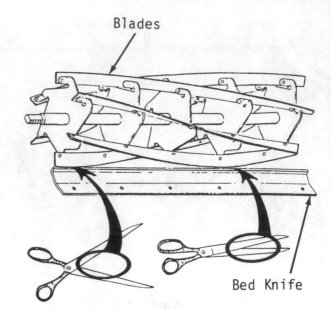

Fig. 13—Two types of rigid blade mounts. Type "D" attaches the blade with three screws. Type "E" attaches blade with one screw but ridges on the mount keep blade from turning.

Fig. 15—The cutting action of the blade and bed knife of a reel mower corresponds to the shearing action of scissors.

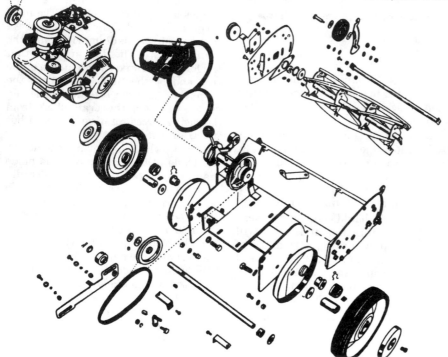

Fig. 14—Exploded view of a typical reel mower. Several different types of drive are used, including the belt drive shown and chain drive with separate clutch.

fer to appropriate repair section for servicing information.

REEL MOWERS

Sharp, properly adjusted reel type mowers (Fig. 14 and Fig. 15) in good operating condition offer several advantages over conventional rotary mowers.

The quality of cut possible with a reel type mower is unequaled, especially for semi-formal/formal turf areas and with certain grass varieties such as fine leaved Bermuda, Bent Grass and Zoysia which require short height. Grooming for best appearance is easily accomplished with a reel type mower without scalping. Reel mowers also require less power to operate than a rotary mower with same width of cut and propulsion type.

The chief disadvantages of reel mowers are: Reel mowers require fairly smooth ground that is free from rocks, sticks, wire and other debris which could cause damage to the mower. The height of the grass to be cut is limited by the diameter of the reel. If grass is too high, the mower will knock the grass down and run over it without cutting. Reel mowers generally required more care while operating and often involve more maintenance than rotary mowers. These disadvantages are usually not very critical when grooming a regularly maintained formal turf area.

A reel mower uses a scissors-like action between each reel blade and the cutter bar to cut grass. The more frequent the "snips" the better and smoother the cut. The frequency of cut will depend upon drive speed, reel speed, reel diameter and number of blades. The clips should be often enough to mow without leaving a riffled or corrugated effect.

ENGINE AND MOWER IDENTIFICATION

The following paragraphs provide information to help determine the manufacturer of the engine used on mowers manufactured by a particular company.

To correctly identify an engine, first determine what company manufactured the engine and then refer to the correct engine section for engine model and serial number locations.

If the manufacturer of the mower being serviced is not listed, identify engine manufacturer and refer to the correct engine section for engine model and serial number locations.

ACE

Ace walk-behind lawn mowers are equipped with four-stroke Briggs & Stratton engines. Mower model and serial number plate is attached to rear portion of mower deck.

Refer to appropriate engine service section for engine model and serial number location.

AIRCAP

Aircap walk-behind lawn mowers are equipped with four-stroke Briggs & Stratton engines. Mower model and serial number plate is attached to rear portion of mower deck. Refer to Fig. AP.

Fig. AP—View showing location of mower model and serial numbers (N) on Aircap walking lawn mowers.

Refer to appropriate engine service section for engine model and serial number location.

ALLIS-CHALMERS

Allis-Chalmers, walk-behind lawn mowers are equipped with four-stroke

Briggs & Stratton engines. Mower model and serial number plate is attached to rear portion of mower deck.

Refer to appropriate engine service section for engine model and serial number location.

ARIENS

Ariens walk-behind lawn mowers are equipped with four-stroke engines manufactured by either Briggs & Stratton or Tecumseh, or a two-stroke engine manufactured by Sachs. Mower model and serial numbers are located on a label on mower deck similar to Fig. AR.

Refer to appropriate engine service section for engine model and serial number location.

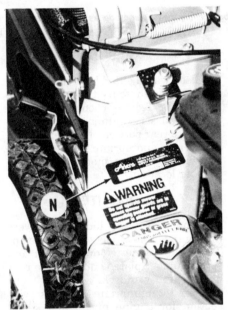

Fig. AR—View showing location of mower model and serial numbers (N) on Ariens walking lawn mowers.

ATLAS

Atlas walk-behind lawn mowers are equipped with Briggs & Stratton or Tecumseh engines. Mower model and serial number plate is attached to rear portion of mower deck.

Refer to appropriate engine service section for engine model and serial number location.

BOLENS

Bolens walk-behind lawn mowers are equipped with four-stroke Briggs & Stratton or Tecumseh engines. Mower

model and serial number plate is attached to rear portion of mower deck.

Refer to appropriate engine service section for engine model and serial number location.

BUNTON/GOODALL

Bunton/Goodall walk-behind lawn mowers are equipped with four-stroke Briggs & Stratton or Tecumseh engines. Mower model and serial number plate is attached to rear portion of mower deck.

Refer to appropriate engine service section for engine model and serial number location.

CUB CADET

Cub Cadet walk-behind lawn mowers are equipped with Briggs & Stratton engines. Refer to the appropriate engine service section for repair to the engine.

The mower serial number is on a plate located on the mower deck or the control panel attached to the handlebar. This number will be required for obtaining service parts. The engine model and serial number is required for determining some service procedures and for obtaining engine parts. Refer to the specific engine service section for engine identification.

For service to the self-propelled drive and the blade brake clutch, refer to the appropriate section for service to similar MTD models.

Some of the Cub Cadet models included in this book are: 074R, 560B, 836B, 836R, 838R, 848B, 848E, 072R110, 074R110, 098R110, 108R110, 118R100, 118R120, 148R120, 149R120, 560B120, 702R100, 838R120, 848B120, 848E120, 848R120, 898E120, 898R120, 899E120 and 899R120.

DEERE

John Deere walk-behind, 21-inch cut, lawn mowers are equipped with Briggs & Stratton, Kawasaki, or Lawn-Boy engines. Refer to the appropriate engine service section for repair to the engine.

The mower serial number consisting of 13 characters is on a plate located on the mower deck or the control panel attached to the handlebar. This number will be required for obtaining service parts. The first seven characters will identify the mower model as described in Fig. JD1. The engine model and serial number is required for determining some service procedures and for obtaining engine parts. Refer to the specific

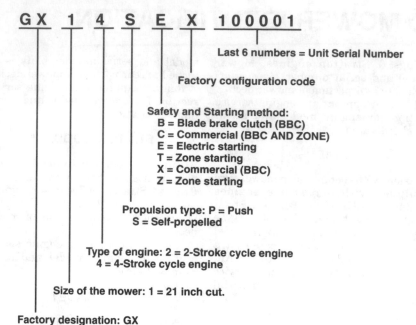

GX 1 4 S E X 100001

Last 6 numbers = Unit Serial Number

Factory configuration code

Safety and Starting method:
B = Blade brake clutch (BBC)
C = Commercial (BBC AND ZONE)
E = Electric starting
T = Zone starting
X = Commercial (BBC)
Z = Zone starting

Propulsion type: P = Push
S = Self-propelled

Type of engine: 2 = 2-Stroke cycle engine
4 = 4-Stroke cycle engine

Size of the mower: 1 = 21 inch cut.

Factory designation: GX

Fig. JD—The first seven numbers of the serial number identify the mower model as described above.

engine service section for engine identification.

Some of the John Deere models included in this book are: 12PB, 12SB, 14PB, 14PT, 14PZ, 14SB, 14SC, 14SE, 14ST, 14SX and 14SZ.

DEUTZ-ALLIS

Deutz-Allis walk-behind lawn mowers are equipped with Briggs & Stratton or Tecumseh engines. Mower model and serial number plate is attached to rear portion of mower deck.

Refer to appropriate engine service section for engine model and serial number location.

DYNAMARK

Dynamark walk-behind lawn mowers are equipped with four-stroke Briggs & Stratton or Tecumseh engines. Mower model and serial number plate is attached to rear portion of mower deck.

Refer to appropriate engine service section for engine model and serial number location.

FORD

Ford walk-behind lawn mowers are equipped with four-stroke Briggs & Stratton engines. Mower model and serial number plate is attached to rear portion of mower deck.

Refer to appropriate engine service section for engine model and serial number location.

GILSON

Gilson walk-behind lawn mowers are equipped with four-stroke Briggs & Stratton or Tecumseh engines. Mower model and serial number plate is attached to rear portion of mower deck.

Refer to appropriate engine service section for engine model and serial number location.

HOMELITE

Homelite walk-behind lawn mowers are equipped with Briggs & Stratton or Tecumseh engines. Mower model and serial number plate is attached to rear portion of mower deck.

Refer to appropriate engine service section for engine model and serial number location.

HONDA

Honda walk-behind lawn mowers are equipped with four-stroke engines manufactured by Honda Motor Com-

pany to metric specifications. Mower model and serial numbers are located as shown in Fig. HN.

Refer to appropriate Honda engine service sections for engine model and serial number.

HUSQVARNA

Husqvarna walk-behind lawn mowers are equipped with Briggs & Stratton or Kawasaki engines. Mower model and serial number plate is attached to rear portion of mower deck.

Refer to appropriate engine service section for engine model and serial number location.

INTERNATIONAL HARVESTER

International Harvester walk-behind lawn mowers are equipped with four-stroke engines manufactured by Briggs & Stratton or two-stroke engines manufactured by Lawn-Boy.

The two-stroke engine used on 1974 and earlier mowers is similar to equivalent Lawn-Boy models. Mower model and serial numbers are located on a plate attached to mower deck or battery box of electric start models. Engine model number is located on plate attached to fin of cylinder head.

The four-stroke engine used on 1975 and later mowers is manufactured by Briggs & Stratton. The engine serial number and model number are stamped on the cooling shroud (blower housing).

Refer to appropriate Briggs & Stratton or Lawn-Boy engine service section.

JACOBSEN

Jacobsen walk-behind lawn mowers are equipped with four-stroke engines manufactured by Briggs & Stratton or Tecumseh, or a two-stroke engine manufactured by Jacobsen. Mower model and serial numbers are located on a label attached to mower deck similar to Fig. JA.

Refer to appropriate engine service section for engine model and serial number location.

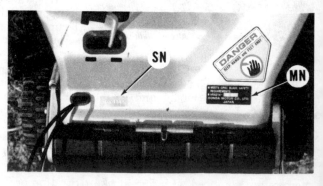

Fig. HN—View showing location of mower serial number (SN) and model number (MN) on Honda walking lawn mowers.

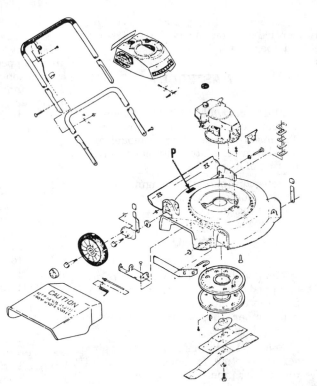

Fig. JA—View of Jacobsen rotary mower showing location of nameplate (P) for identifying mower and engine.

KING O'LAWN

King O'Lawn walk-behind lawn mowers are equipped with four-stroke Briggs & Stratton engine. Mower model and serial number plate is attached to rear of mower deck.

Refer to appropriate engine service section for engine model and serial number location.

KUBOTA

Kubota walk-behind mowers are equipped with four-stroke Kubota engines. Mower model number and serial number plate is attached to rear portion of mower deck.

Refer to Kubota engine service section for engine service procedures.

LAWN-BOY

The mower model and serial number are located on an identification plate attached to the mower deck (Fig. LB1 and Fig. LB2) or under the control panel located between the sides of the handlebars. The mower models and serial number are necessary when ordering parts.

Lawn-Boy walk-behind lawn mowers may be equipped with one of 5 different two-stroke engines manufactured by Lawn-Boy or one of 2 different four-stroke engines. Identify the engine used, then refer to the appropriate engine section for service.

The "L" head, four-stroke engine used on some Gold and Silver Series mowers is similar to either the Briggs & Stratton QUANTUM or Tecumseh TVS115. Refer to the appropriate section in this book for service to the specific engine.

The two-stroke engines used on some Lawn-Boy mowers can be identified for service by locating the engine model number (Fig. LB1) or determining the type by recognizing the construction details as follows.

The model number for series "C" and "D" engines is located on the side of the cylinder fins near the top or on the rewind starter cover (vertical pull starter models). Construction details include:

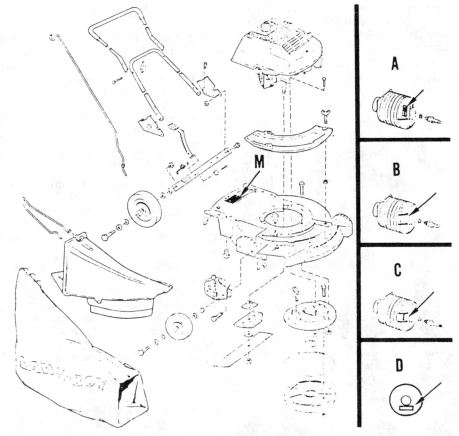

Fig. LB2—View showing plate located at rear of mower deck identifying mower model and serial number. The plate is attached to the handle stanchion above the rear wheel on some later models.

Fig. LB1—View of Lawn-Boy rotary mower showing location of plate (M) identifying mower model. Engine identification numbers are located on identification tag (A), ribs (B and C) or starter cup housing (D).

The carburetor is attached to the engine crankcase opposite the spark plug and the exhaust port is located on the underside of the cylinder. The cylinder and cylinder head are integral, but the cylinder and head assembly is separate from the crankcase.

"F" and "V" series engines are similar. Both series are air-cooled, single-cylinder, two-stroke engines with a vertical crankshaft. Identifiable construction details include: The carburetor is attached to the engine crankcase opposite the spark plug and the exhaust port is located on the underside of the cylinder. The cylinder and head are integral with half of the crankcase on both F and V models. The "F" series engines are used on F-series lawn mowers and some Gold Series mowers. The "V" series engines are used on some Silver Series mowers. The cylinder head on F-Series engines has a generally round shape and the fins are on an angle. The engine model is often stamped on the starter spring cap as shown in Fig. LB1. On V-Series engines, the cylinder and head have a generally square shape and the fins are straight up and down.

The M25 engine, used on "M" series mowers, can be identified by its construction details that are different from the other two-stroke models. The carburetor and the exhaust port are on opposite sides of the engine.

Some of the Lawn-Boy models included in this section are: 4262, 4656, 4861, 5254, 6431, 6461, 7073, 7351, 8073, 8073AE, 8157A, 8243, 8243AE1, 8244, 8431, 8461, 8481, 8481AE, 8861, C20CPR, C20CSR, C21CPN, C21ZMR, C21ZPN, C21ZPR, C21ZSN, L20ZPR, L21ZMR, L21ZPM, L21ZPN, L21ZSM, L21ZSN, M series (M21BMR, M21EMR, M21ZMR, M21ZPR, M21S-715, M21S-725, M21S-735, 10590 and 10591), S19XPN, S19ZPM, S19ZPN, S21BSN, S21BSR, S21BST, S21ESN, S21ESR, S21EST, S21ZPM, S21ZPN, S21ZPR, S21ZPT, S21ZSM, S21ZSN, S21ZSR, S21ZST, S21P-513, S21S-513; Silver series (10200, 10201, 10202, 10212, 10227, 10301, 10302, 10304, 10505, 10310 and 10314); Gold series (10400, 10401, 10415, 10416, 10418, 10420, 10421, 10422, 10515, 10516, 10517, 10518, 10520, 10521, 10522, 10523, 10545 and 10546), 10600 and 10650.

LAWN CHIEF

Lawn Chief walk-behind lawn mowers are equipped with a four-stroke Briggs & Stratton engine. Mower model and serial number plate is attached to rear portion of mower deck.

Refer to the Briggs & Stratton engine service section for model and serial number location.

MASTERCUT

Mastercut walk-behind lawn mowers are equipped with Briggs & Stratton or Tecumseh engines. Mower model and serial number plate is attached to rear portion of mower deck.

Refer to appropriate engine service section for engine model and serial number location.

MONO

Mono walk-behind lawn mowers are equipped with a four-stroke Briggs & Stratton engine. Mower model and serial number plate is attached to rear of mower deck.

Refer to the Briggs & Stratton engine service section for model and serial number location.

MTD

MTD walk-behind lawn mowers are equipped with four-stroke Briggs & Stratton or two-stroke Tecumseh engines. Mower model and serial number plate is attached to rear portion of mower deck.

Refer to appropriate engine service section for engine model and serial number location.

Fig. M—View showing location of model and serial numbers (N) on Murray walking lawn mowers.

MURRAY

Murray walk-behind lawn mowers are equipped with a four-stroke Briggs & Stratton engines. Mower model and serial number plate is attached to rear of mower deck as shown in Fig. M.

Refer to the Briggs & Stratton engine service section for model and serial number location.

PARMI

Parmi walk-behind lawn mowers are equipped with a four-stroke Briggs & Stratton engine. Mower model and serial number plate is attached to rear of mower deck.

Refer to the Briggs & Stratton engine service section for model and serial number location.

J. C. PENNEY

J.C. Penney walk-behind lawn mowers are equipped with a four-stroke Briggs & Stratton engine or a two-stroke Lawn-Boy engine. Mower model and serial number plate is attached to rear of mower deck.

Refer to the appropriate engine service section for model and serial number location.

ROPER

Roper walk-behind lawn mowers are equipped with Briggs & Stratton or Tecumseh engines. Mower model and serial number plate is attached to rear portion of mower deck.

Refer to appropriate engine service section for engine model and serial number location.

SEARS-CRAFTSMAN

Sears-Craftsman walk-behind lawn mowers are equipped with Briggs & Stratton, Honda, Tecumseh or Craftsman engines. Refer to the appropriate engine service section for repair to the engine.

The engine model and serial number is required for determining some service procedures and for obtaining engine parts. Refer to the specific engine service section for engine identification.

For service to the self-propelled drive and the blade brake clutch, refer to the appropriate section for service to similar models.

The mower serial number is on a plate located on the mower deck or the control panel attached to the handlebar. The first three numbers identify the manufacturer and the last number is internal (Sears) coding. The complete number will be required for obtaining service parts. Some of the Sears-Craftsman models included in this book are: 3747, 3786, 3809, 3839, 37204, 37213, 37215, 37218, 37219, 37228, 37234, 37236, 37239, 37242, 37244, 37247, 37250, 37252, 37256, 37265, 37280, 37281, 37282, 37283, 37284, 37285, 37286, 37287, 37288, 37289, 37290, 37291, 37344, 37349, 37452, 37459, 37467, 37471, 37620, 37621, 37627, 37631, 37632, 37635, 37636, 37804, 37814, 37817, 37827, 37860, 37862, 37865, 37869, 37872, 37875, 37903, 38002, 38004, 38007, 38009, 38012, 38023, 38029, 38033, 38034, 38035, 38038, 38039, 38048, 38051, 38054, 38056, 38270, 38271, 38272, 38273, 38274, 38275, 38276, 38277, 38278, 38279, 38284, 38309, 38312, 38314, 38316, 38322, 38324, 38334, 38336, 38337, 38344, 38404, 38421, 38426, 38429, 38434, 38435, 38600, 38601, 38602, 38603, 38604, 38605, 38606, 38612, 38613, 38614 and 38615.

SENSATION

Sensation walk-behind mowers are equipped with four-stroke engines manufactured by Briggs & Stratton, Clinton or Honda, or a two-stroke engine manufactured by Kawasaki. Mower model and serial numbers are located on plate attached to rear of mower deck.

Refer to appropriate engine service section for engine model and serial number location.

SIMPLICITY

Simplicity walk-behind lawn mowers are equipped with four-stroke engines manufactured by Briggs & Stratton or Tecumseh. Mower model and serial number plate is attached to rear of mower deck.

Refer to appropriate engine service section for engine model and serial number location.

SNAPPER

Snapper walk-behind lawn mowers are equipped with four-stroke engines manufactured by Briggs & Stratton or

Fig. S1—View showing plate located at rear of mower deck identifying Snapper mower model and serial number.

Tecumseh. Mower model and serial numbers are located on plate attached to rear of mower deck as shown in Fig. S1.

Refer to appropriate engine service section for engine model and serial number location.

SOUTHLAND

Southland walk-behind mowers are equipped with Briggs & Stratton engines. Mower model and serial number plate is attached to rear portion of mower deck.

Refer to appropriate engine service section for engine model and serial number location.

TORO

Toro walk-behind, lawn mowers may be equipped with Briggs & Stratton, Lawn-Boy, Suzuki, Tecumseh or Toro engines. Refer to the appropriate engine service section for repair to the engine.

The mower serial number is on a plate located on the mower deck or the control panel attached to the handlebar. This number will be required for obtaining service parts. The engine model and serial number is required for determining some service procedures and for obtaining engine parts. Refer to the specific engine service section for engine identification.

Some of the Toro models included in this book are: 16400, 16401, 16402, 16551, 16575, 16585, 16775, 16785, 16793, 20101, 20106, 20107, 20180, 20181, 20210, 20215, 20216, 20217, 20218, 20219, 20321, 20322, 20431, 20432, 20433, 20434, 20435, 20436, 20437, 20438, 20439, 20441, 20442, 20443, 20444, 20453, 20454, 20461, 20462, 20463, 20464, 20465, 20466, 20472, 20473, 20474, 20475, 20476, 20500, 20531, 20532, 20561, 20574, 20581, 20586, 20588, 20684, 20611, 20622, 20631, 20632, 20666, 20667,

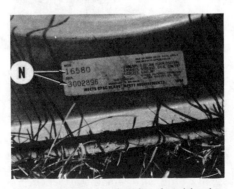

Fig. TO—View showing location of model and serial numbers (N) on some Toro walking lawn mowers. On some models, model and serial numbers are located on underside of handlebar control plate.

20677, 20680, 20692, 22026, 22031, 22040, 22043, 22145, 22150, 22151, 26551, 26562, 26622, 26624, 26641, 26642, 26651, 26682 and 27502.

WARDS

Wards walk-behind lawn mowers are equipped with four-stroke Briggs & Stratton or Tecumseh engines. Mower model and serial number plate is attached to rear of mower deck.

Refer to appropriate engine service section for engine model and serial number location.

WHITE

White walk-behind lawn mowers are equipped with a four-stroke Briggs & Stratton engine. Mower model and serial number plate is attached to rear of mower deck.

Refer to appropriate engine service section for engine model and serial number location.

YARD-MAN

Yard-Man walk-behind lawn mowers are equipped with four-stroke Briggs & Stratton or Tecumseh engines. Mower model and serial number plate is attached to rear of mower deck.

Refer to appropriate engine service section for engine model and serial number location.

STARTING AND OPERATION

Some standard procedures should be carefully followed. Most of the suggested procedures are in the interest of safety; however, some can prevent unnecessary damage to the mower or other property.

1. Never operate the engine in an enclosed area. Exhaust gases contain carbon monoxide, and odorless and deadly poison. Operate engine only where there is adequate ventilation.

2. Do not operate mower on top of loose rocks, sand or other material which may be thrown by the blade. Small objects may be hurled at high velocity by the blade and cause personal injury or property damage. Refer to Fig. 20.

3. Never fill the gas tank while engine is running. Avoid spilling gasoline on hot engine. Rinse all spilled fuel off with water before attempting to start engine. Refer to Fig. 21.

Fig. 20—Never start the mower on top of rocks, sand, gravel, etc. These small objects will be hurled by the blade.

Fig. 21—Be especially careful when filling the fuel tank with gasoline. The tank should be filled when engine is cold whenever possible and never with engine running.

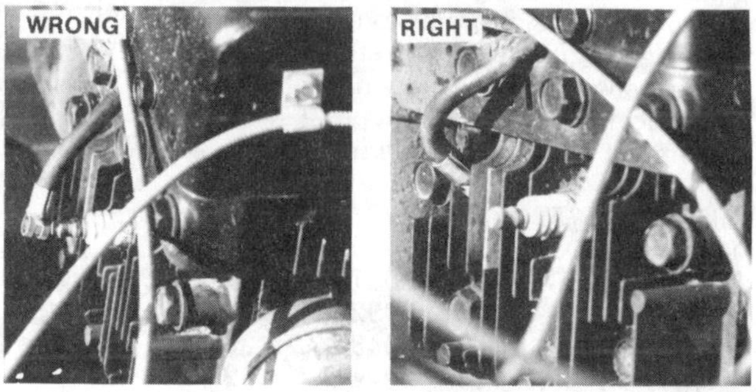

Fig. 22—The purpose of disconnecting the spark plug high tension lead is to keep the engine from accidentally starting. The high voltage can sometimes jump a small gap and allow the engine to start. Firmly grounding the lead to cylinder head is much safer.

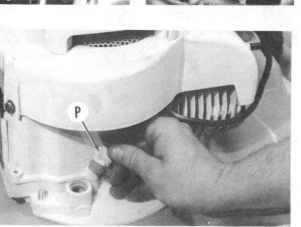

Fig. 23—Always check oil level before starting engine.

4. Always keep nuts, bolts and screws tight. Loose or missing parts can change or interfere with the operation of the engine or mower. Damage or injury can sometimes be easily avoided by making sure that all parts are securely in place.

5. Always disconnect and ground the wire from spark plug before inspecting or repairing any part of mower or engine. The engine may accidentally start causing serious damage or injury if the spark plug wire remains attached. Refer to Fig. 22.

6. Always check the oil level before starting engine. On mowers with four-stroke engine, be sure that crankcase is filled and that mower is level when checking. Total capacity is only about 1 ¼ pints (0.6 L) and the loss of only a small quantity of oil can destroy the engine. On mowers with a two-stroke engine, the oil for engine lubrication is mixed with the fuel. Operating the engine for even a short time without correct amount of oil mixed with the gasoline may extensively damage the engine.

7. Keep the engine clean. The engine is cooled by the circulation of air. Damage can result from overheating if the flow of air is restricted.

Oil and Fuel (4-Stroke Engines). To check oil level, position mower so engine is level. Remove oil level plug (P—Fig. 23) and observe the level of the oil in the threaded hole. The oil should be maintained at top of the hole to the point of overflowing. Total capacity of oil is relatively small, therefore it is important that it is full. Do not attempt to run the engine even for a short time with less than the recommended amount of oil.

Some engines are equipped with a dipstick attached to a fill plug (Fig. 24). Procedure for checking is similar, except that oil should be up to the full mark on dipstick.

On all four-stroke engines, pour oil in slowly. The size of the fill openings and the vent passages are small and some time is required for oil to flow into the engine.

Always use oil recommended by engine manufacturer. Weight and API classification will vary according to ambient temperature and type of engine usage. Used or poor quality oil should never be used. Using less than the best quality oil available will result in shortened engine life and expensive engine repairs or replacement.

Recommended fuel is regular or unleaded gasoline with octane rating of at least 87. Fuel which contains alcohol in any percentage should not be used unless manufacturer specifies that its use is acceptable.

Fuel should be stored in clean, clearly marked containers. Fuel should not be kept for long periods of time as water condensation and fuel deterioration will occur. Octane rating will also be lower in old fuel.

Oil and Fuel (2-Stroke Engines). Internal parts of two-stroke engines are lubricated by oil mixed with the gasoline. Failure to mix the correct amount of type of oil with the gasoline will result in damage. It is important to follow the engine manufacturers recommendation as to oil type and mixing ratio.

Excessive oil or the wrong type oil will cause low power, plug fouling and exces-

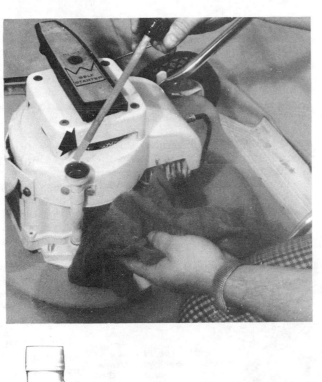

Fig. 24—A dipstick is attached to the fill plug shown for checking level of oil.

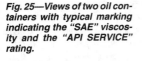

Fig. 25—Views of two oil containers with typical marking indicating the "SAE" viscosity and the "API SERVICE" rating.

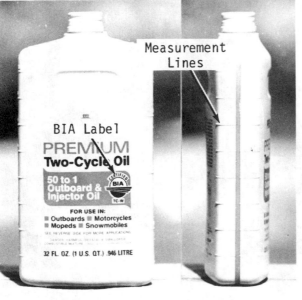

Fig. 26—View showing oil container marked with "TC-W" to indicate oil meets oil standard of NMMA (formerly BIA). Oil containers are also marked with US customary and metric measurements to aid in obtaining proper fuel:oil ratio.

sive carbon build-up. Insufficient amount of oil will result in inadequate lubrication and will result in internal damage similar to any engine operating without oil—Rapid, Severe and Extensive. The recommended ratio of oil to be mixed with the gasoline is listed in the individual engine section of this manual.

Oil should be mixed with gasoline in a separate container before it is poured into the fuel tank. The following table may be useful in mixing correct quantities of oil and gasoline to provide a specific ratio.

Ratio	Gasoline	Oil
10:1	.63 Gallon	1/2 Pint (237mL)
14:1	.88 Gallon	1/2 Pint (237mL)
16:1	1.00 Gallon	1/2 Pint (237mL)
20:1	1.25 Gallons	1.2 Pint (237mL)
30:1	1.88 Gallons	1/2 Pint (237mL)
32:1	2.00 Gallons	1/2 Pint (237mL)
50:1	3.13 Gallons	1/2 Pint (237mL)
10:1	1 Gallon	.79 Pint (379mL)
14:1	1 Gallon	.57 Pint (270mL)
16:1	1 Gallon	.50 Pint (237mL)
20:1	1 Gallon	.40 Pint (189mL)
30:1	1 Gallon	.27 Pint (126mL)
32:1	1 Gallon	.25 Pint (118mL)
50:1	1 Gallon	.16 Pint (76mL)

Often the engine manufacturer recommends a specific type or brand of oil. Other types may perform satisfactorily; however, the type recommended was tested and was proven to be acceptable.

Manufacturer may recommend acceptable oils according to NMMA (National Marine Manufacturers Association), formerly BIA, oil standards. Current standard is TC-WII which can be substituted for previously specified TC and TC-W standards. Oil standard compliance is noted on the oil container (Fig. 26). Most containers are marked on the side to provide a means of properly mixing the correct amount of oil with gasoline to obtain the proper fuel: oil mixture ratio.

Recommended fuel is regular or unleaded gasoline with octane rating of at least 87. Fuel which contains alcohol is any percentage should not be used unless manufacturer specifies that its use is acceptable.

Fuel should be stored in clean, clearly marked containers. Fuel should not be kept for long periods of time as water condensation and fuel deterioration with occur. Octane rating will also be lower in old fuel.

Fill The Fuel Tank. It is much safer to fill the fuel tank when the engine is cold. Refer to Fig. 27. BE SURE to use manufacturers recommended grade of gasoline, at an octane rating minimum or above. On two-stroke engines, be sure that the proper amount of oil has been mixed with the gasoline. Use only clean, fresh gasoline. Always store fuel safely in a properly marked steel container.

Prolonged storage of gasoline may produce deposits in the storage tank (can) or the engine fuel tank which can prevent an engine from running. Gasoline may be stored for short lengths of time, but never use gasoline that has been stored over the winter. Even if the engine runs, the quality of the gasoline is poor and may cause engine damage. Old stale gasoline has a different odor than fresh gasoline, and may be an early clue to the cause of poor performance.

Locate the Mower in a Safe, Practical Area. Mowers are difficult and sometimes impossible to start when standing in tall, thick grasses. Refer to Figs. 28 and 29. The resistance to turn may be enough to prevent the starter from operating fast enough to cause the engine to run. Do not compensate for this condition by starting the mower in a rock roadway. The rocks can be thrown great distances with great force by the rotating blade. Select the place to start the engine carefully with much consideration to safety.

Set The Controls. Make sure all control levers, cables and safety equip-

Fig. 27—The chances of catching fire are greater when refueling a hot engine than with a cold engine.

ment are in good and free working condition. A lever or cable that is damaged or binding may not provide correct engine component control. A faulty safety switch may prevent engine from starting when properly engaged or allow engine to start when safety equipment is not correctly positioned.

Control is required for three basic engine functions: Ignition; Engine Speed (throttle); Starting Enrichment (choke). The ignition must be turned on or, on models so equipped, the safety equipment must be positioned in starting location. On models without controlled carburetor functions, the throttle should be opened slightly and the choke should be actuated unless the engine is already warm. Often a single control (E—Fig. 30) interconnects these three operations and may be operated from the handlebar by a remote control lever.

NOTE: The remote control levers and cable may not move the engine controls correctly, always check for proper movement at engine if engine fails to start.

Operate Starter. The starters used may be as simple as a rope wrapped around a pulley or may be an electric starter operated by turning a key or pressing a switch. Upon operation of the starter the engine should begin to run. Move manual choke controls, if so equipped, to open the choke soon after engine starts. If control was set at an indicated "CHOKE" or "START" position, move the control to "RUN" position.

Stopping The Mower. The mower may have safety controls that stop the engine when a bar attached to the handle is released. Most models also have a

Fig. 28—Tall grass can cause enough resistance to prevent the engine from starting.

Fig. 29—Move the mower to area where blade is not obstructed, when starting the engine.

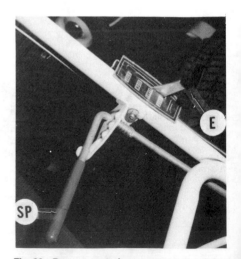

Fig. 30—Be sure controls are properly set before attempting to start.

PROBLEMS AND REMEDIES

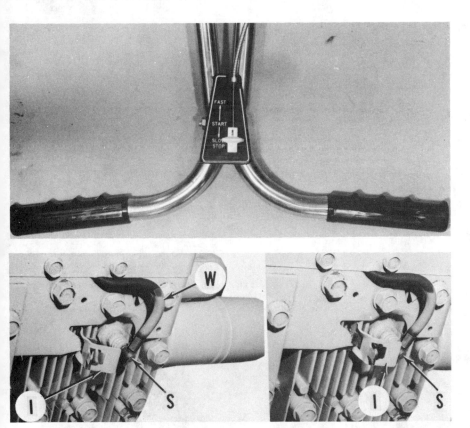

Fig. 31—Stop switch (I) can be against spark plug lead or high tension lead (W) can be shorted out. Either condition will cause engine not to start.

Fig. 32—Dirty mowers may be impossible to inspect. Long accumulations are difficult to remove.

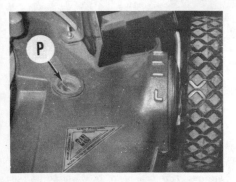

Fig. 33—Many mowers are equipped with a clean out port (P) to help clean the mower.

Repair is divided into three areas: 1. Recognition that a problem exists; 2. Locating the source of the problem; and 3. Correcting the problem.

Recognize Problems. Occasionally, a mower will have a serious problem, but most often the problems will be minor and can be easily remedied. Remember though, minor problems that are not corrected almost always cause major damage. Example: Continuing to run an engine without enough oil will almost certainly result in serious engine damage. Regular scheduled lubrication, cleaning, testing and adjusting will help you locate problems, but the operator can also be a valuable aid in early detection. The operator should be familiar with the proper way to operate the mower so that he/she does not cause the damage, but should also be encouraged to report any changes in the way a mower operates or problems encountered while mowing. If an engine stops while mowing and can not be restarted, it will probably be difficult or impossible to start at the next mowing.

Locate the Problem's Source. Safe and efficient mower operation must include correcting all problems quickly, but to do that effectively you must know the source not just the symptom. See Fig. 34. The next step is to list the possible causes for the problem (symptom) that you have identified. As an example, if the engine will not start, the problem could be:

1. Ignition — No spark, spark at the wrong time, etc.

2. Fuel—No fuel, too much fuel, wrong fuel, etc.

3. Mechanical—Starter not working, broken connecting rod, valve(s) stuck, etc.

4. Electrical—Battery dead, safety switch damaged, wiring short (or open), etc.

Additional tests or inspection(s) may be required to narrow the list of possibilities. Frequently the wrong system is first blamed for the problem. Modern ignition systems have reduced the frequency of failure, but some safety devices and controls (Fig. 31) can prevent ignition. It is important to correctly identify the source of the problem. A quick check of the ignition system using a test plug (Fig. 35) and visually checking the spark plug can quickly determine if the ignition system is able to deliver a spark. Refer to Figs. 36, 37, 38, 39, 40 and 41. If ignition appears normal but the spark plug is still dry after

"STOP" or "OFF" position on the engine controls. See Fig. 31.

Cleaning Mower Deck. Dirty mowers (Fig. 32) are difficult to inspect and service. The complete mower should be cleaned frequently, and some mowers are provided with a hose connection (P—Fig. 33) to assist cleaning under the mower deck. Mowers should, however, be lubricated after cleaning to prevent rusting. The controls, cables, wheels and blade (especially the cutting edges) should be dried, then protected with a coat of oil before storing.

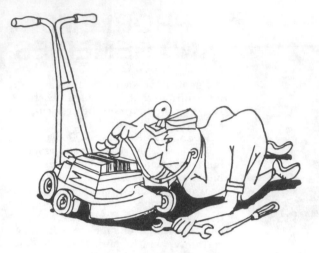

Fig. 34—Locating the cause of problems is important when servicing anything. Installing all new parts is a poor substitute for locating the real source of trouble.

Fig. 38—Normal plug appearance in four-stroke cycle engine. Insulator is light tan to gray in color and electrodes are not burned. Renew plug at regular intervals as recommended by engine manufacturer.

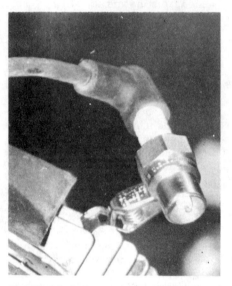

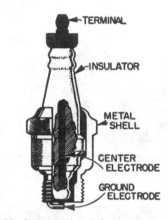

TERMINAL

INSULATOR

METAL SHELL

CENTER ELECTRODE

GROUND ELECTRODE

Fig. 36—Cross-sectional drawing of spark plug showing construction and nomenclature. The gap between ground electrode and center electrode is where spark should occur.

Fig. 39—Appearance of spark plug from four-stroke engine indicating cold fouling. Cause of cold fouling may be use of a too-cold plug, excessive idling or light loads, carburetor adjusted too "rich" or low engine compression. Similar appearance of spark plug from two-stroke engine would be considered normal after several hours of operation.

Fig. 35—A test plug can be connected to spark plug cable to check ignition for spark.

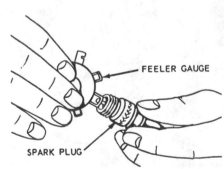

FEELER GAUGE

SPARK PLUG

Fig. 37—Be sure to check spark plug electrode gap with correct thickness gage and adjust gap if necessary. Special spark plug gap gauges are available from most tool sources.

attempting to start, the fuel system should be checked.

The troubleshooting procedures included in this section will help determine the source of most common problems.

Correct the Problem. After determining the cause, follow the service procedures included in this book for the specific make, model and system. Also, check for possible contributing causes or side effects. As an example, if the carburetor fuel passages are clogged with grass or rust, also check the fuel tank, filters, lines and valves for additional contamination. The trouble will probably reoccur if the tank and possibly the storage container are not cleaned also.

It should be pointed out that some troubles may result from more than one cause. As an example, a worn spark plug and improper fuel mixture may combine to prevent the engine from starting.

Sometimes the engine will start after correcting the mixture or installing a new spark plug, but the problem will soon reoccur if both problems are not corrected.

TROUBLESHOOTING

The first clue of a problem may be a noise that is different than usual, an

Fig. 40—Appearance of spark plug indicating wet fouling; a wet, black oily film is over entire firing end of plug. On four-stroke engines, cause may be oil getting by worn valve guides, worn oil rings or plugged breather or breather valve in tappet chamber. On two-stroke engine, cause may be incorrect type or amount of oil mixed with the gasoline or may be caused by wrong (too cold) spark plug installed.

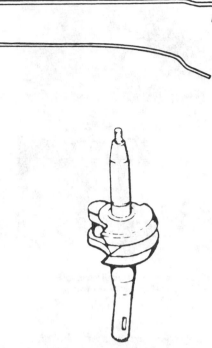

Fig. 43—Be sure that blade is straight and not bent. The blade may be shaped as shown in "A," but obviously bend blades "B" should be discarded.

Fig. 41—Appearance of spark plug indicating overheating. Check for plugged cooling fins, or bent or damage blower housing, engine being operated without all shields in place or other causes of engine overheating. Also can be caused by too lean a fuel-air mixture or spark plug not tightened properly.

CAUTION: The spark plug wire MUST be detached and grounded when examining or working on the underside of the mower to safely prevent the engine from accidentally starting. See Fig. 42. The spark plug wire should be grounded to eliminate the possibility of coil damage even if the spark plug is removed. During the following tests, it is suggested that the spark plug be removed so the engine crankshaft can be turned more easily.

Fig. 44—A bent crankshaft must be renewed to ensure correct and safe operation of engine.

engine that will not start or overall low performance. A systematic approach should be used to determine the source of the problem. The following are not the only effective procedures, but these can be used to help determine the cause of many engine problems.

NOISES

Noise is one of the most significant trouble signals. The mower operator should be constantly alert to changes in sound and should be encouraged to report any noted differences. Listen for any unusual noise, then try to determine which unit causes (caused) the sound. Check to see if the noise only occurs during specific operating conditions, such as when the blade brake clutch is engaged (blade stopped) or the self-propelled drive is engaged.

Knocking or rattling noises may be caused by loose cover, muffler or engine attaching bolts, but sharp knocking noises which seem to be coming from within the engine usually indicate serious trouble. Stop the engine and carefully examine the unit to determine the cause.

A bent or loose blade or a bent engine crankshaft may cause extremely loud noises, which are usually accompanied by severe vibration. A similar noise, but with a higher frequency can be caused by a part (cover, deck, etc.) either bent or loose so the blade hits the part. If you suspect the blade is hitting another part, detach the high tension wire, remove the spark plug, then ground the wire connector to a metal part of the engine before turning the mower upside down. Hold the engine brake lever or blade engaging levers as necessary so the blade can be turned by hand. Turn the blade and observe the position of each blade tip in relation to the mower deck. If the tip of one blade is higher than the other, check for a bent blade (Fig. 43). If the blade is higher on one side of the deck than when the same blade is on the other side, check for a bent crankshaft (Fig. 44). Also check for interference between the blade and any part of the mower deck. A bent cover or deck can sometimes be straightened, but be careful that the part is not broken and never leave a cover off. Never attempt to straighten a bent blade or crankshaft.

ENGINE WILL NOT START

For an engine to start, it needs sufficient fuel in the cylinder and a spark at approximately the right time to ignite that fuel. The starter (regardless of type) must turn the crankshaft fast enough (storing sufficient momentum) to continue the cycle of events.

The condition of the mower when it was last used may help determine the reason it will not start. If the lawn mower hit a solid object and suddenly stopped, then could not be restarted, check the condition of the flywheel key (Fig. 45).

Operate the manual starter slowly and check to feel the resistance of compression. On engine models with compression release, the compression will be light. If the manual starter does not engage properly and turn the crankshaft, refer to the engine section that covers the starting system used on the specific engine. Carefully observe what is happening and what should occur that is not.

Prepare the engine for normal starting. Make sure the fuel tank is filled with the proper type of fuel. Check the oil level and fill with the type recommended by the engine manufacturer. On some models, a switch prevents the engine from starting or stops a running engine if the oil level is too low for safe operation. Be sure the controls, **including the engine brake** on models with zone starting, are in the proper starting

Fig. 42—The purpose of disconnecting the spark plug high tension lead is to keep the engine from accidentally starting. The high voltage can sometimes jump a small gap and allow the engine to start. Firmly grounding the lead to cylinder head is much safer.

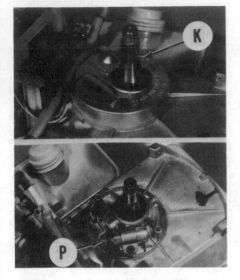

Fig. 45—View of the soft metal flywheel key (K) and the ignition breaker points (P) with flywheel removed.

position, then try to start the engine using the manual starter. Refer to Fig. 46.

If the engine will not start and the starter turns the crankshaft faster than normal, suspect engine damage. The cylinder head may be loose or the gasket may be damaged. If the mower has set for long, a valve may be stuck open or the connecting rod may be broken. If the starter is very difficult to operate, check to be sure the engine brake is not engaged.

If the engine's crankshaft is very hard to turn or impossible to move with the manual starter, suspect serious engine damage. Starter damage can also cause the starter to be difficult to operate.

On models with electric starting, if the engine starts using the manual starter, stop the engine, then try to start the engine using the electric starter. If the engine starts with the manual starter, but not the electric starter, make sure the battery is fully charged. Low battery voltage can cause the starter to spin without engaging the

engine crankshaft or turn the crankshaft more slowly than usual. On electric starting models, don't forget to check the condition of the battery.

The most common cause of not starting is that not enough fuel is reaching the cylinder. Check to be sure that the fuel tank is full and that any fuel shutoff valve is open (ON). If the tank is full, check to make sure the carburetor/intake manifold fasteners are tight. Air leaks in the intake passage can result in an excessively lean fuel:air mixture.

If there is any question about the quality of fuel in the tank, drain all of the fuel from the tank, lines and carburetor, then refill with fresh gasoline. Fuel can be drained into a container and inspected for contamination (Fig. 47). Moisture can condense inside the fuel tank and even a small amount of water can prevent mower engines from starting. Water in the fuel tank can sometimes be seen in at the bottom of the fuel tank.

Make sure the tank is filled with the proper fuel. Fuel used in 4-stroke engines should not have oil mixed with the gasoline. A mix of gasoline and oil in a 4-stroke engine will result in spark plug fouling and low power (if the engine starts). Many 2-stroke engines are lubricated by oil that is mixed with the gasoline and filling the tank with straight gasoline will damage the engine because of lack of lubrication. Some 2-stroke lawn mower engines (including some Lawn-Boy M Series) are equipped with a metering oil pump that injects lubricating oil from a separate tank. The fuel tank of 2-stroke models with metering pump should be filled with straight gasoline. On models requiring a mixture of gasoline and oil, refer to the manufacturer's recommendation to determine the correct amount of oil and gasoline to mix.

When cold, the engine requires a richer mixture (more fuel than for normal running) and chokes or primers are used to provide additional fuel for starting. Check to be sure the starting en-

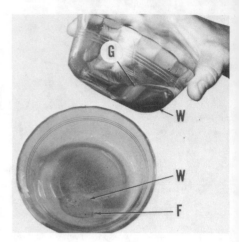

Fig. 47—Water (W) in the fuel (G) can often be noticed visually. Foreign particles (F) including dirt and metal may also be found visually.

richment system is operating properly. If a primer is used, it should squirt fuel into the intake passage. If a choke is used, it should be closed during starting. Refer to the specific engine service section for repair and adjustment of the starting enrichment system.

If the engine starts after operating the primer, then dies or if the engine only runs when the choke is closed, check the fuel delivery system to the carburetor. If the fuel tank, filter, valves and lines deliver sufficient fuel to the carburetor, refer to the specific engine service section to service the carburetor.

NOTE: If the mower has not run for sometime, moisture may have condensed inside the carburetor. Corrosion, varnish or other contamination in the carburetor can prevent the fuel from flowing correctly. The extent of service required will depend upon the degree of damage. Refer to the specific service instructions for the carburetor used in the engine service section.

Remove the spark plug and inspect its condition (Figs. 36, 37, 38, 39, 40 and 41). The removed plug should be reason-

Fig. 46—Be sure engine controls (E) operate properly.

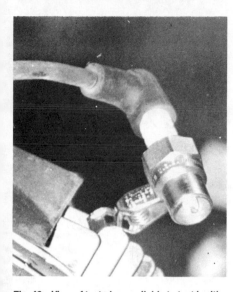

Fig. 48—View of test plug available to test ignition system.

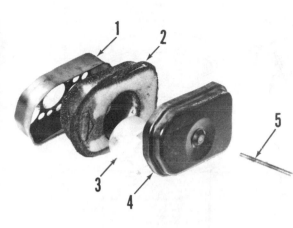

Fig. 49—View showing a typical foam type air cleaner. Clean all parts after 25 hours of normal operation. Clean more often in dusty conditions.

1. Housing
2. Foam element
3. Plastic insert
4. Cover
5. Screw

ably clean and smell of gasoline, but should not be dripping fuel. If the plug and its condition seem normal, check for proper ignition. A simple test plug can be used to test for spark. See Fig. 48. Attach the test plug to the spark plug wire and to the engine ground. Set the controls as required for starting, observe the gap of the test plug and operate the starter. The engine should turn faster than normal with the spark plug removed and a distinct spark should occur at the test plug. It may be necessary to shield light away from the test plug to see the spark. If a spark occurs, the ignition can usually be considered satisfactory. If the test plug does not spark, first check the position of the controls to be sure that switches are not stopping ignition. Some models have safety switches that prevent starting unless certain safety conditions are met.

CAUTION: Do not by-pass any safety switches; they are installed to prevent starting under unsafe conditions. The safety switches sometimes fail and may be incorrectly adjusted, but they are installed by the manufacturer to prevent injury.

If the ignition is determined to be faulty, refer to the specific engine service section for additional troubleshooting and repair. If breaker point ignition is used, the points should be inspected and serviced as required. Most engines used on later mowers are equipped with very dependable solid state ignition systems that require very little service.

ENGINE HARD TO START

Some of the conditions that prevent an engine from starting can cause the engine to be difficult to start. Before starting:

1. Make sure the fuel tank is filled with the correct type of fuel.
2. Check the oil reservoir and fill to the proper level with the recommended type of oil.
3. Locate the mower in an area where it will be safe to start.
4. Set all of the controls properly for starting.

On early mowers and later models with zone starting, the cutting blade is used as a flywheel and the engine may not start with the blade removed. If the engine will not start with the blade removed, install the blade and try again.

To start and run, the mixture of fuel and air drawn into the engine must be ignited by the spark plug. If the fuel and air mixture is too rich (too much fuel) or too lean (not enough fuel), it will not ignite easily and the engine will be hard to start. The most common cause of hard starting is a fuel mixture that is too lean.

Remove the spark plug and inspect its condition. The removed plug should be reasonably clean and smell of gasoline, but should not be dripping fuel. If the plug and its condition seem normal, it can be reinstalled, but a new plug can be installed as easily at this time. Remove the air cleaner and check its condition. If damaged, install a new filter. Some filters (Fig. 49 and 50) can be cleaned as described in the engine service section. A dirty filter may cause the mixture to be too rich, much like running with the choke closed. Check the starting enrichment system before installing the air cleaner. The engine controls should close the choke completely on models so equipped. On models with a primer, its operation can often be viewed with the air cleaner removed.

Check the operation of the engine controls (Fig. 46) to make sure the controls operate throughout the entire range. Adjust controls as described in the engine service section if necessary.

Check the fuel filter for plugging if the engine starts and runs normally for awhile, then slows or dies, but will restart after a short wait.

Most ignition system problems will prevent starting, especially under certain conditions such as when the mower is wet. Some conditions can, however, allow the engine to start, but increase the difficulty of starting. Make sure the spark plug is in good condition and not dirty or damaged. If tests of the ignition system indicates an intermittent lack of spark, check the ignition system as described in the engine service section. Ignition timing, air gaps and other clearances can cause difficult starting. Also, check the safety control systems for proper operation.

Worn out piston rings and cylinder bore or leaking valves can also cause the engine to be difficult to start.

ENGINE PERFORMANCE IS ROUGH AND/OR POWER IS LOW

Lack of power without an apparent miss may be caused by incorrect carburetor adjustment, incorrect governor adjustment (too slow), improper ignition timing, plugged air cleaner or plugged muffler. This condition can also be caused by a dirty or damaged carburetor, malfunctioning governor or worn out rings and cylinder bore.

An intermittent miss may be caused by a malfunctioning ignition system or fuel system, but the presence of a miss rules out the governor or ignition timing as a primary factor.

The most common cause is usually not a lack of power at all, but is a dull blade. More power is required to beat the grass with a dull blade than is required to cut it with a sharp blade.

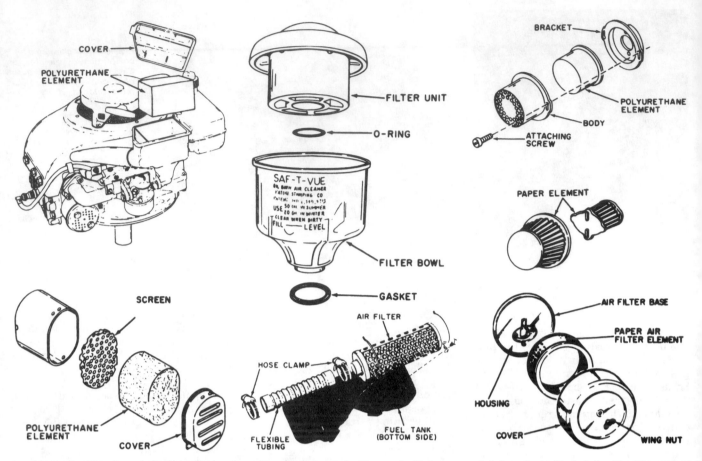

Fig. 50—View showing some typical air cleaners. Paper filter elements can be blown out with compressed air from the inside, but should not be washed. Foam elements can be washed in detergent or solvent, then dried.

The following may help determine the cause and correct the problem of low power or general poor performance.

Fuel Tank Almost Empty. The engine will run poorly just before the tank is out of gas. Be sure the fuel tank is full. This lean condition can be caused by reducing the amount of gasoline or increasing the flow of air. The following problems can affect the engine in ways similar to an empty tank: Fuel filter clogged. Fuel passages or orifices in the carburetor may be clogged. The carburetor or intake manifold mounting screws may be loose. The carburetor fuel mixture needle may be adjusted too lean.

Choke May not Be Open Completely. The choke may be stuck, binding or incorrectly adjusted. This excessively rich (too much gasoline or not enough air) condition is often accompanied by gasoline smell and excessive exhaust smoke.

Air Cleaner Plugged. A clogged air filter will cause an over rich condition by reducing the amount of air very much like closing the choke. The air cleaner can be checked by removing the unit; however, a new or cleaned filter should be installed before using the mower.

Contaminated Fuel. A frequent cause of intermittent miss, loss of power or even failure to start is water or dirt in the system or a plugged fuel filter. If so equipped, close the fuel shut-off valve at the tank, then disconnect the fuel line near the carburetor. If the shut-off valve is operating properly, very little fuel should flow from the detached line. Open the shut-off valve and check fuel flow from the tank. The fuel should flow in a steady stream and be clean. If water, dirt or discolored fuel flow from the detached line, the tank, lines and filter should be cleaned or new parts installed. If very little fuel trickles from the detached line, find and repair the obstruction.

Spark Plug Dirty or Loose. Remove the spark plug and visually inspect its condition. Spark plugs can sometimes be cleaned, but the simplest way to be sure of the spark plug's condition is to install a new plug. Install the type of spark plug recommended by the manufacturer for the specific engine and application. Threads in the cylinder head can be easily damaged by cross threading, over tightening or not tightening the spark plug. Be sure to tighten the spark plug to the correct torque.

Cutting Blade Loose, Dull or Installed Upside Down. The sharp edge (SE—Fig. 51) of the blade must be down and it must be sharp. A dull blade requires much more effort (power) to cut than a sharp blade. An engine in good condition may seem to be low on power if the blade is dull. A loose blade or blade clutch may allow the blade to slip, especially if the blade is dull.

Engine Overheating. Since lawn mowers are not equipped with temperature gauges, almost all overheating conditions will go unnoticed until the combined temperature and accelerated wear keep the engine from running. Overheating can be caused by grass blocking the cooling fins (B—Fig. 52), but is usually the result of several events such as clogged cooling fins, lean fuel mixture, overloaded operation, low oil level and high outside air temperature.

Low Compression. The engine is designed to operate at a specific compression pressure and, if the pressure is lower, the engine will not produce optimum power. The engine may also be harder to start. Normal operation wears the piston rings and cylinder bore, resulting in lowered compression pres-

Fig. 51—View of typical blade installation. Be sure blade is tight and correctly installed.
B. Blade retaining screw
C. Clutch
LE. Lift edge of blade (up)
M. Engine mount bolts
SE. Sharp edge (down)

Fig. 53—Cylinder head screws (S) should be tightened to specified torque in proper sequence. Refer to appropriate engine service section.

Fig. 54—Gas cap should have vent holes (V) to allow entrance of air.

Fig. 52—Grass and dirt (B) packed between cooling fins will cause engine to overheat.

sure. Since lower than new compression caused by normal wear will occur slowly over a long period of time it will usually be unnoticed. Damage or accelerated wear may reduce the compression more quickly and be much more noticeable. Some causes are loose screws (S—Fig. 53) attaching the cylinder head or blown cylinder head gasket. Broken piston rings or damaged valves will also lower the compression pressure.

Engine Vibrates Excessively. Check to make sure the engine mounting bolts (M—Fig. 51) are tight. Vibration can also be caused by a bent crankshaft or a blade that is out of balance. The blade should be balanced each time it is sharpened.

ENGINE SURGES

If the engine surges (rhythmically speeds up and slows down) while run-ning, the trouble is probably caused by incorrect carburetor mixture adjustment. Incorrect governor adjustment, malfunctioning carburetor or damaged governor can also cause surging. Refer to the appropriate engine service section for specific repair and adjustment procedures.

ENGINE STARTS THEN STOPS

If the engine starts, runs a short time, then dies, check for proper flow of fuel from the tank. If so equipped, close the fuel shut-off valve at the tank, then disconnect the fuel line near the carburetor. If the shut-off valve is operating properly, very little fuel should flow from the detached line. Open the shut-off valve and check fuel flow from the tank. The fuel should flow in a steady stream and be clean. The tank, lines and filter should be cleaned or new parts

installed if water, dirt or discolored fuel flow from the detached line. If very little fuel trickles from the detached line, find and repair the obstruction. The cap on the fuel tank (Fig. 54) must be vented. If an unvented cap is installed, it will prevent air from entering the tank as the fuel is used and vacuum will build in the tank. Fuel will stop flowing when sufficient vacuum builds in the tank.

ENGINE USES TOO MUCH OIL

Excessive oil consumption in a 4-stroke engine can easily result in serious engine damage. The total amount of oil is small and loss of only a small amount will increase the operating temperature of the engine. High temperature is especially critical at some of the bearings and sliding surfaces such as the piston skirt and rings. Even moderately high temperatures can cause the engine to lose power and localized hot spots can cause excessive engine damage. Refer to Fig. 55 for some causes of oil consumption. Be sure to check the crankshaft seals (Figs. 56, 57 and 58). Leakage from around the bottom seal under the mower deck may not be noticed except by the loss of oil.

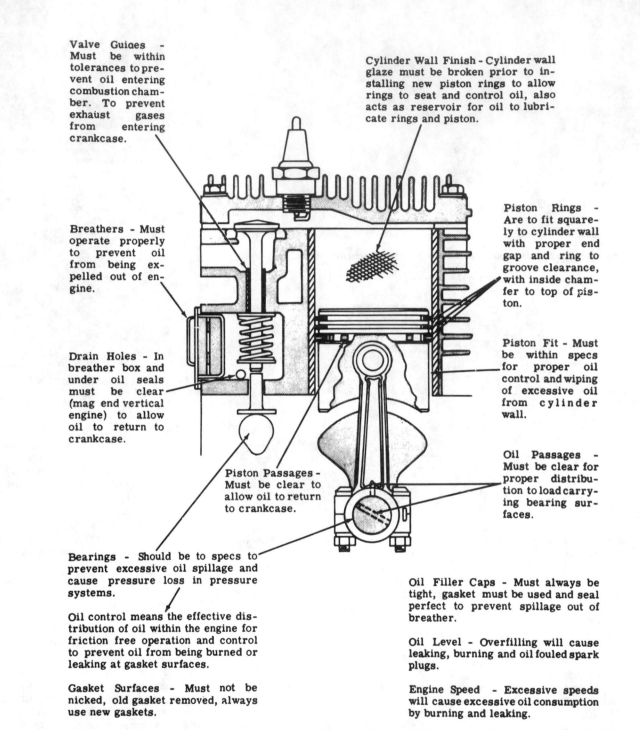

Valve Guides - Must be within tolerances to prevent oil entering combustion chamber. To prevent exhaust gases from entering crankcase.

Cylinder Wall Finish - Cylinder wall glaze must be broken prior to installing new piston rings to allow rings to seat and control oil, also acts as reservoir for oil to lubricate rings and piston.

Breathers - Must operate properly to prevent oil from being expelled out of engine.

Piston Rings - Are to fit squarely to cylinder wall with proper end gap and ring to groove clearance, with inside chamfer to top of piston.

Drain Holes - In breather box and under oil seals must be clear (mag end vertical engine) to allow oil to return to crankcase.

Piston Fit - Must be within specs for proper oil control and wiping of excessive oil from cylinder wall.

Piston Passages - Must be clear to allow oil to return to crankcase.

Oil Passages - Must be clear for proper distribution to load carrying bearing surfaces.

Bearings - Should be to specs to prevent excessive oil spillage and cause pressure loss in pressure systems.

Oil control means the effective distribution of oil within the engine for friction free operation and control to prevent oil from being burned or leaking at gasket surfaces.

Gasket Surfaces - Must not be nicked, old gasket removed, always use new gaskets.

Oil Filler Caps - Must always be tight, gasket must be used and seal perfect to prevent spillage out of breather.

Oil Level - Overfilling will cause leaking, burning and oil fouled spark plugs.

Engine Speed - Excessive speeds will cause excessive oil consumption by burning and leaking.

Fig. 55—In four-stroke engines, the compartments containing oil are sealed to prevent leakage. Damage to any of these seals may permit oil to enter an area of the engine where it does not belong or may permit the oil to leak out of the engine.

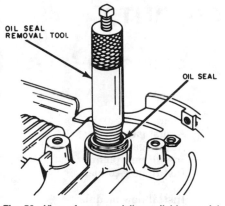

Fig. 56—View of commercially available special seal removal tool to remove oil seals. The only practical repair for a damaged oil seal is installing a new one.

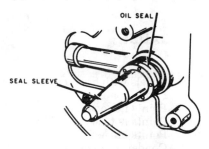

Fig. 58—Use caution when installing new seal. Sharp edges of crankshaft can cut a new seal while installing. Use a sleeve as shown or tape to protect seal from sharp edges of shaft while installing.

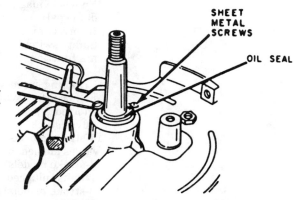

Fig. 57—Two sheet metal screws and a screwdriver may be used to pull the oil seal out of bore without disassembling engine. Refer to Fig. 56 and Fig. 58.

TROUBLESHOOTING CHART

SYMPTOM	CAUSE	CORRECTION
Fails to Start		
No Fuel To Carburetor	No fuel in tank	Fill tank
	Shut-off valve closed	Open valve
	Fuel filter clogged	Clean screen or install new filter
	Fuel line blocked	Install new hose
No Fuel To Cylinder	No fuel to Carburetor	See above
	Float valve stuck	Clean carburetor
	Inlet needle stuck	Clean carburetor
	Incorrect fuel level	Adjust float
	Choke inoperative	Overhaul carb.
	Primer inoperative	Repair primer
	Fuel passages clogged	Overhaul carb.
	No compression	Overhaul engine
	2-Stroke engines- Crankcase leak	Install new seals and gaskets
	Reed valve leaking	Install new valve
	Exhaust plugged	Clean exhaust
Engine flooded	Float stuck open	Clean carburetor
	Incorrect fuel level	Adjust float
	Over choked or primed	Purge engine
	No spark at plug	See below
No spark at plug	Plug fouled	Clean plug
	Incorrect plug gap	Adjust gap
	No spark at plug wire	See below

TROUBLESHOOTING CHART (CONT.)

SYMPTOM	CAUSE	CORRECTION
Fails to Start		
No spark at plug wire		
	Models with breaker point ignition	
	Points coated	Clean points
	Points not opening	Adjust gap
	Points not closing	Adjust gap
	Points burned	Install new points
	Condenser damaged	Install new condenser
	Models with solid state ignition	
	Ignition module bad	Install new module
	All models	
	Flywheel key sheared	Install new key
	Stop switch shorted	Adjust, repair or install new switch
	Coil damaged	Install new coil
	Flywheel magnets damaged	Install new flywheel
	Incorrect air gap	Adjust gap
	Safety switch malfunction	Adjust, repair or install new switch
	Cranking speed slow	Repair starter
	Kill or safety switch shorted	Repair/replace switch
No compression	Valves stuck (4-stroke models)	Free the valves
	Valves burned (4-stroke models)	Install new valves
	Exhaust plugged (2-stroke models)	Clean the exhaust
	Cylinder head loose or gasket leaking	Install new gasket
	Piston/cylinder damaged	Overhaul engine
	Connecting rod damaged	Overhaul engine
Lacks Power		
Engine smokes	Rich fuel mixture	Adjust carburetor or controls
	Air filter plugged	Clean air filter
	Worn piston rings (4-stroke models)	Overhaul engine
	Too much oil in the fuel mix (2-stroke)	Use correct gasoline/oil mixture
Lean fuel mixture	Improper carburetor adjustment	Adjust carburetor
	Carburetor/manifold gasket leaking	Install new gasket
	Tank vent plugged	Clean vent
	Filter plugged	Clean or install new filter
	Crankcase leaking (2-stroke)	Install new seals/gaskets
Engine misses	Ignition/spark plug faulty	Service ignition
Engine Overheats		
	Engine dirty	Clean engine
	Low oil level (4-stroke)	Add oil
	Wrong gasoline/oil mix (2-stroke)	Use correct gasoline/oil mix
	Engine overloaded	Reduce load/sharpen the blade
	Cooling fins, cowling or fan broken/missing	Install new parts
	Lean fuel mixture	See Lean Fuel Mixture above

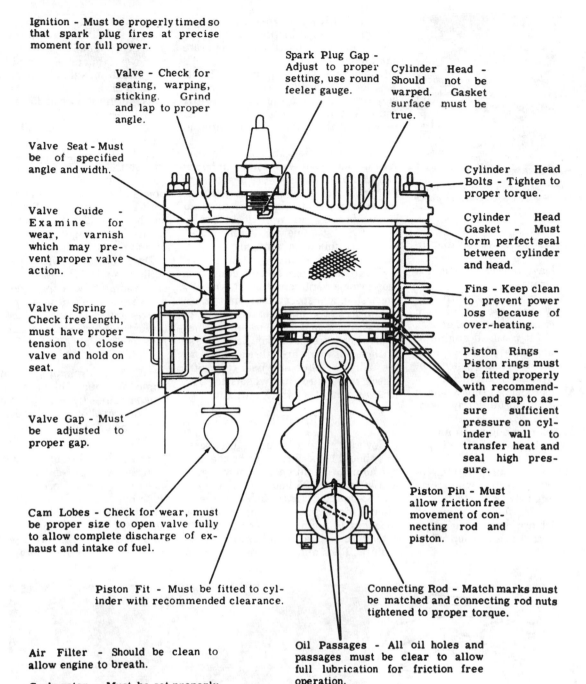

Ignition - Must be properly timed so that spark plug fires at precise moment for full power.

Valve - Check for seating, warping, sticking. Grind and lap to proper angle.

Valve Seat - Must be of specified angle and width.

Valve Guide - Examine for wear, varnish which may prevent proper valve action.

Valve Spring - Check free length, must have proper tension to close valve and hold on seat.

Valve Gap - Must be adjusted to proper gap.

Cam Lobes - Check for wear, must be proper size to open valve fully to allow complete discharge of exhaust and intake of fuel.

Piston Fit - Must be fitted to cylinder with recommended clearance.

Air Filter - Should be clean to allow engine to breath.

Carburetor - Must be set properly to assure proper and sufficient air and fuel.

Spark Plug Gap - Adjust to proper setting, use round feeler gauge.

Cylinder Head - Should not be warped. Gasket surface must be true.

Cylinder Head Bolts - Tighten to proper torque.

Cylinder Head Gasket - Must form perfect seal between cylinder and head.

Fins - Keep clean to prevent power loss because of over-heating.

Piston Rings - Piston rings must be fitted properly with recommended end gap to assure sufficient pressure on cylinder wall to transfer heat and seal high pressure.

Piston Pin - Must allow friction free movement of connecting rod and piston.

Connecting Rod - Match marks must be matched and connecting rod nuts tightened to proper torque.

Oil Passages - All oil holes and passages must be clear to allow full lubrication for friction free operation.

Fig. 59—Some causes of low power from four-stroke engine are indicated above.

SAFETY TIPS

Personal safety for yourself, those around you or those who will operate equipment in the future should be the number one concern when using or servicing power equipment of any type.

Carefully think out every step before performing service work or using power equipment.

There is no substitute for common sense, caution and forethought when working on or using power equipment. The following list of safety suggestions is provided as an aid to develop your own personal safety code to follow when working on or using power equipment.

1. ALWAYS read operator's manual and be thoroughly familiar with all controls and safety features.

2. NEVER remove, alter or disconnect any safety equipment, switches, warning or instructional decals. Never operate, or allow another person to operate equipment which has had safety

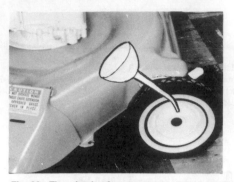

Fig. 60—The wheels of most mowers can be kept lubricated with oil. Some are equipped with grease fittings.

features removed, altered or disconnected.

3. NEVER leave mower unattended while engine is running.

4. NEVER alter engine governor or speed control to increase engine rpm above manufacturer's specifications.

5. ALWAYS wait until all engine or blade motion has stopped before refueling, removing or installing grass catchers, guards or optional equipment.

6. ALWAYS properly ground spark plug wire before performing any maintenance on mower.

7. NEVER operate engine in an enclosed room or where ventilation is not adequate.

8. ALWAYS wear appropriate clothing, shoes and eye protection when servicing or operating mower.

9. ALWAYS store fuel in approved containers which are clearly marked as to contents. Always use caution when handling fuel.

10. NEVER allow irresponsible persons or people not instructed in proper safety and equipment use to operate equipment.

The list of safety suggestions is limitless. Remember, YOU as a service person or as the end user of power equipment are responsible for personal safety and the safety of those around you.

Proper operation and care can prevent damage that would need to be repaired. Lawn mowers were designed to cut grass; not steel, iron, wire, rocks, concrete, rope, etc. Improper use can cause damage, even if accidentally done. Check the mower regularly (but especially following any misuse) and keep the mower clean.

Clean and inspect the complete mower for general condition. It is nearly impossible to inspect a dirty mower.

Lubricate the axles at the center of the wheels. Some wheels are permanently lubricated and some have grease fittings, but many are lubricated by oiling axle at center of wheel (Fig. 60). Check to be sure that wheels are not loose and that they track straight.

ENGINE

Several routine maintenance services should be performed after the first two hours of operation of an new engine and after every 25 hours of engine operation or at least once each year thereafter. This service interval should be considered minimal. Never attempt to extend this time. Small lawns which require fifteen minutes to mow may not

accumulate 25 hours on the mower, but service should be accomplished at least once every year.

Mowers that are operated in dusty or dirty conditions should be serviced more often than every 25 hours of running. This routine service at 25 hour intervals should also be supplemented by normal checks before starting and while cleaning before storing.

At least every 25 hours of operation, change the engine oil and clean the air filter. Oil is necessary for both lubrication and cooling. Running the engine with not enough oil will quickly cause overheating. The heat will, of course, result in damage to internal engine parts.

Drain oil after running engine and while the oil is still warm. Disconnect and ground the wire from the spark plug to prevent accidental starting. Locate mower on level surface above a container suitable for containing oil, then remove drain plug (Fig. 61).

NOTE: Oil drain plug is not used on some engines. Oil is drained from these engines by tipping the mower on its side and allowing oil to drain out the filler tube opening.

Reinstall and tighten the drain plug sufficiently to prevent it from working loose. Fill engine crankcase through filler opening with a good quality oil marked SAE 30, with the latest API SERVICE rating (Fig. 62). Capacity of many engines is only 1-¼ pints (0.6 L) which is slightly less than three-quar-

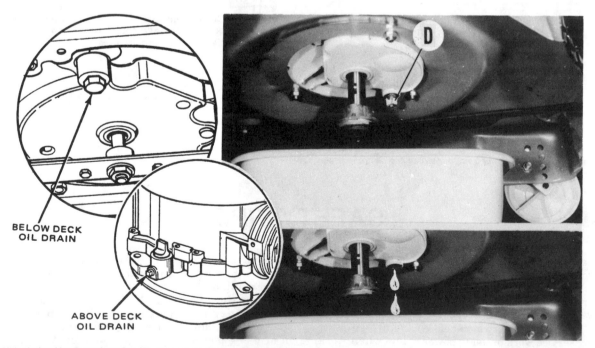

BELOW DECK
OIL DRAIN

ABOVE DECK
OIL DRAIN

Fig. 61—Oil is drained by removing plug (D). Be sure to tighten plug securely before filling with new oil.

Fig. 62—View of two oil containers with typical markings indicating the "SAE" viscosity and "API SERVICE" rating.

Fig. 63—View of typical filler opening (F) with plug (P) removed.

Fig. 64—View showing a typical foam type air cleaner. Clean all parts after 25 hours of normal operation. Clean more often in dusty condition.

1. Housing
2. Foam element
3. Plastic insert
4. Cover
5. Screw

sages become clogged with dirt or with oil, the result is similar to operating with the choke closed. Some mowers may be equipped with oil bath air cleaners which can be cleaned by removing, disassembling, then cleaning with a suitable solvent. Refill the air cleaner cup with engine oil to the level indicated on the side.

Run engine until the fuel tank is completely out of gas before storing the mower for the winter. Any gasoline left in the tank during the off season will begin to evaporate and leave a residue. Some chemical products are available which can be added to the gasoline before storage, but these will not be necessary if the tank is empty.

ROTARY MOWERS

Some adjustments must be correctly set in order to assure proper performance of the mower. The location of the handle can cause the mower to be unsafe or difficult for some people to operate. The rotary cutting blade should be parallel with the ground and the blade should cut the grass at the correct height.

HANDLE POSITION. Handle position is adjustable on most lawn mowers for operator comfort and safety. The mower handle is attached to a bracket on the mower deck. Notice in Fig. 66 that a retaining lug (L) secures the handle in the bracket. The handle height is changed by locating lug (L) in different hole (H).

Height of the handle of some mowers is adjusted with offset holes drilled at attaching ends of handle or lugs are installed off center. Handle height can be changed only by removing handle, then reattaching with ends attached to opposite mounting brackets.

The handle arrangement shown in Fig. 67 is adjusted by loosening retaining bolts (B), relocating the bracket, then tightening the bolts (B).

Several different methods have been used to adjust handle height, but most can be easily understood.

CUTTING HEIGHT. A critical lawn mower adjustment when considering the type of grass being cut is blade height. The blade height determines the cutting height of the mower and is measured from the tip of the cutting blade to the ground on rotary lawn mowers. Refer to Fig. 68. A listing of recommended cuts for some popular grasses is as follow:

ters of one quart. Check oil level after filling.

Do not overfill, but be sure that oil is to "FULL" mark on dipstick or to top of fill plug opening (F—Fig. 63). Install fill plug. Reconnect high tension wire to spark plug after all other service is completed.

Remove any covers necessary, then remove the air cleaner assembly from the engine. Refer to Fig. 64 and Fig. 65

for some typical air cleaner assemblies. Clean the container and element thoroughly. Wash all parts except paper element in detergent or kerosene and dry completely. Saturate foam (polyurethane) element in engine oil, then squeeze out all excess. Foam should have light tint of oil color, but dark appearance indicates too much oil. The foam contains a labyrinth of passages through which air passes. If these pas-

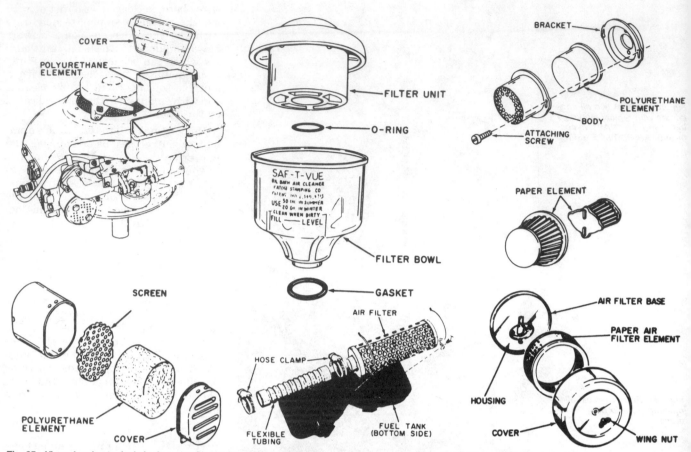

Fig. 65—View showing typical air cleaners. Clean all parts every 25 hours of operation. Paper filter elements can be blown out with compressed air from the inside, but should not be washed. Foam elements can be washed in detergent or solvent, then dried.

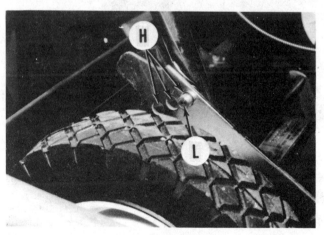

Fig. 66—The handle should be set at a comfortable height. One type of adjustment uses lugs (L) that fit into holes (H).

ness, balance and straightness. Mower vibration may be caused by a bent or unbalanced blade. Unbalanced blades can be balanced, but a bent blade must be replaced. Notice if mower cuts poorly or irregularly which indicates blade damage. Check for poor grass discharge which would indicate lift on blade is not functioning properly.

CAUTION: Ignition wire to spark plug should be disconnected and grounded (Fig. 71) before performing any inspection or servicing of the blade or underside of mower.

Raise the mower and check the blade for firm mounting (Fig. 72). Several different methods for mounting the blade have been used, but none should permit the blade to slip when checking by hand.

Remove blade from mower and clean thoroughly with a wire brush. Inspect cutting and lift areas of blade. Damaged cutting edges can usually be sharpened following procedure in SHARPENING section. Lift areas must not be misshaped or broken. Damaged lift areas affect cutting and blade's ability to discharge grass. Check blade straightness (Fig. 73). Inspect blade mounting hole

Cutting Height	Grass Type
½ to 1 inch	Bermuda, Zoysia
1 to 2 inches	Red fescue, Meadow fescue, Kentucky bluegrass Perennial ryegrass
1 ½ to 3 inches	Bahia grass, Tall fescue, St. Augustine

Note that the preceding list of grasses is only a general guide to some of the commonly grown grasses in home lawn. Special strains of these grasses may re-

quire a different cutting height than shown.

Adjustment is usually accompanied by moving the wheels. Some mowers have wheels that are quickly adjusted by moving the lever (L—Fig. 69) from one notch (N) to another. Others provide several holes (H—Fig. 70) for mounting wheels at different heights. The blade will usually be parallel with the ground if all of the wheels are adjusted alike.

BLADE INSPECTION. Mower blade should be inspected for sharp-

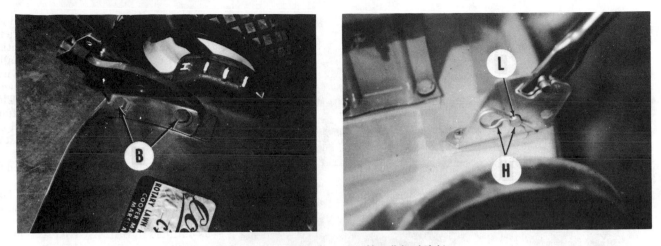

Fig. 67—Handlebar mounting brackets are sometimes slotted to permit adjustment of handlebar height.

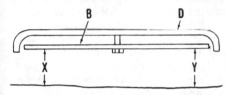

Fig. 68—Blade height (X) should be set correctly for type of grass being cut. Blade is at (B) and mower deck at (D).

Fig. 70—View showing deck with several wheel attachments holes (H) for adjusting blade height.

or holes. Holes should not be deformed as blade can be installed off-center and cause vibration. Inspect retaining bolts or pins. Worn bolts or pins must be replaced with new bolts or pins. Inspect mounting holes in blade and install new blade if holes are worn or damaged.

Visually inspect blade for cracks around mounting hole (or holes) and at the ends. Hang blade by mounting holes and strike blade with another metal object. A solid blade free of cracks will ring like a bell while a cracked blade will emit a dull sound. Discard cracked blades.

SHARPENING. Blade sharpening can be accomplished using a file or grinder. Satisfactory results are ob-

tained using a file, but much more time is required as opposed to using a power tool, especially if the blade is nicked severely. Blade should be removed from mower to properly sharpen blade.

A blade needs to be sharp only at the outer end. A 21-inch blade rotating at 3000 rpm will cut grass with only the outer ½-inch (13 mm) of each blade end when the mower is traveling at normal walking speed. Refer to Fig. 74. A mower with a 21-inch blade rotating at 3000 rpm would have to travel at 18 miles-per-hour if the cutting edges are not to

Fig. 71—The purpose of disconnecting the spark plug high tension lead is to keep the engine from accidentally starting. The high voltage can sometimes jump a small gap shown at right allowing the engine to start. Firmly grounding the lead to cylinder head is much safer.

Fig. 69—Quick blade height adjustment is often accomplished by locating wheel adjustment levers (L) in notches (N).

overlap. It is not necessary, therefore, to sharpen more than the outer three inches of the cutting edge.

Rotary mower blades are usually sharpened to an angle of 30° as shown in Fig. 75. This is an ideal situation which cannot always be attained on a well used or nicked blade without a great deal of sharpening.

Blades wear on the underside which forms a curve into the cutting edge as shown at (A). If the blade is not worn excessively, the desired 30° edge angle and flat underside can be obtained without excessive grinding. If the blade is well worn, be sure to face off the underside as well as sharpening the top face.

quired to remove the gouge as well as grind down the opposite cutting edge to make the two edges symmetrical. Satisfactory cutting performance can usually be obtained by smoothing and removing burrs from the gouge and then sharpening remainder of cutting edge. The blade will cut with no discernible difference and the size of the gouge will be reduced after each sharpening until it is removed.

Cutting edges should be sharpened to be as symmetrical as possible to aid blade balancing. Cutting edge should be sharpened to retain original shape. After sharpening, blade must be balanced as outlined in BALANCING section.

BALANCING. An unbalanced blade can cause severe vibration problems. Blades which are out of balance by only an ounce at one end will create objectionable vibration in a mower.

The most popular blade balancer is the cone type shown in Fig. 76. Before balancing blade, be sure blade is clean and properly sharpened. Place blade on cone with cone located in the center mounting hole of the blade. Blade should be balanced in all directions; end to end and front to back. Heavy parts of blade will be lower than remainder of blade and the heavy part must have metal removed to balance blade. Resharpen cutting edges if necessary for balance. Do not grind away lift edges.

After completing balancing operation, mount blade on mower and tighten mounting bolts. Measure distance from end of mower blade to mower deck, then rotate blade and measure distance from same point on mower deck to other end of blade. For correct dynamic blade balance, distances should be as close as possible.

BLADE TRACKING AND HEIGHT. The rotary blade should cut on a plane parallel to the level mower deck. If the blade or engine crankshaft is bent, the blade will cut unevenly. To check blade track, measure the distance from the end of the blade to the bottom of the mower deck. Rotate the blade and

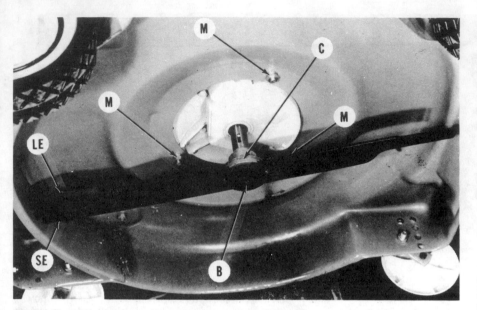

Fig. 72—The cutting blade must be installed securely and correctly.

B. Blade attaching screw
C. Blade clutch
LE. Lift edge of blade (UP)
M. Engine mounting bolts
SE. Sharp cutting edge (down)

Fig. 73—Be sure blade is straight and not bent. The blade may be shaped as shown in "A," but obviously bent blades "B" should be discarded.

½ in. (13 mm)

Fig. 74—At normal walking speeds only the outside edge of a sharp blade is used to cut the grass. A dull blade may never actually cut the grass but only beat it throughout the length of the blade.

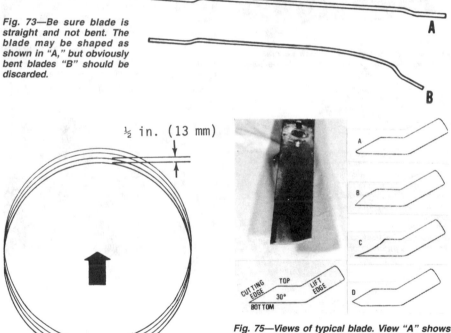

Fig. 75—Views of typical blade. View "A" shows typical cross section of dull blade. View "B" is incorrect because of sharpening at too much angle. View "C" is sharpened at less than 30° angle. View "D" shows incorrect method of sharpening caused by grinding lower edge of blade.

Small nicks to the cutting edge can be removed in the course of normal sharpening, but deep indentations may cause sharpening problems. Most large gouges do not affect cutting operation as they are located towards the center of the blade and not in the outer ½-inch (13 mm) of the blade which does the cutting. A great deal of grinding is re-

Fig. 76—View of a commonly used cone type balancer. Alignment of the two parts of cone indicate balanced blade. The unit shown is available from Frederick Mfg. Co., Inc., 1400 Agnes St., Kansas City, MO. 64127.

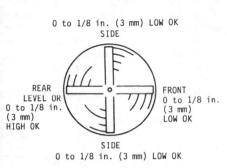

Fig. 77—The blade should be nearly level with the ground. A blade that is ⅛ inch (3 mm) higher in rear is permissible, but blade should never be lower in rear than in front.

measure the distance from the same point on the mower deck to the other end of the blade. Difference in distances should not vary more than $\frac{1}{16}$ inch (1.5 mm) on mowers with straight crankshafts. Check blade for straightness and replace if bent. Blade run-out on a mower with an engine crankshaft which was bent and straightened may exceed $\frac{1}{16}$ inch (1.5 mm) and cutting performance is the only criteria which may be used.

Blade height refers to the position of the blade in the mower deck. The rotary mower blade must always operate within the mower deck and never extend below the deck. Blade height should be the same within ⅛ inch (3 mm) at all points around the mower deck (Fig. 77). This can be measured from the mower deck to the blade end.

Blade height is adjusted by placing washers of required thickness between the engine mounting bosses and the mower deck. Engine mounts bolts must be removed to install or remove washers.

REEL MOWER

The cutting blades (1—Fig. 78) must be kept sharp and the bed knife (2), sometimes called cutter bar, should be properly adjusted. When properly adjusted, the reel should rotate easily with light finger pressure and the reel blades should just touch the bed knife, throughout their entire length. On some models, the reel is moved to adjust the cutting surface, on other mowers the bed knife can be moved to just contact the reel blades. Accurate adjustments is impossible if the mower frame is loose. Be sure frame is firmly assembled and all screws are tight before attempting to adjust reel to bed knife. If adjusted too tight, the cutting surfaces of blades and bed knife will be quickly worn and damaged.

Accurate sharpening requires special equipment to assure that each blade on the reel is equidistant from reel axis throughout the entire length of the blade and that the cutting edge is slightly higher than the trailing edge.

The cutting edge of the bed knife will be rippled if operated with reel adjusted too tight.

Check the cutting surface of each blade and the bed knife. The reel should turn easily by hand with the blades lightly contacting the bed knife.

Small nicks can be removed by carefully using a fine file or stone, but special equipment is necessary for most accurate sharpening. Be sure that drive chains, belts and clutches are correctly adjusted.

Check all assembly and mounting screws to be sure that none are missing or loose. Correct alignment and blade to bed knife adjustment necessitate rigid assembly of the mower frame.

Nicks and other damage to the cutting surfaces of the blades and bed knife can be caused by improper adjustment or some other cause, but are most often the result of trying to mow wire, rocks, sticks, etc. Much damage can be prevented by thoroughly checking the lawn area before mowing and removing debris such as rocks, wire, etc., before beginning to mow.

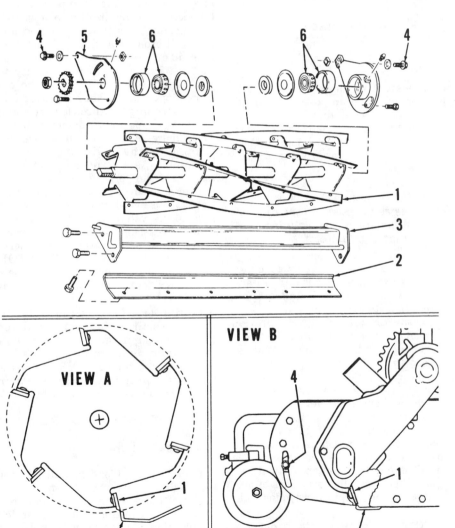

Fig. 78—Views of grass cutting parts of typical reel mower. Adjustment of the mower shown is accomplished by moving the reel after loosening screws (4) so that blades (1) contact bed knife (2) throughout entire length. View "A" shows angle of bed knife and blade cutting surfaces. Partially cut away view "B" shows adjustment of a typical King O'Lawn reel type mower.

1. Reel blade	3. Bed bar	5. Reel bearing holder
2. Bed knife	4. Adjustment screw	6. Reel bearings

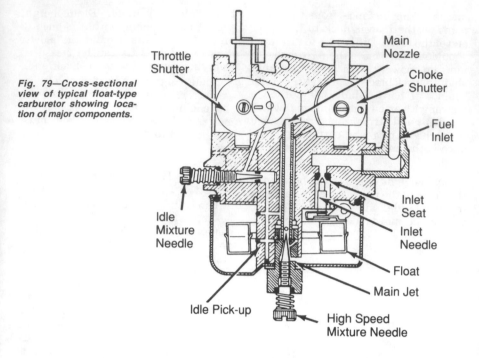

Fig. 79—Cross-sectional view of typical float-type carburetor showing location of major components.

Labels: Throttle Shutter, Main Nozzle, Choke Shutter, Fuel Inlet, Idle Mixture Needle, Inlet Seat, Inlet Needle, Float, Main Jet, Idle Pick-up, High Speed Mixture Needle

Lubricate mower with grease injected into fittings approximately every 16 hours of operation. Chains, wheels and other bushing, not lubricated by grease should be lubricated by coating with SAE 20 oil every eight hours of operation. All suggested lubrication intervals should be reduced if operated in dusty or dirty conditions and should never be left unattended longer than one year even if operated less than recommended times. Dirt accelerates wear and unit should be kept clean at all times. Be especially careful not to allow any oil on "V" belt drives or clutches.

CARBURETOR SERVICE

GENERAL CARBURETOR SERVICE

The bulk of carburetor service consists of cleaning, inspection and adjustment. After considerable service it may become necessary to overhaul the carburetor and renew worn parts to retore origingal operating efficiency. Although carburetor condition affects engine operating economy and power, ignition and engine compression must also be considered to determine and correct causes of poor performance.

Before dismantling carburetor for cleaning or overhaul, clean all external surfaces and remove accumulated dirt and grease. Refer to appropriate engine repair section for carburetor exploded

or cross-sectional views. Dismantle carburetor and note any discrepancies to assure correction during overhaul. Thoroughtly clean all parts and inspect for damage or wear. Wash jets and passages and blow clear with clean, dry, compressed air.

NOTE: Do not use a drill or wire to clean jets as the possible enlargement of calibrated holes will disturb operating balance of carburetor.

The measurement of jets to determine the extent of wear is difficult and new parts are usually installed to assure satisfactory results.

Carburetor manufacturers provide for many of their models an assortment of gaskets and other parts usually needed to do a correct job of cleaning and overhaul. These assortments are usually cataloged as Gasket Kits and Overhaul Kits respectively.

On float type carburetors, inspect float pin and needle valve for wear and renew if necessary. Check metal floats for leaks and where a dual type float is installed, check alignment of float sections. Check cork floats for loss of protective coating and absorption for fuel.

NOTE: Do not attempt to recoat cork floats with shellac or varnish or resolder leaky metal floats. Renew part if defective.

Check the fit of throttle and choke valve shafts. Excessive clearance will cause improper valve plate seating and

will permit dust or grit to be drawn into the engine. Air leaks at throttle shaft bores due to wear will upset carburetor calibration and contribute to uneven engine operation. Rebush valve shaft holes where necessary and renew dust seals. If rebushing is not possible, renew the body part supporting the shaft. Inspect throttle and choke valve plates for proper installation and condition.

Power or idle adjustment needles must not be worn or grooved. Check condition of needle seal packing or "O" ring and renew packing or "O" ring if necessary.

Reinstall or renew jets, using correct size listed for specific model. Adjust power and idle settings as described for specific carburetors in engine service section of this manual.

It is important that the carburetor bore at the idle discharge ports and in the vicinity of the throttle valve be free of deposits. A partially restricted idle port will produce a "flat spot" between idle and mid-range rpm. This is because the restriction makes it necessary to open the throttle wider than the designed opening to obtain proper idle speed. Opening the throttle wider than the design specified amount will uncover more of the port than was intended in the calibration of the carburetor. As a result an insufficient amount of the port will be available as a reserve to cover the transition period (idle to the mod-range rpm) when the high speed system begins to function.

When reassembling float-type carburetors, be sure float position is properly adjusted. Refer to CARBURETOR paragraph in appropriate engine repair section for float level adjustment specifications.

Setting or adjusting the metering control lever (metering diaphragm lever height) on diaphragm-type carburetors necessitates disassembly of the carburetor. Refer to the CARBURETOR section in appropriate engine repair section for adjusting the lever height.

TROUBLESHOOTING

Float-type Carburetor

Refer to Fig. 79 for schematic view of typical float-type carburetor showing location of parts. Normally encountered difficulties resulting from carburetor malfunction, along with possible causes of difficulty for float-type carburetors are listed below.

ENGINE WILL NOT START OR HARD TO START. Could be caused by: (1) incorrect idle mixture screw adjustment, (2) restricted or plugged fuel filter

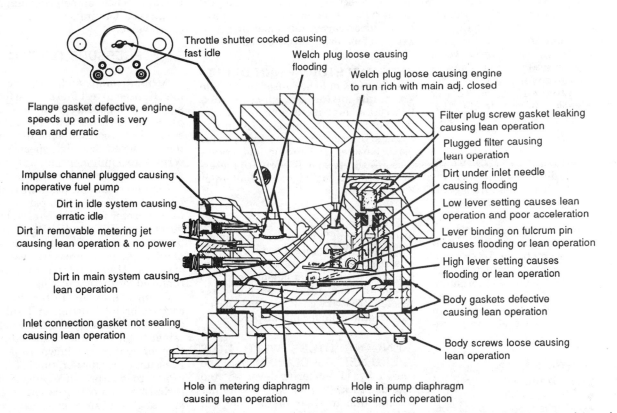

Fig. 80—Schematic cross-sectional view of typical diaphragm-type carburetor illustrating possible causes of malfunction. Refer to appropriate engine repair section for adjustment information and for exploded and/or cross-sectional view of actual carburetors used.

or fuel line, (3) throttle shaft worn, (4) choke shaft worn or not functioning properly, (5) fuel inlet needle valve stuck closed, (6) damaged or worn float or hinge pin, (7) improper float height setting, (8) float chamber atmospheric vent hole restricted or plugged, (9) low speed fuel passages restricted or plugged.

CARBURETOR FLOODS. Could be caused by: (1) Choke not opening fully, (2) dirt or foreign particles preventing inlet fuel needle from seating, (3) damaged or worn fuel inlet needle and/or seat preventing proper seating of needle, (4) damaged or worn float or hinge pin, (5) improper float height setting, (6) restricted or plugged float chamber atmospheric vent hole, (7) Welch plug in fuel chamber is loose.

ENGINE RUNS LEAN. Could be caused by: (1) fuel tank vent plugged, (2) restricted fuel filter or fuel line, (3) high speed fuel passages restricted, (4) improper float height setting, (5) high speed mixture screw incorrectly adjusted, (7) leaky gaskets between carburetor and cylinder intake port.

ENGINE WILL NOT ACCELERATE SMOOTHLY. Could be caused by:

(1) idle or main fuel mixture screws set to lean, (2) restricted low speed air bleed or fuel passages, (3) restricted tank vent, fuel filter or fuel line, (4) plugged air filter.

ENGINE STOPS WHEN DECELERATING. Could be caused by: (1) idle speed, idle mixture or high speed mixture screws incorrectly adjusted, (2) air leaks between carburetor and crankcase, (3) throttle shaft worn, (4) fuel inlet needle binding.

ENGINE WILL NOT IDLE. Could be cause by: (1) damaged or incorrect adjustment of idle fuel and/or idle speed screws, (2) idle discharge or air mixture ports plugged, (3) throttle and/or choke shaft worn, (4) fuel tank vent, filter or fuel line restricted, (5) damaged or worn float or hinge pin, (6) improper float height setting.

ENGINE IDLES WITH LOW SPEED NEEDLE CLOSED. Could be caused by: (1) improper float height setting, (2) fuel inlet needle not seating due to wear or damage.

ENGINE RUNS RICH. Could be caused by: (1) plugged air filter, (2) low

speed or high speed mixture screws incorrectly adjusted or damaged, (3) improper float height setting, (4) damaged or worn float or hinge pin, (5) choke not open fully, (6) fuel inlet needle valve leaking, (7) Welch plug leaking, (8) restricted or plugged air bleed passage.

ENGINE HAS LOW POWER UNDER LOAD. Could be caused by: (1) main mixture screw incorrectly adjusted, (2) plugged fuel tank vent, filter or fuel line, (3) leaky carburetor mounting gasket (4) plugged air filter, (5) throttle shaft worn, (6) air leaks between carburetor and intake manifold, (7) improper float height setting, (8) damaged or worn float or hinge pin, (9) high speed fuel passages restricted.

Diaphragm-type Carburetor

Refer to Fig. 80 for schematic view of typical diaphragm carburetor showing location of parts. Normally encountered difficulties resulting from carburetor malfunction, along with possible causes of difficulty, for diaphragm-type carburetors are listed below.

ENGINE WILL NOT START OR HARD TO START. Could be caused by: (1) incorrect idle mixture screw adjustment, (2) restricted or plugged fuel filter or fuel line, (3) throttle shaft worn, (4) choke shaft worn or not functioning properly, (5) fuel inlet needle valve stuck closed, (6) metering lever worn, bent, binding, or set too low, (7) metering diaphragm cover vent hole restricted or plugged, (8) metering diaphragm, gasket or cover leaking, (9) low speed fuel passages restricted or plugged.

CARBURETOR FLOODS. Could be caused by: (1) dirt or foreign particles preventing inlet fuel needle from seating, (2) damaged or worn fuel inlet needle and/or seat preventing proper seating of needle, (3) diaphragm lever spring not seated correctly on diaphragm lever, (4) metering lever binding or set too high, (5) hole in pump diaphragm, (6) Welch plug in fuel chamber is loose. Also, when fuel tank is located above carburetor, flooding can be caused by leaking fuel pump diaphragm.

ENGINE RUNS LEAN. Could be caused by: (1) fuel tank vent plugged, (2) restricted fuel filter or fuel line, (3) high speed fuel passages restricted, (4) hole in fuel metering diaphragm, (5) metering lever worn, binding, distorted or set too low, (6) high speed mixture screw incorrectly adjusted, (7) leak in pulse passage, (8) leaky gaskets between carburetor and cylinder intake port. Also, check for leaking crankshaft seals, porous or cracked crankcase or other cause for air leak into crankcase.

ENGINE WILL NOT ACCELERATE SMOOTHLY. Could be caused by: (1) idle or main fuel mixture screws set too lean on models without accelerating pump, (2) inoperative accelerating pump, on carburetors so equipped, due to plugged channel, leaking diaphragm, stuck piston, etc., (3) restricted low speed fuel passage, (4) restricted tank vent, fuel filter or fuel line, (5) plugged air filter, (6) restricted vent hole in metering cover, (7) restricted pulse chan-

nel, (8) defective pump diaphragm, (9) metering lever set too low, (10) defective manifold or carburetor mounting gaskets, (11) metering lever set too low.

ENGINE STOPS WHEN DECELERATING. Could be caused by: (1) idle speed, idle mixture or high speed mixture screws incorrectly adjusted, (2) defective pump diaphragm, (3) pulse passage leaking or restricted, (4) air leaks between carburetor and crankcase, (5) throttle shaft worn, (6) metering lever set too high, (7) fuel inlet needle binding.

ENGINE WILL NOT IDLE. Could be caused by: (1) incorrect adjustment of idle fuel and/or idle speed screws, (2) idle discharge or air mixture ports plugged, (3) fuel channel plugged, (4) fuel tank vent, filter or fuel line restricted, (5) leaky gaskets between carburetor and cylinder intake ports.

ENGINE IDLES WITH LOW SPEED NEEDLE CLOSED. Could be caused by: (1) metering lever set too high or stuck, (2) fuel inlet needle not seating due to wear or damage, (3) Welch plug covering idle ports not sealing properly.

ENGINE RUNS RICH. Could be caused by: (1) plugged air filter, (2) low speed or high speed mixture screws incorrectly adjusted or damaged, (3) metering lever worn, binding, distorted or set too high, (4) fuel pump diaphragm defective, (5) fuel inlet needle valve leaking, (6) Welch plug leaking, (7) faulty governor valve (if so equipped).

ENGINE HAS LOW POWER UNDER LOAD. Could be caused by: (1) main mixture screw incorrectly adjusted, (2) plugged fuel tank vent, filter or fuel line, (3) pulse channel leaking or restricted, (4) defective pump diaphragm, (5) plugged air filter, (6) air leaks between carburetor and crankcase, (7) metering lever distorted or set

too low, (8) hole in metering diaphragm or gasket leaking, (9) faulty nozzle check valve.

PRESSURE TESTING

A hand pump and pressure gauge may be used to test fuel system for leakage when diagnosing problems with diaphragm carburetors. With engine stopped and cooled, first adjust carburetor low speed and high speed mixture screws to equipment manufacturer's recommended initial settings.

Connect a suitable pressure tester capable of measuring 0-10 psi (0-70 kPa) to carburetor fuel inlet. Pressurize carburetor until 7 psi (48 kPa) is read on pressure gauge. Pressure should remain constant. If pressure reading decreases, then carburetor must be removed for further testing.

Connect pressure tester directly to carburetor inlet fitting and submerge carburetor assembly into a suitable container filled with a nonflammable solution or water as shown in Fig. 81. Pressurize carburetor until 7 psi (48 kPa) is read on pressure gauge. Observe carburetor and note location of leaking air bubbles. If air bubbles escape from around jet needles or venturi, then inlet needle or metering mechanism is defective. If air bubbles escape at impulse opening, then pump diaphragm is defective. If air bubbles escape from around fuel pump cover, then cover gasket or pump diaphragm is defective.

To check inlet needle and metering mechanism, first rotate low and high speed mixture screws inward until lightly seated. Pressurize system until 7 psi (48 kPa) is read on pressure gauge.

If pressure reading does not remain constant, inlet needle is leaking. If pressure remains constant, depress metering diaphragm with a suitable length and thickness of wire through the vent hole in metering diaphragm cover. This will lift inlet needle off its seat and pressurize the metering chamber. A slight drop in pressure reading should be noted as metering chamber becomes pressurized. If no drop in pressure reading is noted, the inlet needle is sticking. If pressure does not hold after a slight drop, a defective metering mechanism or leaking high or low speed Welch plugs is indicated.

To determine which component is leaking, submerge carburetor as previously outlined. Pressurize carburetor until 7 psi (48 kPa) is read on pressure gauge, then depress metering diaphragm as previously outlined. If pressure reading does not drop off or drops off very slowly, a restriction is indicated. To test high speed circuit, adjust high

Fig. 81—Submerge carburetor in a suitable container filled with solvent or water and pressure test as outlined in text.

speed mixture screw to recommended initial setting and turn low speed mixture screw inward until lightly seated. Pressurize carburetor and depress metering diaphragm as previously outlined and note pressure gauge. If pressure reading does not drop off or drops off very slowly, a restriction is indicated.

Refer to specific carburetor service section and repair defect or renew defective component as needed.

ADJUSTMENT

Initial setting for the mixture adjusting needles is listed in the specific engine section of this manual. Make final carburetor adjustment with engine warm and running. Make certain that engine air filter is clean before performing final adjustment, as a restricted air intake will affect the carburetor settings.

Adjust idle speed screw so that engine is idling at speed specified by equipment manufacturer. Adjust idle fuel mixture needle for best engine idle performance, keeping the mixture as rich as possible (turn needle out to enrich mixture). If necessary, readjust idle speed screw. To adjust main fuel needle, operate engine at wide-open throttle and find the rich and lean drop-off points, and set the mixture between them. Main fuel needle may also be adjusted while engine is under load to obtain optimum performance. Do not operate engine with high speed mixture set too lean as engine damage may occur due to overheating.

If idle mixture is too lean and cannot be properly adjusted, consider the possibility of plugged idle fuel passages, expansion plug for main fuel check valve loose or missing, main fuel check valve not seating, improperly adjusted inlet control lever, leaking metering diaphragm or malfunctioning fuel pump.

If idle mixture is too rich, check idle mixture screw and its seat in carburetor body for damage. Check causes for carburetor flooding.

If high speed mixture is too lean and cannot be properly adjusted, check for dirt or plugging in main fuel passages, improperly adjusted metering lever, malfunctioning metering diaphragm or main fuel check valve. Also check for damaged or missing packing for high speed mixture screw and for malfunctioning fuel pump. If high speed mixture is too rich, check high speed mixture screw and its seat for damage. Check for improperly adjusted metering lever or faulty fuel inlet needle valve. Check for faulty governor valve if carburetor is so equipped.

ENGINE SERVICE

DISASSEMBLY AND ASSEMBLY

Special techniques must be developed in repair of engines of aluminum alloy or magnesium alloy construction.

Soft threads in aluminum or magnesium casting are often damaged by carelessness in over tightening fasteners or in attempting to loosen or remove seized fasteners. Manufacturer's recommended torque values for tightening screw fasteners should be followed closely.

NOTE: If damaged threads are encountered, refer to following paragraph, "REPAIRING DAMAGED THREADS."

A given amount of heat applied to aluminum or magnesium will cause it to expand a greater amount than will steel under similar conditions. Because of the different expansion characteristics, heat is usually recommended for easy installation of bearings, pins, etc., in aluminum or magnesium castings.

Sometimes, heat can be used to free parts that are seized or where an interference fit is used. Heat, therefore, becomes a service tool and the application of heat is one of the required service techniques. An open flame is not usually advised because it destroys the paint and other protective coatings and because a uniform and controlled temperature with open flame is difficult to obtain. Methods commonly used are heating in oil or water, with a heat lamp, electric hot plate, or in an oven or kiln.

The use of water or oil gives a fairly accurate temperature control but is somewhat limited as to the size and type of part that can be handled.

Thermal crayons are available which can be used to determine the temperature of a heated part. These crayons melt when the part reaches a specified temperature, and a number of crayons for different temperatures are available. Temperature indicating crayons are usually available at welding equipment supply houses.

The crankcase and combustion chambers of a two-stroke cycle engine must be sealed against pressure and vacuum. To assure a perfect seal, nicks, scratches and warpage are to be avoided. Slight imperfections can be removed by using a fine-grit sandpaper. Flat surfaces can be lapped by using a surface plate or a smooth piece of plate glass, and a sheet

of 120-grit sandpaper or lapping compound. Use a figure-eight motion with minimum pressure, and remove only enough metal to eliminate the imperfection. Bearing clearances, if any, must not be lessened by removing metal from the joint.

Use only the specified gaskets when reassembling, and use an approved gasket cement or sealing compound unless the contrary is stated. Seal all exposed threads and repaint or retouch with an approved paint.

REPAIRING DAMAGED THREADS

Fastener threads can be damaged for a variety of reasons, and in some cases, restoring the threads is required.

NOTE: Be sure to identify the thread size and type (US or metric) before attempting to restore the threads. The only positive method of identification is to use a screw pitch gauge or known fastener.

Often the threads can be cleaned by running a tap (for internal threads) or die (for external threads) through the threads. To clean or repair spark plug threads, a spark plug tap or "thread chaser" can be used.

If an internal thread is damaged, it may be necessary to install a thread repair insert. Thread repair inserts are available in a wide variety of US and metric thread sizes at auto supply stores and some hardware stores. Note that a specific size drill bit must be used, which must be purchased separately. To install a typical thread repair insert, proceed as follows:

Drill out the old threads using the drill bit recommended for the thread size being repaired. Be sure the hole is straight and the centerline of the hole is not moved while drilling. Cut new threads in the hole using the tap provided in the kit. This is a special tap that cuts threads to fit the outer threads on the thread repair insert. Turn the thread repair insert into the hole using the special tool until the top of the insert is a quarter to one-half turn below the surface. Snap off the insert tang by pushing down on the tang; don't attempt to twist off the tang.

VALVE SERVICE FUNDAMENTALS

When overhauling engines, obtaining proper valve sealing is of primary importance. The following paragraphs cover fundamentals of servicing intake

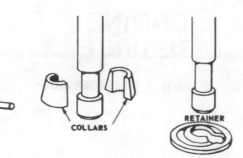

Fig. 82—Drawing showing three types of valve spring keepers used.

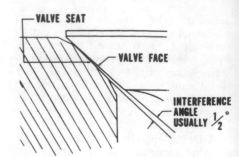

Fig. 84—Drawing showing line contact of valve face with valve seat when valve face is ground at smaller angle than valve seat; this is specified on some engines.

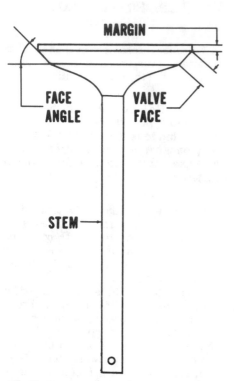

Fig. 83—Drawing showing typical four-stroke cycle engine valve. Face angle is usually 30° or 45°. On some engines, valve face is ground to an angle of ½ or 1° less than seat angle.

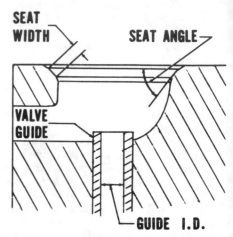

Fig. 85—Cross-sectional drawing of typical valve seat and valve guide as used on small engines. Valve guide may be an insert pressed into cylinder block or an integral part of cylinder block. On some models so constructed, valve guide ID may be reamed out and a valve with oversize stem installed. On other models, a service guide may be installed after counter-boring cylinder block.

will result in increased wear and/or damage.

REMOVING AND INSTALLING VALVES. A valve spring compressor is a valuable aid in removing and installing the engine valves. This tool is used to hold spring compressed while removing or installing pin, collars or retainer from valve stem. Refer to Fig. 82 for illustrations of some of the different methods of retaining valve spring to valve stem.

VALVE REFACING. If valve face (Fig. 83) is slightly worn, burned or pitted, valve can usually be refaced providing proper equipment is available. Many shops will usually renew valves, however, rather than invest in somewhat costly valve refacing tools.

Before attempting to reface a valve, refer to specifications in appropriate engine repair section for valve face angle.

On some engines, manufacturer recommends grinding the valve face to an angle of ½ to 1 degree less than that of the valve seat. See Fig. 84. Also, nominal valve face angle may be either 30° or 45°.

After valve is refaced, measure thickness of valve "margin" (Fig. 83). If margin is less than manufacturer's minimum specification, or is less than one-half the margin of a new valve, renew the valve. Valves having excessive material removed in refacing operation will not give satisfactory service.

When refacing or renewing a valve, the seat should also be reconditioned. Note that valve seat is renewable on some engines. Then, the valve should be "lapped in" to its seat using a fine valve grinding compound. Refer to following paragraph "REFACING OR RENEWING VALVE SEATS."

REFACING OR RENEWING VALVE SEATS. Some engines have the valve seat machined directly in the cylinder block casting. The seat can be reconditioned by using a correct angle seat grinding stone or valve seat cutter. When reconditioning valve seat, care should be taken that only enough mate-

and exhaust valves, valve seats and valve guides.

VALVE CLEARANCE SETTING. Specific settings and procedures for adjusting clearances between valve stem end and tappet or rocker arm are listed in the appropriate individual sections. Valve clearance should not be changed from the clearances listed. When the valves are closed, heat is transferred from the valve to the cylinder head, and valves may burn if valve clearance is set too tight. If the valve clearance is too loose, the engine will have decreased power.

The "rattle" usually accompanying too much valve clearance is caused by metal parts of the valve system hitting. Althought the noise is sometimes not objectionable, the constant pounding

rial is removed to provide a good seating area on valve contact surface. The width of seat should then be measured (Fig. 85) and if width exceeds manufacturer's maximum specifications, seat should be narrowed by using a stone or cutter with an angle 15° greater than or less than seat angle.

When narrowing seat, coat seat lightly with Prussian blue and check where seat contacts valve face by inserting valve in guide and rotating valve lightly against seat. Seat should contact approximately the center of valve face. By using only the narrow angle stone or cutter, seat contact will be moved toward outer edge of valve face.

Some engines have renewable valve seats. The seats are retained in cylinder block counterbore by interference fit; that is, outside diameter of seat is slightly larger than counterbore in block. Refer to appropriate engine repair section in this manual for recommended method of removing old seat and install new seat. Refer to Fig. 86 for

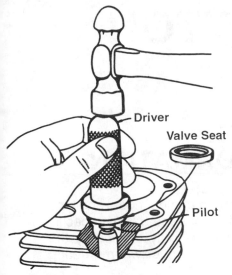

Fig. 86—View showing one method used to install valve seat insert. Refer to appropriate engine repair section for manufacturer's recommended method.

one method of installing new valve seats.

It sometimes occurs that a valve seat will become loose in counterbore, especially on engines with aluminum cylinder block.

Some manufacturers provide oversize valve seat inserts (insert OD larger than standard part) so that if standard size insert fits loosely, counterbore can be cut oversize and a new insert be tightly installed. After installing valve seat insert in engines of aluminum construction, metal around seat should be peened at three equally spaced locations around outer diameter of seat. See Fig. 87.

Where a loose insert is encountered and an oversize insert is not available, loose insert can usually be tightened by center-puching cylinder block material at three equally spaced points around insert, then peening completely around insert as shown in Fig. 87.

INSTALLING OVERSIZE PISTON AND RINGS

Some engine manufacturers have oversize piston and rings sets available for use in repairing engines in which cylinder bore is excessively worn and standard size piston and rings cannot be used. If care and approved procedure are used in oversizing cylinder bore, in-stallation of an oversize piston and ring set should result in a highly satisfactory overhaul.

Where oversize piston and rings are available, it will be noted in appropriate engine repair section of the manual. Also, the standard bore diameter will be given. Before attempting to rebore or hone the cylinder to oversize, carefully measure the cylinder bore and examine for damage. It may be possible cylinder is excessively worn or damaged and bor-ing or honing to larger oversize will not clean up the cylinder surface.

Cylinder bore may be oversized by using either a boring bar or a hone; however, if a boring bar is used, it is recommended that cylinder bore be fin-ished with a hone. Refer to Fig. 88 for illustration showing desired cross-hatch pattern in cylinder that should be obtained when honing cylinder.

After honing is completed, clean cyl-inder bore thoroughly with warm soapy water, dry and lubricate with engine oil.

TWO-STROKE ENGINE CRANKCASE PRESSURE TEST

Pressure testing the crankcase is an important part of troubleshooting and repair of two-stroke cycle engines that is often overlooked. An improperly sealed crankcase allows supplementary air to enter the engine and upsets the fuel:air mixture. This can cause the en-gine to be hard to start, run rough, have low power and overheat.

To test crankcase for leakage, a suit-able hand pump and pressure gauge must be connected to the crankcase as follows: Remove muffler and carburetor. Fabricate a seal using gasket paper to cover the exhaust port, then reinstall muffler. Use either of the following methods to connect a hand pump and pressure gauge to crankcase. Fabricate an adapter plate and install in place of the carburetor to cover and seal the intake manifold port. The adapter plate must have a nipple to connect pressure hose of tester.

An alternate method of testing is as follows: Fabricate a seal using gasket paper to cover the intake port and rein-stall carburetor. Connect a suitable hand pump and pressure gauge to car-buretor pulse line, or plug carburetor end of pulse line and install pressure tester in spark plug hole. If testing leak-age through spark plug hole, position

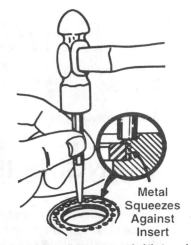

Fig. 87—It is usually recommended that on alumi-num block engines, metal be peened around valve seat insert after insert is installed.

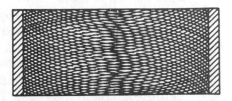

Fig. 88—A cross-hatch pattern as shown should be obtained when honing cylinder. Pattern is ob-tained by moving hone up and down cylinder bore as hone is being turned by slow speed electric drill.

piston at bottom dead center. If testing leakage through intake mainfold or pulse line, position piston at top dead center.

Apply pressure until gauge reads 7 psi (48 kPa) and close pump vent screw. Pressure should remain constant. If pressure drops more than 2 psi (14 kPa) in 30 seconds, leak must be located.

Crankcase seals may also be tested for a vacuum leak using a vacuum pump in place of pressure pump as outlined above. Actuate vacuum pump until gauge indicates vacuum of 7 psi (48 kPa). If vacuum reading remains con-stant or decreases no more than 2 psi (14 kPa), crankcase seals are in good condition. If seals fail to hold a vacuum, even if no pressure leak was indicated, they should be renewed.

If crankcase leakage is indicated, use a soap and water solution to check gas-kets, crankcase seals, pulse line and castings for leakage.

BRIGGS & STRATTON

**BRIGGS & STRATTON CORPORATION
P.O. Box 702
Milwaukee, Wisconsin 53201**

BRIGGS & STRATTON
ENGINE IDENTIFICATION INFORMATION

Before servicing the engine and ordering parts, the Briggs & Stratton engine model and type numbers must be determined. Although engines may be similar in appearance, specific differences that affect service specifications and part configuration are only defined by the model and type numbers. Although rarely required, provide the code number when ordering parts.

Engine identification numbers, including the model number, type number and code number, are located on the blower housing around the flywheel. The numbers are stamped in an identification plate or directly in the metal (Fig. BS1).

The engine model number identifies the basic engine family. Refer to the table on page 47 for a breakdown of Briggs & Stratton engine model numbers. As an example, an engine model number of 92502 would indicate that the engine has an approximate displacement of 9 cubic inches and the design series is "2". The engine is equipped with a vertical crankshaft, Vacu-Jet carburetor, plain main bearings and a rewind starter.

The type number specifies the parts configuration of the engine, as well as cosmetic details such as paint color and decals. The type number also determines governor speed settings depending on the engine's application, i.e., lawn mower, tractor, pump, generator, etc.

The code number provides information concerning the manufacturing of the engine. For instance, a code number of 87031051 indicates the engine was built in 1987, the third month of the year, on the 10th day of the month, in manufacturing plant "01".

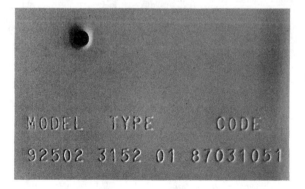

Fig. BS1—Engine model, type and code numbers are stamped in an identification plate or directly in metal of blower housing.

BRIGGS & STRATTON NUMERICAL MODEL NUMBER SYSTEM

CUBIC INCH DISPLACEMENT	BASIC DESIGN SERIES	CRANKSHAFT, CARBURETOR, GOVERNOR	BEARINGS, AUXILIARY DRIVE	TYPE OF STARTER
6, 8, 9, 10, 11, 12, 13, 16, 17, 19, 22, 23, 24, 25, 26, 28, 29, 30, 32, 35, 40 or 42	0 to 9 or A to Z	0 - Horizontal, Diaphragm	0 - Plain bearing starter	0 - Without
		1 - Horizontal, Vacu-Jet	1 - Flange mounted plain bearing	1 - Rope starter
		2 - Horizontal, Pulsa-Jet, Pneumatic	2 - Replaceable bearing	2 - Rewind starter
		3 - Horizontal, Flo-Jet, Mechanical	3 - Flange mounted ball bearing	3 - Electric 110 volt starter
		4 - Horizontal, Flo-Jet	4 - Pressure lube	4 - Belt drive 12 volt starter/gen.
		5 - Vertical, Vacu-Jet	5 - Gear reduction (6 to 1)	5 - Gear drive 12 volt starter
		6 -	6 - Gear (6 to 1) reduction, reverse rotation	6 - Alternator* only
		7 - Vertical, Flo-Jet	7 - Pressure lube	7 - Gear drive 12 volt with alternator
		8 -	8 - Auxiliary drive perpendicular to crankshaft	8 - Vertical-pull starter
		9 - Vertical, pulsa-Jet	9 - Auxiliary drive parallel to crankshaft	9 -

* Indicates Wind-up starter on early 60000, 80000 and 92000 engines.

Model 104772 is:

10	**4**	**7**	**7**	**2**
10 cubic inch displacement	Design series "4"	Vertical crankshaft, Flo-Jet carburetor**	Pressure lubrication	Rewind

** Some models with "7" at this location have a mechanical speed control governor while others are equipped with a pneumatic governor.

Fig. BS2—Explanation of engine model numerical code used by Briggs & Stratton to identify engine and components.

BRIGGS & STRATTON
2-STROKE ENGINES

Model	Bore	Stroke	Displacement	Power Rating
95700, 96700	60 mm	50 mm	141 cc	3.0 kW
	(2.36 in.)	(1.97 in.)	(8.6 cu. in.)	(4.0 hp)

NOTE: Metric fasteners are used throughout engine except threaded hole in pto end of crankshaft which is US threads.

ENGINE INFORMATION

All models are two-stroke, single-cylinder engines utilizing a third-port scavenging system. The engine may be equipped with a chrome plated or cast iron cylinder bore. Refer to table found on page 47 for an interpretation of Briggs & Stratton model numbers.

MAINTENANCE

LUBRICATION. Manufacturer recommends mixing a good quality BIA or NMMA 2-cycle oil certified for TC-WII service with regular or low-lead gasoline at a 50:1 ratio. Do not use an automotive (4-cycle) engine oil. The use of gasoline that contains alcohol is not recommended. However, if gasoline with alcohol is used, it must not contain more than 10 percent ethanol. Do not use gasoline containing methanol. If gasoline containing ethanol is used, it must be drained from the fuel system before storing the engine.

Always mix fuel in a separate container and add only mixed fuel to engine fuel tank. To assure thorough mixing of the oil and gasoline, fill the container partially with gasoline, then add the correct amount of oil per the chart shown in Fig. BS49. Shake the container to mix the oil and gasoline, then add remainder of gasoline and shake the container again.

AIR CLEANER. The air cleaner consists of a cover and a pleated paper cartridge, or a combination of a foam precleaner and a paper cartridge. Under normal operating conditions, filter elements should be cleaned and inspected after every 25 hours of engine operation, or after three months, whichever occurs first. Under extremely dusty conditions, service the filter more often. Tap filter gently to dislodge accumulated dirt. Filter may be washed using warm water and nonsudsing detergent directed from inside of filter to outside. DO NOT use petroleum-based cleaners or solvents to clean filter. DO NOT direct pressurized air towards filter. Let filter air dry thoroughly, then inspect filter and discard it if damaged or uncleanable. DO NOT apply oil to the paper cartridge or the foam precleaner. Clean the filter cover. Inspect and, if necessary, replace any defective gaskets.

FUEL FILTER. The fuel tank is equipped with a filter at the outlet. Check filter annually and periodically during operating season.

CARBURETOR. All models are equipped with the float type carburetor shown in Fig. BS50.

Adjustment. Idle speed at normal operating temperature should be 1200 rpm. Adjust idle speed by turning idle speed screw (IS). Idle mixture is controlled by idle jet (IJ) which is not adjustable. High speed mixture is controlled by main jet (MJ) which is not adjustable. Optional main jets are available for high altitude operation.

Overhaul. To disassemble carburetor, remove float bowl retaining screw (17—Fig. BS50), gasket (16) and float bowl (15). Remove float pin (13) by

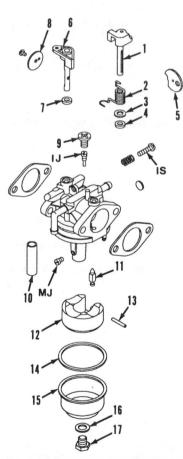

Fig. BS50—Exploded view of carburetor used on Models 95700 and 96700.

IJ. Idle mixture jet	8. Throttle plate
IS. Idle speed screw	9. Plug
MJ. Main jet	10. Vent tube
1. Choke shaft	11. Fuel inlet valve
2. Spring	12. Float
3. Plastic washer	13. Float hinge pin
4. Felt washer	14. Gasket
5. Choke plate	15. Fuel bowl
6. Throttle shaft	16. Gasket
7. Seal	17. Screw

50:1					
U.S.		Imperial		Metric	
Gasoline Gallons	2 Cycle Oil Ounces	Gasoline Gallons	2 Cycle Oil Ounces	Gasoline Liters	2 Cycle Oil Liters
1	2.5	1	3.2	4	.08
2	5	2	6.4	8	.16
5	13	5	16	20	.4

Fig. BS49—Chart for mixing gasoline and oil in the proper ratio.

Illustrations Courtesy of Briggs & Stratton Corp.

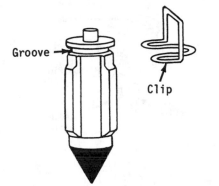

Fig. BS51—When installing fuel inlet valve, be sure round loop of clip fits around groove of valve and square portion of clip fits around float tab.

pushing against round end of pin towards the square end of pin. Remove float (12), fuel inlet needle (11) and clip. Remove throttle and choke shaft assemblies after unscrewing throttle and choke plate retaining screws.

Clean parts in a suitable carburetor cleaner. Do not use wire or drill bits to clean fuel passages as carburetor calibration may be affected if passages are enlarged. Inspect parts for wear or damage and renew as necessary.

When assembling the carburetor, note the following. Place a small drop of nonhardening sealant such as Permatex #2 or equivalent on throttle and choke plate retaining screws. The "U" bend end of choke return spring is on top and fits around choke shaft arm. Install throttle shaft seal with flat side towards carburetor body. Numbers on throttle plate must face out with throttle closed. Be sure inlet needle clip properly engages groove of inlet needle as shown in Fig. BS51 and square portion of clip fits around float tab. Float height is not adjustable.

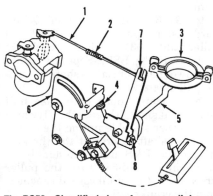

Fig. BS52—Simplified view of governor linkage.

1. Governor lever-to-carburetor rod
2. Spring
3. Flyweight assy.
4. Spring
5. Governor shaft
6. Speed lever
7. Governor lever
8. Clamp bolt

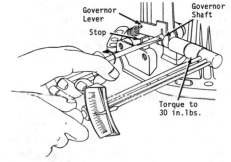

Fig. BS53—Follow procedure outlined in text for governor adjustment.

GOVERNOR. Models 95700 and 96700 are equipped with the centrifugal type governor shown in Fig. BS52.

Maximum engine speed is limited by changing spring (4) and varying location of the spring in holes in speed lever (6). Different tension governor springs are available which allows setting of governed speed from 2600 to 3600 rpm. Governor speed should be adjusted to desired speed specified by the equipment manufacturer.

If governor lever (7—Fig. BS52) is detached or moved on governor shaft, correct lever position on shaft must be established. Detach governor rod (1) from lever (7) and loosen clamp bolt (8). Use a screwdriver and turn slotted end of governor shaft counterclockwise as shown in Fig. BS53 as far as possible. Rotate the governor lever counterclockwise until it strikes the stop. Tighten clamp bolt to 3.4 N•m (30 in.-lbs.) torque.

SPARK PLUG. Recommended spark plug is Autolite 235 or 245 or Champion J19LM or RJ19LM. Spark plug electrode gap should be 0.76 mm (0.030 in.). Tighten spark plug to 18 N•m (160 in.-lbs.) torque.

CAUTION: Briggs & Stratton does not recommend using abrasive blasting to clean spark plugs as this may introduce some abrasive material into the engine which could cause extensive damage.

IGNITION SYSTEM. Models 95700 and 96700 are equipped with a Magnetron ignition system.

To check spark, remove spark plug and connect spark plug cable to B&S tester 19051, then ground remaining tester lead to engine. Spin engine at 350 rpm or more. If spark jumps the 4.2 mm (0.165 in.) tester gap, system is functioning properly.

To remove armature and Magnetron module, remove flywheel shroud and armature retaining screws. Disconnect stop switch wire from module. When installing armature be sure stop switch wire and grommet are properly installed in cylinder fins. Position armature so air gap between armature legs and flywheel surface is 0.20-0.40 mm (0.008-0.016 in.).

If armature coils are suspected faulty, note the following specifications. Primary coil resistance should be 0.2-0.4 ohms and secondary coil resistance should be 2500-3500 ohms.

COMPRESSION PRESSURE. Compression reading for engine should be 620-820 kPa (90-120 psi). A low compression reading could indicate worn cylinder bore, piston and/or rings. A higher than normal compression reading could indicate an excessive accumulation of carbon on the piston and combustion chamber.

FLYWHEEL BRAKE. The engine is equipped with a band type flywheel brake. The brake should stop the engine within three seconds when the operator releases mower safety control and the speed control is in high speed position. Stopping time can be checked using B&S tool 19255.

To check brake band adjustment, remove starter and properly ground spark plug lead to prevent accidental starting. Turn flywheel nut using a torque wrench with brake engaged. Rotating flywheel nut at a steady rate in a clockwise direction should require at least 5.1 N•m (45 in.-lbs.) torque. An insufficient torque reading may indicate misadjustment or damaged components. Renew brake band if friction material of band is damaged or less than 0.76 mm (0.030 in.) thick.

To adjust brake, unscrew brake cable clamp retaining screw so hole (H—Fig. BS54) is vacant. (If a pop rivet secures the cable clamp, do not remove rivet;

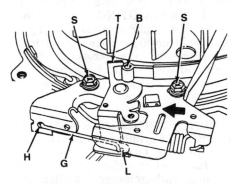

Fig. BS54—View of flywheel band brake and lever assembly.

B. Brake band
G. Gauge link
H. Hole
L. Hole
S. Retaining screws
T. Brake lever tang

gauge tool can be inserted through hole in pop rivet.) Loosen screws (S) securing brake control bracket. Place bayonet end of B&S gauge 19256 (G) in hole (L) of control lever (C). Push against control lever and insert opposite end of gauge (G) in hole (H), or in hole of pop rivet if used to secure cable. Apply pressure against control bracket in direction shown by arrow in Fig. BS54 until tension on gauge is just removed; then while holding pressure, tighten bracket screws (S) to 2.8-3.4 N•m (25-30 in.-lbs.) torque. As gauge is removed a slight friction should be felt and control lever should not move.

Brake band must be renewed if damaged or if friction material thickness is less than 0.76 mm (0.030 in.). Use tool 19229 to bend brake lever tang (T) away from band end (B—Fig. BS54). Release brake lever spring and remove brake band. Install new band with brake material side toward the flywheel. Reconnect brake spring, bend lever retaining tang over band end and adjust brake as outlined above.

REPAIRS

TIGHTENING TORQUES. Recommended tightening torque specifications are as follows:

Carburetor	5.6 N•m (50 in.-lbs.)
Crankcase	6.8 N•m (60 in.-lbs.)
Cylinder	12.4 N•m (110 in.-lbs.)
Flywheel nut	40.7 N•m (30 ft.-lbs.)
Muffler	9.6 N•m (85 in.-lbs.)
Spark plug	19.2 N•m (170 in.-lbs.)

CRANKCASE PRESSURE TEST. An improperly sealed crankcase can cause the engine to be hard to start, run rough, have low power and overheat. Refer to SERVICE SECTION TROUBLE-SHOOTING section of this manual for crankcase pressure test procedure. If crankcase leakage is indicated, pressurize crankcase and use a soap and water solution to check gaskets, seals, carburetor pulse line and casting for leakage.

PISTON, PIN, RINGS AND CYLINDER. The cylinder and head are one piece and may be removed after removing fuel tank, muffler guard, blower housing, carburetor and muffler. Unscrew four 5 mm Allen screws in cylinder base and carefully separate cylinder from crankcase. Remove and discard piston pin retaining clips. If possible,

hand-push piston pin out of rod, otherwise, use a suitable puller to extract piston pin and separate piston from connecting rod. Do not use a hammer to drive out piston pin as damage to connecting rod could result.

Piston ring end gap should not exceed 1.01 mm (0.040 in.). With ring placed 32 mm (1¼ in.) down in cylinder bore, use a feeler gauge to measure ring end gap.

Renew piston pin if diameter is 13.97 mm (0.550 in.) or less. Wear limit for piston pin hole in piston is 14.04 mm (0.553 in.).

Renew piston if it is scored or if diameter at skirt is 59.84 mm (2.356 in.) or less. Piston and rings are available in standard size only.

Wear limit for cylinder bore diameter is 60.14 mm (2.368 in.) for chrome plated bores and 60.17 mm (2.369 in.) for cast iron bores. Renew cylinder if cylinder bore has deep score marks or if chrome plating (if used) is damaged.

Piston rings are pinned and rings must be installed on piston so ring gap indexes with locating pin. Upper piston ring is semi-keystone type and must be installed with "N" toward top (crown) of piston as shown in Fig. BS55. Lower compression ring is rectangular and may be installed either side up.

Piston must be mated to connecting rod so arrow on piston crown will point toward the cylinder exhaust port (Fig. BS56). Use new piston pin retaining clips and install clips so gap of clip is toward either piston crown or crankshaft.

Lubricate piston and rings with clean 2 cycle engine oil, then slide cylinder with a new gasket onto piston and rings. Tighten cylinder base screws to 12.4 N•m (110 in.-lbs.).

CRANKSHAFT AND CRANKCASE. To disassemble crankcase assembly, remove cylinder and remaining components attached to crankcase and crankshaft. Remove four cap screws retaining crankcase halves. Place flywheel-side crankcase half on bottom with flywheel end of crankshaft inserted in flywheel as shown in Fig.

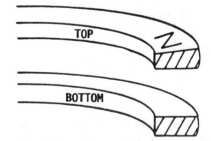

Fig. BS55—Top piston ring is semi-keystone type and must be installed with "N" toward piston crown.

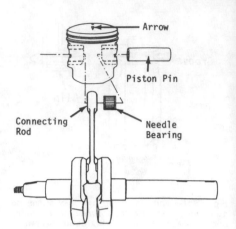

Fig. BS56—Install piston on rod so arrow on piston crown points toward exhaust port.

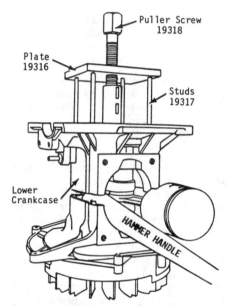

Fig. BS57—View showing B&S tools used to separate pto-side crankcase half from magneto-side crankcase half.

BS57. Insert a small wooden hammer handle into the crankcase to prevent crankshaft rotation. Install B&S puller plate 19136 (with side marked "X" toward piston), puller screw 19138 and puller studs 19317 on lower crankcase as shown in Fig. BS57. Separate crankcase lower half from crankshaft by turning puller screw.

To separate upper crankcase half from crankshaft, thread the flywheel nut or other suitable nut on the end of the crankshaft to protect the threads. Install the B&S puller assembly as shown in Fig. BS58. Turn the puller screw until the crankcase disengages from the crankshaft.

Remove crankcase oil seals and if bearing on pto side is to be removed, remove governor crank. Use B&S tool assembly shown in Fig. BS59 to remove

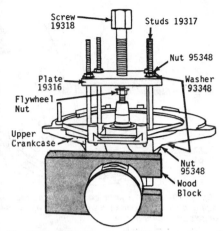

Fig. BS58—View showing B&S tools used to pull magneto-side crankcase half away from crankshaft assembly.

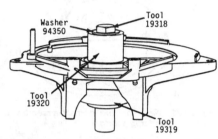

Fig. BS59—The main bearing in each crankcase half can be removed using the B&S tools shown above. Removal of magneto-side bearing is shown, removal of pto-side bearing is similar.

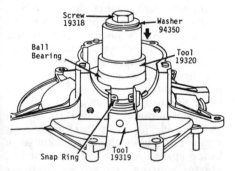

Fig. BS60—View showing B&S tools used to install main bearing in magneto-side crankcase half. Bearing must seat against snap ring.

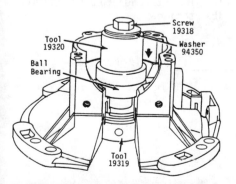

Fig. BS61—Assemble B&S tools as shown to install main bearing in pto-side crankcase half. Bearing must seat against shoulder of crankcase half.

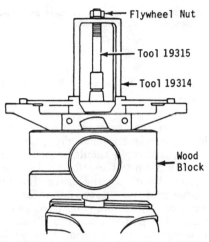

Fig. BS62—The oil seals can be installed in crankcase halves using the B&S tools shown above.

Fig. BS63—Install B&S tools 19314 and 19315 as shown and use flywheel nut or equivalent to pull magneto-side crankcase half onto crankshaft assembly. A wooden block is shown placed between piston and crankcase to prevent crankshaft rotation.

bearings from crankcase halves. Turn screw to force bearing from crankcase. Bearings must be discarded if removed from crankcase.

The crankshaft and connecting rod are a unit assembly and disassembly is not recommended. Renew crankshaft if diameter of main bearing journals is 24.95 mm (0.982 in.) or less, or if out-of-round 0.013 mm (0.0005 in.) or more.

To install magneto-side bearing, assemble B&S tools as shown in Fig. BS60 and turn screw until bearing seats against snap ring. To install pto-side bearing, assemble B&S tools as shown in Fig. BS61 and turn screw until bearing is seated against shoulder of crankcase half. Install oil seals using B&S tool assemblies shown in Fig. BS62. Flat side of seal must be towards outside of engine.

Pull crankshaft into magneto-side crankcase half using B&S tools 19314 and 19315 as shown in Fig. BS63.

NOTE: Crankshaft must not turn while pulling crankshaft into bearings.

Install crankcase gasket then install governor weight assembly as shown in

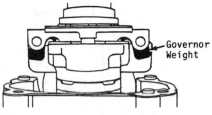

Fig. BS64—Governor weights are incorrectly positioned if they are not in the position shown above.

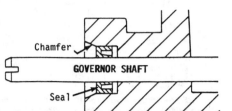

Fig. BS65—View of correctly installed governor shaft seal (seal lip facing inward).

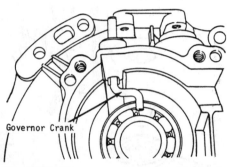

Fig. BS66—The governor crank must be positioned as shown for correct operation.

Fig. BS64 (be sure weights appear as shown). Install governor shaft seal so lip is towards inside of crankcase and face is flush with chamfer (Fig. BS65). Install washer and "E" ring on governor shaft then position governor crank as shown in Fig. BS66.

Position pto-side crankcase half on crankshaft and magneto-side crankcase assembly as shown in Fig. BS67 and install B&S tool 19314. Pull halves together by turning blade adapter bolt; using one of the puller studs threaded into the crankcase will help align the halves. If excessive resistance is felt, disassemble and check for complete seating of the main bearings. Tighten crankcase bolts to 6.8 N•m (60 in.-lbs.) torque. Trim crankcase gasket flush with cylinder mating surface.

It is recommended that the crankcase be pressure tested for leakage before proceeding with remainder of engine reassembly.

REWIND STARTER. Refer to Fig. BS68 for exploded view of rewind starter. The static guard cover above the

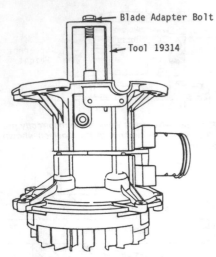

Fig. BS67—Install B&S tool 19314 and use the blade adapter bolt to pull the crankcase halves together.

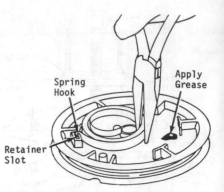

Fig. BS69—Route the starter rope as shown through pulley and rope outlet.

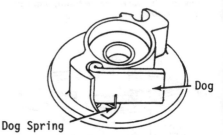

Fig. BS70—Apply a light coating of grease to pulley face. Outer end of rewind spring must engage spring anchor slot.

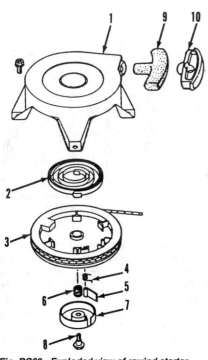

Fig. BS68—Exploded view of rewind starter.

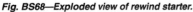

1. Starter housing
2. Rewind spring
3. Pulley
4. Dog spring
5. Dog
6. Brake spring
7. Retainer
8. Screw (L.H. thread)
9. Starter rope insert
10. Starter rope grip

Fig. BS71—View showing correct assembly of starter dog and dog spring.

starter must be removed for access to starter.

To install a new rope, proceed as follows. Rope length for models equipped with a band brake should be 22.6 cm (87 in.), 15.2 cm (60 in.) for engines not equipped with a band brake. Remove starter and pull old rope out as far as it will go. Extract old rope from pulley, then allow pulley to unwind. To install new rope, turn pulley counterclockwise until spring is tightly wound. Then rotate pulley clockwise until rope hole in pulley is aligned with rope outlet in housing. Pass rope through pulley hole and outlet as shown in Fig. BS69 and tie a temporary knot near handle end of rope. Release pulley and allow rope to wind onto pulley. Install rope handle, release temporary knot and allow rope to enter starter.

To disassemble starter, remove rope and allow pulley to totally unwind. Unscrew pulley retaining screw (screw has left-hand threads). Remove retainer (7—Fig. BS68) and brake spring (6). Wear appropriate safety eyewear and gloves before disengaging pulley (3) from starter as spring may uncoil uncontrolled. Place shop towel around pulley and lift pulley out of housing; spring should remain with

pulley. Carefully extract spring from pulley.

Inspect components for wear and damage which may prevent smooth operation. Apply a light coat of grease on pulley face where spring will rub. Install rewind spring (2) on pulley so spring is wound in a counterclockwise direction from outer end. Be sure outer end properly engages spring anchor slot of pulley (Fig. BS70). Install pulley and spring in starter housing and rotate pulley counterclockwise so inner spring end engages anchor of starter housing. Assemble remainder of components while noting correct assembly of dog and dog spring in Fig. BS71. Tighten pulley retaining screw (left-hand threads) to 3.4 N•m (30 in.-lbs.) torque.

BRIGGS & STRATTON
4-STROKE ENGINES
(Except Europa, Quantum & Vanguard)

Model Series	Bore	Stroke	Displacement	Power Rating
90700, 91700, 92500, 92900, 93500, 93900, 94500, 94900, 95500, 95900, 96500, 96900, 98900	2.56 in. (65.0 mm)	1.75 in. (44.5 mm)	9.0 cu. in. (148 cc)	3.5* hp (2.6* kW)
110700, 110900, 111700, 111900, 112700, 112900, 113900, 114700, 114900	2.78 in. (70.6 mm)	1.88 in. (47.6 mm)	11.4 cu. in. (186 cc)	4.0 hp (3 kW)
130700, 130900, 131700, 131900, 132900, 133700, 135700	2.56 in. (65.0 mm)	2.44 in. (62.0 mm)	12.6 cu. in. (206 cc)	5.0 hp (3.8 kW)

* Certain models are rated at 3.75 hp (2.8 kW).

ENGINE IDENTIFICATION

Engines covered in this section have aluminum cylinder blocks with either a plain aluminum cylinder bore or with a cast iron sleeve integrally cast into the block.

Refer to page 47 for Briggs & Stratton engine identification information.

MAINTENANCE

LUBRICATION. All engines are lubricated using splash lubrication. Oil in the oil pan is thrown onto internal engine parts by an oil slinger driven by the camshaft gear for vertical crankshaft engines.

Some engines are equipped with a low-oil level system (Oil Gard) that uses a float which is located inside the crankcase and connected by a wire lead to the ignition. If there is insufficient oil in the crankcase, the ignition is grounded so the engine stops or will not start.

Engine oil should meet or exceed latest API service classification. Use SAE 30 oil for temperatures above 40° F (4° C); use SAE 10W-30 oil for temperatures between 0° F (-18° C) and 40° F (4° C); below 0° F (-18° C) use petroleum based SAE 5W-20 or a suitable synthetic oil. Briggs & Stratton states that

multiviscosity oil should not be used above 40° F (4° C) as engine damage may result due to high running temperature of an air-cooled engine.

Fill engine with oil by pouring oil through oil fill plug opening or opening for the oil dipstick. If engine is equipped with an oil fill plug, unscrew plug and add oil until oil level is even with top threads in plug hole.

Some engines are equipped with an extended oil fill tube and a dipstick attached to oil fill cap. When checking the oil level, screw the dipstick into place until the cap bottoms on the filler tube, then unscrew the dipstick and observe oil level on dipstick. The oil level should be between the ADD and FULL marks on dipstick.

Briggs & Stratton specifies that the engine oil should be changed after the first five hours of operation, and then, if used normally, after every 50 hours of operation or seasonally, whichever is less. If the engine is run in severe conditions, such as under heavy load or in high ambient temperatures, the oil should be changed weekly or after every 25 hours of operation, whichever occurs first.

Approximate oil capacities are listed in the following table:

130700, 130900, 131700, 131900, 132900, 133700
and 135700 . . . . 1¾ pints (0.8 L)
Other models . . . . 1¼ pints (0.6 L)

AIR CLEANER. The air cleaner consists of a canister and the filter element it contains. The canister is secured by one or two wing nuts, screws or knobs. The filter element may be made of foam or paper, or a combination of both foam and paper. The recommended maintenance interval depends on the type of filter element.

Foam Type. Foam type filter elements should be cleaned, inspected and re-oiled after every 25 hours of engine operation, or after three months, whichever occurs first. Clean filter in kerosene or soapy water and squeeze until dry. Inspect filter for tears and holes or any other opening. Discard filter if it cannot be cleaned satisfactorily or if filter is torn or otherwise damaged. Pour clean engine oil into the filter, then squeeze filter to remove excess oil and distribute oil throughout filter. Clean filter canister. Inspect and, if necessary, replace any defective gaskets. Be sure filter element fits properly and any spacers are properly positioned during assembly. If air cleaner has a screen, the screen should be placed on top of the filter.

Paper Type. Paper type filter elements should be cleaned and inspected after every 25 hours of engine operation, or after three months, whichever occurs first. Tap filter gently to dislodge accumulated dirt. Filter may be washed using warm water and nonsudsing detergent, then rinse with clean water directed from inside of filter to outside. DO NOT use petroleum-based cleaners or solvents to clean filter. DO NOT direct pressurized air towards filter. Let filter air dry thoroughly, then inspect filter and discard it if damaged or cannot be cleaned. Clean filter canister. Inspect and, if necessary, replace any defective gaskets.

Combination Foam and Paper Type. The combination type air cleaner consists of a foam type filter, known as the precleaner, wrapped around or in front of a paper type filter. The foam precleaner should be cleaned weekly or after every 25 hours of operation, whichever occurs first. The paper filter should be cleaned yearly or after every 100 hours of operation, whichever occurs first. Clean foam precleaner or paper filter using cleaning methods previously outlined for foam and paper filters.

CRANKCASE BREATHER. The crankcase breather is built into the tappet chamber cover. A fiber disc acts as a one-way valve. The breather allows vapor from the crankcase to be evacuated to the intake manifold, but blocks the return flow of air, thus maintaining a vacuum in the crankcase. The vacuum prevents oil from being forced out of the engine past the piston rings, oil seals and gaskets.

Clearance between fiber disc check valve and breather body (Fig. B1) should not exceed 0.045 inch (1.14 mm). If it is possible to insert a 0.045 inch

(1.14 mm) wire between disc and breather body, renew breather assembly. Do not use excessive force when measuring gap. Disc should not stick or bind during operation. Renew if distorted or damaged. Inspect breather tube for leakage.

SPARK PLUG. The original spark plug may be either 1½ inches or 2 inches long. Briggs & Stratton recommends Champion or Autolite spark plugs.

If a Champion spark plug is used and spark plug is 1½ inches long, recommended spark plug is J19LM or CJ8. Install a Champion RJ19LM or RCJ8 if a resistor type spark plug is required. If spark plug is 2 inches long, recommended spark plug is J19LM or J8C. Install a Champion RJ19LM or RJ8C if a resistor type spark plug is required.

If an Autolite spark plug is used and spark plug is 1½ inches long, recommended spark plug is 235. Install a Autolite 245 if a resistor type spark plug is required. If spark plug is 2 inches long, recommended spark plug is 295. Install a Autolite 306 if a resistor type spark plug is required.

NOTE: Briggs & Stratton does not recommend using abrasive blasting to clean spark plugs as abrasive material may enter engine.

Spark plug electrode gap should be 0.030 inch (0.76 mm). Tighten spark plug to 140-200 in.-lbs. (15.8-22.6 N•m) torque.

CARBURETOR. The engine may be equipped with either a suction type (Pulsa-Jet, Pulsa-Prime, Vacu-Jet) or a float type (Flo-Jet, Walbro) carburetor. The suction type carburetor is identified by its location on top of the fuel tank. Refer to the appropriate following section.

Suction Type Carburetors Except Pulsa-Prime. Pulsa-Jet and Vacu-Jet carburetors are suction type carburetors that are mounted on the fuel tank. The carburetors are differentiated by the presence of one fuel tube (Fig. B2) on Vacu-Jet carburetors and two fuel tubes on Pulsa-Jet carburetors. Some Pulsa-Jet carburetors are identified by the fuel pump (P) mounted on the side of the carburetor. If the carburetor has a primer bulb, it is a Pulsa-Prime carburetor, which is covered in the following section.

OPERATION. The Vacu-Jet carburetor has a fuel tube that extends into the fuel tank as shown in Fig. B3. Atmospheric pressure against the fuel forces fuel up the fuel tube due to the vacuum created in the carburetor bore when the engine runs. A check valve allows fuel to flow up the tube but prevents fuel from draining back into the fuel tank. The mixture screw controls the amount of fuel entering the carburetor bore at high speed. The fuel passes through two metering holes into the bore. The metering holes are different sizes and at idle only the smaller diameter hole passes fuel due to the position of the throttle plate. Fuel mixture in the Vacu-Jet is affected by the amount of fuel in the fuel tank (fuel weight versus

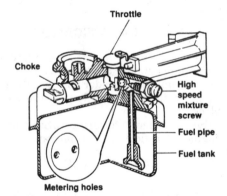

Fig. B3—Cutaway view of a typical Vacu-Jet carburetor. Inset shows fuel metering holes.

Fig.B1—Clearance between fiber disc valve and crankcase breather housing must be less than 0.045 inch (1.15 mm). A spark plug wire gauge may be used to check clearance as shown, but do not apply pressure against disc valve.

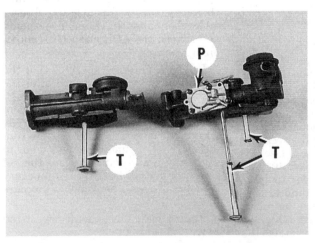

Fig. B2—Vacu-Jet carburetors are equipped with one fuel tube while Pulsa-Jet carburetors have two fuel tubes. Note fuel pump (P) found on the side of some Pulsa-Jet carburetors.

Illustrations Courtesy of Briggs & Stratton Corp.

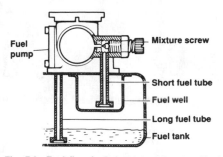

Fig. B4—Fuel flow in Pulsa-Jet carburetor. Fuel pump fills constant level fuel well below carburetor and excess fuel flows back into tank. Fuel is drawn from fuel well through tube to mixture screw.

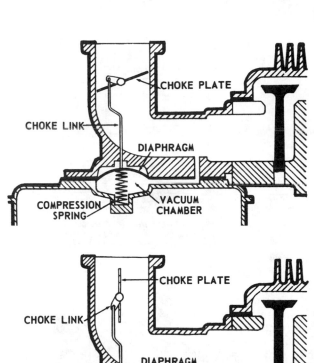

Fig. B6—Drawing of vacuum-operated automatic choke when engine starts. Lack of vacuum allows choke spring to close the choke plate.

Fig. B7—Drawing of vacuum-operated automatic choke with engine running. Vacuum against the diaphragm overcomes spring pressure thereby opening the choke plate.

atmospheric pressure). Carburetor adjustments should be performed with a half-full fuel tank thereby resulting in a satisfactory mixture adjustment whether the tank is near empty or full.

The Pulsa-Jet carburetor operates similarly to the Vacu-Jet except in delivery of the fuel to the carburetor. The fuel tank for a Pulsa-Jet carburetor has a fuel well (Fig. B4) that always contains a constant amount of fuel. Fuel passes through the long fuel tube to a diaphragm type pump on the side of the carburetor which transfers fuel from the fuel tank to the fuel well. The short fuel tube passes fuel from the fuel well to the mixture screw. With a constant amount of fuel present in the fuel well, the fuel mixture in the carburetor remains the same regardless of the amount of fuel in the tank, unlike the Vacu-Jet. On some Pulsa-Jet carburetors, the fuel pump is a part of the fuel tank mating surface with the carburetor.

Most Pulsa-Jet and Vacu-Jet carburetors are equipped with a plate type choke valve. Some models are equipped with an automatic choke plate that is actuated by a link attached to a diaphragm between the carburetor and fuel tank. See Fig. B5. A compression spring works against the diaphragm holding the choke plate in closed position when the engine is not running. See Fig. B6. A vacuum passage leads from the carburetor to a chamber under the

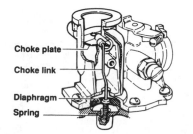

Fig. B5—Cutaway view of vacuum-operated automatic choke. See text and Figs. B6 and B7 for operation.

Fig. B8—View of bimetallic spring (S) used on some Pulsa-Jet and Vacu-Jet carburetors with an automatic choke. Refer to text.

diaphragm. When the engine starts, increased vacuum pulls down the diaphragm with the choke link, thereby opening the choke plate. See Fig. B7. This type automatic choke also operates if the engine loses engine speed under heavy load. The resulting loss of intake vacuum results in the choke plate closing, which provides a rich mixture so the engine will not stall. When engine speed increases, the increased vacuum returns the choke plate to the open position.

The automatic choke on some Pulsa-Jet and Vacu-Jet carburetors may be controlled by a bimetallic spring (S—Fig. B8) that is connected to the choke plate shaft. Air in the breather tube is directed to the bimetallic spring cavity

on the carburetor. Air temperature activates the spring which turns the choke shaft and plate. Cold air causes the spring to contract thereby closing the choke plate, while warm air opens the choke.

Some Pulsa-Jet and Vacu-Jet carburetors may be equipped with a slide type choke. When the choke slide is in (running position), a slot in the tube allows incoming air to flow into the carburetor. When the choke slide is out, incoming air is blocked and the mixture is enriched to enhance starting.

ADJUSTMENT. On all Pulsa-Jet and Vacu-Jet carburetors (except Pulsa-Jet with a fixed jet), the mixture screw controls high speed mixture setting. Turn mixture screw clockwise until it is lightly seated, then turn screw counterclockwise 1½ turns. Run engine until engine is at normal operating temperature. Be sure choke is open. Run engine at full throttle. Turn mixture screw clockwise until engine begins to stumble and note screw position. Turn mixture screw counterclockwise until engine begins to stumble and note screw position. Turn mixture screw clockwise to a position that is midway from the clockwise (lean) and counterclockwise (rich) positions. Adjust idle speed screw so engine speed is 1750 rpm. With engine running at idle, rapidly move speed control to full throttle position. If engine stumbles or hesitates, slightly turn mix-

Fig. B9—Fixed jet Pulsa-Jet carburetors may be identified by the presence of threaded holes (H) in the inlet flange.

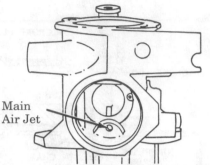

Main Air Jet

Fig. B10—On Pulsa-Jet carburetors with fixed main jet, the main jet air bleed can be removed to improve performance at high altitudes.

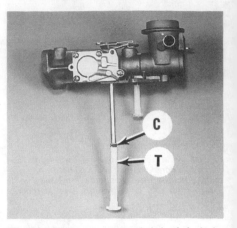

Fig. B12—To remove an extended plastic fuel tube (T), detach the retainer clip (C) then pull the plastic tube off the brass tube.

ture screw counterclockwise and repeat test. Recheck idle speed and, if necessary, readjust idle speed screw.

The mixture screw on Pulsa-Jet carburetors with a fixed jet (carburetor is identified by threaded holes shown in Fig. B9) controls the idle mixture setting. Turn screw clockwise until it is lightly seated, then turn screw counterclockwise 1½ turns. Run engine until engine is at normal operating temperature. Be sure choke is open. Run engine with speed control in slow position and adjust idle speed screw so engine speed is 1750 rpm. Turn mixture screw clockwise until engine begins to stumble and note screw position. Turn idle mixture screw counterclockwise until engine begins to stumble and note screw position. Turn the idle mixture screw clockwise to a position that is midway from the clockwise (lean) and counterclockwise (rich) positions. With engine running at idle, rapidly move speed control to full throttle position. If engine stumbles or hesitates, slightly turn mixture screw counterclockwise and repeat test. Recheck idle speed and, if necessary, readjust idle speed screw.

NOTE: If engine performance is poor when operating at high altitudes, remove the Welch plug from the choke end of the carburetor and remove main air jet (Fig. B10).

R&R AND OVERHAUL. On suction type carburetors, it may be necessary to remove the carburetor and fuel tank as a unit from the engine before separating the carburetor from the fuel tank. Note the position of governor link and springs before removing the carburetor to ensure correct reassembly. Do not bend governor links or stretch springs.

Some engines are equipped with an automatic choke that uses a diaphragm (diaphragm is part of fuel tank gasket) and spring between the carburetor and fuel tank (Fig. B5). Before separating carburetor from fuel tank, remove cover from carburetor body and detach the choke link (Fig. B5). Do not lose the

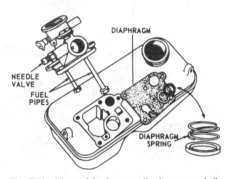

DIAPHRAGM

NEEDLE VALVE

FUEL PIPES

DIAPHRAGM SPRING

Fig. B11—View of fuel pump diaphragm and diaphragm spring found on the underside of some Pulsa-Jet carburetors.

choke spring after separating carburetor and fuel tank.

The fuel pump on some Pulsa-Jet carburetors is located on the underside of the carburetor (fuel pump diaphragm is part of fuel tank gasket). The diaphragm spring and cup (Fig. B11) will be loose when the carburetor is separated from the fuel tank.

Note the following when disassembling the carburetor: DO NOT remove metal fuel feed tubes. Plastic fuel feed tubes with a hex end can be unscrewed from the carburetor body. Fuel feed tubes with a round end can be removed by grasping the tube with pliers and

pulling the tube from the carburetor body.

NOTE: A new fuel feed tube must be the same length as the original tube. When ordering parts, measure and compare the old tube with the new tube.

If equipped with a brass fuel feed tube, the plastic pickup should be replaced if it cannot be cleaned in place with aerosol carburetor cleaner. If equipped with a long tube (Fig. B12), detach the retainer clip (C) then pull the plastic tube (T) from the brass tube. If equipped with a plastic pickup on the brass tube, drive the pickup off of the brass tube.

On Pulsa-Jet carburetors with a side-mounted fuel pump, unscrew and remove the pump cover (Fig. B13), then remove the diaphragm, spring and spring cup.

If equipped with an all-temperature choke, remove rubber elbow (E—Fig. B14), then force out the spring-shaft end of the choke with the spring by pushing against the inner end of the shaft. Note that the spring post on some

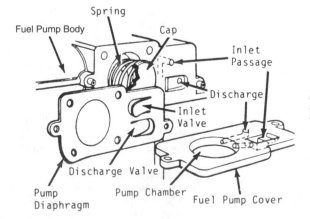

Fuel Pump Body

Spring

Cap

Inlet Passage

Discharge

Inlet Valve

Discharge Valve

Pump Diaphragm

Pump Chamber

Fuel Pump Cover

Fig. B13—Exploded view of Pulsa-Jet fuel pump mounted on side of carburetor.

Illustrations Courtesy of Briggs & Stratton Corp.

Fig. B14—A rubber elbow (E) fits around the choke housing on carburetors with an all-temperature choke.

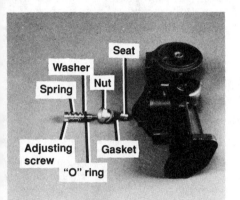

Fig. B15—Exploded view of fuel mixture screw assembly used on some carburetors.

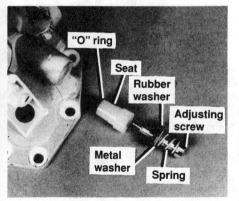

Fig. B16—Exploded view of fuel mixture screw assembly that uses a plastic seat.

carburetors must be dressed down to release the spring end.

Some carburetors are equipped with a plastic choke plate that is bonded to the plastic choke shaft. Use a tool with a sharp edge to cut through the bond along the edge of the shaft to separate shaft from plate.

Some carburetors are equipped with a removable idle mixture screw valve seat (Fig. B15).

Fig. B17—Some carburetors are equipped with a removable spiral insert (I).

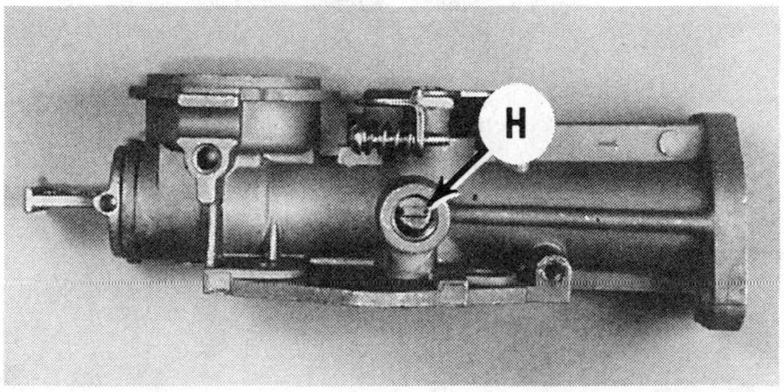

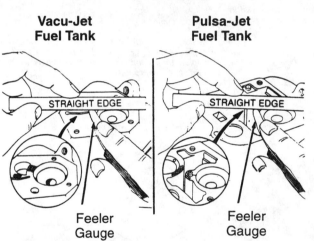

Fig. B18—Fuel metering holes (H) are accessible for cleaning after removing mixture screw. Be careful not to enlarge the holes when cleaning them.

Vacu-Jet Fuel Tank

Pulsa-Jet Fuel Tank

Fig. B19—Use a straightedge and 0.002 inch (0.05 mm) feeler gauge to check machined surface of fuel tank for flatness. Measure at shaded areas shown in insets.

Some carburetors are equipped with a fuel mixture screw assembly that has a plastic seat (Fig. B16). Unscrew adjustment screw four or five turns then pull assembly out of carburetor.

If carburetor is equipped with Welch plugs, pierce the plug with a sharp punch, then pry out the plug. Be careful not to damage underlying metal.

If so equipped, spiral insert (I—Fig. B17) may be pulled from the carburetor bore.

Inspect the carburetor and components. Some carburetor bodies are made of plastic. They must not be soaked in carburetor cleaner for longer than 15 minutes. Metering holes (H—Fig. B18) in the mixture screw cavity are calibrated and should be cleaned with compressed air only. Do not enlarge or damage holes.

Discard any diaphragms that are torn, creased or otherwise damaged. On Pulsa-Jet carburetors, renew fuel pump diaphragm if flap valves (Fig. B13) are damaged. The body must be replaced if there is excessive throttle or choke shaft play as bushings are not available. All gaskets and seals should be replaced.

Check flatness of carburetor mounting surface on fuel tank. If surface is not flat, it is possible for gasoline to pass between the fuel tank surface and diaphragm and enter the carburetor vacuum passage. This will cause a rich air:fuel mixture. To check flatness, place a straightedge on the fuel tank and attempt to slide a 0.002 inch (0.05 mm) feeler gauge between the straightedge and the fuel tank surface as shown in Fig. B19. If the feeler gauge slides under the straightedge, discard the fuel tank. Do not attempt to flatten machined surface of fuel tank by filing. If the carburetor is not equipped with an automatic choke, Briggs & Stratton repair kit 391413 can be used to repair warped Pulsa-Jet fuel tank.

Note color of choke actuating diaphragm spring (S—Fig. B20) and measure spring length. Replace spring and diaphragm if colored red and length is not $1\frac{1}{8}$ to $1\frac{7}{32}$ inches (28.6-30.9 mm), if colored blue and length is not $1\frac{5}{16}$ to $1\frac{3}{8}$ inches (33.3-34.9 mm), or if colored green and length is not $1\frac{7}{64}$ to $1\frac{3}{8}$ inches (28.2-34.9 mm).

Assemble the carburetor by reversing the removal procedure while noting the

Fig. B20—Diaphragm spring (S) is color-coded to indicate length of spring.

Fig. B21—Install a throttle plate with a raised edge (E) so raised edge is toward mixture screw side of carburetor.

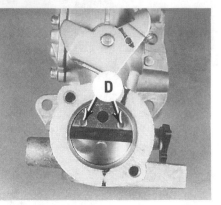

Fig. B23—If equipped with a choke plate that has dimples (D), install choke plate on choke shaft so dimples are up and hole in plate is toward throttle when choke is closed.

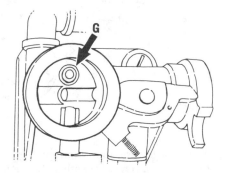

Fig. B24—If equipped with a spring-loaded valve on the choke plate, install choke plate so spring (G) is visible when choke plate is closed.

Fig. B25—If equipped with an all-temperature choke, position choke plate in closed position, then install choke shaft with bimetallic spring so outer spring end is above anchor pin (A).

If equipped with a choke plate that has dimples (Fig. B23), install choke plate on choke shaft so dimples are up and hole in plate is toward throttle when choke is closed. Be sure to install the felt washer on the choke shaft before insertion into the carburetor.

If equipped with a spring-loaded valve (G—Fig. B24) on the choke plate, install choke plate so spring is visible when choke plate is closed.

If equipped with a manual choke using sector gears to rotate the choke, be sure choke operates properly after mating the gears.

If equipped with an all-temperature choke, position choke plate in closed position, then install choke shaft with bimetallic spring so outer spring end is above anchor pin (A—Fig. B25). Rotate spring end counterclockwise and attach to pin. If carburetor is plastic, use a warm soldering iron to flare end of spring anchor pin so spring end cannot slide off pin.

If equipped with a side-mounted fuel pump, install spring cup (C—Fig. B26) so smooth side is towards diaphragm. Tighten fuel pump cover retaining screws evenly in a crossing pattern.

If equipped with a brass fuel feed tube that has a plastic extension tube, heat the plastic tube in hot water before installation.

When installing the carburetor, note the following: If equipped with an all-temperature choke, use the following procedure when installing the carburetor on the fuel tank. Invert carburetor with choke diaphragm and spring in place. If equipped with a fuel pump, the fuel pump spring and spring cup (smooth side towards diaphragm) must be installed as well. Choke link should not be attached to choke lever. Place fuel tank on carburetor while guiding choke diaphragm spring into well of fuel tank (Fig. B27). Install carburetor mounting screws, but do not tighten. Attach choke

Fig. B22—Install a flat throttle plate so mark (M) is on fuel pump side of bore.

following: If so equipped, install throttle shaft seal so lip is out. If throttle plate has a raised edge (E—Fig. B21), install throttle plate with raised edge toward mixture screw side of carburetor. If throttle plate is flat, install throttle plate so mark (M—Fig. B22) is on fuel pump side of bore.

If so equipped, install spiral insert (I—Fig. B17) so end is parallel with fuel tank mounting surface and insert end is flush or just below mounting face of carburetor.

If carburetor is equipped with Welch plugs, apply a nonhardening sealer to outer edge of plug and drive plug into hole with concave side toward carburetor. Be careful not to collapse the plug.

Fig. B26—Install fuel pump spring cup (C) so smooth side is towards diaphragm.

Fig. B27—While inverted, place fuel tank on carburetor while guiding choke diaphragm spring into well of fuel tank. See text.

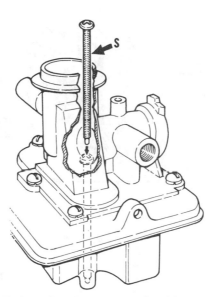

Fig. B28—On carburetors so equipped, be sure to install screw (S) located in carburetor bore.

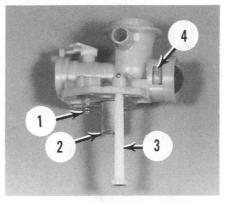

Fig. B29—View of Pulsa-Prime carburetor showing location of fuel pump spring (1), screen (2), long fuel tube (3) and primer retainer tab (4).

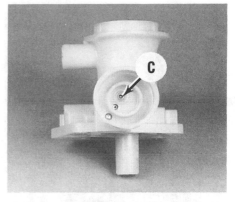

Fig. B30—View of check valve (C) on Pulsa-Prime carburetor.

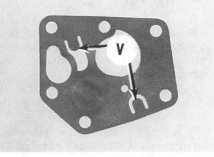

Fig. B31—View of fuel pump diaphragm and valves (V).

link to choke lever, hold choke plate in closed position and tighten carburetor mounting screws. Check choke operation.

On carburetors so equipped, be sure to install screw (S—Fig. B28) located in carburetor bore that is used to secure carburetor to fuel tank.

Pulsa-Prime Suction Type Carburetor. The Pulsa-Prime carburetor is mounted on the fuel tank and is equipped with a primer bulb.

OPERATION. The Pulsa-Prime carburetor has two fuel tubes. A screen (2—Fig. B29) covers the short fuel tube. The longer fuel tube (3) extends into the fuel tank. A diaphragm type fuel pump between the carburetor and fuel tank transfers fuel from the fuel tank into a fuel well that is a part of the fuel tank under the carburetor. The short fuel tube has a jet at the bottom. The tube extends into the fuel well and passes fuel from the fuel well to the carburetor bore. There are no provisions for mixture adjustment on the Pulsa-Prime carburetor. Actuating the primer bulb

forces fuel past check valves in the long fuel tube and primer cavity to prime the fuel pump as well as providing additional fuel for engine starting. Several pushes against the primer bulb are required to fill the fuel system if it is dry.

ADJUSTMENT. There are no adjustments on Pulsa-Prime carburetors.

R&R AND OVERHAUL. The fuel tank and carburetor should be removed and installed as a unit. Note the position of governor link and springs before removing the carburetor to ensure correct reassembly. Do not bend governor links or stretch springs.

After the fuel tank and carburetor are removed, the carburetor can be separated from the fuel tank. Carefully separate the carburetor from the fuel tank so the diaphragm can be reused if undamaged.

When disassembling the carburetor, note the following: Use pliers to pull the

long fuel tube out of the body. Press in tabs (4—Fig. B29) on primer bulb retainer ring and remove retainer ring and primer bulb. Using a suitable tool, extract the check valve seat (C—Fig. B30) in the primer cavity, then remove the check ball and spring. Do not deform the spring. The main jet in the bottom of the short fuel tube is permanently installed and should not be removed. Do not enlarge or damage the main jet hole. Replacement jets are not available.

The carburetor body is made of plastic. It must not be soaked in carburetor cleaner for longer than 15 minutes. Inspect carburetor and components. Discard diaphragm if torn, creased or otherwise damaged, also note condition of flap valves (V—Fig. B31). The body must be replaced if there is excessive throttle shaft play as bushings are not available. Replace long fuel tube or screen around short fuel tube if clogged or damaged.

When reassembling carburetor, note the following: Insert throttle plate in throttle shaft so hole (H—Fig. B32) in plate is out. Convex side of dimples in throttle plate should be toward breather tube side of carburetor.

Install spring and check ball in primer cavity, then install ball seat so groove on seat is out (Fig. B30).

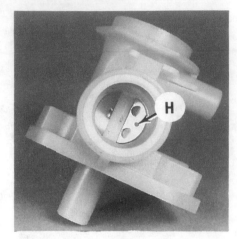

Fig. B32—Insert throttle plate in throttle shaft so hole (H) in plate is out.

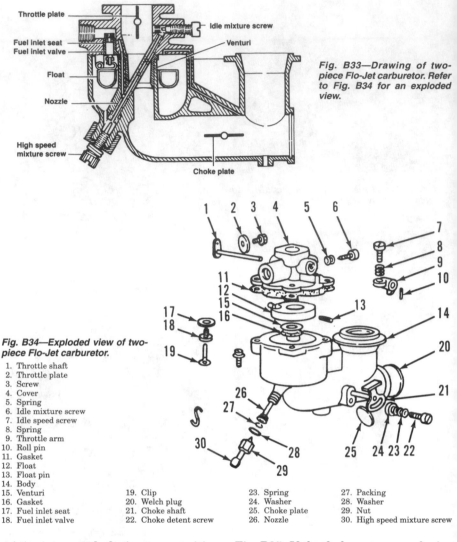

Fig. B33—Drawing of two-piece Flo-Jet carburetor. Refer to Fig. B34 for an exploded view.

Fig. B34—Exploded view of two-piece Flo-Jet carburetor.

1. Throttle shaft
2. Throttle plate
3. Screw
4. Cover
5. Spring
6. Idle mixture screw
7. Idle speed screw
8. Spring
9. Throttle arm
10. Roll pin
11. Gasket
12. Float
13. Float pin
14. Body
15. Venturi
16. Gasket
17. Fuel inlet seat
18. Fuel inlet valve
19. Clip
20. Welch plug
21. Choke shaft
22. Choke detent screw
23. Spring
24. Washer
25. Choke plate
26. Nozzle
27. Packing
28. Washer
29. Nut
30. High speed mixture screw

Moisten inside of primer cavity, then install primer bulb and retainer ring. Push in retainer ring until locking tabs engage slots on body.

Fuel pump spring (1—Fig. B29) fits around a peg on the underside of the carburetor.

To install the carburetor, place diaphragm on fuel tank, then place gasket on diaphragm. Install carburetor on fuel tank and evenly tighten screws in a crossing pattern. Apply a light coat of oil to "O" ring in carburetor bore, then install carburetor and fuel tank on engine.

Two-Piece Flo-Jet Carburetor. The two-piece Flo-Jet carburetor (Fig. B33) is a float type carburetor. The carburetor is identified by the fuel bowl that is integral with the carburetor body. Two castings make up the carburetor. The idle mixture screw and fuel inlet valve are located in the cover, which also serves as the attachment point for the float. The high speed mixture screw and nozzle are located in the body, although the nozzle protrudes into the cover to provide fuel for the idle circuit.

ADJUSTMENT. See Fig. B33 for location of idle mixture screw and high speed mixture screw. To adjust the mixture screws, proceed as follows: Turn idle mixture screw and high speed mixture screw clockwise until lightly seated. Turn idle mixture screw counterclockwise 1¼ turns. Turn high speed mixture screw counterclockwise 1½ turns. Run engine until at normal operating temperature. Be sure choke is open. Run engine with speed control in fast position. Turn high speed mixture screw clockwise until engine begins to stumble and note screw position. Turn high speed mixture screw counterclockwise until engine begins to stumble and note screw position. Turn the high speed

mixture screw clockwise to a position that is midway from the clockwise (lean) and counterclockwise (rich) positions. Run engine at idle and adjust idle speed screw so engine speed is 1750 rpm. Turn idle mixture screw clockwise until engine begins to stumble and note screw position. Turn idle mixture screw counterclockwise until engine begins to stumble and note screw position. Turn the idle mixture screw clockwise to a position that is midway from the clockwise (lean) and counterclockwise (rich) positions. With engine running at idle, rapidly move speed control to full throttle position. If engine stumbles or hesitates, slightly turn idle mixture screw counterclockwise and repeat test. Recheck idle speed and, if necessary, readjust idle speed screw.

OVERHAUL. Refer to Fig. B34 for an exploded view of carburetor. Before servicing the carburetor, check the cover for distortion. Attempt to insert a 0.002 inch (0.05 mm) feeler gauge between the cover and body as shown in

Fig. B35. If the feeler gauge can be inserted, then the body is warped or damaged and must be renewed.

When disassembling the carburetor, note that the nozzle (26—Fig. B34) is angled between the body and cover. **The nozzle must be removed before the cover is removed, otherwise, the nozzle will be damaged.**

Check the throttle shaft and bushing wear before removal. Play in bushings should not exceed 0.010 inch (0.25 mm), otherwise, the throttle shaft and/or bushings must be replaced.

The fuel inlet valve seat may be a threaded or press-in type. If a threaded type, a screwdriver can be used to unscrew valve seat. If valve seat is a press-in type (identified by absence of a screwdriver slot) and replacement is required, thread a ¼-20 self-tapping screw or screw extractor into fuel inlet valve seat and remove valve seat.

Inspect carburetor and components. If throttle shaft bushings are worn and must be replaced, use a ¼-inch tap or screw extractor to extract bushings. Push new bushings into carburetor,

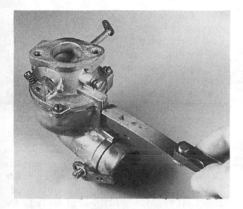

Fig. B35—Attempt to insert a 0.002 inch (0.05 mm) feeler gauge between the cover and body as shown to check the cover for distortion.

Fig. B36—Install throttle plate so dimples (D) are up.

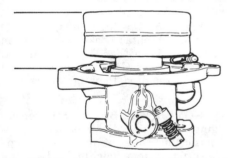

Fig. B37—Float should be parallel with fuel bowl mating surface on carburetor. Bend float tang to adjust float level.

then insert throttle shaft and check for free shaft rotation. If binding occurs, use a 7/32-inch drill bit as a line reamer by passing drill through both bushings.

When assembling carburetor, note the following: If equipped with a pressed-in fuel inlet valve seat, install valve seat so it is flush with carburetor body. Install throttle plate so dimples (D—Fig. B36) are up. If carburetor is equipped with a removable venturi, be sure to align holes in venturi and gasket during assembly.

After installing float on cover, check float level. Float should be parallel with fuel bowl mating surface on carburetor

Fig. B38—Removing the air jet from the right main air bleed hole (H) leans the high speed mixture, which may be desirable if the engine is operated at high altitudes. See text.

(Fig. B37). To adjust float level, bend float tang.

If Welch plug was removed, apply sealant to edge of Welch plug before installation, then swage carburetor body metal around edge of plug in several places to secure plug.

Walbro LMS Carburetor. The Walbro LMS carburetor is a float type carburetor. The carburetor can be identified by the letters "LMS" embossed on the carburetor mounting flange. Three versions of the LMS carburetor have been used. Some carburetors have both idle mixture and high speed mixture screws, some carburetors have a fixed jet instead of a high speed mixture screw, and some carburetors with a fixed jet use a primer system in place of the choke plate.

OPERATION. The Walbro LMS carburetor operates like other typical float type carburetors. If the engine is operated at high altitudes, improved engine performance may be obtained by removing the metal jet in the right main air bleed hole (H—Fig. B38), however, the air jet should be installed if engine is operated at lower altitudes. Removing the air jet leans the high speed mixture.

ADJUSTMENT. Refer to Fig. B39 for location of mixture adjusting screws. Some carburetors are not equipped with the adjustable high speed mixture screw on the bottom of the fuel bowl; a fixed main jet is located inside the carburetor.

To adjust mixture screws, proceed as follows: Turn idle mixture screw and high speed mixture screw, if so equipped, clockwise until they are lightly seated, then turn both screws counterclockwise 1¼ turns. Run engine until normal operating temperature is attained. Be sure choke is open. Run

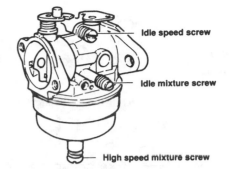

Fig. B39—View of Walbro LMS carburetor showing location of adjusting screws.

engine with speed control in slow position and adjust idle speed screw so engine speed is 1750 rpm. Turn idle mixture screw clockwise until engine begins to stumble and note screw position. Turn idle mixture screw counterclockwise until engine begins to stumble and note screw position. Turn the idle mixture screw clockwise to a position that is midway from clockwise (lean) and counterclockwise (rich) positions.

If carburetor is equipped with a high speed mixture screw, run engine with speed control in fast position. Turn high speed mixture screw clockwise until engine begins to stumble and note screw position. Turn high speed mixture screw counterclockwise until engine begins to stumble and note screw position. Turn high speed mixture screw clockwise to a position that is midway from clockwise (lean) and counterclockwise (rich) positions. With engine running at idle, rapidly move speed control to full throttle position. If engine stumbles or hesitates, slightly turn idle mixture screw counterclockwise and repeat test. Recheck idle speed and, if necessary, readjust idle speed screw.

OVERHAUL. Disassembly of carburetor is evident after inspection and referral to Fig. B40. To remove the Welch plug, pierce the plug with a sharp punch, then pry out the plug, but do not damage underlying metal.

Inspect carburetor and renew any damaged or excessively worn components. The body must be replaced if there is excessive throttle or choke shaft play as bushings are not available. Apply fingernail polish or other suitable nonhardening sealant to outer edge of new Welch plug, then install plug using a pin punch that is slightly smaller in diameter than the plug. Be careful not to indent the plug; the plug should be flat after installation. Use a 3/16-inch (5 mm) diameter rod to install the fuel inlet valve seat. The groove on the seat must be down (towards carburetor

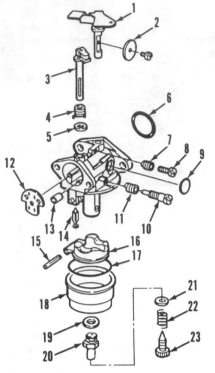

Fig. B40—Exploded view of Walbro LMS carburetor.

1. Throttle shaft	13. Main air jet
2. Throttle plate	14. Fuel inlet valve
3. Choke shaft	15. Float pin
4. Washer	16. Float
5. Seal	17. Gasket
6. Gasket	18. Fuel bowl
7. Spring	19. Washer
8. Idle speed screw	20. Bowl retainer
9. Welch plug	21. "O" ring
10. Idle mixture screw	22. Spring
11. Spring	23. High speed
12. Choke plate	mixture screw

Fig. B41—For proper operation of Choke-A-Matic controls, remote control wire must extend to dimension shown and have a minimum travel of 1-3/8 inches (34.9 mm).

bore). Push in the seat until it bottoms. Install the choke plate so the numbers are visible when the choke is closed. Install the throttle plate so the numbers are visible and towards the idle mixture screw when the throttle is closed. The float level is not adjustable. If the float is not approximately parallel with the body when the carburetor is inverted, then the float, fuel valve and/or valve seat must be replaced. Tighten the fuel bowl retaining screw or high speed mixture nut to 50 in.-lbs. (5.6 N·m) torque.

Tighten carburetor mounting screws to 75 in.-lbs. (8.5 N·m) torque.

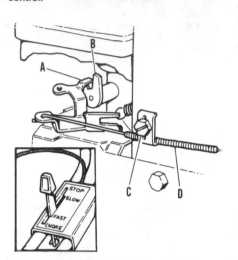

Fig. B42—Refer to text to adjust Choke-A-Matic control on models equipped with a dial speed control.

Fig. B43—If equipped with Choke-A-Matic control shown, refer to text for adjustment.

CHOKE-A-MATIC CARBURETOR CONTROL.
Some engines may be equipped with a control unit with which the carburetor choke, throttle and magneto grounding switch are operated from a single lever (Choke-A-Matic carburetors).

To check the operation of Choke-A-Matic engine control, proceed as follows: Move the speed control lever to the "CHOKE" or "START" position. Remove air cleaner and verify that choke slide or plate is completely closed. Move speed control lever to "RUN", "FAST" and "SLOW" positions; the choke should be open. Reinstall air cleaner. Start engine. Move control lever to "STOP" position. The engine should stop running.

If equipped with a control cable between the remote control and engine,

the remote control cable must move a certain distance for the remote control and carburetor to be synchronized. At full extension, control wire must extend 2 1/8 inches (54 mm) from cable housing as shown in Fig. B41. The wire must travel at least 1 3/8 inches (34.9 mm) from "CHOKE" or "START" to "STOP" positions.

If equipped with a dial type control (Fig. B42), adjust mechanism as follows: Move dial control to "START" position. Loosen ferrule screw shown in Fig. B42. Move carburetor lever fully clockwise. Position remote control arm so it is 1/8 inch (3.2 mm) from bracket. With carburetor lever and remote control arm in positions previously specified, tighten ferrule screw. Start engine. Move control lever to "STOP" position. The engine should stop running.

Several Choke-A-Matic configurations have been used on Briggs & Stratton engines. Refer to Figs. B43, B44 and B45 for some typical setups and the following list for adjustment points:

Fig. B43—On these units, lever (A) should just contact link or arm (B) when control is in "FAST" position. If not, loosen screw (C) and move control wire housing (D) as required, then tighten screw.

Fig. B44—On these units, adjustment is performed by bending choke link at point indicated by arrow so choke is closed when control is in "START" position.

Fig. B45—On these units, lever (A) should just contact choke lever (B) when lever (C) is in "FAST" detent. If not, loosen screws (D) and move control plate as required, then tighten screws.

GOVERNOR.
Briggs & Stratton engines are equipped with either a pneumatic (air vane) or mechanical type governor system. Refer to Fig. B46 for a view of a typical air vane governor and speed control linkage used on vertical crankshaft engines. A view of a typical governor and speed control linkage used on vertical crankshaft engines with a mechanical governor system is shown in Fig. B47.

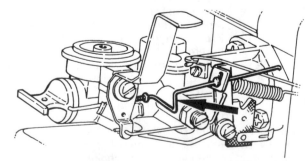

Fig. B44—Bend choke link at point indicated by arrow so choke is closed when control is in "START" position.

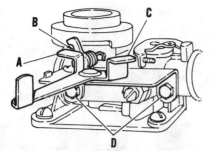

Fig. B45—If equipped with Choke-A-Matic control shown, refer to text for adjustment.

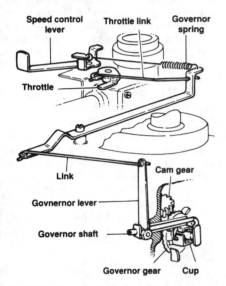

Fig. B46—View of a typical air vane type governor mechanism used on a vertical crankshaft engine.

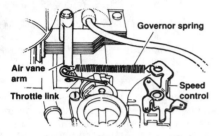

Fig. B47—View of a typical mechanical governor mechanism used on a vertical crankshaft engine.

NOTE: Observe the following when working on governor or speed control linkage. Before disconnecting linkage, mark linkage so it can be reassembled in its original configuration. Do not stretch governor spring during removal or installation. When attaching or detaching a governor spring end with a closed loop, use a twisting motion at spring end. Do not pull spring end with pliers or other tools as spring end may be deformed, which can affect governor operation.

AIR VANE GOVERNOR ADJUSTMENT. Other than checking for disconnected or binding linkage, air vane governor system does not require adjustment.

MECHANICAL GOVERNOR ADJUSTMENT. On some engines with a mechanical governor, idle speed is governed. Refer to previous sections in this chapter for adjustment of governed idle speed screw or tang.

On some engines, maximum governed speed is adjustable. The maximum governed speed is usually specified by the equipment manufacturer according to engine application.

On all engines with a mechanical governor, it may be necessary to adjust position of governor lever on governor shaft. Adjust position of governor lever assembly as follows: Loosen clamp bolt on governor lever (Fig. B48). Move governor lever (L) so carburetor throttle plate is in wide open position. Rotate governor shaft (S) as far as possible clockwise on Models 80000 and 83000 or counterclockwise on all other models. Tighten clamp bolt.

IGNITION. All models are equipped with a Magnetron breakerless ignition system. All components are located outside the flywheel.

To check spark, remove spark plug and connect spark plug cable to B&S tester 19051, then ground remaining tester lead to engine. Spin engine at 350 rpm or more. If spark jumps the 0.165 inch (4.2 mm) tester gap, system is functioning properly.

Armature air gap should be 0.010-0.014 inch (0.25-0.36 mm) for Models 130000, 131000, 132000, 133000 and 135000 and 0.006-0.010 inch (0.15-0.25 mm) for all other models.

FLYWHEEL BRAKE. The engine may be equipped with a band type flywheel brake. The brake should stop the engine within three seconds when the operator releases the mower safety control and the speed control is in high speed position. Stopping time can be checked using tool 19255.

Refer to FLYWHEEL BRAKE in RE-PAIRS section for flywheel brake adjustment and service.

VALVE ADJUSTMENT. To correctly set tappet clearance, remove spark plug and breather/valve tappet chamber cover. Rotate crankshaft in normal direction (clockwise at flywheel) so piston is at top dead center on compression stroke. Continue to rotate crankshaft so piston is 1/4 inch (6.4 mm) down from top dead center. This position places the tappets away from the compression release device on the cam lobes. Using a feeler gauge, measure clearance between intake and exhaust valve stem ends and the tappets.

The intake valve tappet gap should be 0.005-0.007 inch (0.13-0.18 mm). The exhaust valve tappet gap on Models 130000, 131000, 132000, 133000 and 135000 should be 0.009-0.011 inch (0.23-0.28 mm). The exhaust valve tappet gap for all other models should be 0.007-0.009 inch (0.18-0.23 mm).

NOTE: On some 90000 model series engines, the exhaust valve gap should be 0.005-0.007 inch (0.13-0.18 mm). These engines are identified by the specification stamped on the inside of the crankcase breather.

Valve tappet clearance is adjusted on all models by carefully grinding end of valve stem to increase clearance or by grinding valve seats deeper and/or renewing valve or tappet to decrease clearance.

CYLINDER HEAD. After 100 to 300 hours of engine operation, the cylinder head should be removed and any carbon or deposits should be removed.

REPAIRS

Refer to Fig. B49 for an exploded view of a typical vertical crankshaft engine.

Fig. B48—The governor is adjusted by holding governor lever (L) while turning governor shaft (S) in direction specified in text.

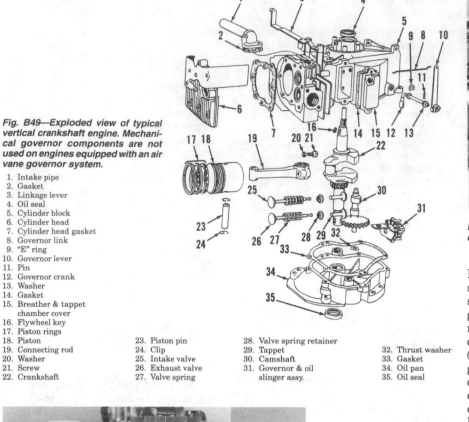

Fig. B49—Exploded view of typical vertical crankshaft engine. Mechanical governor components are not used on engines equipped with an air vane governor system.

1. Intake pipe
2. Gasket
3. Linkage lever
4. Oil seal
5. Cylinder block
6. Cylinder head
7. Cylinder head gasket
8. Governor link
9. "E" ring
10. Governor lever
11. Pin
12. Governor crank
13. Washer
14. Gasket
15. Breather & tappet chamber cover
16. Flywheel key
17. Piston rings
18. Piston
19. Connecting rod
20. Washer
21. Screw
22. Crankshaft

23. Piston pin
24. Clip
25. Intake valve
26. Exhaust valve
27. Valve spring

28. Valve spring retainer
29. Tappet
30. Camshaft
31. Governor & oil slinger assy.

32. Thrust washer
33. Gasket
34. Oil pan
35. Oil seal

Fig. B51—Tighten cylinder head screws in sequence shown.

Fig. B50—Long cylinder head retaining screws (S) are used in positions shown.

TIGHTENING TORQUES. Recommended tightening torque specifications are as follows:

Connecting rod . . . . 100 in.-lbs. (11.3 N•m)

Oil pan:
130000, 131000,
132000, 133000,
135000 . . . . 120 in.-lbs. (13.6 N•m)

All other models . . . . 85 in.-lbs. (9.6 N•m)

Cylinder head . . . . 140 in.-lbs. (15.8 N•m)

Flywheel nut or starter clutch:
130000, 131000,
132000, 133000,
135000 . . . . 65 ft.-lbs. (7.3 N•m)

All other models . . . . 55 ft.-lbs. (6.2 N•m)

Spark plug . . . . 140-200 in.-lbs. (15.8-22.6 N•m)

CYLINDER HEAD. When removing cylinder head, note location and lengths of cylinder head retaining screws so they can be installed in their original positions.

Always install a new cylinder head gasket. Do not apply sealer to head gasket. Note position of three long screws (S—Fig. B50). Lubricate screws with graphite grease and tighten screws in sequence shown in Fig. B51 to 140 in.-lbs. (15.8 N•m) torque.

VALVE SYSTEM. Valve face and seat angles should be ground at 45°. Renew valve if margin is 1/16 inch (1.6 mm) or less. Seat width should be 3/64 to 1/16 inch (1.2-1.6 mm). All models are equipped with valve seat inserts. Peen around insert to secure insert in engine.

The valves operate directly in valve guide bores in the aluminum crankcase.

If original valve guide bores are excessively worn, service guides may be installed. Maximum allowable valve guide inside diameter is 0.266 inch (6.76 mm). If B&S valve guide gauge 19122 can be installed to a depth of 5/16 inch (7.9 mm) in valve guide, then a new guide should be installed. Ream guide out first with B&S reamer 19064 to a depth approximately 1/16 inch (1.6 mm) deeper than length of service guide. Press in service guide with B&S driver 19065, then ream using B&S finish reamer 19066. Reface valve seats after new guides are installed.

Some engines may be equipped with a heavy duty exhaust valve or exhaust valve seat made of Cobalite. The Cobalite exhaust valve is marked on the valve head with letters "TXS," "XS" or "PP-XS." The Cobalite exhaust valve and valve seat can be installed on all engines. Some engines may be equipped with a valve rotator on the exhaust valve.

OIL SUMP REMOVAL, AUXILIARY PTO MODELS. On models equipped with an auxiliary pto, one of the oil sump (engine base) to cylinder retaining screws is installed in the recess in the sump for the pto auxiliary drive gear. To remove the oil sump, remove the cover plate (Fig. B52) and then remove the shaft stop (Fig. B53). The gear and shaft can then be moved as shown to allow removal of the oil pan retaining screws. Reverse procedure to reassemble.

CAMSHAFT. The camshaft rides directly in the aluminum of the crankcase or oil pan. The camshaft gear and shaft are integral, except on models which have a camshaft constructed of metal and plastic.

Illustrations Courtesy of Briggs & Stratton Corp.

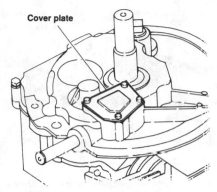

Fig. B52—Remove cover plate on oil pan for access to auxiliary drive shaft and gear.

Shaft stop

Gear and shaft

Oil pan screw

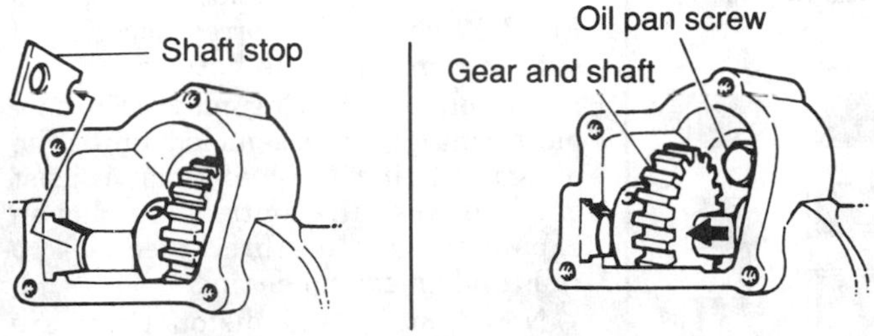

Fig. B53—For access to oil pan retaining screw, pull out shaft stop and move gear in direction of arrow.

Fig. B54—View of yoke type compression release mechanism.

On Models 110000, 111000, 112000, 113000 and 114000, replace camshaft if journal diameter for end that fits into crankcase is 0.436 inch (11.07 mm) or less, or if journal diameter nearer cam gear is 0.498 inch (12.65 mm) or less. Replace camshaft on all other models if either camshaft journal is 0.498 inch (12.65 mm) or less.

Replace camshaft if cam lobe height of either cam lobe is equal or less than following dimension:

Cam Lobe Reject Height

90000, 191000, 92000,
   93000, 94000, 95000,
   96000 . . . . 0.883 in.
                      (22.43 mm)

110000, 111000,
   112000, 113000,
   114000 . . . . 0.870 in.
                      (22.10 mm)

130000, 131000,
   132000, 133000,
   135000 . . . . 0.950 in.
                      (24.13 mm)

Inspect camshaft bearing surfaces in crankcase and oil pan. On model series 110000, 111000, 112000, 113000 and 114000, replace crankcase or oil pan if camshaft bearing diameter in crankcase is 0.443 inch (11.25 mm) or more, or if camshaft bearing diameter in oil pan is greater than 0.504 inch (12.80 mm). For other models, replace crankcase or oil pan if camshaft bearing diameter is greater than 0.504 inch (12.80 mm).

Some camshafts may be equipped with a compression release mechanism, which may be either the yoke type shown in Fig. B54 or the cam-weight type shown in Fig. B55. The mechanism should move freely without binding. No individual components are available.

Some camshafts are also equipped with "Easy-Spin" starting. The intake cam lobe is designed to hold the intake valve slightly open on part of the compression stroke. To check compression, the crankshaft must be turned backwards.

"Easy-Spin" camshafts (cam gears) can be identified by two holes drilled in web of gear. Where part number of an older cam gear and an "Easy-Spin" cam gear are same (except for an "E" following "Easy-Spin" part number), gears are interchangeable.

Some "Easy-Spin" camshafts are also equipped with a mechanically operated compression release on the exhaust lobe. With engine stopped or at cranking speed, the spring holds the actuator cam weight inward against the rocker cam. See Fig. B55. The rocker cam is held slightly above the exhaust cam surface, which in turn holds the exhaust valve open slightly during compression stroke. This compression release greatly reduces power needed for cranking.

When the engine starts and rpm is increased, the actuator cam weight moves outward overcoming spring pressure. See Fig. B56. The rocker cam is rotated below the cam surface to provide normal exhaust valve operation.

On some engines, a worm gear on the camshaft drives an auxiliary drive shaft that is used on self-propelled lawn mowers. The camshaft, worm gear and oil slinger are available only as a unit assembly. A thrust washer (W—Fig. B57) is used to accommodate additional axial

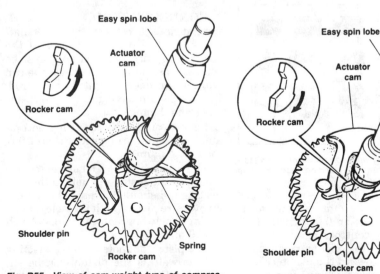

Easy spin lobe

Actuator cam

Rocker cam

Shoulder pin

Spring

Rocker cam

Fig. B55—View of cam-weight type of compression release mechanism. At cranking speed, spring holds actuator cam inward against the rocker cam and rocker cam is forced above exhaust cam surface.

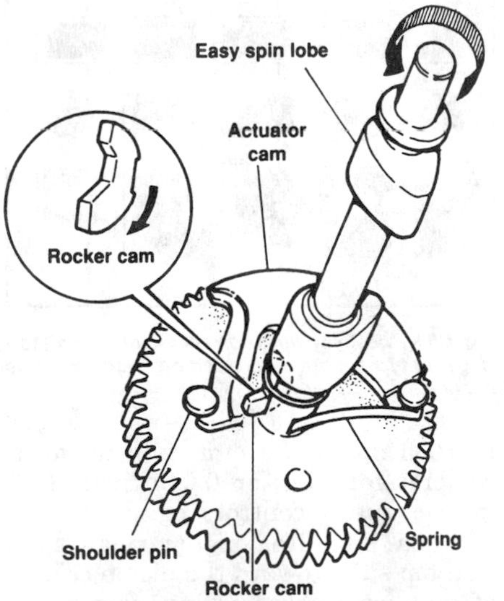

Easy spin lobe

Actuator cam

Rocker cam

Shoulder pin

Spring

Rocker cam

Fig. B56—When engine starts and rpm is increased, actuator cam weight moves outward allowing rocker cam to rotate below exhaust cam surface.

Illustrations Courtesy of Briggs & Stratton Corp.

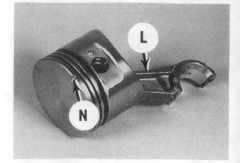

Fig. B57—A thrust washer (W) is located on the end of the auxiliary drive shaft. Shaft rotation determines washer location. See text.

Fig. B58—A tin plated piston is marked with an "L" on the piston crown. The piston is used in an iron cylinder bore.

Fig. B60—If piston crown is notched (N), assemble connecting rod and piston as shown while noting relation of long side of rod (L) and notch (N) in piston crown.

thrust of the camshaft. The thrust washer is located at flywheel end of camshaft if auxiliary drive shaft rotation is clockwise. The thrust washer is located at worm gear end of camshaft if auxiliary shaft rotation is counterclockwise.

PISTON, RINGS AND PIN. Two different types of piston are used depending on the metal used for the cylinder bore. The piston used in an aluminum cylinder bore is chrome plated while the piston used in an iron sleeve is tin plated. The tin plated piston is marked with an "L" on the piston crown (Fig. B58). The pistons are not interchangeable.

Piston diameter sizes are not specified by Briggs & Stratton. The cylinder bore should be measured as outlined in the CYLINDER section.

To check piston ring grooves for wear, install new piston ring in top groove and measure side clearance between ring and ring groove land using a feeler gauge. Renew piston if top piston ring side clearance is 0.007 inch (0.18 mm) or more.

Piston pin is available in a standard size as well as 0.005 inch (0.13 mm) oversize. Renew piston pin if it is out-of-round by 0.0005 inch (0.013 mm) or more. The standard size piston pin should be renewed if it is worn to a diameter of 0.489 inch (12.42 mm) or less.

The piston should be renewed or the piston pin hole in the piston should be reamed to accept an oversize piston pin if the hole diameter is equal to or greater than 0.492 inch (12.50 mm).

Discard piston ring on engines with an iron sleeve if ring end gap is 0.030 inch (0.76 mm) or more for a compression ring or 0.035 inch (0.89 mm) for the oil control ring. Discard piston ring on aluminum bore engines if ring end gap

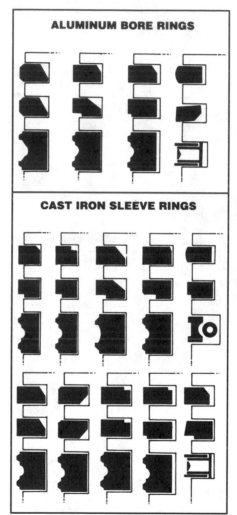

ALUMINUM BORE RINGS

CAST IRON SLEEVE RINGS

Fig. B59—View showing correct location of piston rings for typical ring sets used on engines in this section.

is 0.035 inch (0.89 mm) or more for a compression ring or 0.045 inch (1.14 mm) for the oil control ring.

When installing piston rings, note that top side (toward the piston crown) of some compression rings is marked with a dot to identify the top side of the ring. Several piston ring configurations have been used. Refer to the informa-

tion supplied with the new piston rings for proper ring placement. The chart in Fig. B59 shows the correct location of some piston ring combinations.

The oil control ring may be a one-piece ring or an assembled unit. The assembled oil control ring may consist of two pieces—the control ring plus an expander ring, or three pieces—two rails and an expander ring.

New pistons and piston rings are available in standard size as well as various oversizes to fit a resized cylinder. Be sure the proper size is available before machining or purchasing components.

The piston and connecting rod can be assembled in either direction, except on pistons with a notch used in vertical crankshaft engines. If the piston on a vertical crankshaft engine has a notch in the piston crown, then the piston and connecting rod must be assembled so the notch (N—Fig. B60) and long side of the rod (L) are positioned as shown in Fig. B60.

CONNECTING ROD. The connecting rod rides directly on the crankshaft crankpin. The mating surfaces of the rod and cap are serrated and must be correctly assembled, otherwise the cap will be improperly aligned on the rod. Inspect the connecting rod for excessive wear and damage.

Renew connecting rod if big end diameter is equal to or greater than 1.001 inch (25.43 mm).

The connecting rod should be replaced or the piston pin hole in the connecting rod should be reamed to accept an oversize piston pin if the hole diameter is equal to or greater than 0.492 inch (12.50 mm).

The piston pin hole in the connecting rod, as well as the piston, can be enlarged with a reamer, presuming it is standard size, to accept a piston pin that is 0.005 inch (0.13 mm) larger in diameter than the standard piston pin.

Fig. B61—View of governor and oil slinger assembly used on vertical crankshaft engines so equipped.

Governor flyweights

Oil slinger

M

Fig. B62—Install crankshaft gear so timing mark (M) is out.

Tighten connecting rod screws to 100 in.-lbs. (11.3 N•m) torque.

GOVERNOR. Engines that use a mechanical governor are equipped with a flyweight assembly that is driven by the camshaft gear. The flyweight assembly is mounted on end of camshaft along with oil slinger (Fig. B61). The oil slinger and flyweight assembly are only available as a unit assembly. Inspect flyweight assembly for broken components. Inspect the flyweight assembly for broken or excessively worn components.

CRANKSHAFT AND MAIN BEARINGS. Some crankshafts are equipped with a removable crankshaft gear that is driven by a pin or key in the crankshaft. It may be necessary to pry off gear. Note that gear must be installed on crankshaft so side with timing mark (Fig. B62) is visible (chamfered side is towards crankshaft counterweight). A crankshaft drive pin is not removable, while a crankshaft drive key can be removed.

Inspect all mating surfaces on crankshaft for indications of scoring, scuffing and other damage. Renew crankshaft if crankpin journal diameter is equal to or less than 0.996 inch (25.30 mm).

Renew crankshaft on Models 130000, 131000, 132000, 133000 and 135000 if the pto crankshaft journal diameter is

equal to or less than 0.998 inch (25.35 mm), or if the flywheel end crankshaft journal diameter is equal to or less than 0.873 inch (22.17 mm). Renew crankshaft of all other models if either crankshaft main journal diameter is 0.873 inch (22.17 mm) or less.

NOTE: All models equipped with an auxiliary drive unit have a rejection size for the main bearing journal at the output end of 0.998 inch (25.35 mm).

The crankshaft rides directly in the aluminum of the crankcase and oil pan or in a renewable bushing. On some engines, a bushing can be installed if the aluminum is excessively worn or damaged. Most engines can be repaired using a bushing, but check parts availability on a specific engine.

Tools for reaming and installing service bushings are available from Briggs & Stratton. If the bearings are scored, out-of-round 0.0007 inch (0.018 mm) or more, or are worn larger than the reject size, ream the bearing and install a service bushing.

Main bearing reject size on Models 130000, 131000, 132000, 133000 and 135000 is 1.003 inches (25.48 mm) for the oil pan bearing and 0.878 inch (22.30 mm) for the crankcase bearing. Main bearing reject size on all other models is 0.878 inch (22.30 mm) for either bearing.

NOTE: All models equipped with an auxiliary drive unit have a rejection size for the main bearing in the oil pan of 1.003 inch (25.48 mm).

Install steel-backed aluminum service bushing as follows. Prior to installing bushing, use a chisel to make an indentation in inside edge of bearing bore in crankcase. Install bushing so oil notches are properly aligned and bushing is flush with outer face of bore. Stake bushing into previously made indentation and finish ream bushing. Do not stake where bushing is split.

When installing "DU" type bushing, stake bushing at oil notches in crankcase, but locate bushing so bushing split is not aligned with an oil notch. Bushing should be 1/32 inch (0.8 mm) below face of crankcase bore.

Crankshaft end play is 0.002-0.030 inch (0.05-0.76 mm) on 92500 and 92900 models with a next-to-last digit of "5" in the code number. Crankshaft end play is 0.002-0.008 inch (0.05-0.20 mm) for all other models. At least one 0.015 inch crankcase gasket must be in place when measuring end play. Additional gaskets in several sizes are available to aid in

end play adjustment. If end play is excessive, place shims between crankshaft gear and crankcase.

Refer to VALVE TIMING section for proper timing procedure when installing crankshaft.

CYLINDER. If cylinder bore wear is 0.003 inch (0.08 mm) or more or is 0.0025 inch (0.06 mm) or more out-of-round, cylinder must be bored to next larger oversize.

The standard cylinder bore sizes for each model are given in the following table.

STANDARD CYLINDER
BORE SIZES

Model	Cylinder Diameter
90000, 91000, 92000, 93000, 94000, 95000, 96000	2.5615-2.5625 in. (65.06-65.09 mm)
110000, 111000, 112000, 113000, 114000	2.7802-2.7812 in. (70.62-70.64 mm)
130000, 131000, 132000, 133000, 135000	2.5615-2.5625 in. (65.06-65.09 mm)

A hone is recommended for resizing cylinders. Operate hone at 300-700 rpm and with an up and down movement that will produce a 45° crosshatch pattern. Always check availability of oversize piston and ring sets before honing cylinder.

NOTE: A chrome piston ring set is available for slightly worn standard bore cylinders. No honing or cylinder deglazing is required for these rings. The cylinder bore can be a maximum of 0.005 inch (0.01 mm) oversize when using chrome rings.

VALVE TIMING. Align the timing mark on the camshaft gear with the timing mark on the crankshaft gear as shown in Fig. B63. On engines with a plastic camshaft gear, the dimple on the crankshaft gear tooth should be positioned between the gear teeth on the

Fig. B63—Align timing marks on cam gear and crankshaft gear on plain bearing models.

Fig. B64—On engines with a plastic camshaft gear, the dimple on the crankshaft gear tooth should be positioned between the gear teeth on the camshaft gear marked by the two lines.

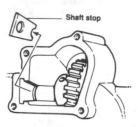

Fig. B65—To remove auxiliary shaft and gear, pull out shaft stop, if not previously removed, and drive pin out of gear hub.

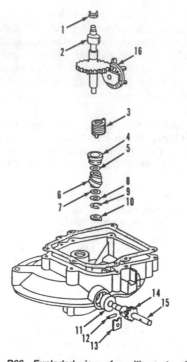

Fig. B66—Exploded view of auxiliary pto shaft assembly used on some model series 110000 engines.

1. Clip washer	9. "E" ring
2. Camshaft assy.	10. Washer
3. Spring	11. Seal
4. Clutch sleeve	12. Pin
5. Thrust washer	13. Shaft stop
6. Worm gear	14. Worm gear
7. Thrust washer	15. Pto shaft
(thick)	16. Governor & oil
8. Copper washer	slinger assy.

camshaft gear marked by the two lines (Fig. B64). Note that other marks (such as "O") on the camshaft gear face are molding impressions.

AUXILIARY PTO. To remove auxiliary pto shaft and gear, refer to Fig. B65 and remove shaft stop, if not previously removed. Drive pin out of gear and shaft then withdraw shaft.

Some model series 110000 engines are equipped with a clutch mechanism on the camshaft to engage the pto shaft assembly. When spring tang of clutch sleeve (4—Fig. B66) is pushed, worm should lock. With spring released, worm should rotate freely in both directions. When assembling clutch and worm, upper end of spring (3) must engage hole in camshaft while lower end of spring must engage hole in clutch sleeve (4). Install lower copper washer (8) so gray coated side is next to thick thrust washer (7). Worm gear end play should be 0.004-0.017 inch (0.10-0.43 mm). Be sure clip of washer (10) properly engages camshaft bearing boss.

FLYWHEEL BRAKE. The engine may be equipped with a band type flywheel brake. To check brake band adjustment, remove starter and properly ground spark plug lead to prevent accidental starting. On electric start models, remove battery. Turn flywheel nut using a torque wrench with brake engaged. Rotating flywheel nut at a steady

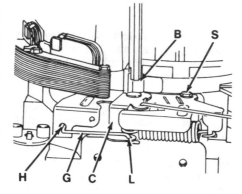

Fig. B67—To adjust flywheel brake, loosen bracket screws (S) and position gauge (G) as outlined in text.

rate in a clockwise direction should require at least 45 in.-lbs. (5.08 N·m) torque. An insufficient torque reading may indicate misadjustment or damaged components. Renew brake band if friction material of band is damaged or less than 0.030 inch (0.76 mm) thick.

To adjust brake, unscrew brake cable retaining screw so hole (H—Fig. B67) is vacant. (If a pop rivet secures the cable, do not remove rivet; gauge tool can be inserted through hole in rivet.) Loosen screws (S) securing brake control

bracket. Place bayonet end of gauge 19256 (G) in hole (L) of control lever (C). Push against control lever and insert opposite end of gauge (G) in hole (H), or in hole of pop rivet if used to secure cable. Apply pressure against bracket until tension on gauge is just removed, then while holding pressure, tighten bracket screws (S) to 25-30 in.-lbs. (2.82-3.39 N·m) torque. As gauge is removed a slight friction should be felt and control lever should not move.

Brake band must be renewed if damaged or if friction material thickness is less than 0.030 inch (0.76 mm). Use tool 19229 to bend retaining tang away from band end (B—Fig. B67).

FLYWHEEL. The flywheel is secured to the crankshaft by a retaining nut or by the starter clutch on engines equipped with a rewind starter on the blower housing. To remove flywheel, remove blower housing and any other components so flywheel is accessible. If equipped with flywheel brake, disconnect brake spring. Secure the flywheel from rotating using Briggs & Stratton or aftermarket flywheel holder, then unscrew starter clutch or retaining nut. Use a suitable puller to remove flywheel from crankshaft.

NOTE: Do not attempt to hold the flywheel by inserting a tool between the fins as damage to flywheel may result.

The tapered portion of flywheel and crankshaft mating surfaces must be clean and smooth with no damage. Renew flywheel if any cracks are evident or any fins are broken. Be sure the keyway in crankshaft and flywheel is not damaged or worn. If flywheel key is replaced, a key made of aluminum must be installed. DO NOT install a steel key.

Install flywheel and key and tighten retaining nut or starter clutch to torque specified in TIGHTENING TORQUES section.

REWIND STARTER. **Rewind Starter On Blower Housing.** A detachable plastic ring may surround the housing of the rewind starter that is mounted on the blower housing. The rope pulley drives a ball-type sprag clutch (Fig. B68) mounted on the flywheel. When the rewind starter is operated, the flywheel rotates and one of the balls will engage a sprag. When the engine runs, the balls are thrown out by centrifugal force to a disengaged position.

To renew a broken rewind spring, proceed as follows: Grasp free outer end of

Fig. B68—View of starter clutch used on engines with a rewind starter mounted on the blower housing.

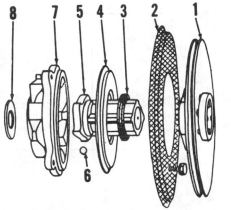

Fig. B71—Exploded view of starter clutch. Refer to Fig. 72 for cutaway view of ratchet (5).

1. Rope pulley
2. Debris screen
3. Rubber seal
4. Ratchet
6. Steel balls
7. Clutch housing (flywheel nut)
8. Spring washer

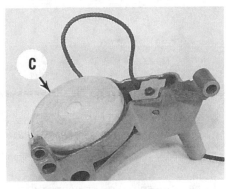

Fig. B73—Pull out rope as shown and rotate pulley counterclockwise to release spring tension. Cover (C) encloses rewind spring.

spring (S—Fig. B69) and pull broken end from starter housing. With blower housing removed, bend up tangs (T) and remove starter pulley from housing. Untie knot in rope and remove rope and inner end of broken spring from pulley. Install rewind spring by threading inner end of spring through notch in starter housing, then engage inner end of spring in pulley hub. Apply a small amount of grease on inner face of pulley and place pulley in housing. Bend the pulley retainer tangs (T—Fig. B69) towards the pulley so the gap between the tang and the pulley is $\frac{1}{16}$ inch (1.6 mm). Insert a ¾ inch bar in pulley hub and turn pulley in a counterclockwise direction until spring is wound tightly. Rotate pulley so rope hole (H—Fig. B70) in pulley is aligned with rope outlet hole in housing, then secure pulley so it cannot rotate. Hook a wire in inner end of rope and thread rope through guide and hole

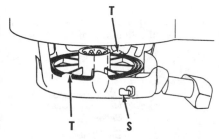

Fig. B69—View of outer rewind spring end (S) and pulley retaining tangs (T).

Fig. B70—Align inner rope hole (H) with rope outlet in housing before inserting rope.

Illustrations Courtesy of Briggs & Stratton Corp.

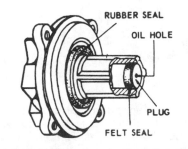

Fig. B72—Cutaway view showing felt seal and plug in end of starter ratchet (5—Fig. B78).

RUBBER SEAL
OIL HOLE
PLUG
FELT SEAL

in pulley; then, tie a knot in rope and release the pulley allowing spring to wind rope into pulley groove.

To renew starter rope only, it is not generally necessary to remove starter pulley and spring. Wind up the spring and install new rope as outlined in preceding paragraph.

To disassemble starter clutch unit, refer to Fig. B71 and proceed as follows: Remove rotating screen (2) and starter ratchet cover (4). Lift ratchet (5) from housing and crankshaft and extract the steel balls (6). If necessary to remove housing (7), hold flywheel and unscrew housing in counterclockwise direction using B&S tool 19224. When installing housing, be sure spring washer (8) is in place on crankshaft with cup (concave) side towards flywheel; then, tighten housing securely. Inspect felt seal and plug in outer end of ratchet (Fig. B72). Renew ratchet if seal or plug is damaged as these parts are not serviced separately. Lubricate the felt with oil and place ratchet on crankshaft. Insert the steel balls and install ratchet cover, rubber seal and rotating screen.

Vertical-Pull Rewind Starter.

Some "L" head Briggs & Stratton engines are equipped with a vertical-pull rewind starter that is mounted on the

Fig. B74—Anchor screw (S) retains spring anchor (A).

side of the engine. When the starter rope is pulled, the starter gear inside the starter housing travels up a helix to engage the ring gear on the flywheel.

To renew rope or spring, first remove all spring tension from rope. Extract rope from starter as shown in Fig. B73, then wind rope and pulley counterclockwise three turns to remove spring tension. Carefully pry off the plastic spring cover (C). Refer to Fig. B74 and remove anchor screw (S) and spring anchor (A). Carefully remove spring from housing. Unscrew and remove rope guide (G—Fig. B75), then remove pulley and gear assembly (Fig. B76).

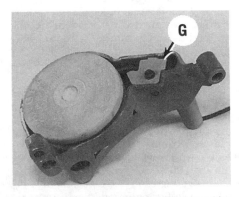

Fig. B75—Unscrew rope guide for access to friction link (L—Fig. B78).

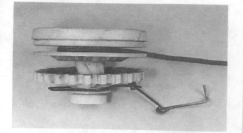

Fig. B76—View of pulley, gear and friction link assembly.

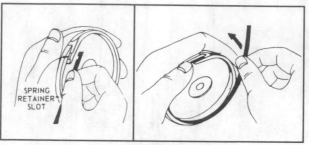

Fig. B77—Hook outer end of spring in retainer slot, then coil the spring counterclockwise in the housing.

It is not necessary to remove the gear retainer unless pulley or gear is damaged and renewal is necessary. Clean and inspect parts. The friction link should move the gear to both extremes of its travel. If not, renew the linkage assembly.

Install new spring by hooking end in retainer slot and winding until spring is coiled in housing (Fig. B77). Insert new rope through the housing and into the pulley. Tie a small knot, heat seal the knot and pull it tight into the recess in pulley. Install pulley assembly in the housing with friction link (L—Fig. B78) in groove in casting as shown. Install rope guide. Rotate pulley counterclockwise until rope is fully wound. Hook free end of spring to anchor, install anchor screw and tighten to 75-90 in.-lbs. (8-11 N·m) torque. Lubricate spring with a small amount of engine oil. Snap the plastic spring cover in place. Preload spring by pulling out about one foot of rope as shown in Fig. B79, then winding rope and pulley two or three turns clockwise. Check starter operation.

ELECTRIC STARTER MOTOR.
Two types of electric starter motors have been used.

The starter shown in Fig. B80 is typical of that used with a 6 or 12-volt battery on models smaller than 12.6 cubic inch displacement. At a no-load minimum speed of 800 rpm measured at end of helix (2), 6-volt starter should draw no more than 18 amps and 12-volt starter should draw no more than 8 amps. Do not run starter for more than five seconds during testing. Starter pinion and helix must move without binding. Do not apply oil to helix (2) or nylon gear (3). Renew brushes if length (L—Fig. B81) is 5/64 inch (2.0 mm) or less.

When assembling starter, install fiber washer (11—Fig. B82), gray plastic washers (15) and steel washer (12) on armature shaft. Install sufficient gray plastic washers (9—Fig. B80) at drive end of armature so armature shaft end play is 0.005-0.025 inch (0.13-0.63 mm). Be sure notches in end cap, housing and end bracket are aligned. Apply approximately ¾ ounce of gear lubricant under

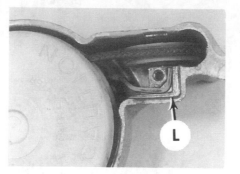

Fig. B78—Friction link (L) must fit in groove in housing.

clutch (7). Tap end cap (14) to seat bearings and tighten through-bolts to 25 in.-lbs. (2.8 N·m) torque. Tighten starter cover screws to 25 in.-lbs. (2.8 N·m) torque.

The starter shown in Fig. B83 is used on 130000 series engines with 12-volt and 110-volt versions available. No-load test of 12-volt starter should indicate a minimum tachometer reading of 5600 rpm at pinion gear (4) with a maximum ammeter reading of 6 amps. No-load test of 110-volt starter should indicate a minimum tachometer reading of 8300

Fig. B79—With rope pulled out as shown, rotate pulley clockwise to apply tension to rewind spring.

rpm at pinion gear (4) with a maximum ammeter reading of 1½ amps.

WARNING: Exercise particular caution when testing 110-volt starter and starter circuit as damaged components may result in a dangerous short circuit.

Do not clamp starter housing (11) in a vise or strike housing of the 110-volt

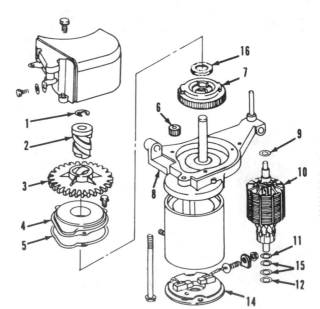

Fig. B80—Exploded view of starter used on System 3 and 4 engines.

1. "E" ring
2. Helix
3. Nylon gear
4. Cover
5. Gasket
6. Pinion gear
7. Clutch gear
8. Drive end bracket
9. Gray plastic washer
10. Armature
11. Fiber washer
12. Steel washer
13. Field housing
14. Brush end cap
15. Gray plastic washers
16. Felt washer

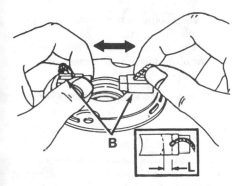

Fig. B81—Minimum brush length (L) is 5/64 inch (2.0 mm).

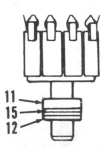

Fig. B82—Install gray plastic washers (15) between fiber washer (11) and steel washer (12).

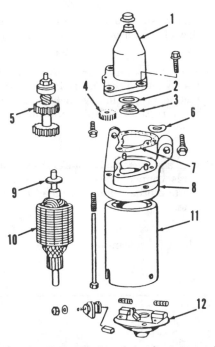

Fig. B83—Exploded view of electric starter used on 130000 series engines.

1. Drive housing
2. Washer
3. Retainer
4. Gear
5. Drive assy.
6. Spring washer
7. Gasket
8. Drive end bracket
9. Thrust washer
10. Armature
11. Field housing
12. Brush end cap

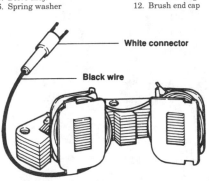

Fig. B84—Drawing of alternator used on System 3 and System 4 engine models.

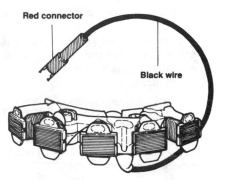

Fig. B85—Drawing of 1.2 amp alternator used on some 130000, 131000, 132000, 133000 and 135000 engine models.

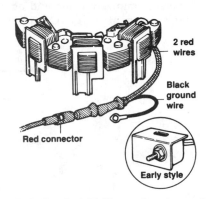

Fig. B86—Drawing of 1-1/2 amp alternator used on some 130000, 131000, 132000, 133000 and 135000 engine models.

starter as ceramic magnets may crack. Make match marks on end bracket (8), housing (11) and end cap (12) before disassembly so they can be reassembled in their original positions. Renew brushes if length is ¼ inch (6.4 mm) or less.

ALTERNATOR. Some Briggs & Stratton engines are equipped with an alternator adjacent to the flywheel to provide electrical energy. A rectifier (diode) must be installed to provide direct current for charging the battery.

Identification. Model 90000, 91000, 92000, 93000, 94000, 110000, 111000, 112000, 113000 and 114000 engines may be equipped with a System 3 or System 4 alternator as shown in Fig. B84. The System 3 and System 4 alternator coils are mounted outside the flywheel. Refer to the following System 3 and System 4 section for testing procedures.

Model 130000, 131000, 132000, 133000 and 135000 engines may be equipped with either the 1.2 amp alternator shown in Fig. B85 or the 1.5 amp alternator shown in Fig. B86. The charging coils for both 1.2 and 1.5 amp alternators are mounted under the flywheel. Refer to the appropriate following 1.2 Amp Alternator or 1.5 Amp Alternator section for testing procedures.

"System 3" and "System 4." Refer to Fig. B84. To test alternator output, disconnect black stator lead at white connector. Connect red lead of a DC ammeter to stator lead and black ammeter lead to a good engine ground. Alternator output should be least 0.5 amps DC with engine running at 2800 rpm. If alternator output is zero or low and stator air gap is correct, replace stator.

The air gap between the stator and the flywheel magnets should be 0.010 inch (0.25 mm). The stator attaching screws should be tightened to 25 in.-lbs. torque.

1.2 Amp Alternator. Refer to Fig. B85. The 1.2 amp alternator provides battery charging current. The stator is located under the flywheel. A 12 ampere hour battery should be used for warm temperature operation and a 24 ampere hour battery should be used for cold temperatures.

To test alternator output, disconnect black stator lead at red connector. Connect red lead of a DC ammeter to stator lead and black ammeter lead to engine. Alternator output should be least 1.0 amps DC with engine running at 3600 rpm. If alternator output is zero or low, replace stator.

1.5 Amp Alternator. Refer to Fig. B86. The 1.5 amp alternator provides battery charging current. The stator is located under the flywheel. A 12 ampere hour battery should be used for warm temperature operation and a 24 ampere hour battery should be used for cold temperatures.

The solid-state rectifier on early models is adjacent to starter drive housing, while on later models the rectifier diodes are contained in the stator wire near the connector. Only later inline type rectifier is available and may be substituted for early type.

To test alternator output, disconnect charging lead from charging terminal on early models, or disconnect stator lead at connector on later models. Connect red lead of a DC ammeter to charging terminal or stator lead and black ammeter lead to engine. Alternator output should be least 1.2 amps DC with engine running at 3600 rpm. Test rectifier if output is low or zero.

Check for a faulty rectifier as follows:

1. With engine stopped, disconnect lead from output terminal on early models, or disconnect stator connector on later models.

2. Insert a pin in one of the stator wires and connect one ohmmeter lead to pin and other ohmmeter lead to output terminal on early models or to end of connector on later models.

3. Check for continuity.

4. Reverse ohmmeter leads and again check for continuity. Ohmmeter should show a continuity reading (low ohms) for one direction only.

5. Repeat test on other stator wire. If tests show no continuity in either direction or continuity in both directions, rectifier is faulty and must be replaced.

6. With a pin inserted in one of the stator wires, connect one ohmmeter lead to pin and other ohmmeter lead to engine.

7. Check for continuity.

8. Reverse ohmmeter leads and again check for continuity. Ohmmeter should show a continuity reading (low ohms) for one direction only.

9. Repeat test on other stator wire.

10. Replace stator lead if tests indicate rectifier diodes are faulty.

The old stator leads must be cut and the new stator leads must be attached using rosin core solder. Mechanical fasteners must not be used to splice the old and new stator leads together.

If rectifier tests satisfactorily, replace stator.

BRIGGS & STRATTON
4-STROKE QUANTUM ENGINES

Model	Bore	Stroke	Displacement	Power Rating
100700	2.56 in.	1.94 in. (65.1 mm)	10 cu.in. (49.3 mm)	3.5 hp (164 cc) (2.6 kW)
12A800, 12D800, 121700, 121800, 122700, 122800, 123700, 123800, 124700, 124800, 125700, 126700, 126800, 127700, 127800, 128700, 128800, 129700, 129800	2.69 in. (68.0 mm)	2.04 in. (51.8 mm)	11.57 cu.in. (190 cc)	3.5, 4.0, 5 hp (2.6, 3.0, 3.8 kW)

ENGINE INFORMATION

These Quantum models are air-cooled, four-stroke, single-cylinder engines. The engine has a vertical crankshaft and utilizes a compression release. Refer to page 47 for a table that outlines the Briggs & Stratton model numbering system.

MAINTENANCE

LUBRICATION. All models are lubricated by an oil slinger that is gear-driven by the camshaft.

It is recommended that the oil be changed after first eight hours of operation and after every 50 hours of operation or at least once each operating season. Change oil weekly or after every 25 hours of operation if equipment undergoes severe usage.

Engine oil should meet or exceed latest API service classification. Use SAE 30 oil for temperatures above 40° F (4° C); use SAE 10W-30 oil for temperatures between 0° F (−18° C) and 100° F (38° C); below 20° F (−7° C) use petroleum based SAE 5W-20 or a suitable synthetic oil.

Crankcase capacity is 1¼ pints (0.6 liters).

AIR CLEANER. The paper type filter element (Fig. BS200) should be cleaned and inspected after every 25 hours of engine operation, or after three months, whichever occurs first. Tap the filter gently to dislodge accumulated dirt. Filter may be washed using warm water and nonsudsing detergent di-

rected from inside of filter to outside. DO NOT use petroleum-based cleaners or solvents to clean filter. DO NOT direct pressurized air towards filter. Let filter air dry thoroughly, then inspect filter and discard it if damaged or cannot be cleaned. Clean filter canister.

A fuel primer system is used on some models which has the primer bulb incorporated into the air filter back plate. Check the condition of the primer bulb and hoses. Replace damaged parts as required. The crankcase breather is at-

tached to the air cleaner base with a hose on all models. Make sure the hoses are properly connected and in good condition. If the air filter back plate is removed, tighten the attaching screws evenly to 40 in.-lbs. (4.5 N•m) torque.

FUEL FILTER. The fuel tank is equipped with a filter at the outlet. On some models, an inline filter may also be installed in the fuel line. Check filters periodically during operating season and clean or renew as necessary.

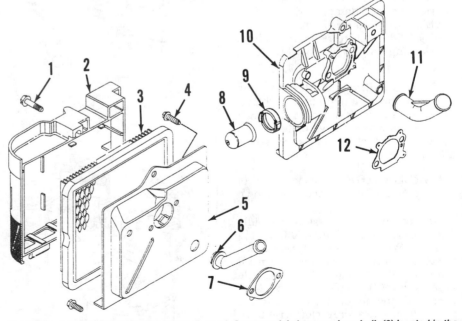

Fig. B200—A flat cartridge type air cleaner is used. Some models have a primer bulb (8) located in the back plate (10).

1. Screw	4. Screw	7. Gasket
2. Cover	5. Back plate	8. Primer bulb
3. Filter cartridge	6. Breather hose	9. Retainer

10. Back plate (w/primer)
11. Breather hose
12. Gasket

Fig. B201—Clearance between fiber disc valve and crankcase breather housing must be less than 0.045 inch (1.15 mm). A spark plug wire gauge may be used to check clearance as shown, but do not apply pressure against disc valve.

CRANKCASE BREATHER. The crankcase breather is built into the tappet chamber cover. A fiber disc acts as a one-way valve. The breather allows vapor from the crankcase to be evacuated to the air filter back plate, but blocks the return flow of air, thus maintaining a vacuum in the crankcase. The vacuum prevents oil from being forced out of the engine past the piston rings, oil seals and gaskets.

Clearance between fiber disc check valve and breather body (Fig. B201) should not exceed 0.045 inch (1.14 mm). If it is possible to insert a 0.045 inch (1.14 mm) wire between disc and breather body, renew breather assembly. Do not use excessive force when measuring gap. Disc should not stick or bind during operation. Renew if distorted or damaged. Inspect breather tube and hose for leakage.

SPARK PLUG. Recommended spark plug is Champion RJ19LM or J19LM. Specified spark plug electrode gap is 0.030 inch (0.76 mm). Tighten spark plug to 165 in.-lbs. (19 N•m) torque.

CAUTION: Briggs & Stratton does not recommend using abrasive blasting to clean spark plugs as this may introduce some abrasive material into the engine which could cause extensive damage.

CARBURETOR. Exploded view of carburetor used on all models is shown in Fig. B202.

Adjustment. Initial setting of idle mixture screw (9—Fig. B203) is 1¼ turn out. With engine at normal operating temperature and equipment control lever in "SLOW" position, adjust idle speed screw (7) so engine idles at 1400 rpm. With engine running at idle speed, turn idle mixture screw clockwise until engine speed just starts to drop. Note screw position. Turn idle mixture screw counterclockwise until engine speed just starts to drop again. Note screw

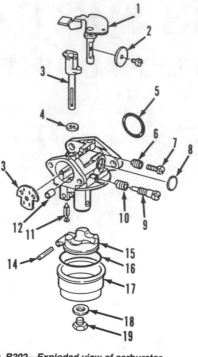

Fig. B202—Exploded view of carburetor.

1. Throttle shaft
2. Throttle plate
3. Choke shaft
4. Washer
5. Gasket
6. Spring
7. Idle speed screw
8. Welch plug
9. Idle mixture screw
10. Spring
11. Fuel inlet valve
12. Main air jet
13. Choke plate
14. Float pin
15. Float
16. Gasket
17. Fuel bowl
18. Gasket
19. Screw

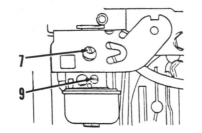

Fig. B203—View showing location of idle speed screw (7) and idle mixture screw (9).

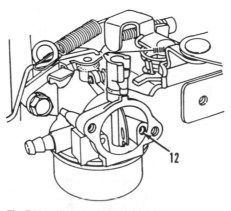

Fig. B204—Remove main air jet (12) if engine does not run properly at high altitudes.

position, then turn screw to midpoint between the noted screw positions. If engine will not accelerate cleanly, slightly enrich mixture by turning idle mixture screw counterclockwise. If necessary, readjust idle speed screw.

High speed mixture is controlled by a fixed main jet. On some models, the main jet is a drilled passage in the fuel bowl retaining screw (19—Fig. B202).

On early models, the main jet size cannot be changed from the standard size. If the engine does not run properly at high altitude, remove main air jet (12—Fig. B204) and install a similar jet with a larger size to adjust the mixture for smooth operation.

On later models, the fuel bowl retaining screw (19--Fig. B202) is available with optional main jet sizes. The standard size is correct for most applications, but a smaller size may be required for operation at high altitude. An identifying number or letter may be stamped on the outside of the main jet indicating the size of the main jet passage. Smaller numbers or letters nearer the first of the alphabet indicate smaller jet sizes.

Overhaul. To disassemble, remove fuel bowl screw (19—Fig. B202) and separate fuel bowl (17), float (15) and fuel inlet valve (11) from carburetor body. Unscrew idle mixture screw (9). A ⁵⁄₃₂ inch (4 mm) diameter punch ground flat at the end makes a suitable tool for removing Welch plug (8). Clean components with suitable carburetor cleaning solvent. Discard any parts which are damaged or excessively worn.

When reassembling the carburetor, observe the following: Do not deform Welch plug (8) during installation. When installed properly, it should be flat. Seal outer edges of plug with non-hardening sealer. Install choke and throttle plates so numbers are on outer face when choke or throttle plate is in closed position. Install fuel inlet seat using B&S driver 19057 or a suitable tool so grooved face of seat is toward the inside. Float height is not adjustable. Install a new gasket (16) and fiber washer (18). Tighten fuel bowl retaining screw (19) to 50 in.-lbs. (5.6 N•m) torque. Tighten the two carburetor mounting nuts to 75 in.-lbs. (8.5 N•m) torque. Tighten the screws attaching the air cleaner back plate evenly to 40 in.-lbs. (4.5 N•m) torque.

ENGINE CONTROLS. The engine may be equipped with a control unit that adjusts engine speed and stops the engine with a grounding switch. On models with a choke, the same controls open/close the carburetor choke.

On models with remote control, the control wire must travel at least

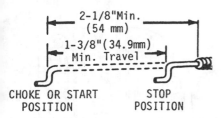

Fig. B205—For proper operation of Choke-A-Matic controls, remote control wire must extend to dimension shown and have a minimum travel of 1-3/8 inches (34.9 mm).

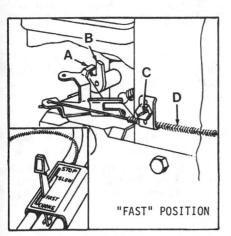

Fig. B206—On Choke-A-Matic controls shown, lever (A) should just contact choke shaft arm (B) when control is in "FAST" position. If not, loosen screw (C) and move control wire housing (D) as required, then tighten screw.

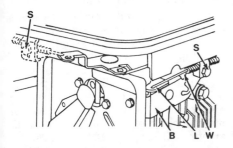

Fig. B207—View of Choke-A-Matic controls used on 121000, 122000, 123000, 124000, 125000 and 126000 models. Cable housing screw may be located at either location (S).

1⅜inches (35 mm) for proper Choke-A-Matic operation. See Fig. B205.

Model 100700. To check operation of Choke-A-Matic carburetor control, move control lever to "CHOKE" position. Carburetor choke plate must be completely closed. Move control lever to "STOP" position. Magneto grounding switch should be making contact. With the control lever in "RUN", "FAST" or "SLOW" position, carburetor choke should be completely open. On units with remote control, synchronize movement of remote lever to carburetor control lever by loosening screw (C—Fig. B206) and moving control wire housing (D) as required; then, tighten screw to

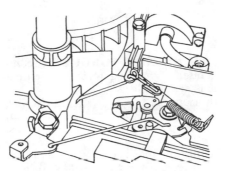

Fig. B208—View of governor linkage on Model 100700.

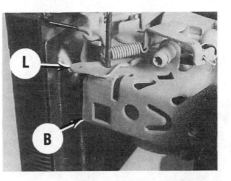

Fig. B209—To adjust governor on Models 121000, 122000, 123000, 124000, 125000 and 126000, move equipment control lever to "FAST" position and place an 1/8-inch rod through holes in governor control lever (L) and bracket (B), then refer to Fig. B210.

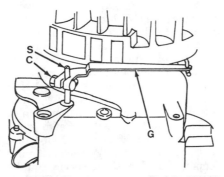

Fig. B210—The governor on Models 121000, 122000, 123000, 124000, 125000 and 126000 is adjusted by holding governor lever (G) while turning governor shaft (S) counterclockwise as outlined in text.

clamp the housing securely. Check for proper operation.

All 12 Cubic Inch Displacement Models. If equipment control lever has detents, proceed as follows: Move equipment control lever to "FAST" position and loosen cable clamp screw (S—Fig. B207). Move cable so 1/8 inch (3 mm) holes in governor control lever (L) and bracket (B) are aligned and tighten cable clamp screw (S). Check for proper operation. If equipped with stop switch, switch (W) should contact governor control lever when equipment control lever is in "STOP" position.

If equipment control lever does not have detents proceed as follows: Move equipment control lever to "CHOKE" position and loosen cable clamp screw (S—Fig. B207). Move cable so carburetor choke plate is closed and tighten clamp screw (S). Check for proper operation. If equipped with stop switch, switch (W) should contact governor control lever when equipment control lever is in "STOP" position.

On models equipped with a primer bulb (8--Fig. B200) incorporated in the air cleaner back plate, adjustment procedure is similar to models with choke. The controls must move freely and completely from "FAST" to "STOP" positions.

GOVERNOR. An air vane type governor is used on Model 107000; other (all 12 cid models) are equipped with a mechanical governor.

Model 107000. Refer to Fig. B208 for view of the air vane governor control linkage. No adjustment is required. The governor mechanism should not bind. Renew any damaged or worn components.

All 12 CID Models. These engines are equipped with a mechanical governor. The governor gear and flyweight assembly is driven by the camshaft and located inside the crankcase. Refer to REPAIRS section for service information.

To adjust governor, move equipment control lever to "FAST" position and place an ⅛ inch (3 mm) diameter rod through holes in governor control lever (L—Fig. B209) and bracket (B). Loosen clamp bolt (C—Fig. B210) then rotate governor shaft (S) counterclockwise until it stops. Hold shaft and tighten clamp bolt to 35-45 in.-lbs. (4-5 N•m) torque.

IGNITION. All models are equipped with a Magnetron breakerless ignition system. All components are located outside the flywheel.

To check spark, remove spark plug and connect spark plug cable to B&S tester 19051, then ground remaining tester lead to engine. Spin engine at 350 rpm or more. If spark jumps the 0.165 inch (4.2 mm) tester gap, system is functioning properly.

To remove armature and Magnetron module, remove flywheel shroud and armature retaining screws. Disconnect stop switch wire from module. When reinstalling armature, position armature so air gap between armature legs and flywheel surface is 0.006-0.010 inch (0.15-0.25 mm).

On models equipped with a flywheel brake, stop switch (S—Figs. B211 and B212) should ground ignition system

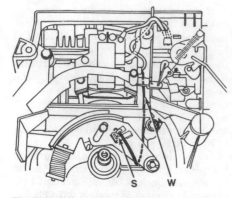

Fig. B211—View showing location of stop switch (S) and proper routing of stop switch wire (W) on Model 100700.

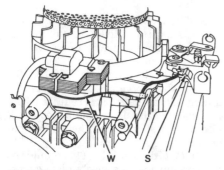

Fig. B212—View showing location of stop switch (S) and proper routing of stop switch wire (W) on Models 121000, 122000, 123000, 124000, 125000 and 126000.

when flywheel brake is activated. Note in Figs. B211 and B212 correct routing for stop switch wire (W) of models equipped with flywheel brake system.

VALVE ADJUSTMENT. To correctly set tappet clearance, remove spark plug and breather/valve tappet chamber cover. Rotate crankshaft in normal direction (clockwise at flywheel) so piston is at top dead center on compression stroke. Continue to rotate crankshaft so piston is 1/4 inch (6.4 mm) down from top dead center. Using a feeler gauge, measure clearance between intake and exhaust valve stem ends and the tappets.

Valve tappet clearance (engine cold) should be 0.005-0.007 inch (0.13-0.18 mm) for intake valve and 0.007-0.009 inch (0.18-0.23 mm) for exhaust valve. Adjust tappet clearance by grinding end of valve stem to increase clearance or grind valve seat deeper to decrease clearance.

CYLINDER HEAD. Manufacturer recommends that after every 100-300 hours of operation the cylinder head is removed and cleaned of deposits.

REPAIRS

TIGHTENING TORQUES. Recommended tightening torque specifications are as follows:

Alternator	25 in.-lbs. (2.8 N•m)
Carburetor mounting nuts	90 in.-lbs. (10.2 N•m)
Connecting rod	100 in.-lbs. (11.3 N•m)
Crankcase cover	85 in.-lbs. (9.6 N•m)
Cylinder head	140 in.-lbs. (16 N•m)
Spark plug	165 in.-lbs. (19 N•m)

CYLINDER HEAD. Lubricate cylinder head screws with graphite grease before installation. Do not apply sealant to the head gasket. Tighten screws hand-tight, then tighten in sequence shown in Fig. B213 or Fig. B214 to 140 in.-lbs. (16 N•m) torque.

VALVE SYSTEM. Valve face and seat angles should be ground at 45°. Renew valve if margin is 1/16 inch (1.6 mm) or less. Seat width should be 3/64 to 1/16 inch (1.2-1.6 mm).

The valves operate directly in valve guide bores in the aluminum crankcase. If original valve guide bores are excessively worn, service guides may be installed. Maximum allowable valve guide inside diameter is 0.266 inch (6.76 mm). If B&S valve guide gauge 19122 can be installed to a depth of 5/16 inch (7.9 mm) in valve guide, then a new guide should be installed. Ream guide out first with B&S reamer 19064 to a depth approximately 1/16 inch (1.6 mm) deeper than length of service guide. Press in service guide with B&S driver 19065 then ream using B&S finish reamer 19066. Reface valve seats after new guides are installed.

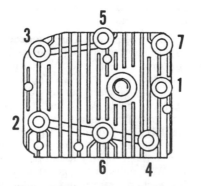

Fig. B213—Tighten cylinder head screws on Model 100700 in sequence shown.

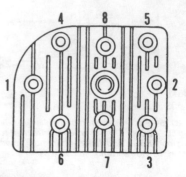

Fig. B214—Tighten cylinder head screws on Models 121000, 122000, 123000, 124000, 125000 and 126000 in sequence shown.

CAMSHAFT. Some models are equipped with a camshaft (22—Figs. B215 and B216) constructed of metal and plastic. The camshaft and gear should be inspected for wear and damage on journals, cam lobes and gear teeth. Renew camshaft if bearing journals are 0.498 inch (12.65 mm) or less.

When installing camshaft, align timing mark on camshaft gear with mark on crankshaft gear as shown in Fig. B217.

PISTON, PIN, RINGS AND CONNECTING ROD. The connecting rod and piston may be removed as an assembly after removing the cylinder head and lower crankcase.

Renew piston if it shows visible signs of wear, scoring or scuffing. If, after cleaning carbon from top ring groove, a new top ring has a side clearance of 0.007 inch (0.18 mm) or more, renew the piston. Renew piston or hone piston pin hole to 0.005 inch (0.13 mm) oversize if pin hole is 0.0005 inch (0.013 mm) or more out-of-round, or is worn to a diameter of 0.491 inch (12.47 mm).

If piston pin is 0.0005 inch (0.013 mm) or more out-of-round, or is worn to a diameter of 0.489 inch (12.42 mm), renew piston pin. A piston pin that is 0.005 inch (0.13 mm) oversize is available.

Piston and piston rings are available in standard size and oversizes of 0.010, 0.020 and 0.030 inch.

Connecting rod reject size for crankpin hole is 1.001 inch (25.43 mm). Renew rod if piston pin hole is scored or out-of-round more than 0.0005 inch (0.013 mm) or pin hole is 0.492 inch (12.50 mm) or greater. The connecting rod piston pin hole can be reamed to accept a 0.005 inch (0.13 mm) oversize piston pin. A connecting rod with 0.020 inch (0.51 mm) undersize big end diameter is available to accommodate a worn crankpin (machining instructions are included with new rod).

Install piston on connecting rod so notch in piston crown will be toward flywheel as shown in Fig. B218. Be sure that offset connecting rod is positioned as shown on rod and that match marks on rod and cap are aligned. Refer to Fig. B219 and install piston rings according to type of ring set to be installed on piston.

Tighten connecting rod screws to 100 in.-lbs. (11.3 N•m) torque.

CRANKSHAFT AND MAIN BEARINGS. The crankshaft rides directly in the crankcase bores. Rejection sizes for crankshaft are: pto-end bearing journal 1.060 inch (26.92 mm); flywheel-end bearing journal 0.873 inch (22.17 mm); crankpin 0.996 inch (25.30 mm). A connecting rod with 0.020 inch (0.51 mm) undersize big end diameter is available to accommodate a worn crankpin (machining instructions are included with new rod).

The crankcase main bearing bore rejection size is 0.878 inch (22.30 mm). The crankcase cover or oil pan main bearing bore rejection size is 1.065 inch (27.05 mm). A service bushing is available for installation in the flywheel-side crankcase if the bearing bore requires service. No bushing is available for the

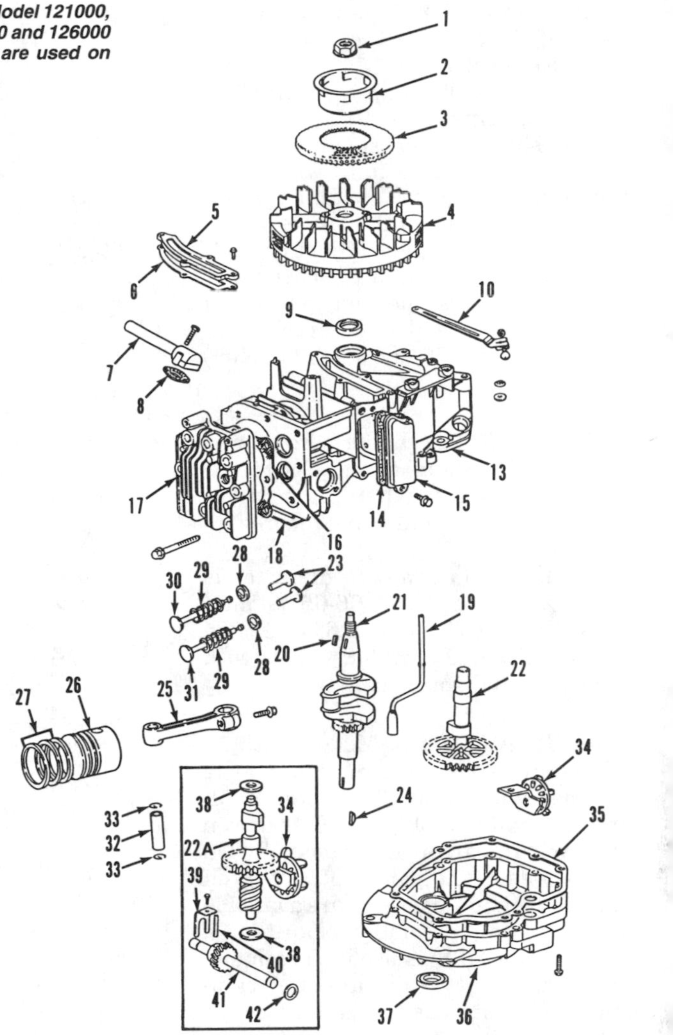

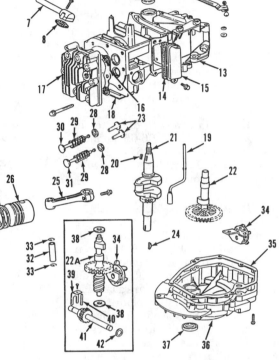

Fig. B216—Exploded view of Model 121000, 122000, 123000, 124000, 125000 and 126000 engine. Components in inset are used on models with an auxiliary pto.

1. Nut
2. Starter cup
3. Screen
4. Flywheel
5. Baffle
6. Gasket
7. Intake manifold tube
8. Gasket
9. Seal
10. Governor lever
11. Push nut
12. Washer
13. Cylinder block
14. Gasket
15. Breather & tappet cover
16. Head gasket
17. Cylinder head
18. Shroud
19. Governor shaft
20. Key
21. Crankshaft
22. Camshaft
22A. Camshaft, auxiliary pto gear
23. Tappets
24. Key
25. Connecting rod
26. Piston
27. Piston rings
28. Valve retainers
29. Valve springs
30. Intake valve
31. Exhaust valve
32. Piston pin
33. Clips
34. Governor & oil slinger
35. Gasket
36. Crankcase
37. Seal
38. Washer
39. Shaft stop
40. Roll pin
41. Auxiliary pto shaft
42. Seal

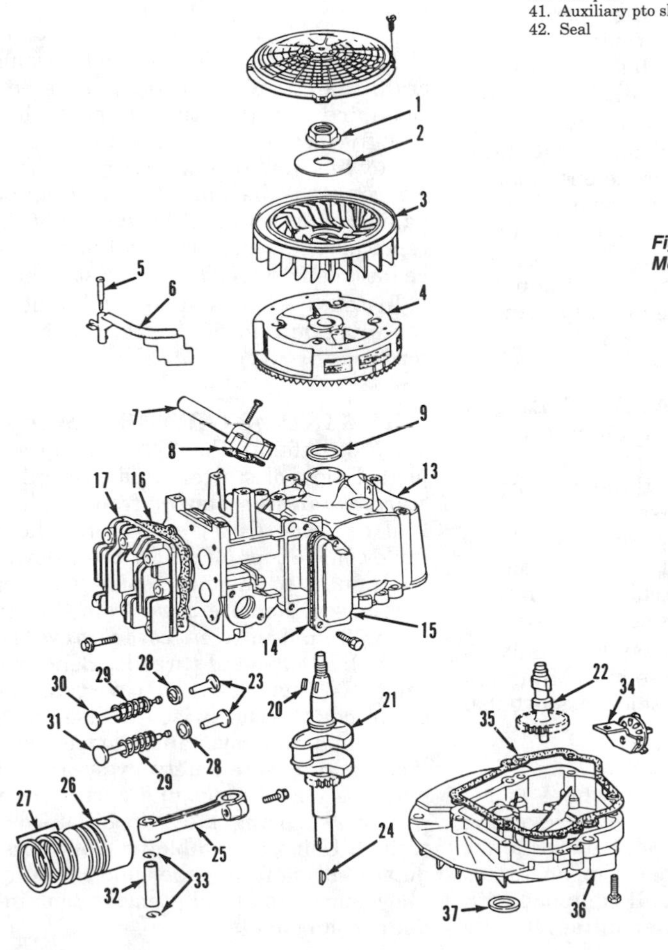

Fig. B215—Exploded view of Model 100700 engine.

1. Nut
2. Washer
3. Fan
4. Flywheel
5. Pivot pin
6. Governor air vane
7. Intake manifold tube
8. Gasket
9. Seal
13. Cylinder block
14. Gasket
15. Breather & tappet cover
16. Head gasket
17. Cylinder head
20. Key
21. Crankshaft
22. Camshaft
23. Tappets
24. Key
25. Connecting rod
26. Piston
27. Piston rings
28. Valve retainers
29. Valve springs
30. Intake valve
31. Exhaust valve
32. Piston pin
33. Clips
34. Governor & oil slinger
35. Gasket
36. Crankcase
37. Seal

Fig. B217—Align timing marks (M) on camshaft gear and crankshaft gear.

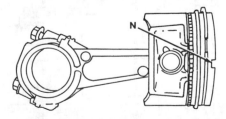

Fig. B218—Notch (N) in piston crown must be toward flywheel.

pto-side crankcase so it must be renewed if bearing bore is damaged or worn excessively.

Install oil seals so lip is towards inside of crankcase.

Crankshaft end play should be 0.002-0.030 inch (0.05-0.76 mm) with 0.015 inch crankcase gasket installed. Additional gaskets of several thicknesses are available for end play adjustment. If end play is excessive, a thrust washer which can be installed on pto end of crankshaft is available. Tighten crankcase screws to 85 in.-lbs. (9.6 N•m) torque.

CYLINDER. If cylinder bore wear is 0.003 inch (0.76 mm) or more, or out-of-round is 0.0025 inch (0.04 mm) or greater, cylinder must be rebored to next oversize.

Standard cylinder bore diameter is 2.5615-2.5625 inch (65.06-65.09 mm) for Model 100700 and 2.6875-2.6885 inch (68.26-68.29 mm) for models with 12 cubic inch displacement.

AUXILIARY PTO. Models with 12 cubic inch displacement may be equipped with an auxiliary pto. Auxiliary pto shaft (41—Fig. B220) is driven by a worm gear on the camshaft. On these models, the camshaft (22A), oil slinger (34) and worm gear are available only as a unit assembly. Note that a thrust washer (38) is used to accommodate additional axial thrust of camshaft. Thrust washer is located at flywheel end of camshaft if pto shaft rotation is clockwise, while thrust washer is located at gear end of camshaft if pto shaft rotation is counterclockwise.

To remove auxiliary pto shaft and gear, unscrew Allen screw (S—Fig. B221) on bottom of crankcase. Insert a punch through the screw hole and drive out pin (40) retaining gear. Unfasten shaft stop (39) and withdraw auxiliary pto shaft.

FLYWHEEL BRAKE. Model 100700. The engine is equipped with a pad type flywheel brake (Fig. B211).

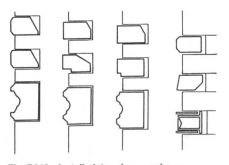

Fig. B219—Install piston rings as shown.

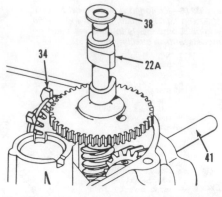

Fig. B220—View of auxiliary pto assembly used on some Models 121000, 122000, 123000, 124000, 125000 and 126000.

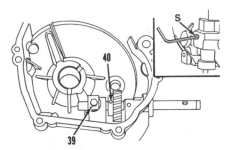

Fig. B221—Drive out roll pin (40) and unfasten shaft stop (39) to remove auxiliary pto shaft.

The brake should stop the engine within three seconds when the operator releases mower safety control and the speed control is in high speed position. Stopping time can be checked using tool 19255. Adjustment is not required.

The brake mechanism is located under the flywheel. If brake operation is unsatisfactory, remove flywheel and renew any components which are damaged or excessively worn. Brake pad and arm must be renewed if the pad is damaged or friction material thickness is less than 0.090 inch (2.3 mm).

FLYWHEEL BRAKE. All 12 CID Models. The engine is equipped with a pad type flywheel brake (Fig. B222). The brake should stop the engine within three seconds when the operator releases mower safety control and the speed control is in high speed position. Stopping time can be checked using tool 19255. Adjustment is not required.

The brake pad is available only as part of the bracket assembly. Minimum allowable brake pad thickness is 0.090 inch (2.3 mm).

FLYWHEEL. The flywheel is secured to the crankshaft by a retaining nut. To remove flywheel, remove blower housing and any other components so flywheel is accessible. If equipped with flywheel brake, disconnect brake

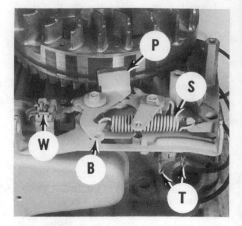

Fig. B222—View of flywheel brake mechanism used on Models 121000, 122000, 123000, 124000, 125000 and 126000 showing bracket (B), brake pad (P), brake spring (S), electric starter motor terminals (T) and stop switch (W).

spring. Secure the flywheel from rotating using Briggs & Stratton or aftermarket flywheel holder, then unscrew retaining nut. Use a suitable puller to remove flywheel from crankshaft.

NOTE: Do not attempt to hold the flywheel by inserting a tool between the fins as damage to flywheel may result.

The tapered portion of flywheel and crankshaft mating surfaces must be clean and smooth with no damage. Renew flywheel if any cracks are evident or any fins are broken. Be sure the keyway in crankshaft and flywheel is not damaged or worn. If flywheel key is replaced, a key made of aluminum must be installed. DO NOT install a steel key.

Install flywheel and key and tighten retaining nut to 55 ft.-lbs. (75 N•m) torque.

REWIND STARTER. Model 100700. Refer to Fig. B223 for an exploded view of starter. To disassemble starter, unfasten starter from engine. Pull out rope as far as possible, hold pulley, move rope off pulley, then slowly allow pulley to unwind so spring tension is released. Remove decal from starter cover (3) and unscrew cover screw (1); screw has left-hand threads. Bend out tang (T—Fig. B224) in cover, rotate cover counterclockwise to disengage spring end from cover and remove cover. Wear appropriate safety eyewear and gloves before disengaging spring from pulley as spring may uncoil uncontrolled. Using a suitable pair of pliers, detach spring from pulley and carefully allow spring to uncoil. Remove remainder of components.

Inspect components and renew any which are damaged or excessively worn. Assemble as shown in Fig. B223. Be sure steel washer (10) is installed first on starter shaft (11), then the plastic washer (9). Install brake spring (8) so looped end of spring is toward and between fingers of starter shaft (11). Attach clip (7) to ends of brake spring. Install rewind spring so outer end is attached to notch in periphery of pulley and coil direction is clockwise from outer spring end. Before installing cover (3), apply a light coat of grease to inner face. Before tightening cover screw (left-hand threads), rotate cover clockwise so arrow or "O" on cover is aligned with starter cam (Fig. B225) if rope handle is situated on top of engine, or rotate cover clockwise so arrow or "O" on cover is 90 degrees from starter cam (Fig. B226) if starter rope is situated or runs through a rope guide adjacent to cylinder head. Tighten cover screw to 55 in.-lbs. (6.2 N•m) torque. Turn gear against spring tension until spring is tightly wound. Align pulley rope knot pocket and rope outlet in cover, then install rope in pulley and through cover opening. Tie a temporary knot in rope end and allow rope to wind onto pulley. Install starter on engine and install rope handle.

REWIND STARTER. All 12 CID Models. Refer to Fig. B227 for exploded view of rewind starter. To remove starter proceed as follows: Remove starter cover, detach fuel line, remove fuel tank and oil fill tube. Detach starter from shroud.

To install a new rope, proceed as follows. Remove starter and extract old rope from pulley. Allow pulley to unwind, then turn pulley counterclockwise until spring is tightly wound. Rotate pulley clockwise until rope hole in pulley is aligned with rope outlet in housing. Pass rope through pulley hole and housing outlet and tie a temporary knot near handle end of rope. Release

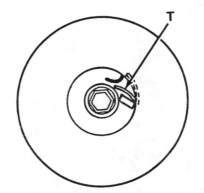

Fig. B224—Tang (T) engages inner end of rewind spring.

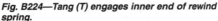
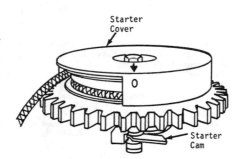

Fig. B225—Arrow or "O" on starter cover must be positioned in line with starter cam on engines with rope handle on top of engine.

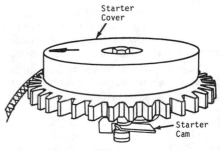

Fig. B226—Arrow or "O" on starter cover must be positioned 90° from starter cam on engines with rope adjacent to cylinder head.

pulley and allow rope to wind onto pulley. Install rope handle, release temporary knot and allow rope to enter starter.

To disassemble starter, remove rope and allow pulley to totally unwind. Position a suitable hollow sleeve support under pulley. Using pin punch, drive out retainer pin (11). Remove retainer (7), dogs (6), springs (5) and brake spring (9). Wear appropriate safety eyewear and gloves before disengaging pulley from starter housing as spring may uncoil uncontrolled. Place shop towel around pulley and lift pulley out of housing; spring should remain with pul-

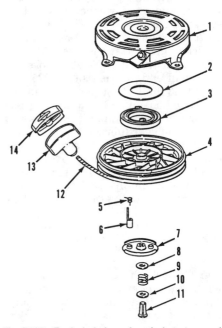

Fig. B227—Exploded view of rewind starter used on Models 121000, 122000, 123000, 124000, 125000 and 126000.

1. Starter housing
2. Spring cover
3. Rewind spring
4. Pulley
5. Springs
6. Dogs
7. Retainer
8. Plastic washer
9. Spring
10. Steel washer
11. Pin
12. Rope
13. Handle
14. Insert

ley. Do not attempt to separate spring from pulley as they are a unit assembly.

Inspect components for damage and excessive wear. Reverse disassembly procedure to install components. Be sure inner end of rewind spring engages spring retainer adjacent to housing center post. Pin (11) should be driven or pressed until flush with retainer (7). Install rope as previously outlined.

ELECTRIC STARTER. Some models may be equipped with the 12-volt DC electric starter motor shown in Fig. B228. The starter pinion engages gear teeth on the flywheel.

Starter should draw no more than 8 amps at a no-load minimum speed of 800 rpm measured at end of helix (2).

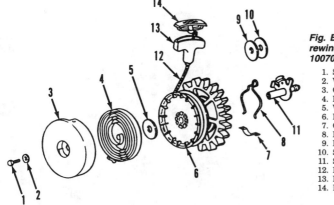

Fig. B223—Exploded view of rewind starter used on Model 100700.

1. Screw (L.H.)
2. Washer
3. Cover
4. Rewind spring
5. Washer
6. Pulley & gear
7. Clip
8. Brake spring
9. Plastic washer
10. Steel washer
11. Starter shaft
12. Rope
13. Handle
14. Insert

Starter pinion and helix must move without binding. Do not apply oil to helix or pinion. Do not engage starter for more than five seconds during testing.

Remove gear assembly at drive end of starter, then unscrew through-bolts to disassemble remainder of starter. Be sure positive terminal remains with end cap assembly (14) when detaching housing (13). Renew brushes if length (L—Fig. B229) is 5/64 inch (2.0 mm) or less.

When assembling starter, install fiber washer (11) and steel washer (12) on armature shaft with needed number of gray plastic washers (9) between fiber washer and steel washer to obtain a stack height (H—Fig. B230) equal to 0.200-0.225 inch (5.08-5.71 mm). Install sufficient gray plastic washers (9—Fig. B228) at drive end of armature so armature shaft end play is 0.005-0.025 inch (0.13-0.63 mm). Be sure notches in end cap (14), housing (13) and end bracket (8) are aligned. Apply approximately 3/4 ounce of gear lubricant under clutch (7). Tap end cap (14) to seat bearings and tighten through-bolts to 25 in.-lbs. (2.8 N•m) torque. Tighten starter cover screws to 25 in.-lbs. (2.8 N•m) torque. Tighten 5/16-inch starter mounting screw to 140 in.-lbs. (15.8 N•m) torque. Tighten 1/4-inch starter mounting screw to 90 in.-lbs. (10.2 N•m) torque.

ALTERNATOR. Models equipped with an electric starter are also equipped with an alternator for charging the battery. A rectifier, necessary to

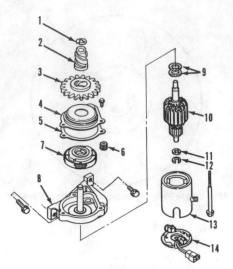

Fig. B228—Exploded view of electric starter motor used on some 121000, 122000, 123000, 124000, 125000 and 126000 models.

1. "E" ring		8. Drive end bracket
2. Helix		9. Plastic washers
3. Pinion		10. Armature
4. Cover		11. Fiber washer
5. Gasket		12. Steel washer
6. Gear		13. Field housing
7. Clutch		14. End cap

provide direct current, is part of the alternator stator assembly.

Air gap between alternator stator legs and flywheel should be 0.007 inch (0.18 mm). Loosen alternator mounting screws and move alternator to obtain desired air gap. Tighten screws to 25 in.-lbs. (2.8 N•m) torque.

Alternator output can be checked by connecting a suitable ammeter to out-

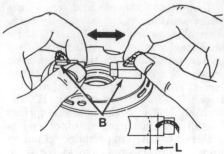

Fig. B229—Minimum brush length (L) is 5/64 inch (2.0 mm).

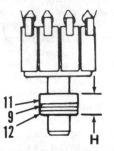

Fig. B230—Install gray plastic washers (9) between fiber washer (11) and steel washer (12) so stack height (H) is 0.200-0.225 inch (5.08-5.71 mm).

put lead from the alternator and to engine ground. Alternator output with engine running at 2800 rpm (or faster) should be no less than 0.5 amps DC. If low or no output is found, check to be sure stator air gap is set correctly. If air gap is within specification, the stator coil or rectifier (diode) may be faulty. Install a new stator assembly.

BRIGGS & STRATTON

4-STROKE VANGUARD OHV ENGINES

Model	Bore	Stroke	Displacement	Rated Power
104700	65.1 mm	49.3 mm	164 cc	3.7 kW
	(2.56 in.)	(1.94 in.)	(10 cu.in.)	(5.0 hp)

NOTE: Metric fasteners are used throughout engine except threaded hole in pto end of crankshaft, flange mounting holes and flywheel puller holes which are US threads.

ENGINE INFORMATION

The 104700 Vanguard models are air-cooled, four-stroke, single-cylinder engines. The engine has a vertical crankshaft and utilizes an overhead valve system. Refer to page 47 for a table that outlines the Briggs & Stratton model numbering system.

MAINTENANCE

LUBRICATION. The engine is lubricated by oil supplied by a rotor type oil pump located in the bottom of the crankcase.

Periodically check oil level; do not overfill. Oil dipstick should be screwed in until bottomed for correct oil level reading. Change engine oil after first eight hours of operation and every 50 hours thereafter under normal operating conditions. Recommended oil change interval is 25 hours if severe service is encountered. Note location of three drain plugs in Fig. B401.

The engine may be equipped with a spin-on type oil filter. If so equipped, manufacturer recommends changing oil filter after every 100 hours of operation. Filter should be changed more frequently if engine is operated in a severe environment.

Engine oil should meet or exceed latest API service classification. Use SAE 30 oil for temperatures above 40° F (4° C); use SAE 10W-30 oil for temperatures between 0° F (–18° C) and 40° F (4° C); below 0° F (–18° C) use petroleum based SAE 5W-20 or a suitable synthetic oil.

Crankcase capacity is 0.9 liter (29 fl. oz.) if equipped with an oil filter, 0.7 liter (24 fl. oz.) if not equipped with a filter.

A low oil pressure switch may be located on the sump or on the oil filter housing, if so equipped. Switch should be closed at zero pressure and open at 28-41 kPa (4-6 psi). If switch does not open before engine reaches 2000 rpm, cause must be identified.

AIR CLEANER. The air cleaner consists of a canister and the filter element it contains. The filter element is made of paper. A foam precleaner surrounds the filter element.

The foam precleaner should be cleaned weekly or after every 25 hours of operation, whichever occurs first. The paper filter should be cleaned yearly or after every 100 hours of operation, whichever occurs first.

Tap paper filter gently to dislodge accumulated dirt. Filter may be washed using warm water and nonsudsing detergent directed from inside of filter to outside. DO NOT use petroleum-based cleaners or solvents to clean filter. DO NOT direct pressurized air towards filter. Let filter air dry thoroughly, then inspect filter and discard it if damaged or cannot be cleaned. Clean filter canister. Inspect and, if necessary, replace any defective gaskets.

Clean foam precleaner in soapy water and squeeze until dry. Inspect filter for tears and holes or any other opening. Discard precleaner if it cannot be cleaned satisfactorily or if precleaner is torn or otherwise damaged. Pour clean engine oil into the precleaner, then squeeze to remove excess oil and distribute oil throughout.

FUEL FILTER. The fuel tank is equipped with a filter at the outlet and an inline filter may also be installed in

fuel line. Check filters annually and periodically during operating season.

CRANKCASE BREATHER. The engine is equipped with a crankcase breather that provides a vacuum for the crankcase. Vapor from the crankcase is evacuated to the intake manifold. A fiber disk acts as a one-way valve to maintain crankcase vacuum. The breather system must operate properly or excessive oil consumption may result.

The breather valve is located in the top of the crankcase. Remove the flywheel for access to breather cover. Remove cover and inspect the fiber disk valve (V—Fig. B402) should be renewed if warped, damaged or excessively worn. Inspect breather tube (T) for cracks and damage which can cause leakage. Tighten breather cover screws to 6 N•m (55 in.-lbs.) torque.

SPARK PLUG. Recommended spark plug is either an Autolite 3924 or Champion RC12YC. Specified spark plug electrode gap is 0.76 mm (0.030 in.). Tighten spark plug to 19 N•m (165 in.-lbs.) torque.

CAUTION: Briggs & Stratton does not recommend using abrasive blasting to clean spark plugs as this may introduce some abrasive material into the engine which could cause extensive damage.

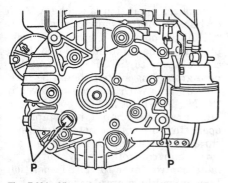

Fig. B401—View of three crankcase drain plugs (P).

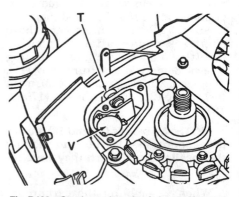

Fig. B402—Crankcase breather is located beneath flywheel. Be sure breather tube (T) and disc valve (V) are not damaged and seal properly.

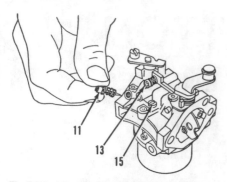

Fig. B403—Idle speed is adjusted by turning screw (13) and idle mixture is adjusted by turning idle mixture screw (11). Idle mixture jet (15) is not adjustable.

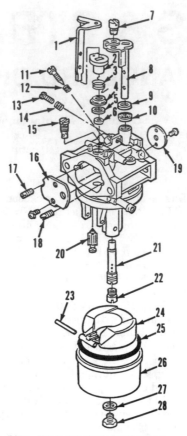

Fig. B404—Exploded view of carburetor.

1. Choke shaft & lever	15. Idle mixture jet
2. Bushing	16. Choke plate
3. Spring	17. Idle air bleed
4. Washer	18. Main air bleed
5. Seal	19. Throttle plate
6. Bushing	20. Fuel inlet valve
7. Link retainer	21. Main fuel nozzle
8. Throttle shaft & lever	22. Main jet
9. Washer	23. Float pin
10. Seal	24. Float
11. Idle mixture screw	25. Gasket
12. Spring	26. Fuel bowl
13. Idle speed screw	27. Washer
14. Spring	28. Screw

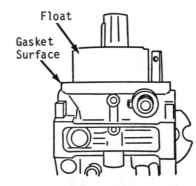

Fig. B405—Float must be parallel with gasket surface when carburetor is inverted. Float height is not adjustable so components must be replaced if not parallel.

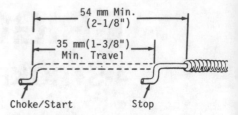

Fig. B406—Control wire must be capable of travel shown above for proper operation.

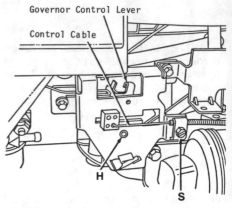

Fig. B407—Loosen cable clamp screw (S) and align holes (H) of governor lever and bracket to synchronize remote control and carburetor as outlined in text.

CARBURETOR. The engine is equipped with the float type carburetor shown in Fig. B404.

Adjustment. Idle speed at normal operating temperature should be 1500 rpm. Adjust idle speed by turning idle speed screw (13—Fig. B403). Idle mixture is controlled by the pilot jet nozzle (15) and idle mixture screw (11). To adjust idle mixture, turn idle mixture screw clockwise to lean mixture until engine speed just starts to slow, then turn screw counterclockwise to enrich mixture just until engine speed begins to slow. Turn idle screw to halfway point between lean and rich positions. Turn idle mixture screw counterclockwise in small increments to enrich mixture if engine stumbles when accelerating. Only one size of pilot jet nozzle is available and it is not adjustable. Fuel/air mixture at high speed is controlled by the size of main jet (22—Fig. B404). Only one size of main jet is suggested for normal operation, but an optional size (smaller) is available for high altitude operation. The main jet of early models is at the bottom as shown (22—Fig. B404). On later models, the main jet is installed on the side.

Overhaul. To disassemble carburetor, remove fuel bowl retaining screw (28—Fig. B404) and fuel bowl (26). Remove float pin (23) by pushing against round end of pin toward the square end of pin. Remove float (24) and fuel inlet needle (20). Remove throttle and choke shaft assemblies after unscrewing throttle and choke plate retaining screws. Remove idle mixture screw (11), pilot jet nozzle (15), main jet (22), main fuel nozzle (21) and air bleeds (17 and 18).

NOTE: Air bleeds (17 and 18) are not interchangeable. Be sure to identify the location from which they were removed.

When assembling the carburetor, note the following. Place a small drop of nonhardening sealant such as Per-matex #2 or equivalent on throttle and choke plate retaining screws. Numbers on choke plate (16) must face out and be on fuel inlet side of carburetor. Install throttle shaft seal (10) with flat side toward carburetor. Numbers on throttle plate (19) must face out and be on fuel inlet side of carburetor. Be sure groove of fuel inlet valve (20) engages slot in float tab. Float should be parallel with body when carburetor is inverted as shown in Fig. B405. Float height is not adjustable; replace components necessary so float is parallel.

If removed, install spacer between carburetor and manifold so circular opening is toward carburetor and "D" shaped opening is toward engine. Tighten carburetor mounting nuts to 5.1 N·m (45 in.-lbs.) torque.

CHOKE-A-MATIC CARBURETOR CONTROLS. The engine may be equipped with a control unit that controls the throttle, choke and grounding switch.

The remote control wire must travel at least 35 mm (1⅜ in.) for proper Choke-A-Matic operation. See Fig. B406.

To check operation of Choke-A-Matic carburetor control, move control lever to "CHOKE" position. Carburetor choke plate must be completely closed. Move control lever to "STOP" position. Magneto grounding switch should be making contact. With the control lever in "RUN", "FAST" or "SLOW" position, carburetor choke should be completely open. On units with remote control, synchronize movement of remote lever to carburetor control lever by moving remote control lever to "FAST" position. Loosen cable clamp screw (S—Fig. B407) and move cable so holes (H) in

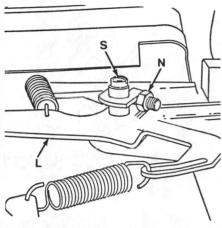

Fig. B408—View of governor shaft and lever. Adjust linkage as outlined in text.

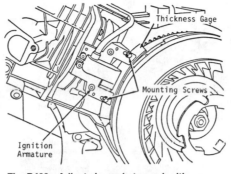

Fig. B409—Adjust air gap between ignition armature and flywheel to 0.20-0.30 mm (0.008-0.012 in.).

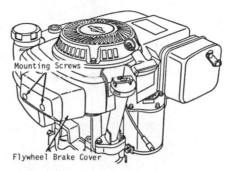

Fig. B410—The flywheel brake cover may be removed after unscrewing two mounting screws.

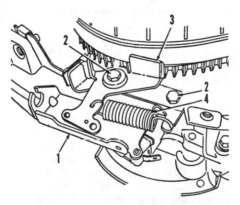

Fig. B411—Flywheel rotation is stopped when brake pad (3) contacts flywheel.

1. Brake lever bracket
2. Mounting screws
3. Brake lever & pad
4. Brake spring

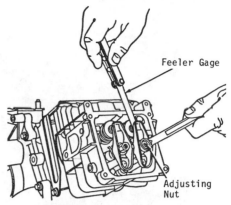

Fig. B412—Use a feeler gauge to check clearance between valve stem and rocker arm.

governor lever and bracket are aligned. Tighten clamp screw. Check for proper operation.

GOVERNOR. The engine is equipped with a mechanical, flyweight type governor. To adjust governor linkage, proceed as follows: Loosen governor lever clamp nut (N—Fig. B408), rotate governor lever (L) so throttle plate is fully open and hold lever in place. Turn governor shaft (S) clockwise as far as possible, then tighten nut (N) to 4 N•m (35 in.-lbs.) torque.

If internal governor assembly must be serviced, refer to REPAIRS section.

IGNITION SYSTEM. The engine is equipped with a Magnetron ignition system.

To check spark, remove spark plug and connect spark plug cable to B&S tester 19051, then ground remaining tester lead to engine. Spin engine at 350 rpm or more. If spark jumps the 4.2 mm (0.165 in.) tester gap, system is functioning properly.

To remove armature and Magnetron module, remove flywheel shroud and armature retaining screws. Disconnect stop switch wire from module. When installing armature, position armature so air gap between armature legs and flywheel surface (Fig. B409) is 0.20-0.30 mm (0.008-0.012 in.).

FLYWHEEL BRAKE. The engine is equipped with a flywheel brake that utilizes a pad which is forced against the flywheel's circumference. The brake should stop the engine within three seconds when the operator releases mower safety control and the speed control is in high speed position. Stopping time can be checked using tool 19255.

To check brake adjustment, remove starter and properly ground spark plug

lead to prevent accidental starting. Turn flywheel nut using a torque wrench with brake engaged. Rotating flywheel nut at a steady rate in a clockwise direction should require at least 3.4 N•m (30 in.-lbs.) torque.

An insufficient torque reading may indicate misadjustment or damaged components. Remove flywheel brake cover shown in Fig. B410 for access to brake mechanism (Fig. B411). Inspect components for damage and excessive wear. Renew brake arm and pad assembly (3—Fig. B411) if friction material of pad is damaged or less than 2.28 mm (0.090 in.) thick. If condition of mecha-

nism is satisfactory, reduce clearance between pad and flywheel by repositioning control cable housing (1). Recheck brake action.

VALVE ADJUSTMENT. Remove rocker arm cover. Remove spark plug. Rotate crankshaft so piston is at top dead center on compression stroke. Then, using a suitable measuring device inserted through spark plug hole, rotate crankshaft clockwise as viewed at flywheel end so piston is 6.35 mm (0.250 in.) below TDC to prevent interference by the compression release mechanism with the exhaust valve. Clearance between rocker arm pad and valve stem end (Fig. B412) should be 0.08-0.12 mm (0.003-0.005 in.) for intake and exhaust. Loosen lock screw and turn rocker arm adjusting nut to obtain desired clearance. Tighten lock screw to 5.6 N•m (50 in.-lbs.) torque.

CYLINDER HEAD. Manufacturer recommends that after every 100-300 hours of operation the cylinder head is removed and cleaned of deposits.

REPAIRS

TIGHTENING TORQUES. Recommended tightening torque specifications are as follows:

Carburetor mounting nuts . . . 5.1 N•m (45 in.-lbs.)
Connecting rod. . . . . 10 N•m (90 in.-lbs.)
Cylinder head. . . . . 8.5 N•m (75 in.-lbs.)
Flywheel nut . . . . 88 N•m (65 ft.-lbs.)
Oil pan . . . . 16 N•m (140 in.-lbs.)
Oil pump cover. . . . . 6.2 N•m (55 in.-lbs.)
Rocker arm lock screw . . . . . . 5.6 N•m (50 in.-lbs.)
Rocker arm stud . . . . 9.6 N•m (85 in.-lbs.)

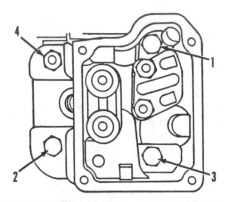

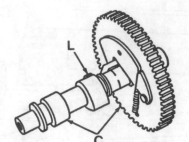

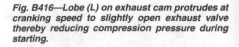

Fig. B413—Exploded view of cylinder head assembly.

1. Rocker cover
2. Lock screw
3. Adjusting nut
4. Rocker arm
5. Stud
6. Push rod guide
7. Gasket
8. Cylinder head
9. Head gasket
10. Valve cap
11. Valve retainer
12. Valve spring
13. Valve seal
14. Exhaust valve
15. Intake valve
16. Exhaust gasket
17. Push rod
18. Cam follower (tappet)

Fig. B416—Lobe (L) on exhaust cam protrudes at cranking speed to slightly open exhaust valve thereby reducing compression pressure during starting.

Fig. B417—Install camshaft so timing marks on camshaft and crankshaft gears are aligned. The model shown is typical

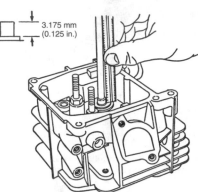

3.175 mm (0.125 in.)

Fig. B414—Tighten cylinder head bolts in steps following sequence shown above.

Fig. B415—Valve guide height (H) should be 3.175 mm (0.125 in.).

CYLINDER HEAD. To remove the cylinder head, first remove blower housing, carburetor, muffler, exhaust manifold and rocker arm cover. Loosen lock screws (2—Fig. B413) and remove rocker arm adjusting nuts (3), rocker arms (4) and push rods (17); mark all parts so they can be returned to original location. Unscrew cylinder head bolts and remove cylinder head (8). Clean cylinder head thoroughly, then check for cracks, distortion or other damage.

Note the following when reinstalling cylinder head: Do not apply sealer to cylinder head gasket. Tighten cylinder head bolts progressively in three steps using sequence shown in Fig. B414 until final torque reading of 8.5 N·m (75 in.-lbs.) is obtained.

VALVE SYSTEM. Valves are actuated by rocker arms mounted on a stud threaded into the cylinder head. Remove valve wear caps (10—Fig. B413). Depress valve springs until slot in valve spring retainer (11) can be aligned with end of valve stem. Release spring pressure and remove retainer, spring and valve from cylinder head. Clean cylinder head thoroughly, then check for cracks, distortion or other damage.

Valve face and seat angles are 45° for intake and exhaust. Specified seat width is 0.8-1.2 mm (0.031-0.047 in.). Minimum allowable valve margin is 0.38 mm (0.015 in.).

The cylinder head is equipped with renewable valve guides for both valves. Maximum allowable inside diameter of guide is 6.10 mm (0.240 in.). Use B&S tool 19367 to remove and install guides. Guides may be installed either way up. Top of guide should protrude 3.175 mm (0.125 in.) as shown in Fig. B415. Use B&S tools 19345 and 19346 to ream valve guide to correct size.

Rocker arm studs (5—Fig. B413) are screwed into cylinder head. Hardening sealant should be applied to threads contacting cylinder head. When installing studs, tighten to 9.6 N·m (85 in.-lbs.) torque.

CAMSHAFT. Camshaft and camshaft gear (C—Fig. B416) are an integral casting which is equipped with a compression release mechanism. The compression release lobe (L) extends at cranking speed to hold the exhaust valve open slightly thereby reducing compression pressure.

To remove camshaft proceed as follows: Drain crankcase oil and remove engine from equipment. Clean pto end of crankshaft and remove any burrs or rust. Remove rocker arm cover, rocker arms and push rods; mark all parts so they can be returned to original position. Unscrew fasteners and remove oil pan. Rotate crankshaft so timing marks on crankshaft and camshaft gears are aligned (this will position valve tappets out of way). Withdraw camshaft and remove tappets.

Reject size for bearing journal at flywheel end of camshaft is 12.65 mm (0.498 in.); reject size for pto end bearing journal is 17.45 mm (0.687 in.). Reject size for camshaft lobes is 28.85 mm (1.136 in.). With compression release lobe (L—Fig. B416) fully extended, lobe protrusion should be 0.51-0.64 mm (0.020-0.025 in.). If not, renew camshaft. Compression release mechanism must operate freely without binding.

Reverse removal procedure to reassemble components. Install camshaft while aligning timing marks (Fig. B417) on crankshaft and camshaft gears. Be sure governor arm is in proper position to contact governor, and camshaft end will properly engage oil pump drive. Install oil pan and tighten cover screws to 16 N·m (140 in.-lbs.) torque in sequence shown in Fig. B418. Do not force mating of oil pan with crankcase. Reassemble remainder of components.

PISTON, PIN AND RINGS. To remove piston and rod assembly, drain

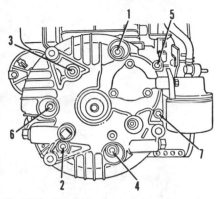

Fig. B418—Use tightening sequence shown above when tightening oil pan screws.

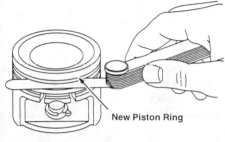

New Piston Ring

Fig. B419—Checking piston ring groove for wear.

engine oil and remove engine from equipment. Remove cylinder head and camshaft as previously outlined. Unscrew connecting rod screws and remove piston and rod.

Insert each piston ring (one at a time) squarely in top of cylinder and use a feeler gauge to measure ring end gap. Maximum allowable piston ring end gap is 0.76 mm (0.030 in.) for compression rings and 1.65 mm (0.065 in.) for oil ring. Check piston skirt for score marks and wear and renew as necessary. To check piston ring grooves for wear, insert a new ring in piston ring groove and use a feeler gauge to measure side clearance between ring and piston land. Renew piston if ring side clearance exceeds 0.10 mm (0.004 in.) for compression

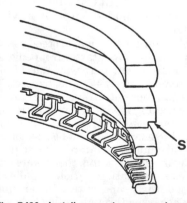

Fig. B420—Install second compression piston ring so step (S) is toward piston skirt.

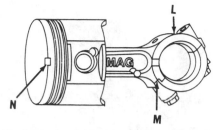

Fig. B421—Assemble rod and piston so long side of rod (L) and notch (N) in piston crown are positioned as shown. Piston must be installed so notch (N) in piston crown is toward flywheel side of engine.

rings and 0.20 mm (0.008 in.) for oil ring. Piston and rings are available in oversizes as well as standard size.

Piston pin is a slip fit in piston and rod. Renew piston if piston pin bore diameter is 14.02 mm (0.552 in.) or greater. Renew piston pin if diameter is 14.00 mm (0.551 in.) or less. A piston pin 0.012 mm (0.0005 in.) oversize is available.

Top piston ring may be installed with either side up. Second piston ring must be installed with stepped edge (S—Fig. B420) toward piston skirt.

When assembling piston and rod, note relation of notch in piston crown and long side of rod as shown in Fig. B421 ("MAG" is marked on flywheel side of some rods). Install piston and rod assembly in engine with notch on piston crown toward flywheel. Install rod cap so match marks (M—Fig. B421) are aligned and tighten rod screws to 10 N·m (90 in.-lbs.) torque.

Install camshaft and cylinder head as previously outlined.

CONNECTING ROD. The connecting rod rides directly on crankpin. Connecting rod and piston are removed as an assembly as outlined in previous section.

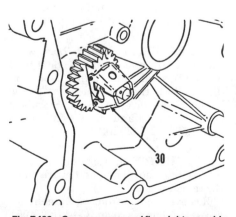

Fig. B422—Governor gear and flyweight assembly (30) is mounted inside the crankcase cover.

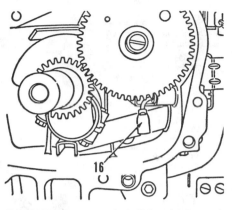

Fig. B423—Governor shaft (16) must be positioned as shown before installing oil pan.

Connecting rod reject size for crankpin hole is 31.33 mm (1.233 in.). Renew connecting rod if piston pin bore diameter is 14.02 mm (0.552 in.) or greater. A connecting rod with 14.02 (0.552 in.) undersize big end diameter is available to accommodate a worn crankpin (machining instructions are included with new rod).

GOVERNOR. The governor gear and flyweight assembly (30—Fig. B422) is located on the inside of the oil pan. The plunger in the gear assembly contacts the governor arm and shaft (16—Fig. B423) in the crankcase. The governor shaft and arm transfer governor action to the external governor linkage.

To gain access to the governor gear assembly, drain crankcase oil and remove engine from equipment. Clean pto end of crankshaft and remove any burrs or rust. Unscrew fasteners and remove oil pan.

Flyweight assembly must operate freely for proper governor action. The governor shaft and arm ride in a bushing (7—Fig. B424) in the crankcase. The bushing should be renewed if worn excessively. B&S reamer 19333 will size new bushing to desired diameter.

To reassemble, position governor gear assembly in oil pan. Be sure that governor arm is in proper position to contact governor as shown in Fig. B423 and that camshaft end will properly engage oil pump drive. Install oil pan and tighten retaining screws to 16 N·m (140 in.-lbs.) torque in sequence shown in Fig. B418. Do not force mating of oil pan with crankcase. Reassemble remainder of components.

CRANKSHAFT AND MAIN BEARINGS. To remove crankshaft, first remove flywheel and camshaft. Rotate crankshaft so piston is at top dead

Illustrations Courtesy of Briggs & Stratton Corp.

Fig. B424—Exploded view of engine crankcase and cylinder assembly.

1. Oil seal
2. Breather cover
3. Breather valve
4. Gasket
5. Crankcase
7. Governor shaft bushing
8. Seal
9. Washer
10. Cotter pin
11. Washers
12. Governor lever
13. Dowel pin
14. Dowel pin
16. Governor shaft
17. Crankshaft
18. Key
19. Connecting rod
20. Piston pin
21. Clips
22. Piston
23. Piston rings
24. Key
25. Gear
26. Snap ring
27. Camshaft
28. Compression release spring
29. Oil pump drive pin
30. Governor gear & flyweight
31. Snap ring
32. Washer
33. Oil screen
34. Spring
35. Oil pressure relief valve
36. Gasket
37. Oil pan
38. Oil seal
39. Drain plug
40. Oil pump inner rotor
41. Outer rotor
42. "O" ring
43. Oil pump cover

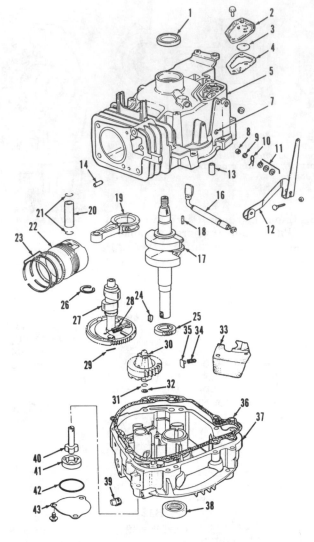

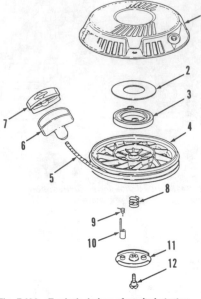

Fig. B426—Exploded view of rewind starter.

1. Starter housing
2. Spring cover
3. Rewind spring
4. Pulley
5. Rope
6. Handle
7. Insert
8. Brake spring
9. Dog springs
10. Dogs
11. Retainer
12. Screw

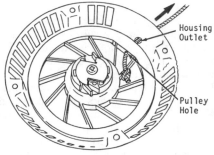

Fig. B427—Rope should extend through hole in pulley and housing outlet.

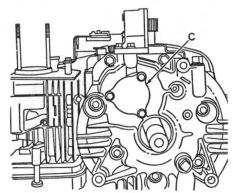

Fig. B425—Remove oil pump cover (C) for access to oil pump components.

center and remove connecting rod cap. Rotate crankshaft so it will clear connecting rod and withdraw crankshaft from crankcase.

Renew crankshaft if main bearing journal diameter is 29.94 mm (1.179 in.) or less. Wear limit for crankpin is 31.19 mm (1.228 in.). A connecting rod with 0.51 mm (0.020 in.) undersize big end diameter is available to accommodate a worn crankpin (machining instructions are included with new rod).

Main bearing located in crankcase is a renewable bushing. The pto end of crankshaft rides directly in the aluminum bore of oil pan. If crankcase bushing diameter is 30.07 mm (1.184 in.) or greater, renew bushing. When installing new main bearing, be sure that oil hole in bearing is aligned with oil hole in crankcase. Renew oil pan if diameter is 30.07 mm (1.184 in.) or greater.

CYLINDER. If cylinder bore wear exceeds 0.076 mm (0.003 in.) or if bore is out-of-round more than 0.038 mm (0.0015 in.), then cylinder should be bored to the next oversize. Standard cylinder bore diameter is 65.06-65.09 mm (2.5615-2.5625 in.).

OIL PUMP. The rotor type oil pump is located in the oil pan and is driven by the camshaft.

Remove engine from equipment for access to oil pump cover (C—Fig. B425). Remove cover and extract pump rotors

(40 and 41—Fig. B424). Mark rotors so they can be reinstalled in their original position. Renew any components which are damaged or excessively worn. Tighten oil pump cover screws to 6.2 N·m (55 in.-lbs.) torque.

REWIND STARTER. Refer to Fig. B426 for exploded view of rewind starter.

To install a new rope, proceed as follows. First remove starter from engine. Pull old rope out part way, untie knot and remove insert (7) and handle (6). Then pull rope out as far as it will go and while holding rewind pulley, extract old rope from pulley. Allow pulley to unwind. Rope length should be 234 cm (92 in.). Turn pulley counterclockwise until spring is tightly wound, then rotate pulley clockwise until rope hole in pulley is aligned with rope outlet in housing. Pass new rope through pulley hole and housing outlet as shown in Fig. B427

Illustrations Courtesy of Briggs & Stratton Corp.

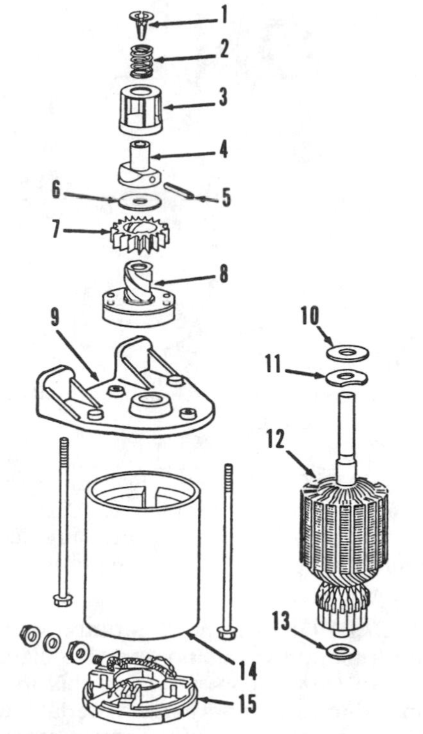

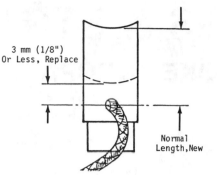

Fig. B428—Exploded view of optional electric starter motor.

1. Spring retainer
2. Return spring
3. Cover
4. Clutch retainer
5. Roll pin
6. Washer
7. Pinion gear
8. Helix
9. Drive end cap
10. Thrust washer
11. Spring washer
12. Armature
13. Washer
14. Starter housing
15. Brush end cap

and tie a temporary knot near handle end of rope. Release pulley and allow rope to wind onto pulley. Install rope handle, release temporary knot and allow rope to enter starter.

To disassemble starter, remove rope handle and allow pulley to totally unwind. Unscrew pulley retaining screw (12—Fig. B426). Remove retainer (11), dogs (10), springs (9) and brake spring (8). Wear appropriate safety eyewear and gloves before disengaging pulley from starter as spring may uncoil uncontrolled. Place shop cloth around pul-

Fig. B429—Renew brush if worn to 3 mm (1/8 in.) or less.

ley and lift pulley out of housing; spring should remain with pulley. Do not attempt to separate spring from pulley as they are a unit assembly.

Inspect components for damage and excessive wear. Reverse disassembly procedure to install components. Be sure inner end of rewind spring engages spring retainer adjacent to housing center post. Tighten screw (12) to 7.9 N·m (70 in.-lbs.) torque. Install rope as previously outlined.

When installing the starter, position starter on blower housing then pull out starter rope until dogs engage starter cup. Continue to place tension on rope and tighten starter mounting screws to 6.2 N·m (55 in.-lbs.) torque.

ELECTRIC STARTER. The engine may be equipped with a 12-volt DC electric starter motor. Refer to Fig. B428 for an exploded view of starter motor.

Under no load, the starter should draw no more than 20 amps at a minimum speed of 5000 rpm.

When disassembling starter, do not clamp starter housing (14) in a vise or strike housing as ceramic magnets may crack. Place alignment marks on drive end cap (9) and starter housing before disassembly. Drive roll pin (5) out of starter drive retainer (4) and remove starter drive assembly. Remove through-bolts and withdraw drive end

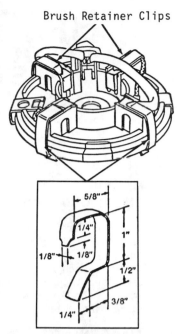

Fig. B430—Use suitable metal, such as a rewind starter spring, to construct brush retainer clips for use in assembling starter motor.

cap (9), brush end cap (15) and armature (12) from field housing (14).

Install new brushes if existing brushes are worn to less than 3 mm (1/8 in.) as shown in Fig. B429. Brush spring pressure should be at least 113-170 grams (4-6 ounces). Minimum allowable commutator diameter is 31.24 mm (1.230 in.).

When reassembling starter, brush retainer clips shown in Fig. B430 may be constructed from spring steel (such as scrap rewind starter springs) and used to retain brushes in end cap. Lubricate bearings in both end caps with a small amount of SAE 20W oil. Notch in starter housing must index with protruding terminal on brush end cap (15—Fig. B428). Apply Lubriplate to inside diameter of gear (7). Install gear with chamfered edges of teeth toward end of shaft. A new roll pin (5) should be installed. Pin must be centered in shaft.

BRIGGS & STRATTON

4-STROKE EUROPA ENGINES

Model	Bore	Stroke	Displacement	Power Rating
99700	2.56 in.	1.74 in.	8.9 cu.in.	5 hp
		(65.0 mm)	(44.2 mm)	(147 cc) (3.7 kW)

ENGINE INFORMATION

The 99700-99799 Europa models are air-cooled, four-stroke, single-cylinder engines. The engine has a vertical crankshaft and utilizes an overhead valve system. Refer to page 47 for a table that outlines the Briggs & Stratton model numbering system.

MAINTENANCE

LUBRICATION. The engine is lubricated by oil supplied by a rotor type oil pump located in the bottom of the crankcase, as well as by a slinger driven by the camshaft gear.

Change oil after first eight hours of operation and after every 50 hours of operation or at least once each operating season. Change oil weekly or after every 25 hours of operation if equipment undergoes severe usage.

Engine oil level should be maintained at full mark on dipstick. Engine oil should meet or exceed latest API service classification. Use SAE 30 oil for temperatures above 40° F (4° C); use SAE 10W-30 oil for temperatures between 0° F (−18° C) and 40° F (4° C); below 20° F (−7° C) use petroleum based SAE 5W-20 or a suitable synthetic oil.

Crankcase capacity is 22 fl. oz. (0.65 L). Fill engine with oil so oil level reaches, but does not exceed, full mark on dipstick.

AIR CLEANER. The air cleaner consists of a canister and the filter element it contains. The filter element is made of paper. A foam precleaner surrounds the filter element.

The foam precleaner should be cleaned weekly or after every 25 hours of operation, whichever occurs first. The paper filter should be cleaned yearly or after every 100 hours of operation, whichever occurs first.

Tap paper filter gently to dislodge accumulated dirt. Filter may be washed using warm water and nonsudsing detergent directed from inside of filter to outside. DO NOT use petroleum-based cleaners or solvents to clean filter. DO NOT direct pressurized air towards filter. Let filter air dry thoroughly, then inspect filter and discard it if damaged or cannot be cleaned. Clean filter canister. Inspect and, if necessary, replace any defective gaskets.

Clean foam precleaner in soapy water and squeeze until dry. Inspect filter for tears and holes or any other opening. Discard precleaner if it cannot be cleaned satisfactorily or if precleaner is torn or otherwise damaged. Pour clean engine oil into the precleaner, then squeeze to remove excess oil and distribute oil throughout.

CRANKCASE BREATHER. The engine is equipped with a crankcase breather that provides a vacuum for the crankcase. Vapor from the crankcase is evacuated to the air cleaner housing. A fiber disk acts as a one-way valve to maintain crankcase vacuum. The breather system must operate properly or excessive oil consumption may result.

The crankcase breather is built into the tappet cover. A fiber disc acts as a one-way valve. Clearance between fiber disc valve and breather body should not exceed 0.045 inch (1.14 mm). If it is possible to insert a 0.045 inch (1.14 mm) diameter wire (W—Fig. B501) between disc and breather body, renew breather assembly. Do not use excessive force when measuring gap. Disc should not stick or bind during operation. Renew if distorted or damaged. Inspect breather tube for leakage.

SPARK PLUG. Recommended spark plug is Champion RC12YC or Autolite 3924. Specified spark plug electrode gap is 0.030 inch (0.76 mm).

CAUTION: Briggs & Stratton does not recommend using abrasive blasting to clean spark plugs as this may introduce some abrasive material into the engine which could cause extensive damage.

CARBURETOR. The engine is equipped with a Walbro LMS float type carburetor.

The Walbro LMS carburetor operates like other typical float type carburetors. If the engine is operated at high altitudes, improved engine performance may be obtained by removing the metal jet in the right main air bleed hole (H—Fig. B502), however, the air jet should be installed if engine is operated at lower altitudes. Removing the air jet leans the high speed mixture.

Adjustment. Initial setting of idle mixture screw (9—Fig. B503) is 1¼ turns out from a lightly seated position. Run engine until normal operating temperature is attained. Be sure choke is open. Run engine with speed control in

Fig. B501—Clearance between fiber disc valve and crankcase breather housing must be less than 0.045 inch (1.15 mm). A spark plug wire gauge (W) may be used to check clearance as shown, but do not apply pressure against disc valve.

Fig. B502—Removing the air jet from the right main air bleed hole (H) leans the high speed mixture, which may be desirable if the engine is operated at high altitudes. See text.

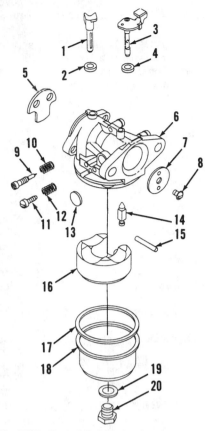

Fig. B503—Exploded view of carburetor.

1. Choke shaft		11. Idle speed screw
2. Washer		12. Spring
3. Throttle shaft		13. Welch plug
4. Washer		14. Fuel inlet valve
5. Choke plate		15. Pin
6. Body		16. Float
7. Throttle plate		17. Gasket
8. Screw		18. Fuel bowl
9. Idle mixture screw		19. Gasket
10. Spring		20. Main jet nut

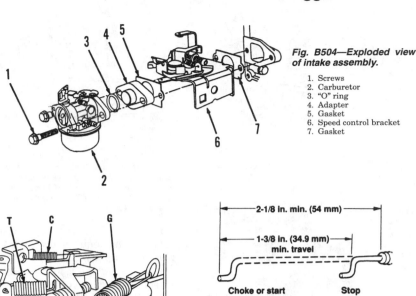

Fig. B504—Exploded view of intake assembly.

1. Screws
2. Carburetor
3. "O" ring
4. Adapter
5. Gasket
6. Speed control bracket
7. Gasket

Fig. B505—Drawing of speed control assembly showing location of choke spring (C), throttle spring (T) and governor spring (G).

Fig. B506—For proper operation of Choke-A-Matic controls, remote control wire must extend to dimension shown and have a minimum travel of 1-3/8 inches (34.9 mm).

slow position and adjust idle speed screw so engine speed is 1500 rpm. Turn idle mixture screw clockwise until engine begins to stumble and note screw position. Turn idle mixture screw counterclockwise until engine begins to stumble and note screw position. Turn the idle mixture screw clockwise to a position that is midway from clockwise (lean) and counterclockwise (rich) positions. With engine running at idle, rapidly move speed control to full throttle position. If engine stumbles or hesitates, slightly turn idle mixture screw counterclockwise and repeat test. Recheck idle speed and, if necessary, readjust idle speed screw.

High speed mixture is controlled by the jet in the fuel bowl retaining nut (20—Fig. B503) and is not adjustable. A nut with a jet for high altitude operation is available.

R&R And Overhaul. When removing or installing carburetor, note location of components shown in Fig. B504. Also note the location of governor link-age and springs to ensure correct reassembly. Tighten carburetor mounting screws to 75 in.-lbs. (8.5 N•m) torque.

To disassemble carburetor refer to Fig. B503 and remove bowl nut (20) and float bowl (18). Remove float pin (15), float (16) and fuel inlet valve (14). If necessary to remove inlet valve seat, use a stiff wire with a hook on one end to pull seat from carburetor body. To remove the Welch plug (13), pierce the plug with a sharp pin punch, then pry out the plug, but do not damage underlying metal. Remove idle mixture needle (9). Remove retaining screws from throttle plate (7) and choke plate (5) and withdraw throttle and choke shafts.

Inspect carburetor and renew any damaged or excessively worn components. The body must be replaced if there is excessive throttle or choke shaft play as bushings are not available. Install Welch plug while being careful not to indent the plug; the plug should be flat after installation. Apply a nonhardening sealant around the plug. Use a 3/16 inch (5 mm) diameter rod to install the fuel inlet valve seat. The groove on the seat must be down (towards carburetor bore). Push in the seat until it bottoms. Install the choke plate so the numbers are visible when the choke is closed. Install the throttle plate so the numbers are visible and towards the idle mixture screw when the throttle is closed. The float level is not adjustable.

If the float is not approximately parallel with the body when the carburetor is inverted, then the float, fuel valve and/or valve seat must be replaced. Tighten the high speed mixture nut to 50 in.-lbs. (5.6 N•m) torque.

Refer to Fig. B505 for view of speed control panel.

CHOKE-A-MATIC CARBURETOR CONTROL. The engine may be equipped with a control unit with which the carburetor choke, throttle and magneto grounding switch are operated from a single lever (Choke-A-Matic).

If equipped with a control cable between the remote control and engine, the remote control cable must move a certain distance for the remote control and carburetor to be synchronized. At full extension, control wire must extend 2⅛ inches (54 mm) from cable housing as shown in Fig. B506. The wire must travel at least 1⅜ inches (34.9 mm) from "CHOKE" or "START" to "STOP" positions.

To synchronize the control cable and speed control, loosen cable clamp screw (W—Fig. B507). Move the equipment speed control to the fast position. Move the speed control lever (L) so a ⅛ inch (3 mm) diameter rod (R) can be inserted in holes in the lever and control bracket (B). Tighten clamp screw (W).

GOVERNOR. Remove blower housing and fuel tank for access to governor linkage. To adjust governor linkage, loosen governor lever clamp nut (N—Fig. B508). Move speed control lever (L—Fig. B507) to fast position and in-

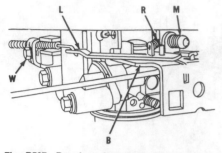

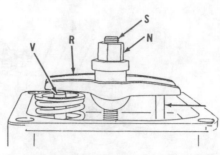

Fig. B507—Drawing of speed control assembly. Refer to text for adjustments.

Fig. B510—Loosen lock screw (S) and rotate adjusting nut (N) to adjust valve clearance. Clearance between rocker arm (R) and valve stem cap (V) should be 0.005-0.007 inch (0.12-0.18 mm) for intake and exhaust.

(5.1 N·m) torque. Tighten valve cover screws to 85 in.-lbs. (9.6 N·m) torque.

CYLINDER HEAD. Manufacturer recommends that after every 100-300 hours of operation the cylinder head is removed and cleaned of deposits.

REPAIRS

TIGHTENING TORQUES. Recommended tightening torque specifications are as follows:

Connecting rod	100 in.-lbs. (11.3 N·m)
Cylinder head	160 in.-lbs. (18.1 N·m)
Flywheel nut	60 ft.-lbs. (81.6 N·m)
Oil pan	85 in.-lbs. (9.6 N·m)
Oil pump cover	80 in.-lbs. (9 N·m)
Rocker arm cover	85 in.-lbs. (9.6 N·m)
Rocker arm lock screw	45 in.-lbs. (5.1 N·m)
Rocker arm stud	110 in.-lbs. (12.4 N·m)

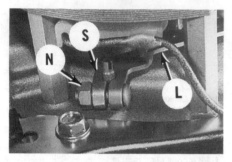

Fig. B508—Drawing of governor lever (L), shaft (S) and clamp nut (N). Refer to text for adjustment.

sert a 1/8 inch (3 mm) diameter rod (R) into holes in the lever and control bracket (B). Rotate governor shaft (S—Fig. B508) counterclockwise as far as possible, hold shaft and tighten clamp nut.

Maximum governed speed is adjusted by turning screw (M—Fig. B507). Maximum governed speed is usually specified by the equipment manufacturer according to engine application.

IGNITION. The engine is equipped with a Magnetron breakerless ignition system. All components are located outside the flywheel.

To check spark, remove spark plug and connect spark plug cable to B&S tester 19051, then ground remaining tester lead to engine. Spin engine at 350 rpm or more. If spark jumps the 0.165 inch (4.2 mm) tester gap, system is functioning properly.

Armature air gap should be 0.006-0.012 inch (0.15-0.30 mm).

On models equipped with a flywheel brake, stop switch (S—Fig. B509) should ground ignition system when flywheel brake is activated.

VALVE ADJUSTMENT. Remove rocker arm cover. Remove spark plug. Rotate crankshaft so piston is at top dead center on compression stroke. Insert a suitable measuring device through spark plug hole, then rotate crankshaft clockwise as viewed at flywheel end so piston is 1/4 inch (6.4 mm) below TDC to prevent interference by the compression release mechanism with the exhaust valve. Measure clearance between rocker arm (R—Fig. B510) and valve stem cap (V) using a feeler gauge. Clearance should be 0.005-0.007 inch (0.12-0.18 mm) for intake and exhaust. Loosen lock screw (S) and turn rocker arm pivot nut (N) to obtain desired clearance.

NOTE: Pivot nut is 10 mm and lock screw is either Torx design or metric Allen design.

After clearance is adjusted, hold pivot nut and tighten lock screw to 45 in.-lbs.

CYLINDER HEAD. To remove the cylinder head, first remove fuel tank, air cleaner, blower housing, carburetor, speed control bracket, muffler, and rocker arm cover. Loosen lock screws (10—Fig. B511) and remove rocker arm adjusting nuts (11), rocker arms (12) and push rods (15); mark all parts so they can be returned to original location. Unscrew cylinder head screws and remove cylinder head (16). Clean cylinder head thoroughly, then check for cracks, distortion or other damage.

When reinstalling cylinder head, do not apply sealer to cylinder head gasket. Tighten cylinder head bolts progressively in three steps using a crossing

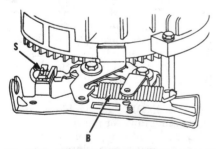

Fig. B509—Drawing of flywheel brake assembly used on some engines showing location of stop switch (S) and brake spring (B).

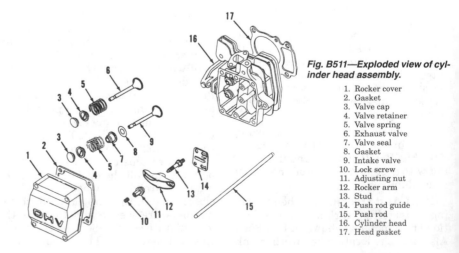

Fig. B511—Exploded view of cylinder head assembly.

1. Rocker cover
2. Gasket
3. Valve cap
4. Valve retainer
5. Valve spring
6. Exhaust valve
7. Valve seal
8. Gasket
9. Intake valve
10. Lock screw
11. Adjusting nut
12. Rocker arm
13. Stud
14. Push rod guide
15. Push rod
16. Cylinder head
17. Head gasket

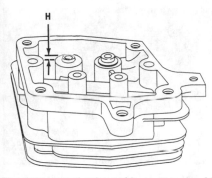

Fig. B512—Install valve guide so top of guide protrudes (H) above boss 0.120-0.150 inch (3.05-3.81 mm).

pattern until final torque reading of 160 in.-lbs. (18.1 N•m) is obtained.

VALVE SYSTEM. Valves are actuated by rocker arms mounted on a stud threaded into the cylinder head. Remove valve wear caps (3—Fig. B511). Depress valve springs until slot in valve spring retainer (4) can be aligned with end of valve stem. Release spring pressure and remove retainer, spring and valve from cylinder head.

Valve face and seat angles are 45 degrees for intake and exhaust. Specified seat width is 0.047-0.063 inch (1.2-1.6 mm). Minimum allowable valve margin is 0.015 inch (0.38 mm).

The cylinder head is equipped with renewable valve guides for both valves. Renew valve guide if inside diameter is 0.240 inch (6.10 mm) or more. Use B&S tool 19367 to remove and install guides. Guides may be installed either way up. Top of guide should protrude 0.120-0.150 inch (3.05-3.81 mm) as shown in Fig. B512. Use B&S tools 19345 and 19346 to ream valve guide to correct size.

Install push rod guide plate (P—Fig. B513) so "TOP" mark is toward flywheel side of cylinder head. Rocker arm studs (D) are screwed into cylinder head. Hardening sealant should be applied to threads contacting cylinder head. When

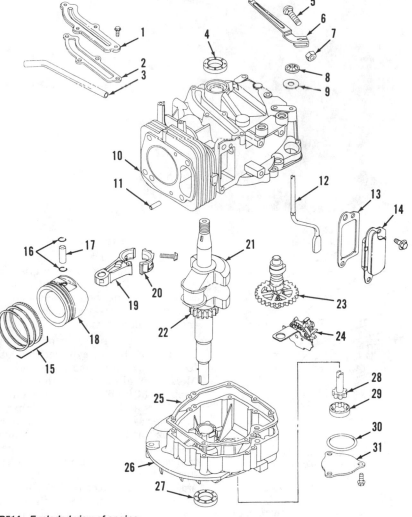

Fig. B514—Exploded view of engine.

1. Cover	9. Washer	17. Piston pin	25. Gasket
2. Gasket	10. Crankcase	18. Piston	26. Oil pan
3. Breather tube	11. Dowel pin	19. Connecting rod	27. Oil seal
4. Oil seal	12. Governor shaft	20. Rod cap	28. Oil pump inner rotor
5. Clamp bolt	13. Gasket	21. Crankshaft	29. Outer rotor
6. Governor lever	14. Tappet cover	22. Gear	30. "O" ring
7. Nut	15. Piston rings	23. Camshaft	31. Cover
8. Push nut	16. Retaining rings	24. Governor	

installing studs, tighten to 110 in.-lbs. (12.4 N•m) torque.

Install gasket (8—Fig. B511) and valve seal (7) on intake valve. Do not lubricate wear caps (3).

CAMSHAFT. To remove camshaft (23—Fig. B514) proceed as follows: Remove engine from equipment and drain crankcase oil. Clean pto end of crankshaft and remove any burrs or rust. Remove rocker arm cover, rocker arms and push rods; mark all parts so they can be returned to original position. Unscrew fasteners and remove oil pan. Remove governor assembly (24). Rotate crankshaft so timing marks on crankshaft and camshaft gears (Fig. B515) are aligned (this will position valve tappets out of way). Withdraw camshaft and remove tappets.

Renew camshaft if either camshaft bearing journal diameter is 0.615 inch (15.62 mm) or less. Renew camshaft if lobes are excessively worn or scored.

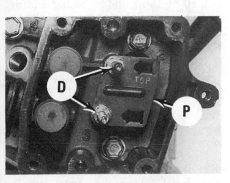

Fig. B513—Install push rod guide plate (P) so "TOP" is toward flywheel side of head.

Fig. B515—Install camshaft so timing marks (M) on camshaft and crankshaft gears are aligned. Pin (P) in camshaft end must engage slot in oil pump drive shaft when installing crankcase cover.

Illustrations Courtesy of Briggs & Stratton Corp.

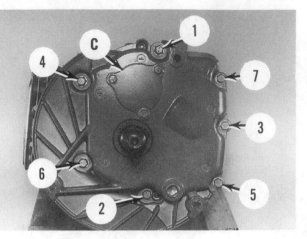

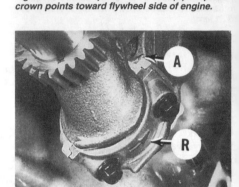

Fig. B519—Install piston so arrow (A) on piston crown points toward flywheel side of engine.

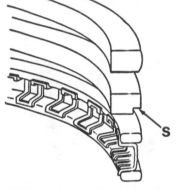

Fig. B517—Install second compression piston ring so step (S) is toward piston skirt.

Reverse removal procedure to reassemble components. Install camshaft while aligning timing marks (M—Fig. B515) on crankshaft and camshaft gears. Install governor assembly on camshaft. Note that roll pin in end of camshaft (Fig. B515) must engage oil pump drive shaft in oil pan during assembly. Install oil pan and apply nonhardening sealant such as Permatex #2 to screw (4—Fig. B516). Tighten cover screws to 85 in.-lbs. (9.6 N•m) torque in sequence shown in Fig. B516. Do not force mating of oil pan with crankcase. Reassemble remainder of components.

PISTON, PIN AND RINGS. To remove piston and rod assembly, drain engine oil and remove engine from equipment. Remove cylinder head and camshaft as previously outlined. Unscrew connecting rod screws and remove piston and rod.

Insert each piston ring (one at a time) squarely in top of cylinder and use a feeler gauge to measure ring end gap. Maximum allowable piston ring end gap is 0.030 inch (0.76 mm) for compression rings and 0.060 inch (1.52 mm) for oil ring rails. To check piston ring grooves for wear, insert a new ring in piston top groove and use a feeler gauge to measure side clearance between ring and piston land. Renew piston if ring side clearance exceeds 0.005 inch (0.12 mm) with a new piston ring installed in groove. Oversize as well as standard size piston and rings are available.

Piston pin is a slip fit in piston and rod. Renew piston if piston pin bore diameter is 0.552 inch (14.02 mm) or greater. Renew piston pin if diameter is 0.551 inch (14.00 mm) or less.

Top piston ring may be installed with either side up. Second piston ring must be installed with stepped edge (S—Fig. B517) toward piston skirt.

When assembling piston and rod, note that arrow on piston crown and "MAG" on connecting rod must be on

Fig. B520—Install rod cap so arrow on cap (R) points in same direction as arrow (A) on rod.

same side. See Fig. B518. Install piston and rod assembly in engine with arrow on piston crown toward flywheel as shown in Fig. B519. Install rod cap so arrow on cap (R—Fig. B520) points in same direction as arrow (A) on rod. Tighten rod screws to 100 in.-lbs. (11.3 N•m) torque.

Install camshaft and cylinder head as previously outlined.

CONNECTING ROD. The connecting rod rides directly on crankpin. Connecting rod and piston are removed as an assembly as outlined in previous section.

Connecting rod reject size for crankpin hole is 1.127 inch (28.63 mm). Renew connecting rod if piston pin bore diameter is 0.5525 inch (14.03 mm) or greater. A connecting rod with 0.020 inch (0.51 mm) undersize big end diameter is available to accommodate a worn crankpin (machining instructions are included with new rod).

GOVERNOR. The engine is equipped with a mechanical governor that is driven by the camshaft gear. Remove engine from the equipment, drain oil and remove oil pan for access to governor unit.

The flyweight assembly is mounted on end of camshaft along with oil slinger (Fig. B521). The oil slinger and flyweight assembly are only available as a

Fig. B518—Assemble piston and rod so arrow (A) on piston crown and "MAG" on side of rod are positioned as shown.

Fig. B521—View of governor and oil slinger assembly.

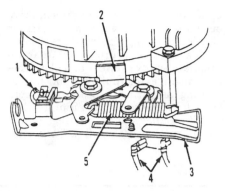

Fig. B523—View of flywheel brake assembly.

1. Stop switch wire
2. Brake pad & arm
3. Brake bracket
4. Starter interlock switch wires
5. Brake spring

unit assembly. Inspect flyweight assembly for broken components.

CRANKSHAFT AND MAIN BEARINGS.

The crankshaft rides directly in the crankcase bores. Rejection sizes for crankshaft are: pto-end bearing journal 1.060 inch (26.92 mm); flywheel-end bearing journal 0.873 inch (22.17 mm); crankpin 1.122 inch (28.50 mm). A connecting rod with 0.020 inch (0.51 mm) undersize big end diameter is available to accommodate a worn crankpin (machining instructions are included with new rod).

The crankcase main bearing bore rejection size is 0.878 inch (22.30 mm). The oil pan main bearing bore rejection size is 1.065 inch (27.05 mm). A service bushing is available for installation in the crankcase if the bearing bore requires service. No bushing is available for the oil pan so it must be renewed if bearing bore is damaged or worn excessively.

Install oil seals so lip is toward inside of crankcase.

Crankshaft end play should be 0.002-0.034 inch (0.05-0.86 mm) with 0.015 inch crankcase gasket installed. Additional gaskets of several thicknesses are available for end play adjustment. If end play is excessive, renew the oil pan. Tighten oil pan screws to 85 in.-lbs. (9.6 N•m) torque.

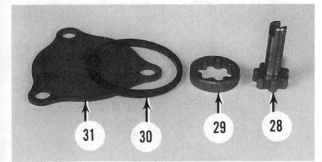

Fig. B522—View of oil pump components.

28. Oil pump inner rotor
29. Outer rotor
30. "O" ring
31. Cover

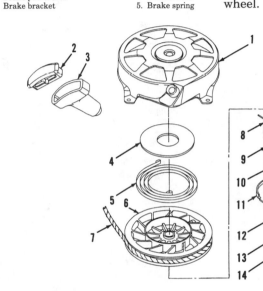

Fig. B524—Exploded view of rewind starter.

1. Starter housing
2. Insert
3. Handle
4. Spring cover
5. Rewind spring
6. Pulley
7. Rope
8. Springs
9. Pawls
10. Plastic washer
11. Retainer
12. Spring
13. Steel washer
14. Pin

CYLINDER.

If cylinder bore wear is 0.003 inch (0.76 mm) or more, or out-of-round is 0.0015 inch (0.038 mm) or greater, cylinder must be rebored to next oversize.

Standard cylinder bore diameter is 2.5615-2.5625 inch (65.06-65.09 mm).

OIL PUMP.

A rotor type oil pump driven by the camshaft is located in the bottom of the oil pan.

Remove engine from equipment for access to oil pump cover (C—Fig. B516). Remove cover and extract pump rotors (28 and 29—Fig. B522). Mark rotors so they can be reinstalled in their original

position. Renew any components which are damaged or excessively worn. Tighten oil pump cover screws to 80 in.-lbs. (9 N•m) torque.

FLYWHEEL BRAKE.

Some engines are equipped with a pad type flywheel brake (2—Fig. B523). The brake should stop the engine within three seconds when the operator releases mower safety control and the speed control is in high speed position. Stopping time can be checked using tool 19255.

Adjustment may be possible on some applications by adjusting control cable position so brake pad is closer to flywheel.

To service flywheel brake, remove fuel tank, dipstick and oil fill tube, blower housing and rewind starter. Disconnect brake spring (5—Fig. B523). Disconnect stop switch wire (1) and safety interlock wires (4) if so equipped. Remove two retaining screws from brake pad arm and brake bracket.

The brake pad is available only as part of the bracket assembly. Minimum allowable brake pad thickness is 0.090 inch (2.3 mm). When installing brake assembly, tighten retaining screws to 40 in.-lbs. (4.5 N•m) torque.

REWIND STARTER.

Refer to Fig. B524 for exploded view of rewind starter.

To install a new rope, proceed as follows. Remove fuel tank, dipstick and oil fill tube, and blower housing for access to starter assembly. Extract old rope from starter pulley. Allow pulley to unwind, then turn pulley counterclockwise until spring is tightly wound. Rotate pulley clockwise until rope hole in pulley is aligned with rope outlet in housing. Be sure that the new rope is the same diameter and length as the old rope. Pass new rope through pulley hole and housing outlet and tie a temporary knot near handle end of rope. Release pulley and allow rope to wind onto pulley. Install rope handle, release temporary knot and allow rope to enter starter.

To disassemble starter, remove rope and allow pulley to totally unwind. Position a suitable hollow sleeve support under pulley. Using a pin punch, drive out retainer pin (14). Remove retainer (11), brake spring (12), washers (10 and 13), pawls (9) and springs (8). Wear appropriate safety eyewear and gloves before disengaging pulley from starter housing as spring may uncoil uncontrolled. Place shop towel around pulley and lift pulley out of housing; spring should remain with pulley. Do not attempt to separate spring from pulley as they are a unit assembly.

Inspect components for damage and excessive wear. Reverse disassembly procedure to install components. Be sure inner end of rewind spring engages spring retainer adjacent to housing center post. Pin (14) should be driven or pressed until flush with retainer (11). Install rope as previously outlined.

Illustrations Courtesy of Briggs & Stratton Corp.

BRIGGS & STRATTON SPECIAL TOOLS

The following special tools are available from Briggs & Stratton Central
Parts Distributors.

TOOL KITS

19158—Main bearing service kit for most engines with 6 to 13 cubic inch displacement.

PLUG GAGES

19055—Check breaker plunger hole for early models with breaker point ignition.
19122—Check valve guide bore for most engines with 6 to 13 cubic inch displacement.
19164—Check camshaft bearings for most engines with aluminum cylinders.
19166—Check main bearing bore for most engines with 6 to 13 cubic inch displacement.
19375—Check pto main bearing bore on Series 92000, 99700, 104700 and 120000.
19381—Check valve guide bore on Series 85400, 99700, 104700 and 115400.
19387—Check camshaft bearings on Series 99700.

REAMERS

19064—Ream valve guide bore to install bushing in most engines with 6 to 13 cubic inch displacement.
19066—Finish ream valve guide bushing on same models as 19064 reamer.
19095—Finish ream flywheel main bearing of some models with 10, 12 and 13 cubic inch siaplacement and both main bearings of some 6, 8, 9 and 11 cubic inch diaplacement.
19099—Ream counterbore for main bearings on same models as 19095 reamer.
19172—Ream counterbore for pto main bearing of some models with 13 cubic inch displacement.
19173—Finish ream main bearings on same models as 19172 reamer.
19346—Finish ream valve guide of Series 85400, 99700, 104700 and 115400.

GUIDE BUSHINGS FOR VALVE GUIDE REAMERS

19191—For some models with 6, 8, 9, 11, 12 and 13 cubic inch displacement.
19345—For Series 85400, 99700, 104700 and 115400.

PILOTS

19096—Pilot for main bearing reamer of some models with 6, 8, 9, 10, 11, 12 and 13 cubic inch displacement.
19126—Expansion pilot for valve seat counterbore cutter on some models with 6, 8, 9, 10, 10, 11, 12 and 13 cubic inch displacement.
19395—Main bearing removal and installation on Series 85400 and 115400.
19396—Main bearing removal and installation on Series 115400.

DRIVERS

19057—To install breaker plunger bushing for 6, 8, 9, 10, 11 and 13 cubic inch displacement models with breaker point ignition.
19367—To install valve guide bushings for some models with 6, 8, 9, 10, 11, 12 and 13 cubic inch displacement.
19124—To install main bearing bushings for some models with 6, 8, 9, 10, 11, 12 and 13 cubic inch displacement.
19136—To install valve seat inserts.
19204—To install governor shaft bushing on Series 104700.
19274—To install valve guides on Series 104700.
19349—Remove and install main bearings on Series 104700.

GUIDE BUSHINGS FOR MAIN BEARING REAMERS

19094—For pto main bearing pilot on some models with 6, 8, 9, 10, 11, 12 and 13 cubic inch displacement and for flywheel main bearing pilot on some models with 6, 8, 9 and 11 cubic inch displacement.
19100—For pto main bearing reamer on some models with 6, 8 or 9 cubic inch displacement.
19101—For flywheel main bearing reamer on some models with 6, 8, 9, 10, 11, 12 and 13 cubic inch displacement.
19168—For pto main bearing pilot on some models with 13 cubic inch displacement.
19186—For pto main bearing reamer on some vertical shaft 13 cubic inch displacement models.

19373—For pto main bearing reamer on Series 99700, 100700 and some 12 cubich inch displacement.

FLYWHEEL HOLDER

19167—For some models with 6, 8 and 9 cubic inch displacement.

VALVE SPRING COMPRESSOR

19063—For all except OHV models.
19347—For OHV models.

PISTON RING COMPRESSOR

19070—For all engines with 6, 8, 9, 10, 11, 13 and 13 cubic inch displacement.

FLYWHEEL PULLERS

19069—For most models with 6, 8, 9 11, 12 and 13 cubic inch displacement.
19203—For Series 85400, 104700 and 115400.

CRANKCASE SUPPORT JACK

19123—Cylinder support for engines with 6, 8, 9, 10, 11, 12 and 13 cubic inch displacement.

IGNITION SPARK TESTER

19051—For all engines.

VALVE SEAT REPAIR TOOLS

19137—T-handle for expansion pilots.
19138—Valve seat puller kit.
19237—Valve seat cutter kit.
19182—Puller nut adapter.
19269—Valve guide repair kit for 1/4 inch valve guides.

PULLER KIT

19332—Remove and install seals, bearings and crankshaft on Models 95700 and 96700.

STARTER CLUTCH WRENCH

19244—All engines equipped with rewind starter clutch.

BRIGGS AND STRATTON
CENTRAL PARTS DISTRIBUTORS

(Arranged Alphabetically by States)
These franchised firms carry extensive stocks of repair parts.
Contact them for name of the nearest service distributor.

BEBCO, Inc.
Phone (205) 251-4600
2221 Second Avenue, South
Birmingham, Alabama 35233

Power Equipment Company
Phone (602) 272-3936
#7 North 43rd Avenue
Phoenix, Arizona 85107

Pacific Western Power
Phone (415) 692-3254
1565 Adrain Road
Burlingame, California 94010

Power Equipment Company
Phone (805) 684-6637
1045 Cindy Lane
Carpinteria, California 93013

Pacific Power Equipment Company
Phone (303) 744-7891
1441 W. Bayaud Avenue #4
Denver, Colorado 80223

Spencer Engine, Inc.
Phone (813) 253-6035
1114 W. Cass St.
Tampa, Florida 33606

Sedco, Inc.
Phone (404) 925-4706
4305 Steve Reynolds Blvd.
Norcross, Georgia 30093

Small Engine Clinic, Inc.
Phone (808)488-0711
98019 Kam Highway
Aiea, Hawaii 96701

Midwest Engine Warehouse
Phone (708) 833-1200
515 Roman Road
Elmhurst, Illinois 60126

Commonwealth Engine, Inc.
Phone (502) 267-7883
11421 Electron Drive
 Louisville, Kentucky 40229

Delta Power Equipment
Phone (504) 465-9222
755 E. Airline Highway
Kenner, Louisiana 70062

Atlantic Power
Phone (508) 543-6911
77 Green Street
Foxboro, Massachusetts 02035

Wisconsin Magneto, Inc.
Phone (612) 780-5585
8010 Ranchers Road
Minneapolis, Minnesota 55432

Diamond Engine Sales
Phone (314) 652-2202
3134 Washington
St. Louis, Missouri 63103

Original Equipment, Inc.
Phone (406) 245-3081
905 Second Avenue, North
Billings, Montana 59101

Midwest Engine Warehouse of Omaha
Phone (402) 339-4700
7706-30 "I" Plaza
Omaha, Nebraska 68127

Atlantic Power
Phone (908) 356-8400
650 Howard Avenue
Somerset, New Jersey 08873

Power Equipment Company
Phone (505) 345-8851
7209 Washington Street, North East
Albuquerque, New Mexico 87109

AEA, Inc.
Phone (704) 377-6991
700 West 28th Street
Charlotte, North Carolina 28206

Central Power Systems
Phone (614) 876-3533
2555 International Street
Columbus, Ohio 43228

Engine Warehouse, Inc.
Phone (405) 946-7800
 4200 Highline Blvd.
Oklahoma City, Oklahoma 73108

Brown & Wiser, Inc.
Phone (503) 692-0330
9991 South West Avery Street
Tualatin, Oregon 97062

Three Rivers Engine Distributors
Phone (412) 321-4111
1411 Beaver Avenue
Pittsburgh, Pennsylvania 15233

Automotive Electric Corporation
Phone (901) 345-0300
3250 Millbranch Road
Memphis, Tennessee 38116

Grayson Company, Inc.
Phone (214) 630-3272
1234 Motor Street
Dallas, Texas 75207

Engine Warehouse, Inc.
Phone (713) 937-4000
7415 Empire Central Drive
Houston, Texas 77040

Frank Edwards Company
Phone (801) 972-0128
1284 South 500 West
Salt Lake City, Utah 84101

RBI Corporation
Phone (804) 550-2210
101 Cedar Ridge Drive
Ashland, Virginia 23005

Wisconsin Magneto, Inc.
Phone (414) 445-2800
4727 North Teutonia Avenue
Milwaukee, Wisconsin 53209

CANADIAN DISTRIBUTORS

Briggs & Stratton Canada, Inc.
Phone (403) 435-9265
9519 49th Avenue
Edmonton, Alberta T6E 5Z5

Briggs & Stratton Canada, Inc.
Phone (604) 520-1294
1360 Cliveden Avenue
Delta, British Columbia V3M 6K2

Briggs & Stratton Canada, Inc.
Phone (204) 633-5400
89 Paramount Road
Winnipeg, Manitoba R2X 2W6

Briggs & Stratton Canada, Inc.
Phone (416) 625-6557
1815 Sismet Road
Mississauga, Ontario L4W 1P9

Briggs & Stratton Canada, Inc.
Phone (514) 366-6891
112-116 Lindsay Avenue
Dorval, Quebec H9P 2T8

CLINTON

CLINTON ENGINES CORPORATION
Maquoketa, Iowa

CLINTON ENGINE IDENTIFICATION INFORMATION

To obtain the correct service replacement parts when overhauling Clinton engines, it is important that the engine be properly identified as to:

1. Model number
2. Variation number
3. Type letter

A typical nameplate from the model number series engines prior to 1961 is shown in Fig. CL1. In this example, the following information is noted from the nameplate:

1. Model number – **B-760**
2. Variation number – **AOB**
3. Type letter – **B**

In some cases, the model number may be shown as in the following example:

D-790-2124

Thus, "D-790" would be the model number of a D-700-2000 series engine in which the digits "2124" would be the variation number.

In late 1961, the identification system for Clinton engines was changed to be acceptable for use with IBM inventory record systems. A typical nameplate from a late production engine is shown in Fig. CL2. In this example, the following information is noted from the nameplate:

1. Model number – 405-0000-000
2. Variation number – 070
3. Type letter – D

In addition, the following information may be obtained from the model number on the nameplate:

First digit – identifies type of engine, i.e., 4 means four-stroke engine and 5 means two-stroke engine.

Second and third digits – completes basic identification of engine. Odd numbers will be used for vertical shaft engines and even numbers for horizontal shaft engines; i.e., 405 would indicate a four-stroke vertical shaft engine and 500 would indicate a two-stroke horizontal shaft engine.

Fourth digit – indicates type of starter as follows:

0 – Rewind starter
1 – Rope starter
2 – Impluse starter
3 – Crank starter
4 – 12 Volt electric starter
5 – 12 Volt starter-generator
6 – 110 Volt electric starter
7 – 12 Volt generator
8 – unassigned to date
9 – Short block assembly.

Fifth digit – indicates bearing type, etc., as follows:

0 – Standard bearing
1 – Aluminum or bronze sleeve bearing with flange mounting

surface and pilot diameter on engine mounting face for mounting equipment concentric to crankshaft center line

2 – Ball or roller bearing
3 – Ball or roller bearing with flange mounting surface and pilot diameter on engine mounting face for mounting equipment concentric to crankshaft center line
4 – Numbers 4 through 9 are unassigned to date

Sixth digit – indicates auxiliary power takeoff and speed reducers as follows:

0 – Without auxiliary power pto or speed reducer
1 – Auxiliary power takeoff
2 – 2:1 speed reducer
3 – not assigned to date
4 – 4:1 speed reducer
5 – not assigned to date
6 – 6:1 speed reducer
7 – numbers 7 through 9 are unassigned to date

Seventh digit – if other than "0" will indicate a major design change.

Eighth, ninth & tenth digits – identifies model variations.

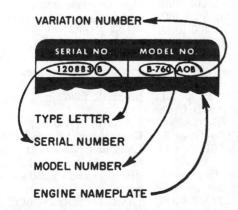

Fig. CL1—Typical nameplate from Clinton Engine manufactured prior to late 1961.

TYPE LETTER

MFD BY CLINTON ENGINES CORP.
MAQUOKETA, IOWA U.S.A.

SERIAL NO.   10278904   D
MODEL NO.   405 0000 070

DIGITS   1-2-3   4-5-6-7   8-9-10
  VARIATION

Fig. CL2—Typical nameplate from Clinton engine after model identification system was changed in late 1961. First seven digits indicate basic features of engine. Engines with "Mylar" (plastic) nameplate have engine model and serial numbers stamped on the cylinder air deflector next to the nameplate.

CLINTON

Model	Bore	Stroke	Displacement
E-65 CW, E-65 CCW	2.125 in. (53.2 mm)	1.625 in. (41.3 mm)	5.8 cu. in. (92 cc)
200, A-200, AVS-200-1000, VS-200, VA-200-1000, VS-200-2000, VS-200-3000	1.875 in. (47.6 mm)	1.625 in. (41.3 mm)	4.5 cu. in. (74 cc)
VS-200-4000	2.125 in. (53.2 mm)	1.625 in. (41.3 mm)	5.8 cu. in. (92 cc)
290	1.875 in. (47.6 mm)	1.625 in. (41.3 mm)	4.5 cu. in. (74 cc)
A-400	2.125 in. (53.2 mm)	1.625 in. (41.3 mm)	5.8 cu. in. (92 cc)
A-400-1000, AVS-400, CVS-400-1000, VS-400, VS-400-1000, VS-400-2000, VS-400-3000, VS-400-4000	2.125 in. (53.2 mm)	1.625 in. (41.3 mm)	5.8 cu. in. (92 cc)
A-460*	2.125 in. (53.2 mm)	1.625 in. (41.3 mm)	5.8 cu. in. (92 cc)
490, A-490	2.125 in. (53.2 mm)	1.625 in. (41.3 mm)	5.8 cu. in. (92 cc)
500-0100-000, 501-0000-000, 501-0001-000, GK-590	2.125 in. (53.2 mm)	1.625 in. (41.3 mm)	5.8 cu. in. (92 cc)
502-0308-000, 503-0308-000	2.375 in. (60.3 mm)	1.750 in. (44.5 mm)	7.8 cu. in. (127 cc)
502-0309-000, 503-0309-000	2.500 in. (63.5 mm)	1.750 in. (44.5 mm)	8.6 cu. in. (141 cc)

*Reduction gear

ENGINE IDENTIFICATION

Clinton two-stroke engines are of aluminum alloy die-cast construction with an integral cast-in iron cylinder sleeve. Reed type inlet valves are used on all models. Refer to CLINTON ENGINE IDENTIFICATION INFORMATION section preceding this section.

MAINTENANCE

SPARK PLUG. Champion H10J or equivalent spark plug is recommended for use in E-65 CW and E-65 CCW models.

Champion H11 or H11J or equivalent spark plug is recommended for use in 200, A-200, AVS-200, AVS-200-1000, VS-200, VS-200-1000, VS-200-2000, VS-200-3000 (types A and B), 290, A-400, A-400-1000 (type A), AVS-400, AVS-400-1000, BVS-400, VS-400-1000, VS-400-2000, VS-400-3000, VS-400-4000 (types A and B), 490 and A-490-1000 (type A) models.

Champion J12J or equivalent plug is recommended for VS-200-3000 (type C), VS-200-4000, A-400-1000 (types B, C, D, E, F), CVS-400-1000, VS-400-4000 (types C, D, E, F), A-490-1000 (types B, C, D, E, F), 500-0100-000, 501-000-000 and 501-001-000 models.

Autolite A7NX or equivalent spark plug is recommended for use in 502-0308-000, 502-0309-000, 503-0308-000 and 503-0309-000 models.

On all models, set electrode gap at 0.030 inch (0.76 mm). Use graphite on threads when installing spark plug and tighten spark plug to 275-300 in.-lbs. (31-34 N·m).

CARBURETOR. Several different carburetors have been used on Clinton two-stroke engines. Refer to the appropriate following paragraphs.

Clinton (Walbro) LM Float Type Carburetor. Clinton (Walbro designed) LMB and LMG float type carburetors are used. Refer to Fig. CL5 for identification and exploded view of typical model.

Initial adjustment of idle (9) and main (22) fuel needles from a lightly seated position is 1¼ turns open for each nee-

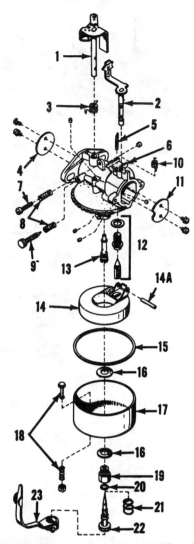

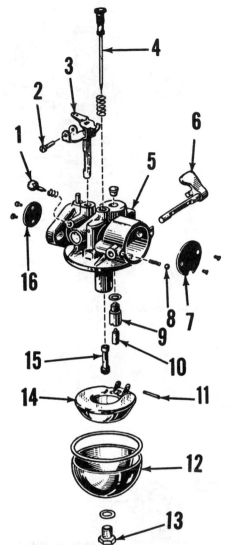

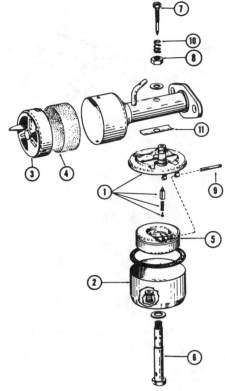

Fig. CL5—Exploded view of typical LMG series carburetor. LMV and LMB series are similar.

1. Throttle shaft
2. Choke shaft
3. Spring
4. Throttle plate
5. Spring
6. Carburetor body
7. Idle stop screw
8. Springs
9. Idle fuel needle
10. Spring
11. Choke plate
12. Inlet needle & seat
13. Main nozzle
14. Float
14A. Float pin
15. Gasket
16. Gaskets
17. Float bowl
18. Drain valve
19. Retainer
20. Seal
21. Spring
22. Main fuel needle
23. Lever (optional)

Fig CL7—Exploded view of a typical Carter Model N carburetor. Design of float and float bowl may vary from that shown.

1. Idle fuel needle
2. Idle stop screw
3. Throttle shaft
4. Main fuel needle
5. Carburetor body
6. Choke shaft
7. Choke plate
8. Detent ball
9. Inlet valve seat
10. Inlet needle
11. Float pin
12. Float bowl
13. Retainer
14. Float
15. Main nozzle
16. Throttle plate

Fig. CL8—Exploded view of float type carburetor used on 501-000-000 model series engine.

1. Inlet valve & seat
2. Float bowl
3. Choke assy.
4. Air cleaner element
5. Float
6. Main nozzle
7. Fuel needle
8. Nut
9. Float pin
10. Spring
11. Gasket

Float drop should be 3/16 inch (4.76 mm). Carefully bend tabs on float hinge to adjust float drop.

Carter Model N Float Type Carburetor. Refer to Fig. CL7 for identification and exploded view of Carter Model N float type carburetor. The following models have been used:

N-2003-S
N-2029-S
N-2087-S
N-2171-S
N-2457-S

Initial adjustment of fuel mixture needles on Models N-2003-S and N-2029-S from a lightly seated position is ¾ turn open for idle fuel needle (1) and 1 turn open for main fuel mixture needle (4).

Initial adjustment of fuel mixture needles on Models N-2087-S, N-2171-S and N-2457-S is 1½ turns open for idle mixture needle (1) and ½ turn open for main mixture needle (4).

Final adjustments on all models are made with engine at operating temperature and running. Operate engine at rated speed under load and adjust main fuel mixture needle for smoothest engine operation. Operate

dle. Final adjustments are made with engine at operating temperature and running. Operate engine at rated speed under load and adjust main fuel mixture needle for smoothest engine operation. Operate engine at idle speed and adjust idle fuel mixture needle for smoothest

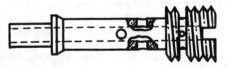

Fig. CL6—When original main fuel nozzle is removed from a LM series carburetor, it must be discarded and service type nozzle shown installed.

engine idle. Check acceleration from slow to fast idle and open idle needle approximately 1/8 turn (counterclockwise) if necessary for proper acceleration.

When overhauling LMB or LMG carburetors, discard main fuel nozzle (13) if removed and install a service type nozzle (see Fig. CL6). Do not install old nozzle.

To check float setting, invert carburetor throttle body and float assembly. Measure distance between top of free side of float and float bowl mating surface of carburetor. Measurement should be 5/32 inch (3.97 mm). Carefully bend float lever tang which contacts fuel inlet needle if necessary to obtain correct float level.

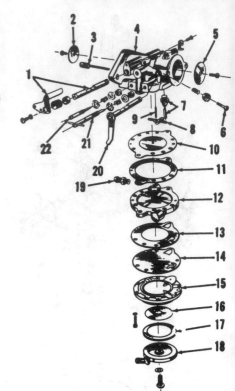

Fig. CL9—Exploded view of Tillotson HL diaphragm type carburetor.

1. Choke plate	11. Gasket
2. Idle stop screw	12. Cover
3. Choke shaft	13. Gasket
4. Throttle shaft	14. Pump diaphragm
5. Main fuel needle	15. Pump body
6. Idle fuel needle	16. Screen
7. Throttle plate	17. Gasket
8. Inlet lever pivot	18. Cover
9. Inlet lever	19. Welch plug
10. Diaphragm	20. Inlet valve & seat

Fig. CL10—Exploded view of Brown CP carburetor.

1. Choke plate	13. Gasket
2. Idle stop screw	14. Diaphragm
3. Filter plug	15. Pump cover
4. Throttle shaft	16. Gasket
5. Gasket	17. Inlet fitting
6. Carburetor body	18. Inlet lever
7. Idle jet	19. Inlet valve
8. Throttle plate	20. Idle fuel needle
9. Inlet lever spring	21. Choke shaft
10. Gasket	22. Main fuel needle
11. Diaphragm	23. Inlet lever pivot
12. Cover	

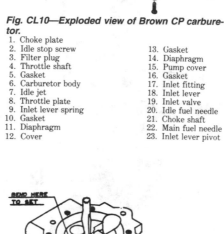

Fig. CL11—Method of checking and setting fuel inlet lever on Brown diaphragm type carburetors.

Fig. CL12—Exploded view of Brown CS carburetor.

1. Throttle shaft	12. Cover
2. Throttle plate	13. Gasket
3. Inlet lever pivot	14. Pump diaphragm
4. Carburetor body	15. Pump cover
5. Choke plate	16. Screen
6. Idle stop screw	17. Gasket
7. Inlet needle valve & seat	18. Inlet fitting
8. Inlet lever	19. Connection
9. Inlet lever spring	20. Choke shaft
10. Diaphragm	21. Main fuel nozzle
11. Gasket	22. Idle fuel needle

engine at idle speed and adjust idle needle for smooth engine idle then open needle slightly to run a slightly over-rich mixture.

Float setting on Models N-2003-S and N-2457-S is 13/64-inch (5.16 mm) clearance between outer edge of casting and free end of flat. Float setting on Models N-2029-S, N-2087-S and N-2171-S is 11/64-inch (4.37 mm) clearance between outer edge of casting and free end of float. On all models, carefully bend lip on float hinge if necessary to obtain correct float level.

On Model N-2457-S, low speed jet and high speed fuel nozzle are permanently installed. Do not attempt to remove these parts.

Carter Model NS Float Type Carburetor. Refer to Fig. CL8 for identification and exploded view of Carter Model NS float type carburetor. This carburetor is designed for engine operation between 3000 and 3800 rpm and is not equipped with an idle fuel mixture adjusting needle.

Initial adjustment of main fuel mixture needle (7) from a lightly seated position is 1 turn open. Final adjustments are made with engine at operating temperature. Operate engine at rated speed and adjust main fuel mixture nee-

dle to obtain smoothest engine operation and acceleration.

To check float level, invert carburetor throttle body. Measure between outer edge of bowl cover and top surface of free end of float. Measurement should be 13/64 inch (5.16 mm). Fuel inlet needle, seat and spring are integral parts of bowl cover and available as an assembly only.

Tillotson HL Diaphragm Type Carburetor. Refer to Fig. CL9 for identification and exploded view of Tillotson HL diaphragm type carburetor. Models HL-13A and Hl-44A are used. Clockwise rotation of mixture needles on all models leans the fuel mixture.

Initial adjustment of idle (6) and main (5) fuel mixture needles from a lightly seated position is ¾ turn open for idle mixture needle and 1 to 1¼ turns open for main fuel mixture needle.

Final adjustments are made with engine at operating temperature and running. Operate engine at rated speed and adjust main fuel mixture needle for smoothest engine operation, then open needle slightly to provide an over-rich fuel mixture. Operate engine at idle speed and adjust idle mixture screw for smoothest engine idle. If engine fails to accelerate smoothly, open idle mixture needle slightly as necessary.

Brown CP Diaphragm Type Carburetor. Refer to Fig. CL10 for identification and exploded view of Brown Model 3-CP diaphragm type carburetor. Idle mixture needle has a slotted head and main fuel mixture needle has a "T" head. Note fuel must pass through a felt filter and screen, located under plug (3), to enter the diaphragm chamber.

Initial adjustment of idle (20) and main (22) fuel mixture needles from a lightly seated position is ½ to ¾ turn open for each needle.

Final adjustments are made with engine at operating temperature and running. Operate engine at rated speed

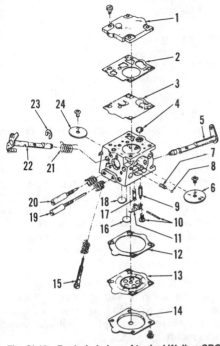

Fig. CL13—Exploded view of typical Walbro SDC, diaphragm type carburetor. Model SDC-35 used on 502-0308-000 engines has choke (5) and throttle (22) levers of slightly different configuration from those shown. Also, an additional diaphragm check valve (not shown) is fitted between gasket (2) and pump diaphragm (3).

1. Fuel pump cover
2. Gasket
3. Pump diaphragm
4. Fuel inlet screen
5. Choke shaft
6. Choke plate
7. Choke detent spring
8. Choke detent ball
9. Inlet valve needle
10. Lever pin retainer
11. Metering lever
12. Metering diaphragm gasket
13. Metering diaphragm
14. Diaphragm cover
15. Idle speed screw & spring
16. Welch plug
17. Metering lever spring
18. Welch plug
19. Main fuel needle & spring
20. Idle mixture needle & spring
21. Throttle return spring
22. Throttle shaft
23. Shaft retainer
24. Throttle plate

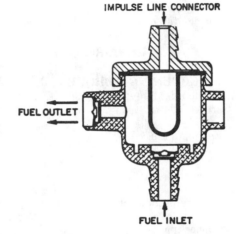

Fig. CL14—View of metering lever adjustment procedure on SDC-34 carburetors. Check engagement of inlet valve needle and diaphragm hook to lever. Ensure spring under lever is correctly seated. Metering lever should just touch straightedge (A).

IMPULSE LINE CONNECTOR

FUEL OUTLET

FUEL INLET

Fig. CL15—Cross section view of impulse type fuel pump used on some engines. Renew complete pump assembly if inoperative.

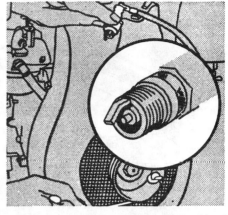

Fig. CL16—Magneto condition may be considered satisfactory if it will fire an 18 mm spark plug with electrode gap set at 0.156-0.187 inch (3.97-4.76 mm).

Final adjustments are made with engine at operating temperature and running. Operate engine at rated speed and adjust main fuel mixture needle for smoothest engine performance. Operate engine at idle speed and adjust idle fuel mixture for smooth engine idle. Note that very slight adjustments to idle and main fuel mixture needles may be necessary to obtain satisfactory engine acceleration.

Model 502-0308-000 engines rely on throttle position changes to control speed only and are not equipped with governor.

Refer to Fig. CL14 for adjustment procedure for metering lever. Be sure metering lever spring is properly seated and hook on diaphragm and inlet valve needle are correctly engaged.

FUEL PUMP. Some models are equipped with a diaphragm type fuel pump as shown in the cross-sectional view in Fig. CL15. The pump diaphragm is actuated by pressure pulsations in the engine crankcase transmitted via an impulse tube connected between the fuel pump and crankcase. The pump is

and adjust main fuel mixture needle for smoothest engine operation, then open mixture needle slightly to provide an over-rich fuel mixture. Operate engine at idle speed and adjust idle mixture needle for smooth engine idle. Check acceleration and open main fuel needle slightly if necessary to obtain smooth acceleration.

Refer to Fig. CL11 for proper diaphragm lever setting. Always renew the copper sealing gasket if inlet needle seat is removed.

Brown CS Diaphragm Type Carburetor. Refer to Fig. CL12 for identification and exploded view of Brown CS-15 diaphragm type carburetor. Idle fuel mixture needle has slotted adjustment head and main fuel adjustment needle has a "T" head.

Initial adjustment of idle (22) and main (21) fuel mixture needles from a lightly seated position is ¾ turn open for each screw.

Final adjustments are made with engine at operating temperature and running. Operate engine at rated speed and adjust main fuel mixture needle for smoothest engine operation, then open mixture needle slightly to provide an over-rich fuel mixture. Operate engine at idle speed and adjust idle mixture needle for smooth engine idle and proper acceleration.

Refer to Fig. CL11 for proper diaphragm lever setting. Always renew the copper sealing gasket if inlet needle is removed.

Walbro Model SDC-34 Diaphragm Type Carburetor. Refer to Fig. CL13 for identification and exploded view of Walbro Model SDC-34 carburetor used on Model 502-0308-000 engine.

Initial adjustment of idle (20) and main (19) fuel mixture needles from a lightly seated position is 1 turn open for each needle.

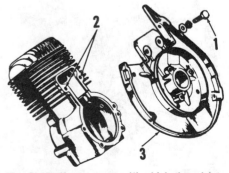

Fig. CL17—If cap screws (1) which thread into holes (2) are too long, they may bottom and damage cylinder walls.

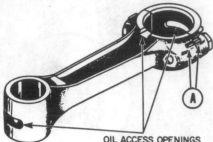

OIL ACCESS OPENINGS

Fig. CL18—Be sure embossments (A) are aligned when assembling cap to connecting rod.

designed to lift fuel approximately 6 inches (152 mm). Service consists of renewing the complete fuel pump assembly.

GOVERNOR. Speed control is maintained by an air vane type governor. Renew bent or worn governor vane or linkage and be sure linkage does not bind in any position when moved through full range of travel.

On models with speed control lever, adjust lever stop so maximum speed does not exceed 3600 rpm. On models without speed control, renew or retension governor spring to limit maximum speed to 3600 rpm. On all models (so equipped), make sure blower housing is clean and free of dents that would cause binding of air vane.

MAGNETO AND TIMING. Ignition timing is 27° BTDC and is nonadjustable. Armature air gap should be 0.007-0.017 inch (0.18-0.43 mm). Adjust breaker point gap to 0.018-0.021 inch (0.46-0.53 mm) on all models.

Magneto may be considered satisfactory if it will fire an 18 mm spark plug with gap set at 0.156-0.187 inch (3.97-4.76 mm). Refer to Fig. CL16.

LUBRICATION. Engine is lubricated by mixing a good quality two-stroke air-cooled engine oil with regular gasoline.

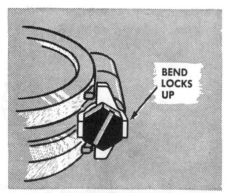

BEND LOCKS UP

Fig. CL19—Bend connecting rod cap retaining screw locks up as shown.

Oil to gasoline mixing ratio is determined by type of bearings installed in a particular two-stroke engine. Plain sleeve main and connecting rod bearings require 0.75 pint (0.36 L) of oil for each gallon of gasoline. Engines equipped with needle bearings require 0.50 pint (0.24 L) of oil for each gallon of gasoline. During break-in (first five hours of operation) a 50% increase of oil portion is advisable, especially if engine will be operated at or near maximum load or rpm.

CARBON. Power loss on two-stroke engines can often be corrected by cleaning the exhaust ports and muffler. To clean the exhaust ports, remove the muffler and turn engine until piston is below ports. Use a dull tool to scrape carbon from ports. Take care not to damage top of piston or cylinder walls.

REPAIRS

TIGHTENING TORQUES. Recommended tightening torque specifications are as follows:

Bearing plate to block	75-95 in.-lbs. (8-11 N·m)
Blower housing	65-70 in.-lbs. (7-8 N·m)
Carburetor mounting	60-65 in.-lbs. (7 N·m)
Connecting rod:	
E65, GK590, 502, 503 (aluminum)	70-80 in.-lbs. (8-9 N·m)
E65, GK590 (steel)	90-100 in.-lbs. (10-11 N·m)
All others (aluminum)	35-45 in.-lbs. (4-5 N·m)
Cylinder head (502 & 503)	140-160 in.-lbs. (16-18 N·m)
Engine base	125-150 in.-lbs. (14-17 N·m)
Flywheel:	
E65 & GK590	250-300 in.-lbs. (28-34 N·m)
All others	375-400 in.-lbs. (42-45 N·m)
Muffler	40-60 in.-lbs. (4-7 N·m)
Spark plug	275-300 in.-lbs. (31-34 N·m)
Stator plate to bearing plate	50-60 in.-lbs. (5-7 N·m)

BEARING PLATE. Because of the pressure and vacuum pulsations in crankcase, bearing plate and gasket must form an airtight seal when installed. Inspect bearing plate gasket surface for cracks, nicks or warpage. Ensure oil passages in crankcase, gasket and plate are aligned and that correct number and thickness of thrust washers are used. Also make certain cap screws of the correct length are installed when engine is reassembled.

CAUTION: Cap screws (1—Fig. C17) may bottom in threaded holes (2) if incorrect screws are used. When long screws are tightened, damage to cylinder walls can result.

FLYWHEEL. On vertical shaft engines, both a lightweight aluminum flywheel and a cast iron flywheel are available. The lightweight aluminum flywheel should be used only on rotary lawnmower engines where the blade is attached directly to the engine crankshaft. The cast iron flywheel should be used on engines with belt pulley drive, etc.

Some kart engine owners will prefer using the lightweight aluminum flywheel due to the increase in accelerating performance.

CONNECTING ROD. Connecting rod and piston unit can be removed after removing the reed plate and crankshaft.

On E-65 and GK590 models (karting engines), and on 502 and 503 models, needle roller bearings are used at crankpin end of connecting rod. Renew crankshaft and/or connecting rod if bearing surfaces are scored or rough. When reassembling, place the thirteen needle rollers between connecting rod and crankpin. Using a low melting point grease, stick the remaining twelve needle rollers to connecting rod cap. Install

Fig. CL20—View showing method of installing ring locking wires on three-ring pistons and placement of rings on two- and three-ring pistons. Some two-ring pistons do not have ring locking pins.

cap with the embossments (see A – Fig. CL18) on cap and rod properly aligned.

On all other models, an aluminum connecting rod with bronze bearing surfaces is used. Standard diameter of connecting rod crankpin bearing bore (plain bearing) is 0.7820-0.7827 inch (19.863-19.881 mm).

Clearance between connecting rod and crankpin journal should be 0.0026-0.0040 inch (0.07-0.10 mm). Renew connecting rod and/or crankshaft if clearance exceeds 0.0055 inch (0.14 mm).

Clearance between piston pin and connecting rod piston pin bore should be 0.0004-0.0011 inch (0.010-0.028 mm). Renew connecting and/or piston pin if

clearance exceeds 0.002 inch (0.05 mm).

Reinstall cap to connecting rod with embossments (A – Fig. CL18) aligned and carefully tighten screws to recommended specification. Bend the locking tabs against screw heads as shown in Fig. CL19.

PISTON, PIN AND RINGS. Pistons may be equipped with either two or three compression rings. On three-ring pistons, a locking wire is fitted in a small groove behind each piston ring to prevent ring rotation on the piston. To install the three locking wires, refer to Fig. CL20 and hold piston with top up and intake side of piston to right. Install

top and bottom locking wires with locking tab (end of wire ring bent outward) to right of locating hole in ring groove. Install center locking wire with locking tab to left of locating hole.

Piston and rings are available in several oversizes as well as standard size. Piston pin is available in standard size only.

When installing pistons with ring locating pins or locking wires, be sure end gaps of rings are properly located over the pins or the locking tabs and install piston using a ring compressor. Refer to Fig. CL20.

Be sure to reinstall piston and connecting rod assembly with exhaust side of

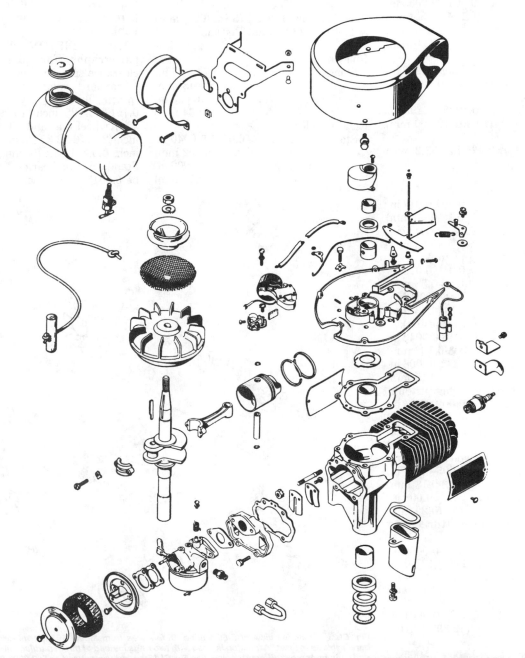

Fig. CL21—Exploded view of typical vertical shaft two-stroke engine. Model 503 differs in type of starter (see Fig. CL102—ACCESSORIES), use of an eight-petal rossette type reed valve, a detachable cylinder head and has ball and roller bearings to support crankshaft with needle bearing at crankpin.

piston (long sloping side of piston dome) towards exhaust ports in cylinder.

Check piston, pin and rings against the following specifications:

Specifications For 1.875 in. (47.6 mm) Pistons

Ring end gap:
Standard . . . . 0.005-0.013 in.
(0.13-0.33 mm)
Maximum . . . . 0.020 in.
(0.51 mm)

Ring side clearance:
Standard . . . . 0.0015-0.0040 in.
(0.038-0.102 mm)
Maximum . . . . 0.006 in.
(0.15 mm)

Piston skirt clearance:
Standard . . . . 0.0045-0.0065 in.
(0.114-0.165 mm)
Maximum . . . . 0.008 in.
(0.20 mm)

Piston pin
diameter . . . . 0.4294-0.4296 in.
(10.899-10.904 mm)

Piston pin bore
diameter . . . . 0.4295-0.4298 in.
(10.901-10.909 mm)

Specifications For 2.125 in. (53.2 mm) Piston

Ring end gap (two-ring piston):
Standard . . . . 0.007-0.017 in.
(0.18-0.43 mm)
Maximum . . . . 0.025 in.
(0.64 mm)

Ring end gap (three-ring piston):
Standard . . . . 0.010-0.015 in.
(0.25-0.38 mm)
Maximum . . . . 0.017 in.
(0.43 mm)

Ring side clearance (two-ring piston):
Standard . . . . 0.0015-0.0040 in.
(0.038-0.102 mm)
Maximum . . . . 0.006 in.
(0.15 mm)

Ring side clearance (three-ring piston):
Standard . . . . 0.002-0.004 in.
(0.05-0.10 mm)
Maximum . . . . 0.0055 in.
(0.140 mm)

Piston skirt clearance (two-ring piston):
Standard . . . . 0.005-0.007 in.
(0.13-0.18 mm)
Maximum . . . . 0.008 in.
(0.20 mm)

Piston skirt clearance (three-ring piston):
Standard . . . . 0.0045-0.0050 in.
(0.114-0.127 mm)
Maximum . . . . 0.007 in.
(0.18 mm)

Piston pin
diameter . . . . 0.4999-0.5001 in.
(12.698-12.703)

Piston pin
bore diameter . . . . . . 0.5000-0.5003 in.
(0.127-0.135 mm)

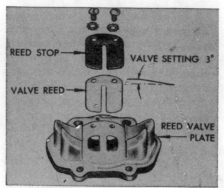

Fig. CL22—Details of two-petal reed inlet valve used on some models. Eight-petal rosette style reed valve is also used. See. Fig. CL23.

Specifications For 2.375 in. (60.3 mm) & 2.500 in. (63.5 mm) Pistons

Ring end gap:
Standard . . . . 0.007-0.017 in.
(0.18-0.43 mm)
Maximum . . . . 0.025 in.
(0.64 mm)

Ring side clearance:
Standard . . . . 0.0015-0.0040 in.
(0.038-0.102 mm)
Maximum . . . . 0.006 in.
(0.15 mm)

Piston skirt clearance:
Standard . . . . 0.005-0.007 in.
(0.13-0.18 mm)
Maximum . . . . 0.008 in.
(0.20 mm)

CYLINDER AND CRANKCASE.

The one-piece aluminum alloy cylinder and crankcase unit is integrally die-cast around a cast iron sleeve (cylinder liner). Cylinder can be rebored if worn beyond specifications. Standard cylinder bore diameter for models with 1.875 inch (47.63 mm) bore is 1.875-1.876 inches (47.63-57.65 mm); with 2.125 inch (53.98 mm) bore is 2.125-2.126 inches (53.98-54.00 mm); with 2.375 inch (60.33 mm) bore is 2.375-2.376 inches (60.33-60.35 mm) and with 2.500 inch (63.50 mm) bore is 2.500-2.501 inches (63.50-63.53 mm).

Refer to PISTON, PIN AND RINGS paragraphs for piston-to-cylinder clearance specifications.

Standard main bearing diameters (plain bushing type) should be 0.7517-0.7525 inch (19.093-19.114 mm) at flywheel end and either 0.877-0.878 inch (22.276-22.301 mm) or 1.002-1.003 inch (25.451-25.476 mm) at pto end. Standard main bearing clearance should be 0.0015-0.0030 inch (0.038-0.076 mm)

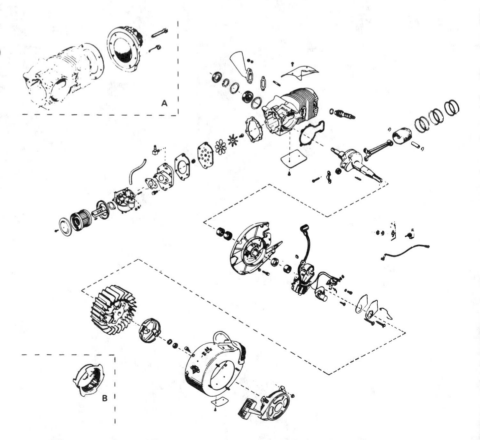

Fig. CL23—Exploded view of E-65 engine. Differences from Model 502 are minor: Cylinder head is detachable as in inset "A"; piston is fitted with two rings instead of three; muffler, starter cup (inset "B") and carburetor are of different design. See Fig. CL13 for carburetor used on 502-0308-000 engines. Model 502-0309-000 engines are equipped with float type carburetor.

and crankcase should be renewed if worn beyond specification or if out-of-round 0.0015 inch (0.038 mm) or more.

Main bearing bushings, bushing remover and driver, reamers and reamer alignment plate are available through Clinton parts sources for renewing bushings in crankcase and bearing plate. On vertical crankshaft engines having two bushings in the crankcase, the outer bushing must be removed towards inside of crankcase.

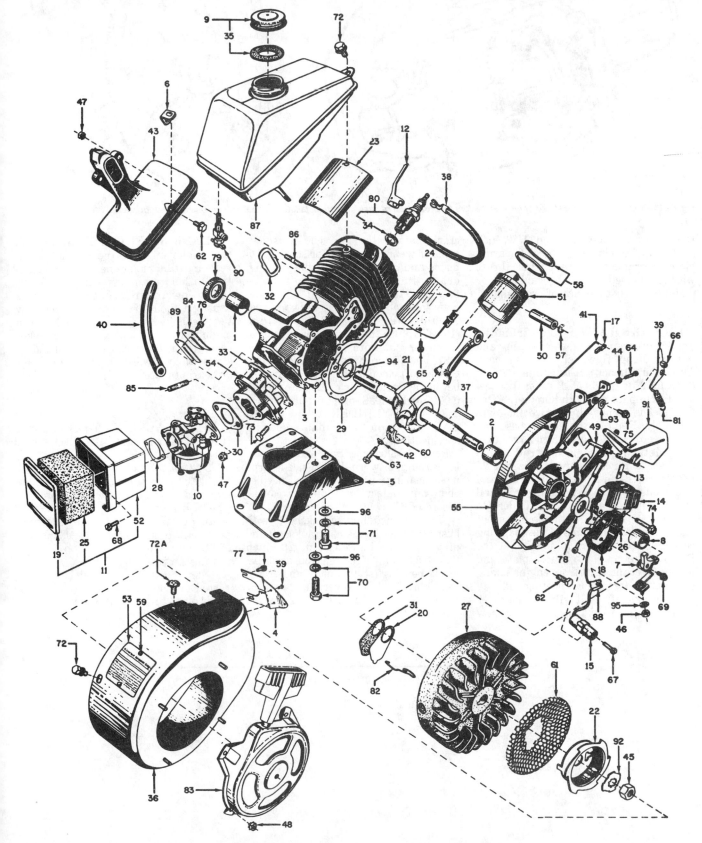

Fig. CL24—Exploded view of typical horizontal crankshaft engine.

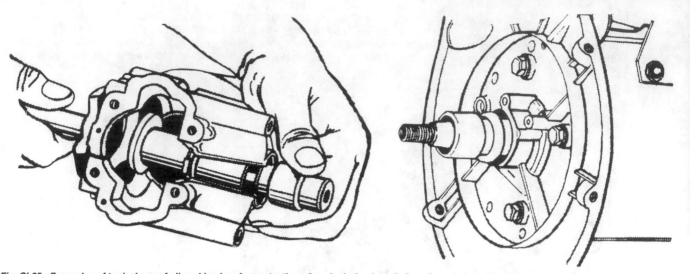

Fig. CL25—Examples of typical use of oil seal loaders for protection of seals during installation of crankshaft. Use ample lubrication.

Bushings must be recessed 1/32 inch (0.79 mm) from inside surface of bearing plate or crankcase except when thrust washer is used between crankcase or plate and thrust surface of crankshaft.

CRANKSHAFT. To remove crankshaft, remove blower housing and nut retaining flywheel to crankshaft. Thread an impact nut to within 1/8 inch (3.18 mm) of flywheel. Pull on flywheel and tap impact nut with hammer. After flywheel is removed, remove magneto assembly. Remove the engine base and inlet reed valve plate from crankcase and detach connecting rod from crankshaft. Be careful not to lose the 25 needle rollers on E-65, GK-590, 502 and 503 models. Push connecting rod and piston unit up against top of cylinder. On models with ball bearing main on output end of crankshaft, remove the snap ring retaining ball bearing in crankcase. Remove the magneto stator plate and withdraw crankshaft from engine taking care not to damage connecting rod.

On crankshaft used with needle roller main or crankpin bearings, renew crankshaft if bearing surface shows signs of wear, roughness or scoring. On mains and/or cast-in crankpin bearing, crankpin diameter should be 0.7788-0.7795 inch (19.782-19.799 mm). Main journal diameter at flywheel end should be 0.7495-0.7502 inch (19.037-19.055 mm) and main journal diameter at pto end should be 0.8745-0.8752 inch (22.212-22.230 mm). Crankshaft should be renewed if worn beyond specifications or if out-of-round 0.0015 inch (0.038 mm) or more.

Refer to CYLINDER AND CRANK-CASE section for main bearing specifications.

Renew ball bearing type mains if bearing is rough or worn. Renew needle type main bearings if one or more needles show any defect or if needles can be separated the width of one roller.

When reinstalling crankshaft with bushing or needle mains, crankshaft end play should be 0.005-0.020 inch (0.13-0.51 mm). The gasket used between bearing (stator) plate and crankcase is available in several thicknesses. It may also be necessary to renew the crankshaft thrust washer.

CRANKSHAFT OIL SEALS. On all two-stroke engines, the crankshaft oil seals must be maintained in good condition to hold crankcase compression on the downward stroke of the piston. It is usually a good service practice to renew the seals whenever overhauling an engine. Apply a small amount of gasket sealer to the outer rim of the seal and install with lip towards inside of crankcase or bearing plate.

REED VALVE. Either a dual reed (Fig. CL21) or eight-petal rosette reed (Fig. CL23) is used.

The 3° setting of the dual reed shown in Fig. CL22 is the design of the reed as stamped in the manufacturing process. The 3° bend should be towards the reed seating surface. The reed stop should be adjusted to approximately 0.280 inch (7.11 mm) from tip of stop to reed seating surface.

Renew reed if any petal is cracked, rusted or does not lay flat against the reed plate. Renew the reed plate if rusted, pitted or worn.

CLINTON

Horizontal Crankshaft Engines

Model	Bore	Stroke	Displacement
100, 2100,A-2100, 400-0100-000, 402-0100-000	2.375 in. (60.3 mm)	1.625 in. (41.3 mm)	7.2 cu. in. (118 cc)
3100,4100, 404-0100-000, 406-0100-000, 408-0100-000, 424-0100-000, 426-0100-000, 492-0000-000	2.375 in. (60.3 mm)	1.875 in. (47.6 mm)	8.3 cu. in. (136 cc)
410-0000-000	2.500 in. (63.5 mm)	1.875 in. (47.6 mm)	9.2 cu. in. (151 cc)

Vertical Crankshaft Engines

Model	Bore	Stroke	Displacement
V-100,VS-100, VS-2100,VS300, 403-0000-000, 405-0000-000, 411-0002-000	2.375 in. (60.3 mm)	1.625 in. (41.3 mm)	7.2 cu. in. (118 cc)
AFV-3100, AV-3100, AVS-3100, FV-3100, V-3100, VS-3100, AVS-4100, VS-4100, 405-0000-000, 407-0000-000, 409-0000-000, 415-0000-000, 417-0000-000, 435-0000-000, 455-0000-000	2.375 in. (60.3 mm)	1.875 in. (47.6 mm)	8.3 cu. in. (136 mm)
419-0000-000, 429-0000-000, 431-0003-000	2.500 in. (63.5 mm)	1.875 in. (47.6 mm)	9.2 cu. in. (151 cc)

MAINTENANCE

SPARK PLUG. Recommended spark plug for all models is a Champion H10 or equivalent. Electrode gap is 0.025-0.028 inch (0.64-0.71 mm). Tighten spark plug to specified torque.

CARBURETOR. Either Clinton (Walbro) float type or Clinton suction type carburetor is used. Refer to the appropriate paragraph.

Clinton (Walbro) Float Type Carburetor. A variety of Clinton (Walbro) LMB, LMG and LMV series carburetors have been used. To identify carburetor, refer to Fig. CL61 for identification number.

Initial adjustment of idle (9) and main (22) fuel mixture needles from a lightly seated position is 1¼ turns open for each needle.

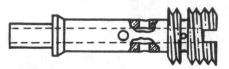

Fig. CL60—Views showing location of identification numbes on LMB, LMG and LMV series carburetors. Identification numbers must be used when ordering service parts.

Final adjustment is made with engine at operating temperature and running. Operate engine at rated speed and adjust main fuel mixture needle for smoothest engine operation. Operate engine at idle speed and adjust idle fuel mixture needle for smooth engine idle. If engine fails to accelerate smoothly it may be necessary to slightly richen main fuel needle adjustment.

When overhauling carburetor, do not remove the main fuel nozzle (13) unless necessary. If nozzle is removed, it must be discarded and a service type nozzle (Fig. CL61A) installed.

Choke plate (11 – Fig. CL61) should be installed with the "W" or part number to outside. Install throttle plate with the side marked "W" facing towards mounting flange and with the part number towards idle needle side of carburetor bore when plate is in closed position. When installing throttle plate, back idle speed adjustment screw out, turn plate and throttle shaft to closed position and seat plate by gently tapping wtih small screwdriver before tightening plate retaining screws.

If either the float valve or seat is damaged, install a new matched valve and seat assembly (12) and tighten seat to 40-50 in.-lbs. (5-6 N·m).

To check float level, invert carburetor throttle body and float assembly. Distance between free side of float and float bowl mating surface of carburetor surface should be 5/32 inch (3.97 mm). Carefully bend float lever tang which contacts fuel inlet needle if necessary to obtain correct float level.

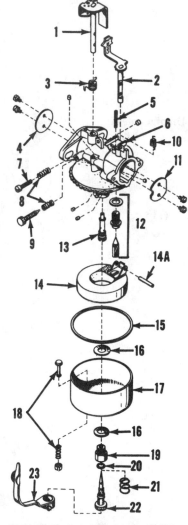

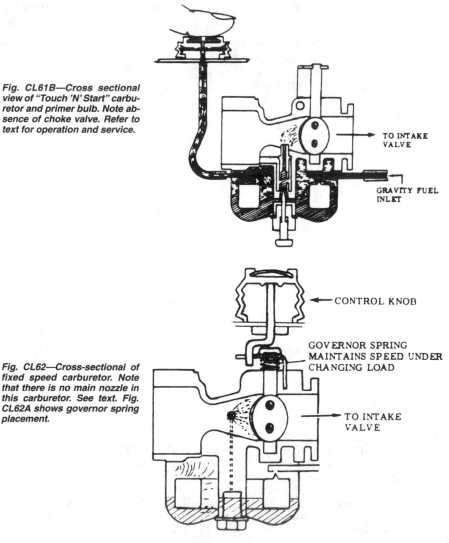

Fig. CL61A–When original main fuel nozzle is removed from LM series carburetors, it must be discarded and service type nozzle shown must be installed.

Fig. CL61B—Cross sectional view of "Touch 'N' Start" carburetor and primer bulb. Note absence of choke valve. Refer to text for operation and service.

Fig. CL62—Cross-sectional of fixed speed carburetor. Note that there is no main nozzle in this carburetor. See text. Fig. CL62A shows governor spring placement.

TO INTAKE VALVE

GRAVITY FUEL INLET

CONTROL KNOB

GOVERNOR SPRING MAINTAINS SPEED UNDER CHANGING LOAD

TO INTAKE VALVE

Fig. CL61—Exploded view of typical LMG series carburetor. LMB and LMV series are similar.

1. Throttle shaft
2. Choke shaft
3. Spring
4. Throttle plate
5. Spring
6. Carburetor body
7. Idle stop screw
8. Springs
9. Idle fuel needle
10. Spring
11. Choke plate
12. Inlet needle
13. Main nozzle
14. Float
14A. Float pin
15. Gasket
16. Gaskets
17. Float bowl
18. Drain valve
19. Retainer
20. Seal
21. Spring
22. Main fuel needle
23. Lever (optional)

Clinton "Touch 'N' Start" Carburetor. Refer to Fig. CL61B for identification and cross-sectional view of "Touch 'N' Start" carburetor. Instead of choke valve (11–Fig. CL61) carburetor is furnished with a flexible primer bulb.

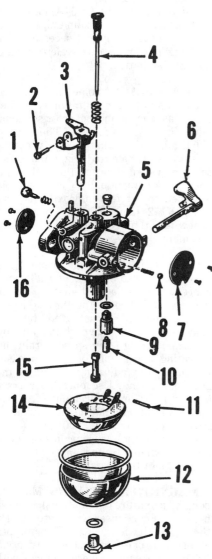

which provides a rich charging mixture to carburetor venturi and intake manifold for easier starting. Float bowl is vented through primer tube to flexible bulb and vent is closed when operator's finger depresses primer bulb. Service procedures and specifications are the same as for Clinton (Walbro) float type carburetor.

Fig. CL62A—Top view of fixed speed carburetor showing correct installation of governor link and spring.

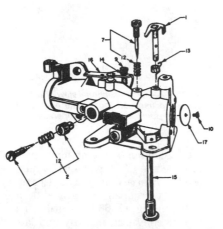

Fig. CL64—Exploded view of Clinton suction lift carburetor. On late production models, idle adjustment screw is threaded directly into carburetor body and does not have the threaded bushing shown. Choke plate (17) and throttle plate (not shown) may be attached with one screw as shown although later models have two holes for attaching screws in each plate and shaft.

1. Choke shaft	12. Springs
2. Idle fuel needle & bushing	13. Spring
	14. Spring
7. Main fuel needle	16. Throttle shaft
9. Idle stop screw	17. Choke plate
10. Screw	

Fixed Speed Carburetor. Refer to Fig. CL62 for identification and sectional view of LMB, LMG and LMV carburetors equipped with constant speed control. These carburetors have no main nozzle (13–Fig. CL61) and are without an idle current. Speed control knob is turned clockwise to close throttle and stop engine.

Engine speed is controlled at 3000-3400 rpm (no load) by throttle governor spring. See Fig. CL62A for spring placement.

Initial adjustment of idle and main fuel adjustment needles are the same as for Clinton (Walbro) float type carburetor with the exception that main fuel needle initial adjustment is 1¼ to 1½ turns open. Refer to CLINTON (WALBRO) CARBURETORS section for service specifications.

Carter Float Type Carburetor. Refer to Fig. CL63 for identification and ex-

28° REVISED LEVER
45°
ORIGINAL LEVER

Fig. CL65—Choke lever for later production of Clinton suction lift carburetor shown in Fig. CL64 is modified as shown here to prevent breakage. Early models should have choke lever (1—Fig. CL64) modified as shown.

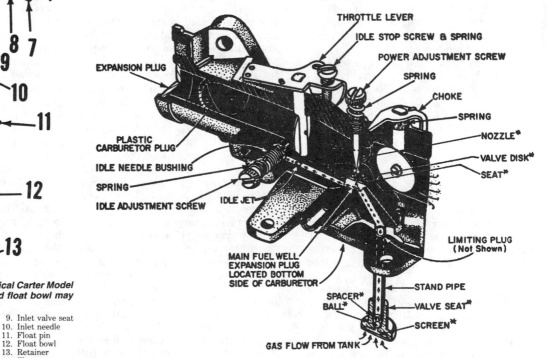

Fig. CL64A—Cut-away view of Clinton suction lift carburetor. Refer to test for disassembly procedure.

Fig. CL63—Exploded view of typical Carter Model N carburetor. Design of float and float bowl may vary from that shown.

1. Idle fuel needle	9. Inlet valve seat
2. Idle stop screw	10. Inlet needle
3. Throttle shaft	11. Float pin
4. Main fuel needle	12. Float bowl
5. Carburetor body	13. Retainer
6. Choke shaft	14. Float
7. Choke plate	15. Main nozzle
8. Detent ball	16. Throttle plate

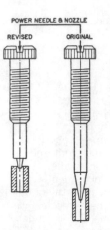

Fig. CL66—View showing early production and late production main fuel needles for Clinton suction lift carburetors. Original and revised needles are not interchangeable. Needle seats are nonrenewable; renew carburetor if seat is damaged.

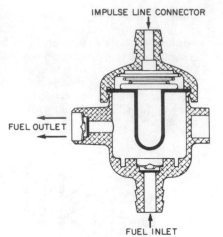

Fig. CL66A—Cross-sectional view of impulse type fuel pump used on four-stroke engines. Renew complete pump assembly if inoperative.

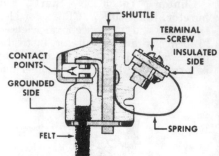

Fig. CL67—Shuttle type breaker points shown are used in early production models.

ploded view of Carter N series carburetors used on some models. Design of float and float bowl may vary.

Initial adjustment of idle (1) and main (4) fuel mixture needles from a lightly seated position is 1 turn open for idle mixture screw and 1½ turns open for main fuel mixture screw on N-2264S and N-2459S models or 1 turn open for idle fuel mixture needle and 2 turns open for main fuel mixture needles on N-2236S and N-2458S models.

Final adjustment is made with engine at operating temperature and running. Operate engine at rated speed and adjust main fuel mixture needle for smoothest engine operation. Operate engine at idle speed and adjust idle fuel mixture needle for smooth engine idle. If engine fails to accelerate smoothly it may be necessary to slightly richen main fuel needle adjustment.

To check float level, invert carburetor throttle body and float assembly. Distance between free side of float and float bowl mating surface on carburetor should be 11/64 inch (4.37 mm). Carefully bend float lever tang which contacts fuel inlet needle as necessary to obtain correct float level.

Clinton Suction Type Carburetors. Refer to Fig. CL64 for identification and exploded view of Clinton suction type carburetor used on vertical crankshaft engines. Carburetor used on horizontal crankshaft engines is similar except that expansion plug and plastic plug shown in cut-away view (Fig. CL64A) are not used.

Initial adjustment of idle fuel mixture needle (2 – Fig. CL64) from a lightly seated position is 1½ turns open for mixture needle threaded directly into carburetor body or 4 to 4¼ turns open for mixture needle which thread into a bushing, and bushing is threaded into carburetor body.

Initial adjustment of main fuel mixture needle (7 – Fig. CL64) adjustment needle from a lightly seated position is ¾ to 1 turn open for early style needle (refer to Fig. CL66 to identify fuel mixture needle used in early and late carburetors) or 1¼ to 1½ turns open for late style needle (Fig. CL64).

Final adjustments are made with engine at operating temperature and running with fuel tank approximately ½ full. Operate engine at rated speed (fully loaded) and adjust main fuel mixture needle for smoothest engine operation. Note that engine main fuel adjustments cannot be made without engine under load. Engine high speed operation must be adjusted for a richer fuel mixture which may not produce smooth engine operation until load is applied. Operate engine at idle speed and adjust idle fuel mixture needle for smoothest engine idle.

To remove throttle shaft on carburetors from vertical crankshaft engines, drill through the expansion plug at rear of carburetor body, insert punch in drilled hole and pry plug out. Remove plastic plug, throttle valve screws, throttle valve and the throttle shaft. When reassembling, use new expansion plug and seal plug with sealer.

Test check valve in the fuel stand pipe by alternately blowing and sucking air through pipe. Stand pipe can be removed by clamping pipe in vise and prying carburetor from pipe. Apply sealer to stem of new stand pipe and install so it projects 1.895-1.985 inches (48.13-50.32 mm) from carburetor body.

To remove idle jet (Fig. CL64A), remove expansion plug from bottom of carburetor, idle needle and if so equipped, idle needle bushing. Insert a 1/16 inch (1.59 mm) rod through fuel well and up through idle passage to push jet out into idle reservoir. To install

new jet, place mark on the rod exactly 1¼ inches (31.75 mm) from end and push new jet into passage until mark on rod is in exact center of fuel well.

Limiting plug (Fig. CL64A) located in fuel passageway from stand pipe should not be removed unless necessary for cleaning purposes. Use sealer on plug during installation.

FUEL PUMP. Some models are equipped with a diaphragm type fuel pump as shown in the cross-sectional view in Fig. CL66A. The pump diaphragm is actuated by pressure pulsations transmitted via an impulse tube connected between the fuel pump and intake manifold. The pump is designed to lift fuel approximately six inches (152 mm). Service consists of renewing the complete fuel pump assembly.

GOVERNOR. An air vane type governor is used on all models. The air vane, which is located in the blower housing, is linked to the throttle lever. The governor is actuated by air delivered by the flywheel fan and by governor spring. Any speed within the operating speed range of the engine can be obtained by adjusting tension on the governor spring. Use only the correct Clinton part for replacement of governor spring and do not adjust maximum governed speed above 3600 rpm.

Make sure the governor linkage does not bind when linkage is moved through full range of travel.

MAGNETO AND TIMING. Magneto coil and armature (laminations), breaker points and condenser are located under the engine flywheel. Two different types of breaker point assemblies are used. Early model engines were equipped with shuttle type breaker points as shown in Fig. CL67. Early type breaker points are enclosed in a box which is an integral part of the engine crankcase and are covered by a plate and gasket. Some shuttle type points may also be enclosed in a sealed unit within the breaker box. Magneto edge gap for models with shut-

Fig. CL67A—Magneto can be considered in satisfactory condition if it will fire an 18 mm spark plug with electrode gap set at 0.156-0.187 inch (3.96-4.75 mm).

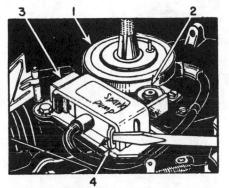

Fig. CL68—After installing spark pump assembly, remove clip (4) with screwdriver as shown. Clip (4) or a 0.10 inch (2.54 mm) spacer should be placed between spark pump lever and frame prior to removing the spark pump from engine. Refer to text.

1. Timing switch
2. Eccentric bearing
3. Spark pump
4. Spacer clip

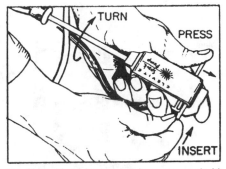

Fig. CL70—If spark pump has been removed without installing clip or spacer (Fig. CL68), before reinstalling pump, turn load adjusting screw about ½ turn in a counterclockwise direction and hold screw in this position. Press actuating lever in direction shown and insert a 0.10 inch (2.54 mm) spacer between inner end of lever and spark pump frame.

tle type points .is 0.156-0.187 inch (3.96-4.75 mm). Lubricate felt with a high melting point grease.

Later engine models are equipped with rocker type breaker points and the points are enclosed in a breaker box which is attached to the engine crankcase. Magneto edge gap for systems with rocker type breaker points is 0.094-0.250 inch (2.39-6.35 mm).

Breaker point gap for all models is 0.018-0.021 inch (0.46-0.53 mm). Ignition timing is 21° BTDC and is nonadjustable.

SPARK PUMP. On a limited number of engines, a Dyna-Spark ignition system (spark pump or "piezo-electric" ignition system) is used instead of the conventional flywheel type magneto. The system consists of a spark pump (3 – Fig. CL68) and a timing switch (1).

The spark pump is actuated by an eccentric bearing (2) on the entended end of the engine camshaft and the timing switch is driven by the crankshaft. A spark is generated whenever the cam lever on the spark pump is moved.

As with the conventional magneto, the Dyna-Spark ignition system may be considered in satisfactory condition if it will fire a spark plug with electrode gap set at 0.156-0.187 inch (3.96-4.75 mm). See Fig. CL67A.

If system is inoperative, inspect wire from spark pump to timing switch and from timing switch to spark plug for shorts or breaks in wire. If inspection does not reveal open or shorted condition, the complete Dyna-Spark unit must be renewed.

To remove Dyna-Spark unit, disconnect spark plug and remove engine blower housing and flywheel. Turn engine slowly until eccentric bearing (2 – Fig. CL68) on end of camshaft is at maximum lift position and install a 0.10 inch (2.54 mm) spacer between spark

pump actuating lever and spark pump frame. Turn engine so the eccentric bearing is at minimum lift position and remove the spark pump and timing switch from engine. The eccentric bearing may be removed from the camshaft after removing the retaining snap ring.

To install Dyna-Spark unit, turn engine so eccentric bearing is at minimum lift position and install the spark pump and timing switch on engine. Turn engine so eccentric bearing is at maximum lift position and remove the clip (4) or spacer from spark pump. Turn the load screw (6 – Fig. CL69) counterclockwise with slotted tool (7) or needle nose pliers to release tension on the spark generating element. Lever on spark pump should then follow eccentric bearing closely and smoothly as the engine is turned. Be sure pin (5) properly engages engine flywheel when reinstalling flywheel.

Fig. CL69—Turn load adjusting screw (6) counterclockwise with slotted tool (7) to remove pressure from spark generating cell; spring within spark pump will turn screw back clockwise to apply correct pressure. CAUTION: Never turn load adjusting screw in a clockwise direction. Timing switch is driven by pin (5) which engages engine flywheel.

CAUTION: Never turn load screw (6) in a clockwise direction. A coil spring within the spark pump unit will return the load screw to correct tension.

If the spark pump has been removed without a 0.10 inch (2.54 mm) spacer (or the clip as provided in a new spark pump) installed, refer to Fig. CL70 prior to installation of spark pump on engine.

LUBRICATION. Manufacturer recommends oil with an API service classification SE or SF. Use SAE 30 oil for temperatures above 32° F (0° C), SAE 10W oil for temperatures between –10° F (–23° C) and 32° F (0° C) and SAE 5W oil for temperatures below –10° F (–23° C).

On models equipped with reduction gearing, use SAE 30 oil in gearbox.

CRANKCASE BREATHER. Crankcase breather assembly located in or behind valve chamber cover should be cleaned if difficulty is experienced with oil loss through breather. Be sure the breather is correctly reassembled and reinstalled.

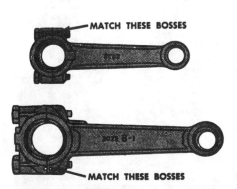

Fig. CL71—When assembling cap to connecting rod, be sure embossments on rod and cap are aligned as shown.

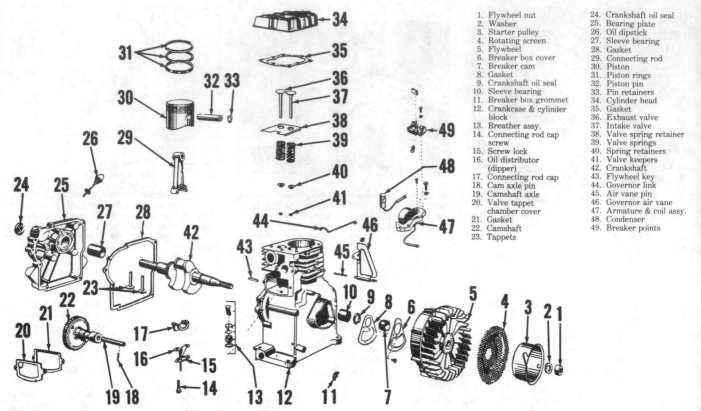

1. Flywheel nut	24. Crankshaft oil seal
2. Washer	25. Bearing plate
3. Starter pulley	26. Oil dipstick
4. Rotating screen	27. Sleeve bearing
5. Flywheel	28. Gasket
6. Breaker box cover	29. Connecting rod
7. Breaker cam	30. Piston
8. Gasket	31. Piston rings
9. Crankshaft oil seal	32. Piston pin
10. Sleeve bearing	33. Pin retainers
11. Breaker box grommet	34. Cylinder head
12. Crankcase & cylinder block	35. Gasket
13. Breather assy.	36. Exhaust valve
14. Connecting rod cap screw	37. Intake valve
15. Screw lock	38. Valve spring retainer
16. Oil distributor (dipper)	39. Valve springs
17. Connecting rod cap	40. Spring retainers
18. Cam axle pin	41. Valve keepers
19. Camshaft axle	42. Crankshaft
20. Valve tappet chamber cover	43. Flywheel key
21. Gasket	44. Governor link
22. Camshaft	45. Air vane pin
23. Tappets	46. Governor air vane
	47. Armature & coil assy.
	48. Condenser
	49. Breaker points

Fig. CL71A—Exploded view of early production horizontal crankshaft model. Camshaft (22) rotates on cam axle (19). Breather assembly (13) is located inside valve chamber. Breaker box is integral part of crankcase and breaker points (49) are accessible after removing flywheel and cover (6). Refer to Fig. CL71B for exploded view of late production horizontal crankshaft mode.

REPAIRS

TIGHTENING TORQUES. Recommended tightening torque specifications are as follows:

Base plate or side cover	75-80 in.-lbs. (8.5-9 N·m)
Blower housing	60-70 in.-lbs. (6.7-8 N·m)
Carburetor to manifold	35-50 in.-lbs. (4-6 N·m)
Carburetor (manifold) to block	60-65 in.-lbs. (6.7-7.3 N·m)

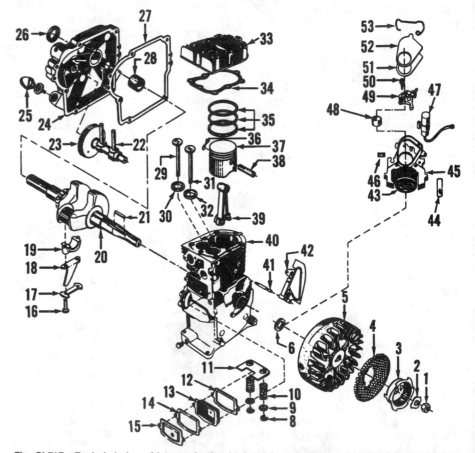

1. Flywheel nut	28. Sleeve bearing
2. Washer	29. Exhaust valve
3. Starter cup	30. Exhaust valve seat
4. Rotating screen	31. Intake valve
5. Flywheel	32. Intake valve seat
6. Crankshaft oil seal	33. Cylinder head
8. Valve keeper	34. Gasket
9. Spring retainer	35. Piston rings
10. Valve springs	36. Piston pin retainers
11. Spring retainer plate	37. Piston
12. Gasket	38. Piston pin
13. Breather assy.	39. Connecting rod
14. Gasket	40. Crankcase & cylinder block
15. Tappet chamber cover	41. Air vane pin
16. Connecting rod cap screws	42. Governor air vane
17. Cap screw lock	43. Ignition coil
18. Oil distributor	44. Coil retaining clips
19. Connecting rod cap	45. Armature & stator assy.
20. Crankshaft	46. Cam wiper felt
21. Flywheel key	47. Condenser
22. Tappets	48. Breaker cam
23. Camshaft	49. Breaker points
24. Bearing plate	50. Screw
25. Oil dipstick	51. Gasket
26. Crankshaft oil seal	52. Breaker box cover
27. Gasket	53. Retainer spring

Fig. CL71B—Exploded view of late production horizontal crankshaft model with die-cast aluminum crankcase and cylinder block assembly. Models with cast iron cylinder block are similar except for valve seat inserts (30 and 32).

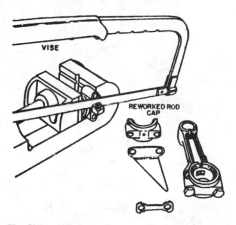

Fig. CL72—When necessary to install late type oil distributor on early type connecting rod, saw oil cup from rod cap as shown. Take care not to damage crankpin bearing surface and smooth off any burrs.

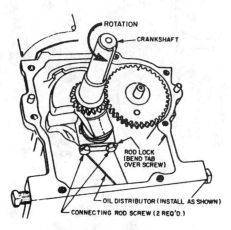

Fig. CL73—View showing correct installation of oil distributor in relation to crankshaft rotation.

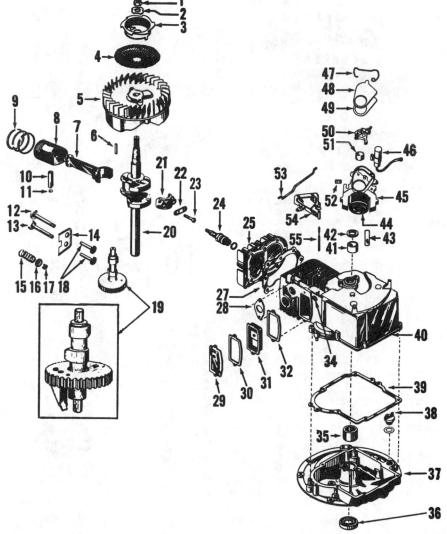

Fig. CL73A—Exploded view of vertical crankshaft model with splash lubrication system. Note oil dipper attached to lower side of camshaft gear (insert 19). Refer to Fig. CL76A for exploded view of vertical crankshaft model with oil pump.

1. Flywheel nut	15. Valve springs	29. Tappet chamber cover	43. Coil retaining clips
2. Washer	16. Spring retainer	30. Gasket	44. Ignition coil
3. Starter cup	17. Valve keepers	31. Breather assy.	45. Armature & coil
4. Rotating screen	18. Valve tappets	32. Gasket	assy.
5. Flywheel	19. Camshaft	34. Grommet	46. Condenser
6. Flywheel key	20. Crankshaft	35. Sleeve bearing	47. Retainer spring
7. Connecting rod	21. Connecting rod cap	36. Crankshaft oil seal	48. Breaker box cover
8. Piston	22. Cap screw lock	37. Engine base	49. Gasket
9. Piston rings	23. Connecting rod cap	38. Oil filler plug	50. Breaker points
10. Piston	screws	39. Gasket	51. Breaker cam
11. Pin retainers	24. Spark plug	40. Crankcase & cylinder	52. Felt cam wiper
12. Intake valve	25. Cylinder head	block	53. Governor link
13. Exhaust valve	27. Gasket	41. Sleeve bearing	54. Governor air vane
14. Spring retainer plate	28. Gasket	42. Crankshaft oil seal	55. Air vane pin

Connecting rod	100-125 in. lbs.
	(11-14 N·m)
Cylinder head	225-250 in.-lbs.
	(25-28 N·m)
Flywheel	375-400 in.-lbs.
	(42-45 N·m)*
Spark plug	275-300 in.-lbs.
	(31-34 N·m)

*Flywheel for "Touch 'N' Start" brake is tightened to 650-700 in.-lbs. (73-79 N·m).

CONNECTING ROD. Connecting rod and piston assembly can be removed after removing cylinder head and engine base (vertical crankshaft models). On horizontal crankshaft engines having ball bearing mains, oil seal and snap ring must be removed from side cover and crankshaft before side cover can be removed from engine.

The aluminum alloy connecting rod rides directly on the crankpin. Recommended connecting rod-to-crankpin clearance is 0.0015-0.0030 inch (0.04-0.08 mm). If clearance is 0.004 inch (0.10 mm) or more, connecting rod and/or crankshaft must be renewed.

Standard connecting rod bearing bore diameter may be 0.8140-0.8145 inch (20.68-20.69 mm) or 0.8770-0.8775 inch (22.28-22.29 mm) according to model and application.

Standard connecting rod-to-piston pin clearance is 0.0004-0.0011 inch (0.01-0.03 mm) on all models. Renew piston pin and/or connecting rod if clearance is 0.002 inch (0.05 mm) or more.

Standard piston pin bore diameter in connecting rod is 0.5630-0.5635 inch (14.30-14.31 mm).

Install connecting rod with oil hole towards flywheel side of engine and with embossments on rod and cap aligned as shown in Fig. CL71.

Connecting rods on early horizontal crankshaft models had an oil cup on rod cap which was designed for use with an oil distributor which is no longer available. If necessary to renew this oil distributor, a new distributor, Clinton part 220-147, and two new rod locks,

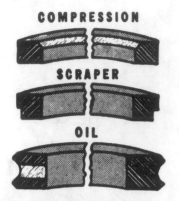

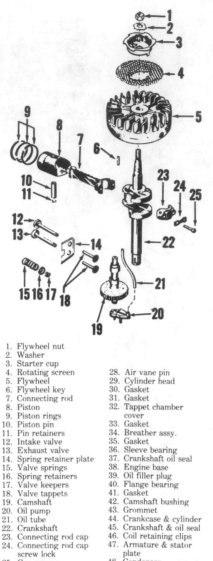

Fig. CL76—Drawing showing proper placement of piston rings. Note bevel at top of ring on inside diameter on top compression ring and notch in lower side of outside diameter of second compression (scraper) ring. Oil ring may be installed with either side up.

part 31038 must be used. If connecting rod with oil cup is to be reused, it must be reworked as shown in Fig. CL72. Install oil distributor and rod locks as shown in Fig. CL73.

PISTON, PIN AND RINGS. Piston is equipped with two compression rings and one oil control ring.

Standard ring side clearance in groove is 0.002-0.005 inch (0.05-0.12 mm). If side clearance is 0.006 inch (0.15 mm), renew rings and/or piston.

Standard piston ring end gap is 0.007-0.017 inch (0.18-0.26 mm). If ring end gap is 0.025 inch (0.64 mm) or more, renew rings and/or recondition cylinder bore.

Standard piston skirt-to-cylinder bore clearance is 0.0045-0.0065 inch (0.114-0.165 mm). If clearance is 0.008 inch (0.203 mm) or more, renew piston and/or recondition cylinder bore.

Standard pin bore diameter in piston is 0.5625-0.5628 inch (14.29-14.30 mm). Standard piston pin diameter is 0.5624-0.5626 inch (14.288-14.295 mm). Piston pin is a 0.0001 inch (0.003 mm) interference to a 0.0004 inch (0.010 mm) loose fit in piston pin bore.

Piston and rings are available in a variety of oversizes as well as standard and a special chrome ring set is available for cylinders having up to 0.010 inch (0.25 mm) taper and/or out-of-round condition.

CLYINDER AND CRANKCASE. Cylinder and crankcase are an integral unit of either an aluminum alloy die-casting with a cast-in iron cylinder liner or a shell casting of cast iron.

Standard cylinder bore diameter for 419-0003-000, 429-0003-000 and 431-0003-000 models is 2.499-2.500 inch (63.48-63.50 mm). Standard cylinder bore diameter for all other models is 2.3745-2.3755 inch (60.31-60.34 mm).

1. Flywheel nut	
2. Washer	
3. Starter cup	
4. Rotating screen	28. Air vane pin
5. Flywheel	29. Cylinder head
6. Flywheel key	30. Gasket
7. Connecting rod	31. Gasket
8. Piston	32. Tappet chamber
9. Piston rings	cover
10. Piston pin	33. Gasket
11. Pin retainers	34. Breather assy.
12. Intake valve	35. Gasket
13. Exhaust valve	36. Sleeve bearing
14. Spring retainer plate	37. Crankshaft oil seal
15. Valve springs	38. Engine base
16. Spring retainers	39. Oil filler plug
17. Valve keepers	40. Flange bearing
18. Valve tappets	41. Flange bearing
19. Camshaft	42. Camshaft bushing
20. Oil pump	43. Grommet
21. Oil tube	44. Crankcase & cylinder
22. Crankshaft	45. Crankshaft & oil seal
23. Connecting rod cap	46. Coil retaining clips
24. Connecting rod cap	47. Armature & stator
screw lock	plate
25. Cap screws	48. Condenser
26. Spark plug	49. Retaining clip
27. Governor air vane	50. Breaker box cover
51. Gasket	
52. Breaker points	
53. Breaker cam	
54. Cam wiper felt	
55. Ignition coil	

Fig. CL76A—Exploded view of vertical crankshaft model with lubricating oil pump (20). Refer to Fig. CL73A for vertical crankshaft model with spash lubrication.

Refer to PISTON, PIN AND RINGS section for piston-to-cylinder specifications.

CRANKSHAFT, MAIN BEARINGS AND SEAL. Crankshaft may be supported in-bushing type, integral bushing type or ball bearing type main bearings.

Standard crankpin diameter is either 0.8119-0.8125 inch (20.62-20.64 mm) or 0.8745-0.8752 inch (22.21-22.23 mm) according to model and application. If crankshaft main journal is 0.001 inch (0.03 mm) or more out-or-round, or if crankpin journal is 0.0015 inch (0.04 mm) or more out-of-round, renew crankshaft.

Standard clearance between crankshaft main bearing journals and bushing or integral type main bearings is 0.0018-0.0035 inch (0.05-0.09 mm). If clearance is 0.005 inch (0.13 mm) or

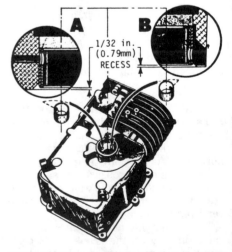

Fig. CL77—When installing crankshaft bushing in crankcase be sure oil holes are aligned as shown and that inner edge of bushing is 1/32 inch (0.79 mm) below thrust face of block.

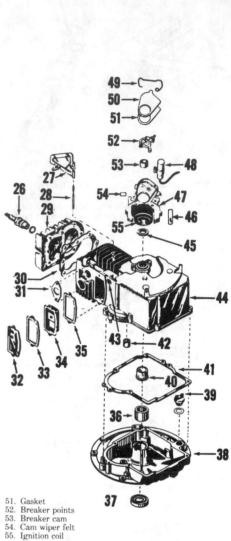

more, renew bearings and/or crankshaft. Refer to Fig. CL77 for proper placement of bushing in crankcase bore. On models where the crankshaft rides directly in the aluminum alloy crankcase, side plate or base plate (integral type), bearing can be renewed by reaming out the bore to accept a service bushing. Contact nearest Clinton Central Parts Distributor for correct tools, reamers and parts.

Standard crankshaft end play for models with bushing type bearings is 0.008-0.018 inch (0.20-0.46 mm). If end play is 0.025 inch (0.64 mm) or more, end play must be adjusted by varying thickness and number of shims between crankcase and side plate/base plate. Gaskets are available in a variety of thicknesses.

On horizontal crankshaft models with ball bearing type main bearings, bearing on pto (side plate) end of crankshaft is retained in the side plate with a snap ring and is also retained on the crankshaft with a snap ring. To remove the side plate, first pry crankshaft seal from side plate and remove snap ring retaining bearing to crankshaft. Separate side plate with bearing from crankcase and

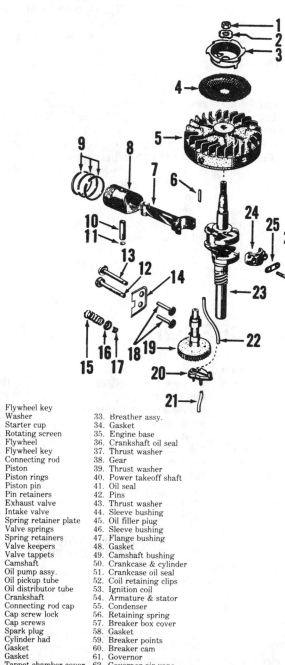

INSTALL OIL SEAL FLUSH TO 0.010 in. ABOVE CASTING (0.25 mm)

0.060 in. (1.52 mm) CHAMFER ALLOWABLE FOR PROPER INSTALLATION OF OIL SEAL

GEM OR CLINTALLOY BLOCK

SOME BLOCKS MAY HAVE CAST COUNTER BORE AS SHOWN, OR MAY BE MACHINED FULL DEPTH AS INDICATED BY DOTTED LINE

Fig. CL78—Install oil seal in block (crankcase) as shown.

1. Flywheel key
2. Washer
3. Starter cup
4. Rotating screen
5. Flywheel
6. Flywheel key
7. Connecting rod
8. Piston
9. Piston rings
10. Piston pin
11. Pin retainers
12. Exhaust valve
13. Intake valve
14. Spring retainer plate
15. Valve springs
16. Spring retainers
17. Valve keepers
18. Valve tappets
19. Camshaft
20. Oil pump assy.
21. Oil pickup tube
22. Oil distributor tube
23. Crankshaft
24. Connecting rod cap
25. Cap screw lock
26. Cap screws
27. Spark plug
28. Cylinder had
29. Gasket
30. Gasket
31. Tappet chamber cover
32. Gasket
33. Breather assy.
34. Gasket
35. Engine base
36. Crankshaft oil seal
37. Thrust washer
38. Gear
39. Thrust washer
40. Power takeoff shaft
41. Oil seal
42. Pins
43. Thrust washer
44. Sleeve bushing
45. Oil filler piug
46. Sleeve bushing
47. Flange bushing
48. Gasket
49. Camshaft bushing
50. Crankcase & cylinder
51. Crankcase oil seal
52. Coil retaining clips
53. Ignition coil
54. Armature & stator
55. Condenser
56. Retaining spring
57. Breaker box cover
58. Gasket
59. Breaker points
60. Breaker cam
61. Governor
62. Governor air vane
63. Governor pin

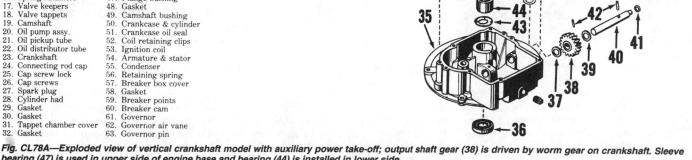

Fig. CL78A—Exploded view of vertical crankshaft model with auxiliary power take-off; output shaft gear (38) is driven by worm gear on crankshaft. Sleeve bearing (47) is used in upper side of engine base and bearing (44) is installed in lower side.

crankshaft. Ball bearing and retaining snap ring can then be removed from the side plate. Bearing should be renewed if rough, loose or damaged.

When installing crankshaft seal in crankcase, refer to Fig. CL78 for proper placement of seal. When installing crankshaft, make certain crankshaft and camshaft gear timing marks are aligned as shown in Fig. CL79.

CAMSHAFT. On early models, integral camshaft and gear turned on a stationary axle. Later models are equipped with a solid integral camshaft and gear which is supported at each end in bearings which are an integral part of crankcase or side plate/baseplate assemblies.

On early models, clearance between camshaft and cam axle is 0.001-0.003 inch (0.03-0.08 mm). If clearance is 0.005 inch (0.13 mm) or more, camshaft and/or axle must be renewed.

Standard axle diameter is 0.3740-0.3744 inch (9.50-9.51 mm). Axle should be a 0.0009 inch (0.02 mm) tight to 0.001 inch (0.03 mm) loose fit in crankcase and side plate/base plate.

On models where camshaft turns in bores in crankcase and base or side plate, standard clearance between camshaft journals and bearing bore is 0.001-0.003 inch (0.03-0.08 mm). If

Fig. CL79—Valves are correctly timed when marks on camshaft gear and crankshaft gear are aligned as shown.

clearance is 0.006 inch (0.15 mm) or more, renew camshaft and/or crankcase, side plate or base plate.

When installing camshaft, align camshaft and crankshaft gear timing marks as shown in Fig. CL79.

VALVE SYSTEM. Recommended valve tappet gap for intake and exhaust valves on all models is 0.009-0.011 inch (0.23-0.28 mm). Adjust valve clearance by grinding off end of valve stem to increase clearance or by renewing valve and/or grinding valve seat deeper into block to reduce clearance.

Valve face angle is 45° and valve seat angle is 44°. If valve face margin is 1/64 inch (0.4 mm) or less, renew valve. On models with aluminum alloy cylinder block, seat inserts are standard. On models with cast iron cylinder block, seats are ground directly into cylinder block surface. Standard valve seat width is 0.030-0.045 inch (0.76-1.29 mm). If seat width is 0.060 inch (1.52 mm) or more, seat must be narrowed.

Standard valve stem-to-guide clearance is 0.0015-0.0045 inch (0.04-0.11 mm). If clearance is 0.006 inch (0.15 mm) or more, guide may be reamed to 0.260 inch (6.60 mm) and a valve with a 0.010 inch (0.25 mm) oversize stem installed.

LUBRICATING SYSTEM. All horizontal crankshaft models and some vertical crankshaft models are splash lubricated. An oil distributor is attached to the connecting rod cap on horizontal crankshaft models and an oil scoop is riveted to the lower side of the camshaft gear on vertical crankshaft models. Refer to CONNECTING ROD section for additional information on oil distributor on connecting rod cap.

A gear type oil pump, driven by a pin on the lower end of the engine camshaft, is used on some vertical crankshaft models. When reassembling these engines, be sure the oil tube fits into the recesses in cylinder block and oil pump before installing base plate.

SERVICING CLINTON ACCESSORIES

IMPULSE STARTERS
(EARLY PRODUCTION)

Difficulty in starting engine equipped with impulse type starter may be caused by improper starting procedure or adjustment. The throttle lever must be in the full choke position and left there until engine starts. After impulse starter is fully wound, move handle to start position and push handle down against stop until starter releases. Occasionally there is a hesitation because the engine is on the compression stroke. If engine does not start readily (within 5 releases of the starter), make the following checks:

1. Remove air cleaner and be sure choke is fully closed when throttle lever is in full choke position. If not, adjust controls so choke can be fully closed.

2. Check the idle and high speed fuel mixture adjustment needles. See engine servicing section for recommended initial adjustment for appropriate model being serviced.

3. Check magneto for spark.

To disassemble unit, make certain starter spring is released, remove the four phillips head screws (3 – Fig. CL100) and invert the assembly. Holding the assembly at arms length, lightly tap the legs of the starter frame against work bench to remove bottom cover, power springs and cups, plunger assembly and the large gear. Carefully separate the spring and cup assemblies from the plunger. Hold plunger and unscrew ratchet using a ⅜-inch Allen wrench. Remove the snap ring (9) and disassemble plunger unit. Renew all damaged parts or assemblies.

Prior to reassembly, coat all internal parts with light grease. Install large gear with beveled edge of teeth to bottom (open) side of starter and engage the lock pawl as shown in Fig. CL100A. Assemble the plunger unit and install it through the large gear so release button protrudes through top of starter frame. Install power spring and cup assembly with closed side of cup towards large gear and carefully work inner end of spring over the plunger. If two power springs are used, install second spring and cup assembly with closed side of cup towards first spring and cup unit. In some starters, an empty spring cup is used as a spacer. Install cup with closed side toward power spring. Install the bottom cover (4 – Fig. CL100) and spring (2); then, screw ratchet into plunger bushing. It is not necessary to tighten the ratchet as normal action of the starter will do this.

IMPULSE STARTER
(LATE PRODUCTION)

Troubleshooting procedure for late type impulse starter unit shown in Fig. CL101 will be similar to that for early unit.

Service is limited to renewal of handle (3), pawl (6) and/or pawl spring (9). If power spring is broken, or if drive gear that engages starter cup (2) is worn or damaged, a complete new starter assembly must be installed. Starter cup

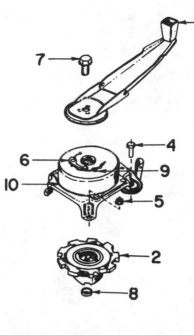

(2) is not included as part of the starter assembly.

REWIND STARTERS

Exploded view of rewind starter currently used on most Clinton engines is shown in Fig. CL102. Other starters used are shown in Figs. CL102A through CL110. Care should be taken when reassembling all starters to be sure the rewind spring is not wound too tightly. The spring should be wound tight enough to rewind the rope, but not so tight that the spring is fully wound before the rope is pulled out to full length. Coat spring and all internal parts with Lubriplate or equivalent grease when reassembling. Be sure spring, pulley and related parts are assembled for correct rotation.

12 VOLT STARTER AND LIGHTING COIL

Refer to Figs. CL113, CL114, CL115 and CL116. Service and/or parts for the 12 volt starter are available at American Bosch Service Centers.

The 12 volt lighting coils are mounted on the magneto armature core as shown in Fig. CL115 and CL116. Wiring diagram when unit is used for lighting circuit only is shown in Fig. CL115.

Fig. CL101—Exploded view of late type Clinton impulse starter. Starter is serviced only in parts indicated by callouts (1) through (9).

1. Starter cup adapter
2. Starter cup
3. Handle assy.
4. Barrel nut
5. Nut
6. Starter pawl
7. Cap screw & washer
8. Starter cup spacer
9. Pawl spring
10. Housing, power spring & gear assy.

Fig. CL102—Exploded view of late production Clinton rewind starter.

1. Starter cup
2. Snap ring
3. Actuator
4. Snap ring
5. Nut
6. Pawl & pin assy.
7. Actuator spring
8. Pulley
9. Pan head screw
10. Housing
11. Handle
12. Rope
13. Nut & washer assy.
14. Rewind spring

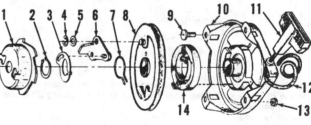

Fig. CL100—Exploded view of early type Clinton impulse type starter. Some starters having only one power spring (5) used an empty power spring cup as a spacer.

1. Ratchet
2. Spring
3. Cap screws
4. Cover plate
5. Power spring & cup assy.
6. Plunger hub
7. Steel balls (2)
8. Plunger
9. Snap ring
10. Gear
11. Housing, crank & pinion assy.

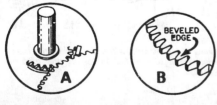
Fig. CL100A—When reinstalling large gear (10—Fig. CL10), be sure beveled edge of gear is towards open side of housing and lock engages gear as shown.

Fig. CL102A—Exploded view of Deluxe Model of Clinton rewind starter of the type used on chain saws and some engines. Starter will operate in either rotation by interchanging springs (5) and inverting pawls (6) and rewind spring (12).

1. Flywheel
2. Plate
3. Flywheel nut
4. Spacer
5. Spring
6. Pawl
7. Snap ring
8. Washer
9. Wave washer
10. Pulley
11. Cup
12. Rewind spring
13. Handle
14. Guide
15. Housing
16. Screen
17. Retainer

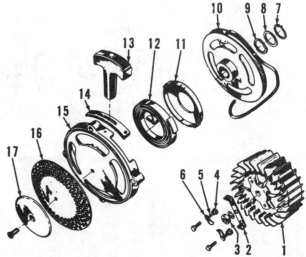

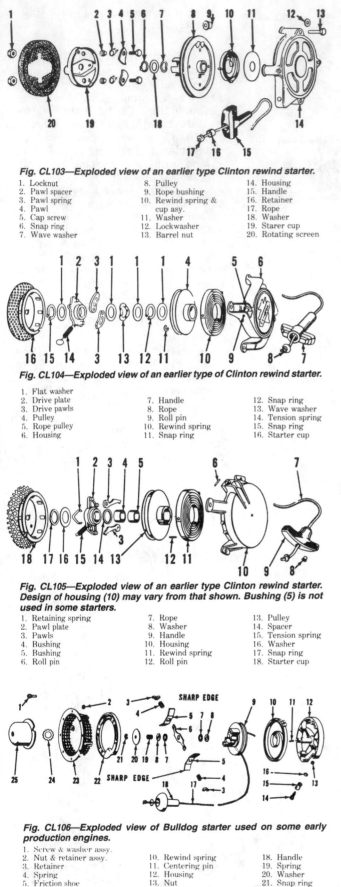

Fig. CL103—Exploded view of an earlier type Clinton rewind starter.

1. Locknut	8. Pulley	14. Housing
2. Pawl spacer	9. Rope bushing	15. Handle
3. Pawl spring	10. Rewind spring &	16. Retainer
4. Pawl	cup asy.	17. Rope
5. Cap screw	11. Washer	18. Washer
6. Snap ring	12. Lockwasher	19. Starer cup
7. Wave washer	13. Barrel nut	20. Rotating screen

Fig. CL104—Exploded view of an earlier type of Clinton rewind starter.

1. Flat washer	7. Handle	12. Snap ring
2. Drive plate	8. Rope	13. Wave washer
3. Drive pawls	9. Roll pin	14. Tension spring
4. Pulley	10. Rewind spring	15. Snap ring
5. Rope pulley	11. Snap ring	16. Starter cup
6. Housing		

Fig. CL105—Exploded view of an earlier type Clinton rewind starter. Design of housing (10) may vary from that shown. Bushing (5) is not used in some starters.

1. Retaining spring	7. Rope	13. Pulley
2. Pawl plate	8. Washer	14. Spacer
3. Pawls	9. Handle	15. Tension spring
4. Bushing	10. Housing	16. Washer
5. Bushing	11. Rewind spring	17. Snap ring
6. Roll pin	12. Roll pin	18. Starter cup

Fig. CL106—Exploded view of Bulldog starter used on some early production engines.

1. Screw & washer assy.	10. Rewind spring	18. Handle
2. Nut & retainer assy.	11. Centering pin	19. Spring
3. Retainer	12. Housing	20. Washer
4. Spring	13. Nut	21. Snap ring
5. Friction shoe	14. Shoulder screw	22. Flange
6. Brake lever	15. Roller	23. Base
7. Washer	16. Washer	24. Lockwasher
8. Slotted washer	17. Rope	25. Pulley (cup)
9. Pulley		

When unit is used to provide a battery charging current, a rectifier must be installed in the circuit to convert the AC current into DC current as shown in Fig. CL116.

110 VOLT ELECTRIC STARTERS

Exploded views of the two types of 110 volt electric starters are shown in Figs. CL117 and CL118. Always connect starter cord at engine before connecting cord to 110 volt power source.

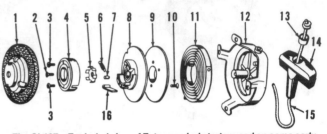

Fig. CL107—Exploded view of Eaton rewind starter used on some early production engines.

1. Starter pulley	6. Tension spring	11. Rewind spring
2. Screws	7. Spring retainer	12. Housing
3. Screws (2)	8. Hub	13. Cup
4. Retainer	9. Plate	14. Handle
5. Brake	10. Screw	15. Rope

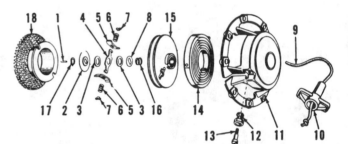

Fig. CL108—Exploded view of Fairbanks-Morse rewind starter used on early production engines. Refer to Fig. CL109 for a second type of Fairbanks-Morse starter used on other Clinton models.

1. Centering pin	7. Retainer	13. Screw
2. Washer	8. Washer	14. Rewind spring
3. Fiber washer	9. Rope	15. Pulley
4. Brake lever	10. Handle	16. Spring
5. Friction shoe	11. Housing	17. Snap ring
6. Spring	12. Roller	18. Pulley (cup)

Fig. CL109—Exploded view of a Fairbanks-Morse rewind starter used on some Clinton engines. Refer to Fig. CL108 for another tpye of Fairbanks-Morse starter used.

1. Centering pin	9. Middle flange	16. Screws
2. Washer	10. Housing	17. Rewind spring
3. Washer	11. Rope	18. Pulley
4. Fiber washer	12. Handle	19. Brake lever
5. Friction shoe	13. Cup	20. Spring
6. Retainer	14. Screw	21. Snap ring
7. Spring	15. Roller	22. Pulley (cup)
8. Mounting flange		

ELECTRA-START

Electra-Start models have a built-in battery, starter and flywheel mounted alternator. Early models used a wet cell 12 volt battey mounted on mower deck. Late models use a 12-cell, nickel-cadmium battery which attaches to crankcase, making the unit fully self-contained.

Electra-Start models are equipped with the bulb type fuel primer which pressurizes the carburetor float chamber when bulb is depressed, forcing a small amount of fuel out main nozzle.

Nominal voltage of the nickel-cadmium battery is 15 volts. Charging rate of the flywheel alternator is 0.2-0.25 DC amps. About 40-125 amp-seconds are normally required to start the engine and recovery time to full charge should be 3-10 minutes of operation. About 20 minutes running time should be allowed when battery or engine is first put into service.

Fig. CL113—View of American Bosch 12 volt starter mounted on a later production horizontal crankshaft engine. Square-shaped unit below starter motor is a rectifier to convert AC current from lighting coil on magneto armature core to DC current.

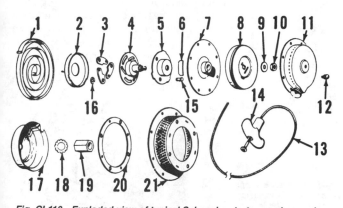

1. Rewind spring
2. Cover
3. Pawls
4. Cam plate & axle
5. Drive plate*
6. Spring*
7. Plate
8. Drum
9. Washer
10. Nut
11. Housing
12. Screws
13. Rope
14. Handle
15. Pin
16. Snap ring
17. Rope pulley
18. Lockwasher
19. Driven nut
20. Ring
21. Housing

Fig. CL110—Exploded view of typical Schnacke starter used on early production engines. Asterisk indicates part not used on all starters.

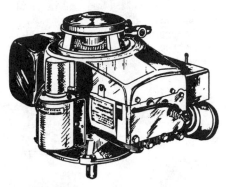

Fig. CL114—View of American Bosch 12 volt starter mounted on a late production vertical crankshaft engine.

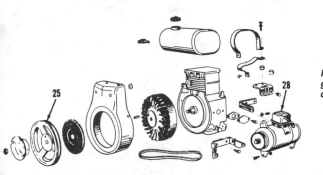

Fig. CL111—The 12 volt starter-generator (28) is driven (and drives) by a belt and pulley (25).

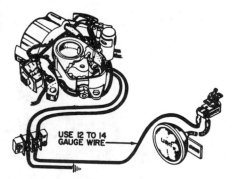

Fig. CL115—View showing wiring circuit from lighting coils when used for lighting purposes only.

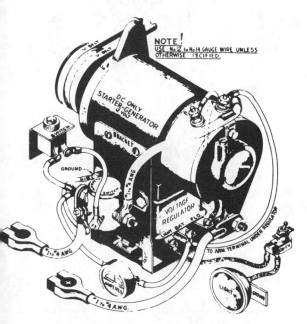

Fig. CL112—Wiring diagram for 12 volt DC starter-generator.

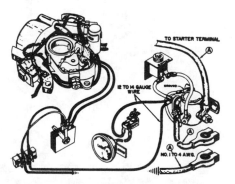

Fig. CL116—View showing wiring circuit from lighting coils. A rectifier is included in circuit to provide DC current for charging a 12 volt battery.

The alternator output (200-250 milliamperes) cannot be measured with regular shop equipment. If trouble is encountered, start the engine and operate at rated speed. Disconnect generator lead from red (positive) battery lead and check generator output using one of the following methods:

1. Connect one lead of a voltmeter or small test light to generator lead and ground the remaining lead. Voltmeter should indicate charging current or test light should glow, indicating charging current.

2. In the absence of test equipment, momentarily touch the disconnected generator lead to a suitable ground and watch for a spark.

If test equipment or spark indicated charging current, the generator should be considered satisfactory.

If a charging current is not indicated, remove the flywheel and renew the generator coil which is mounted on one leg of magneto pole shoe. The halfwave rectifier is built into magneto coil and is not renewable separately.

POLYURETHANE AIR CLEANER

Some Clinton models are equipped with a polyurethane air filter element. Element should be removed and washed in nonflammable solvent (mild solution of detergent and water) after every 10 hours of operation. Reoil element with SAE 10 motor oil and wring out excess oil. Insert the element evenly into air cleaner housing and snap cover in place. Refer to Fig. CL119.

REMOTE CONTROLS

Several different remote control options are available. Refer to Fig. CL122. Views A through G are for engines with following basic numbers: IMB basic numbers 494 and 498; old basic numbers 900, 960 990, B1260 and B1290.

View A shows standard fixed speed for hoizontal shaft engine. B, C and F show available remote control options. Typical cable and handle assembly is shown in view D. Detail of pivot pin to block is shown in E. View G shows method of securing control wire to lever on some applications.

The remote control allows the engine speed to be regulated by movement of the remove control lever some distance away from the engine. The engine speed will be maintained by the engine governor at any setting of the remote control lever within the prescribed speed range of the engine. Maximum engine speed should not exceed 3600 rpm.

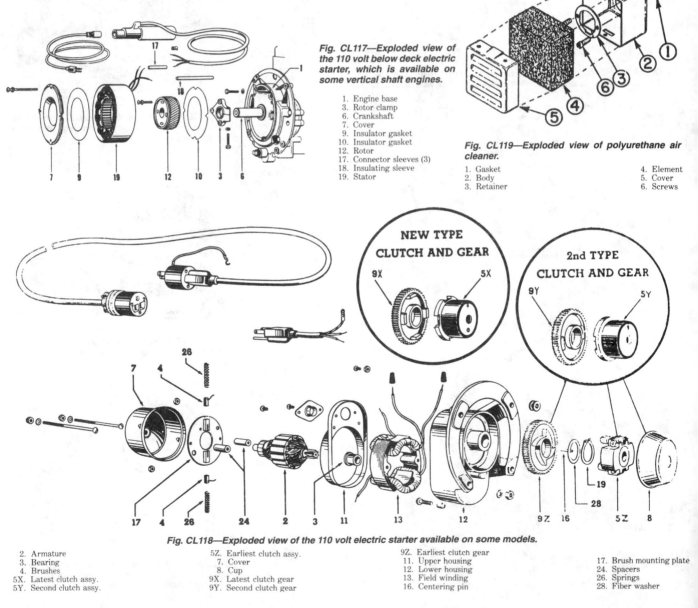

Fig. CL117—Exploded view of the 110 volt below deck electric starter, which is available on some vertical shaft engines.

1. Engine base
3. Rotor clamp
6. Crankshaft
7. Cover
9. Insulator gasket
10. Insulator gasket
12. Rotor
17. Connector sleeves (3)
18. Insulating sleeve
19. Stator

Fig. CL119—Exploded view of polyurethane air cleaner.

1. Gasket
2. Body
3. Retainer
4. Element
5. Cover
6. Screws

NEW TYPE CLUTCH AND GEAR

2nd TYPE CLUTCH AND GEAR

Fig. CL118—Exploded view of the 110 volt electric starter available on some models.

2. Armature
3. Bearing
4. Brushes
5X. Latest clutch assy.
5Y. Second clutch assy.

5Z. Earliest clutch assy.
7. Cover
8. Cup
9X. Latest clutch gear
9Y. Second clutch gear

9Z. Earliest clutch gear
11. Upper housing
12. Lower housing
13. Field winding
16. Centering pin

17. Brush mounting plate
24. Spacers
26. Springs
28. Fiber washer

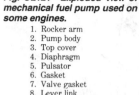
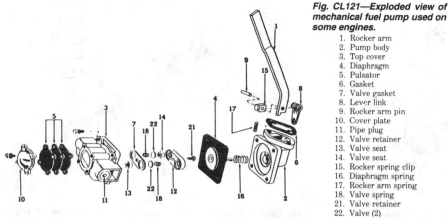

Fig. CL121—Exploded view of mechanical fuel pump used on some engines.

1. Rocker arm
2. Pump body
3. Top cover
4. Diaphragm
5. Pulsator
6. Gasket
7. Valve gasket
8. Lever link
9. Rocker arm pin
10. Cover plate
11. Pipe plug
12. Valve retainer
13. Valve seat
14. Valve seat
15. Rocker spring clip
16. Diaphragm spring
17. Rocker arm spring
18. Valve spring
21. Valve retainer
22. Valve (2)

SPEED REDUCERS. Speed reducers (gear reduction units) with ratios of 2:1, 4:1 and 6:1 are available on a number of horizontal shaft engines.

Refer to Fig. CL124 for exploded view of typical speed reducer for engines of less than 5 horsepower (3.7 kW). Unit should be lubricated by filling with SAE 30 oil to the level plug. Oil level should be checked after every 10 hours of operation. Drain and refill the reduction unit with clean SAE 30 oil after every 100 hours of operation.

Use Fig. CL124 as disassembly and reassembly guide. Unit can be mounted on engine in any of four positions; however, be sure outer housing is installed so filler plug is up.

An exploded view of typical speed reducer used on engines of 5 horsepower (3.7 kW) and larger is shown in Fig. CL125. Units used on early engines support output end of crankshaft in sleeve bearing (1) as shown. Late units support output end of crankshaft in a tapered roller bearing.

To adjust remote control with the engine running:

1. Loosen screw in swivel nut on control lever.

2. Move control lever to high speed position (view B–Fig. CL122).

3. Move control wire through control casing and swivel nut until maximum desired engine speed is obtained. Do not exceed maximum engine speed of 3600 rpm. Lever should remain in high speed position.

4. Tighten screw in swivel nut to hold control wire.

5. Move control lever to slow speed position to be sure engine can slow down to idle speed.

PTO AND SPEED REDUCER UNITS

AUXILIARY PTO. Some vertical crankshaft models are equipped with an auxiliary pto as shown in Fig. CL123.

Unit is lubricated by oil in engine crankcase. To disassemble unit, drive the pins (6, 7 and 22) partially out of shaft (11), turn shaft half-turn and pull pins. Remove shaft and gears (2 and 4). Remove output shaft (12) and gear (21) in similar manner.

Fig. CL123—Exploded view of auxiliary pto unit used on some vertical crankshaft engines. Gear ratio is either 15:1 or 30:1.

1. Flange bearing
2. Drive gear
3. Gasket
4. Worm gear
5. Thrust washer
6. Pin
7. Pin
8. Pin
9. Expansion plug
10. Needle bearing
11. Worm shaft
12. Pto shaft
13. Oil seal
14. Housing
15. Oil filler cap
16. Gasket
17. Oil drain plug
18. Cap screw
19. Expansion plug
20. Sleeve bearing
21. Pto gear
22. Pin

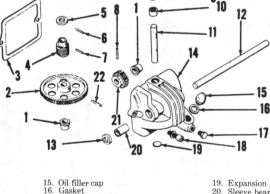

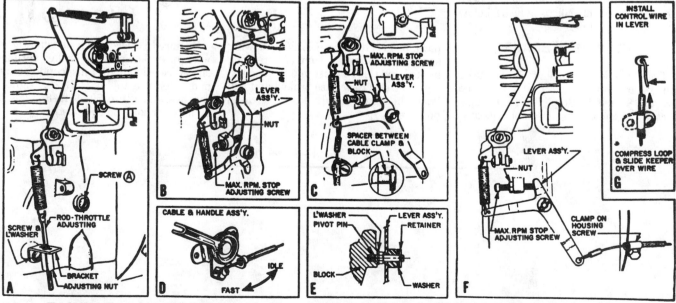

Fig. CL122—Remote control hook-ups for various Clinton engines. Refer to text for engine application and adjustment procedures.

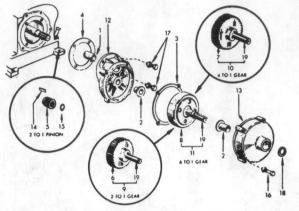

Fig. CL124—Exploded view of gear reduction unit used on engines of less than 5 horsepower (3.7 kW). Gear ratio may be 2:1, 4:1 or 6:1. Sleeve bearings must be reamed after installation.

1. Sleeve bearing	15. Nut & washer assy.
2. Sleeve bearing	16. Breather plug
3. Gasket	17. Expansion plug
4. Gasket	18. Oil level plug
5. 2:1 pinion	19. Snap ring
6. 2:1 gear	20. Screw
7. 4:1 gear	21. Screw
8. 6:1 gear	22. Oil seal
9. Gear & shaft	23. Shaft
10. Gear & shaft	24. Thrust washer
11. Gear & shaft	25. Thrust washer
12. Inner housing	26. Flat washer
13. Outer housing	27. Lockwasher
14. Key	

Fig. CL125—Exploded view of gear reduction unit used on engines larger than 5 horsepower (3.7 kW). Gear ratio may be 2:1, 4:1 or 6:1. Sleeve bearing (1) must be finish reamed after installation. Units used on late production engine have tapered roller engine main bearing instead of sleeve bearing (1) shown.

1. Sleeve bearing	11. Gear & shaft
2. Flange bearing	12. Inner housing
3. Gasket	13. Outer housing
4. Gasket	14. Key
5. 2:1 pinion	15. Snap ring
6. 2:1 gear	16. Screw & washer
7. 4:1 gear	17. Screw & washer
8. 6:1 gear	18. Oil seal
9. Gear & shaft	19. Shaft
10. Gear & shaft	

After unit has been drained of oil or after reassembly, initially fill unit with same oil as used in engine. Lubricating oil supply is thereafter maintained from engine crankcase through passage drilled in inner housing (12). Gaskets (4) used between inner housing and engine crankcase or bearing plate are available in several thicknesses. Use proper thickness gasket to maintain specified crankshaft end play.

As unit can be mounted on engine in any of four different positions, be sure outer housing (13) is installed with filler plug to top and oil level drain plugs down. Note that after engine has been started, oil level will usually be below level of oil level plug.

FLYWHEEL BRAKE

Some vertical crankshaft models used on rotary lawnmowers are equipped with a "Touch 'N' Stop" flywheel brake. Actuating the control assembly releases

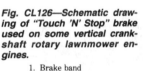

Fig. CL126—Schematic drawing of "Touch 'N' Stop" brake used on some vertical crankshaft rotary lawnmower engines.

1. Brake band
2. Flywheel nut
3. Flywheel
4. Pin
5. Pivot bolt
6. Screw
7. Cam
8. Spring
9. Spring
10. Pawl lever
11. Cocking lever
12. Flat spring

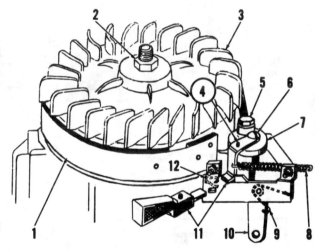

pawl lever (10–Fig. CL126) allowing spring (8) to rotate cam (7) applying brake band (1). To reset, move the cocking lever (11) to release brake band and latch the pawl with brake in released position.

Required service, such as renewal of worn or broken parts or broken springs, should be evident after inspection of unit and reference to Fig. CL126. Tighten flywheel nut (2) to 50-58 ft.-lbs. (68-79 N·m) on models so equipped.

CRAFTSMAN

The following Craftsman engines were manufactured by the Tecumseh Products Company. The accompanying cross-reference chart will assist in identifying an engine for service requirements. Much of the service will be identical to service on similar Tecumseh engines. The Craftsman service section which follows the cross reference charts includes service which is different than repairing Tecumseh engines.

TWO-STROKE MODELS

Craftsman Model Number	Tecumseh Engine Number
143.17112	638-07(AV520)
143.171112	638-07(AV520)
143.171122	638-01A(AV520)
143.171272	638-51(AV520)
200.183112	638-07A(AV520)
200.183122	638-17A(AV520)
200.193132	638-07B(AV520)
200.193142	17B(AV520)
200.193152	650-44(AV520)
200.193162	650-29A(AV520)
200.203112	670-100(AV520)
200.203172	670-39(AV520)
200.203182	670-32(AV520)
200.203192	670-18(AV520)
200.213112	670-39A(AV520)
200.213122	670-32A(AV520)
200.233112	661-30(TVS600)
200.243112	670-83(AV520)
200.283012	670-100(AV520)
200.2131128	653-01(AV520)
200.2132228	661-24(TVS600)
200.503111	1525A(AH520)
200.583111	1499(AH520)
200.593121	1525(AH520)
200.602112	1617(AH520)
200.613111	1553(AH520)
200.633111	1625(AH600)
200.643121	1625A(AH600)
200.651001	2019C(TC200)
200.653111	1643(AH600)
200.663111	1643M(AH600)
200.673111	1649M(AH600)
200.681001	3010A(TC300)
200.681011	2019D(TC200)
200.681021	3013A(TC300)
200.681031	1649N(AH600)
200.681041	1658N(AH600)
200.681051	1627N(AH600)
200.681061	3021A(TC300)
200.691001	3019A(TC300)
200.691011	2040D(TC200)
200.692112	1596A(AH520)
200.692122	1604(AH520)
200.692132	1610(AH520)

Craftsman Model Number	Tecumseh Engine Number
200-701001	1665N(AH600)
200-701011	2045E(TC200)
200-701021	3027B(TC300)
200-701031	3013B(TC300)
200-701041	3305(TCH300)
200-701051	3031B(TC300)
200-711001	1665P(HSK600)
200-711011	8208(HSK840)
200-711021	3305A(TCH300)
200-711031	3013C(TC300)
200-721001	2103(TC200)
200-731001	1686R(HSK600)
200-731011	1687R(HSK600)
200-731021	8216(HSK840)
200-731031	3013E(TC300)

FOUR-STROKE ENGINES
Vertical Crankshaft

Craftsman Model Number	Basic Tecumseh Number
143.V20A-1-1WA	V 20 D
143.V25A-5-1-1WA	V 25 D
143.V27A-3-1-1WA	V 27 D
143.09300	LAV 25 B
143.09301	LAV 25 B
143.09302	LAV 25 B
143.10250	LAV 22 B
143.10251	LAV 22 B
143.10300	LAV 25 B
143.10301	LAV 25 B
143.11300	LAV 25 B
143.11301	LAV 25 B
143.11302	LAV 25 B
143.11350	LAV 30 B
143.11351	LAV 30 B
143.11352	LAV 30 B
143.12300	LAV 25 B
143.12301	LAV 25 B
143.12302	LAV 25 B
143.12303	LAV 25 B
143.12304	LAV 25 B
143.12350	LAV 30 B
143.12351	LAV 30 B
143.13250	LAV 22 B
143.13251	LAV 22 B
143.13300	LAV 25 B
143.13301	LAV 25 B
143.14350	LAV 30 B
143.14351	LAV 30 B
143.15300	LAV 25 B
143.15301	LAV 25 B
143.16350	LAV 30 B
143.16351	LAV 30 B
143.17350	LAV 30 B

Craftsman Model Number	Basic Tecumseh Number
143.17351	LAV 30 B
143.18350	LAV 30 B
143.18351	LAV 30 B
143.19400	LAV 35 B
143.19401	LAV 35 B
143.20100	V 20 D
143.20400	V 35 D
143.20401	V 35 D
143.20500	V 45 B
143.20501	V 45 B
143.20502	V 45 C
143.20503	V 45 C
143.23250	HA 22 C
143.23251	HA 22 C
143.24250	HA 22 C
143.24251	HA 22 C
143.25100	V 25 D
143.25250	HA 22 C
143.25251	HA 22 C
143.27100	V 27 D
143.27200	V 20 D
143.30250	LAV 22 B
143.30350	LAV 30 B
143.30351	LAV 30 B
143.31600	V 55 B
143.31601	V 55 C
143.36250	HA 22 C
143.36251	HA 22 C
143.36252	H 22 D
143.36253	H 22 H
143.36255	H 22 H
143.39250	LAV 22 B
143.39251	LAV 22 B
143.40250	H 22 D
143.40251	H 22 D
143.40300	LAV 25 B
143.40301	LAV 25 B
143.40350	LAV 30 B
143.40351	LAV 30 B
143.40500	V 45 B
143.40501	V 45 B
143.40502	V 45 C
143.40503	V 45 C
143.40600	V 55 B
143.41300	LAV 25 B
143.41301	LAV 25 B
143.41302	LAV 25 B
143.41350	LAV 30 B
143.41351	LAV 30 B
143.41352	LAV 30 B
143.42200	V 22 H-8
143.42201	V 22 H-8P
143.42202	V 22 H-37
143.42203	V 22 H-8
143.42205	V 22 H-8B
143.42500	V 22 H-8
143.42501	V 25 H-8P

Craftsman Model Number	Basic Tecumseh Number	Craftsman Model Number	Basic Tecumseh Number	Craftsman Model Number	Basic Tecumseh Number
143.42700	V 25 H-8	143.56253	HA 22 A	143.76252	LAV 22 B
143.42701	V 25 H-8P	143.58250	HA 22 C	143.82000	H 20 B-15
143.43004	V 30 H-3P	143.58251	HA 22 C	143.82001	H 20 B-15P
143.43200	V 30 H-8	143.59250	H 22 D	143.82002	H 20 B-15
143.43201	V 30 H-29	143.59251	H 22 D	143.82003	H 20 B-15P
143.43202	V 30 H-40	143.60020	V 20 G-8	143.82004	H 20 B-15
143.43203	V 30 H-8P	143.60021	V 20 G-8P	143.82005	H 20 B-15P
143.43204	V 30 H-29P	143.60025	V 25 G-14	143.82006	H 20 B-15
143.43205	V 30 H-40P	143.60026	V 25 G-14P	143.82007	H 20 G-15P
143.43250	H 22 H	143.60030	V 30 G-8	143.83000	H 30 B-15
143.43251	H 22 H	143.60031	V 30 G-8P	143.83001	H 30 B-15P
143.43300	V 30 H-8	143.60040	VX 40 A-19	143.83250	LAV 22 B
143.43301	V 30 H-8P	143.60125	V 25 G-8	143.83251	LAV 22 B
143.43500	V 45 B	143.60126	V 25 G-8P	143.83252	LAV 22 B
143.43501	V 45 B	143.60130	V 30 G-8	143.84300	LAV 25 B
143.43700	V 32 A-28	143.60131	V 30 G-8P	143.84301	LAV 25 B
143.43701	V 32 A-28P	143.60140	VX 40 A-24	143.84302	LAV 25 B
143.44000	V 32 A-28P	143.60225	V 25 G-8	143.86400	LAV 35 B
143.44400	H 35 D	143.60226	V 25 G-8P	143.86401	LAV 36 B
143.44401	H 35 D	143.60231	V 30 G-4P	143.86402	LAV 35 B
143.50020	V 20 G-8	143.60240	VX 40 A-19	143.90020	H 20 A-15
143.50021	V 20 G-8P	143.60325	V 25 G-14	143.90021	H 20 A-15P
143.50025	V 25 G-8	143.60326	V 25 G-14	143.91250	H 22 H
143.50026	V 25 G-8P	143.60326	V 25 G-14F	143.91251	H 22 H
143.50030	V 30 G-14	143.60327	V 27 G-16	143.93000	H 30 B-15P
143.50031	V 30 G-14P	143.60328	V 27 G-16P	143.97250	H 22 H
143.50040	V 40 A-4	143.60330	V 27 G-2	143.97251	H 22 H
143.50045	V 40 B-4	143.60331	V 27 G-2P	143.101010	LAV 30 E
143.50125	V 25 G-3	143.60340	VX 40 A-19	143.101011	LAV 30 E
143.50126	V 25 G-3P	143.60351	LV 30 B	143.101012	LAV 30 E
143.50130	V 30 G-8	143.60401	LV 35 B	143.101020	LAV 30 E
143.50131	V 30 G-8P	143.62200	V 22 H-8	143.101021	LAV 30 E
143.50230	V 30 G-3	143.62201	V 22 H-8P	143.101022	LAV 30 E
143.50231	V 30 G-3P	143.62700	V 25 H-8	143.101030	LAV 30 E
143.50250	HA 22 A	143.62701	V 25 H-14	143.101031	LAV 30 E
143.50251	HA 22 A	143.62702	V 25 H-3	143.101032	LAV 30 E
143.50300	H 30 D	143.62703	V 25 H-8P	143.102010	LAV 30 E
143.50301	H 30 D	143.62704	V 25 H-14P	143.102011	LAV 30 E
143.50400	H 35 D	143.62705	V 25 H-3P	143.102012	LAV 30 E
143.50401	H 35 D	143.63200	V 30 H-8	143.102020	LAV 30 E
143.50402	H 35 H	143.63201	V 30 H-14	143.102021	LAV 30 E
143.50403	H 35 H	143.63202	V 30 H-3	143.102022	LAV 30 E
143.50700	V 25 H-8	143.63203	V 30 H-8P	143.102030	LAV 30 E
14352200	V 22 H-8	143.63204	V 30 H-14P	143.102031	LAV 30 E
143.52201	V 22 H-8P	143.63205	V 30 H-3P	143.102040	LAV 30 E
143.52701	V 25 H-8P	143.64000	V 40 B-4	143.102041	LAV 30 E
143.52702	V 25 H-8	143.64500	V 45 A-4	143.102041	LAV 30 E
143.52703	V 25 H-8P	143.65250	H 22 H	143.102050	LAV 30 E
143.53001	V 30 H-4P	143.65251	H 22 H	143.102051	LAV 30 E
143.53200	V 30 H-8	143.66250	H 22 H	143.102060	LAV 30 E
143.53201	V 30 H-8P	143.66251	H 22 H	143.102061	LAV 30 E
143.53300	V 30 H-8	143.66500	V 45 B	143.102062	LAV 30 E
143.53301	V 30 H-8P	143.66501	V 45 B	143.102070	LV 30 E
143.54500	VX-45 A-24	143.67250	H 22 H	143.102071	LV 30 E
143.54502	V 45 A-4	143.67251	H 22 H	143.102072	LV 30 E
143.55250	HA 22 A	143.71250	LAV 22 B	143.102100	LAV 30 E
143.55251	HA 22 A	143.71251	LAV 22 B	143.102101	LAV 30 E
143.55300	H 30 D	143.75250	LAV 22 B	143.102102	LAV 30 E
143.56250	HA 22 A	143.75251	LAV 22 B	143.102110	LAV 30 E
143.56251	HA 22 A	143.76250	LAV 22 B	143.102111	LAV 30 E
143.56252	HA 22 A	143.76251	LAV 22 B	143.102112	LAV 30 E

Craftsman Model Number	Basic Tecumseh Number	Craftsman Model Number	Basic Tecumseh Number	Craftsman Model Number	Basic Tecumseh Number
143.102120	LAV 30 E	143.105030	V 45 D	143.122321	LAV 30 L
143.102121	LAV 30 E	143.105031	V 45 D	143.122322	LAV 30 L
143.102130	LAV 30 E	143.105040	V 55 D	143.123021	LAVR 30 L
143.102131	LAV 30 E	143.105041	V 55 D	143.123022	LAVR 30 L
143.102132	LAV 30 E	143.105050	V 45 D	143.123031	LAVR 30 L
143.102140	LAV 30 E	143.105051	V 45 D	143.123041	LAVR 30 L
143.102141	LAV 30 E	143.105060	V 45 D	143.123051	LAVR 30 L
143.102150	LAV 30 E	143.105061	V 45 D	143.123052	LAVR 30 L
143.102151	LAV 30 E	143.105070	V 45 D	143.123071	LAVR 30 L
143.102152	LAV 30 E	143.105071	V 45 D	143.123091	LAVR 30 L
143.102160	LAV 25 E	143.105090	V 45 D	143.123092	LAVR 30 L
143.102161	LAV 25 E	143.105091	V 45 D	143.124011	LV 35 L
143.102162	LAV 25 E	143.105100	V 45 D	143.124021	LAV 35 L
143.102170	LAV 30 E	143.105101	V 45 D	143.124031	LAV 35 L
143.102171	LAV 30 E	143.105110	V 55 D	143.124041	LV 35 M
143.102172	LAV 30 E	143.105120	V 45 D	143.124051	LV 35 N
143.102190	LAV 30 E	143.105121	V 45 D	143.124061	LAVT 35 C
143.102191	LAV 30 E	143.106010	LAV 30 E	143.124071	LV 35 N
143.102200	LAV 30 E	143.106011	LAV 30 E	143.125011	VT 45 A
143.102201	LAV 30 E	143.106012	LAV 30 E	143.125021	VT 45 C
143.102202	LAV 30 E	143.106020	LAV 30 E	143.125031	VT 45 A
143.102210	LV 30 E	143.106021	LAV 30 E	143.125041	VT 45 C
143.102211	LV 30 E	143.106030	LAV 30 E	143.125051	VT 45 C
143.102212	LV 30 E	143.106031	LAV 30 E	143.125061	VT 45 C
143.102220	LAV 30 E	143.122011	LV 30 L	143.126011	VT 55 A
143.102221	LAV 30 E	143.122012	LV 30 L	143.126021	VT 55 B
143.102222	LAV 30 E	143.122021	LAV 30 L	143.126031	VT 55 B
143.103010	LAV 30 E	143.122022	LAV 30 L	143.126041	VT 55 C
143.103011	LAV 30 E	143.122031	LAV 30 L	143.126051	VT 55 C
143.103012	LAV 30 E	143.122032	LAV 30 L	143.126061	VT 55 C
143.103020	LAV 30 E	143.122041	LAV 30 L	143.131022	LAV 30
143.103021	LAV 30 E	143.122042	LAV 30 L	143.131032	LAV 30
143.103050	LAV 30 E	143.122051	LAV 30 L	143.131042	LAV 30
143.103051	LAV 30 E	143.122052	LAV 30 L	143.131052	LAV 30
143.103052	LAV 30 E	143.122061	LAV 30 L	143.131062	LAV 30
143.103060	LAV 30 E	143.122071	LAV 30 L	143.131072	LAV 30
143.103061	LAV 30 E	143.122081	LAV 30 L	143.131082	LAV 30
143.104010	LAV 35 E	143.122082	LAV 30 L	143.131092	LAV 30
143.104011	LAV 35 E	143.122091	LAV 30 L	143.131102	LAV 30
143.104020	LAV 35 E	143.122092	LAV 30 L	143.131112	LAV 22
143.104021	LAV 35 E	143.122101	LAV 25 L	143.131122	LAV 30
143.104030	LV 35 E	143.122102	LAV 25 L	143.131132	LAV 30
143.104031	LV 35 E	143.122201	LAV 30 L	143.131142	LAV 30
143.104040	LV 35 E	143.122202	LAV 30 L	143.131152	LAV 30
143.104041	LV 35 E	143.122211	LAV 30 M	143.131162	LAV 30
143.104050	LV 35 E	143.122212	LAV 30 M	143.131172	LAV 30
143.104051	LV 35 E	143.122221	LAV 30 M	143.131182	LAV 30
143.104080	LAV 35 E	143.122222	LAV 30 M	143.133012	LAV 30
143.104081	LAV 35 E	143.122231	LAV 30 M	143.133022	LAV 30
143.104090	LAV 35 E	143.122232	LAV 30 M	143.133032	LAV 30
143.104091	LAV 35 E	143.122242	LAV 35 M	143.133042	LV 35
143.104100	LV 35 E	143.122251	LV 30 M	143.133052	LAV 30
143.104101	LV 35 E	143.122252	LV 30 M	143.134012	LV 35
143.104110	LV 35 E	143.122261	LAV 30 M	143.13402	LV 35
143.104111	LV 35 E	143.122262	LAV 30 M	143.134032	LAV 35
143.104120	LV 35 E	143.122271	LAV 30 M	143.134042	LV 35
143.104121	LV 35 E	143.122272	LAV 30 M	143.134052	LV 35
143.105010	V 45 D	143.122281	LAV 30 M	143.135012	V 50
143.105011	V 45 D	143.122282	LAV 30 M	143.135022	V 50
143.105020	V 45 D	143.122291	LAVT 30 C	143.135042	V 50
143.105021	V 45 D	143.122311	LV 30 N	143.135052	V 50

Craftsman Model Number	Basic Tecumseh Number	Craftsman Model Number	Basic Tecumseh Number	Craftsman Model Number	Basic Tecumseh Number
143.135062	V 50	143.145042	V 50	143.161102	LAV 30
143.135072	V 50	143.145052	V 50	143.161112	LAV 30
143.135082	V 50	143.145062	V 50	143.161132	LAV 30
143.135092	V 50	143.145072	V 50	143.161142	LAV 30
143.136012	V 60	143.146012	V 60	143.161152	LAV 30
143.135112	V 50	143.146022	V 60	143.161162	LAV 30
143.136012	V 60	143.147012	V 40	143.161172	LAV 30
143.136052	V 60	143.147022	V 40	143.161182	LAV 30
143.136042	V 60	143.147032	V 40	143.161192	LAV 30
143.136052	V 60	143.151012	LAV 30	143.161202	LAV 30
143.137012	V 40	143.151022	LAV 30	143.161212	LAV 30
143.137032	V 40	143.151032	LAV 30	143.161222	LAV 30
143.141012	LAV 30	143.151042	LAV 30	143.161232	LAV 30
143.141022	LAV 30	143.151052	LAV 30	143.161242	LAV 30
143.141032	LAV 30	143.151072	LAV 30	143.161262	LAV 30
143.141042	LAV 30	143.151082	LAV 30	143.162022	LAV 35
143.141052	LAV 30	143.151092	LAV 30	143.162032	LAV 35
143.141062	LAV 30	143.151102	LAV 30	143.162092	LAV 35
143.141072	LAV 30	143.151103	LAV 30	143.163012	LAV 30
143.141082	LAV 30	143.151104	LAV 30	143.163022	LAV 30
143.141092	LAV 25	143.151105	LAV 30	143.163032	LAV 30
143.141102	LAV 30	143.151142	LAV 30	143.163042	LAV 30
143.141112	LAV 30	143.151152	LAV 30	143.163052	LAV 30
143.141122	LAV 30	143.151162	LAV 30	143.163062	LAV 30
143.141132	LAV 25	143.153012	LAV 30	143.164012	LAV 35
143.141142	LAV 30	143.153022	LAV 30	143.164022	LAV 35
143.141152	LAV 30	443.153032	LAV 30	143.164032	LAV 35
143.141162	LAV 30	143.154012	LAV 35	143.164042	LAV 35
143.141172	LAV 30	143.154022	LAV 35	143.164052	LAV 35
143.141182	LAV 30	143.154032	LAV 35	143.164062	LAV 35
143.141192	LAV 30	143.154042	LAV 35	143.164072	LAV 35
143.141202	LAV 30	143.154052	LAV 35	143.174082	LAV 35
143.141212	LAV 30	143.154062	LAV 35	143.164102	LAV 35
143.141222	LAV 30	143.154072	LAV 35	143.164112	LAV 35
143.141232	LAV 30	143.154082	LAV 35	143.164122	LAV 35
143.141242	LAV 30	143.154092	LAV 35	143.164132	LAV 35
143.141252	LAV 30	143.154102	LAV 35	143.164142	LAV 35
143.141262	LAV 30	143.154112	LAV 35	143.164152	LAV 35
143.141272	LAV 30	143.154132	LAV 35	143.164162	LAV 35
143.141282	LAV 30	143.154142	LAV 35	143.164172	LAV 35
143.141292	LAV 30	143.155012	V 50	143.164182	LAV 35
143.141302	LAV 30	143.155022	V 50	143.164202	LAV 35
143.143012	LAV 30	143.155032	V 50	143.165012	V 50
143.143022	LAV 30	143.155042	V 50	143.165022	V 50
143.143032	LAV 30	143.155052	V 50	143.165032	V 50
143.144012	LV 35	143.155062	V 50	143.165042	V 50
143.144022	LV 35	143.156012	V 60	143.165052	V 50
143.144032	VL 35	143.156022	V 60	143.166012	V 60
143.144042	VL 35	143.156032	V 60	143.166022	V 60
143.144052	VL 35	143.157012	V 40	143.166032	V 60
143.144062	LV 35	143.157022	V 40	143.166042	V 60
143.144072	LV 35	143.157032	V 40	143.166052	V 60
143.144082	LV 35	143.161012	LAV 30	143.167012	V 40
143.144092	LV 35	143.161022	LAV 30	143.167022	V 40
143.144102	LV 35	143.161032	LAV 30	143.167032	V 40
143.144112	LV 35	143.161042	LAV 30	143.167042	V 40
143.144122	LV 35	143.161052	LAV 30	143.171012	LAV 30
143.144132	LV 35	143.161062	LAV 30	143.171022	LAV 30
143.145012	V 50	143.161072	LAV 30	143.171032	LAV 30
143.145022	V 50	143.161082	LAV 30	143.171042	LAV 30
143.145032	V 50	143.161092	LAV 30	143.171052	LAV 30

Craftsman Model Number	Basic Tecumseh Number	Craftsman Model Number	Basic Tecumseh Number	Craftsman Model Number	Basic Tecumseh Number
143.171062	LAV 30	143.171032	LAV 30	143.176082	V 60
143.171072	LAV 30	143.171042	LAV 30	143.176092	V 60
143.171082	LAV 30	143.171052	LAV 30	143.176102	V 60
143.171092	LAV 30	143.171062	LAV 30	143.177012	V 40
143.171102	LAV 30	143.171072	LAV 30	143.177022	V 40
143.171132	LAV 30	143.171082	LAV 30	143.177032	V 40
143.171142	LAV 30	143.171092	LAV 30	143.177042	V 40
143.161152	LAV 30	143.171102	LAV 30	143.177062	V 40
143.161162	LAV 30	143.171132	LAV 30	143.177072	V 40
143.161172	LAV 30	143.171142	LAV 30	143.181042	LAV 30
143.161182	LAV 30	143.171152	LAV 30	143.181052	LAV 30
143.161192	LAV 30	143.171162	LAV 30	143.181062	LAV 30
143.161202	LAV 30	143.171172	LAV 30	143.181082	LAV 30
143.161212	LAV 30	143.171202	LAV 35	143.181092	LAV 30
143.161222	LAV 30	143.171212	LAV 30	143.181102	LAV 30
143.161232	LAV 30	143.171232	LAV 30	143.181112	LAV 30
143.161242	LAV 30	143.171242	LAV 30	143.181122	LAV 30
143.161262	LAV 30	143.171252	LAV 30	143.181132	LAV 30
143.162022	LAV 35	143.171262	LAV 30	143.183042	LAV 30
143.162032	LAV 35	143.171302	LAV 30	143.184012	LAV 35
143.162092	LAV 35	143.171312	LAV 30	143.184052	LAV 35
143.163012	LAV 30	143.171322	LAV 30	143.184082	LAV 35
143.163022	LAV 30	143.171332	LAV 30	143.184092	LAV 35
143.163032	LAV 30	143.173012	LAV 30	143.184102	LAV 35
143.163042	LAV 30	143.173042	LAV 30	143.184112	LAV 35
143.163052	LAV 30	143.174012	LAV 35	143.184122	LAV 35
143.163062	LAV 30	143.174022	LAV 35	143.184132	LAV 35
143.164012	LAV 35	143.174032	LAV 35	143.184142	LAV 35
143.164022	LAV 35	143.174042	LAV 35	143.184152	LAV 35
143.164032	LAV 35	143.174052	LAV 35	143.184162	LAV 35
143.164042	LAV 35	143.174062	LAV 35	143.184172	LAV 35
143.164052	LAV 35	143.174072	LAV 35	143.184182	LAV 35
143.164062	LAV 35	143.174082	LAV 35	143.184192	LAV 35
143.164072	LAV 35	143.174092	LAV 35	143.184202	LAV 35
143.174082	LAV 35	143.174102	LAV 35	143.184212	LAV 35
143.164102	LAV 35	143.174132	LAV 35	143.184232	ECV 100
143.164112	LAV 35	143.174142	LAV 35	143.184242	ECV 100
143.164122	LAV 35	143.174152	LAV 35	143.184252	ECV 100
143.164132	LAV 35	143.174162	LAV 35	143.184262	LAV 35
143.164142	LAV 35	143.174172	LAV 35	143.184272	LAV 35
143.164152	LAV 35	143.174182	LAV 35	143.184282	LAV 35
143.164162	LAV 35	143.174192	LAV 35	143.184292	LAV 35
143.164172	LAV 35	143.174232	LAV 35	143.184302	LAV 35
143.164182	LAV 35	143.174242	LAV 35	143.184402	LAV 35
143.164202	LAV 35	143.174252	LAV 35	143.185012	V 50
143.165012	V 50	143.174272	LAV 35	143.185022	V 50
143.165022	V 50	143.174292	LAV 35	143.185032	V 50
143.165032	V 50	143.175012	V 50	143.185042	V 50
143.165042	V 50	143.175022	V 50	143.185052	V 50
143.165052	V 50	143.175032	V 50	143.186012	V 60
143.166012	V 60	143.175042	V 50	143.186052	V 60
143.166022	V 60	143.175052	V 50	143.186062	V 60
143.166032	V 60	143.175062	V 50	143.186082	V 60
143.166042	V 60	143.175072	V 50	143.186092	V 60
143.166052	V 60	143.176012	V 60	143.186102	V 60
143.167012	V 40	143.176022	V 60	143.186112	V 60
143.167022	V 40	143.176032	V 60	143.186122	V 60
143.167032	V 40	143.176042	V 60	143.187022	LAV 40
143.167042	V 40	143.176052	V 60	143.187042	LAV 40
143.171012	LAV 30	143.176062	V 60	143.187052	LAV 40
143.171022	LAV 30	143.176072	V 60	143.187062	LAV 40

Craftsman Model Number	Basic Tecumseh Number	Craftsman Model Number	Basic Tecumseh Number	Craftsman Model Number	Basic Tecumseh Number
143.187072	LAV 40	143.207032	LAV 40	143.206032	V 60
143.187082	LAV 40	143.207052	LAV 40	143.207012	LAV 40
143.187094	LAV 40	143.187062	LAV 40	143.207022	LAV 40
143.187102	EVC 105	143.187072	LAV 40	143.207032	LAV 40
143.191012	LAV 30	143.187082	LAV 40	143.207052	LAV 40
143.191022	LAV 30	143.187094	LAV 40	143.207062	ECV 105
143.191032	LAV 30	143.187102	EVC 105	143.207072	LAV 40
143.191042	LAV 30	143.191012	LAV 30	143.207082	ECV 105
143.191052	LAV 30	143.191022	LAV 30	143.213012	LAV 30
143.194012	LAV 35	143.191032	LAV 30	143.213022	LAV 30
143.194022	LAV 35	143.191042	LAV 30	143.213042	LAV 30
143.194032	LAV 35	143.191052	LAV 30	143.214012	LAV 35
143.194042	LAV 35	143.194012	LAV 35	143.214022	LAV 35
143.194052	LAV 35	143.194022	LAV 35	143.214032	LAV 35
143.194062	ECV 100	143.194032	LAV 35	143.214042	ECV 100
143.194072	LAV 35	143.194042	LAV 35	143.214052	ECV 100
143.194082	LAV 35	143.194052	LAV 35	143.214062	ECV 100
143.194092	LA V35	143.194062	ECV 100	143.214072	ECV 100
143.194102	ECV 100	143.194072	LAV 35	143.214082	LAV 35
143.194112	LAV 35	143.194082	LAV 35	143.214092	LAV 35
143.194122	LAV 35	143.194092	LAV 35	143.214102	LAV 35
143.194132	LAV 35	143.194102	ECV 100	143.214112	LAV 35
143.194142	LAV 35	143.194112	LAV 35	143.214122	LAV 35
143.195012	V 50	143.194122	LAV 35	1432.214132	LAV 35
143.195022	V 50	143.194132	LAV 35	143.214192	LAV 35
143.196012	V 60	143.194142	LAV 35	143.214202	LAV 35
143.190622	V 60	143.195012	V 50	143.214212	LAV 35
143.196032	V 60	143.195022	V 50	143.214222	LAV 35
143.196082	V 60	143.196012	V 60	143.214232	LAV 35
143.17012	LAV 40	143.190622	V 60	143.214242	LAV 35
143.197022	ECV 105	143.196032	V 60	143.214252	LAV 35
143.197032	ECV 105	143.196082	V 60	143.214262	ECV 100
143.197042	LAV 40	143.17012	LAV 40	143.214272	ECV 100
143.197052	LAV 40	143.197022	ECV 105	143.214282	ECV 100
143.197062	LAV 40	143.197032	ECV 105	143.214292	LAV 35
143.197072	LAV 40	143.197042	LAV 40	143.214302	LAV 35
143.197082	ECV 105	143.197052	LAV 40	143.214312	ECV 100
143.201032	LAV 30	143.197062	LAV 40	143.214322	ECV 100
143.201042	LAV 30	143.197072	LAV 40	143.214332	LAV 35
143.203012	LAV 30	143.197082	ECV 105	143.214342	LAV 35
143.204022	ECV 100	143.201032	LAV 30	143.214352	ECV 100
143.204032	LAV 35	143.201042	LAV 30	143.216042	V 60
143.204042	LAV 35	143.203012	LAV 30	143.216052	V 60
143.204052	LAV 35	143.204022	ECV 100	143.216122	V 60
143.204062	ECV 100	143.204032	LAV 35	143.216142	V 60
143.204072	LAV 35	143.204042	LAV 35	143.216182	V 60
143.204082	LAV 35	143.204052	LAV 35	143.217012	ECV 105
143.204092	LAV 35	143.204062	ECV 100	143.217022	ECV 105
143.204102	EVC 100	143.204072	LAV 35	143.217032	ECV 105
143.204132	ECV 100	143.204082	LAV 35	143.217042	LAV 40
143.204142	LAC 35	143.204092	LAV 35	143.217052	LAV 40
143.204162	LAV 35	143.204102	ECV 100	143.217062	LAV 40
143.204172	LAV 35	143.204132	ECV 100	143.217072	LAV 40
143.204182	LAV 35	143.204142	LAC 35	143.217092	ECV 105
143.204192	LAV 35	143.204162	LAV 35	143.217102	LAV 40
143.204202	ECV 100	143.204172	LAV 35	143.223012	LAV 30
143.205022	V 50	143.204182	LAV 35	143.223022	LAV 30
143.206012	V 60	143.204192	LAV 35	143.223032	LAV 30
143.206032	V 60	143.204202	ECV 100	14.3223042	LAV 30
143.207012	LAV 40	143.205022	V 50	143.223052	LAV 30
143.207022	LAV 40	143.206012	V 60	143.224012	LAV 35

Craftsman Model Number	Basic Tecumseh Number	Craftsman Model Number	Basic Tecumseh Number	Craftsman Model Number	Basic Tecumseh Number
143.224022	LAV 35	143.233012	LAV 30	143.244122	ECV 100
143.224032	ECV 100	143.233032	LAV 30	143.244132	ECV 100
143.224062	LAV 35	143.233042	LAV 30	143.244142	ECV 100
143.224092	LAV 35	143.234022	LAV 35	143.244202	LAV 35
143.224102	LAV 35	143.234042	LAV 35	143.244212	ECV 100
143.224112	LAV 35	143.234052	LAV 35	143.244222	LAV 35
143.224122	LAV 35	143.234062	ECV 100	143.244232	LAV 35
143.224132	LAV 35	143.234072	ECV 100	143.244242	ECV 100
143.224142	LAV 30	143.234082	ECV 100	143.244252	ECV 100
143.224162	LAV 35	143.234092	ECV 100	143.244262	LAV 35
143.224172	LAV 35	143.234102	LAV 35	143.244272	LAV 35
143.224182	LAV 35	143.234112	LAV 35	143.244282	LAV 35
143.224192	LAV 35	143.234122	LAV 35	143.244292	ECV 100
143.224202	LAV 35	143.234132	LAV 35	143.244302	ECV 100
143.224212	LAV 35	143.234142	LAV 35	143.244312	ECV 100
143.224222	LAV 35	143.234162	LAV 35	143.244322	ECV 100
143.224232	ECV 100	143.234182	ECV 100	143.244332	ECV 100
143.224242	ECV 100	143.234192	LAV 35	143.245012	LAV 50
143.224252	LAV 35	143.234202	LAV 35	143.245042	V 50
143.224262	LAV 35	143.234212	ECV 100	143.245052	ECV 120
143.224272	LAV 35	143.234222	ECV 100	143.245062	ECV 120
143.224282	LAV 35	143.234232	ECV 100	143.245072	ECV 120
143.224292	ECV 100	143.234242	LAV 35	143.245082	ECV 120
143.224302	ECV 100	143.234252	LAV 35	143.245092	LAV 50
143.224312	LAV 35	143.234262	LAV 35	143.245102	ECV 120
143.224322	LAV 35	143.235012	ECV 120	143.245112	ECV 120
143.224332	LAV 35	143.235022	ECV 120	143.245122	ECV 120
143.224342	LAV 35	143.235032	LAV 50	143.245132	ECV 120
143.224352	ECV 100	143.235042	ECV 120	143.245142	LAV 50
143.224362	ECV 100	143.235052	ECV 120	143.245152	LAV 50
143.224372	LAV 35	143.235062	V 50	143.245162	ECV 120
143.224392	LAV 35	143.235072	LAV 50	143.245172	LAV 50
143.224402	LAV 35	143.236012	V 60	143.245182	LAV 50
143.224411	LAV 35	143.236052	V 60	143.245192	ECV 120
143.224422	LAV 35	143.236082	V 60	143.246012	V 60
143.225012	ECV 120	143.236102	V 60	143.246042	V 60
143.225022	ECV 120	143.236112	V 60	143.246352	V 60
143.225032	V 50	143.236132	V 60	143.246392	V 60
143.225042	V 50	143.236152	V 60	143.254012	LAV 35
143.225052	V 50	143.237012	ECV 110	143.254022	LAV 35
143.225062	ECV 120	143.237022	ECV 110	143.254032	LAV 35
143.225072	ECV 120	143.237032	ECV 105	143.254042	LAV 35
143.225082	V 50	143.237042	LAV 40	143.254052	LAV 35
143.225092	V 50	143.243012	LAV 30	143.254062	ECV 100
143.225102	V 50	143.243022	LAV 30	143.254072	LAV 35
143.226012	V 60	143.242042	LAV 30	143.254082	LAV 35
143.226032	V 60	143.243052	LAV 30	143.254092	LAV 35
143.266132	V 60	143.243062	LAV 30	143.254102	LAV 35
143.226152	V 60	143.243072	LAV 30	143.254112	LAV 35
143.226162	V 60	143.243082	LAV 30	143.254122	LAV 35
143.226182	V 60	143.244012	LAV 35	143.254142	ECV 100
143.226222	V 60	143.244022	LAV 35	143.254152	ECV 100
143.226232	V 60	143.244032	LAV 35	143.264162	ECV 100
143.226242	V 60	143.244042	ECV 100	143.254172	ECV 100
143.226262	V 60	143.244052	ECV 100	143.254182	ECV 100
143.262322	V 60	143.244062	ECV 100	143.254192	ECV 100
143.226332	V 60	143.244072	LAV 35	143.254212	LAV 35
143.227012	ECV 110	143.244082	LAV 35	143.254222	LAV 35
143.227022	ECV 110	143.244092	LAV 35	143.254232	ECV 100
143.227062	ECV 110	143.244102	LAV 35	143.254242	ECV 100
143.227072	ECV 110	143.244112	LAV 35	143.254252	ECV 100

Craftsman Model Number	Basic Tecumseh Number	Craftsman Model Number	Basic Tecumseh Number	Craftsman Model Number	Basic Tecumseh Number
143.254262	ECV 100	143.264272	LAV 35	143.266432	V 60
143.254272	ECV 100	143.264282	LAV 35	143.266442	V 60
143.254282	ECV 100	143.264292	LAV 35	143.266452	V 60
143.254292	ECV 100	143.264302	LAV 35	143.267012	LAV 40
143.254302	LAV 35	143.264312	LAV 35	143.267022	LAV 40
143.254312	LAV 35	143.264322	LAV 35	143.267042	LAV 40
143.254322	ECV 100	143.264332	LAV 35	143.274022	ECV 100
143.254332	LAV 35	143.265352	ECV 100	143.274032	ECV 100
143.254342	ECV 100	143.264362	ECV 100	143.274042	ECV 100
143.254352	ECV 100	143.264372	ECV 100	143.274052	ECV 100
143.254362	LAV 35	143.264382	LAV 35	143.274062	ECV 100
143.254372	ECV 100	143.264392	ECV 100	143.274072	ECV 100
143.254382	ECV 100	143.264402	ECV 100	143.274092	LAV 35
143.254392	LAV 35	143.264412	ECV 100	143.274102	LAV 35
143.254402	ECV 100	143.264422	LAV 35	143.274112	LAV 35
143.254412	ECV 100	143.264432	ECV 100	143.274122	LAV 35
143.254432	LAV 30	143.264452	ECV 100	143.274132	LAV 35
143.254442	ECV 100	143.264462	ECV 100	143.274142	ECV 100
143.254452	LAV 35	143.264482	ECV 100	143.274162	LAV 35
143.254462	ECV 100	143.264492	LAV 35	143.274172	LAV 35
143.254472	LAV 35	143.264052	LAV 35	143.274182	LAV 35
143.254482	LAV 35	143.264512	ECV 100	143.274202	ECV 100
143.254492	ECV 100	143.264522	LAV 35	143.274212	ECV 100
143.254502	LAV 35	143.264542	LAV 35	143.274222	ECV 100
143.254512	LAV 35	143.264562	ECV 100	143.274232	ECV 100
143.254522	LAV 35	143.264572	ECV 100	143.274242	ECV 100
143.254532	LAV 35	143.264582	ECV 100	143.274252	LAV 35
143.255012	LAV 50	143.264592	ECV 100	143.274262	ECV 100
143.255022	LAV 50	143.264602	ECV 100	143.274272	LAV 35
143.255042	LAV 50	143.264612	ECV 100	143.274282	LAV 35
143.255052	LAV 50	143.264622	ECV 100	143.274292	LAV 35
143.255062	LAV 50	143.264632	ECV 100	143.274302	LAV 35
143.255072	LAV 50	143.264642	ECV 100	143.274312	LAV 35
143.255092	LAV 50	143.264652	ECV 100	143.274322	LAV 35
143.255112	LAV 50	143.264672	ECV 100	143.274332	LAV 35
143.256022	V 60	143.264682	LAV 35	143.274342	ECV 100
143.256052	V 60	143.265012	LAV 50	143.274352	LAV 35
143.256082	V 60	143.265032	LAV 50	143.274362	ECV 100
143.256092	V 60	143.265042	LAV 50	143.274372	LAV 35
143.256122	V 60	143.265052	LAV 50	143.274392	ECV 100
143.257012	LAV 40	143.265062	LAV 50	143.274402	ECV 100
143.257022	LAV 40	143.265072	LAV 50	143.274412	ECV 100
143.257032	LAV 40	143.265082	LAV 50	143.274422	ECV 100
143.257042	LAV 40	143.265092	LAV 50	143.274432	ECV 100
143.257052	LAV 40	143.265112	LAV 50	143.274442	ECV 100
143.257062	LAV 40	143.265122	LAV 50	143.274452	ECV 100
143.257072	LAV 40	143.265132	LAV 50	143.274462	ECV 100
143.264012	LAV 35	143.265142	LAV 50	143.274472	LAV 35
143.264022	LAV 35	143.265152	LAV 50	143.274482	ECV 100
143.264032	LAV 35	143.265162	LAV 50	143.274492	LAV 35
143.264042	LAV 35	143.265172	LAV 50	143.274502	ECV 100
143.264052	ECV 100	143.265192	LAV 50	143.274512	ECV 100
143.264062	ECV 100	143.266032	V 60	143.274522	ECV 100
143.264072	ECV 100	143.266062	V 60	143.274542	ECV 100
143.264082	ECV 100	143.266082	V 60	143.274552	LAV 35
143.264092	LAV 35	143.266252	V 60	143.274562	ECV 100
143.264102	ECV 100	143.266372	V 60	143.274582	ECV 100
143.264232	LAV 35	143.266382	V 60	143.274592	LAV 35
143.264242	LAV 35	143.266392	V 60	143.274602	ECV 100
143.264252	LAV 35	143.266402	V 60	143.274612	EVC 100
143.264262	LAV 35	143.266412	V 60	143.274622	EVC 100

Craftsman Model Number	Basic Tecumseh Number	Craftsman Model Number	Basic Tecumseh Number	Craftsman Model Number	Basic Tecumseh Number
143.274632.	EVC 100	143.284382.	ECV 100	143.294072.	TVS 90
143.274642.	LAV 35	143.284392.	LAV 35	143.294092.	TVS 90
143.274652.	LAV 35	143.284402.	LAV 35	143.294102.	TVS 90
143.274672.	ECV 100	143.284412.	LAV 35	143.294112.	TVS 90
143.274682.	LAV 35	143.284422.	LAV 35	143.294122.	TVS 90
143.274692.	ECV 100	143.284432.	ECV 100	143.294132.	TVS 90
143.274702.	LAV 35	143.284442.	LAV 30	143.294142.	ECV 100
143.274712.	ECV 100	143.284452.	ECV 100	143.294152.	ECV 100
143.274722.	ECV 100	143.284462.	ECV 100	143.294162.	ECV 100
143.274732.	ECV 100	143.284472.	ECV 100	143.294172.	ECV 100
143.274742.	ECV 100	143.284482.	LAV 35	143.294182.	TVS 90
143.274752.	ECV 100	143.284492.	ECV 100	143.294192.	TVS 90
143.274762.	ECV 100	143.284502.	ECV 100	143.294202.	TVS 90
143.274772.	LAV 35	143.284512.	LAV 35	143.294212.	TVS 90
143.274782.	ECV 100	143.284522.	LAV 35	143.294222.	ECV 100
143.274792.	LAV 35	143.284532.	ECV 100	143.294232.	ECV 100
143.275012.	LAV 50	143.284542.	LAV 35	143.294242.	TVS 90
143.275022.	LAV 50	143.284552.	LAV 35	143.294252.	TVS 90
143.275042.	LAV 50	143.284562.	LAV 35	143.294262.	TVS 90
143.275052.	LAV 50	143.284572.	LAV 35	143.294272.	TVS90
143.275062.	LAV 50	143.284582.	ECV 100	143.294282.	TVS 90
143.275072.	LAV 50	143.284592.	LAV 35	143.294292.	TVS 90
143.275082.	LAV 50	143.284602.	ECV 100	143.294302.	TVS 90
143.276182.	V 60	143.284612.	ECV 100	143.294312.	TVS 90
143.276202.	V 60	143.284622.	ECV 100	143.294322.	TVS 90
143.276252.	V 60	143.284632.	LAV 35	143.294332.	ECV 100
143.276412.	V 60	143.284642.	ECV 100	143.294342.	TVS 90
143.277012.	LAV 40	143.284652.	LAV 35	143.294352.	ECV 100
143.277022.	LAV 40	143.284672.	ECV 100	143.294362.	ECV 100
143.284012.	LAV 35	143.284682.	ECV 100	143.294372.	ECV 100
143.284022.	LAV 35	143.284692.	ECV 100	143.294382.	ECV 100
143.284032.	LAV 35	143.284702.	ECV 100	143.294392.	ECV 100
143.284042.	ECV 100	143.284712.	LAV 35	143.294402.	ECV 100
143.284052.	LAV 35	143.284722.	LAV 35	143.294412.	ECV 100
143.284062.	LAV 35	143.284732.	LAV 35	143.294422.	ECV 100
143.284072.	ECV 100	143.284742.	ECV 100	143.294432.	TVS 90
143.284082.	LAV 35	143.284752.	ECV 100	143.294442.	TVS 90
143.284092.	LAV 35	143.284762.	LAV 35	143.294452.	TVS 90
143.284102.	ECV 100	143.284772.	ECV 100	143.294462.	TVS 90
143.284112.	LAV 35	143.284782.	ECV 100	143.294472.	ECV 100
143.284142.	LAV 35	143.285012.	LAV 50	143.294482.	ECV 100
143.284152.	LAV 35	143.285022.	LAV 50	143.294492.	TVS 90
143.284162.	LAV 35	143.285032.	LAV 50	143.294502.	TVS 90
143.284182.	LAV 35	143.285042.	LAV 50	143.294512.	TVS 90
143.284212.	ECV 100	143.285052.	LAV 50	143.294522.	TVS 90
143.284222.	LAV 30	143.285062.	LAV 50	143.294532.	TVS 90
143.284232.	TVS 90	143.285072.	LAV 50	143.294542.	ECV 100
143.284242.	LAV 35	143.285082.	LAV 50	143.294552.	TVS 105
143.284252.	LAV 35	143.285092.	LAV 50	143.294562.	TVS 105
143.284262.	ECV 100	143.285102.	LAV 50	143.294572.	ECV 100
143.284272.	TVS 90	143.286012.	V 50	143.294582.	ECV 100
143.284282.	LAV 35	143.286022.	V 60	143.294592.	ECV 100
143.284292.	LAV 35	143.286342.	V 60	143.294602.	TVS 90
143.284302.	LAV 35	143.287012.	LAV 40	143.294612.	TVS 90
143.284312.	LAV 35	143.293012.	TVS 75	143.294632.	TVS 105
143.284322.	LAV 35	143.294012.	TVS 90	143.294642.	TVS 105
143.284332.	ECV 100	143.294022.	TVS 90	143.294652.	TVS 90
143.284342.	ECV 100	143.294032.	TVS 90	143.294662.	ECV 100
143.284352.	ECV 100	143.294042.	TVS 90	143.294672.	ECV 100
143.284362.	ECV 100	143.294052.	TVS 90	143.294682.	ECV 100
143.284372.	ECV 100	143.294062.	TVS 90	143.294692.	TVS 90

Craftsman Model Number	Basic Tecumseh Number	Craftsman Model Number	Basic Tecumseh Number	Craftsman Model Number	Basic Tecumseh Number
143.294702	TVS 105	143.314382	TVS 90	143.324232	ECV 100
143.294712	TVS 90	143.314392	ECV 100	143.326012	TVM 195
143.294722	ECV 100	143.314402	TVS 90	143.331012	TVS 75
143.294732	ECV 100	143.314412	TVS 90	143.331022	TVS 75
143.294742	ECV 100	143.314422	ECV 100	143.334032	TVS 90
143.295012	LAV 50	143.314432	LAV 35	143.334042	ECV 100
143.295022	LAV 50	143.314442	ECV 100	143.334052	TVXL 105
143.295032	LAV 50	143.314452	ECV 100	143.334062	VS 90
143.295042	ECV 120	143.314462	ECV 100	143.334072	TVS 90
143.297012	TVS 105	143.314472	ECV 100	143.334082	ECV 100
143.304012	TVS 90	143.314152	ECV 100	143.334102	ECV 100
143.304032	ECV 100	143.314522	ECV 100	143.334112	TVS 90
143.304042	ECV 100	143.314532	LAV 35	143.334122	TVS 90
143.304052	TVS 90	143.314542	TVS 90	143.334132	ECV 100
143.304072	ECV 100	143.314552	TVS 90	143.334142	TVS 90
143.304092	TVS 90	143.314562	TVS 90	143.334152	TVS 90
143.304102	ECV 100	143.314572	TVS 90	143.334162	TVS 90
143.304112	ECV 100	143.314582	ECV 100	143.334172	ECV 100
143.304122	ECV 100	143.314592	ECV 100	143.334182	ECV 100
143.305012	ECV 120	143.314612	ECV 100	143.334192	LAV 35
143.305022	ECV 120	143.314622	ECV 100	143.334202	TVS 90
143.305032	ECV 120	143.314632	ECV 100	143.334212	ECV 100
143.305042	LAV 50	143.314642	ECV 100	143.334222	ECV 100
143.305052	ECV 120	143.314652	ECV 100	143.334232	ECV 100
143.305062	LAV 50	143.314662	ECV 100	143.334242	ECV 100
143.313012	TVS 75	143.314672	ECV 100	143.334252	ECV 100
143.314012	ECV 100	143.314682	ECV 100	143.334262	TVS 90
143.314022	ECV 100	143.314692	ECV 100	143.334272	TVS 90
143.314032	TVS 90	143.314702	LAV 35	143.334282	TVS 90
143.314042	TVS 90	143.315012	ECV 120	143.334292	TVS 90
143.314052	TVS 90	143.315022	LAV 50	143.334302	TVS 90
143.314062	TVS 90	143.315032	TVS 105	143.334312	TVS 90
143.314072	TVS 90	143.315042	TVS 105	143.334322	ECV 100
143.314082	TVS 90	143.315062	LAV 50	143.334332	TVS 90
143.314092	TVS 90	143.315072	TVS 105	143.334342	ECV 100
143.314102	TVS 90	143.315082	ECV 120	143.334352	TVS 90
143.314112	TVS 90	143.315092	LAV 50	143.334362	TVS 90
143.314122	ECV 100	143.315102	LAV 50	143.334372	TVS 90
143.314132	ECV 100	143.315112	LAV 50	143.334382	TVS 90
143.314142	ECV 100	143.315122	LAV 50	143.335012	ECV 120
143.314152	ECV 100	143.321012	TVS 75	143.335022	ECV 120
143.314162	ECV 100	143.321022	TVS 75	143.335032	LAV 50
143.314172	ECV 100	143.324012	ECV 100	143.335042	LAV 50
143.314182	TVS 90	143.324022	ECV 100	143.335052	TVS 120
143.314192	ECV 100	143.324042	ECV 100	143.341012	TVS 75
143.314202	ECV 100	143.324052	TVS 90	143.344022	TVS 90
143.314212	ECV 100	143.324062	ECV 100	143.344032	TVS 90
143.314222	ECV 100	143.324072	ECV 100	143.344042	TVS 90
143.314232	ECV 100	143.324082	ECV 100	143.344052	ECV 100
143.314242	ECV 100	143.324102	ECV 100	143.344062	ECV 100
143.314252	ECV 100	143.324112	TVS 90	143.344072	TVS 90
143.314262	TVS 90	143.324132	ECV 100	143.344082	ECV 100
143.314272	TVS 90	143.324142	TVS 90	143.344092	ECV 100
143.314282	TVS 90	143.324152	TVS 90	143.344102	TVS 90
143.314292	TVS 90	143.324162	TVS 90	143.344112	TVXL 105
143.314302	TVS 90	143.324172	TVS 90	143.344122	ECV 100
143.314312	ECV 100	143.324182	TVXL 105	143.344132	ECV 100
143.314322	TVS 90	143.324192	TVS 90	143.344142	TVS 90
143.314332	TVS 90	143.324202	ECV 100	143.344152	ECV 100
143.314342	TVS 90	143.324212	ECV 100	143.344162	TVS 90
143.314372	ECV 100	143.324222	ECV 100	143.344172	ECV 100

Craftsman Model Number	Basic Tecumseh Number	Craftsman Model Number	Basic Tecumseh Number	Craftsman Model Number	Basic Tecumseh Number
143.344182	TVS 90	143.354252	ECV 100	143.364302	ECV100
143.344192	TVS 90	143.354262	ECV 100	143.364312	ECV100
143.344202	TVS 90	143.354272	ECV 100	143.364322	ECV100
143.344212	TVS 90	143.354282	LAV 35	143.364332	ECV100
143.344222	TVS 90	143.354292	TVS 90	143.364342	ECV100
143.344232	ECV 100	143.354302	ECV 100	143.364352	TVS90
143.344242	ECV 100	143.354312	TVS90	143.364362	TVS90
143.344262	ECV 100	143.354322	TVS90	143.364372	TVS90
143.344272	ECV 100	143.354332	TVS90	143.364382	ECV100
143.344282	ECV 100	143.354342	TVS90	143.364392	TVS90
143.344292	ECV 100	143.354352	TVS90	143.364402	TVS105
143.344302	ECV 100	143.354362	ECV 100	143.365012	ECV120
143.344312	ECV 100	143.354372	ECV 100	143.365022	ECV120
143.344322	ECV 100	143.354382	ECV 100	143.366082	TVM125
143.344332	ECV 100	143.354392	ECV 100	143.366182	TVM125
143.344342	ECV 100	143.354402	ECV 100	143.371012	TVS75
143.334352	ECV 100	143.354412	ECV 100	143.371022	TVS75
143.344362	ECV 100	143.354422	ECV 100	143.371032	TVS75
143.344372	ECV 100	143.354432	ECV 100	143.374012	TVS90
143.344382	ECV 100	143.354442	ECV 100	143.374022	TVS90
143.344392	ECV 100	143.354452	ECV 100	143.371032	TVS90
143.344402	TVXL 105	143.354462	ECV 100	143.374052	TVS90
143.344412	TVXL 105	143.354482	TVS105	143.374062	TVS90
143.344422	TVS 90	143.354492	TVS105	143.374072	TVS90
143.344432	TVS 90	143.354502	TVS105	143.374082	TVS90
143.344442	TVS 105	143.355012	ECV 120	143.374092	ECV100
143.344452	ECV 100	143.355022	ECV 120	143.374102	ECV100
143.344462	TVS 105	143.355032	LAV50	143.374112	ECV100
143.344472	ECV 100	143.356022	TVM125	143.374122	ECV100
143.345012	ECV 120	143.356062	TVM125	143.374132	ECV100
143.345022	ECV 120	143.356362	TVM125	143.374142	ECV100
143.345032	TVS 120	143.361012	TVS75	143.374152	ECV100
143.345042	LAV 50	143.364012	TVS90	143.374162	ECV100
143.345052	ECV 120	143.364022	ECV100	143.374172	ECV100
143.345062	ECV 120	143.364032	ECV100	143.37182	ECV100
143.346202	TVM 125	143.364042	ECV100	143.374192	ECV100
143.351012	TVS 75	143.364052	ECV100	143.374202	ECV100
143.354012	TVS 90	143.364062	ECV100	143.374212	TVS90
143.354022	ECV 100	143.364072	ECV100	143.374222	TVS90
143.354032	ECV 100	143.364082	TVS90	143.374232	TVS90
143.345042	ECV 100	143.364092	ECV100	143.374282	TVS90
143.354052	ECV 100	143.364102	TVS90	143.374292	TVS105
143.354062	TVS 90	143.364112	TVS90	143.374302	TVS90
143.354072	ECV 100	143.364122	TVS90	143.374312	TVS105
143.354082	ECV 100	143.364132	TVS90	143.374322	TVS90
143.354092	TVS 90	143.364142	TVS90	143.374332	TVS90
143.354102	TVS 90	143.364152	TVXL105	143.374342	ECV100
143.354112	TVS 100	143.364162	ECV100	143.374362	TVS90
143.354122	TVS 90	143.364172	ECV100	143.374372	TVS105
143.354132	TVXL 105	143.364182	ECV100	143.374382	TVS90
143.354142	TVS 90	143.364192	ECV100	143.374402	ECV100
143.354152	EVC 100	143.364202	TVS90	143.374412	ECV100
143.354162	TVS 90	143.364212	ECV100	143.374422	TVS105
143.354172	TVS 90	143.364222	TVS90	143.374432	TVS90
143.354182	TVS 90	143.364232	ECV100	143.374452	ECV100
143.354192	TVS 90	143.364242	ECV100	143.375012	ECV120
143.354202	TVS 90	143.364252	ECV100	143.375022	ECV120
143.354212	TVS 90	143.364262	TVS105	143.375032	LAV50
143.354222	ECV 100	143.364272	ECV100	143.375042	LAV50
143.345232	TVS 90	143.364282	ECV100	143.375052	ECV120
143.354242	ECV 100	143.364292	ECV100	143.381012	TVS75

Craftsman Model Number	Basic Tecumseh Number	Craftsman Model Number	Basic Tecumseh Number	Craftsman Model Number	Basic Tecumseh Number
143.381022	TVS75	143.385032	ECV120	143.404292	TVS120
143.384012	TVS90	143.382042	LAV50	143.404312	TVS105
143.384022	TVS90	143.385052	LAV50	143.404322	TVS105
143.384032	TVS90	143.391012	TVS75	143.404332	TVS105
143.384042,TTVS90		143.391022	TVS75	143.404342	TVS90
143.384052	TVS90	143.394012	ECV100	143.404352	TVS90
143.384062	TVS90	143.394022	ECV100	143.404362	TVS105
143.384072	TVS90	143.394022	TVS90	143.404372	TVS105
143.384082	TVS90	143.394032	TVS90	143.404382	TVS105
143.384092	ECV100	143.394042	TVS90	143.404392	TVS105
143.384102	ECV100	143.394052	TVS90	143.404402	TVS120
143.384112	ECV100	143.394062	TVS90	143.404412	TVS105
143.384122	ECV100	143.394072	TVS90	143.404422	TVS105
143.384132	OVRM40	143.394082	ECV100	143.404432	TVS105
143.384142	OVRM40	143.394092	OVRM40	143.404442	TVS105
143.384142	OVRM40	143.394102	OVRM40	143.404452	TVS105
143.384152	OVRM40	143.394112	OVRM40	143.404462	TVS105
143.384162	OVRM40	143.394122	TVS90	143.404472	TVS120
143.384172	ECV100	143.394132	TVS90	143.404482	TVS120
143.384182	OVRM40	143.394142	TVS90	143.404502	TVS90
143.384192	OVRM40	143394152	TVS90	143.404532	TVS90
143.384202	ECV100	143.394162	ECV100	143.406082	TVM125
143.384212	ECV100	143.394172	ECV100	143.414012	TVS90
143.384222	ECV100	143394182	ECV100	143.414022	TVS105
143.384232	ECV100	143.394192	OVRM40	143.414032	TVS90
143.384242	ECV100	143.394202	OVRM40	143.414042	TVS90
143.384252	ECV100	143.394212	OVRM40	143.414052	TVS90
143.384262	ECV100	143.394222	ECV100	143.414062	TVS105
143.384272	TVS90	143.394232	ECV100	143.414072	TVS105
143.384282	TVS90	143.394242	TVS90	143.414082	TVS90
143.384292	TVS90	143.394252	ECV100	143.414092	ECV100
143.384302	TVS90	143.394272	ECV100	143.414102	ECV100
143.384312	TVS90	143.394272	ECV100	143.414112	ECV100
143.384322	ECV100	143.394282	ECV100	143.414122	ECV100
143.384332	ECV100	143.394302	TVS90	143.414132	ECV100
143.384342	TVS90	143.394322	TVS90	143.414142	ECV100
143.384352	ECV100	143.394372	ECV100	143.414152	ECV100
143.384362	ECV100	143.394492	TVS90	143.414162	ECV100
143.384372	ECV100	143.394502	LAV35	143.414172	TVS90
143.384382	TVS90	143.395012	ECV120	143.414182	TVS90
143.384392	TVS90	143.395022	ECV120	143.414192	ECV100
143.384402	TVS105	143.396102	TVM125	143.414202	ECV100
143.384412	TVS105	143.401012	TVS75	143.414212	TVS90
143.384422	TVS105	143.404022	TVS75	143.414232	TVS90
143.384432	TVS100	143.404032	TVS90	143.414242	TVS90
143.384442	TVS90	143.404042	TVS105	143.414252	TVS90
143.384452	TVS90	143.404082	TVS105	143.414262	ECV100
143.384462	ECV100	143.404092	TVS105	143.414272	ECV100
143.384472	ECV100	143.404122	TVS120	143.414282	TVS90
143.384485	ECV100	143.404132	TVS105	143.414292	TVS105
143.384492	ECV100	143.404142	TVS105	143.414302	TVS120
143.384502	ECV100	143.404152	TVS120	143.414312	TVS105
143.384512	ECV100	143.404162	TVS105	143.414322	TVS105
143.384522	ECV100	143.404172	TVS105	143.414332	TVS90
143.384532	ECV100	143.404182	TVS120	143.414342	TVS105
143.384542	ECV100	143.404202	TVS105	143.414352	TVS120
143.384552	TVS90	143.404222	TVS105	143.414362	TVS105
143.384562	ECV100	143.404232	TVS105	143.414372	TVS105
143.384572	TVS90	143.404242	TVS105	143.414382	TVS105
143.385012	ECV120	143.404252	TVS105	143.414392	TVS120
143.385022	ECV120	143.404282	TVS105	143.414402	TVS105

Craftsman Model Number	Basic Tecumseh Number	Craftsman Model Number	Basic Tecumseh Number	Craftsman Model Number	Basic Tecumseh Number
143.414412	TVS105	143.414612	TVS90	143.424112	TVS100
143.414422	TVS120	143.414622	TVS120	143.424122	TVS100
143.414432	OVRM50	143.414632	TVS105	143.424132	TVS100
143.414442	TVS105	143.414642	TVS120	143.424142	TVS105
143.414452	TVS105	143.414652	TVS105	143.424152	TVS120
143.414462	TVS105	143.414662	TVS105	143.424162	TVS105
143.414472	TVS120	143.414672	TVS105	143.424172	TVS120
143.414482	TVS105	143.414682	ECV100	143.424182	TVS100
143.414492	TVS120	143.414692	TVS100	143.424202	TVS90
143.414502	TVS90	143.416052	TVM125	143.424312	TVS105
143.414512	TVS90	143.416062	TVM125	143.424322	TVS105
143.414522	TVS90	143.424012	TVS90	143.424332	TVS120
143.414532	TVS90	143.424022	TVS105	143.424342	TVS120
143.414542	TVS105	143.424032	TVS90	143.424352	TVS105
143.414552	TVS120	143.424042	TVS105	143.424362	TVS90
143.414562	TVS105	143.424052	TVS90	143.424372	TVS90
143.414572	TVS120	143.424062	TVS120	143.424382	TVS105
143.414582	TVS105	143.424072	TVS120	143.424392	TVS105
143.414592	TVS105	143.424082	TVS105	143.424402	TVS120
143.414602	TVS105	143.424102	TVS120		

CRAFTSMAN

ENGINE IDENTIFICATION

Engines must be identified by the complete model number, including the serial number and type number in order to obtain correct repair parts. These numbers are located on the name plate as shown in Fig. C1A. If short block renewal is necessary, original identification plate must be transferred to replacement short block assemblies so unit can be identified when servicing at a later date.

PARTS PROCUREMENT

Parts for Craftsman engines are available from all Sears Service Centers. Be sure to give complete Craftsman model, serial and type number of engine when ordering parts or service material.

SERVICE NOTES (FOUR-STROKE)

CARBURETOR. The carburetors used on many Craftsman engines are the same as used on similar Tecumseh engines. Special Craftsman fuel systems are used on some models. The tank mounted suction carburetor is shown in view (A—Fig. C1).

The Craftsman float carburetor without speed control shown in view (B) is used without a mechanical or air vane governor.

Some engines use a mechanical governor (15, 16 and 17) which controls engine speed using a throttle valve (7 and 8) located in the intake manifold (6).

Refer to the appropriate following paragraphs for servicing Craftsman fuel systems.

Fuel Tank Mounted Carburetor. Early carburetors are equipped with a Bowden wire control as shown in Fig. C2. Later fuel tank mounted carburetors have a manual control knob and a positioning spring as shown in Fig. C3. Other differences are also noted and it is important to identify the type used before servicing.

On all tank mounted carburetors, turn the control valve clockwise to the position shown in Fig. C4, then withdraw the valve. There are no check valves or check balls in the carburetor pickup tube, but the tube can be removed for more thorough cleaning. To reinstall

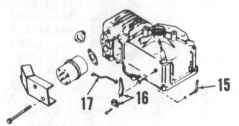

Fig. C1—Craftsman fuel systems are (A) tank mounted suction carburetor, (B) special float carburetor without governor or (C) the special float carburetor with mechanical governor linkage (15, 16 and 17) hooked up to a throttle (7 and 8) located in the intake manifold (6).

1. Control valve
2. Suction tube
3. Fuel tank
4. Intake manifold
5. Float carburetor
6. Intake manifold
7. Governor throttle shaft
8. Governor throttle plate
9. Return spring
10. Bellcrank
11. Linkage (10 to 12)
12. Governor spring
15. Internal lever
16. External lever
17. Linkage (16 to 7)

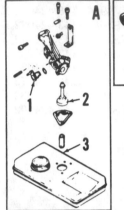
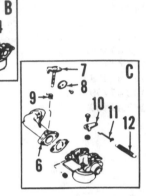
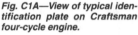

Fig. C1A—View of typical identification plate on Craftsman four-cycle engine.

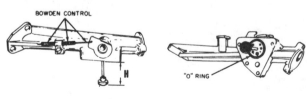

Fig. C2—View of early tank mounted suction carburetor. Notice the Bowden control cable and groove for "O" ring on lower surface. Refer to Fig. C3 for later type.

Fig. C3—View of later tank mounted suction carburetor. The unit is controlled by moving the manual control on carburetor. The lower surface is sealed with a gasket and the "O" ring used on early models is not used. The pickup tube has a collar to make sure it is installed at the correct depth.

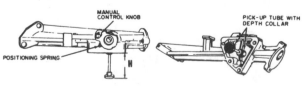

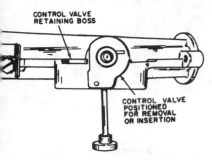

C4—The control valve must be turned clock-
to the position shown to clear the retaining

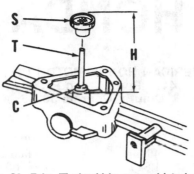

Fig. C6—Tube (T) should be pressed into bore
until collar (C) contacts body of late carburetor.
Press strainer (S) onto tube until height (H) is
correct.

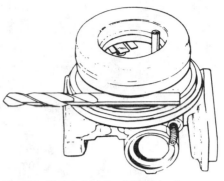

Fig. C11—Float height should be set using a number 4 drill bit positioned as shown. Drill size is 0.2
inch (5.31 mm) diameter.

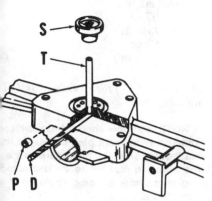

C5—A ¼-inch drill bit (D) should be used to
the correct installed depth of tube (T). New
(P) should be used when assembling.

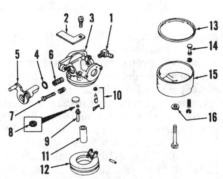

Fig. C10—Exploded view of Craftsman float type
carburetor. Refer to text for service procedure.

1. Fuel inlet fitting	9. Fuel pickup tube
2. Retaining plate	10. Fuel inlet valve
3. Carburetor body	11. Bowl spacer
4. "O" ring	12. Float
5. Control valve	13. Gasket
6. Positioning spring	14. Bowl drain
7. High speed stop	15. Float bowl
8. Screen	16. Gasket

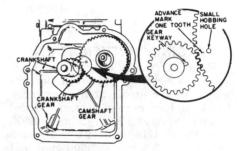

Fig. C12—Camshaft timing marks should be advanced one tooth when engine is not equipped
with mechanical governor.

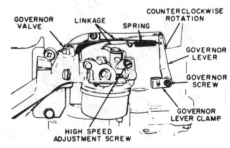

Fig. C13—View of Craftsman float type carburetor
installed. The model shown uses mechanical governor controlling the governor throttle valve located in the intake manifold. This system is shown
at (C—Fig. C1).

kup tube in early models, it is
cessary to remove plug (P – Fig. C5).
sert ⅛ inch drill into passage as shown
d press tube into bore until seated
ainst drill bit. Leave drill in place and
ess strainer (S) onto pickup tube until
ight (H—Fig. C2) is 1-27/64 to 1-7/16
ches (36.1-36.5 mm). Remove drill bit
d install new cap plug.

On late carburetors, the tube (T—Fig.
) has a collar near the top end. Press
e tube into bore until the collar is
ainst carburetor body casting; then
ess the strainer (S) onto strainer until dis-
nce (H) is 1-15/32 inches (27.3 mm).

The reservoir tube in the fuel tank
uld have slotted end toward bottom
tank on all models.

uel mixture is nonadjustable, but the
xture will be changed by dirty or miss-
g air filter. Be sure air filter is in good
ndition and clean.

NOTE: The camshaft timing should be
vanced one tooth for engines with this
rburetor. Refer to Fig. C12.

Craftsman Float Carburetor. The
carburetor is serviced in manner similar
to other float type carburetors. Refer to
Fig. C10.

The carburetor is equipped with mixture adjustment. It is important that
float height is correct. The air filter
must be in good condition and clean.
Refer to Fig. C11 for measuring float
height with drill bit.

The fuel pickup tube (9) should be
pressed into bore until collar is against
carburetor body.

**NOTE: Some engines equipped with
this carburetor are not equipped with a
variable speed governor. These models
are equipped with a plain intake manifold
as shown (B—Fig. C1). The camshaft tim-**

**ing should be advanced one tooth for
engines without governor as shown in Fig.
C12.**

Camshaft timing marks should be
aligned for models with variable speed
governor. The governed high speed is
adjusted by turning the adjustment
screw shown in Fig. C13.

HONDA

AMERICAN HONDA MOTOR CO., INC.
4475 River Green Parkway
Duluth, Georgia 30136

Model	Bore	Stroke	Displacement
G100	46 mm	46 mm	76 cc
	(1.84 in.)	(1.84 in.)	(4.6 cu. in.)
G150	64 mm	45 mm	144 cc
	(2.5 in.)	(1.8 in.)	(8.8 cu. in.)
GV150	64 mm	45 mm	144 cc
	(2.5 in.)	(1.8 in.)	(8.8 cu. in.)
G200	67 mm	56 mm	197 cc
	(2.6 in.)	(2.2 in.)	(12.0 cu. in.)
GV200	67 mm	56 mm	197 cc
	(2.6 in.)	(2.2 in.)	(12.0 cu. in.)

ENGINE IDENTIFICATION

Honda G series engines are four-stroke, air-cooled, single-cylinder engines. Valves are located in cylinder block and crankcase casting. Model G100 is rated at 1.5 kW (2 hp) at 3600 rpm, Models G150 and GV150 are rated at 2.6 kW (3.5 hp) at 3600 rpm and

Models G200 and GV200 are rated at 3.7 kW (5 hp) at 3600 rpm.

The "G" prefix indicates horizontal crankshaft model and "GV" prefix indicates vertical crankshaft model.

Engine model number decal is located on cooling shroud just above or beside recoil starter. Engine serial number for Models G100, G150 (after serial number 1181478), G200 (after serial number 1286400) and all GV200 engines is located on crankcase or crankcase cover near oil filler and dipstick opening. Engine serial number for all Model GV150 engines is located on oil pan just below cylinder head. Engine serial number for all other models is located on lower left edge (facing pto side) of crankcase. See Fig. HN1.

Always furnish engine model and serial number when ordering parts or service information.

MAINTENANCE

SPARK PLUG. Recommended spark plug is as follows:

Model	Standard	Resistor
G100	NGK BM4A	NGK BMR4A
G150*	NGK B4HS	NGK BR4HS
GV150*	NGK BM6A	NGK BMR6A
G200*	NGK B4HS	NGK BR4HS
G150**	NGK BP4HS	NGK BPR4HS
GV150**	NGK BPM6A	NGK BPMR6A
G200*	NGK BP4HS	NGK BPR4HS
GV200*	NGK BM6A	NGK BMR6A
GV200**	NGK BPM6A	NGK BPMR6A

*Breaker point ignition system
**CDI ignition system

Spark plug should be removed and cleaned after every 100 hours of operation. Set electrode gap at 0.6-0.7 mm (0.024-0.028 in.) for models with breaker point ignition system or 0.9-1.0 mm

(0.035-0.039 in.) for models with CDI nition system.

NOTE: Caution should be exercise abrasive type spark plug cleaner is us Inadequate cleaning procedure may all the abrasive cleaner to be deposited engine cylinder causing rapid wear a part failure.

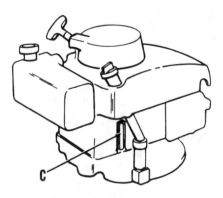

Fig. HN1—View showing serial number locations for all models. (A)—All Model G100, Models G150 (after serial number 1181478) and G200 (after serial number 1286400), (B)—Models G150 (prior to serial number 1181479) and G200 (prior to serial number 1286401). (C)—All model GV200.

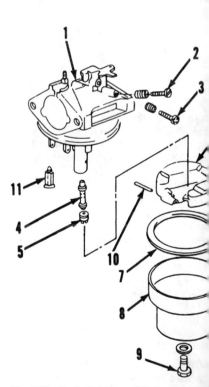

Fig. HN2—Exploded view of carburetor use Models G150, G200, GV150 and GV200. Carbu. used on Model G100 is similar.
1. Carburetor throttle body
2. Idle mixture screw
3. Throttle stop screw
4. Nozzle
5. Main jet
6. Float
7. Gasket
8. Float bowl
9. Bolt
10. Float pin
11. Fuel inlet ne

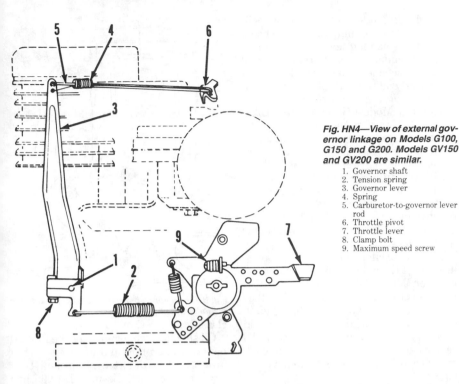

Fig. HN4—View of external governor linkage on Models G100, G150 and G200. Models GV150 and GV200 are similar.

1. Governor shaft
2. Tension spring
3. Governor lever
4. Spring
5. Carburetor-to-governor lever rod
6. Throttle pivot
7. Throttle lever
8. Clamp bolt
9. Maximum speed screw

CARBURETOR. All models are equipped with a float type side draft carburetor. Carburetor is equipped with idle fuel mixture screw. High speed fuel mixture is controlled by a fixed jet.

Engine idle speed is 1400 rpm for Models G100, G150 and G200 and 1700 rpm for Models GV150 and GV200. Idle speed is adjusted by turning throttle stop screw (3 – Fig. HN2). Initial adjustment of idle fuel mixture screw (2) from a lightly seated position is 1⅜ turns open on Models G100 and G150, 3¼ turns open on Model G200 and 1¾ turns open on Models GV150 and GV200. On all models, final adjustment is made with engine at operating temperature and running. Adjust idle mixture screw to attain smoothest engine operation. Recheck engine idle speed and adjust if necessary.

Main jet (5) controls fuel mixture for high speed operation. Standard main jet size is #55 for Model G100, #65 for Models G150 and GV150, #72 for Model G200 and #75 for Model GV200.

Float level should be 6.7-9.7 mm (0.26-0.38 in.) on Models G100 and GV200 and 8.2 mm (0.32 in.) on Models G100, G150 and G200. To measure float level, invert carburetor throttle body and float assembly. Measure distance from top of float to float bowl mating surface. If dimension is not as specified, renew float.

FUEL FILTER. A fuel filter screen is located in sediment bowl below fuel shut-off valve. To remove sediment bowl, shut off fuel, unscrew threaded ring and remove ring, sediment bowl and gasket. Make certain gasket is in place before reassembly. To clean screen, fuel shut-off valve must be disconnected from fuel line and unscrewed from fuel tank.

AIR FILTER. Engines may be equipped with one of four different types of air cleaner (filter); single element type, dual element type, foam (semidry) type or oil bath type. On all models, air filter should be removed and serviced after every 20 hours of operation. Refer to appropriate paragraph for model being serviced.

Dry Type Air Filter. To remove element, loosen the two wing nuts and remove air cleaner cover. Remove element and separate foam element from paper element. Direct low pressure air from inside filter elements toward the outside to remove all loose dirt and foreign material. Reinstall elements.

Dual Element Type Air Filter. Remove wing nut, cover and elements. Separate foam outer element from paper element. Wash foam element in warm soapy water and thoroughly rinse. Allow element to air dry. Dip dry foam element in clean engine oil and gently squeeze out excess oil.

Direct low pressure air from inside paper element toward the outside to remove all loose dirt and foreign material. Reassemble elements and reinstall.

Foam (Semi-dry) Type Air Filter. Remove air cleaner cover and element. Clean element in nonflammable solvent and squeeze dry. Soak element in new engine oil and gently squeeze out excess oil. Reinstall element and cover.

Oil Bath Type Air Filter. Remove air cleaner assembly and separate cover, element and housing. Clean element in nonflammable solvent and air dry. Drain old oil and thoroughly clean housing. Fill housing to oil level mark with new engine oil and reassemble air cleaner.

GOVERNOR. The internal centrifugal flyweight governor assembly is located inside crankcase and is either gear or chain driven.

To adjust governor, first stop engine and make certain all linkage is in good condition and tension spring (2 – Fig. HN4) is not stretched or damaged. Spring (4) must pull governor lever (3) toward throttle pivot (6).

On all models except Models GV150 and GV200, loosen clamp bolt (8) and

Fig. HN5—"F" mark on flywheel should align with timing (index) mark on crankcase when points just begin to open. Timing tool number 07974-8830001 is available to adjust timing with flywheel removed.

"F" Mark on Flywheel

Timing (Index) Mark

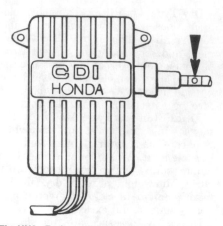

Fig. HN6—Exciter coil must be timed according to timing number on CDI unit.

turn governor shaft clockwise as far as it will go and move governor lever as far to the right as it will go. Tighten retaining bolt. Start and run engine until it reaches operating temperature. Adjust stop screw to obtain 3000-3200 rpm.

On Models GV150 and GV200, loosen clamp bolt, pull governor shaft all the way to the right and rotate governor shaft clockwise as far as possible. Tighten clamp bolt. With engine stopped, governor is assembled properly when governor lever is spring-loaded and moves freely. Recommended engine speed is 3000-3200 rpm.

IGNITION SYSTEM. Engines may be ·equipped with a breaker point ignition system or a capacitor discharge ignition (CDI) system. Refer to appropriate paragraph for model being serviced.

Breaker Point Ignition System. Breaker points and ignition coil are located underneath the flywheel on all models. Breaker points should be checked after every 300 hours of operation. Initial breaker point gap should be 0.3-0.4 mm (0.012-0.016 in.) and can be varied to obtain 20° BTDC timing setting.

NOTE: Timing tool number 07974-8830001 is available from Honda Motor Company to allow timing adjustment with flywheel removed.

To check ignition timing, connect positive ohmmeter lead to engine stop switch wire and connect remaining lead to engine ground. Rotate flywheel until ohmmeter needle deflects. "F" mark on flywheel should align with index mark on crankcase (Fig. HN5). Remove flywheel and vary point gap to obtain correct timing setting. If timing tool is used, ignition timing can be checked with flywheel removed.

To check Model G100 ignition coil, connect positive ohmmeter lead to black wire and remaining lead to coil laminations. Ohmmeter should register 0.49 ohms. Disconnect positive lead and reconnect lead to spark plug wire. Ohmmeter should register 4 ohms.

To check Models G150, GV150, G200 and GV200 ignition coil, connect positive ohmmeter lead to spark plug wire and remaining lead to coil laminations. Ohmmeter should register 6.6 ohms.

CDI Ignition System. The capacitor discharge ignition (CDI) system consists of the flywheel magnets, exciter coil (located under flywheel) and CDI unit. CDI system does not require regular maintenance.

To test exciter coil on all models, disconnect the blue and black exciter coil leads on Model GV200 or the red and black exciter coil leads on all other models. Connect an ohmmeter lead to each exciter coil lead. Ohmmeter should register continuity, if not, renew coil. To renew exciter coil, remove engine cooling shrouds and flywheel. Remove exciter coil.

NOTE: Exciter coil must be installed and timed according to timing number on CDI unit. Refer to Fig. HN6.

Determine CDI unit timing number (Fig. HN6) and position coil so its inner edge aligns with scale position indicated by the CDI unit timing number (Fig. HN7). Distance between scale ridges indicates 2°. Tighten exciter coil mounting bolts and recheck alignment. Reinstall flywheel and cooling shrouds.

If timing, ignition stop switch and exciter coil check satisfactory, but an ignition system problem is still suspected, renew CDI unit. Make certain ground terminal on CDI unit is making an adequate connection.

VALVE ADJUSTMENT. Valves and seats should be refaced and stem clearance adjusted after every 300 hours of operation. Refer to REPAIRS section for service procedures and specifications.

CYLINDER HEAD AND COMBUSTION CHAMBER. Cylinder head, combustion chamber and piston should be cleaned and carbon and other deposits removed after every 300 hours of operation. Refer to REPAIRS section for service procedure.

LUBRICATION. Engine oil should be checked prior to each operating interval. Oil level should be maintained between reference marks on dipstick with dipstick just touching first threads. Do not screw dipstick in to check oil level. Manufacturer recommends SAE 10W-40 oil with an API service

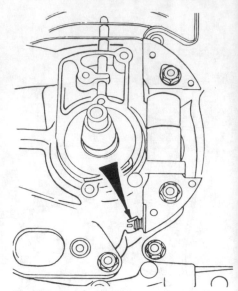

Fig. HN7—Distance between scale ridges indicate 2° ignition timing positions.

classification SE or SF.

Oil should be changed after the first 20 hours of operation and after every 100 hours of operation thereafter. Crankcase capacity is 0.45 L (0.95 pt.) for Model G100 and 0.7 L (1.48 pt.) for all other models.

GENERAL MAINTENANCE. Check and tighten all loose bolts, nuts and clamps prior to each operating interval. Check for fuel and oil leakage and repair if necessary.

Clean dust, dirt, grease and any foreign material from cylinder head and cylinder block cooling fins after every 100 hours of operation. Inspect fins for damage and repair if necessary.

REPAIRS

TIGHTENING TORQUES. Recommended tightening torque specifications are as follows:

Flywheel nut:
  G100 . . . . 4.8 N·m
                        (3.5 ft.-lbs.)
  All others . . . . 73 N·m
                        (54 ft.-lbs.)
Crankcase cover . . . . 8-12 N·m
                        (6-8 ft.-lbs.)
Cylinder head bolts:
  G100 . . . . 10 N·m
                        (7 ft.-lbs.)
  All others . . . . 24-26 N·m
                        (18-19 ft.-lbs.)
Connecting rod bolts:
  G100 . . . . 3 N·m
                        (2.2 ft.-lbs.)
  All others . . . . 9-11 N·m
                        (6-9 ft.-lbs.)
Oil pump cover
(GV150 & GV200) . . . . 10 N·m
                        (7 ft.-lbs.)

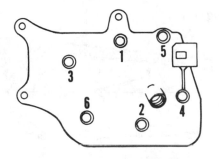

Fig. HN8—Tighten head bolts on Model G100 to specified torque following sequence shown.

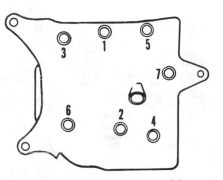

Fig. HN9—Tighten head bolts on all models except Model G100 to specified torque following sequence shown.

Standard piston diameters and service limits are as follows:

Model	Standard Diameter	Service Limit
G100	45.98-46.00 mm (1.810-1.811 in.)	45.92 mm (1.808 in.)
G150, GV150	63.98-64.00 mm (2.518-2.520 in.)	63.99 mm (2.515 in.)
G200, GV200	66.98-67.00 mm (2.637-2.638 in.)	66.88 mm (2.633 in.)

If piston diameter is less than service limit, renew piston.

Before installing rings, install piston in cylinder bore and use a suitable feeler gage to measure clearance between piston and cylinder bore. Standard clearance and service limits are as follows:

Model	Standard Clearance	Service Limit
G100	0.030 mm (0.001 in.)	0.130 mm (0.005 in.)
G150, GV150	0.060 mm (0.0024 in.)	0.285 mm (0.0112 in.)
G200, GV200	0.040 mm (0.0016 in.)	0.045 mm (0.0018 in.)

CYLINDER HEAD. To remove cylinder head, first remove cooling shrouds. Clean engine to prevent entrance of foreign material. Remove spark plug. Loosen cylinder head bolts in ¼ turn increments following the sequence shown in Fig. HN8 for Model G100 or Fig. HN9 for all other models until all bolts are loose enough to remove by hand. Remove cylinder head. Clean carbon and deposits from cylinder head.

Reinstall cylinder head and new gasket. Tighten head bolts to specified torque using the correct sequence shown (Fig. HN8 or HN9) according to model being serviced.

CONNECTING ROD. Connecting rod rides directly on crankshaft crankpin journal on all models. Piston and connecting rod are accessible after cylinder head removal and crankcase cover or oil pan is separated from crankcase. Remove the two connecting rod bolts, lock plate and connecting rod cap. Push piston and connecting rod assembly out through the top of cylinder block. Remove snap rings and piston pin to separate piston from connecting rod.

Standard diameter for piston pin bore in connecting rod small end is 10.006-10.017 mm (0.3939-0.3944 in.) for Model G100 or 15.005-15.020 mm (0.5907-0.5913 in.) for all other models. If dimension exceeds 10.050 mm (0.3957 in.) for Model G100 or 15.070 mm (0.5933 in.) for all other models, renew connecting rod.

Standard clearance between connecting rod bearing surface and crankpin journal is 0.016-0.033 mm (0.0006-0.0013 in.) for Model G100 and 0.040-0.066 mm (0.0016-0.0026 in.) for all other models. If clearance exceeds 0.1 mm (0.004 in.) for Model G100 or 0.120 mm (0.0047 in.) for all other models, renew connecting rod and/or recondition crankshaft.

Standard connecting rod side play on crankpin journal is 0.2-0.9 mm

(0.008-0.035 in.) for Model G100 or 0.10-0.80 mm (0.004-0.031 in.) for all other models. If side play exceeds 1.1 mm (0.043 in.) for Model G100 or 1.20 mm (0.047 in.) for all other models, renew connecting rod.

To install piston on connecting rod, refer to appropriate paragraph for model being serviced.

Model G100. Install piston on connecting rod so number 896 stamped on top of piston is toward long side of connecting rod (Fig. HN10). With match marks on connecting rod and cap aligned, long side of rod is installed toward valve side of engine.

Models G150, GV150 And G200. Piston may be installed on connecting rod either way. Install connecting rod and piston assembly in engine so marked side of piston top is toward valve side of engine. Align match marks on connecting rod and rod cap.

Model GV200. Install piston on connecting rod with mark on top of piston toward ribbed side of connecting rod. Install connecting rod so ribbed side is towards oil pan. Align connecting rod and rod cap match marks.

All models. Install oil dipper if equipped. Tighten connecting rod bolts to specified torque and lock bolts with lock plate if equipped.

PISTON, PIN AND RINGS. Piston and connecting rod are removed as an assembly. Refer to CONNECTING ROD section for removal and installation procedure.

After separating piston and connecting rod, carefully remove rings. Clean carbon and deposits from piston surface and ring lands.

CAUTION: Extreme care should be exercised when cleaning ring lands. Do not damage squared edges or widen ring grooves. If ring lands are damaged, piston must be renewed.

Measure piston diameter at piston thrust surfaces, 90° from piston pin.

If clearance exceeds service limit dimension, renew piston and/or recondition cylinder bore.

Standard piston bore diameter in piston is 10.000-10.006 mm (0.3937-0.3939 in.) for Model G100 or 15.000-15.006 mm (0.5906-0.5908 in.) for all other models. Service limit for piston pin bore diameter is 10.046 mm (0.4096 in.) for Model G100 or 15.046 mm (0.5924 in.) for all other models. If diameter exceeds service limit, renew piston.

Standard piston pin outside diameter is 9.994-10.000 mm (0.3935-0.3937 in.) for Model G100 or 14.994-15.000 mm (0.5903-0.5906 in.) for all other models. Service limit for piston pin outside diameter is 9.950 mm (0.3917 in.) for Model G100 or 14.954 mm (0.5887 in.) for all other models. If diameter is less than service limit, renew piston pin.

Standard piston ring to piston groove side clearance for Model G100 is 0.025-0.055 mm (0.0009-0.0022 in.) for top ring and 0.010-0.040 mm (0.0004-0.0016 in.) for all remaining rings. Standard piston ring to piston groove side clearance for all other models is 0.01-0.05 mm (0.0004-0.0020 in.). If ring side clearance exceeds 0.10 mm (0.0039 in.) on Model G100 or 0.15 mm (0.0059 in.) on all other models, renew rings and/or piston.

On all models, if piston ring end gap exceeds 1.0 mm (0.039 in.) with ring

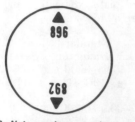

Fig. HN10—Note numbers on piston crown and install piston of Model G100 so "896" on piston is towards long side of rod.

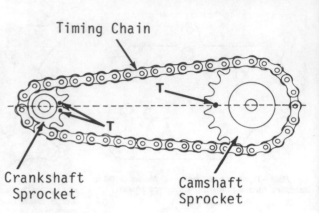

Fig. HN12—On models with extended camshaft for pto drive shaft, engines are equipped with timing sprockets and timing chain. Timing sprockets must be aligned with timing dot "T" as shown before installing timing chain and sprocket assembly on crankshaft and camshaft.

squarely installed in cylinder bore, renew ring and/or recondition cylinder bore.

Install piston rings with marked side towards top of piston. Stagger ring end gaps equally around circumference of piston.

CYLINDER AND CRANKCASE. Cylinder and crankcase are an integral casting. Standard cylinder bore diameters are as follows:

Model	Standard Diameter	Service Limit
G100	46.00-46.01 mm	46.05 mm
	(1.811-1.812 in.)	(1.813 in.)
G150,		
GV150	64.00-64.02 mm	64.17 mm
	(2.519-2.520 in.)	(2.526 in.)
G200,		
GV200	67.00-67.02 mm	67.17 mm
	(2.638-2.639 in.)	(2.644 in.)

If cylinder bore diameter at any point in cylinder bore exceeds the service limit, recondition cylinder bore.

CRANKSHAFT, MAIN BEARINGS AND SEALS. Crankshaft is supported by ball bearing type main bearings at each end. To remove crankshaft, remove all cooling shrouds, flywheel, cylinder head and crankcase cover or oil pan. Remove piston and connecting rod assembly. Carefully remove crankshaft and camshaft. Remove main bearings

and crankshaft oil seals if necessary.

Standard crankpin diameter is 17.973-17.984 mm (0.7076-0.7080 in.) for Model G100 or 25.967-25.980 mm (1.0223-1.0228 in.) for all other models. If crankpin diameter is less than 17.940 mm (0.7063 in.) for Model G100 or 25.197 mm (1.0204 in.) for all other models, renew or recondition crankshaft.

Main bearings are a light press fit on crankshaft and in bearing bores of crankcase and crankcase cover. It may be necessary to slightly heat crankcase or crankcase cover to reinstall bearings.

Inspect main bearings for roughness and looseness. Also check bearings for a loose fit on crankshaft journals or in crankcase and crankcase cover. Renew bearings if any of the previously described conditions are evident.

If crankshaft oil seals have been removed, use suitable seal driver to install new seals. Seals should be pressed in evenly until 4.5 mm (0.18 in.) below flush for seal in crankcase cover or oil pan and until 2.00 mm (0.08 in.) below flush for seal in crankcase.

Make certain crankshaft gear (sprocket) and camshaft gear (sprocket) timing marks are aligned (Fig. HN11 or Fig. HN12) during crankshaft installation.

CAMSHAFT, BEARINGS AND SEAL. Camshaft is supported at each end by bearings which are an integral

part of crankcase or crankcase cover casting. An extended camshaft pto which utilizes a ball bearing for crankcase bearing, is available on some models. Refer to CRANKSHAFT, MAIN BEARINGS AND SEALS section for camshaft removal procedure.

Standard camshaft lobe height is 18.1-18.5 mm (0.71-0.73 in.) for intake and exhaust lobes on Model G100 or 33.4-33.6 mm (1.31-1.32 in.) for intake lobe, and 33.7-33.9 mm (1.33-1.34 in.) for exhaust lobe on all other models. If intake or exhaust lobe on Model G100 is less than 17.940 mm (0.7063 in.), renew camshaft. On all other models, if intake lobe is less than 33.25 mm (1.309 in.) or exhaust lobe is less than 33.55 mm (1.321 in.) renew camshaft.

Standard clearance between camshaft bearing journal and integral type bearings is 0.013-0.043 mm (0.0005-0.0017 in.). If clearance exceeds 0.1 mm (0.004 in.), renew camshaft and/or crankcase and crankcase cover.

On models with extended camshaft, ball bearing should be a light press fit on camshaft journal and in crankcase cover. Camshaft seal should be pressed into crankcase cover 2.0 mm (0.08 in.).

Make certain camshaft gear (sprocket) and crankshaft gear sprocket timing marks are aligned during installation.

GOVERNOR. The internal centrifugal flyweight governor is gear driven off of the camshaft gear on Model

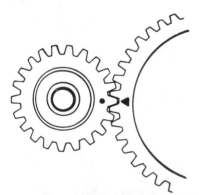

Fig. HN11—When installing crankshaft or camshaft, make certain timing marks on gears are aligned as shown.

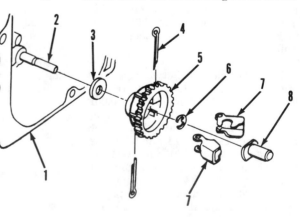

Fig. HN13—Exploded view of governor assembly used on Model G100. On all other models, governor weight assembly is mounted on camshaft gear or sprocket.

1. Crankcase cover
2. Governor stud
3. Thrust washer
4. Pin
5. Gear
6. "E" clip
7. Weights
8. Sleeve

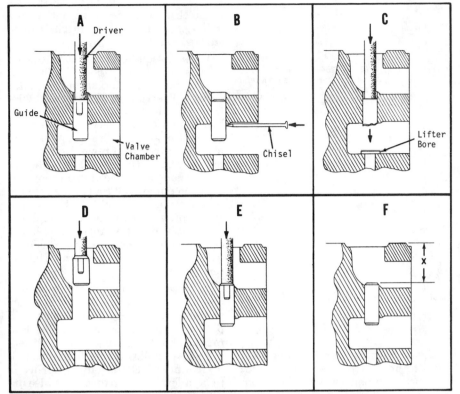

Fig. HN14—View showing valve guide removal and installation sequence on all models except Model G100. Refer to text.

G100 and is located on camshaft gear (sprocket) for all other models. Refer to GOVERNOR paragraphs in MAINTENANCE section for external governor adjustments.

To remove governor assembly, remove external linkage, metal cooling shrouds and crankcase cover or oil pan. On G100 models, remove "E" clip (Fig. HN13) and slide governor assembly off of shaft. On all other models, governor assembly is mounted on camshaft gear or sprocket.

When reassembling, make certain governor sliding sleeve and internal governor linkage is correctly positioned.

OIL PUMP. Models GV150 and GV200 are equipped with an internal oil pump located inside crankcase. All other models are splash lubricated.

Oil pump rotors may be removed and checked without disassembling the engine. Remove oil pump cover and withdraw outer and inner rotors. Remove "O" ring. Make certain oil passages are clear and pump body is thoroughly clean. Inner-to-outer rotor clearance should be 0.15 mm (0.006 in.). If clearance is 0.20 mm (0.008 in.) or more, renew rotors. Clearance between oil pump body and outer rotor diameter should be 0.15 mm (0.006 in.). If clearance is 0.26 mm (0.010 in.) or more,

renew rotors and/or oil pan. Outside diameter of outer rotor should be 23.15-23.28 mm (0.911-0.917 in.). If diameter is 23.23 mm (0.915 in.) or less, renew rotors.

Reverse disassembly procedure for reassembly and tighten oil pump cover bolts to specified torque.

VALVE SYSTEM. Clearance between valve stem and valve tappet (cold) should be 0.04-0.10 mm (0.002-0.004 in.) for intake and exhaust valves on Model G100; 0.04-0.12 mm (0.002-0.005 in.) for intake and exhaust valves on Models G150 (prior to serial number 1100543) and G200 (prior to serial number 1168820); 0.05-0.11 mm (0.002-0.004 in.) for intake valve and 0.09-0.15 mm (0.004-0.006 in.) for exhaust valve on Models G150 (serial number 1100543 to 1380694) and G200 (serial number 1168820 to 1556007); 0.08-0.16 mm (0.003-0.006 in.) for intake valve and 0.16-0.24 mm (0.006-0.009 in.) for exhaust valve on Models G150 (after serial number 1380694) and G200 (after serial number 1556007); or 0.05-0.11 mm (0.002-0.004 in.) for intake valve and 0.09-0.015 mm (0.004-0.006 in.) for exhaust valve on all GV200 models.

On all models, valve clearance is adjusted as follows: To increase valve clearance, grind off end of stem. To

reduce valve clearance, renew valve and/or grind valve seat deeper.

Valve face and seat angles are 45° for all models. Standard valve seat width is 0.42-0.78 mm (0.016-0.031 in.) for Model G100 while standard valve seat width is 0.7 mm (0.028 in.) for all other models. If valve seat width exceeds 1.0 mm (0.039 in.) for Model G100 or 2.0 mm (0.08 in.) for all other models, seats must be narrowed.

Standard valve stem diameters on Model G100 are 5.480-5.490 mm (0.2157-0.2161 in.) for intake valve stem and 5.435-5.445 mm (0.2140-0.2144 in.) for exhaust valve stem. If intake valve stem diameter is less than 5.450 mm (0.2146 in.) or exhaust valve stem diameter is less than 5.400 mm (0.2126 in.), renew valve.

Standard valve stem diameters on all models except Model G100 are 6.955-6.970 mm (0.2738-0.2744 in.) for intake valve stem and 6.910-6.925 mm (0.2720-0.2726 in.) for exhaust valve stem. If intake valve stem diameter is less than 6.805 mm (0.2679 in.) or exhaust valve stem diameter is less than 6.760 mm (0.2661 in.), renew valve.

Standard valve guide inside diameter for both intake and exhaust valve guides is 5.500-5.512 mm (0.2165-0.2170 in.) for Model G100 and 7.00-7.015 mm (0.2756-0.2762 in.) for all other models. If inside diameter of guide exceeds 5.560 mm (0.2189 in.) for Model G100 or 7.080 mm (0.2787 in.) for all other models, guides must be renewed.

To remove and install Model G100 valve guides, use Honda valve guide tool 07969-8960000 to pull guide out of guide bore and press new guide in. New guide is pressed in to a depth of 18 mm (0.7 in.) measured from end of guide to cylinder head surface as shown in section (F – Fig. HN14) at (X). Finish ream guide after installation with reamer 07984-2000000.

To remove and install valve guides on all models except Model G100, use the following procedure and refer to the sequence of illustrations in Fig. HN14. Use driver 07942-8230000 and drive valve guide down into valve chamber slightly (A). Use a suitable cold chisel and sever guide adjacent to guide bore (B). Cover tappet opening to prevent fragments from entering crankcase. Drive remaining piece of guide into valve chamber (C) and remove from chamber. Place new guide on driver and start guide into guide bore (D). Alternate between driving guide into bore and measuring guide depth below cylinder head surface (E). Guide is driven in to a depth of 27.5 mm (1.08 in.) measured from end of guide to cylinder head surface as shown in section (F) at (X). Finish ream guide after installation with reamer 07984-5900000.

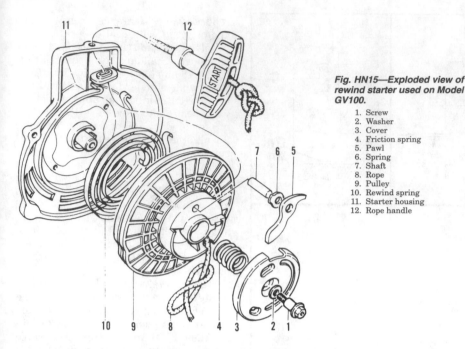

Fig. HN15—Exploded view of rewind starter used on Model GV100.

1. Screw
2. Washer
3. Cover
4. Friction spring
5. Pawl
6. Spring
7. Shaft
8. Rope
9. Pulley
10. Rewind spring
11. Starter housing
12. Rope handle

til notch aligns with rope outlet, and disengage rope from notch. Check starter operation.

When assembling starter used on models other than Model GV100 (Fig. HN16), install rewind spring on pulley so coil direction is counterclockwise from outer end. Wrap rope around pulley in counterclockwise direction viewed from flywheel side of pulley. Apply grease to side of rewind spring and pulley shaft, then install pulley in starter housing so end of spring engages notch on pulley, and route rope through rope outlet in housing. Attach rope handle. Apply grease to pawl shaft and friction plates (6 and 9). Install remainder of starter components. Convex sides of friction plates should be facing. Tighten center nut to 20-28 N.m (15-20 ft.-lbs.).

To place tension on starter rope, pull rope out of housing until notch in pulley is aligned with rope outlet, then hold pulley to prevent pulley rotation. Pull rope back into housing while positioning rope in pulley notch. Turn rope pulley counterclockwise until spring is tight, allow pulley to turn clockwise until notch aligns with rope outlet, and disengage rope from notch. Check starter operation.

REWIND STARTER. Model GV100 may be equipped with the rewind starter shown in Fig. HN15 while the starter shown in Fig. HN16 may be used on other models.

To disassemble starter, remove rope handle and allow rope to wind into starter. Remove pulley cover, if so equipped. Unscrew center retaining screw or nut. Wear appropriate safety eyewear and gloves before disengaging pulley from starter as spring may uncoil uncontrolled. Place shop towel around pulley and lift pulley out of housing. Use caution when detaching rewind spring from pulley or housing. If spring must be removed from pulley or housing, position pulley or housing so spring side is down and against floor.

Tap pulley or housing to dislodge spring.

When assembling starter used on Model GV100 (Fig. HN15), install rewind spring on pulley so coil direction is counterclockwise from outer end. Wrap rope around pulley in counterclockwise direction viewed from flywheel side of pulley. Apply grease to side of rewind spring, then install pulley in starter housing so end of spring engages notch on pulley, and route rope through rope outlet in housing. Apply grease to pawl shaft and install remainder of starter components.

To place tension on starter rope, pull rope out of housing until notch in pulley

is aligned with rope outlet, then hold pulley to prevent pulley rotation. Pull rope back into housing while positioning rope in pulley notch. Turn rope pulley counterclockwise until spring is tight, allow pulley to turn clockwise un-

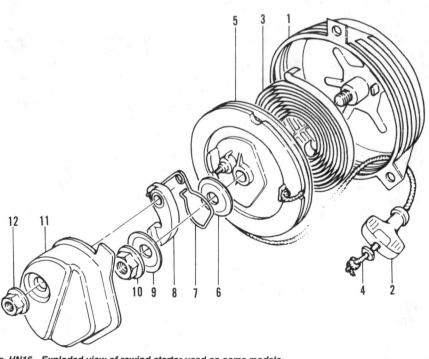

Fig. HN16—Exploded view of rewind starter used on some models.

1. Starter housing
2. Rope handle
3. Rewind spring
4. Rope
5. Pulley
6. Friction plate
7. Spring
8. Pawl
9. Friction plate
10. Nut
11. Cover
12. Nut

HONDA

Model	Bore	Stroke	Displacement
GX110	57 mm	42 mm	107 cc
	(2.2 in.)	(1.7 in.)	(6.6 cu. in.)
GX140	64 mm	45 mm	144 cc
	(2.5 in.)	(1.8 in.)	(8.8 cu. in.)
GX240	73 mm	58 mm	242 cc
	(2.9 in.)	(2.3 in.)	(14.8 cu. in.)
GXV120	60 mm	42 mm	118 cc
	(2.4 in.)	(1.7 in.)	(7.2 cu. in.)
GXV140	64 mm	42 mm	135 cc
	(2.5 in.)	(1.7 in.)	(8.2 cu. in.)
GXV160	68 mm	45 mm	163 cc
	(2.7 in.)	(1.8 in.)	(10.0 cu. in.)

ENGINE INFORMATION

All models are four-stroke, overhead valve, single-cylinder, air-cooled engines. Models GXV120, GXV140 and GXV160 are vertical crankshaft engines. All other models are horizontal crankshaft engines with the cylinder inclined 25 degrees.

Horsepower ratings at 3600 rpm are as follows: Model GX110—2.6 kW (3.5 hp); Model GX140—3.8 kW (5.0 hp); Model GX240—5.9 kW (8.0 hp); Model GXV120—2.9kW (4.0 hp); Model GXV140—3.3 kW (4.4 hp); Model GXV160—4.1 kW (5.5 hp).

Engine model number is cast into side of crankcase (Fig. HN30). Engine serial number is stamped into crankcase (Fig. HN31). Always furnish engine model and serial number when ordering parts.

MAINTENANCE

SPARK PLUG. Spark plug should be removed, cleaned and inspected after every 100 hours of use.

Recommended spark plug is a NGK BP5ES or ND W16EP-U. A resistor type spark plug may be required in some locations. Spark plug electrode gap should be 0.7-0.8 mm (0.028-0.031 inch) for all models.

When installing spark plug, manufacturer recommends installing spark plug finger tight, then for a new plug, tighten an additional 1/2 turn. For a used plug, tighten an additional 1/4 turn.

CARBURETOR. All models are equipped with a Keihin float type carburetor with a fixed main fuel jet and an adjustable low speed fuel mixture needle.

Initial adjustment of low speed fuel mixture screw (LS—Fig. HN32) from a lightly seated position is 3 turns open for Models GX110 and GXV120, 1-5/8 turns open for Model GX140, 2-1/2 turns open for Model GX240, 1-1/4 turn open for Model GXV140 (some California models require 1-3/4 turns) and 2 to 2-1/2 turns open for Model GXV160.

Adjust effective throttle cable length by loosening jam nuts and turning adjuster at handlebar end of cable. The choke should be fully open when throttle lever is in "CHOKE" position, and engine should stop when throttle lever is in "STOP" position.

For final adjustment engine must be at normal operating temperature and running. Operate engine at idle speed and adjust low speed mixture screw (LS) to obtain a smooth idle and satisfactory acceleration. Adjust idle speed by turning throttle stop screw (TS) to obtain idle speed of 1850-2150 rpm.

To check float level, remove fuel bowl and invert carburetor. Measure from top edge of float to fuel bowl mating edge of carburetor body. Measurement should be 13.7 mm (0.54 inch) on Model GXV140 and 12.2-15.2 mm (0.48-0.60 inch) for all other models. Renew float if float height is incorrect.

Standard main jet is #65 for Models GX110, GXV120 and GXV140, #68 for Model GX140 and #88 for Model GX240. Optional jet sizes are available for high altitude operation.

AIR CLEANER. Engine air filter should be cleaned and inspected after every 50 hours of operation, or more often if operating in extremely dusty conditions.

Remove foam and paper air filter elements from air filter housing. Foam element should be washed in a mild detergent and water solution, rinsed in

Fig. HN32—View of Keihin float type carburetor used on all models showing location of low speed mixture screw (LS) and throttle stop screw (TS).

Fig. HN30—Engine model number (MN) is cast into side of engine crankcase.

Fig. HN31— Engine serial number (SN) is stamped on raised portion of crankcase.

clean water and allowed to air dry. Soak foam element in clean engine oil. Squeeze out excess oil.

Paper element may be cleaned by directing low pressure compressed air stream from inside filter toward the outside. Reinstall elements.

FLYWHEEL BRAKE. Some models may be equipped with a flywheel brake that should stop the engine within three seconds after the safety handle is released. When the flywheel brake is activated, an engine stop switch grounds the ignition.

Be sure the flywheel brake operates properly. Check free play of operating handle at top of handle. Free play should be 5-10 mm (3/16 to 3/8 inch) for lawn mower Models HR194, HR214 and HRA214, and 20-25 mm (3/4 to 1 inch) for Models HR195, HR215, HRA215, HRC215 and HRC216. Loosen jam nuts and turn adjuster at handlebar end of control cable to adjust free play.

GOVERNOR. The mechanical flyweight type governor is located inside engine crankcase. To adjust external linkage, stop engine and make certain all linkage is in good condition and tension spring (5—Fig. HN33) is not stretched or damaged. Spring (2) must pull governor lever (3) and throttle pivot toward each other. Loosen clamp bolt (7) and move governor lever (3) so throttle is completely open. Hold governor lever in this position and rotate governor shaft (6) in the same direction until it stops. Tighten clamp bolt.

Start engine and operate at an idle until operating temperature has been reached. Attach a tachometer to engine and move throttle so engine is operating at maximum speed (3100 rpm for lawn mower). Adjust throttle stop screw (8) so throttle movement is limited to correct maximum engine rpm.

IGNITION SYSTEM. The breakerless ignition system requires no regular maintenance. Ignition coil unit is mounted outside the flywheel. Air gap between flywheel and coil should be 0.2-0.6 mm (0.008-0.024 inch).

To check ignition coil primary side, connect one ohmmeter lead to primary (black) coil lead and touch iron coil laminations with remaining lead. Ohmmeter should register 1.0-1.2 ohms on GXV120 and 0.7-0.9 ohm on other models.

To check ignition coil secondary side, connect one ohmmeter lead to the spark plug lead wire and remaining lead to the iron core laminations. Ohmmeter should read 10k-14k ohms on GXV120 and 6.3k-7.7k ohms on other models. If ohmmeter readings are not as specified, renew ignition coil.

VALVE ADJUSTMENT. Valve-to-rocker arm clearance should be checked and adjusted after every 300 hours of operation.

To adjust valve clearance, remove rocker arm cover. Rotate engine so piston is at top dead center (TDC) on compression stroke. Insert a feeler gage between rocker arm (3—Fig. HN34) and end of valve stem (4). Loosen rocker arm jam nut (1) and turn adjusting nut (2) to obtain desired clearance. Specified

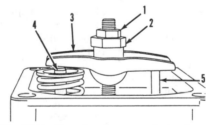

Fig. HN34—View of rocker arm and related parts.
1. Jam nut
2. Adjustment nut
3. Rocker arm
4. Valve stem clearance
5. Push rod

clearance for Model GXV120 is 0.10 mm (0.004 inch) for intake and 0.15 mm (0.006 inch) for exhaust. Specified clearance for Model GX240 is 0.10 mm (0.004 inch) for intake and 0.05 mm (0.002 inch) for exhaust. Clearance for all other models is 0.15 mm (0.006 inch) for intake and 0.20 mm (0.008 inch) for exhaust. Tighten jam nut and recheck clearance. Install rocker arm cover.

CYLINDER HEAD AND COMBUSTION CHAMBER. Manufacturer recommends removal of carbon and lead deposits from cylinder head combustion chamber, valves and valve seats after every 300 hours of operation. Refer to CYLINDER HEAD paragraph in REPAIRS section for service procedure.

LUBRICATION. Engine oil level should be checked prior to operating engine. Maintain oil level at top of reference marks (Fig. HN35) when checked with cap not screwed in, but just touching first threads.

Oil should be changed after the first 20 hours of engine operation and after every 100 hours thereafter.

Manufacturer recommends oil with an API service classification SE or SF. Use SAE ·10W-30 or 10W-40 oil; use SAE 10W-40 if temperature is above 32° C (90° F).

Crankcase capacity is 0.6 liter (0.63 quart) for all models except Model GX240. Crankcase capacity for Model GX240 is 1.1 liters (1.16 quarts).

REPAIRS

ENGINE REMOVAL. If engine must be separated from deck, refer to sections in this manual related to the self-propelled drive system and blade brake clutch.

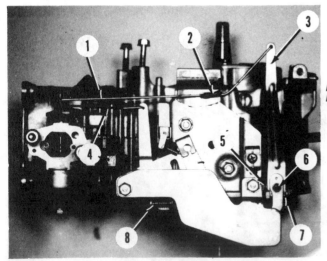

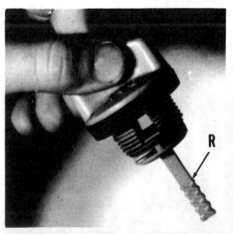

Fig. HN33—View of governor linkage.
1. Governor-to-carburetor rod
2. Spring
3. Governor lever
4. Choke rod
5. Tension spring (behind plate & lever)
6. Governor shaft
7. Clamp bolt
8. Throttle stop screw

Fig. HN35—Do not screw in dipstick plug when checking oil level. Maintain oil level at top edge of reference marks (R) on dipstick.

TIGHTENING TORQUES. Recommended tightening torque specifications are as follows:

Connecting rod:
Models GX110,
GX140, GXV120,
GXV140, GXV160 . . . . 12 N·m
(106 in.-lbs.)

Model GX240 serial
number 1000001-
1020232 . . . . 32-34 N·m
(16-19 ft.-lbs.)

Model GX240 after
serial number
1020232 . . . . 12-16 N·m
(106-141 in.-lbs.)

Crankcase cover . . . . 22-26 N·m
(16-19 ft.-lbs.)

Cylinder head:
Models GX110,
GX140, GXV120,
GXV140, GXV160 . . . . 24 N·m
(18 ft.-lbs.)

Model GX240 . . . . 32-38 N·m
(23-27 ft.-lbs.)

Flywheel nut:
Models GX110,
GX140, GXV120,
GXV140, GXV160 . . . . 75 N·m
(55 ft.-lbs.)

Model GX240 . . . . 110-120 N·m
(80-86 ft.-lbs.)

Oil drain plug . . . . 18 N·m
(160 in.-lbs.)

Oil pan . . . . 12 N·m
(106 in.-lbs.)

Rocker arm cover . . . . 8-12 N·m
(71-106 in.-lbs.)

Rocker arm jam nut . . . . . . 8-12 N·m
(71-106 in.-lbs.)

CYLINDER HEAD. To remove cylinder head, remove blower shroud. Disconnect carburetor linkage and remove carburetor. Remove heat shield and muffler. Remove rocker arm cover and the four head bolts. Remove cylinder head. Use care not to lose push rods.

Remove rocker arms, compress valve springs and remove valve retainers. Note exhaust valve on Models GX110, GX140 and GX240 is equipped with a valve rotator on valve stem. Remove valves and springs. Remove push rod guide plate if necessary.

Valve face and seat angles are 45 degrees. Standard valve seat width is 0.8 mm (0.032 inch). Narrow seat if seat width is 2.0 mm (0.079 inch) or more.

Standard valve spring free length for Model GX240 is 39.0 mm (1.54 inches). Renew valve spring if free length is 37.5 mm (1.48 inches) or less. Standard valve spring free length for all other models is 34.0 mm (1.339 inches). Renew valve spring if free length is 32.5 mm (1.280 inches) or less.

Standard valve guide inside diameter for Model GX240 is 6.60 mm (0.260 inch). Renew guide if inside diameter is 6.66 mm (0.262 inch) or more. Standard valve guide inside diameter for all other models is 5.50-5.51 mm (0.2165-0.2170 inch). Renew guide if inside diameter is 5.562 mm (0.219 inch) or more.

Valve stem-to-guide clearance for all models except Model GX240 should be 0.02-0.04 mm (0.0008-0.0016 inch) for intake valve and 0.06-0.09 mm (0.0024-0.0035 inch) for exhaust valve. Renew valve and/or guide if clearance is 0.10 mm (0.004 inch) or more for intake valve or 0.12 mm (0.005 inch) or more for exhaust valve.

Valve stem-to-guide clearance for Model GX240 should be 0.010-0.037 mm (0.0004-0.0015 inch) for intake valve and 0.050-0.077 mm (0.002-0.003 inch) for exhaust valve. Renew valve and/or guide if clearance is 0.10 mm (0.004 inch) or more for intake valve or 0.12 mm (0.005 inch) or more for exhaust valve.

To renew valve guide on all models except Model GX240, heat entire cylinder head to 150° C (300° F) and use valve guide driver 07942-8920000 to remove and install guides. DO NOT heat head above recommended temperature as valve seats may loosen. Drive guides out toward rocker arm end of head. Note if exhaust valve guide has a locating clip around the top. If there is NO clip, drive guides into cylinder head until distance from end of guide to cylinder head mounting surface is 23.0 mm (0.905 inch) for Models GX110 and GXV120 or 25.5 mm (1.004 inch) for Models GX140, GXV140 and GXV160. If there is a clip around the exhaust valve guide, drive in the exhaust valve guide so the clip (C—Fig. HN36) is bottomed in the head, and drive in the intake valve guide so the top of the guide (S) stands 3.0 mm (0.12 inch) above the cylinder head boss. On all models, new valve guides must be reamed after installation to obtain specified valve stem clearance.

To renew valve guide on Model GX240, heat entire cylinder head to

150° C (300° F) and use valve guide driver 07942-6570100 to remove and install guides. Drive guides into cylinder head until top of intake valve guide is 9.0 mm (0.35 inch) from top of valve guide bore and exhaust valve guide is 7.0 mm (0.28 inch) from top of valve guide bore. New valve guides must be reamed after installation.

When installing cylinder head on all models, tighten head bolts to specified torque following sequence shown in Fig. HN37. Adjust valves as outlined in VALVE ADJUSTMENT paragraph.

CAMSHAFT. Camshaft and camshaft gear are an integral casting equipped with a compression release mechanism (Fig. HN38). To remove camshaft, first remove engine from equipment. Remove crankcase cover or oil pan. Rotate crankshaft so piston is at top dead center on compression stroke. Withdraw camshaft from crankcase.

Standard camshaft bearing journal diameter for Models GX110, GX120, GX140, GX160, GXV120, GXV140 and GXV160 is 13.984 mm (0.5506 in.). Renew camshaft if journal diameter is 13.916 mm (0.5479 in.) or less.

Standard camshaft lobe height (Fig. HN39) for all models is 27.7 mm (1.091 in.) for intake lobe and 27.75 mm (1.093 in.) for exhaust lobe. If intake lobe measures 27.45 mm (1.081 in.) or less, or exhaust lobe measures 27.50 mm (1.083 in.) or less, renew camshaft.

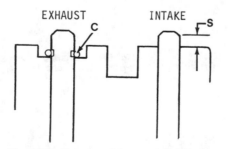

Fig. HN36—Some models are equipped with a locating clip (C) around the top of the exhaust valve guide. On these models, install intake valve guide so standout (S) above cylinder head boss is 3.0 mm (0.12 inch).

Fig. HN37—Tighten cylinder head bolts in sequence shown.

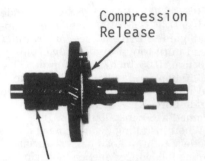

Fig. HN38—Camshaft and gear are an integral casting equipped with a compression release mechanism. Camshaft shown is for models with an auxiliary drive shaft.

Fig. HN40—Compression release mechanism spring (1) and weight (2) installed on camshaft gear.

Model	Piston Diameter
GX110	56.965-56.985 mm (2.2427-2.2435 in.)
Wear limit	56.55 mm (2.226 in.)
GX120	59.985 mm (2.3616 in.)
Wear limit	59.845 mm (2.3561 in.)
GX140	63.985 mm (2.5191 in.)
Wear limit	63.815 mm (2.5124 in.)
GX160	67.985 mm (2.6766 in.)
Wear limit	67.845 mm (2.6711 in.)
GXV120	59.985 mm (2.3616 in.)
Wear limit	59.845 mm (2.3561 in.)

Inspect compression release mechanism (Fig. HN40) for damage. Spring must pull weight tightly against camshaft so decompressor lobe holds exhaust valve slightly open. Weight overcomes spring tension at 1000 rpm and moves decompressor lobe away from cam lobe to release exhaust valve.

When installing camshaft, make certain camshaft and crankshaft gear timing marks are aligned as shown in Fig. HN41.

PISTON, PIN AND RINGS. Piston and connecting rod are removed as an assembly. To remove piston and connecting rod, remove cylinder head, crankcase cover or oil pan, and camshaft. Remove connecting rod cap screws and cap. Push connecting rod and piston assembly out of cylinder. Remove piston pin retaining rings and separate piston from connecting rod.

Standard piston diameter measured 10 mm (0.4 in.) from lower edge of skirt and 90° from piston pin is listed in the following table:

Fig. HN41—Align crankshaft gear and camshaft gear timing marks (F) during installation.

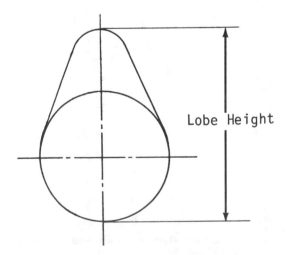

Fig. HN39—Drawing showing camshaft lobe height measurement.

GXV140	63.985 mm (2.5191 in.)
Wear limit	63.815 mm (2.5124 in.)
GXV160	67.985 mm (2.6766 in.)
Wear limit	67.845 mm (2.6711 in.)

Standard piston pin bore diameter in piston is 13.002 mm (0.5119 in.) for Models GX110, GX120 and GXV120, and 18.002 mm (0.7087 in.) for remaining models. Renew piston if diameter exceeds 13.048 mm (0.5137 in.) on Models GX110, GX120 and GXV120, or 18.048 mm (0.7105 in.) on remaining models.

Standard piston pin diameter is 13.000 mm (0.5118 in.) for Models

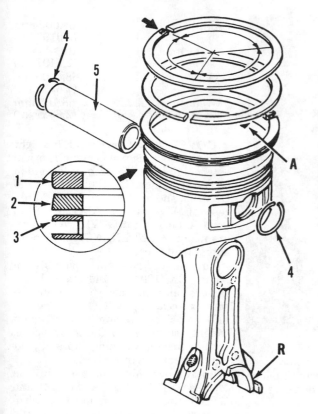

Fig. HN42—View of rod and piston assembly. Long side of connection rod (R) and arrowhead (A) on piston crown must be on the same side. Install piston ring with marked side toward piston crown.

1. Top ring (chrome plated)
2. Second ring (tapered face)
3. Oil control ring
4. Retaining rings
5. Piston pin

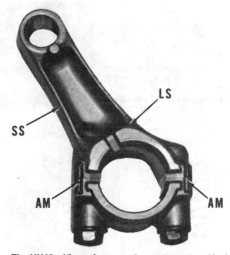

Fig. HN43—View of connecting rod used on Models GXV120, GXV140 and GXV160. Models GX110, GX140 and GX240 are equipped with an oil dipper on connecting rod cap.

GX110, GX120 and GXV120, and 18.000 mm (0.7087 in.) for remaining models.

For Models GX110, GX120 and GXV120, renew piston pin if diameter is 12.954 mm (0.510 in.) or less. For Models GX140, GX160, GXV140 and GXV160, renew piston pin if piston pin diameter is 17.954 mm (0.7068 in.) or less. Standard clearance between piston pin and pin bore in piston is 0.002-0.014 mm (0.0001-0.0006 in.) for all models. If clearance is 0.08 mm (0.003 in.) or greater, renew piston and/or pin.

Ring side clearance in piston ring groove should be 0.030-0.065 mm (0.0012-0.0026 in.) on Model GXV160 and 0.015-0.045 mm (0.0006-0.0018 in.) on all other models. Ring end gap for compression rings on all models should be 0.2-0.4 mm (0.008-0.016 in.). Ring end gap for oil control ring on all models should be 0.15-0.35 mm (0.006-0.014 in.). If ring end gap for any ring is 1.0 mm (0.039 in.) or more, renew ring and/or cylinder. Oversize piston rings are available for some models.

Refer to Fig. HN42 for correct installation of piston rings. Note that top ring is chrome plated and that second ring has a tapered face. Install marked piston rings with marked side toward piston crown and stagger ring end gaps equally around piston as shown in Fig. HN42. Lubricate piston and rings with engine oil prior to installation.

When reassembling piston on connecting rod, long side of connecting rod (R) and arrowhead (A) on piston crown must be on the same side as shown in Fig. HN42.

When installing piston pin retaining rings, do not align the end gap of the ring with the cutout in the piston pin bore.

When reinstalling piston and connecting rod assembly in cylinder, arrowhead on piston crown must be on camshaft side of engine. Align connecting rod cap and connecting rod match marks (AM--Fig. HN43), install connecting rod bolts and tighten to specified torque.

CONNECTING ROD. The aluminum alloy connecting rod rides directly on crankpin journal on all models. Connecting rod cap for all horizontal crankshaft models is equipped with an oil dipper. There is no dipper on vertical crankshaft models (Fig. HN43).

Refer to previous PISTON, PIN AND RINGS section for removal and installation procedure.

Standard piston pin bore diameter in connecting rod is 13.005 mm (0.512 in.) for Models GX110, GX120 and GXV120, 18.002 mm (0.7087 in.) for Models GX140, GX160 and GXV140, and 18.005 mm (0.7089 in.) for Model GXV160. Renew connecting rod if diameter exceeds 13.07 mm (0.515 in.) on Models GX110, GX120 and GXV120, or 18.07 mm (0.711 in.) on Models GX140, GX160, GXV140, GXV160 or GX240.

Standard connecting rod bearing bore-to-crankpin clearance is 0.040-0.063 mm (0.0015-0.0025 in.) for all models. Renew connecting rod and/or crankshaft if clearance is 0.12 mm (0.0047 in.) or more. An undersize connecting rod is available for some models.

Connecting rod side play on crankpin should be 0.1-0.7 mm (0.004-0.028 in.) for all models. Renew connecting rod if side play is 1.1 mm (0.043 in.) or more.

Standard connecting rod big end diameter is 26.02 mm (1.0244 in.) for Models GX110, GX120 and GXV120, 30.02 mm (1.1819 in.) for Models GX140, GX160, GXV140 and GXV160. Renew connecting rod if big end diameter exceeds 26.066 mm (1.0262 in.) on Models GX110, GX120 and GXV120, 30.066 mm (1.1837 in.) on Models GX140, GX160, GXV140 and GXV160.

CRANKSHAFT, MAIN BEARINGS AND SEALS. Crankshaft for Models GX110, Gx120, GX140 and GX160 is supported at each end in ball bearing type main bearings. Crankshaft for Models GXV120, GXV140 and GXV160 is supported at flywheel end in a ball bearing main bearing and at pto end in a bushing type main bearing that is an integral part of the oil pan casting.

To remove crankshaft, first remove engine from equipment. Remove blower housing, flywheel, cylinder head, crankcase cover or oil pan, camshaft, connecting rod and piston assembly. Withdraw crankshaft from crankcase.

Fig. HN44—Governor assembly on Models GXV120, GXV140 and GXV160 is mounted in crankcase cover. Refer to Fig. HN45 also. Governor assembly for all other models is similar except assembly is located in crankcase.

G. Auxiliary drive gear
P. Retaining hair pin
W. Thrust washers
1. Bolt
2. Governor gear
3. Weight
4. Governor gear shaft
5. Crankcase cover
6. Auxiliary drive shaft.

GXV140	64.000 mm
	(2.5197 in.)
Wear limit	64.165 mm
	(2.5197 in.)
GXV160	68.000 mm
	(2.6772 in.)
Wear limit	68.165 mm
	(2.6837 in.)

GOVERNOR. Centrifugal flyweight type governor controls engine rpm via external linkage. Governor is located in oil pan on Models GXV120, GXV140 and GXV160, and on flywheel side of crankcase on Models GX110, GX120, GX140 and GX160. Refer to GOVERNOR paragraphs in MAINTENANCE section for adjustment procedure.

To remove governor assembly on Models GXV120, GXV140 and GXV160, remove oil pan. Remove governor assembly retaining bolt (1--Fig. HN44) and remove governor gear (2) and weight assembly (3). Governor sleeve, thrust washer, retaining clip and gear may be removed from shaft.

To remove governor assembly on Models GX110, GX120, And GX140 and GX160, the crankshaft must be withdrawn. Remove governor sleeve and washer. Remove retaining clip for governor gear shaft, then remove gear and weight assembly and remaining thrust washer.

Reinstall governor assemblies by reversing removal procedure. Adjust external linkage as outlined under GOVERNOR in MAINTENANCE section.

AUXILIARY DRIVE. Models GXV120, GXV140 and GXV160 may be equipped with an auxiliary drive. The auxiliary drive shaft (Fig. HN44 and HN45) is mounted in crankcase cover and driven by a gear which is an integral part of the camshaft.

Drive shaft is retained in crankcase cover by retaining pin (P--Fig. HN44). When reassembling, carefully slide

Standard crankpin journal diameter is 25.98 mm (1.023 in.) for Models GX110, GX120 and GXV120; 29.980 mm (1.1803 in.) for Models GX140, GXV140 and GXV160. Renew crankshaft if crankpin diameter is 25.92 mm (1.178 in.) or less for Models GX110, GX120 and GXV120. Renew crankshaft if crankpin diameter is 29.92 mm (1.178) or less for Models GX140, GX160, GXV140 or GXV160. On some models an undersize connecting rod is available to fit a reground crankshaft.

On some models, the timing gear is a press fit on the crankshaft. Prior to removal of timing gear, mark position of gear on crankshaft using the timing mark on the gear as a reference point. Transfer marks to new timing gear so it can be installed in same position as old gear.

Ball bearing type main bearings are a press fit on crankshaft journals and in bearing bores of crankcase and cover.

Renew bearings if loose, rough or fit loosely on crankshaft or in bearing bores.

Bushing type bearing in crankcase cover of vertical crankshaft models in an integral part of oil pan. Renew crankcase cover if bearing is worn, scored or damaged.

Seals should be pressed into seal bores until outer edge of seal is flush with seal bore.

When installing crankshaft, make certain crankshaft gear and camshaft gear timing marks are aligned as shown in Fig. HN41.

CYLINDER AND CRANKCASE. Cylinder and crankcase are an integral casting. Refer to following table for standard cylinder bore size and wear limit. Bore cylinder for oversize piston or renew cylinder if cylinder bore exceeds wear limit.

Model	Cylinder Diameter
GX110	57.000-257.015 mm
	(2.2441-2.2447 in.)
Wear limit.	57.165 mm
	(2.2506 in.)
GX120	60.000 mm
	(2.3622 in.)
Wear limit.	60.165 mm
	(2.3687 in.)
GX140	64.000 mm
	(2.5197 in.)
Wear limit.	64.165 mm
	(2.5162 in.)
GX160	68.000 in.
	(2.6772 in.)
Wear limit.	68.165 mm
	(2.6837 in.)
GXV120	60.000 mm
	(2.3622 in.)
Wear limit.	60.165 mm
	(2.3687 in.)

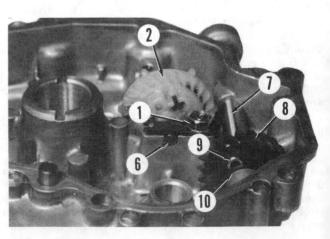

Fig. HN45—Auxiliary drive shaft is mounted in crankcase cover and driven by a gear which is an integral part of camshaft. See Fig. HN38.

1. Bolt
2. Governor gear
6. Governor gear shaft
7. Auxiliary drive shaft
8. Auxiliary drive gear
9. Retaining hair pin
10. Thrust washer

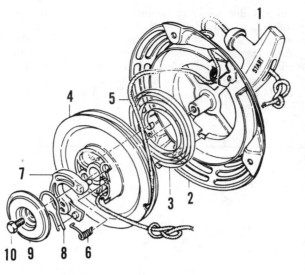

Fig. HN46—Exploded view of single-pawl rewind starter used on some engines.

1. Rope handle
2. Starter housing
3. Rewind spring
4. Pulley
5. Rope
6. Spring
7. Pawl
8. Friction spring
9. Friction plate
10. Screw

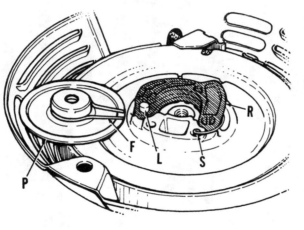

Fig. HN47—View of rewind starter showing correct installation of pawl (R) and spring (S). Install spring (F) in groove of friction plate (P). Ends of spring must fit around lug (L) on pawl.

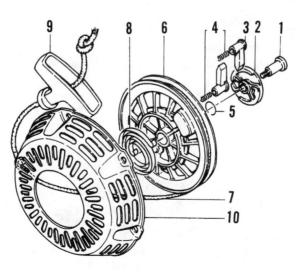

Fig. HN48—Exploded view of dual-pawl rewind starter used on some engines.

1. Screw
2. Retainer
3. Pawl
4. Friction spring
5. Snap ring
6. Pulley
7. Rope
8. Rewind spring
9. Rope handle
10. Starter housing

drive shaft through cover oil seal, thrust washer, gear and remaining thrust washer. Insert retaining hairpin in hole in drive shaft so it is located between gear (G) and outer thrust washer (W).

REWIND STARTER. The engine may be equipped with the rewind starter shown in Fig. HN46 or HN48. To disassemble starter remove rope handle and allow rope to wind into starter. Un-

screw center retaining screw. Wear appropriate safety eyewear and gloves before disengaging pulley from starter as spring may uncoil uncontrolled.

Place shop towel around pulley and lift pulley out of housing. Use caution when detaching rewind spring from pulley or housing. If spring must be removed from housing, position housing so spring side is down and against floor, then tap housing to dislodge spring.

On both types of starter, apply light grease to pulley shaft and sliding surfaces of rewind spring, pawls and friction spring.

On single-pawl starter (Fig. HN46), install rewind spring (3) so outer end engages starter housing notch and coils are in counterclockwise direction from outer end. Wrap rope around pulley in counterclockwise direction viewed from flywheel side of pulley. Install pulley in starter housing so inner end of spring engages notch on pulley and route rope through rope outlet in housing. Attach rope handle. Install pawl as shown in Fig. HN47 and hook outer end of pawl spring (S) under pawl. Apply a light coat of grease to friction spring (F) and install spring in groove of friction plate (P). Install friction plate so the two ends of friction spring fit around lug (L) on pawl. Install center screw (10—Fig. HN46). Pretension rewind spring by turning pulley two turns counterclockwise before passing rope through rope outlet of housing and attaching handle.

On dual-pawl starter (Fig. HN48), wrap rope around pulley in counterclockwise direction viewed from flywheel side of pulley. Install rewind spring (8) in spring cavity in pulley in a counterclockwise direction from outer end. Install pulley in starter housing so inner end of spring engages tab on starter housing and route rope through rope outlet in housing. Attach rope handle. Install snap ring (5) on shaft. Install springs (4), pawls (3), retainer (2) and screw (1).

To place tension on starter rope, pull rope out of housing until notch in pulley is aligned with rope outlet, then hold pulley to prevent pulley rotation. Pull rope back into housing while positioning rope in pulley notch. Turn rope pulley two turns counterclockwise, disengage rope from notch and allow rope to wind onto pulley. Check starter operation.

ELECTRIC STARTER. Some engines may be equipped with a 12 volt DC starter.

Test specifications for electric starter on Models GXV120 are: under load at more than 320 rpm and with a cranking voltage of 10.8 volts DC, the current draw should be less than 30 amps; under no load with a cranking voltage of 11.7 volts DC, the current draw should be less than 15 amps.

Test specifications for electric starter on Models GX120 and GX160 are: under load at more than 474 rpm and with a cranking voltage of 10.24 volts DC, the current draw should be less than 50 amps; under no load with a cranking voltage of 11.4 volts DC, the current draw should be less than 25 amps. Minimum brush length is 6 mm (0.24 in.).

Test specifications for electric starter on Models GXV120 and GXV160 are: under load at more than 367 rpm and with a cranking voltage of 9.8 volts DC, the current draw should be less than 150 amps; under no load with a cranking voltage of 11.0 volts DC, the current draw should be less than 18 amps. Minimum brush length is 6 mm (0.24 in.).

JACOBSEN

Model	Bore	Stroke	Displacement
J-125	2.00 in.	1.50 in.	4.7 cu. in.
	(50.8 mm)	(38.1 mm)	(77 cc)
J-175	2.125 in.	1.75 in.	6.2 cu. in.
	(54.0 mm)	(44.5 mm)	(102 cc)
J-225	2.25 in.	2.00 in.	8.0 cu. in.
	(57.2 mm)	(50.8 mm)	(131 cc)
J-321	2.125 in.	1.75 in.	6.2 cu. in.
	(54.0 mm)	(44.5 mm)	(102 cc)
J-501	2.125 in.	1.75 in.	6.2 cu. in.
	(54.0 mm)	(44.5 mm)	(102 cc)

ENGINE INFORMATION

All models are two-stroke, air-cooled engines. Models with letter "V" suffix have vertical crankshafts. Models with letter "H" suffix have horizontal crankshafts.

MAINTENANCE

SPARK PLUG. Refer to the following chart for recommended Champion spark plug.

J-125, rotary mower J12J
J-125, reel mower UJ12
J-175, rotary mower J8J
J-225, rotary mower J8J
J-321 & J-501, rotary mower . . . J-17LM
J-321 & J-501, reel mower* UJ12
*For short spark plug, use TJ8.

Set electrode gap to 0.030 inch (0.76 mm) for all models and applications.

CARBURETOR. Tillotson MT58A carburetor is used on Model J-125, Tillotson MT59A carburetor is used on Model J-175, Tillotson MT54A carburetor is used on Model J-225 and either a Walbro LMB or LMG carburetor is used on Models J-321 and J-501. Refer to appropriate paragraph for model being serviced.

Tillotson Carburetors. Initial adjustment of fuel mixture screws from a lightly seated position, is 1 turn open for idle mixture screw (23 – Fig. JAC8) and 1¼ turns open for main fuel mixture screw (26).

Make final adjustments with engine at operating temperature and running. Operate engine at ½ throttle and turn main fuel adjustment screw in until engine loses speed. Turn main fuel screw counterclockwise until maximum rpm is obtained. Operate engine just above idle speed. Turn idle mixture screw in until engine loses speed and misses, then back screw out until engine is idling smoothly. Set idle speed as listed in chart (Fig. JAC7) for model and application by adjusting idle speed screw (18).

Carburetor inlet needle is spring loaded. Float setting is 1/16 to 3/32 inch

Engine Application	Engine RPM Idle Speed	Top Speed
9" Edge-R-Trim (32A9, 32B9 & 32C9)	1500-2000	3000-3300
9" Edge-R-Trim (50012)	1500-1800	Up to 3600
10" Trimo (3110-8610, 86A & 86B)	1500-2000	3400-3600
10" Trimo (50035) .		3500-3700
18" Pacer (52C18, 42D18 & 42E-18)	1300-1600	3500 max.
18" Pacer (11814) .	1500-1800	Up to 3600
18" Turbo-Cut (3418, 34B18, 34C18 & 34D18)	1300-1800	3400-3500
18" Turbo-Cut (7518, 75A18 & 75B18)	1500-2000	3400-3500
18" Turbo-Vac (31817)	1500-1800	3200-3400
18" Turbo-Vac (31819)*	1500-1800	3200-3400
18" Turbo-Vac (31819)	2400-2600	3200-3400
18" 4-Blade Rotary (31809)	2400-2600	3200-3400
18" Turbo Cone (117-18)	1500-1600	3200-3400
20" Scepter (8020 & 80A20)	1500-1800	3000-3200
20" Commercial Rotary (35025) . .	1500-1600	3200-3400
20" Commercial Rotary (32028) . .	2400-2600	3200-3400
20" Commercial Rotary (32028)* .	1500-1600	3200-3400
20" Robust (32031)	1500-1700	3200-3400
20" Snow Jet (9620 & 96A20)	1500-1800	3600-3800
20" Snow Jet (52002, 52003) . .	1700-1900	3600-3800
21" 4-Blade Rotary (32114)	2400-2600	3200-3400
21" 4-Blade Rotary S.P. (42114, 42118, 42119) . . .	2400-2600	3200-3400

*Speed control on handle.

Engine Application	Engine RPM Idle Speed	Top Speed
21" Turbo-Cut (3921, 39B21 & 39C21)	1500-1800	3200-3400
21" Turbo Cone (119-21)	1500-1600	3200-3400
21" Turbo-Cut (3521, 35C21, 35D21, 35E21 & 35F21)	1500-1800	3500 max.
21" Turbo Cone (121-21)	1500-1600	3200-3400
21" Lawn Queen (2C21, 2D21 & 2E21)	1300-1600	3500 max.
21" Lawn Queen (12113)	1500-1800	Up to 3600
21" Manor (28F21 & 28G21)	1300-1600	3500 max.
21" Manor (22114, 32121-7B1)	1500-1800	Up to 3600
22" Putting Green (9A22 & 9B22) . .	1500-1800	3400 max.
22" Greensmower (62203, 62208) . .	1500-1800	Up to 3800
22" Scepter (8022 & 80A22)	1500-1800	3000-3200
24" Estate (8A24 & 8B24)	1300-1600	3800 max.
24" Rotary S. P. (40A24)	1900-2100	3000 max.
26" Estate (8A26, 8B26, 8C26 & 8D26)	1300-1600	3800 max.
26" Estate R.R. (22601, 22605-7B1)	1500-1800	Up to 3800
26" Estate F.R. (22611, 22615-7B1)	1500-1800	Up to 3800
26" Lawn King (12A26 & 12B26)	1300-1600	3200 max.
26" Lawn King (12601)	1500-1800	Up to 3800

*Speed control on handle.

Fig. JAC7—Chart showing engine idle and top speed for various engine applications. Refer to text.

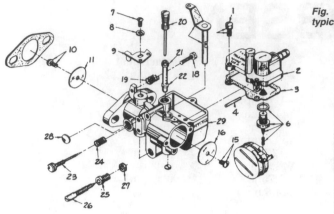

Fig. JAC8—Exploded view of typical Tillotson carburetor.

Fig. JAC8—Exploded view of typical Tillotson carburetor.

1. Screw & lockwasher
2. Bowl cover
3. Gasket
4. Lever pin
6. Inlet needle assy.
9. Throttle stop lever
10. Shutter screw
11. Throttle shutter
15. Shutter screw
16. Choke shutter
18. Idle speed screw
19. Spring
20. Idle tube
21. Main nozzle
22. Gasket
23. Idle mixture screw
24. Spring
25. Packing nut
26. Main adjusting screw
27. Packing
28. Welch plug
29. Carburetor body

engine begins to lose speed, then turn idle fuel screw counterclockwise 1/8 to 1/4 turn. Engine will have a slight "stutter" or intermittent exhaust sound at both idle and high speed when fuel mixture adjustments are correct.

Idle speed is controlled by proper adjustment of the governor rather than by adjustment of the idle speed stop screw on carburetor throttle. This is to prevent engine stalling when traction and/or reel clutch is engaged with engine at idle speed. Refer to GOVERNOR section.

To check float setting on Walbro carburetor, invert the body casting and float level should be 5/32 inch (3.97mm)

(1.59-2.38 mm) from bowl cover flange to top of float with bowl cover assembly inverted and float resting lightly on inlet needle. Refer to Fig. JAC9. Float level should be 5/16 inch (7.94 mm) if a plastic float is used. Bend tab on float if necessary to obtain correct setting.

Walbro Carburetor. Refer to Figs. JAC10, JAC11 and JAC12 for exploded view of typical Walbro carburetors used on J-321 and J-501 models.

Walbro carburetor shown in Fig. JAC12 does not have adjustable idle or main fuel orifices. Note some carburetors shown in Fig. JAC10 or JAC11 are not equipped with an idle mixture adjusting screw. Refer to the following paragraphs for carburetor adjustments on carburetors equipped with idle adjusting screw and/or main fuel mixture screw.

For initial adjustment, open the idle and/or main fuel adjustment screw 1 to 1¼ turns from a lightly seated position. Make final adjustments with engine at operating temperature and running at "FAST" throttle position. Slowly turn main fuel mixture screw clockwise until engine begins to lose speed, then turn the main screw counterclockwise 1/8 to 1/4 turn. Move throttle to "IDLE" position and slowly turn idle fuel screw on carburetors so equipped, clockwise until

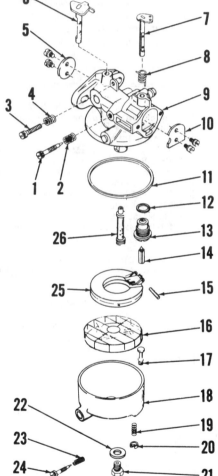

Fig. JAC10—Exploded view of Walbro series LMB float carburetor used on some J-321 and J-501 models. Note the fuel bowl screen (16) used on this type carburetor.

1. Idle fuel needle
2. Spring
3. Idle speed screw
4. Spring
5. Throttle plate
6. Throttle shaft
7. Choke shaft
8. Choke return spring
9. Carburetor body
10. Choke plate
11. Gasket
12. Gasket
13. Inlet valve seat
14. Inlet valve
15. Float pin
16. Fuel bowl screen
17. Drain valve
18. Fuel bowl
19. Spring
20. Retainer
21. Bowl retainer
22. Gasket
23. Spring
24. Main fuel nozzle
25. Float
26. Main nozzle

Fig. JAC11—Exploded view of typical Walbro series LMG carburetor used on some Model J-321 and J-501 engines.

2. Main fuel nozzle
3. Spring
4. Seals
5. Bowl retainer
6. Washer
7. Adapter
8. Seal
9. Washer
10. Float bowl
11. Gasket
12. Retainer
13. Spring
14. Drain valve
15. Gasket
16. Float pin
17. Float
18. Main nozzle
19. Inlet valve
21. Gasket
22. Idle fuel needle
23. Spring
24. Idle stop screw
25. Spring
27. Throttle plate
28. Throttle shaft
30. Choke plate
31. Choke shaft
32. Choke spring
33. Carburetor body

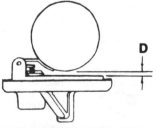

Fig. JAC9—Distance (D) between bowl cover flange and nearest edge of float with bowl cover assembly inverted should be 1/16 to 3/32 inch (1.59-2.38 mm).

Illustrations Courtesy of Jacobsen Div. of Textron, Inc

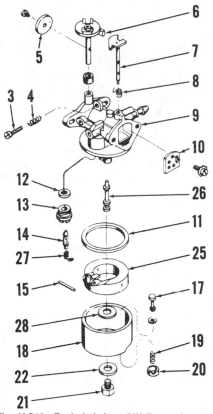

Fig. JAC12—Exploded view of Walbro carburetor with fixed idle and main fuel jets. Refer to Fig. JAC10 for parts identification except for retainer (27) and gasket (28).

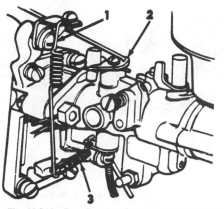

Fig. JAC14—Drawing showing correct installation of Tillotson carburetor control. Refer to text.

measured between carburetor body casting and free side of float. On carburetor with fixed main fuel orifice, float level should be 1/16-3/32 inch (1.59-2.38 mm). Adjust clearance by bending tab on float which contacts fuel inlet needle on all models.

Check float free travel. Float should have 3/16 inch (4.76 mm) of free movement. Adjust free travel by bending tab on float which contacts float stop.

Fixed main fuel orifice on carburetors so equipped, may be cleaned with a #63 drill bit. Be careful not to damage orifice during cleaning.

GOVERNOR. Speed control on all models is maintained by a pneumatic (air vane) type governor. The air vane which is linked directly to the carburetor upper throttle lever is actuated by air from the flywheel fan. Make certain the linkage does not bind in any position when moved through the full range of travel.

To adjust governor linkage, refer to chart (Fig. JAC7) for recommended idle and top speed for various engine applications and refer to appropriate paragraphs for model being serviced.

Models J-321 And J-501 With Fixed Speed. Governor adjustment on models with fixed governed speed is accomplished by turning governor adjustment screw shown in Fig. JAC13. Turning adjustment screw provides adjustment range of approximately 400 rpm. Refer to recommended governor speeds.

Governor Adjustments With Tillotson Carburetor. With engine stopped,

close the throttle control lever. The upper throttle shaft lever (2–Fig. JAC14) should be in the ½ open position. If not in this position, bend the balance spring (1) at upper end until the desired position is obtained. The lower throttle shaft lever is connected to the governor balance spring (1) by a small antisurge spring (3). Correct spring (3) installation is accomplished by hooking one end into the inner hole of the lower throttle shaft lever from the top side. Hook the other end into the governor balance spring loop so it is underneath the throttle lever link.

Governor Adjustment With Remote Control Walbro Carburetor. Set the throttle control to "FAST" position. The hook in the choke lever (link) should just touch the first loop in choke spring, or clear the first loop by 1/16 inch (1.59 mm) as shown in Fig. JAC15. If choke is partially closed, or clearance between hook in link and loop in spring exceeds 1/16 inch (1.59 mm), loosen the engine control cable clamp. Slide cable back or forward until choke control lever (link) just touches the loop in choke spring, then tighten the control cable clamp. Test setting by moving control to "STOP" position. The carburetor control lever should touch the contact point of "STOP" switch. Move the control to "CHOKE (START)" position. Carburetor choke should be completely closed.

MAGNETO AND TIMING. Model J-321 may be equipped with a breakerless ignition system. All other models are equipped with a flywheel magneto ignition system with breaker points. Refer to appropriate section for model being serviced.

Breakerless Ignition System. A Blaser ignition system is used on some engines and is identified by use of a

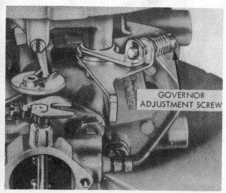

Fig. JAC13—View of governor adjustment screw on Model J-321 or J-501 engine.

Fig. JAC15—Drawing showing correct installation of Walbro carburetor controls. Refer to text.

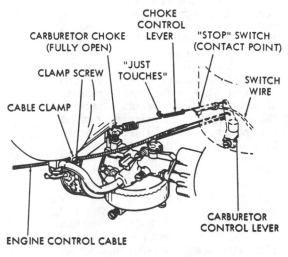

FAST (HIGH SPEED) POSITION

CHARGING COIL &
ELECTRONICS GROUP

D

TRIGGER
COIL
1

BOTTOM

A

B

TOP

C

HIGH
TENSION
COIL

TRIGGER COIL 2

Fig. JAC16—Top and bottom views of CD ignition system used on some J-321 engines.

D

EARLY PRODUCTION

D

LATE PRODUCTION

Fig. JAC17—Location of terminal (D) will identify early and late production CD ignition systems. Refer also to Fig. JAC16 for location of terminal (D).

single trigger coil instead of two trigger coils used in CD ignition system shown in Fig. JAC16. Individual components and complete assembly are not available for Blaser unit. Blaser ignition must be replaced with either a standard breaker type ignition system or with other CD ignition system if renewal is necessary. Flywheel must be renewed when installing different ignition system.

Some J-321 engines are equipped with the CD ignition system shown in Fig. JAC16. Components are available for this ignition. If service is required, the following troubleshooting procedure may be used. Be sure ignition is defective by using Wico test plug #14281 and rotating engine with starter. If test plug does not fire, ignition should be tested.

Remove ignition system from engine. To test high tension coil, connect positive lead of an ohmmeter to coil terminal (B–JAC16) and connect negative lead to ground screw (C). Ohmmeter should read 0.1-0.5 ohms. Disconnect ohmmeter and connect positive lead to high tension lead of coil and connect negative lead to ground screw (C). Ohmmeter should read 900-1100 ohms. Renew high tension coil if coil fails either of the two tests. Disconnect leads to each trigger coil. Connect ohmmeter leads to the leads of a trigger coil and read resistance of each coil. Ohmmeter should indicate 15-25 ohms resistance. Renew trigger coil if incorrect reading was obtained. Check connections and leads of trigger coils for continuity.

Before checking charging coil and electronic unit, note difference in early and late production units as shown in Fig. JAC17. Remove plug-in terminal (B–Fig. JAC16) from coil tower and disconnect "ENGINE STOP" wire from terminal (D). Connect positive lead of ohmmeter to terminal (A) and negative lead to terminal (D). Ohmmeter should

read 5-25 ohms on early units and 1 megohm to infinity on late units. Reverse leads of ohmmeter. Ohmmeter should read infinity on early units and 1 megohm to infinity on late units. Disconnect ohmmeter leads and connect positive meter lead to terminal (D) and

negative meter lead to ground screw (C). Ohmmeter should read infinity on early production units and 560-760 ohms on late units. Reverse meter lead connections. Ohmmeter should read 1500-2000 ohms on early units. On late units, ohmmeter reading should be slightly less than reading (560-760) obtained previously. If any of these tests are failed, charging coil windings are defective and charging coil and electronic unit must be renewed. Electronic circuit of unit cannot be tested except by substitution with a new charging coil and electronic unit.

Ignition timing on models with CD or Blaser ignition system is fixed and cannot be adjusted.

Breaker Point Ignition. Some J-321 models and all other models are equipped with a flywheel magneto ignition system using ignition breaker points. Magneto components are accessible after removing flywheel.

Breaker point gap for all models is 0.020 inch (0.51 mm). Recommended ignition timing is 30° BTDC on J-125 models, 28° BTDC on J-175 models and 27° BTDC on J-225 models. On Model

Fig. JAC18—View showing use of special Wico Test Plug number S14281 to check magneto output. Refer to text.

IF SPARK JUMPS ACROSS TEST PLUG WHEN ENGINE IS CRANKED—MAGNETO IS OK.

Fig. JAC19—Typical magneto installation. Note location of 1/8-inch (3.18 mm) vent hole referred to in text.

HIGH TENSION WIRE

CONDENSER

VENT HOLE LOCATION

CAM

CAM WIPER FELT

BREAKER POINTS

IGNITION COIL

J-321 engine used on Snow Jet, rotate stator to full counterclockwise (advanced) position. On J-501 models and all other J-321 models with breaker point ignitions, rotate stator plate to full clockwise (retarded) position.

On J-125, J-175 and J-225 models, ignition timing is satisfactory if breaker points just begin to open when piston is 0.125 inch (3.18 mm) BTDC. Piston position can be determined by inserting a suitable dial indicator through spark plug hole. Reposition magneto stator plate if necessary to obtain desired timing.

Magneto output at starting speeds can be checked without removing magneto from engine using a special Wico Test Plug S14281. Refer to Fig. JAC18. Note engine spark plug remains in place when using test plug.

On early models, the manufacturer recommends drilling an ⅛-inch (3.18 mm) vent hole in the lower left-hand corner of magneto breaker box to aid in ventilating the contact points (refer to Fig. JAC19).

AIR CLEANER. If the engine is operated under dry or dusty conditions, the manufacturer recommends servicing the air cleaner after every 25 hours of operation. Refer to the appropriate paragraphs for type being serviced.

Foil Type Cleaner. Wash and rinse thoroughly in a suitable nonflammable solvent. Shake off solvent and immerse in clean SAE 30 oil. Allow excess oil to drain off before reinstallation.

Paper Filter. Brush or wipe outside of cleaner. Tap gently to loosen dirt from inside of filter. Do not oil or wash filter. Filter can also be cleaned by gently blowing compressed air from the inside. If, after extended use, filter is too dirty to clean properly, renew the filter.

Oil Bath Air Cleaner. Remove cover from oil reservoir and discard old oil. Wash cleaner in a suitable nonflammable solvent. Dry cleaner thoroughly. Refill to level indicated by arrow with clean SAE 30 motor oil.

Foam Type Filter. Remove filter and wash and rinse thoroughly in a nonflammable solvent. Soak in clean SAE 30 engine oil and carefully compress element to remove excess oil.

LUBRICATION. A good quality two-stroke, air-cooled engine oil should be mixed with regular grade gasoline at a ratio of 50:1 for Model J-501; 30:1 for Model J-321 and 16:1 for all other models.

Use SAE 10 oil in the reduction gear box on models so equipped. Gearbox is fitted with an oil level plug.

CLEANING CARBON. Power loss can often be corrected by cleaning carbon from exhaust ports and muffler. To clean, remove spark plug and muffler. Turn engine so piston is below bottom of exhaust ports and remove carbon from ports with a dull knife or similar tool. Clean out the muffler openings, then replace muffler and spark plug.

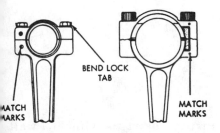

Fig. JAC20—Be sure match marks are aligned when reassembling rod cap to connecting rod. Bend lock tab against screw heads on models so equipped.

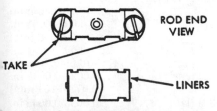

Fig. JAC21—On Model J-321 and J-501 engines with aluminum connecting rod, be sure bearing liners fit together as shown. Stake cap retaining screws as shown.

Illustrations Courtesy of Jacobsen Div. of Textron, Inc.

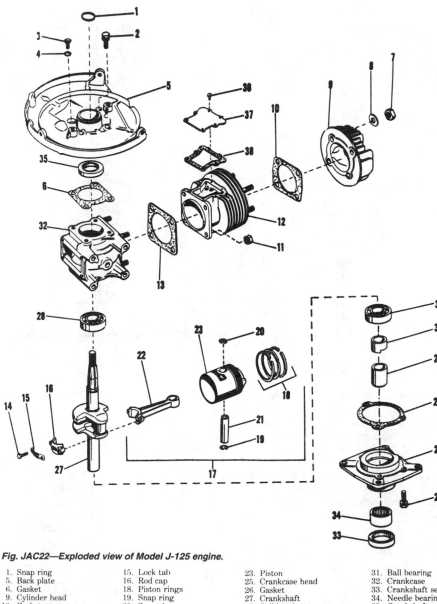

Fig. JAC22—Exploded view of Model J-125 engine.

1. Snap ring	15. Lock tab	23. Piston	31. Ball bearing
5. Back plate	16. Rod cap	25. Crankcase head	32. Crankcase
6. Gasket	18. Piston rings	26. Gasket	33. Crankshaft seal
9. Cylinder head	19. Snap ring	27. Crankshaft	34. Needle bearing
10. Gasket	20. Snap ring	28. Ball bearing	35. Crankshaft seal
12. Cylinder	21. Piston pin	29. Bearing race	37. Transfer cover
13. Gasket	22. Connecting rod	30. Spacer	38. Gasket

REPAIRS

TIGHTENING TORQUES. Recommended tightening torques are as follows:

Back plate screws . . . . 60-80 in.-lbs.
(7-9 N·m)

Carburetor adapter screws:
J-321 & J-501 with needle
bearing connecting rod . . 60-80 in.-lbs.
(7-9 N·m)

All other models . . . . 30-50 in.-lbs.
(3-6 N·m)

Connecting rod screws:
J-321 & J-501 with needle bearing
connecting rod . . . . 45-50 in.-lbs.
(5-6 N·m)

All other models . . . . . . 65-75 in.-lbs.
(7-9 N·m)

Crankcase bearing
plate bolts . . . . 80-100 in.-lbs.
(9-11 N·m)

Cylinder to crankcase
nuts (J-125) . . . . 150-180 in.-lbs.
(17-20 N·m)

Cylinder head bolts
or nuts . . . . 150-180 in.-lbs.
(17-20 N·m)

Engine mounting
bolts . . . . 120-150 in.-lbs.
(13-17 N·m)

Muffler mounting bolts:
Rotary mower engine . . . 60-80 in.-lbs.
(7-9 N·m)

Reel mower engine . . . . 80-100 in.-lbs.
(9-11 N·m)

Fan housing screws . . . . . . 60-80 in.-lbs.
(7-9 N·m)

Flywheel nut . . . . 300-360 in.-lbs.
(34-41 N·m)

Gearbox cover:
¼ inch screws . . . . 60-80 in.-lbs.
(7-9 N·m)

5/16 inch screws . . . . . . 80-100 in.-lbs.
(9-11 N·m)

Spark plug . . . . 180-200 in.-lbs.
(20-23 N·m)

Stator plate screws . . . . . . 60-80 in.-lbs.
(7-9 N·m)

PISTON, PIN AND RINGS. To remove piston, remove gas tank, air cleaner and interfering shrouds preventing access to cylinder head or carburetor. Disconnect governor link to carburetor and remove carburetor and reed valve plate. Remove cylinder head. Unscrew connecting rod cap screws and remove connecting rod and piston. Be careful not to lose loose bearing rollers on models so equipped. Refer to CONNECTING ROD section to service connecting rod.

The cam ground aluminum piston is fitted with either two or three compression rings depending upon engine model. Renew piston if badly worn or scored, or if side clearance of new ring in top ring groove is 0.010 inch (0.25 mm) or more. Install top ring with chamfer down and

Fig. JAC23—Exploded view of Model J-175 engine.

1. Spark plug
3. Air deflector
5. Air deflector
7. Air baffle
10. Cylinder head
11. Gasket
13. Lock tab
14. Rod cap
16. Piston rings
17. Snap ring
18. Snap ring
19. Piston pin
20. Piston
21. Connecting rod
24. Back plate
25. Gasket
26. Thrust washer
27. Crankshaft
28. Thrust washer
30. Cylinder & crankcase
31. Needle bearing
32. Crankshaft seal
34. Needle bearing
35. Needle bearing
36. Crankshaft seal
37. Gasket
38. Crankcase head

second ring with chamfer up.

Piston skirt diameters (measured at right angle to piston pin) are listed in the following table.

J-125 . . . . 1.9965-1.9970 in.
(50.711-50.724 mm)
J-175 . . . . 2.1235-2.1240 in.
(53.937-53.950 mm)
J-225 . . . . 2.2475-2.2480 in.
(57.087-57.099 mm)
J-321 (early) . . . . 2.1225-2.2480 in.
(53.912-53.929 mm)
J-321 (late) . . . . 2.1220-2.1227 in.
(53.899-53.917 mm)
J-501 . . . . 2.1220-2.1227 in.
(53.899-53.917 mm)

Piston skirt-to-cylinder wall clearances (new, measured at right angle to piston pin) are shown in the following table.

J-125 . . . . 0.004-0.005 in.
(0.10-0.30 mm)
J-175 . . . . 0.002-0.003 in.
(0.05-0.08 mm)
J-225 . . . . 0.003-0.004 in.
(0.08-0.10 mm)
J-321 (early) . . . . 0.0028-0.0040 in.
(0.071-0.101 mm)
J-321 (late) . . . . 0.0033-0.0045 in.
(0.084-0.114 mm)
J-501 . . . . 0.0033-0.0045 in.
(0.084-0.114 mm)

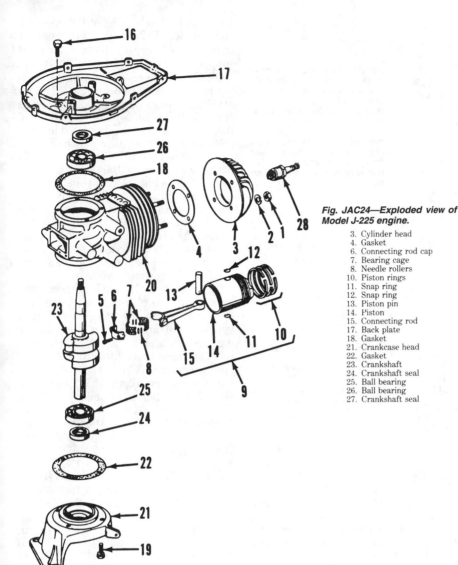

Fig. JAC24—Exploded view of Model J-225 engine.

3. Cylinder head
4. Gasket
6. Connecting rod cap
7. Bearing cage
8. Needle rollers
10. Piston rings
11. Snap ring
12. Snap ring
13. Piston pin
14. Piston
15. Connecting rod
17. Back plate
18. Gasket
21. Crankcase head
22. Gasket
23. Crankshaft
24. Crankshaft seal
25. Ball bearing
26. Ball bearing
27. Crankshaft seal

CONNECTING ROD. Connecting rod and piston unit can be removed from above after removing cylinder head and carburetor adapter.

Several types of connecting rods have been used according to engine model and application. Refer to appropriate paragraphs for model being serviced.

MODEL J-225. Model J-225 engine is equipped with a connecting rod which has needle roller crankpin and piston pin bearings. The crankpin needle rollers are separated by a split type cage and use crankpin and connecting rod surfaces as bearing races. The caged piston pin needle bearing is not renewable except by renewing connecting rod assembly.

Renew connecting rod is crankpin bearing surface is worn or scored and if any of the piston pin needle rollers have a flat spot or if two needles can be separated the width of one needle. Connecting rod crankpin bearing bore diameter is 0.9399-0.9403 inch (23.874-23.884 mm). Connecting rod side play on crankpin is 0.008-0.018 inch (0.20-0.46 mm).

MODELS J-321 AND J-501. Models J-321 and J-501 engines may be equipped with either a plain bearing bronze connecting rod (see All Other Models paragraphs) or an aluminum connecting rod with needle roller crankpin bearing and plain piston pin bearing. Model J-501 is equipped with an aluminum connecting rod.

The aluminum connecting rod has renewable steel bearing inserts for needle roller outer race. Twenty eight loose needle bearing rollers are used. Bearing guides (10 – Fig. JAC25) are used to center bearing rollers on crankpin. Bearing rollers and guides may be held on crankpin with grease before installation of connecting rod.

Piston pin-to-connecting rod bearing bore clearance should be 0.0007-0.0016 inch (0.018-0.041 mm) on all models. On bronze connecting rod, crankpin-to-connecting rod clearance is 0.0035-0.0045 inch (0.09-0.11 mm) and connecting rod side play on crankpin should be 0.004-0.017 inch (0.10-0.43 mm).

On aluminum connecting rods, rod should have a crankpin bore diameter of 0.9819-0.9824 inch (24.940-24.953 mm). Connecting rod side play on crankpin should be 0.005-0.008 inch (0.13-0.46 mm).

ALL OTHER MODELS. A bronze connecting rod with plain crankpin and piston pin bearings is used in all models except J-225, J-501 and some J-321 engines.

Piston pin-to-connecting rod clearance should be 0.0005-0.0015 inch (0.013-0.038 mm) on Models J-125H and

Piston ring end gap specifications are shown in the following table.

J-125 . . . . 0.005-0.010 in.
(0.13-0.25 mm)
J-175 (un-pinned ring) . . . 0.005-0.013 in.
(0.13-0.33 mm)
J-175 (pinned ring) . . . . . . 0.052-0.060 in.
(1.32-1.52 mm)
J-225, J-321, J-501 . . . . . . 0.005-0.013 in.
(0.13-0.33 mm)

Piston pin diameter for Model J-321 and J-501 engines is 0.4999-0.5001 inch (12.697-12.726 mm). Piston pin diameter for all other models is 0.49975-0.50025 in. (12.693-12.705 mm).

On Model J-225 engines (needle bearing in connecting rod) renew piston pin if scoring or excessive wear evident.

Piston pin-to-connecting rod clearances for all models without needle

bearings are listed in the following table.

J-125 . . . . 0.0005-0.0015 in.
(0.013-0.038 mm)
J-175 . . . . 0.00055-0.00175 in.
(0.0140-0.0445 mm)
J-321, J-501 . . . . 0.0007-0.0016 in.
(0.018-0.041 mm)

On Models J-321 and J-501, piston pin should be 0.0003 inch (0.008 mm) tight to 0.0002 inch (0.005 mm) loose fit in pin bore of piston. On all other models, piston pin should be 0.00025 inch (0.006 mm) tight to 0.00055 inch (0.013 mm) loose fit in pin bore of piston.

Piston pins are available in several oversizes as well as standard size. If oversize pin is used, refer to previous paragraphs for the appropriate pin to piston and rod bore specifications and ream the bores accordingly.

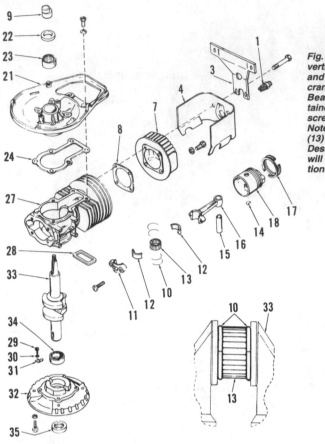

Fig. JAC25—Exploded view of vertical crankshaft Model J-321 and J-501 engine. Horizontal crankshaft models are similar. Bearing (34) on J-501 is retained by a snap ring and not screw retainer (29, 30 and 31). Note location of bearing rollers (13) and guides (10) in inset. Design of crankcase head (32) will vary with engine application.

1. Spark plug
3. Bracket
4. Air deflector
7. Cylinder head
8. Gasket
9. Breaker cam
10. Bearing roller guides
11. Rod cap
13. Bearing rollers (28)
14. Snap rings
15. Piston pin
16. Connecting rod
17. Piston rings
18. Piston
21. Back plate
22. Crankshaft seal
23. Needle bearing
24. Gasket
27. Cylinder & crankcase
28. Gasket
31. Bearing retainer
32. Crankcase head
33. Crankshaft
34. Ball bearing
35. Crankshaft seal

a ball type main bearing at the opposite end. Model J-125 and J-175 engines have a third bearing (needle bearing) supporting outer end of crankshaft.

On all models, use an approved bearing puller to remove bearings. When installing new bearings, be sure crankshaft is supported between the throws and the bearing is heated in oil to prevent bending of the crankshaft.

On Model J-321 engines, it is necessary to remove the two bearing retainers (31 – Fig. JAC25) before the crankcase head (32) can be removed from the crankshaft. Remove snap ring which retains bearing on Model J-501.

Install crankcase head (32) on crankcase (27) of Model J-321 or J-501 so flat spot on inner portion of crankcase head will be towards cylinder.

On Model J-175 engines, maintain crankshaft end play of 0.004-0.018 inch (0.10-0.46 mm) by renewing thrust washers (26 and 28 – Fig. JAC23); or gaskets (25 and 37) are available with less thickness than standard gaskets to reduce crankshaft end play.

Standard crankpin diameters are shown in the following table.

Model J-125H . . . . 0.6240-0.6245 in.
(15.850-15.862 mm)
Model J-125V . . . . 0.6230-0.6235 in.
(15.824-15.837 mm)
Model J-175 . . . . 0.7485-0.7490 in.
(19.012-19.025 mm)
Model J-225 . . . . 0.7500-0.7503 in.
(19.050-19.058 mm)
Model J-321 . . . . 0.7485-0.7490 in.
(19.012-19.025 mm)
Model J-501 . . . . 0.7496-0.7501 in.
(19.040-19.053 mm)

On all models with direct drive, install crankcase seals so lip faces toward inside of engine. On models with speed reducer, the crankcase oil seal on the speed reducer side should be installed with lip facing the reducer.

REED VALVE. On all models the carburetor is mounted on an adapter plate. The plate carries a small spring steel leaf or reed, on the engine side, which acts as an inlet valve. The reed has a bend in it and must be installed so reed is forced firmly against the mounting plate. Blow-back through the carburetor may be caused by foreign matter holding reed valve open or by a damaged or improperly installed reed.

J-125V and 0.00055-0.00175 inch (0.0140-0.0445 mm) on Model J-175.

Crankpin-to-connecting rod bearing clearance should be 0.0015-0.0030 inch (0.038-0.076 mm) for Model J-125H, 0.0025-0.0040 inch (0.064-0.102 mm) for Model J-125V and 0.0035-0.0045 inch (0.090-0.114 mm) for Model J-175.

Connecting rod side play on crankpin for Models J-125H, J-125V and J-175 should be 0.004-0.017 inch (0.10-0.43 mm).

On all models, make certain match marks on connecting rod and cap are aligned as shown in Fig. JAC20 during installation. Bend lock tabs, if equipped, against cap screw heads. On Model J-321 and J-501 with aluminum connecting rod, steel bearing inserts must be installed correctly and screw heads staked as shown in Fig. JAC21.

CYLINDER. Cylinder bore should be resized if scored, out-of-round more than 0.0015 inch (0.038 mm) or worn

more than 0.002 inch (0.05 mm). Standard cylinder bore diameter is 2.0010-2.0015 inch (50.825-50.838 mm) for Model J-125 engines, 2.1260-2.1265 inch (54.000-54.013 mm) for Model J-175 engines, 2.2510-2.2515 inch (57.175-57.188 mm) for Model J-225 engines and 2.1260-2.1265 inch (54.000-54.013 mm) for Models J-321 and J-501 engines.

Several oversize pistons as well as standard size are available. If reboring is not necessary, the manufacturer recommends deglazing the bore to aid in seating new rings.

CRANKSHAFT AND SEALS. On all models except Models J-175, J-321 and J-501, crankshaft is supported at each end by ball type main bearings which are pressed onto crankshaft. On Models J-175, crankshaft is supported by needle type main bearings and on Models J-321 and J-501, crankshaft is supported by a needle type main bearing at one end and

SERVICING JACOBSEN ACCESSORIES

REWIND STARTER

All models may be equipped with one of the rewind starters shown in Fig. JAC26, Fig. JAC27 or Fig. JAC28. Refer to the appropriate following paragraph and exploded view when servicing rewind starter.

To disassemble dog type starter shown in Fig. JAC26, remove starter from engine and pull starter rope out of starter approximately 12 inches (305 mm). Prevent pulley (3) from rewinding and pull slack rope back through rope outlet. Hold rope away from pulley and allow rope pulley to unwind. Unscrew retaining screw (11) and remove dog assembly and rope pulley being careful not to disturb rewind spring (2) in cover. Note direction of spring winding and carefully remove spring from cover.

To reassemble starter, reverse disassembly procedure. Rewind spring must be preloaded by installing rope through rope outlet of housing and hole in rope pulley, tie a knot at each end of rope and turn rope pulley approximately four turns in direction that places load on rewind spring. Hold pulley and pull remainder of rope through rope pulley. Attach handle to rope end and allow rope to rewind into starter. If spring is properly preloaded, rope will fully rewind.

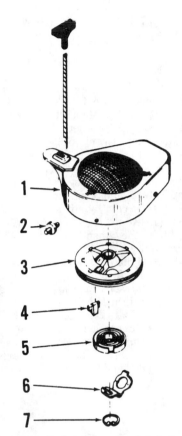

To disassemble starter shown in Fig. JAC27, remove rope handle and allow rope to wind into starter. Remove roll pin (1) and washers (2 and 3). Remove rope pulley and remainder of starter components. When reassembling starter, turn rope pulley approximately 4 turns counterclockwise (viewed from open side) before connecting rope to rope pulley. Clip at rope end should have open side facing outward. After assembling starter, check operation and note if rope is fully rewound into starter.

Rewind starter shown in Fig. JAC28 is a pawl type starter with pawl (4) engaging a flywheel fin when the starter rope is pulled. To disassemble starter, remove rope handle and allow rope to rewind into starter. Remove snap ring (7) and remove starter components from starter housing. Inspect components for wear and damage and install in reverse order of disassembly. Spring cup (5) should be installed so spring attachment point on cup is 180° from rope entry hole in starter housing (1). Turn rope pulley approximately 3½ turns against spring tension before passing end of rope through hole in starter housing. Note that four embossed projections on starter housing adjacent to rope pulley are friction devices and should not be lubricated.

GEAR REDUCTION UNIT

Before the housing can be removed from the engine, the reduction gear cover and gear must be removed. Crankcase oil seal on the speed reducer side should be installed with the lip facing the reducer. On the power takeoff side of the reducer unit, the oil seal lip faces the reduction unit. Refer to Fig. JAC29.

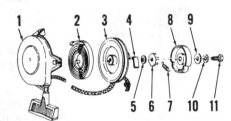

Fig. JAC26—Exploded view of dog type rewind starter.

1. Cover	7. Spring
2. Rewind spring	8. Retainer
3. Rope pulley	9. Washer
4. Dog	10. Washer
5. Washer	11. Screw
6. Brake	

Fig. JAC28—Exploded view of rewind starter used on some later models.

1. Starter housing	5. Rewind spring & Cup
2. Rope guide	6. Pawl plate
3. Rope pulley	7. Snap ring
4. Pawl	

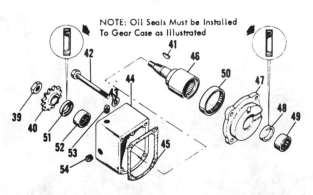

Fig. JAC27—Exploded view of rewind starter used on some engines. Some models use a snap ring in place of pin (1).

1. Pin	4. Cover	6. Washer
2. Washer	5. Spring	7. Rope pulley
3. Washer		

Fig. JAC29—Exploded view of reduction gear assembly used on horizontal crankshaft engines.

NOTE: Oil Seals Must be Installed To Gear Case as Illustrated

40. Drive sprocket	47. Crankcase head	51. Oil seal
41. Woodruff key	48. Crankshaft seal	52. Needle bearing
44. Housing	49. Needle bearing	53. Oil filler plug
45. Gasket	50. Needle bearing	54. Oil level plug
46. Drive gear		

KAWASAKI

KAWASAKI MOTORS CORP. USA
P.O. Box 504
Shakopee, Minnesota 55379

Model	Bore	Stroke	Displacement
KT43	54 mm	48 mm	110 cc
	(2.13 in.)	(1.89 in.)	(6.7 cu. in.)

ENGINE INFORMATION

KT43 models are two-stroke, air-cooled engines. Cylinder head and cylinder bore are bolted to an aluminum die-cast crankcase. The three-piece crankshaft is supported at each end by ball bearing type main bearings.

Model KT43 is rated at 3.2 kW (4.3 hp) at 5000 rpm.

Engine model identification decal is located on cooling shroud and serial number is stamped in crankcase (Fig. KW1). Always furnish engine model and serial number when ordering parts or service material.

MAINTENANCE

SPARK PLUG. Recommended spark plug is NGK BM7, or equivalent.

Spark plug should be removed and cleaned and electrode gap set at 0.6-0.7 mm (0.024-0.027 in.) after every 25 hours of operation. Renew spark plug if electrode is severely burnt or damaged. Tighten spark plug to 27 N·m (20 ft.-lbs.).

NOTE: Caution should be exercised if abrasive type spark plug cleaner is used. Inadequate cleaning procedure may allow the abrasive cleaner to be deposited in engine cylinder accelerating wear and part failures.

CARBURETOR. Model KT43 is equipped with a Mikuni float type carburetor equipped with idle mixture adjustment needle. Main fuel mixture is controlled by a fixed jet.

Initial adjustment of idle mixture screw (2 – Fig. KW2) is 1 turn open from a lightly seated position. Make final adjustment with engine at operating temperature and running. Set engine idle at 1400 rpm by adjusting idle stop screw (1). Adjust idle mixture screw (2) to obtain the smoothest idle and acceleration.

Standard main jet size is #82.5.

To check float level, remove carburetor and separate float bowl from carburetor throttle body. Invert throttle body and float assembly (Fig. KW3). Float should contact float valve lever when bottom edge of float is just level with edge of throttle body. Float lever is spring-loaded and float should just touch lever, but not compress fuel inlet valve spring.

GOVERNOR. Model KT43 is equipped with a flyweight type governor. To adjust external linkage, stop engine. Make certain all linkage is in good condition and tension spring (3 – Fig. KW4) is not stretched. Spring (2) around governor-to-carburetor rod (1) must pull governor lever (4) and throttle arm toward each other. Loosen clamp bolt (5) and push governor lever until throttle is in full open position. Hold lever in this position and use a screwdriver in governor shaft slot to rotate governor shaft (6) clockwise until it stops (range is very slight). Tighten governor clamp bolt (5).

To set minimum speed, engine should be at operating temperature and running, no-load. Close throttle valve by hand until it hits throttle stop screw (1 – Fig. KW2). Adjust throttle stop screw so engine is running at 1400 rpm.

To set maximum speed, engine should be at operating temperature and running, no-load. Attach a tachometer to engine. Slowly move throttle lever increasing engine speed while observing tachometer.

CAUTION: At no time, even during adjustment, should engine be allowed to run above 5000 rpm. Stop throttle movement when engine reaches 4950 rpm and continue as outlined.

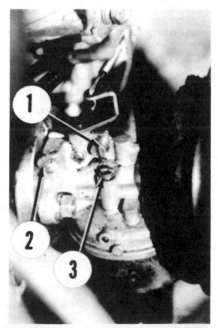

Fig. KW2—Model KT43 engines are equipped with Mikuni float type carburetor.
1. Throttle stop screw
2. Idle mixture screw
3. Pilot air jet

Fig. KW1—View showing location of engine serial number.

Fig. KW3—Carburetor float must be level with lower edge of carburetor throttle body without compressing fuel inlet needle spring.

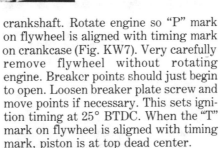

Fig. KW4—View of external governor linkage.

1. Carburetor-to-governor rod
2. Spring
3. Tension spring
4. Governor lever
5. Clamp bolt
6. Governor shaft
7. Throttle & lock
8. Maximum speed limit bolt

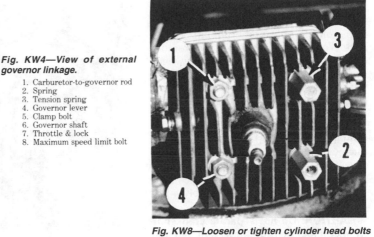

Fig. KW8—Loosen or tighten cylinder head bolts in sequence shown. Refer to text for torque specifications.

Adjust maximum speed limit screw (8—Fig. KW4) to obtain 3200 rpm and lock it securely in place with jam nut.

IGNITION SYSTEM. A breaker point ignition system is standard. Ignition coil, breaker points and condenser are located behind flywheel (Fig. KW5). Flywheel must be removed to perform service or adjustment. Breaker point gap should be 0.3-0.5 mm (0.012-0.020 in.).

To check timing, first remove flywheel, then gently place flywheel on

Fig. KW5—View of ignition coil (1), breaker points (2) and crankshaft (4). Condenser is not shown but is attached to wire leads (3).

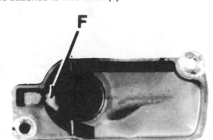

Fig. KW6—Lubricating felt (F) in point cover should receive a drop of oil whenever points are renewed.

crankshaft. Rotate engine so "P" mark on flywheel is aligned with timing mark on crankcase (Fig. KW7). Very carefully remove flywheel without rotating engine. Breaker points should just begin to open. Loosen breaker plate screw and move points if necessary. This sets ignition timing at 25° BTDC. When the "T" mark on flywheel is aligned with timing mark, piston is at top dead center.

CYLINDER HEAD AND COMBUSTION CHAMBER. Cylinder head, combustion chamber and piston should be cleaned and carbon and other deposits removed after every 300 hours of operation. Refer to REPAIR section of this manual for service procedure.

LUBRICATION. Manufacturer recommends mixing a good quality two-stroke, air-cooled engine oil with regular grade gasoline at a 25:1 ratio. Always mix fuel in a separate container and add only mixed fuel to engine fuel tank.

GENERAL MAINTENANCE. Check and tighten all loose bolts, nuts or clamps prior to each day of operation. Check for fuel or oil leakage and repair if necessary.

Clean dust, dirt, grease or any foreign material from cylinder head and cylinder

Fig. KW7—When "P" mark on flywheel is aligned with timing mark on crankcase cover. Breaker points should just begin to open.

block cooling fins after every 100 hours of operation. Inspect fins for damage and repair if necessary.

REPAIRS

TIGHTENING TORQUES. Recommended tightening torques are as follows:

Spark plug . . . . .27 N·m
                (20 ft.-lbs.)
Flywheel nut . . . . .39-44 N·m
                (30-33 ft.-lbs.)
Cylinder head . . . . .20-22 N·m
                (15-16 ft.-lbs.)
Crankcase . . . . .7-9 N·m
                (5-6 ft.-lbs.)

CYLINDER HEAD. To remove cylinder head, disconnect spark plug. Remove rewind starter and cooling shroud assembly. Unbolt cylinder head retaining bolts in sequence shown in Fig. KW8.

Reinstall by reversing removal procedure and tighten head retaining bolts to specified torque in sequence shown in Fig. KW8.

CONNECTING ROD. Connecting rod is forged steel with needle bearings in piston pin bore and crankpin bearing bore. To remove connecting rod, remove cylinder head, cylinder and flywheel. Remove piston pin retainers and piston pin. Separate piston from connecting rod. Use care not to lose needle bearings in connecting rod piston pin bore. Loosen upper crankcase cover bolts in sequence shown in fig. KW9. Loosen lower crankcase cover bolts in a criss-cross pattern and separate crankcase from crankcase covers. Remove connecting rod and crankshaft assembly.

CAUTION: Do not separate crankshaft from connecting rod. Crankshaft and connecting rod are available only as an assembly. Kawasaki does not recommend crankshaft disassembly.

If connecting rod side play at crankpin bearing is 0.5 mm (0.02 in.) or more, or if radial play at piston pin bearing or crankpin bearing is 0.05 mm (0.002 in.) or more, renew crankshaft and connecting rod assembly.

Use light grease to retain needle bearings in their bore during reassembly. Tighten crankcase cover bolts evenly, in graduated steps, to specified torque in sequence shown in Fig. KW9 for upper crankcase bolts. Use a criss-cross pattern when tightening lower crankcase cover bolts.

PISTON, PIN AND RINGS. Piston may be removed after removing cylinder head and cylinder. Refer to CONNECTING ROD paragraphs.

Check clearance between piston and cylinder. If clearance is 0.2 mm (0.008 in.) or more, renew piston and/or cylinder. Maximum side clearance for new ring in ring groove is 0.15 mm (0.006 in.). Maximum ring end gap is 1.0 mm (0.04 in.). Maximum clearance between piston pin and piston is 0.03 mm

Fig. KW9—Upper crankcase bolts must be tightened evenly, in graduated steps, in sequence shown. Refer to text for torque specifications.

(0.001 in.). Renew piston if specifications are not as specified.

When installing piston rings, marked side of ring is towards top of piston. Align ring end gaps with pins in piston ring grooves.

Piston should be installed on connecting rod with the arrow mark on piston top toward the exhaust port side of engine. Lubricate and install piston pin and retaining rings. Use a suitable ring compressor to avoid damaging rings and very carefully install cylinder over piston and ring assembly.

CYLINDER. The cylinder is a low pressure aluminum alloy with iron sleeve. To remove cylinder, remove cylinder head and carefully work cylinder up off of piston.

Standard cylinder bore diameter is 54 mm (2.126 in.) with a service limit of 0.1 mm (0.004 in.). If cylinder bore wear exceeds service limit, renew cylinder.

Refer to PISTON, PIN AND RINGS section for piston-to-cylinder clearance and reassembly procedure.

CRANKSHAFT, MAIN BEARINGS AND SEALS. Refer to CONNECTING ROD section for crankshaft removal. Note that Kawasaki does not recommend separating connecting rod from crankshaft and that crankshaft and connecting rod are available as an assembly only. Ball bearing type main bearings are a slight press fit in crankcase covers. It may be necessary to slightly heat crankcase covers for removal and installation. Maximum axial play for main bearings is 0.15 mm (0.006 in.). Renew main bearings if loose, rough or a loose fit on crankshaft.

GOVERNOR. Refer to MAINTENANCE section for adjustment procedure of external governor linkage.

To remove governor, remove crankcase cover, loosening bolts in sequence shown in Fig. KW9. Separate cover from crankcase. Slide governor holder off the crankshaft and remove the pin which will allow governor sleeve and thrust washer removal.

Check governor tip contact surface and governor weight contact surface of the thrust washer for wear and roughness.

Remove governor lever from external end of governor shaft and governor tip from internal end of governor shaft. Pull governor shaft from crankcase bore. Check governor sleeve contact surface of governor tip for wear. Check governor shaft for wear where it is supported by crankcase bushing bore.

When reassembling governor, lubricate all parts with engine oil and make certain pin is correctly positioned in notch of governor sleeve. Tighten lower crankcase cover bolts equally in sequence shown in Fig. KW9 to specified torque.

KAWASAKI

Model	Bore	Stroke	Displacement	Power Rating
FC150V	65 mm	46 mm	153 cc	3.35 kW
	(2.56 in.)	(1.81 in.)	(9.3 cu.in.)	(4.5 hp)

NOTE: Metric fasteners are used throughout engine.

ENGINE INFORMATION

Model FC150V is an air-cooled, four-stroke, single-cylinder engine. The engine has a vertical crankshaft and utilizes an overhead valve system.

MAINTENANCE

LUBRICATION. All models are lubricated by an oil slinger that is gear-driven by the governor gear.

Change oil after first five hours of operation and after every 50 hours of operation or at least once each operating season. Change oil weekly or after every 25 hours of operation if equipment undergoes severe usage.

Engine oil should meet or exceed latest API service classification. Use SAE 40 oil for temperatures above 68° F (20° C); use SAE 30 oil for temperatures between 32° F (0° C) and 95° F (35° C); use SAE 10W-30 or 10W-40 oil for temperatures between –4° F (–20° C) and 95° F (35° C); below 32° F (0° C) SAE 5W-20 may be used.

Crankcase capacity is 0.55 liters (1.16 U.S. pints).

FUEL FILTER. The fuel tank is equipped with a filter at the outlet. Check filter annually and periodically during operating season.

SPARK PLUG. Recommended spark plug is a NGK BP6ES; install a comparative resistor plug if required. Specified spark plug electrode gap is 0.7-0.8 mm (0.028-0.031 in.).

CARBURETOR. Adjustment. Idle speed at normal operating temperature should be 1400-1600 rpm. Adjust idle speed by turning idle speed screw (10—Fig. KW201). Idle mixture is controlled by idle jet (1) and idle mixture screw (8). Initial setting of idle mixture screw is one turn out. Turning screw clockwise will lean idle mixture. Adjust idle mixture screw so engine runs at maximum idle speed, then turn screw out an additional ¼ turn. Readjust idle speed screw. Idle mixture jet is not adjustable.

High speed operation is controlled by fixed main jet (12).

Overhaul. To disassemble carburetor, remove fuel bowl retaining screw (22), gasket (21) and fuel bowl (18). Remove float pin (16) by pushing against small end of pin toward the large end of pin. Remove float (15) and fuel inlet needle (13). Remove throttle and choke shaft assemblies after unscrewing throttle and choke plate retaining screws. Remove idle mixture screw (8), idle mixture jet (1), main jet (12) and main fuel nozzle (14). Note that main jet must be removed before the nozzle as the jet blocks the nozzle.

When assembling the carburetor note the following. Place a small drop of nonhardening sealant such as Permatex #2 or equivalent on throttle and

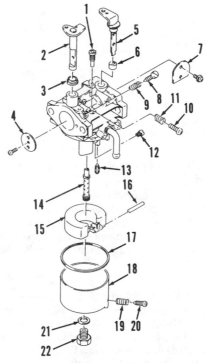

Fig. KW201—Exploded view of carburetor.

1. Idle jet		12. Main jet	
2. Throttle shaft		13. Fuel inlet valve	
3. Collar		14. Nozzle	
4. Throttle plate		15. Float	
5. Choke shaft		16. Float pin	
6. Ring		17. Gasket	
7. Choke plate		18. Fuel bowl	
8. Idle mixture screw		19. Spring	
9. Spring		20. Drain screw	
10. Idle speed screw		21. Washer	
11. Spring		22. Screw	

choke plate retaining screws. Float height is not adjustable; replace any components which are damaged or excessively worn and adversely affect float position.

If removed, install carburetor insulator spacer and gaskets so gasket with square-shaped opening is toward cylinder and gasket with round opening is toward carburetor. Tighten carburetor mounting nuts to 7 N•m (62 in.-lbs.) torque.

CARBURETOR CONTROLS. Operate engine until normal operating temperature is reached and stop engine. Move throttle control to "FAST" position and loosen throttle cable clamp screw (C—Fig. KW202). Rotate speed control lever (T) so holes (H) in lever and plate (P) are aligned and insert a 6 mm (0.24 in.) rod or bolt into holes to maintain alignment. Start and run engine at fast, no-load idle speed specified by equipment manufacturer. Loosen screws (S) and move plate (P) to adjust engine speed. Stop engine and tighten screws. With throttle control in "FAST" position, tighten throttle cable clamp screw (C).

To adjust choke, insert a 6 mm (0.24 in.) diameter rod through holes (H) in speed control lever and control plate. Back out choke screw (K) so it does not touch lever (L), then turn screw in so it just touches lever. Remove the 6 mm (0.24 in.) rod from control lever. With throttle control in "CHOKE" position, the carburetor choke plate should be closed.

GOVERNOR. The engine is equipped with a mechanical, flyweight type governor. To adjust governor linkage, proceed as follows: Loosen governor lever clamp nut (N—Fig. KW203), rotate governor lever (L) so throttle plate is fully open and hold lever in place. Turn governor shaft (S) counterclockwise as far as possible, then tighten nut (N).

If internal governor assembly must be serviced, refer to REPAIRS section.

IGNITION SYSTEM. The engine is equipped with an electronic ignition system and periodic maintenance is not required. All components are located

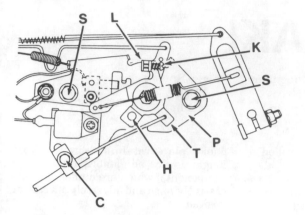

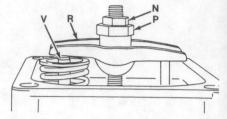

Fig. KW202—View of carburetor and governor control linkage. Refer to text for adjustment.

Fig. KW206—Loosen lock nut (N) and turn pivot nut (P) to adjust clearance between rocker arm (R) and valve stem end (V) which should be 0.12 mm (0.005 in.).

VALVE ADJUSTMENT. Engine must be cold for valve adjustment. Rotate crankshaft so piston is at top dead center on compression stroke. Remove rocker arm cover. Clearance between rocker arm (R—Fig. KW206) and valve stem end (V) should be 0.12 mm (0.005 in.) for both the intake and exhaust valves. Loosen lock nut (N) and turn pivot nut (P) to obtain desired clearance. Tighten lock screw to 7.0 N•m (62 in.-lbs.) torque.

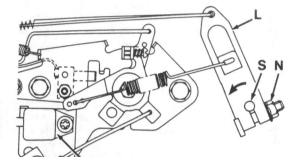

Fig. KW203—View showing location of ignition control unit (ECU) and governor linkage.

COMPRESSION PRESSURE. Minimum allowable compression pressure is 343 kPa (50 psi).

CYLINDER HEAD. Manufacturer recommends that after every 100 hours of operation the cylinder head is removed and cleaned of deposits.

REPAIRS

Fig. KW204—Control unit wire (2) and stop switch wire (3) must be connected to stud terminal (8) as shown. Note 45° angle of wires.

1. Nuts
2. Control unit wire
3. Stop switch wire
5. Washer
6. Insulator
7. Insulator
8. Stud

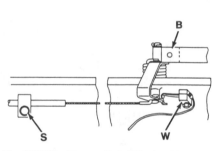

Fig. KW205—Stop switch (W) should contact brake lever when safety handle is released.

outside the flywheel. Ignition timing is not adjustable.

Ignition coil armature leg air gap should be 0.3 mm (0.012 in.). Adjust air gap by loosening ignition coil mounting screws and repositioning ignition coil. Primary side ignition coil resistance should be 0.67-1.10 ohms; secondary side resistance should be 6000-10000 ohms.

The ignition control unit (ECU) is located adjacent to the carburetor and governor controls shown in Fig. KW203. The only positive way of determining if the control unit is faulty is to install a good control unit and check ignition performance. Note in Fig. KW204 the correct attachment of wires from the stop

switch and control unit to the stud terminal.

An ignition stop switch is located adjacent to the flywheel band brake actuating lever on the engine. Be sure stop switch operates properly and stops ignition when the equipment safety handle is released.

FLYWHEEL BRAKE. Mower engines may be equipped with a brake band (B—Fig. KW205) that contacts the flywheel when the mower safety handle is released. Stop switch (W) contacts the brake lever and grounds the ignition when the brake is activated. The brake should stop the engine within three seconds after the safety handle is released.

Adjust brake cable by releasing the equipment safety handle, loosening cable clamp screw (S) and pulling slack out of outer cable housing. Retighten clamp screw.

TIGHTENING TORQUES. Recommended tightening torque specifications are as follows:

Blade brake mounting bolt (M8)	18 N•m (160 in.-lbs.)
Carburetor mounting screw	7 N•m (62 in.-lbs.)
Connecting rod	12 N•m (106 in.-lbs.)
Crankcase cover	7 N•m (62 in.-lbs.)
Crankshaft (pto end)	38 N•m (28 ft.-lbs.)
Cylinder head	23 N•m (204 in.-lbs.)
Flywheel	45 N•m (33 ft.-lbs.)
Muffler	7 N•m (62 in.-lbs.)
Oil drain plug	21 N•m (186 in.-lbs.)
Rocker arm stud	7 N•m (62 in.-lbs.)
Standard screws:	
M5	3.5 N•m (31 in.-lbs.)
M6	6 N•m (53 in.-lbs.)
M8	15 N•m (133 in.-lbs.)

CRANKCASE BREATHER.

Crankcase pressure is vented to the cylinder head where two reed valves are located. One reed valve is found in the rocker arm chamber while the other reed valve is situated in a breather chamber on the top side of the cylinder head. Renew reed valve if tip of reed stands up more than 0.2 mm (0.008 in.), or if reed is damaged or worn excessively.

CYLINDER HEAD AND VALVE

SYSTEM. To remove cylinder head, first remove engine cover as follows: Disconnect fuel line from carburetor inlet and drain fuel into suitable container. Disconnect fuel line from fuel shut-off valve. Remove oil filler cap. Unbolt and remove rewind starter. Remove flywheel nut and starting pulley. Lift engine cover and disconnect intake pipe adapter from air cleaner outlet. Remove engine cover.

Remove carburetor and muffler. Remove rocker arm cover. Unscrew cylinder head screws and remove head. Push rods, rocker arms and pivot nuts should be marked so they can be reinstalled in their original position.

Clean deposits from cylinder head and inspect for cracks or other damage. Check flatness of cylinder head gasket surface using a straightedge and feeler gauge. Renew head if warped more than 0.07 mm (0.003 in.).

Valve face and seat angles are 45 degrees. Specified seat width is 0.53-1.16 mm (0.021-0.046 in.). Minimum allowable valve margin is 0.5 mm (0.020 in.). Minimum allowable valve stem diameter is 5.435 mm (0.2319 in.) for intake valve and 5.420 mm (0.2133 in.) for exhaust valve. Renew valve if runout exceeds 0.03 mm (0.0012 in.) measured at midpoint of stem. Renew valve if valve stem end is worn so length from stem

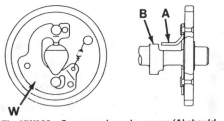

Fig. KW208—Compression release arm (A) should protrude above cam lobe base (B) when weight (W) is in innermost (starting) position.

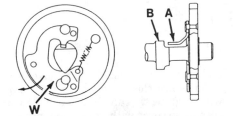

Fig. KW209—Compression release arm (A) should be beneath surface of cam lobe base (B) when weight (W) is extended to running position.

end to groove in valve stem is less than 3.8 mm (0.15 in.).

Valve guides are not renewable. If valve guide inner diameter is larger than 5.550 mm (0.2185 in.) for intake or 5.560 mm (0.2189 in.) for exhaust, renew cylinder head.

Renew push rod if runout exceeds 0.6 mm (0.024 in.) measured at midpoint of push rod.

Rocker arm studs are threaded into cylinder head. When installing studs, apply Loctite to threads and tighten to 7 N·m (62 in.-lbs.) torque.

Note the following when reinstalling cylinder head: Do not apply sealer to cylinder head gasket. Piston should be at top dead center on compression stroke. Tighten cylinder head bolts evenly in three steps using sequence shown in Fig. KW207 until final torque reading of 23 N·m (204 in.-lbs.) is obtained.

CAMSHAFT. Camshaft and camshaft gear are an integral casting which is equipped with a compression release mechanism. The compression release arm (A—Fig. KW208) extends at cranking speed to hold the exhaust valve open slightly thereby reducing compression pressure.

To remove camshaft proceed as follows: Drain crankcase oil and remove engine from equipment. Clean pto end of crankshaft and remove any burrs or rust. Remove rocker arms and push rods and mark them so they can be returned to original position. Unscrew fasteners and remove crankcase cover (oil sump). Rotate crankshaft so timing marks on crankshaft and camshaft gears are aligned (this will position

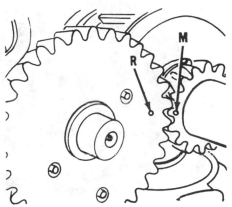

Fig. KW210—Align timing mark (R) on camshaft with timing mark (M) on crankshaft.

valve tappets out of way). Withdraw camshaft and remove tappets.

Minimum allowable camshaft bearing journal diameter is 13.920 mm (0.5480 in.) for both ends. Renew camshaft if either cam lobe height is less than 22.80 mm (0.898 in.). Minimum allowable inside diameter of bearing bore in crankcase or crankcase cover (oil sump) is 14.070 mm (0.554 in.).

Refer to Figs. KW208 and KW209 to check compression release mechanism. With weight (W) in starting position (Fig. KW208), arm (A) should protrude above cam lobe base. With weight (W) extended in running position (Fig. KW209), arm (A) should be beneath surface of cam lobe base.

Install camshaft while aligning timing marks (Fig. KW210) on crankshaft and camshaft gears. Be sure governor weights are closed and governor gear will align with camshaft gear. Mate crankcase cover with crankcase, but do not force. Tighten crankcase screws evenly in steps using sequence shown in Fig. KW211 to 7 N·m (62 in.-lbs.) torque. Reassemble remainder of components.

PISTON, PIN, RINGS AND CONNECTING ROD. To remove piston and rod assembly, drain engine oil and remove engine from equipment. Remove cylinder head as previously outlined. Clean pto end of crankshaft and remove any burrs or rust. Unscrew fasteners and remove crankcase cover (oil sump). Rotate crankshaft so timing marks on crankshaft and camshaft gears are aligned (this will position valve tappets out of the way). Withdraw camshaft from cylinder block. Remove carbon or ring ridge, if present, from top of cylinder prior to removing piston. Unscrew connecting rod screws, remove rod cap and push piston and rod out of cylinder block.

Renew piston if top or second ring side clearance in piston ring groove ex-

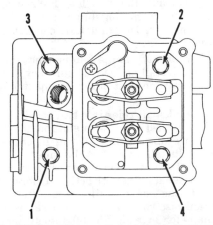

Fig. KW207—Tighten cylinder head screws to a torque of 23 N·m (204 in.-lbs.) in sequence shown above.

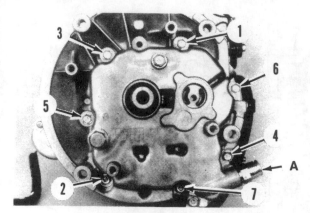

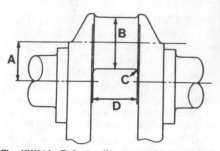

Fig. KW214—Refer to diagram and following dimensions to grind crankpin for 0.5 mm undersize connecting rod.

A. 22.950-23.000 mm (0.9035-0.9055 in.)	C. 1.5-1.8 mm (0.059-0.071 in.)
B. 27.467-27.480 mm (1.0814-1.0819 in.)	D. 24.00-24.10 mm (0.945-0.949 in.)

and camshaft gears. Be sure governor weights are closed and governor gear will align with camshaft gear. Mate crankcase cover with crankcase, but do not force. Tighten crankcase screws evenly in steps using sequence shown in Fig. KW211 to 7 N·m (62 in.-lbs.) torque. Reassemble remainder of components.

GOVERNOR. The governor gear and flyweight assembly is located on the inside of the crankcase cover (oil sump). The plunger in the gear assembly contacts the governor arm and shaft in the crankcase. The governor shaft and arm transfer governor action to the external governor linkage.

To gain access to the governor gear assembly, drain crankcase oil and remove engine from equipment. Clean pto end of crankshaft and remove any burrs or rust. Unscrew fasteners and remove crankcase cover.

Governor assembly rides on a stud pressed into the crankcase cover. The governor assembly must be pried loose from the stud which damages the assembly so it must be discarded. When installing a new governor assembly, assemble plunger in governor gear before installing gear on crankcase cover stud. Place a thrust washer around the stud, then position governor gear assembly on stud so step in governor bore indexes on groove of stud. Check governor and flyweight movement which must be free without binding.

If removed, install governor shaft and arm in side of crankcase and attach cotter pin as shown in Fig. KW213.

To reassemble, position governor gear assembly in crankcase cover. Be sure governor arm is in proper position to contact governor, and camshaft end will properly engage oil pump drive. Install crankcase cover and tighten cover screws to 16 N·m (140 in.-lbs.) torque in sequence shown in Fig. KW211. Do not force mating of cover with crankcase. Reassemble remainder of components.

CRANKSHAFT AND MAIN BEARINGS. To remove crankshaft, first drain crankcase oil and remove engine from equipment. Clean pto end of crankshaft and remove any burrs or rust. Remove cylinder head, flywheel, crankcase cover and camshaft. Unscrew connecting rod cap and remove piston and rod. Withdraw crankshaft.

Renew crankshaft if main bearing journal diameter is less than 24.920 mm (0.9811 in.) for either end. With crankshaft supported at ends, runout measured at bearing journals must not exceed 0.20 mm (0.008 in.). Crankshaft must be renewed or reground if crankpin diameter is less than 27.920 mm (1.0992 in.). Refer to Fig. KW214 for crankpin regrinding dimensions to fit a 0.5 mm (0.020 in.) undersize connecting rod.

Crankshaft timing gear is removable. When installing gear be sure key does not protrude past outer face of timing gear.

Crankshaft rides in a ball bearing at the flywheel end. Use a suitable tool to remove and install bearing in crankcase. Install oil seal so flat side is out and flush with crankcase surface. Crankshaft rides directly in bore in crankcase cover (oil sump). Renew crankcase cover if bearing bore inside diameter exceeds 25.100 mm (0.9882 in.). Install oil seal so flat side is out and flush with crankcase surface.

Fig. KW212—Install piston rings as shown above with "N" on ring toward piston crown.

ceeds 0.10 mm (0.004 in.). Maximum piston ring end gap is 1.0 mm (0.040 in.) for top or second ring and 1.5 mm (0.060 in.) for oil ring. Maximum allowable piston pin hole diameter is 15.050 mm (0.5925 in.). Minimum allowable piston pin diameter is 14.975 mm (0.5896 in.). Pistons are available in oversizes of 0.25, 0.50 and 0.75 mm.

Renew connecting rod if small end inner diameter is greater than 15.050 mm (0.5925 in.) or big end inner diameter exceeds 28.070 mm (1.1051 in.). A connecting rod with 0.5 mm (0.020 in.) undersize big end hole is available to fit a crankshaft with a reground crankpin.

When assembling piston and rod, arrow on piston crown must be on same side as "MADE IN JAPAN" on rod. Renew piston pin retaining rings whenever they are removed. Install piston rings on piston as shown in Fig. KW212, making sure that "N" mark on top and second ring faces up. Assemble piston and rod in cylinder block with arrow mark on piston crown toward flywheel side of engine. Install rod cap so index grooves on rod and cap align. Tighten connecting rod screws to 12 N·m (106 in.-lbs.) torque.

Install camshaft while aligning timing marks (Fig. KW210) on crankshaft

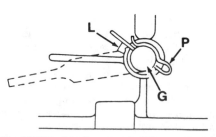

Fig. KW213—Install cotter pin (P) on governor shaft (G) as shown. Note location of lug (L).

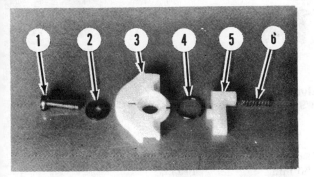

Fig. KW215—Note position of recoil starter pawl (5) before removing it from starter.

1. Screw
2. Washer
3. Retainer
4. Snap ring
5. Pawl
6. Spring

CYLINDER. If cylinder bore exceeds 65.060 mm (2.5614 in.) or if out-of-round of bore exceeds 0.060 mm (0.0024 in.), cylinder should be bored to the next oversize of 0.25, 0.50 or 0.75 mm. Bore cylinder to following diameter:

Piston Oversize	Bore Diameter
0.25 mm	65.230-65.250 mm (2.5681-2.5689 in.)
0.50 mm	65.480-65.500 mm (2.5779-2.5787 in.)
0.75 mm	65.730-65.750 mm (2.5878-2.5886 in.)

REWIND STARTER. To disassemble starter, remove starter from engine. Remove rope handle and allow rope to wind slowly into starter. Note position of pawl (5—Fig. KW215), then unscrew center screw and remove retainer and pawl assembly. Wear appropriate safety eyewear and gloves before disengaging pulley from starter as spring may uncoil uncontrolled. Place shop cloth around pulley and lift pulley out of housing; spring should remain with pulley. If spring must be removed from pulley, position pulley so spring side is down and against floor, then tap pulley to dislodge spring.

Reassemble starter by reversing disassembly procedure while noting the following. Lightly grease sides of rewind spring and pulley. Install spring in pulley so coil direction is counterclockwise from outer spring end. Wind rope around pulley in counterclockwise direction as viewed from pawl side of pulley. Position pulley in starter housing and turn pulley counterclockwise until spring tension is felt. Apply thread locking compound to threads of screw (1—Fig. KW215), then install pawl (5) and retainer (3). Tighten retainer screw to 3.5 N•m (30 in.-lbs.) torque; do not over tighten. After installing retainer, hold rope in notch and preload spring by turning pulley three turns counterclockwise, then pass rope through rope outlet in housing and install handle.

ELECTRICAL SYSTEM. Some engines may be equipped with a 12-volt electrical system that is separate from the ignition system. The electrical system comprises an electric starter, alternator and battery. Starter and alternator are considered unit assemblies. No service specifications are available for starter. The alternator is located under the flywheel and should be renewed if output is less than 8 volts DC.

KUBOTA

KUBOTA
550 W. Artesia Blvd.
Compton, California 90220

Model	Bore	Stroke	Displacement
GH150V	61 mm	50 mm	146 cc
	(2.4 in.)	(2.0 in.)	(8.9 cu. in.)

ENGINE INFORMATION

The Model GH150V is a four-stroke, overhead valve, single-cylinder, air-cooled engine. The engine is equipped with a vertical crankshaft. The engine power rating at 3600 rpm is 3.73 kW (5.0 hp).

MAINTENANCE

SPARK PLUG. Spark plug should be removed, cleaned and inspected after every 100 hours of use.
Recommended spark plug is a NGK BR5ES. Spark plug electrode gap should be 0.7-0.8 mm (0.028-0.031 inch) for all models.

FUEL FILTER. Some models are equipped with a fuel filter in the fuel tank that is attached to the fuel valve. Other models are equipped with an in-line filter in the fuel line.

AIR CLEANER. The air cleaner consists of a paper element and a urethane element. Discard paper element if low-pressure air from a compressor will not dislodge dirt. The urethane element can be washed with soapy water then air dried. Do not apply oil to urethane element.

CARBURETOR. All models are equipped with a Mikuni float type carburetor with a fixed main fuel jet.
Remove fuel bowl for access to main fuel jet and fuel inlet valve. When assembling the carburetor note the following. Place a small drop of nonhardening sealant such as Permatex #2 or equivalent on throttle and choke plate retaining screws. Float height is not adjustable; replace any components which are damaged or excessively worn and adversely affect float position.
Refer to Fig. KU1 and adjust position of choke rod retaining screw. Move throttle lever to wide open position. Loosen choke rod retaining screw (K) and move choke to wide open position. Move screw (K) so distance (D) from center of screw to end of slot is 2-3 mm (0.08-0.12 inch).

GOVERNOR. The mechanical flyweight type governor is located inside engine crankcase. To adjust external linkage, stop engine and make certain all linkage is in good condition and springs are not stretched or damaged. Loosen clamp bolt (B—Fig. KU1) and move governor lever (L) so throttle is completely open. Hold governor lever in this position and rotate governor shaft (S) in clockwise direction until it stops. Tighten clamp bolt.
Start engine and operate at an idle until operating temperature has been reached. Attach a tachometer to engine and move throttle so engine is operating at maximum speed of 3050 rpm. Adjust throttle stop screw (W) so throttle movement is limited to correct maximum engine rpm.

IGNITION SYSTEM. The breakerless ignition system requires no regular maintenance. Ignition coil unit is mounted outside the flywheel. Air gap (G—Fig. KU2) between flywheel magnet (M) and coil (C) should be 0.5 mm (0.020 inch).
To check ignition coil primary side, connect one ohmmeter lead to primary coil lead and touch iron coil laminations with remaining lead. Ohmmeter should register approximately 0.6 ohms.

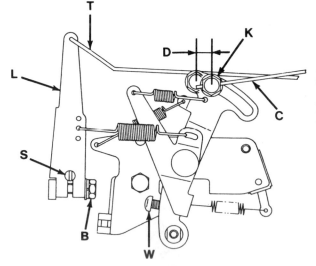

Fig. KU1—Drawing of governor and carburetor linkage. Distance (D) from center of choke rod retaining screw (K) and end of slot should be 2-3 mm (0.08-0.12 inch).

B. Clamp bolt
C. Choke rod
K. Choke rod retaining screw
L. Governor lever
S. Governor shaft
T. Throttle rod
W. Throttle stop screw

Fig. KU2—Gap (G) between ignition unit core (C) and flywheel magnet (M) should be 0.5 mm (0.020 inch).

To check ignition coil secondary side, connect one ohmmeter lead to the spark plug lead wire and remaining lead to the iron core laminations. Ohmmeter should read approximately 12.6k ohms. If ohmmeter readings are not as specified, renew ignition coil.

VALVE ADJUSTMENT. Valve-to-rocker arm clearance should be checked and adjusted after every 300 hours of operation. Clearance should be checked when engine is cold.

To adjust valve clearance, remove rocker arm cover and rotate engine so piston is at top dead center (TDC) on compression stroke. Insert a feeler gage between rocker arm and end of valve stem as shown in Fig. KU3. Loosen rocker arm lock nut and turn adjusting nut to obtain desired clearance. Specified clearance for both valves with engine cold is 0.05-0.10 mm (0.002-0.004 in.). Tighten lock nut and recheck clearance. Install rocker arm cover.

LUBRICATION. Read oil level on dipstick after dipstick is fully screwed into engine. Oil should be changed after the first 20 hours of engine operation and after every 100 hours thereafter.

Manufacturer recommends using oil with an API service classification of SE or SF. Use SAE 30 oil for temperatures above 80° F (27° C); use SAE 10W-30 or SAE 10W-40 oil for temperatures between 0° F (-18° C) and 80° F (27° C).

Crankcase capacity is 0.6 liter (0.6 quarts).

REPAIRS

ENGINE REMOVAL. If engine must be separated from deck, refer to sections in this manual related to the self-propelled drive system and blade brake clutch.

TIGHTENING TORQUES. Recommended tightening torque specifications are as follows:

Connecting rod . . . . .13.7-19.6 N·m
       (121-173 in.-lbs.)
Crankcase cover . . . . . . .9.8-14.7 N·m
       (87-130 in.-lbs.)
Cylinder head . . . . .25-32 N·m
       (18-24 ft.-lbs.)
Flywheel nut . . . . .59-68 N·m
       (43-50 ft.-lbs.)
Rocker arm lock nut . . . .7.8-12.7 N·m
       (69-112 in.-lbs.)

CYLINDER HEAD. To remove cylinder head, first remove recoil starter, air cleaner assembly, blower housing and muffler. Drain the fuel and remove fuel tank. Disconnect throttle and choke linkage, then unbolt and remove carburetor. Remove rocker arm cover. Remove rocker arm adjusting nuts, rocker arms and push rods. Remove cylinder head bolts and separate cylinder head and gasket from cylinder block.

Compress valve springs and remove spring retainers, valve springs and valves from cylinder head. Identify all parts so they can be installed in original positions if reused. Clean carbon from cylinder head and valves. Inspect all parts for wear or damage and renew as necessary.

Valve face and seat angles are 45 degrees for intake and exhaust. Standard valve seat width is 0.6-0.8 mm (0.024-0.031 inch). Narrow seat if seat width is 1.3 mm (0.051 inch) or more.

Standard valve spring free length is 33.0-33.5 mm (1.30-1.32 inches). Renew valve spring if free length is 32.5 mm (1.28 inches) or less.

Standard valve guide inside diameter is 5.500-5.512 mm (0.2165-0.2170 inch). Standard intake valve stem diameter is 5.448-5.460 mm (0.2145-0.2150 inch). Standard exhaust valve stem diameter is 5.428-5.440 mm (0.2137-0.2141 inch).

Valve stem-to-guide clearance should be 0.040-0.064 mm (0.0016-0.0025 inch) for intake valve and 0.060-0.084 mm (0.0024-0.0033 inch) for exhaust valve. Renew valve and/or guide if clearance is 0.10 mm (0.004 inch) or more.

When renewing valve guides, use suitable installing tool to prevent damage to valve guide bore. Valve guides should be pressed into cylinder head from the top so intake valve guide is 24.5-25.1 mm (0.965-0.988 inch) from cylinder head mating surface. Press in exhaust valve guide so guide is 24.2-24.8 mm (0.952-0.976 inch) from cylinder head mating surface. See Fig. KU4.

To install cylinder head, reverse the removal procedure using a new head gasket. Tighten head bolts to 25-32 N·m (18-24 ft.-lbs.). Adjust valve clearance as outlined in VALVE ADJUSTMENT paragraph.

CONNECTING ROD. The aluminum alloy connecting rod rides directly on crankpin journal. To remove connecting rod, remove engine from mower deck. Remove mower blade clutch from crankshaft. Remove cylinder head assembly. Remove crankcase cover retaining screws, then tap cover with plastic hammer to remove cover from locating dowel pins. Be sure to note location of shims (1 and 2—Fig. KU5) so they can be reinstalled in original positions. Remove carbon and ring ridge (if present) from top of cylinder prior to removing piston. Remove connecting rod cap screws and cap. Push connecting rod and piston assembly out of cylinder. Remove piston pin retaining rings and separate piston from connecting rod.

Standard piston pin bore diameter in connecting rod is 13.015-13.025 mm (0.5124-0.5128 inch). Renew connecting rod if diameter is 13.07 mm (0.515 inch).

Standard connecting rod big end diameter is 25.500-25.516 mm (1.0039-1.0046 inch). Connecting rod bearing bore-to-crankpin clearance should be 0.016-0.047 mm (0.0006-0.0018 inch). Renew connecting rod and/or crankshaft if clearance is 0.1 mm (0.004 inch) or more. An undersize connecting rod is available.

Connecting rod side play on crankpin should be 0.2-0.9 mm (0.008-0.035 inch). Renew connecting rod if side play is 1.5 mm (0.059 inch) or more.

When reassembling piston on connecting rod, arrowhead on piston crown

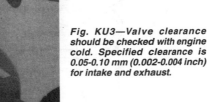

Fig. KU3—Valve clearance should be checked with engine cold. Specified clearance is 0.05-0.10 mm (0.002-0.004 inch) for intake and exhaust.

Fig. KU4—Install valve guides so distance (E) from exhaust guide to cylinder head surface is 24.2-24.8 mm (0.952-0.976 inch) and distance (I) from intake valve guide to cylinder head surface is 24.5-25.1 mm (0.965-0.988 inch).

(Fig. KU6) must be on the same side as rod and cap locating marks (M). Heat piston to approximately 212° F (100° C) before inserting piston pin.

When reinstalling piston and connecting rod assembly in cylinder, arrowhead (A—Fig. KU6) on piston crown and casting number (N) on connecting rod must point toward blade end of crankshaft. Align connecting rod and cap match marks (M), install connecting rod bolts and tighten to 13.7-19.6 N·m (121-173 in.-lbs.).

PISTON, PIN AND RINGS. Piston and connecting rod are removed as an assembly. Refer to previous CONNECTING ROD paragraphs for removal and installation procedure.

Standard piston diameter measured 10 mm (0.4 inch) from lower edge of skirt and 90 degrees from piston pin is 60.95-60.97 mm (2.3996-2.4004 inches).

Renew piston if diameter is less than 60.85 mm (2.3957 inches). Pistons 0.25 and 0.50 mm oversize are available.

Standard piston pin bore diameter is 13.009-13.017 mm (0.5121-0.5125 inch). Renew piston pin if diameter is 13.04 mm (0.5134 inch) or less.

Ring side clearance in piston ring groove should be 0.02-0.06 mm (0.0008-0.0024 inch) for all rings. Renew piston if ring side clearance exceeds 0.1 mm (0.004 inch). Ring end gap for all rings should be 0.2-0.4 mm (0.008-0.016 inch). If ring end gap for any ring is 1.0 mm (0.039 inch) or more, rebore cylinder for installation of oversize piston and rings.

Install marked piston rings with marked side (M—Fig. KU7) toward piston crown. Stagger ring end gaps at 120 degree intervals around piston, with end gap of top ring (A) positioned so that it will be toward camshaft side of cylinder block.

CYLINDER AND CRANKCASE. Cylinder and crankcase are an integral casting. Standard cylinder bore diameter is 61.00-61.02 mm (2.4016-2.4024 inches). Resize cylinder if diameter exceeds 61.12 mm (2.4063 inches). The cylinder may be bored to accommodate a 0.25 or 0.50 mm oversize piston.

CRANKSHAFT, MAIN BEARINGS AND SEALS. The crankshaft is supported at the flywheel end by a ball bearing. The crankshaft rides directly in the crankcase cover at the pto end. To remove crankshaft, first remove engine from mower deck. Remove blade brake, flywheel, cylinder head and crankcase cover. Turn cylinder block so tappets fall away from camshaft, then withdraw camshaft. Remove connecting rod and piston assembly. Pull crankshaft out of cylinder block.

Renew ball bearing, crankcase cover or crankshaft if components are damaged or worn excessively. Maximum allowable crankshaft end play is 0.2 mm (0.008 inch). Install shims as needed to obtain desired end play.

Standard crankpin journal diameter is 25.469-25.484 mm (1.0027-1.0033 inch). The crankshaft may be reground to fit a 0.25 or 0.50 mm undersize connecting rod.

When installing crankshaft, make certain that crankshaft gear and camshaft gear timing marks are aligned as shown in Fig. KU8.

CAMSHAFT. Camshaft and camshaft gear are an integral casting equipped with a compression release mechanism. The camshaft is accessible after removing crankcase cover.

Standard camshaft lobe height is 27.335-27.365 mm (1.0762-1.0774 inches) for intake and exhaust lobes. Renew camshaft if either lobe height is less than 27.15 mm (1.069 inches).

Inspect compression release mechanism for damage. Spring must pull weight tightly against camshaft so decompressor pin holds exhaust valve slightly open. Weight overcomes spring tension at 1000 rpm and moves decompressor pin away from cam lobe to release exhaust valve. If pin (P—Fig. KU9) does not protrude 0.52-0.92 mm (0.020-0.036 inch) above exhaust lobe, renew pin.

When installing camshaft, make certain camshaft and crankshaft gear timing marks are aligned as shown in Fig. KU8.

GOVERNOR. A centrifugal flyweight type governor controls engine rpm via external linkage. Governor is located in crankcase cover. Refer to GOVERNOR paragraphs in MAINTENANCE section

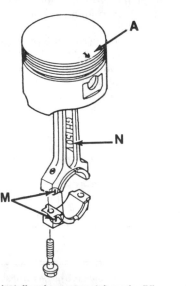

Fig. KU5—View of engine with crankcase cover (3) removed. Shims (1 and 2) are used to adjust crankshaft and camshaft end play.

Fig. KU6—Install rod cap so match marks (M) on rod and cap are aligned. Arrow (A) on piston crown, match marks (M) and casting number (N) must be on same side as shown.

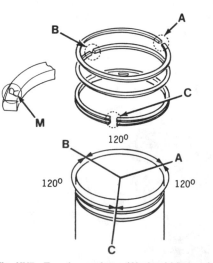

Fig. KU7—Top ring end gap (A) should be positioned on piston so that it faces camshaft side of engine. Install rings with manufacturer's mark (M) facing up.

Illustrations Courtesy of Kubota Tractor Corp.

Fig. KU8—Align timing marks (TM) on crankshaft and camshaft gears. Note two marks on crankshaft gear. With one mark at 12 o'clock position, align mark at 3 o'clock position with camshaft timing mark.

meter lead connected to rectifier negative terminal and positive lead connected to positive terminal, the ohmmeter should indicate some resistance. With negative ohmmeter lead connected to rectifier positive terminal and positive ohmmeter lead connected to rectifier negative terminal, the ohmmeter should indicate infinite resistance. If correct readings are not obtained, renew rectifier.

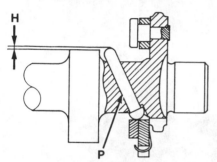

Fig. KU9—Height (H) of decompressor pin (P) should be 0.52-0.92 mm (0.020-0.036 inch).

Minimum allowable brush length (L—Fig. KU12) is 3.5 mm (0.14 inch). Minimum allowable commutator diameter is 21 mm (0.827 inch).

CHARGING SYSTEM. Models equipped with a battery are equipped with an alternator and rectifier to charge the battery. Resistance between the two alternator leads should be 0.34-0.46 ohms.

To test rectifier, disconnect wires to rectifier and check resistance between rectifier terminals. With negative ohm-

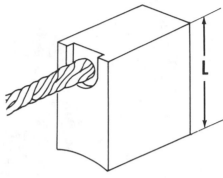

Fig. KU12—Minimum allowable brush length (L) is 3.5 mm (0.14 inch).

for adjustment procedure. Refer to Fig. KU10 for view of governor components.

AUXILIARY DRIVE. Some engines are equipped with the auxiliary drive shaft (11—Fig. KU10). The shaft is mounted in crankcase cover and is splined to driven gear (9) which is driven by a gear on lower end of the camshaft. The shaft is retained by spring pin (8).

ELECTRIC STARTER. Some models may be equipped with the electric starter shown in Fig. KU11.

To check starter relay connect an ohmmeter to terminals C and D on starter relay. When battery is not connected to relay, there should be infinite resistance between C and D terminals. When battery is connected to A and B relay terminals, there should be zero ohms indicated between C and D terminals.

To disassemble starter, refer to Fig. KU11 and remove snap ring (1), washers (2), stopper (3), spring (4) and pinion gear assembly (5). Remove through-bolts (11) and separate end cover (10) and front bracket (6) from armature (8) and field housing (9).

Fig. KU10—Exploded view of governor, oil slinger and auxiliary drive shaft. Note that shim (7) is 1 mm thick and shim (10) is 3 mm thick.

1. Retainer
2. Governor sleeve
3. Washer
4. Stopper
5. Governor assy.
6. Oil slinger
7. Shim
8. Spring pin
9. Gear
10. Shim
11. Auxiliary drive shaft
12. Oil seal

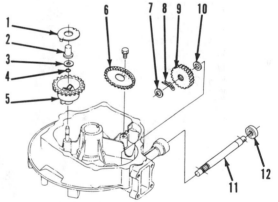

Fig. KU11—Exploded view of optional electric starter motor.

1. "E" ring
2. Washer
3. Stopper
4. Spring
5. Drive pinion
6. Drive housing
7. Washer
8. Armature
9. Frame
10. End cover
11. Through-bolt

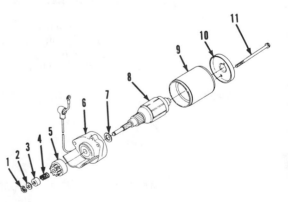

LAWN-BOY

LAWN-BOY, INC.
8111 Lyndale Avenue South
Bloomington, Minnesota 55420

Model	Bore	Stroke	Displacement
C-10, C-12, C-20, C-21, C-22, C-70, C-71, C-72, C-73, C-75	1.94 in. (49.2 mm)	1.50 in. (38.1 mm)	4.43 cu. in. (72.4 cc)
C-13 through C-17, C-40, C-41, C-42, C-50, C-51, C-60, C-61, C-74, C-76, C-77, C-78, C-80, C-81	2.13 in. (54.1 mm)	1.50 in. (38.1 mm)	5.22 cu. in. (86.9 cc)
C-18, C-44, D-400 through D-408, D405E through D-408E, D-409, D-430, D-431, D-432, D-433, D-440, through D-448, D-445E through D-448E, D-449, D-450, D-451, D-452, D-460, D-461, D-462, D-475, D-476, D-480, D-481, D-570, D-600, D-600E, D-601, D-640, D-640E, D-641, D-641E	2.38 in. (60.4 mm)	1.50 in. (38.1 mm)	6.65 cu. in. (108.8 cc)

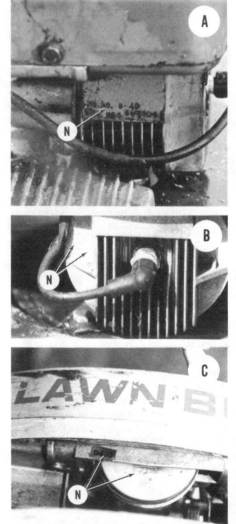

ENGINE INFORMATION

On 1960 and earlier models, engine model and serial numbers will be found on engine shroud or gas tank strap (Fig. LB1). On later models, engine model and serial number are located on either starter spring cap or cylinder (Fig. LB1).

Fig. LB1—Engine model and serial number locations (N) on 1960 and earlier models are shown in views "A" and "B". On newer models, engine model number is located as shown in view "C".

MAINTENANCE

SPARK PLUG. Recommended spark plug for 4.43 cu. in. (72.4 cc) and 5.22 cu. in. (86.9 cc) engines is a Champion J14J, or equivalent. Recommended spark plug for 6.65 cu. in. (108.8 cc) engine is a Champion CJ14, or equivalent.

Electrode gap should be set at 0.025 inch (0.6 mm) for all models except D-600 series (solid state ignition) which calls for a gap of 0.035 inch (0.9 mm). Tighten plugs on all models to 12-15 ft.-lbs. (16-20 N·m).

CARBURETOR. Lawn Boy float type carburetors are used on all engine models. Figure LB2 shows an exploded view of carburetor used on C-series engines. Figure LB3 shows an exploded view of carburetor used on early D-series engines. Later D-series do not have a low speed mixture needle (6 – Fig. LB3), but are equipped instead with a fixed jet requiring no adjustments. D-600 series and Modular D-series carburetors are fully automatic with no external adjustments to regulate normal fuel intake. However, these carburetors are equipped with an altitude compensation needle which is covered later in this section.

Removal of C and early D-series carburetors require removal of reed plate. D-series engines equipped with plastic modular carburetors are secured by externally mounted screws.

C AND D-SERIES CARBURETORS. On C and D-series carburetors equipped with idle (low speed) needle, initial adjustment is approximately ¾-turn out from seated position. Initial adjustment on main fuel needle is approximately 2½ turns out from seated position. After engine is started, adjust main fuel needle so engine runs smoothly until pro-

perly warmed up (about five minutes). Turn main fuel needle in (clockwise) until engine begins to lose speed, then turn

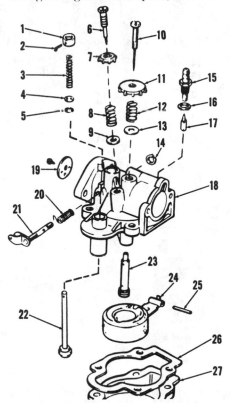

Fig. LB3—Exploded view of carburetor typical of type used on D-series engines. Late D models are not equipped with idle fuel needle (6).

1. Knob	15. Float valve seat
2. Cotter pin	16. Washer
3. Spring	17. Float valve
4. Washer	18. Carburetor body
5. "O" ring	19. Throttle disc
6. Idle fuel needle	20. Throttle spring
7. Knob	21. Throttle shaft
8. Spring	22. Primer plunger
9. Washer	23. Nozzle
10. Main fuel needle	24. Float
11. Knob	25. Float pin
12. Spring	26. Gasket
13. Washer	27. Float bowl
14. Snap ring	

needle out ⅛-¼ turn. Adjust idle needle when engine is at normal operating temperature for smoothest idle performance. If idle mixture is too lean, engine is likely to surge at low speed.

Float setting (H – Fig. LB3A) for C and D-series carburetors is 15/32 inch (12 mm) above carburetor body flange. Adjust float level by bending float arm using needle nose pliers. Do not apply strain or pressure to cork float. If float shows signs of damage or if epoxy varnish is flaked off or chipped, renew float assembly.

Do not use commercial carburetor cleaners. Use a mild solvent to clean and clear carburetor parts and passages. Do not dry carburetor parts with a cloth. Loose lint may be the cause of a later problem.

When reassembling carburetor, reinstall main fuel nozzle (94 – Fig. LB2 or 23 – Fig. LB3) before installing fuel needle (104 – Fig. LB2 or 10 – Fig. LB3) to prevent jamming needle into nozzle seat. Be sure to set a light preload on throttle spring (103 – Fig. LB2 or 20 – Fig. LB3) by adding about ½-turn tension when attaching spring to throttle shaft lever.

SERIES D-600 CARBURETOR. See Fig. LB4 for exploded view of Series D-600 carburetor. Difference between this and preceding models is elimination of external adjustments for main and idle circuits.

Altitude adjustment needle (15 – Fig. LB4) is designed to compensate for differences in atmospheric pressure if engine is to be operated at elevations which are higher or lower in relation to sea level. To adjust, preset altitude needle 1½ turns (counterclockwise) from fully seated position. Start engine and

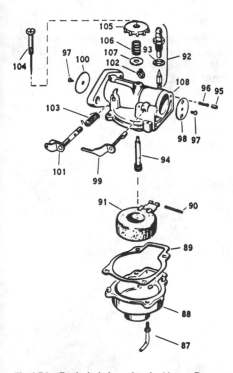

Fig. LB2—Exploded view of typical Lawn-Boy carburetor used on C-series engines. Refer to Fig. LB3 for carburetor used on D-series engines.

87. Bowl retaining screws	98. Choke disc
88. Float bowl	99. Choke shaft
89. Gasket	100. Throttle disc
90. Float pin	101. Throttle shaft
91. Float	103. Throttle spring
92. Inlet valve assy.	104. Fuel adjustment needle
93. Gasket	105. Knob
94. Nozzle	106. Spring
95. Choke detent	107. Washer
96. Spring	108. Carburetor body

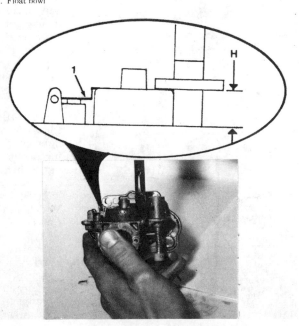

Fig. LB3A—Correct float setting (H) for C and D-series carburetors is 15/32 inch (12 mm). Adjust float setting by bending float arm (1).

Fig. LB4—Exploded view of D-600 series carburetor.

1. Gasket	13. Throttle spring
2. Float bowl	14. Throttle shaft
3. Dump valve stem	15. Altitude screw
4. Valve seat	16. Spring
5. Valve keeper	17. Fuel tube
6. Valve spring	18. Connector
8. Float	19. Body assy.
9. Float valve	20. Washer
assy.	21. Plug
10. Clip	22. Float pin
11. Washer	23. Throttle shaft
12. Throttle disc	retainer

Fig. LB6—Exploded view of "Hinged Float" style modular carburetor used on some later Model D-series engines.

1. Filter cover	
2. Filter element	13. Screw
3. "O" ring	14. Main body
4. Air screw	15. Retainer
5. Return spring	16. Bowl gasket
6. Screw	17. Clip
7. Throttle disc	18. Valve seat
8. Throttle shaft	19. Needle
9. "O" ring	20. Pin
10. Reed plate	21. Float
11. Reed	22. Bowl
12. Reed retainer	23. Screw

Fig. LB7—Correct float height setting for hinged float style modular carburetor.

run 3 to 5 minutes to warm up. Place speed control lever in low speed position. Slowly turn altitude needle in (clockwise) until engine begins to surge or slow down. Turn altitude needle out slowly until engine runs smoothly, then allow engine to run a few minutes while observing engine performance. If engine does not run smoothly repeat altitude needle adjustment procedure. Set speed control to high speed position. If engine is not running smoothly, turn altitude needle out (counterclockwise) in ¼-turn increments until engine runs smoothly.

Shut off engine and restart immediately. If difficulty in restarting is encountered, turn altitude needle out an additional ⅛-¼ turn to richen mixture.

Carburetor servicing is limited to visual inspection, cleaning with a mild solvent (**DO NOT** use a standard carburetor cleaner) and adjustment of float height. Adjust float height to 15/32 inch (12 mm) above carburetor body flange as shown in Fig. LB3. Adjust float lever only by bending float arm using needle nose pliers. Do not apply strain or pressure to cork float. If float shows signs of damage or if epoxy varnish is flaked off or chipped, renew float assembly.

Early 1972 production was fitted with a plastic throttle shaft and disc. If renewal becomes necessary, use assembly number 681008 which contains bronze parts.

If throttle shaft and disc are removed for servicing or renewal, be sure to set a light preload on throttle spring by adding about ½-turn tension when attaching spring.

MODULAR CARBURETOR. Engine Models D-409, D-481, D-601, D-641 and D-641E may be equipped with a modular-type carburetor. There are two styles, the "Free Float" style as shown in Fig. LB5 and the "Hinged Float" style as shown in Fig. LB6. These carburetors are fully automatic and require no external adjustments except for the altitude adjustment needle.

On "Free Float" style carburetor, the specific free length of float spring (12—Fig. LB5) should be ⅝ inch (16 mm). If length is incorrect, renew spring.

On "Hinged Float" style carburetors, the correct float height should be 11/16 inch (17 mm) measured above carburetor body flange as shown in Fig. LB7. Adjust float level by bending float arm using needle nose pliers. Do not bend arm by applying pressure on cork float.

Altitude adjustment needle should be opened ¾-turn from fully seated for elevations from 500-1500 feet above sea level.

Check all parts for excessive wear or damage and renew as needed. **DO NOT** use standard carburetor cleaners, use only a mild grease solvent to clean carburetor parts and blow dry with compressed air. **DO NOT** dry carburetor parts with a cloth, as lint from cloth could plug fuel passage and cause a performance problem.

PRIMER. D-series carburetors are equipped with priming devices to aid in starting. C-series carburetors are equipped with a standard manual choke butterfly. D-series carburetor uses a mechanical primer as shown in Fig. LB8. Primer plunger lifts fuel into car-

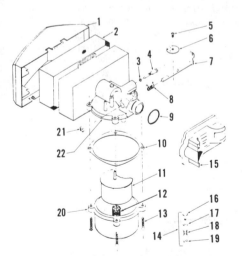

Fig. LB5—Exploded view of "Free Float" style modular carburetor used on some later Model D-series engines.

1. Filter cover	12. Spring
2. Filter element	13. Screw
3. "O" ring	14. Dump valve assy.
4. Air screw	15. Reed plate
5. Screw	16. Valve stem
6. Disc	17. Valve seat
7. Throttle shaft	18. Valve spring
8. Return spring	19. Valve keeper
9. "O" ring	20. Float bowl
10. Bowl gasket	21. Retainer
11. Float	22. Main body

Fig. LB8—View showing primer plunger assembly used on D-series carburetors.

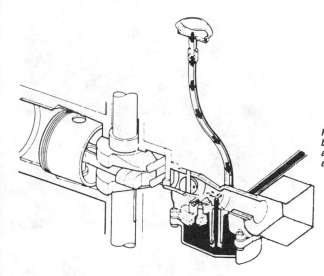

Fig. LB9—Cutaway view of carburetor showing priming pump assembly used on modular style carburetors.

Fig. LB12—View showing installation of governor yoke, weights and collar as a unit.

buretor chamber. Modular carburetors use a pneumatic bulb type primer as shown in Fig. LB9. Depressing primer bulb forces air in float chamber which forces fuel through main jet into carburetor venturi. **DO NOT** over-prime; one priming stroke is normally sufficient.

REED VALVE. Reed valves permit fuel-air mixture to enter crankcase on the compression stroke and seal fuel-air mixture in crankcase on the power stroke. Reeds are attached to reed plate on C and D-series engines and can be cleaned and serviced after removal of reed plate and carburetor. Reeds can be cleaned with solvent or carburetor cleaner. **DO NOT** use compressed air on reed assemblies or distortion may occur resulting in hard starting or loss of power. Bent or distorted reeds cannot be repaired. Rough edge of reed must be positioned away from machined surface of mounting plate. Check reed-to-plate clearance as shown in Fig. LB10. Clearance of 0.015 inch (0.38 mm) between reed tip and machined surface is allowable. Renew if clearance is excessive.

cessive. Coat reed mounting screws with Lawn Boy Nut & Screw Lock (Part 682301) or a suitable equivalent and tighten to 10-13 in.-lbs. (1 N·m).

GOVERNOR. All C and D-series engines are equipped with a mechanical governor. The governor weight unit is located under the flywheel. View of a typical engine governor assembly is shown in Fig. LB11. Most D-series engines are also equipped with a variable speed spring and governor lever which will be explained later. Engine speed is controlled by compression of coil spring under governor weight unit as shown in Fig. LB12.

Two different governor springs are available on C-series engines providing governed speeds of 2800 rpm and 3200 rpm. Data on governor springs is as follows:

C-Series Engines

Rpm	Free Length	Color
2800	0.750-0.780 in. (19-20 mm)	Red
3200	0.735-0.765 in. (18.67-19.44 mm)	....

On D-series engines, all models except D-430 and D-460 are equipped with a

variable speed spring located between speed control lever and governor lever (See Fig. LB16) to provide a variable speed governor. Governor spring color is green. Models D-430 and D-460 are equipped with a unpainted (Natural) governor spring to provide a governed speed of 3200 rpm. Data on governor springs is as follows:

D-Series Engines

Rpm	Free Length	Color
Variable (2500-3200)	0.735-0.765 in. (18.67-19.44 mm)	Green
3200	0.735-0.765 in. (18.67-19.44 mm)	Natural

Shown in Fig. LB13 is procedure for checking governor adjustment on D-series engines. On D-600 series engines turn variable speed control to "light" position and rotate thrust collar clockwise against its stop on governor lever. On all D-series engines, place Lawn Boy special tool 604541 (1) over crankshaft end. Push governor weight unit as far down on crankshaft as possible and hold carburetor throttle shaft (4) in closed position. Gap (G) between governor lever (2) and end of governor rod (3) should be 1/16-inch (1.6 mm). If

Fig. LB10—View showing a typical reed plate assembly. Clearance of 0.015 inch (0.38 mm) measured as shown is allowable. Renew reed valve if clearance is excessive or if bent or distorted so as to prevent sealing under pressure.

Fig. LB11—View showing components of a typical engine governor assembly used on all C and D-series engines.
1. Governor yoke
2. Weights
3. Collar
4. Wear block
5. Lever
6. Rod

Fig. LB15—View showing governor lever (2) installed in thrust collar (1) on D-series engines equipped with variable speed governor.

Fig. LB13—View showing procedure for checking governor adjustment on D-series engine. C-series engine is similar. Measure gap (G) and refer to text.

1. Special tool
2. Governor lever
3. Governor rod
4. Throttle shaft

Fig. LB16—Hooking variable speed spring (1) into governor lever (2) on so equipped D-series engines.

not, bend governor lever at crease in lever near point where it contacts governor rod.

Governor adjustment procedures for C-series engine are the same as for D-series engine except for the following: Lawn Boy special tool 602885 should be used over crankshaft end. Gap between governor lever and end of governor rod should be ⅛ inch (3.2 mm).

Governor lever thrust collars on D-400 and D-600 series engines are different as shown in Fig. LB14. D-600 collar is designed to prevent engine from starting and running backward due to preignition, combustion chamber hot spot or other malfunction. D-400 and D-600 thrust collars are **NOT** interchangeable.

When reassembling governor on D-series engines with variable speed governor, place web in groove of plastic thrust collar (See Fig. LB15) between arms on governor lever with lugs on arms inserted in groove of collar. Engage tabs on governor lever in slots on breaker point dust cover. Hook governor spring into lever as shown in Fig. LB16. Apply a light coat of Lawn Boy "A" grease or a suitable equivalent to both faces of steel thrust washer and place washer on top of plastic collar.

On all C and D-series engines place governor spring over crankshaft. Install

Fig. LB17—Lug (1) on flywheel drives governor weight unit on C-series and early D-400 series engines. Late D-400 and D-600 series engines are equipped with two "dimples" on top of governor yoke.

governor yoke, weights and collar assembly over end of crankshaft and governor spring. Turn governor yoke to position word "Key" located on top of yoke under flywheel key, then install key and flywheel.

NOTE: Bore in flywheel and end of crankshaft should be clean and dry before installing flywheel.

Lug on flywheel (1 – Fig. LB17) on C and early D-400 engines drives governor

weight unit. On late D-400 and D-600 series engines, governor yokes have two "dimples" located on top which engage bottom side of flywheel to drive governor.

MAGNETO AND TIMING. Refer to the following paragraphs for magneto service information on each Lawn Boy engine series.

C-SERIES MAGNETOS. All C-series engines use similar magnetos, refer to

D-400   D-600

Fig. LB14—D-400 and D-600 governor thrust collars shown for comparison. They cannot be interchanged. Refer to text.

Fig. LB18. On all models, timing is fixed and nonadjustable.

Armature air gap should be 0.010 inch (0.25 mm). Air gap can be considered correct if heels of armature core are flush with machined rim on armature plate as shown in Fig. LB19. Breaker point gap should be 0.020 inch (0.51 mm). When installing breaker points and/or condenser, wires from coil and

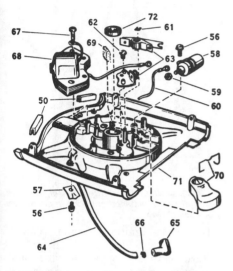

Fig. LB18—Exploded view of magneto used on C-series engines. Design of armature plate (71) is different on some models of C engines.

58. Condenser
60. Stop switch wire
63. Breaker points
68. Coil
69. Cam oiler felt
70. Dust cover
71. Armature plate

Fig. LB19—To set armature air gap on C-series engines, loosen mounting screws and set coil heels flush with rim of armature plate as shown.

Fig. LB20—View showing ignition grounding switch components used on C-series engines.

1. Spring
2. Upper insulator
3. Switch lead
4. Lower insulator
5. Mounting screw

stop switch should be installed under breaker point spring.

For reference in disassembling ignition grounding switch refer to Fig. LB20. Figure LB21 shows grounding switch correctly assembled and installed.

Fig. LB21—View showing grounding switch correctly assembled and installed on C-series engines.

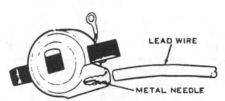

Fig. LB22—Push high tension lead firmly onto metal needle in ignition coil and be sure lead retaining clamp is tight.

Fig. LB23—Flyweight (1) is shown in starting position.

Fig. LB24—View showing movement of flyweight as centrifugal force moves flyweight against spring pressure as engine rpm increases.

Be sure high tension lead is pushed firmly onto metal needle in ignition coil as shown in Fig. LB22 and tighten clamp securing high tension lead to armature plate. Ground lead from ignition coil should be pressed down flat against armature core to prevent governor weights from striking wire.

D-SERIES MAGNETOS. The magneto breaker cam on D-series engines is driven by a flyweight (1-Fig. LB23) to provide an automatic timing advance. The flyweight is retained in position by a pin through a hole in crankshaft which engages small end of flyweight. A coil spring surrounds the pin and forces small end of flyweight away from crankshaft when engine is not running as shown in Fig. LB23. When engine speed reaches approximately 1000 rpm, centrifugal force moves the flyweight against spring pressure which advances breaker cam to running position as shown in Fig. LB24. At starting position, ignition occurs at 6° BTDC; at running position, the timing is advanced to 26° BTDC.

The breaker points, condenser, cam and flyweight are enclosed by a dust cover under the flywheel and governor assembly.

Fig. LB25—Remove flyweight and breaker cam as outlined in text.

To remove flyweight and breaker cam, withdraw flywheel, governor assembly and dust cover. Refer to Fig. LB25 and proceed as follows: Push small end of flyweight towards crankshaft, hold pin and spring in this position, and disengage small end of flyweight from pin and withdraw pin and spring from crankshaft. Lift flyweight and cam from crankshaft.

To adjust breaker points, install breaker cam on crankshaft and turn cam to position of widest breaker point gap. Pull upper end of crankshaft toward carburetor. Adjust breaker point gap to 0.020 inch (0.51 mm) on all later models with flywheel part number 678355 and 0.016 inch (0.41 mm) on early models with flywheel part number 678103. Flywheel part number is located on flywheel. Later flywheel is used in servicing early engines.

NOTE: When servicing magneto, always reinstall wire leads on condenser terminal first, then install breaker point spring and secure with nut. Wire from coil to condenser terminal should be under breaker point base.

When reinstalling cam and flyweight assembly, hold breaker points open and slip cam and flyweight as a unit on crankshaft. Turn cam and flyweight to position small end of flyweight on keyway side of crankshaft. Install spring on pin, push small end of flyweight down and insert inner end of pin in crankshaft hole. Push pin in against spring and engage outer end of pin in small end of flyweight.

When reinstalling flywheel on crankshaft, be sure Woodruff key is installed correctly in crankshaft groove as shown in Fig. LB26.

Armature air gap should be 0.010 inch (0.25 mm). With flywheel installed, place Lawn Boy air gap gage 604659 or a suitable piece of 0.010 inch (0.25 mm) nonmetallic shim stock as shown in Fig.

LB27 between armature core and flywheel magnets. Loosen armature core mounting screws and allow magnets to pull core against flywheel. Tighten armature core mounting screws and remove shim stock.

NOTE: Excessive clearance between crankshaft and top main bearing will affect armature air gap and breaker point gap resulting in faulty ignition.

Top main bearing on 1965 and later models is a renewable needle bearing. The bushing, integral with armature plate on earlier production models, is serviced by installing late type armature plate and needle bearing.

D-600 SERIES CAPACITIVE DISCHARGE IGNITION SYSTEM. Lawn Boy's solid-state (capacitive discharge) ignition design eliminates all moving parts which are normally associated with magneto ignition. On these models, there is no spark advance assembly, breaker cam, breaker point set, condenser or coil. Complete system is electronic, contained in a single, sealed module which is dust and moisture proofed and serviced only as an assembly.

Maintenance is confined to setting air gap between flywheel magnets and CD module, checking for spark output by use of a test spark plug grounded to cylinder and isolation test of ignition switch for continuity. No procedures for troubleshooting or testing ignition pack are offered by manufacturer. If unit will not produce a spark at electrodes of test spark plug and ignition switch and spark plug cable check out to be good, then renewal of module assembly is necessary. Substitution of a spare ignition pack known to be good is an ideal test procedure.

Ignition timing is fixed. System design is set up for 9° retarded spark timing for ease of starting. After engine starts, spark is advanced electronically to 29° BTDC as crankshaft speed reaches 800 rpm.

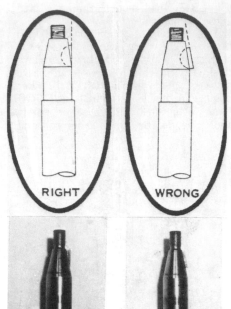

Fig. LB26—When installing flywheel, be sure Woodruff key is installed correctly in crankshaft groove as shown.

To service ignition module, remove three screws holding air baffle to armature plate and separate kill switch lead from ignition switch. Primer and starter need not be removed. With CD ignition pack exposed, 0.010 inch (0.25 mm) air gap may be checked. To do so, rotate flywheel to align flywheel magnets with laminated core heels of ignition module, then insert Lawn Boy Air Gap Gage 604659 or a suitable piece of 0.010 inch (0.25 mm) nonmetallic shim stock as shown in Fig. LB27. With gage in position, when module mounting screws are loosened, magnets will pull module snug against gage. Retighten screws and remove gage.

Operators of this engine should be cautioned to allow 10-15 seconds after shutdown before removing spark plug lead. This is to allow high voltage (approximately 30,000 volts) from CD pack secondary to leak off.

LUBRICATION. Engine is lubricated by premixing oil and gasoline in a separate container before filling engine

Fig. LB27—Adjust air gap using Air Gap Gage between flywheel magnets and coil heels on D-400 series engines. D-600 series engines with capacitive discharge ignition are adjusted following the same procedure. Air gap should be 0.010 inch (0.25 mm). Refer to text.

tank. Manufacturer recommends using Special Lawn Boy lubricant or a suitable good quality two-stroke oil. **DO NOT** use oil additives or standard automotive oils.

The use of regular gasoline (minimum octane rating of 89), unleaded or no-lead (minimum octane rating of 86) is recommended. **DO NOT** use gasoline additives except OMC 2+4 fuel conditioner. When using Special Lawn Boy lubricant mix fuel on 1971 and earlier engines at a ratio of 16:1 or one gallon of gasoline to eight ounces of lubricant. On 1972 and later engines mix fuel at a ratio of 32:1 or two gallons of gasoline to eight ounces of lubricant. When using a different brand of two-stroke oil mix fuel at a ratio of 16:1 on all models.

CARBON. If ignition, fuel supply to combustion chamber and compression check out as satisfactory, but engine will not run or runs poorly, it is likely that there is heavy carbon build-up in exhaust ports and muffler. A common symptom is "four-cycling" or firing every other power stroke.

Manufacturer recommends cleaning out carbon every 35 operating hours. Carbon cleaning procedure is as follows: On all models except D-600, remove two retaining nuts and muffler cover. On D-600 engines, muffler cover is secured by four nuts and mower blade and stiffener must first be removed from lower end of crankshaft. On all models, rotate crankshaft so piston wall blocks exhaust ports, then use a ⅜-inch wooden dowel to break carbon away from port openings. Clean carbon from muffler chamber and cover plate before reassembling.

REPAIRS

TIGHTENING TORQUES. Recommended tightening torques are as follows:

Spark plug............144-180 in.-lbs.
(16-20 N·m)
Carburetor to reed plate..63-75 in.-lbs.
(7-8 N·m)
Reed to reed plate........10-13 in.-lbs.
(1-1.5 N·m)
Reed plate to crankcase...63-75 in.-lbs.
(7-8 N·m)
Breaker point base.......20-25 in.-lbs.
(2-3 N·m)
Coil to armature.........20-25 in.-lbs.
(2-3 N·m)
Condenser to armature...20-25 in.-lbs.
(2-3 N·m)
High tension cable
clamp screw...........20-25 in.-lbs.
(2-3 N·m)
Armature to crankcase...63-75 in.-lbs.
(7-8 N·m)
Shroud to armature
(front)...............25-30 in.-lbs.
(3-3.4 N·m)
Shroud to armature
(side)................10-15 in.-lbs.
(1-1.7 N·m)

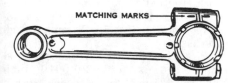

Fig. LB28—When reassembling cap to connecting rod, be sure match marks are aligned as shown.

Fig. LB29—Connecting rod screws are locked into place by either staking screw heads or bending locking tabs.

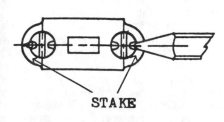

Fig. LB30—Exploded view of C-20, C-21 and C-22 engine. Armature plate (A) is different on other C-series engines. Some models use needle bearings in connecting rod as shown at 7N, 8L and 8R.

A. Armature plate		14. Governor weight
F. Flywheel	5. Cylinder	15. Governor yoke
T. Fuel tank	6. Gasket	8R. Bearing rollers (33)	16. Wear block
1. Reed plate	7. Connecting rod	9. Crankshaft	17. Governor lever
2. Carburetor	(plain bearing)	10. Seal	18. Screws
3. Valve reeds	7N. Connecting rod	11. Shim	19. Carburetor link rod
4. Gasket	8L. Bearing liners	12. Governor spring	20. Sleeve
		13. Governor collar	21. Gasket

Connecting rod.........58-70 in.-lbs.
(6.6-8 N·m)
Cylinder to crankcase...105-115 in.-lbs.
(12-13 N·m)
Engine mounting
screws ....142-170 in.-lbs.
(16-19 N·m)
Tank to shroud ....63-75 in.-lbs.
(7-8 N·m)
Flywheel (C series).....190-225 in.-lbs.
(21-25 N·m)
Flywheel (D series)....335-400 in.-lbs.
(38-45 N·m)
Starter mounting.......58-63 in.-lbs.
(6-6.7 N·m)
Starter pulley..........16-19 in.-lbs.
(1.8-2 N·m)
Blade nut ....450-550 in.-lbs.
(51-62 N·m)
Engine to muffler
plate ....200-240 in.-lbs.
(22.5-27 N·m)
Muffler to muffler plate ...58-63 in.-lbs.
(6.6-7 N·m)

CONNECTING ROD. Rod and piston assembly can be removed after removing reed valve plate and cylinder from crankcase. Early C-series engine were equipped with an aluminum connecting rod with cast-in crankpin bearing surfaces in rod and cap. Late C-series engines and all D-series engines have a needle roller crankpin bearing; the aluminum connecting rod is fitted with renewable steel inserts.

Crankpin diameter is 0.7495-0.7500 inch (19.04-19.05 mm) for C-series engines with plain connecting rod bearing and recommended clearance between bearing and crankpin journal is 0.0025-0.0035 inch (0.064-0.089 mm).

Crankpin diameter is 0.7425-0.7430 inch (18.86-18.87 mm) for C-series engines with needle bearing connecting rod bearing and all D-series engines.

When reassembling plain bearing connecting rod to crankpin, oil bearing surfaces and be sure alignment marks on rod and cap match up as shown in Fig. LB28. After tightening cap retaining screws, be sure rod is free on crankpin. If screws have recesses in head in addition to screwdriver slot, stake cap metal into recesses with dull screwdriver as shown in Fig. LB29.

On needle bearing rods, press needle bearing liners into rod and cap so dovetail ends of liners (8L–Fig. LB30 or LB31) will fit together when rod and cap alignment marks match up. If installing new needle roller set, lay strip of 33 rollers on forefinger and carefully peel backing off rollers. Curl forefinger around crankpin to transfer rollers from finger to journal. Grease on rollers will hold them together and to crankpin. If reinstalling used needle rollers, make certain that rollers are in good condition. Coat surfaces with a layer of OMC Needle Bearing Grease (number 378642) or a suitable equivalent and stick rollers to connecting rod end and cap. Fit 17 rollers to rod cap and 16 to rod end.

Carefully fit rod and cap to crankpin bearing and install cap retaining screws and screw lock tabs. After tightening screws, check to be sure rod assembly is free on crankpin and none of the rollers dropped out during assembly. Bend lock tabs up against flat of screw heads as shown in Fig. LB29.

PISTON, PIN AND RINGS. Piston, pin and rings are available in standard size only. Recommended piston to cylinder clearance is 0.004-0.0055 inch (0.10-0.14 mm) for models with 1.94 inch 49.2 mm) bore, 0.0045-0.006 inch (0.11-0.15 mm) for models with 2.13 inch (54.1 mm) bore or 0.005-0.0065 inch (0.13-0.17 mm) for models with 2.38 inch (60.4 mm) bore.

Piston pin is a push fit in piston. Pin is retained by snap rings at each end of pin bore in piston. Heat piston to facilitate removal and installation of pin.

Piston pin diameter is 0.4270-0.4272 inch (10.84-10.85 mm) for models with 1.94 inch (49.2 mm) bore or 0.4898-0.4900 inch (12.44-12.45 mm) for all models.

Piston pin clearance in connecting rod pin bore is 0.0003-0.0010 inch (0.008-0.025 mm) for all models. Piston pin clearance in piston pin bore is 0.0005 inch (0.013 mm) for models with 1.94 inch (49.2 mm) bore or 0.0007 inch (0.018 mm) for all other models.

Piston ring end gap is 0.015-0.025 inch (0.38-0.64 mm) for all models. Renew piston rings if end gap exceeds 0.025 inch (0.64 mm).

Prior to 1970, all engines were equipped with 3-ring pistons and a plain bronze bearing in wrist pin end of connecting rod. Since 1970, two rings are fitted to all pistons and connecting rod small end contains 27 loose needle roller bearings as shown in Fig. LB32. Great care must be taken to prevent loss of needles during removal as they are not serviced separately.

CYLINDER. Piston and rings are available in standard size only. Renew cylinder if bore is excessively worn or

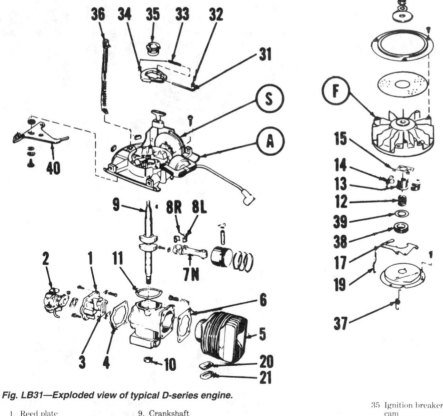

Fig. LB31—Exploded view of typical D-series engine.

1. Reed plate
2. Carburetor
3. Reed valve
4. Gasket
5. Cylinder
6. Gasket
7N. Connecting rod
8L. Bearing liners
8R. Bearing rollers (33)
9. Crankshaft
10. Lower seal
11. Shim
12. Governor spring
13. Governor collar
14. Governor weights
15. Governor yoke
17. Governor lever
19. Carburetor link rod
20. Sleeve
21. Gasket
31. Flyweight pin
32. Retainer
33. Ignition advance spring
34. Ignition advance flyweight
35. Ignition breaker cam
36. Primer plunger & shut-off bar
37. Variable speed spring
38. Thrust collar
39. Thrust washer
40. Governor control lever

Fig. LB32—New style piston and connecting rod assembly with needle bearing set in small end of connecting rod. Assembly shown is interchangeable for all "C" and "D" engines, but components (wrist pin, bearings, etc.) DO NOT interchange. Service as a complete assembly.

Fig. LB33—Needle roller bearing A (25 needles) was installed in armature plates through 1969 production. Bearings B and C have been used since 1970. Note that new Bremen bearing has 32 needles and that Torrington bearing has 33. Be sure to place installing tool against lettered side of cage.

scored. Standard and (new) cylinder bore diameters are 1.940-1.941 inch (49.28-49.30 mm), 2.125-2.126 inch (53.98-54.00 mm) or 2.377-2.378 inch (60.38-60.40 mm). In 1967 production only, Model C-78 and entire "D" series have 2.380-2.381 inch (60.45-60.48 mm) cylinder bore.

When reinstalling cylinder, be sure that the new cylinder to crankcase gasket is properly aligned so that it will not close the transfer ports. Loose cylinder retaining screws can cause considerable power loss. Lawn Boy recommends use of regular split type lock washers under screw heads even if screw is fitted with a serrated type washer.

Because of similarity of appearance, it is possible that cylinders for D-400 and D-600 engines might be confused. D-600 (high compression) cylinders have an "H"-shaped web cast between horizontal and vertical cooling fins. If this cylinder were installed on a D-400 engine, overheating and seizure would result.

CRANKSHAFT AND SEALS. All C-series engines have plain nonrenewable main bearings; magneto end bearing is plain bore in armature plate and pto end bearing is in plain bore of crankcase. Crankshaft main journal diameter is 0.8737-0.8742 inch (22.19-22.20 mm) for both journals. Recommended clearance at magneto end bearing is 0.002-0.0033 inch (0.05-0.08 mm) with maximum allowable clearance of 0.005 inch (0.13 mm). Recommended clearance at pto end bearing is 0.0038-0.0068 inch (0.10-0.17 mm). Crankshaft must be renewed if crankpin journal or main bearing journals are out-of-round 0.0015 inch (0.038 mm) or more.

The production top main bearing on 1964 and earlier D-series engines was a nonrenewable bronze bushing in the armature plate (A – Fig. LB31). Excessive clearance between the crankshaft and the top main bearing will affect both armature air gap and breaker point gap and result in faulty ignition. If the early

Fig. LB34—Exploded view of typical D-600 series engine. If installed, electric starter mounts on crankcase directly opposite recoil type starter. Cylinder (30) is high compression type. Note "H" shaped web cast between fins at top of cylinder. Primer (66) and fuel shut-off (78) are also different on these models.

4. Flywheel	21. Screw	34. Crankshaft	61. Air baffle
5. Governor yoke	22. Lockplate	35. Reed plate gasket	63. Fastener
6. Governor collar	23. Bearing liners	36. Crankcase (includes	64. Cap
7. Governor weights	24. Needle bearings (33)	bearings & seals)	65. Primer base
8. Governor spring	25. Piston pin retainer	46. Reed plate	66. Primer bulb
9. Washer	(2)	48. Retainer	67. Mounting bracket
10. Thrust collar	26. Piston (wrist) pin	49. Reed assy.	69. Fuel line
11. Governor lever	27. Piston	51. Carburetor gasket	71. Control rod & knob
12. Governor rod	28. Piston rings (2)	52. Carburetor	76. Fuel line
16. Variable speed spring	30. Cylinder	53. Gasket	77. Spring clip
18. Flywheel key	31. Cylinder gasket	54. Air filter case	78. Fuel shut-off
20. Connecting rod	33. Armature plate	56. Filter element	79. Washer
assy.	gasket	57. Washer	80. Gasket

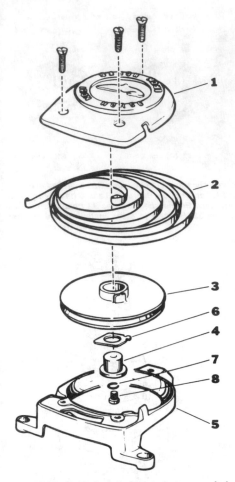

Fig. LB35—Exploded view of early type rewind starter used on some models. Very early models used bead on rope as retainer instead of plate (6). Refer to Fig. LB36 for method of adapting rope retaining plate to early production units.

1. Cover
2. Rewind spring
3. Rope pulley
4. Pulley bearing
5. Housing
6. Rope retainer
7. Lockwasher
8. Screw, pulley to cover

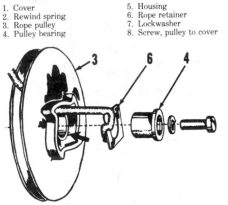

Fig. LB36—When renewing rope in early rewind starter, it is recommended that rope retainer plate (clamp) be installed. To install clamp, first remove 3/64 inch (1 mm) material from boss indicated by arrow; then assemble unit as shown.

Fig. LB37—Old and new rewind spring installations for starter (C-10) shown in Fig. LB35. Note change of spring attachment for C-12 spring shown in Fig. LB38.

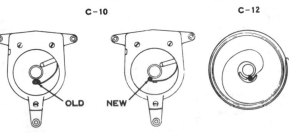

bushing type top main bearing is worn, the later armature plate and needle bearing must be installed. Refer to Fig. LB33 for current change in armature plate bearings. Bearing removal tool 605082 is recommended for driving out old bearings. Hold armature plate in palm of hand for support, not on hard surface during removal to prevent breakage. Use tool 605081 to install new bearing assembly.

Crankpin diameter is 0.7495-0.7500 inch (19.04-19.05 mm) for C-series engines with plain connecting rod bearing and recommended clearance between bearing and crankpin journal is 0.0025-0.0035 inch (0.064-0.089 mm).

Crankpin diameter is 0.7425-0.7430 inch (18.86-18.87 mm) for C-series engines with needle bearing connecting rod bearing in all D-series engines. Crankshaft must be renewed if crankpin journal or main bearing journals show signs of wear, scoring or overheating.

On C and D-series engines, recommended crankshaft end play is 0.012 inch (0.30 mm). Gasket (11 – Fig. LB30 or LB31) used between crankcase and armature plate is available in thicknesses of 0.005 and 0.10 inch for controlling end play.

As in all two-stroke engines, crankshaft seals must be maintained in good condition to prevent loss of crankcase compression and resulting loss of power. Install new seals with lips (grooved side of seal) to inside of crankcase. When installing crankshaft, use an installing sleeve or wrap tape over keyways and sharp shoulders on crankshaft.

RECOIL STARTERS (C-Series Engines). On early recoil starters, starter rope should be attached with retainer as shown at (6 – Fig. LB36). Rope installation on late type starters is shown in Fig. LB39. Refer to Fig. LB37 when installing late type recoil spring in early type starter.

On QUIETFLITE mowers, starter is similar to that shown in Fig. LB38; however, top cover (1) is not used. The rewind spring is anchored on starter bracket as shown in Fig. LB40.

Be sure rewind spring is not overtightened. Never wind pulley over two turns after spring tension begins to be felt.

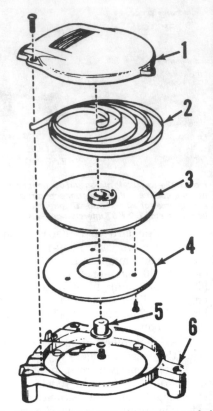

Fig. LB38—Exploded view of later type rewind starter. Refer to Fig. LB39 for rope installation.

1. Cover
2. Rewind spring
3. Rope pulley
4. Plate
5. Bushing
6. Housing

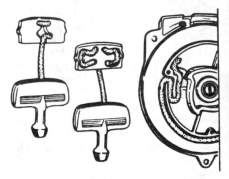

Fig. LB39—View showing method of retaining rope ends in rewind starter shown in Fig. LB36. Singe (heat) about 3/4 inch (19 mm) of each end of nylon rope to be sure it will hold securely.

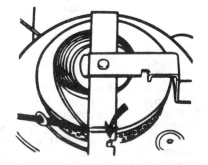

Fig. LB40—On QUIETFLITE models, be sure outer end of rewind spring is anchored at position indicated by arrow.

NOTE: Flywheel pulley must be installed with pulley lug (1—Fig. LB41) positioned in flywheel hole (2). Drive pin or pins (3) on flywheel pulley must be outside starter pulley ratchet before screws holding starter to shroud are tightened.

D-Series Engines. To remove recoil starter, remove cooling shroud and starter handle, then allow rope to slowly recoil. On D-600 series engines, carburetor and reed plate assembly must first be removed from crankcase to

allow access to starter retainer screw in bottom side of armature plate. Remove starter assembly retaining screw and clamp, then withdraw starter assembly.

NOTE: Hold assembly together to prevent recoil spring from unwinding.

Release spring tension, then inspect all components and renew as needed. For reference and identification of parts refer to Fig. LB42 for D-400 series engines and Fig. LB43 for D-600 series engines.

When assembling, apply a light coat of grease to starter spring. **Do not** apply lubricant on starter worm gear or nylon pinion. Attach inner end of starter spring to pulley and position on starter cup with outer end of spring through slot in spring cup. Attach end of rope to pulley and install pulley plate. With pinion spring removed, ends of spring should be less than 1/4-inch (6.4 mm) apart as

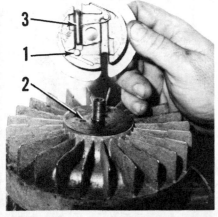

Fig. LB41—View showing a typical flywheel starter pulley used on C-series engines. Pulley lug (1) must engage flywheel hole (2) and drive pin (3) must be positioned outside starter pulley ratchet.

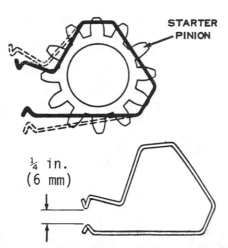

Fig. LB44—Ends of starter pinion spring should be less than ¼ inch (6.4 mm) apart when spring is removed.

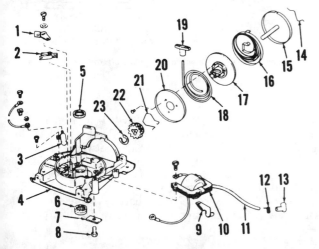

1. Breaker point base
2. Breaker point arm
3. Condenser
4. Armature plate
5. Crankshaft oil seal
6. Needle bearing
7. Starter pin clamp
8. Clamp screw
9. High tension wire clip
10. Coil & lamination assy.
11. High tension wire
12. Spring terminal
13. Spark plug cover
14. Rope retainer spring
15. Starter spring cup
16. Starter spring
17. Starter pulley
18. Starter rope
19. Starter handle
20. Starter pulley plate
21. Starter pinion spring
22. Starter pinion
23. Push-on retainer

Fig. LB42—Exploded view of D-400 series engine starter and magneto assembly. Starter pinion (22) engages teeth in lower side of flywheel; refer to view of flywheel in Fig. LB17. Needle bearing (6) is used in late engines; early production engines have plain bearing bore in armature plate (4) for upper cranksahft journal.

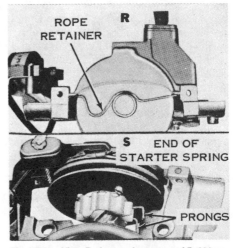

Fig. LB45—View R shows placement of D-400 series starter rope retainer locked in position with starter installed in armature plate. View S shows correct installation of starter pinion spring with one prong above and one below armature plate. Note location of end of recoil spring.

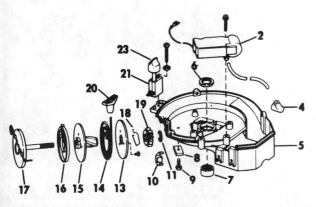

2. CD ignition spark
4. Spark plug boot
5. Armature plate
6. Crankshaft seal
7. Upper main bearing
8. Starter clamp
9. Clamp screw
10. Rope clip
11. Retainer
13. Plate
14. Rope
15. Pulley
16. Recoil spring
17. Cup & pin
18. Pinion spring
19. Pinion
20. Rope handle
21. Shorting switch
23. Knob

Fig. LB43—Exploded view of armature plate and starter used on D-600 series engines. When installed, electric starter is fitted to crankcase, engaging flywheel directly opposite manual starter.

Fig. LB46—View showing positioning of rope retainer spring on starter cup for D-400 series engines.

Fig. LB47—Position pinion spring prongs so one is above and one is below armature plate.

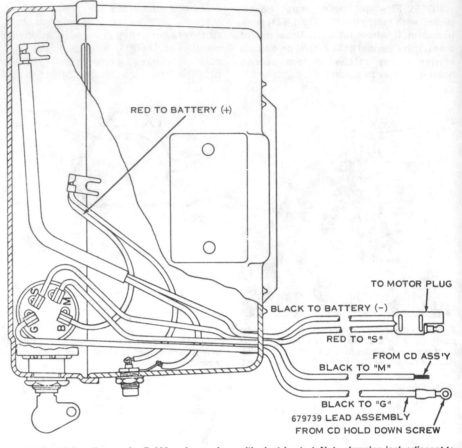

Fig. LB49—Wiring diagram for D-600 series engines with electric start. Note charging jack adjacent to ignition key switch. Refer to text.

shown in Fig. LB44. Install spring in pinion groove with prongs toward pinion teeth as shown in Fig. LB45, being careful not to spread ends of spring excessively apart. Position pinion on pulley, then install retaining snap ring. Wind rope around pulley, then on D-400 series engines position rope retainer springs as shown in Figs. LB45 and LB46 and install assembly. On D-600 series engines rope retainer spring is permanently attached to starter cup. Turn pulley until starter spring "hook" is positioned at top. Position pinion spring prongs so one is above and one is below armature plate as shown in Fig. LB47. Preload starter spring ½-1½ turns, then route starter rope and install handle.

12-VOLT ELECTRIC STARTER. Models equipped with electric start are identified by letter "E" following model number.

D-400 Series. The electric starter pinion (27–Fig. LB48) is located across

from recoil starter pinion (22). The electric starter pinion assembly can be removed after removing drive belt, flywheel and set screw (24–Fig. LB50). When installing, clearance between snap ring and pulley should be 0.010 inch. Clearance is adjusted by moving pulley shaft before tightening set screw (24).

The starter drive belt should have ⅛-inch (3.2 mm) deflection with 1½ lbs. (0.68 Kg.) pressure between pulley. Adjustment is accomplished by moving the starter and bracket after loosening the three screws.

To charge battery, connect trickle charger leads (red to positive post) to

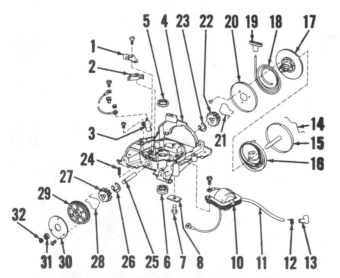

Fig. LB48—Exploded view of armature plate and starter pinions used on D-400 series engines with 12-volt electric starter.

1. Breaker point base
2. Breaker point arm
3. Condenser
4. Armature plate
5. Crankshaft oil seal
6. Needle bearing
7. Starter pin clamp
8. Clamp screw
9. High tension wire clip
10. Coil & lamination assy.
11. High tension wire
12. Spring terminal
13. Spark plug cover
14. Rope retainer spring
15. Starter spring cup
16. Starter spring
17. Starter pulley
18. Starter rope
19. Starter handle
20. Starter pulley plate
21. Starter pinion spring
22. Starter pinion
23. Push-on retainer
24. Set screw
25. Starter shaft
26. Snap ring
27. Starter pinion
28. Pinion spring
29. Pulley
30. Pulley plate
31. Pulley bearing
32. Snap ring

Fig. LB50—End play of starter assembly on starter shaft should be 0.010 inch (0.25 mm). End play is set by inserting feeler gage (F) between snap ring and pulley then pushing shaft in before tightening set screw (24).

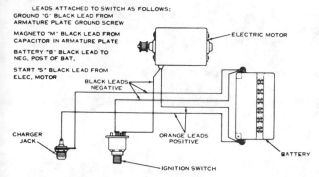

LEADS ATTACHED TO SWITCH AS FOLLOWS:
GROUND "G" BLACK LEAD FROM
ARMATURE PLATE GROUND SCREW

MAGNETO "M" BLACK LEAD FROM
CAPACITOR IN ARMATURE PLATE

BATTERY "B" BLACK LEAD TO
NEG. POST OF BAT.

START "S" BLACK LEAD FROM
ELEC. MOTOR

Fig. LB51—Starter circuit with 12-volt battery on D-400 series engines. Some models do not have charger jack circuit. Refer to text.

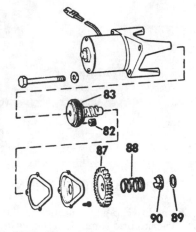

Fig. LB52—View of electric starting motor and drive used on D-600 series engines.

82. Motor pinion
83. Driven gear
87. Starter pinion
88. Spring
89. Retainer
90. Pinion stop washer

battery before connecting charger to 120V outlet. Some later models have a charger connecting jack installed in battery case. Plug charger cable into jack of these models before connecting charger cord to power outlet. Refer to Fig. LB51 for starter-battery circuit layout.

D-600 Series. Refer to Fig. LB49 for wiring diagram of starter-battery charger circuits with ignition switch. On these models, ignition key must be "ON" if manual starter is used and will then function as a kill switch.

Arrangement of starter and drive is shown in Fig. LB52. Pinion (82) and driven gear (83) enclosed in case require light lubrication; OMC Type A lube is recommended. No lubrication should be applied to starter worm gear or nylon starter pinion gear (87). Note that starter moter housing has three mounting legs which attach by long cap screws to engine crankcase. Two of these three bolt holes are oversized so casting can be pivoted to adjust depth of pinion mesh in flywheel. Allow a small amount of backlash when mounting

starter assembly so pinion can engage teeth of flywheel without clashing or binding.

LAWN-BOY

Model	Bore	Stroke	Displacement	Power Rating
F-Series	2.38 in.	1.75 in.	7.78 cu.in.	4.5 hp
	(60.4 mm)	(44.4 mm)	(127 cc)	(3.3 kW)
V-Series	2.38 in.	1.75 in.	7.78 cu.in.	4.5 hp
	(60.4 mm)	(44.4 mm)	(127 cc)	(3.3 kW)

ENGINE IDENTIFICATION

Lawn-Boy F-Series engines are used on "F" Series and some Gold Series lawn mowers. The V-Series engine is used on some Silver Series mowers. Both series are air-cooled, single-cylinder, two-stroke engines with a vertical crankshaft. Construction details of both models include: The carburetor is attached to the engine crankcase opposite the spark plug and the exhaust port is located on the underside of the cylinder. The cylinder and head are integral with half of the crankcase.

The engine model of F-Series is often stamped on the starter spring cap as shown in Fig. LB69. On F-Series engines, the cylinder head has a generally round shape and the fins are on an angle. On V-Series engines, the cylinder and head have a generally square shape and the fins are straight up and down.

MAINTENANCE

LUBRICATION. Engine is lubricated by mixing gasoline and oil at a ratio of 32:1. Gasoline and oil should be mixed in a separate container before filling engine fuel tank. Lawn-Boy recommends using Lawn-Boy 2-CYCLE ASHLESS OIL and advises against mixing different oil brands if another oil is used. DO NOT use automotive (4-cycle) engine oil.

Manufacturer recommends unleaded gasoline with an 85 octane rating or higher. Gasoline containing methanol is not recommended, although gasoline containing 10 percent or less of ethanol may be used. If gasoline containing ethanol is used, it must be drained from the fuel system before storing the engine.

Lawn-Boy Fuel Conditioner is recommended if fuel is stored for an extended period.

AIR FILTER. The foam type filter element should be cleaned, inspected and re-oiled after every 25 hours of engine operation or annually, whichever occurs first. To remove filter element, unsnap filter cover latch and swing filter cover to the side. Clean the filter element in soapy water then squeeze the filter until dry (don't twist the filter).

Inspect the filter for tears and holes or any other opening. Discard the filter if it cannot be cleaned satisfactorily or if the filter is torn or otherwise damaged.

Pour approximately one tablespoon of clean SAE 30 engine oil into the filter, then squeeze the filter to remove the excess oil and distribute oil throughout the filter. Be sure filter fits properly in filter box.

SPARK PLUG. Recommended spark plug is a Champion CJ14 or equivalent. Electrode gap should be 0.035 inch (0.9 mm). Tighten spark plug to 15 ft.-lbs. (20.4 N•m) torque.

CARBURETOR. Different float type carburetors have been used, but the service principles are the same for all. The governor air vane is attached to the carburetor throttle shaft. On F-series engines, lift the carburetor from the engine after removing air filter element, then removing the screw attaching the air filter base and the two screws attaching the carburetor to the crankcase (Fig. LB70). On V-series engines, lift the carburetor from the engine after removing the air filter element and the two carburetor mounting screws.

To adjust idle fuel mixture on F-series engines, turn idle mixture needle (8—Fig. LB71) in (clockwise) until lightly seated, then turn needle out ¾ turn. Start engine and run until normal operating temperature is reached. Set speed control lever to "Low Speed" position, turn fuel flow needle in slowly until engine starts surging or slowing down, then turn needle slowly out until engine runs smoothly. Allow engine to run a few minutes at this setting to make certain fuel mixture is not too lean. With engine running at idle, rapidly move speed control to full throttle position. If engine stumbles or hesitates, slightly turn idle mixture screw ⅛ turn counterclockwise and repeat test.

Fuel mixture on V-series models is not adjustable.

On all models, check to make sure that grass or other foreign matter does not restrict fuel delivery by clogging the filter, main jet, fuel line or fuel inlet needle.

To disassemble carburetor, refer to Fig. LB71 or Fig. LB72 and remove bowl screw(s) and float bowl (18). Remove float pin (11), float (16) and fuel inlet valve (15). If necessary to remove inlet valve seat from the carburetor shown in Fig. LB71, use a stiff wire with a hook on one end to pull the seat (14) from carburetor body. On all models, the fuel inlet valve and seat should be serviced as a set. To remove any Welch plugs, pierce the plug with a sharp pin punch, then pry out the plug, but do not damage underlying metal. Remove idle mixture needle (8—Fig. LB71) from models so equipped. If necessary to remove the throttle plate or shaft, remove throttle plate retaining screw, remove throttle plate (12—Fig. LB71 or Fig. LB72) and

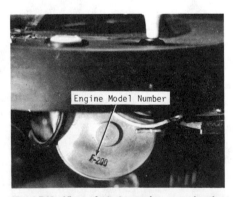

Fig. LB69—View of starter spring cap showing location of engine model number.

Fig. LB70—View showing carburetor air filter and access holes (H) in filter chamber.

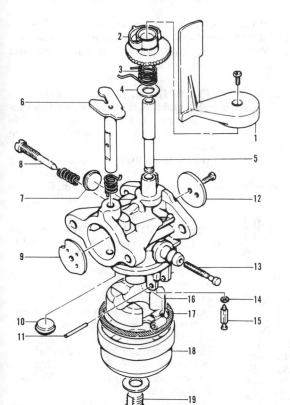

Fig. LB71—Exploded view of carburetor used on F-series engines.

1. Governor air vane
2. Collar
3. Spring
4. Washer
5. Throttle shaft
6. Choke shaft
7. Welch plug
8. Idle mixture screw
9. Choke plate
10. Welch plug
11. Float shaft
12. Throttle plate
13. Fuel filter
14. Valve seat
15. Fuel inlet valve
16. Float
17. Gasket
18. Float bowl
19. Screw

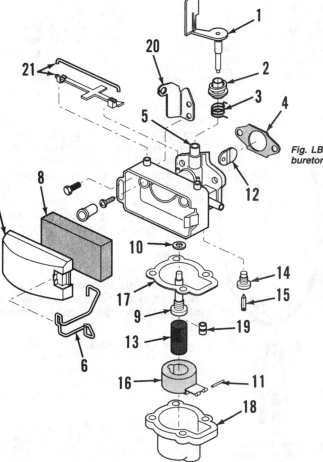

Fig. LB72—Exploded view of carburetor used on V-series engines.

1. Governor air vane
2. Collar
3. Spring
4. Gasket
5. Carburetor body
6. Cover latch
7. Filter cover
8. Filter element
9. Nozzle
10. Gasket
11. Float shaft
12. Throttle plate
13. Fuel filter
14. Valve seat
15. Fuel inlet valve
16. Float
17. Gasket
18. Float bowl
19. Main jet
20. Bracket
21. Throttle linkage

withdraw throttle shaft (5). If removal is required, pull choke plate (9) from the slot in choke shaft (6), then withdraw shaft.

Inspect carburetor and renew any damaged or excessively worn components. The body must be replaced if there is excessive throttle or choke shaft play as bushings are not available. Use a 3/16 inch (5 mm) diameter rod to install the fuel inlet valve seat. The groove on the seat must be down (towards carburetor bore). Push in the seat until it bottoms. If removed, install new Welch plugs being careful not to indent the plugs; the plugs should be flat after installation. Apply a nonhardening sealant around the plug. The float should be approximately parallel with the body when the carburetor is inverted. Bend float hinge tang to adjust float level, or renew float and/or fuel inlet valve.

GOVERNOR. Governor is an air vane (pneumatic) type that is attached to the carburetor throttle shaft. Air vane (A—Fig. LB73) extends through cooling shroud base and responds to air flow created by the flywheel fan. Fluctuation in engine speed, due to change in engine load, opens or closes throttle plate to maintain desired engine rpm. Recommended governor high speed is 3100-3300 rpm.

To adjust governor, hold base of air vane and turn collar (C—Fig. LB73) to obtain desired engine speed. Each click represents approximately 50 rpm. Clockwise rotation of collar increases engine speed, while counterclockwise rotation decreases engine speed.

IGNITION SYSTEM. A solid-state ignition system is used on all models. All ignition components including the ignition coil are contained in a module located outside the flywheel. Ignition timing is not adjustable. The air gap between the ignition module and fly-

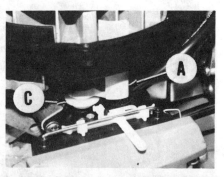

Fig. LB73—Governor air vane (A) extends through cooling shroud base and responds to air flow created by flywheel fan. View shows round-shaped adjusting collar (C). Refer to text.

wheel should be 0.010 inch (0.25 mm). Insert Lawn-Boy gauge 604659 or correct thickness plastic strip between module and flywheel magnets to check air gap. Loosen module mounting screws and reposition module if necessary.

If an ignition malfunction is suspected, first be sure spark plug and high tension wire lead are in good condition. The high tension lead is available separately. There are no test procedures for ignition module. If module is suspected, install a module that is known to be good and recheck ignition performance.

CARBON. If ignition, fuel supply to combustion chamber and compression are satisfactory, but engine will not run or runs poorly, it is likely that there is heavy carbon buildup in exhaust ports and muffler. A common symptom is "four-cycling" or firing every other power stroke.

Manufacturer recommends cleaning out carbon after every 50 hours of operation. Before undertaking carbon cleaning procedure, drain fuel from fuel tank and, if so equipped, remove battery. Tip mower on its side and block in position.

WARNING: Be sure spark plug wire is disconnected from spark plug and wire is properly grounded.

Remove mower blade nut, blade and blade mounting plate. Strike mounting plate in a counterclockwise direction to break plate loose from crankshaft. Remove three screws securing muffler. Refer to Fig. LB74 for view of muffler plate (1) and engine exhaust ports (2). Rotate crankshaft so piston blocks exhaust ports, then use a ⅜-inch (10 mm) diameter wooden dowel to break carbon away from port openings. Clean muffler openings.

CAUTION: Particular care must be used when cleaning exhaust ports so piston is not damaged. Metal tools must not be used.

When reassembling, tighten muffler screws to 155 in.-lbs. (17.5 N•m). Tighten blade nut to 47 ft.-lbs. (64 N•m).

REPAIRS

TIGHTENING TORQUES. Recommended tightening torques are as follows:

Blade nut	47 ft.-lbs. (64 N•m).
Carburetor mounting screw	65 in.-lbs. (7.3 N•m).
Connecting rod	55-65 in.-lbs. (6.2-7.3 N•m).
Crankcase cover	100-120 in.-lbs. (11-13 N•m).
Flywheel nut	33 ft.-lbs. (44.8 N•m).
Muffler	155 in.-lbs. (17.5 N•m).
Spark plug	15 ft.-lbs. (20.4 N•m).

CRANKCASE PRESSURE TEST. An improperly sealed crankcase can cause the engine to be hard to start, run rough, have low power and overheat. Refer to ENGINE SERVICE in the FUNDAMENTALS SECTION of this manual for crankcase pressure test procedure. If crankcase leakage is indi-

cated, pressurize crankcase and use a soap and water solution to check gaskets, seals, carburetor pulse line and casting for leakage.

FLYWHEEL. Remove starter assembly and fuel tank and shroud assembly for access to flywheel. Use suitable puller to remove flywheel from tapered crankshaft.

When installing flywheel, be sure that flywheel key is installed correctly as shown in Fig. LB75. Tighten flywheel nut to 33 ft.-lbs. (44.8 N•m) torque.

PISTON, PIN AND RINGS. Engine must be removed from the equipment to service piston (6—Fig. LB76), pin (4) and rings (3). Piston and rod assembly can be removed after removing flywheel (1), carburetor and crankcase cover half (17). Do not lose the loose bearing rollers (10) when disconnecting rod and cap from crankshaft.

Piston, pin and rings are available in standard size only. Recommended piston-to-cylinder clearance is 0.003-0.004 inch (0.08-0.10 mm).

Piston pin is retained by snap rings at each end of pin bore in piston. Use Lawn-Boy tool 602884 or a suitable wooden dowel to drive piston pin out. Piston pin diameter is 0.4998-0.5000 inch (12.695-12.700 mm).

Top piston ring end gap should be 0.007-0.017 inch (0.18-0.43 mm) and bottom ring end gap should be 0.015-0.025 inch (0.38-0.64 mm). Renew rings if end gap is excessive. Note that a semi-keystone ring is used in top ring groove. When installing rings, stagger ring gaps at least 30 degree apart. Reassemble connecting rod to piston and install piston pin retaining rings. Position piston pin retaining rings (5) so beveled side is toward pin and opening faces upward toward piston crown to prevent ring from popping out during operation.

Before installing piston and rod assembly, place Lawn-Boy stop tool 677389 or a suitable equivalent in spark plug hole.

NOTE: Without piston stop, piston could enter cylinder too far allowing top ring to become stuck in cylinder.

Install piston and connecting rod in cylinder so "BTM" letters on piston skirt are facing toward exhaust ports in cylinder. Attach connecting rod to crankshaft as outlined in following section.

CONNECTING ROD. The aluminum connecting rod rides on renewable steel inserts and 33 needle roller bearings surrounding the crankpin as

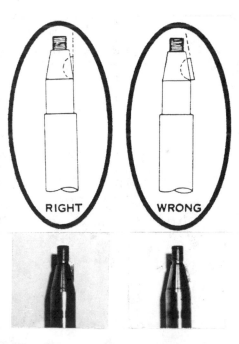

Fig. LB75—When installing flywheel, be sure that Woodruff key is installed correctly in crankshaft groove as shown.

Fig. LB74—View showing muffler plate (1) and engine exhaust ports (2).

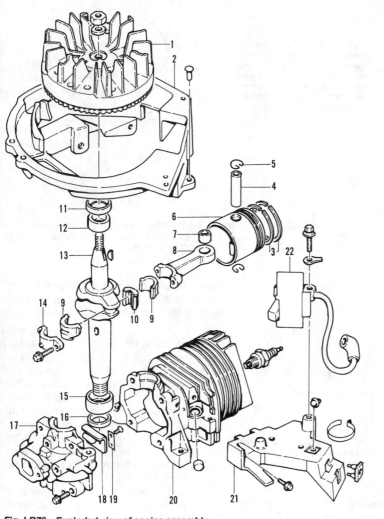

Fig. LB76—Exploded view of engine assembly.

1. Flywheel
2. Base shroud
3. Piston rings
4. Piston pin
5. Retaining ring
6. Piston
7. Bearing
8. Connecting rod
9. Split liner
10. Needle bearings
11. Oil seal
12. Upper main bearing
13. Crankshaft
14. Rod cap
15. Lower main bearing
16. Oil seal
17. Crankcase cover
18. Reed
19. Reed plate
20. Cylinder & crankcase assy.
21. Ignition bracket
22. Ignition module

and stick rollers to connecting rod and cap. Fit 17 rollers to rod cap and 16 rollers to rod.

If installing a new bearing roller set, lay strip of 33 rollers on forefinger and carefully peel backing off rollers. Curl forefinger around crankpin to transfer rollers from finger to journal. Grease on rollers will hold them together and to crankpin journal.

Install connecting rod cap; BE SURE rod and cap mating marks (Fig. LB78) are aligned. Tighten rod cap screws to initial torque of 15-20 in.-lbs. (1.7-2.3 N•m), then alternately tighten screws in two steps to a final torque of 55-65 in.-lbs. (6.2-7.3 N•m). Bend locking tabs (Fig. LB79) snugly against flats on head of screws. Check to be sure that rod assembly is free on crankpin and that none of the rollers dropped out during assembly.

REED VALVE. Reed valves permit air:fuel mixture to enter crankcase on the compression stroke and seal the air:fuel mixture in crankcase on the power stroke. Reed valves are mounted in crankcase cover as shown in Fig. LB80. Reeds can be cleaned with solvent or carburetor cleaner. DO NOT use compressed air on reed assemblies or distortion may occur resulting in hard starting or loss of power. Bent or distorted reeds cannot be repaired. Rough edge of reed must be positioned away from machined surface of mounting plate. Check reed-to-plate clearance as shown Fig. LB80. If clearance between reed tip and machined surface exceeds 0.015 inch (0.38 mm), renew reed. Coat reed mounting screws with Loctite and tighten to 10-13 in.-lbs. (1.12-1.47 N•m) torque.

shown in Fig. LB77. Piston and rod assembly can be removed after separating crankcase cover half from cylinder. Do not lose the loose bearing rollers when disconnecting rod from crankshaft.

When reassembling connecting rod to crankpin, install steel inserts in connecting rod end and cap making sure they are centered and dovetail guides will mate correctly when assembled. If bearing rollers are being reused, be sure that none are damaged. Coat insert surfaces with Lawn-Boy needle bearing grease 378642 or a suitable equivalent

CRANKCASE, CRANKSHAFT, BEARINGS AND SEALS. Crankcase, cylinder and cylinder head are an integral assembly (20—Fig. LB76). Cylinder bore cannot be bored for oversize piston. Crankcase cover (17) houses reed valve assembly. The crankshaft (13) is supported by caged roller bearings that contain 20 bearing rollers each. Top main bearing is shorter than lower bearing.

Crankshaft main bearing journal diameter at either end should be 0.8773-0.8778 inch (22.283-22.296 mm). Diametral clearance between crankshaft journal and roller bearing should be 0.002-0.003 inch (0.05-0.08 mm). Maximum allowable clearance is 0.005 inch (0.13 mm).

Crankpin diameter should be 0.742-0.743 inch (18.85-18.87 mm) with a diametral clearance of 0.0025-0.0035 inch (0.064-0.089 mm) between pin and con-

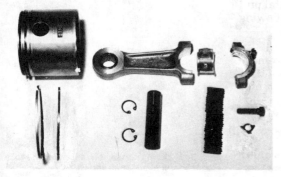

Fig. LB77—View showing connecting rod and piston assembly. Note semi-keystone ring used in top groove.

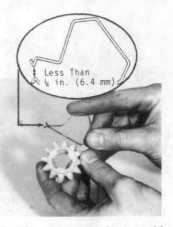

Fig. LB78—View showing connecting rod and piston assembled on crankshaft. Note connecting rod end and cap alignment marks and semikeystone ring used in top piston groove.

Fig. LB82—When pinion spring is removed from pinion gear, ends of spring should be less than ¼ inch (6 mm) apart.

LOCKING TABS

Fig. LB79—Bend locking tabs snugly up against connecting rod cap screws to secure.

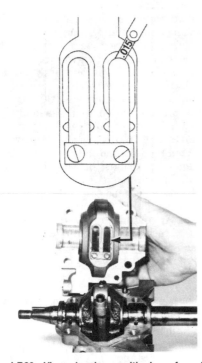

Fig. LB80—View showing positioning of reed valves in crankcase cover. Maximum clearance of 0.015 inch (0.38 mm) between reed tip and machined surface is allowed.

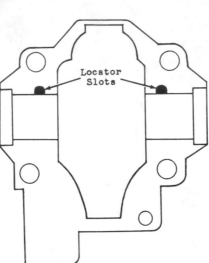

Locator Slots

Fig. LB81—View showing crankcase locator slots used in aligning crankshaft main bearings. Be sure main bearing dowels align in slots.

sonal injury if spring is released accidentally. Wear eye and hand protection during disassembly and reassembly.

When disassembling recoil starter, hold starter cup and pulley together to prevent starter halves from separating. Using needle nose pliers, withdraw retaining clip from cup shaft. Slide washer, pinion gear and drag spring off shaft end. To release spring tension, point shaft end downward allow starter halves to fall onto a suitable solid surface. Halves will separate on impact and spring will unwind.

Inspect all parts for excessive wear or any other damage and renew as needed. With pinion spring removed, ends of spring should be less than ¼ inch (6 mm) apart as shown in Fig. LB82.

When assembling, apply a thin coat of Lawn-Boy type "A" grease 610726 or a suitable equivalent over entire length of starter spring. Attach inner end of spring to pulley as shown in Fig. LB83. Install cup and shaft assembly with spring guided through slot in cup. Install pinion gear, thrust washer and retaining clip. Hold assembly securely

Before assembly, remove any gasket material on mating surfaces of crankcase and cover, then apply a thin coat of Lawn-Boy Gasket Maker 682302 or a suitable equivalent to sealing surface of crankcase cover. Before installing crankcase cover, be sure crankshaft main bearing dowels align in crankcase locator slots as shown in Fig. LB81. Install crankcase cover and securing screws, then using a crossing pattern, tighten screws in small increments until a final torque of 100-120 in.-lbs. (11.3-13.6 N•m) is obtained. Check crankshaft for free rotation.

REWIND STARTER. Early models are equipped with a vertical pull starter while later models use a horizontal pull starter. Refer to appropriate following section.

Vertical Pull Starter. To remove starter, first remove rope handle, then allow rope to wind slowly through hole in air baffle. Loosen crankcase Allen head screws securing starter and remove starter from engine.

CAUTION: Starter spring is wound in cup housing and may cause per-

Fig. LB83—During reassembly, attach inner end of starter spring to pulley as shown.

necting rod assembly. Renew crankshaft if crankpin is out-of-round more than 0.0015 inch (0.38 mm). Crankshaft end play should be 0.006-0.016 inch (0.15-0.41 mm).

Install crankshaft seals (11 and 16—Fig. LB76) with lips (grooved side of seal) to inside of crankcase. When installing crankshaft seals, use a protective sleeve or wrap tape over keyway and sharp shoulders on crankshaft to prevent damage to seals.

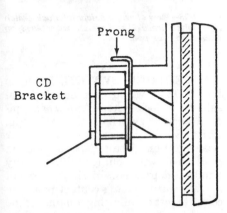

Fig. LB84—During reassembly, wind starter spring until spring hook is secured in cup slot.

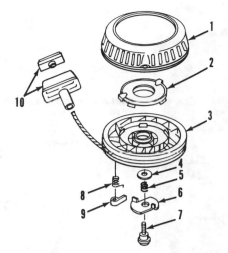

Fig. LB88—Exploded view of horizontal pull rewind starter used on F-series engines.

1. Starter housing
2. Spring cup
3. Pulley
4. Washer
5. Brake spring
6. Retainer
7. Screw
8. Spring
9. Dog
10. Handle & insert

Fig. LB85—Position pinion spring prongs so one is above and one is below flange of CD bracket.

Fig. LB86—Align rope retainer (1) with CD bracket (2) during reassembly.

and turn pinion gear clockwise to wind spring into housing. Wind spring until hook is secured in cup slot as shown in Fig. LB84. Carefully allow spring to unwind against inside of cup.

Install starter assembly in crankcase, then position drag springs so prongs on spring are positioned one above and one below flange of CD bracket as shown in Fig. LB85. Align rope retainer (1—Fig. LB86) with CD bracket (2), then tighten crankcase Allen screws to secure starter.

Wind rope fully on pulley, then note if rope end is in the "A" or "B" portion of the pulley as shown in Fig. LB87. If rope end is in portion "A," pull rope out enough to allow one additional wrap around pulley. If rope end is in portion "B," pull rope out enough to allow two additional wraps around pulley. Thread rope through guide and attach handle. Be sure that starter handle has tension against it and that starter spring is not fully wound tight when starter rope is completely withdrawn.

Horizontal Pull Starter. To disassemble starter, first remove starter assembly from engine. Pull rope partially out of starter and remove rope handle, then allow pulley to unwind slowly. Unscrew pulley retaining screw (7—Fig. LB88 or Fig. LB89). Remove retainer (6), dogs (9), springs (8), brake spring (5) and washer (4). Wear appropriate safety eyewear and gloves before disengaging pulley from starter as spring may uncoil uncontrolled. Place shop towel around pulley (3) and lift pulley out of housing (1); spring and cup may remain in housing or stay in pulley. Do not attempt to separate spring from cup as they are a unit assembly.

Inspect components for damage and excessive wear. Reverse disassembly procedure to install components. Apply a light coat of grease to rewind spring and spring contact area on inside of pulley. Note that spring cup (2) will only fit in pulley if lugs are properly engaged.

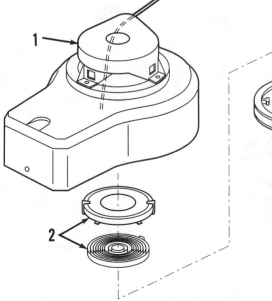

Fig. LB89—Exploded view of horizontal pull rewind starter used on V-series engines.

1. Starter housing
2. Spring assy.
3. Pulley
5. Brake spring
6. Retainer
7. Screw
8. Spring
9. Dog
10. Rope

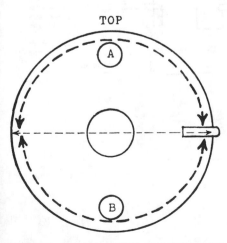

Fig. LB87—Note "A" and "B" halves of starter cup. Refer to text.

Fig. LB90—Install dog spring (8) so long end is up and outside the dog as shown. Spring should force dog toward center of starter.

Fig. LB93—View showing safety interlock switch (1), flywheel brake (2) and adjustment cable (3) on models so equipped.

Fig. LB91—After rotating pulley to place tension on rewind spring, insert rope through housing outlet (O) and pulley hole and tie a knot in pulley end of rope.

Apply grease to ends of brake spring. Flanges of retainer must be toward rewind spring. Tighten center screw to 70 in.-lbs. (7.9 N·m) torque. Rotate pulley counterclockwise until spring is wound tight. Let pulley unwind just until rope holes in pulley and starter housing are aligned. Insert rope through holes and tie knot at pulley end (Fig. LB91). Install rope handle on outer end of rope, then allow pulley to unwind to wind rope onto pulley.

When installing starter on engine, pull out rope so dogs engage starter cup and center starter before tightening starter mounting screws. Tighten starter mounting screws to 25 in.-lbs. (2.8 N·m) torque.

INTERLOCK SWITCH. Refer to Fig. LB92 for wiring diagram of typical safety interlock system. A view of a typical interlock switch is shown in Fig. LB93. Switch is designed to open or close ignition circuit depending upon position of switch plunger. When safety handle is depressed, switch plunger will move inward causing contact points to come together allowing engine to be started and run. When safety handle is released, plunger is forced away from contact point preventing engine from being started.

NOTE: Switch must be in good operating condition to ensure safe operation of mower. Never bypass the interlock switch when operating the mower.

To assemble pulley, spring cup and housing, install spring cup with spring in pulley and hold pulley so spring cup is on top. Place starter housing on top of pulley. Rotate pulley counterclockwise until spring tension is felt indicating inner end of spring has engaged spring anchor. Install dog springs (8) so long end is up and spring forces dog toward center of starter as shown in Fig. LB90.

Fig. LB92—Wiring diagram for electric start models showing three switch positions.

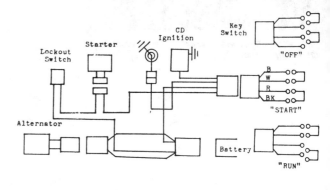

LAWN-BOY

Model	Bore	Stroke	Displacement	Power Rating
M25	2.380 in.	2.00 in. (60.4 mm)	8.9 cu.in. (50.8 mm)	4.5 hp (145.6 cc)

ENGINE INFORMATION

"M" Series lawn mowers (including M21BMR, M21EMR, M21ZMR and M21ZPR) are equipped with a two-stroke, single-cylinder Lawn-Boy Model M25 engine. The engine is air cooled and has a vertical crankshaft.

MAINTENANCE

LUBRICATION. Some models are equipped with an oil pump (known as "FreshLube") that injects oil into the incoming air-fuel mixture through a passage in spacer (11—Fig. LB201). Lawn-Boy recommends using Lawn-Boy 2-CYCLE ASHLESS OIL and advises against mixing different oil brands if another oil is used.

On engines equipped with an oil pump, oil is contained in an oil tank; do not add oil to fuel. Later models are equipped with an oil level sensor in the oil tank that stops the engine if the oil level is low. Early models do not have an oil level sensor and the engine will be damaged if all oil is consumed while the engine is running.

NOTE: Tipping the mower over may allow air to enter the oil line if the oil tank filter is exposed. If bubbles in the oil line are more than ¾ inch (19 mm) long, empty fuel tank, fill fuel tank with a fuel:oil mix of 64:1, be sure oil tank contains oil, and start and run mower. This will insure that there is sufficient lubrication while air bubbles are purged.

If oil pump control linkage has been disturbed, refer to OIL PUMP section for adjustment.

On models not equipped with an oil pump, the oil must be mixed with the fuel. Manufacturer recommends using Lawn-Boy oil. Fuel:oil ratio when using Lawn-Boy oil is 64:1. DO NOT use automotive (4-cycle) engine oil.

Manufacturer advises that using gasoline with alcohol (gasohol) may adversely affect some engine components. If gasoline containing ethanol is used, it must be drained from the fuel system before storing the engine. The use of premium gasoline or gasoline containing methanol is not recommended.

SPARK PLUG. Recommended spark plug is a Champion CJ14 or equivalent. Electrode gap should be 0.035 inch (0.9 mm). Tighten spark plug to 15-18 ft.-lbs. (20-24 N•m).

CARBURETOR. Adjustment. Idle speed at normal operating temperature should be 2100-2300 rpm. Adjust idle speed by turning idle speed screw (16—Fig. LB202). Idle mixture is controlled by idle jet (6) and idle mixture screw (14). Initial setting of idle mixture screw is one turn out. Make final adjustment with engine running and at operating temperature. To adjust idle mixture, turn idle mixture screw clockwise and lean mixture until engine speed just starts to slow, then turn screw counterclockwise and enrich mixture just until engine speed begins to slow. Turn idle screw to halfway point between lean and rich positions. Turn idle screw counterclockwise in small increments to enrich mixture if engine will not accelerate without stumbling. Idle mixture jet is not adjustable. High speed operation is controlled by main jet (19—Fig. LB201) and is not adjustable. Standard size main jet only is available.

Overhaul. To disassemble carburetor, remove fuel bowl retaining screw

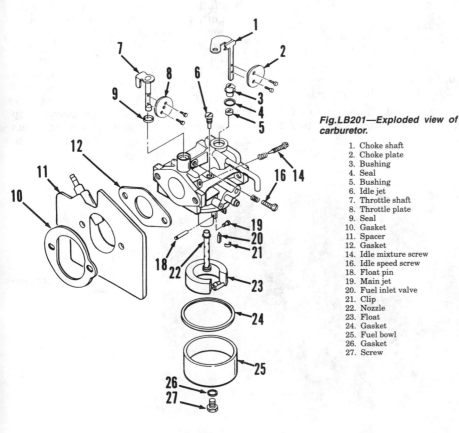

Fig. LB201—Exploded view of carburetor.

1. Choke shaft
2. Choke plate
3. Bushing
4. Seal
5. Bushing
6. Idle jet
7. Throttle shaft
8. Throttle plate
9. Seal
10. Gasket
11. Spacer
12. Gasket
14. Idle mixture screw
16. Idle speed screw
18. Float pin
19. Main jet
20. Fuel inlet valve
21. Clip
22. Nozzle
23. Float
24. Gasket
25. Fuel bowl
26. Gasket
27. Screw

Fig. LB202—View showing location of idle jet (6), idle mixture screw (14) and idle speed screw (16).

Fig. LB203—View showing location of air jets (AJ). Jets are not available except with carburetor body.

Fig. LB205—Install throttle plate so numbers are out and on side opposite to fuel inlet.

Fig. LB204—Install choke plate with flat side toward fuel inlet.

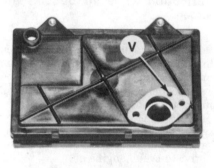

Fig. LB206—Air filter base gasket must be installed so vent hole (V) matches holes in carburetor and filter base.

properly matches opening in spacer. When installing air filter base gasket, be sure vent hole (V—Fig. LB206) matches holes in filter base and carburetor.

GOVERNOR. All models are equipped with a ball type mechanical governor located internally on the crankshaft. As engine speed increases, the internal governor assembly rotates governor shaft (S—Fig. LB207) which in turn rotates governor lever (L) and closes the throttle. The movement of governor lever is counterbalanced by tension of governor spring (G) which tends to open the throttle. When the two forces balance, governed engine speed is obtained.

To adjust governor, loosen governor shaft clamp bolt (B—Fig. LB207). Move throttle control so carburetor throttle plate is in full open position. Turn governor shaft (S) clockwise as far as possible and retighten clamp bolt (be sure throttle is in full open position). With engine warm, maximum engine speed at full throttle should be 3100-3300 rpm. Adjust maximum engine speed by bending governor spring arm (A). Bending the arm up will decrease spring tension and reduce engine speed. DO NOT exceed specified maximum engine speed.

IGNITION SYSTEM. A solid-state ignition system is used on all models. All ignition components including the ignition coil are contained in a module located outside the flywheel. Ignition timing is not adjustable. The air gap (G—Fig. LB208) between the ignition module and flywheel should be 0.010 inch (0.25 mm). Insert Lawn-Boy gauge 604659 or correct thickness plastic strip between module and flywheel magnets and tighten module mounting screws to 100 in.-lbs. (11.3 N•m).

LB201) to 7 in.-lbs. (0.8 N•m) and tighten idle jet (6) and main jet (19) to 6 in.-lbs. (0.7 N•m). Retaining clip (21) for fuel inlet valve must engage groove of fuel inlet valve and fit around tab of float. Float height is not adjustable.

If removed, install spacer (11—Fig. LB201) so "D" shaped opening is toward cylinder and oil fitting (if so equipped) is up. Be sure opening in gasket (10)

(27—Fig. LB201), gasket (26) and fuel bowl (25). Remove float pin (18) by pushing against round end of pin toward the square end of pin. Remove float (23) and fuel inlet needle (20). Remove throttle and choke shaft assemblies after unscrewing throttle and choke plate retaining screws. Remove idle mixture screw (14), idle mixture jet (6), main jet (19) and main fuel nozzle (22). Air jets shown in Fig. LB203 are only available as part of body unit assembly.

When assembling the carburetor note the following. Place a small drop of nonhardening sealant such as Permatex #2 or equivalent on throttle and choke plate retaining screws. Flat side of choke plate must be on fuel inlet side of carburetor (Fig. LB204). Numbers on throttle plate must face out and be on side of carburetor opposite of fuel inlet (Fig. LB205). Tighten nozzle (22—Fig.

Fig. LB207—View of governor linkage.

A. Spring arm
B. Clamp bolt
C. Choke rod
G. Governor spring
H. Throttle/choke control cable
L. Governor lever
S. Governor shaft
T. Throttle rod

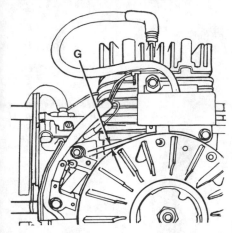

Fig. LB208—Air gap (G) between ignition module and flywheel should be 0.010 inch (0.25 mm).

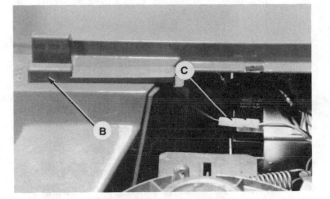

Fig. LB210—View showing location of chute interlock switch (B) and connector (C).

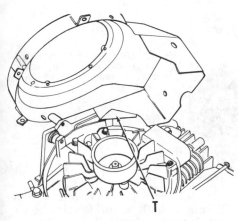

Fig. LB209—Tab (T) on blower shroud must be under ignition and alternator wires.

If an ignition malfunction is suspected, first be sure spark plug and high tension wire lead are in good condition. The high tension lead is available separately. There are no test procedures for ignition module. If module is suspected to be faulty, install a module that is known to be good and recheck ignition performance.

Note that when installing blower shroud the tab (T—Fig. LB209) must be beneath the ignition and alternator wires.

An interlock system is used to prevent unsafe mower operation. Various devices are used to ground the ignition system, either stopping the engine while running or preventing starting. Depending on the components installed, a chute interlock switch (Fig. LB210), blade brake clutch switch or throttle switch may be present. A wiring diagram for electric start models is shown in Fig. LB211.

CAUTION: Be sure all safety related devices work properly; DO NOT run engine otherwise.

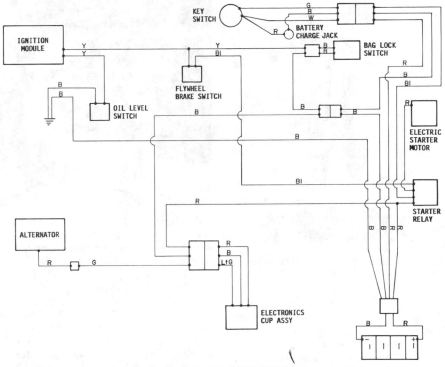

Fig. LB211—Wiring schematic for M25 engine on Model M21EMR lawn mower.

B. Black	G. Green	W. White
Bl. Blue	R. Red	Y. Yellow

REPAIRS

TIGHTENING TORQUES. Recommended tightening torques are as follows:

Alternator . . . . 75 in.-lbs.
(8.5 N•m)
Carburetor mounting screw 65 in.-lbs.
(7.3 N•m)
Crankcase screws . . . . 170 in.-lbs.
(19.2 N•m)
Cylinder head . . . . 190 in.-lbs.
(21.5 N•m)
Electric starter . . . . 170 in.-lbs.
(19.2 N•m)
Engine plate . . . . 155 in.-lbs.
(17.5 N•m)
Flywheel nut . . . . 33 ft.-lbs.
(44.8 N•m)
Ignition module . . . . 100 in.-lbs.
(11.3 N•m)

Muffler mounting screw . . 170 in.-lbs.
(19.2 N•m)
Oil pump mounting screw . . 75 in.-lbs.
(8.5 N•m)
Spark plug . . . . 15 ft.-lbs.
(20.4 N•m)

CRANKCASE PRESSURE TEST. An improperly sealed crankcase can cause the engine to be hard to start, run rough, have low power and overheat. Refer to SERVICE SECTION TROUBLE-SHOOTING section of this manual for crankcase pressure test procedure. If crankcase leakage is indicated, pressurize crankcase and use a soap and water solution to check gaskets, seals, carburetor pulse line and casting for leakage.

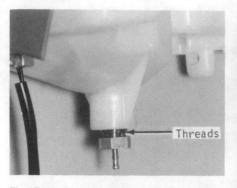

Fig. LB212—To prevent damage to "O" ring, there should be one to two threads exposed on oil tank fitting.

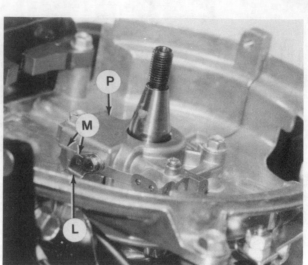

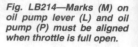

Fig. LB214—Marks (M) on oil pump lever (L) and oil pump (P) must be aligned when throttle is full open.

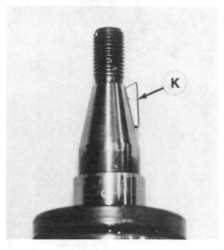

Fig. LB213—Straight edge of crankshaft key (K) must be parallel to crankshaft.

Fig. LB215—Loosen screw (S) and relocate oil pump link end to align oil pump marks shown in Fig. LB214.

OIL TANK. An oil tank is attached to engines equipped with an oil pump. If oil tank fitting is removed, do not screw fitting all the way into tank but leave one or two threads exposed as shown in Fig. LB212. Screwing fitting in completely may damage "O" ring at upper end of fitting.

FLYWHEEL. To remove flywheel, first drain fuel and oil tanks. On later models equipped with oil injection, disconnect oil sensor lead located beneath tanks. Unscrew mounting screws, detach retaining clip on underside and remove fuel and oil tank module. Remove air filter and unscrew top screw securing air filter base to blower shroud. Unscrew top screw securing muffler guard to blower shroud. Detach flywheel brake spring. Remove rewind starter. Remove blower shroud. Use Lawn-Boy tool 613593 or another suitable tool to hold flywheel and unscrew flywheel nut. Use Lawn-Boy tool 611600 or other suitable tool and pull flywheel off crankshaft. If holes in flywheel are not threaded, use a $5/16$-18 tap and cut threads in flywheel puller holes.

Discard flywheel if damaged. Note that flywheel surface contacting flywheel brake must be smooth and free of grease and oil. Be sure flywheel key is parallel with shaft as shown in Fig. LB213, and NOT parallel with taper. Note that when installing blower shroud, the tab (T—Fig. LB209) must be positioned beneath ignition and alternator wires. Tighten flywheel nut to 31-33 ft.-lbs. (42-45 N·m). On Models M21BMR and M21EMR, refer to LUBRICATION section and purge air from oil line as noted.

OIL PUMP. The oil pump (P—Fig. LB214) is located under the flywheel and driven by a worm on the crankshaft.

Adjust. Maximum oil pump output must occur at full throttle. To adjust pump output the flywheel must be removed. Push governor lever so carburetor is fully open. Alignment marks (M) on oil pump and control lever should match as shown in Fig. LB214. To align marks, loosen screw (S—Fig. LB215) and relocate end of control link. Tighten screw and recheck alignment.

Overhaul. Remove flywheel for access to oil pump. Detach oil lines from tank and injection fitting; do not attempt to pull lines from oil pump.

Oil pump and worm are available only as a unit assembly. Individual oil pump components are not available.

Install worm on crankshaft so flat (F—Fig. LB216) on inside corresponds with flat on crankshaft. Install oil pump and tighten mounting screws to 75 in.-lbs. (8.5 N·m).

Note that holes in crankcase for oil lines are marked "IN" and "OUT" (see Fig. LB217). Oil line passing through "IN" hole connects to oil tank fitting while oil line passing through "OUT" hole connects with injection fitting (oil lines will cross).

After assembly, refer to LUBRICATION section and purge air from oil line as noted.

Fig. LB216—Flats (F) on crankshaft and oil pump worm must index when installing worm.

Fig. LB217—Crankcase has "IN" and "OUT" cast on side to identify oil lines.

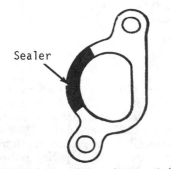

Fig. LB218—Apply sealer to exhaust port side of muffler gasket on rounded portion of gasket indicated.

OIL INJECTION CHECK VALVE.

On models equipped with the FreshLube oil injection system, a check valve is located in the oil injection fitting. The fitting is attached to the spacer plate between the carburetor and engine. The check valve prevents entry of oil into the engine when it is not running. To test the check valve, connect a pressure tester with an oil-filled line to the fitting (there must be oil in the test line or the check valve will not operate properly). The check valve must hold at least 1 psi (6.9 kPa) but require no more than 3-4 psi (20.7-27.6 kPa) before flowing.

MUFFLER. When installing muffler, apply gasket sealer to muffler gasket in area shown in Fig. LB218 on side that contacts muffler. Tighten muffler mounting screws to 170 in.-lbs. (19.2 N•m).

CYLINDER HEAD. The blower shroud must be removed for access to cylinder head. To remove shroud, first drain fuel and oil tanks. On later models equipped with oil injection, disconnect oil sensor lead located beneath tanks. Unscrew mounting screws, detach retaining clip on underside and remove fuel and oil tank module. Remove air filter and unscrew top screw securing air filter base to blower shroud. Unscrew top screw securing muffler guard to blower shroud. Remove rewind

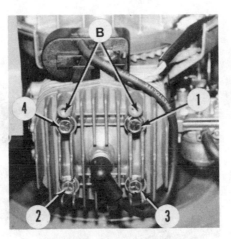

Fig. LB219—Cylinder head must be installed so bosses (B) are toward flywheel. Tighten cylinder head bolts in sequence shown.

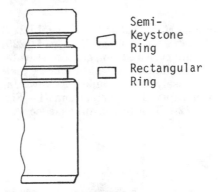

Fig. LB220—Install rectangular piston ring in second piston ring groove and semi-keystone piston ring in top piston ring groove with bevel toward piston crown.

starter. Remove blower shroud. Unscrew cylinder head screws and remove head.

Inspect cylinder head and discard if cracked or otherwise damaged. Remove carbon using a tool that will not damage cylinder head surface.

Install cylinder head so blower shroud screw bosses (B—Fig. LB219) are up. Tighten cylinder head screws in three steps to final torque of 190 in.-lbs. (21.5 N•m) using crossing pattern shown in Fig. LB219. On models equipped with oil pump, refer to LUBRICATION section and purge air from oil line as noted.

PISTON, PIN AND RINGS. To remove piston it is necessary to separate crankcase halves as outlined in CRANKSHAFT AND CRANKCASE section. Detach snap ring and use a suitable puller to extract piston pin so piston can be separated from connecting rod.

Piston diameter at bottom of skirt at right angle to piston pin is 2.3782-2.3792 inch (60.406-60.432 mm). Piston diameter at bottom of skirt inline with

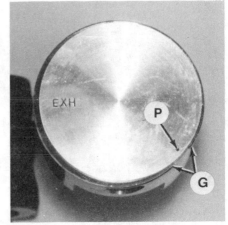

Fig. LB221—Piston must be installed on rod so "EXH" on piston crown will be toward exhaust port side of engine. Piston ring end gaps (G) must align with locating pin (P).

piston pin is 2.3742-2.3752 inch (60.305-60.330 mm). Specified piston pin hole diameter in piston is 0.5631-0.5635 inch (14.303-14.313 mm). Piston pin is available in standard size only. Piston ring end gap should be 0.005-0.015 inch (0.13-0.38 mm).

Piston and rings are available in standard size and 0.020 inch (0.51 mm) oversize. Piston ring nearer the piston crown is a semi-keystone type and the bevel must be toward the piston crown (see Fig. LB220). Second piston ring is rectangular and may be installed either direction.

Install piston on rod so "EXH" on piston crown (see Fig. LB221) will be toward exhaust port. Be sure piston ring end gaps (G) are aligned with locating pin (P) in piston ring grooves when installing piston in cylinder.

CRANKSHAFT AND CRANKCASE. To disassemble crankcase, remove blade and blade clutch if so equipped. Disconnect flywheel brake cable if so equipped. Disconnect throttle cable. On electric start model, disconnect battery. Remove flywheel as previously outlined. Remove air filter, carburetor, muffler, governor linkage and ignition module. On models so equipped, remove alternator and electric starter. Withdraw wiring from engine. On self-propelled models, remove belt cover behind engine. Remove oil pump and worm. Unscrew fasteners securing engine plate to lawn mower deck and remove engine.

Remove engine plate from engine. Remove taper pin (P—Fig. LB222) by driving pin away from cylinder as shown in Fig. LB222. Unscrew crankcase screws and separate crankcase by carefully prying between halves. Do not damage crankcase mating surfaces. When removing crankshaft assembly

Fig. LB222—Tapered alignment pin (P) is removed by driving away from cylinder (direction of arrow).

Fig. LB225—Governor arm (A) must be toward pto end of crankcase. Bearing retaining rings must fit into grooves (G) in both crankcase halves.

from crankcase, note that there are four governor balls that will be loose when governor sleeve (S—Fig. LB223) slides away from crankpin.

Specified main bearing journal diameter for both ends is 0.9835-0.9840 inch (24.981-24.994 mm). Main bearing bore in crankcase should be 2.0462-2.0469 inches (51.973-51.991 mm). Connecting rod small end diameter should be 0.7870-0.7874 inch (19.990-20.000 mm).

Crankshaft and connecting rod are available only as a unit assembly. Bearings (B—Fig. LB223) and seals (L) will fit either end. Top retainer ring (TR) at flywheel end is 0.030 inch (0.76 mm) thick while retainer ring (BR) at blade end is 0.050 inch (1.27 mm) thick.

When assembling crankshaft, install governor so balls are next to crankpin and pin (P—Fig. LB224) engages hole in crank throw. Do not install seals until crankcase is fastened together. Position governor arm (A—Fig. LB225) so arm is toward blade end of crankcase. Use a suitable gasket removing solvent and be sure crankcase mating surfaces are clean, flat and free of burrs or other damage. Apply Loctite 515 to mating surface of crankcase and spread evenly. Install crankshaft and piston assembly being sure piston ring gaps properly engage pin in ring grooves. Bearing re-

taining rings (BR and TR—Fig. LB223) must engage grooves (G—Fig. LB225) in crankcase and ring gaps must be toward cylinder. Install crankcase half and loosely install crankcase screws. Install tapered alignment pin (P—Fig. LB222). Tighten crankcase screws

Fig. LB224—Pin (P) of governor sleeve (S) must index in hole in crankpin.

evenly to 170 in.-lbs. (19.2 N·m). Rotate crankshaft and check for binding. Install oil seals with flat side out using protector 613598 and driver 613594. On self-propelled models, install belt pulley so set screw end of pulley is toward blade and belt groove is toward engine. Pin end of pulley set screw must index in hole in crankshaft. Apply Loctite to set screw threads. Complete reassembly while referring to appropriate component sections.

REWIND STARTER. To disassemble starter, first remove starter assembly from engine. Pull rope partially out of starter, remove rope handle and allow pulley to unwind slowly. Unscrew pulley retaining screw (7—Fig. LB226). Remove retainer (6), dogs (9), springs (8), brake spring (5) and washer (4). Wear appropriate safety eyewear and gloves before disengaging pulley from starter

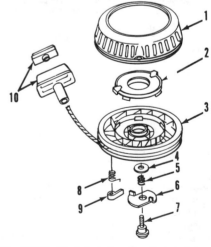

Fig. LB226—Exploded view of rewind starter.

1. Starter housing
2. Spring cup
3. Pulley
4. Washer
5. Brake spring
6. Retainer
7. Screw
8. Spring
9. Dog
10. Rope handle

Fig. LB223—View of crankshaft assembly after removal of crankcase half.

  B. Bearing
BR. Retaining ring
  C. Crankshaft
  L. Seal
TR. Retaining ring
  S. Governor sleeve

Fig. LB227—Install dog spring (8) so long end is up and outside the dog as shown. Spring should force dog toward center of starter.

Fig. LB228—After rotating pulley to place tension on rewind spring, insert rope through housing outlet (O) and pulley hole and tie a knot in pulley end of rope.

as spring may uncoil uncontrolled. Place shop towels around pulley (3) and lift pulley out of housing; spring and cup (2) may remain in housing or stay in pulley. Do not attempt to separate spring from cup as they are a unit assembly.

Inspect components for damage and excessive wear. Reverse disassembly procedure to install components. Apply a light coat of grease to rewind spring and spring contact area on inside of pulley. Note that spring cup (2) will only fit in pulley if lugs are properly engaged.

To assemble pulley, spring cup and housing, install spring cup with spring in pulley and hold pulley so spring cup is on top. Place starter housing on top of pulley. Rotate pulley counterclockwise until spring tension is felt indicating inner end of spring has engaged spring

anchor. Install dog springs (8) so long end is up and spring forces dog toward center of starter as shown in Fig. LB227. Apply grease to ends of brake spring. Flanges of retainer must be toward rewind spring. Tighten center screw to 70 in.-lbs. (7.9 N•m). Rotate pulley counterclockwise until spring is wound tight. Let pulley unwind just until rope holes in pulley and starter housing are aligned. Insert rope through holes and tie knot at pulley end (Fig. LB228). Attach handle to outer end of rope, then allow pulley to wind rope onto pulley.

When installing starter on engine, pull out rope so dogs engage starter cup and center starter before tightening starter mounting screws. Tighten starter mounting screws to 25 in.-lbs. (2.8 N•m).

ELECTRIC STARTER. Engine may be equipped with an electric

starter. To remove starter, tilt rear access door back and disconnect battery connector. Drain fuel, then remove spring clip and screws retaining fuel and oil tank assembly to mounting bracket and position tank assembly on top of blower shroud. Disconnect wire from starter. Remove starter retaining screws and withdraw starter from engine.

To disassemble starter drive components, detach "E" ring (E—Fig. LB229) and lift off pinion assembly. Remove cover (C) for access to gears (Fig. LB230). The remainder of the starter is available only as a unit assembly.

To test starter windings, disconnect starter lead and connect an ohmmeter to starter lead. Ground other ohmmeter lead to starter frame. Slowly rotate starter shaft at least one complete revolution (rapid rotation will give false readings). Resistance should be less than 10 ohms. Renew starter if tester displays high resistance or infinity.

When assembling drive components, note the following: Coat spur gears with Lubriplate; do not lubricate any other drive components. Loop end of drag spring (DS—Fig. LB229) must be around stud. Large end of spring (S) must be next to plastic gear (G). Fingers on washer (W) must engage slots on helix (H).

After installation, rotate starter gear to fully engaged position. Check gap (G—Fig. LB231) between base of flywheel gear teeth and top of starter gear teeth. Gap should be 0.078 inch (1.98 mm). Adjust starter position to obtain desired gap and tighten starter mounting screws to 170 in.-lbs. (19.2 N•m).

ALTERNATOR. Models with an electric starter are equipped with an alternator to charge the battery. The air

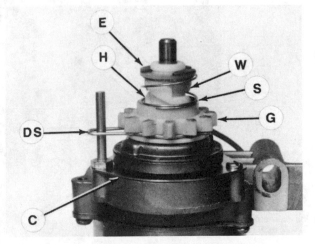

Fig. LB229—View of electric starter.

C. Cover
DS. Drag spring
E. "E" ring
G. Pinion gear
H. Helix & clutch assy.
S. Spring
W. Flanged washer

Fig. LB230—View of electric starter drive gears.

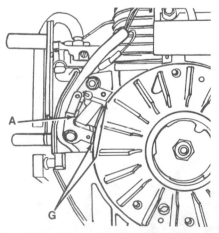

Fig. LB231—Gap (G) between base of flywheel and top of starter gear teeth should be 0.078 inch (1.98 mm).

connected but black wires are not. Connect negative ammeter lead to male end of two black wires and positive lead to female end of one black wire. Ammeter should read 190-450 mA.

NOTE: DO NOT start engine with electric starter when meter is connected as meter will be damaged.

With engine stopped, resistance reading between alternator green lead and ground should be 2.7-3.3 ohms.

FLYWHEEL BRAKE. A flywheel brake is used on some models which are not equipped with the blade brake clutch. Refer to the BLADE BRAKE CLUTCH section in this book for service to that system used on other Lawn-Boy mowers. Refer to the following for service to the flywheel brake.

The flywheel brake will stop the engine within three seconds when the equipment safety handle is released. The ignition circuit is also grounded when the brake is actuated.

Detach spring (S—Fig. LB234) to deactivate brake. Inspect mechanism for excessive wear and damage. Renew brake if brake pad thickness is less than 0.031 inch (0.78 mm) at narrowest point. Brake pad must be clean and free of grease and oil. Flywheel surface must be clean and smooth. Tighten large retaining screw to 155 in.-lbs. (17.5 N•m) and smaller retaining screw and nut to 75 in.-lbs. (8.5 N•m).

To adjust flywheel brake cable, turn adjusting nuts (N—Fig. LB235) so distance (D) from bracket to brake lever is 2⅜ inches (60.3 mm) when the safety bail is pulled against the handlebar.

gap (G—Fig. LB232) between the alternator (A) and flywheel should be 0.010 inch (0.25 mm). Insert Lawn-Boy gauge 604659 or correct thickness plastic strip between module and flywheel magnets and tighten module mounting screws to 75 in.-lbs. (8.5 N•m).

To check alternator output, first be sure air gap is correct. Run engine at 3100-3300 rpm, then disconnect battery at connector. Attach the connector as shown in Fig. LB233 so red wires are

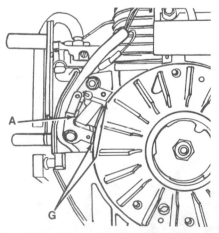

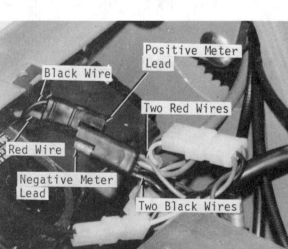

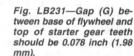

Fig. LB233—Reconnect battery connector so red wires are connected and black wires are disconnected, then check alternator using an ammeter as outlined in text.

Fig. LB232—Air gap (G) between the alternator (A) and flywheel should be 0.010 inch (0.25 mm).

Fig. LB234—Disable flywheel brake by detaching spring (S).

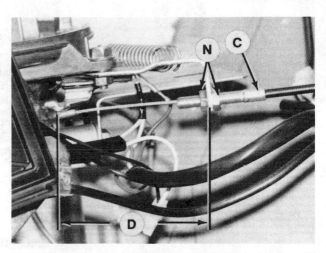

Fig. LB235—When safety bail is pulled against handlebar, distance (D) from bracket to brake lever must be 2-3/8 inches (60.3 mm). Turn nuts (N) to adjust distance.

SACHS

SACHS MOTOR CORP., LTD.
9615 Cote De Liesse
Dorval, Quebec, Canada H9P 1A3

FICHTEL & SACHS AG
852 Schweinfurt Postfach 52
West Germany

Model	Bore	Stroke	Displacement
SB140	60 mm	50 mm	142 cc
	(2.4 in.)	(2.0 in.)	(8.7 cu. in.)

ENGINE INFORMATION

Model SB140 engines are two-stroke, vertical crankshaft type rated at 2.8kW (3.8 hp) at 2850 rpm.

Engine model and serial number identification plate is attached to engine crankcase as shown in Fig. SA1. Always furnish engine model and serial number when ordering parts or service material.

Fig. SA1—Engine model and serial number plate location.

MAINTENANCE

SPARK PLUG. Spark plug should be removed, cleaned and inspected at 100-hour intervals.

Recommended spark plug is a Champion RJ17LM, or equivalent. Recommended spark plug electrode gap is 0.5 mm (0.020 in.).

CAUTION: Manufacturer does not recommend using abrasive blast method to clean spark plugs as this may introduce some abrasive material into the engine which could cause extensive damage. Use commercial cleaning solvent only.

CARBURETOR. All models are equipped with a float type carburetor with a fixed main fuel jet. Carburetor butterfly valve and upper body are an integral part of the fuel tank and cooling shroud assembly. Float bowl assembly can be removed by inserting screwdriver and pushing lock tabs inward while pulling downward on float bowl. Refer to Fig. SA2.

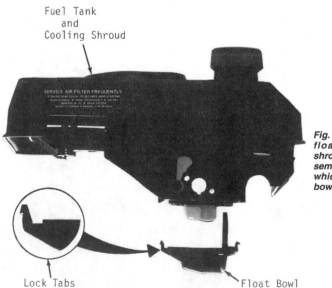

Fuel Tank
and
Cooling Shroud

Lock Tabs

Float Bowl

Fig. SA2—Fuel tank, carburetor float section and cooling shroud are one complete assembly. Inset shows lock tabs which retain carburetor float bowl. Refer to text.

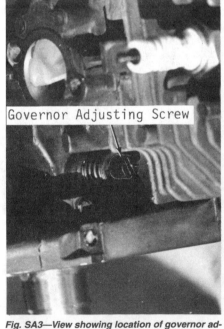

Governor Adjusting Screw

Fig. SA3—View showing location of governor adjusting screw.

Engine speed should be 2850 rpm and is adjusted by pushing governor adjustment screw (Fig. SA3) in slightly and turning it clockwise to increase engine speed or counterclockwise to reduce engine speed. Refer to GOVERNOR paragraphs in REPAIRS section.

Main jet size is 0.93 and is an integral part of jet holder (Fig. SA4). Correct jet holder and jet are identified by "1.1" stamped in flange. Main jet and jet holder are serviced as an assembly only. When reinstalling jet holder, make certain "O" ring is in good condition.

To check float level, invert fuel tank, cooling shroud and upper carburetor assembly. Float edge should be parallel with carburetor to float bowl mating surface. Refer to Fig. SA5. Carefully bend float hinge to obtain correct float level.

Choke lever should be adjusted at cable nuts at control so choke just contacts the metal tang on main jet holder with choke control at "ON" position. Place choke control at "OFF" position. Choke should be fully open.

FUEL FILTER. A fuel filter screen is an integral part of the fuel tank and is not visible. Clean by removing fuel tank and cooling shroud assembly and flush with clean fuel. Use low air pressure to blow through fuel line with fuel cap removed.

AIR CLEANER. Engine is equipped with a coco fiber air cleaner element (Fig. SA7). Filter should be inspected at 8- to 10-hour intervals of normal operation.

To clean felt frame, carefully blow dust off with low air pressure. Clean coco fiber element in warm water and detergent solution. Rinse thoroughly, shake out excess water and allow to air dry. Immerse fiber element in SAE 30 oil for 5 minutes, then allow excess oil to drain before reinstalling element. Make certain cover is firmly seated.

GOVERNOR. The mechanical ball type governor is located inside engine crankcase and is attached to the crankshaft. Use an accurate tachometer to determine engine speed. Correct engine speed is 2850 rpm. To adjust, push governor adjustment screw (Fig. SA3) in slightly and turn screw clockwise to increase engine speed or counterclockwise to reduce engine speed. Also refer to GOVERNOR paragraphs in REPAIRS section.

IGNITION SYSTEM. The breakerless ignition system requires no regular maintenance. Ignition coil unit is mounted outside the flywheel and air gap between flywheel and coil should be 0.05-0.2 mm (0.002-0.008 in.).

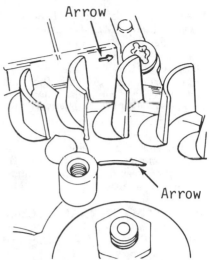

Fig. SA8—When installing ignition coil, arrow on the ignition coil and arrow on flywheel must point in the same direction.

If ignition coil has been removed, make certain arrow on ignition coil and arrow on flywheel are pointing the same direction after installation (Fig. SA8).

To check ignition coil, disconnect lead from stop switch and remove spark plug insulating cap. Position spark plug lead 4-6 mm (0.157-0.236 in.) from engine ground and spin engine flywheel. If strong spark does not occur, check insulation of stop switch lead, spark plug lead or ground contact of ignition coil at crankcase. If insulation and connections are good, and spark does not occur, renew ignition coil.

CARBON. Carbon should be removed when engine performance drops or when engine begins to four-stroke despite correct carburetor settings. To clean, remove muffler and carefully remove carbon deposits from combustion chamber and transfer ports. DO NOT attempt to remove all deposits from piston to obtain a bright surface. Remove only the large carbon deposits. Use a 3 mm (0.118 in.) drill bit to clean decompression hole (Fig. SA10). Muffler

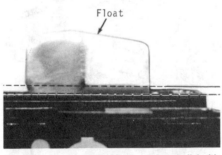

Fig. SA5—Lower edge of float mut be parallel with carburetor to float bowl mating surface for correct float level.

Fig. SA4—View showing main jet holder and location of jet identification number "1.1" stamped on flange.

Fig. SA7—View of air filter component parts.

1. Felt frame   2. Element   3. Cover

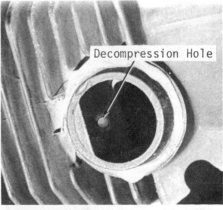

Fig. SA10—View showing location of decompression hole. Refer to text.

is filled with basalt wool and must be renewed if faulty. DO NOT attempt to clean muffler.

LUBRICATION. Engine is lubricated by premixing oil with the fuel. Manufacturer recommends thoroughly mixing one part BIA TC approved oil for every 100 parts of a good grade leaded or lead free gasoline. DO NOT use any form of premium gasoline or any gasoline that contains alcohol. Use of lead free gasoline results in fewer combustion chamber deposits.

GENERAL MAINTENANCE. Check and tighten all loose bolts, nuts or clamps daily. Check for fuel leakage and repair as necessary.

Clean dust, dirt, grease or any foreign material from cylinder head and cylinder block cooling fins at 100-hour intervals. Inspect fins for damage and repair as necessary.

REPAIRS

TIGHTENING TORQUES. Recommended tightening torque specifications are as follows:

Flywheel nut.............30-35 N·m
(20-25 ft.-lbs.)
Crankcase screws.........9-12 N·m
(6-9 ft.-lbs.)

CYLINDER. Cylinder is an integral part of one of the crankcase halves (Fig. SA11). Cylinder should be renewed if scored, flaking or severely out-of-round.

PISTON, PIN AND RING. A single ring piston is used and ring is pinned into position to prevent ring rotation (Fig. SA12). It is necessary to split crankcase and remove piston, connecting rod and crankshaft as an assembly to renew piston. Refer to CRANKCASE section.

CRANKCASE. A split crankcase design with the cylinder as an integral part of one crankcase half is used. It is necessary to split crankcase to renew piston, connecting rod or crankshaft.

To split crankcase, remove fuel tank and cooling shroud assembly. Remove flywheel and recoil starter, ignition coil and flywheel brake assembly. Remove the eight socket head cap screws (Fig. SA13) and carefully separate crankcase halves leaving crankshaft assembly in the cylinder portion of crankcase. Very carefully lift crankshaft and piston assembly from cylinder portion of crankcase while guiding governor lever up off of its pin. Use care during this procedure so ring and piston are not damaged.

To remove piston, remove piston pin retaining rings (12 – Fig. SA17) and use suitable pin extractor to remove piston

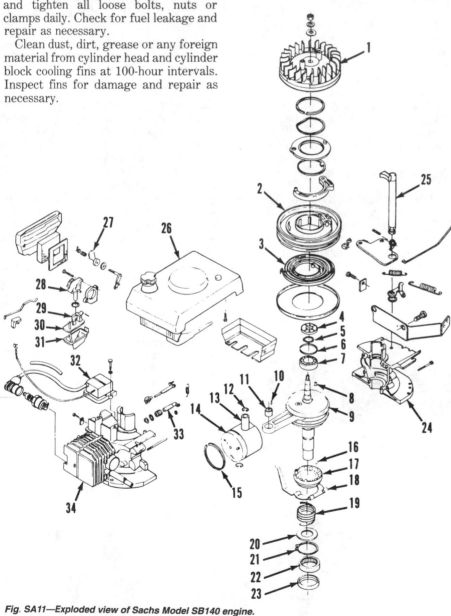

Fig. SA12—View showing location of pin on piston to prevent ring rotation. Make certain ring end gap aligns with pin.

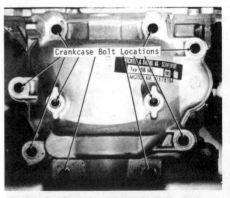

Fig. SA13—View showing location of crankcase retaining bolts. Loosen or tighten in a criss-cross pattern. Tighten to specified torque.

Fig. SA11—Exploded view of Sachs Model SB140 engine.

1. Flywheel	10. Needle bearing (25)	19. Spring
2. Pulley	11. Needle bearing race	20. Washer
3. Recoil spring	12. Retaining ring	21. Snap ring
4. Seal	13. Piston pin	22. Needle bearing
5. Snap ring	14. Piston	23. Seal
6. Retaining ring	15. Ring	24. Crankcase half
7. Bearing	16. Governor balls	25. Brake lining
8. Key	17. Governor cup	& shaft
9. Connecting rod &	18. Governor fork	26. Fuel tank & cool-
crankshaft assy.		ing shroud assy.

27. Choke	
28. Main jet holder	
29. Float	
30. Gasket	
31. Float bowl	
32. Ignition coil	
33. Governor adjustment	
screw	
34. Crankcase half	
(cylinder side)	

pin (13). Remove the 25 needle bearings (10) and press out the needle bearing race (11). New needle bearing is supplied with a plastic sleeve as an assembly aid and bearing should be pressed into connecting rod until it is centered in bore. When reassembling piston to connecting rod, arrow on piston top (Fig. SA14) should be toward exhaust side of engine. Piston pin should be a slight push fit in piston pin bore and needle bearing. Warm piston if necessary to aid pin installation.

CAUTION: Piston top will be stamped with either an "A", "B" or "C" (Fig. SA14) and cylinder top will be stamped with a corresponding "A", "B" or "C" (Fig. SA15). If piston or cylinder are renewed, piston and cylinder MUST HAVE the same letter identification. When ordering piston or cylinder, always specify letter identification needed.

To reassemble crankcase, lightly oil cylinder wall. Make certain side of ring marked "TOP" is up, ring end gap is around positioning pin (Fig. SA12) and governor fork is on crankshaft. Carefully work piston into cylinder (cylinder is tapered to compress ring) while guiding governor fork onto pin. Governor fork lever is positioned against pin of throttle valve shaft as shown in Fig. SA16. Coat mating surfaces of crankcase halves with Loctite 572. Make certain seals and retaining rings are properly seated in grooves and place remaining crankcase half in position. Tighten crankcase retaining screws in a criss-cross pattern to specified torque. Continue to reverse disassembly procedure for reassembly.

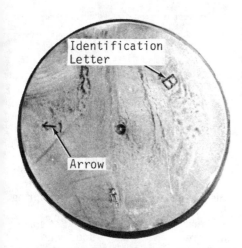

Fig. SA14—After piston installation, arrow must point toward exhaust side of engine. Piston identification letter wil be either an "A", "B" (as shown) or "C". Correctly match piston with cylinder. Refer to Fig. SA15.

Fig. SA15—View showing location of cylinder identification letter required to correctly match piston to cylinder. Refer to text.

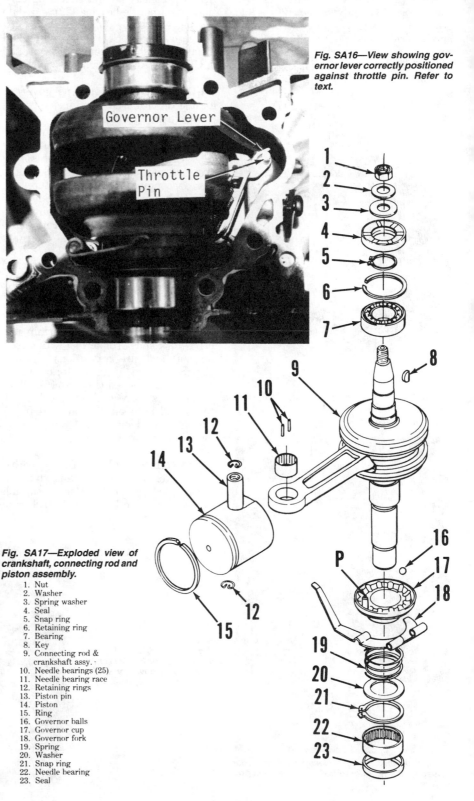

Fig. SA16—View showing governor lever correctly positioned against throttle pin. Refer to text.

Fig. SA17—Exploded view of crankshaft, connecting rod and piston assembly.

1. Nut
2. Washer
3. Spring washer
4. Seal
5. Snap ring
6. Retaining ring
7. Bearing
8. Key
9. Connecting rod & crankshaft assy.
10. Needle bearings (25)
11. Needle bearing race
12. Retaining rings
13. Piston pin
14. Piston
15. Ring
16. Governor balls
17. Governor cup
18. Governor fork
19. Spring
20. Washer
21. Snap ring
22. Needle bearing
23. Seal

CRANKSHAFT, MAIN BEARINGS AND SEALS. Crankshaft and connecting rod are serviced as an assembly only and crankshaft and connecting rod are not available separately.

To remove crankshaft and connecting rod assembly, refer to CRANKCASE section. Remove governor fork (18–Fig. SA17). Slide seal (23) and needle bearing (22) from crankshaft. Remove snap ring (21) and washer (20). Hold governor cup (17) against crankshaft and remove spring (19). Stand crankshaft up so balls (16) will not fall out of cup (17) and remove cup (17). Slide seal (4) and retaining ring (6) off of crankshaft. Remove snap ring (5). Use a suitable puller to remove bearing (7).

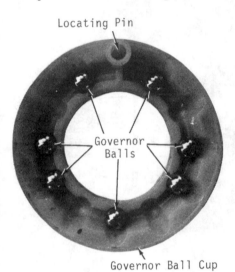

Fig. SA18—View showing governor ball placement in governor cup.

To reassemble, slightly heat bearing (7) and press onto crankshaft. Install snap ring (5), retaining ring (6) and seal (4). Install balls (16) into cup (17) as shown in Fig. SA18. Hold crankshaft in vertical position and slide cup and ball assembly up against crankshaft making sure locating pin (Fig. SA18) enters hole in crankshaft. Install spring (19–Fig. SA17), washer (20) and snap ring (21). Lightly oil needle bearing (22) and slide bearing and seal (23) onto crankshaft. Place governor fork (18) in position and install crankshaft assembly as outlined in CRANKCASE section.

GOVERNOR. A ball type governor located on crankshaft and inside crankcase is used to maintain 2850 rpm engine speed. Speed adjustments are made by pushing governor adjustment screw (Fig. SA19) in slightly against spring pressure and turning screw clockwise to increase engine speed or counterclockwise to reduce engine speed. Governor adjustment screw setting is maintained by spring pressure holding lever seated in notches cast on the inside of crankcase (Fig. SA20).

To remove governor assembly refer to CRANKCASE section. Governor adjustment screw is removed by removing "E" clip and sliding component parts out of crankcase bore.

During reassembly, make certain governor fork ends are parallel with governor cup, balls are in positions shown in Fig. SA18 and governor fork lever is correctly positioned (Fig. SA16). When governor is correct, throttle valve butterfly will be open 0.5 mm (0.020 in.). Carefully bend long arm of governor lever to obtain correct setting.

RECOIL STARTER. To remove recoil starter, remove fuel tank and cooling shroud assembly. Use a suitable puller to remove flywheel. Detach rope

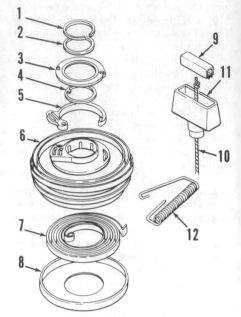

Fig. SA22—Exploded view of recoil starter assembly.

1. Retaining ring	7. Recoil spring
2. Wave washer	8. Cover
3. Brake disc	9. Knot retainer
4. Tab washer	10. Rope
5. Pawl	11. Handle
6. Pulley	12. Guide spring

handle, then remove snap ring (1–Fig. SA22), spring washer (2) and brake disc (3). Remove tab washer (4) and pawl (5). Remove rope pulley (6), rope, spring (7) and cover (8) as an assembly.

To remove spring (7), remove cover (8). Lift spring end while holding spring. Slowly release pressure to allow spring to expand to the outside.

To renew spring, insert end of spring into recess of pulley and wind into pulley. Inner end of spring must be correctly preloaded. Loop should be bent toward center of pulley. Fill lubricating grooves in bearing bore with light grease. Spring must be flat after in-

Fig. SA19—View showing location of governor adjusting screw. Refer to text for adjustment procedure.

Fig. SA20—View showing notches cast on inside of crankcase to vary governor setting. Refer to text for adjustment procedure.

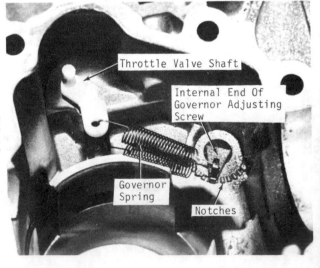

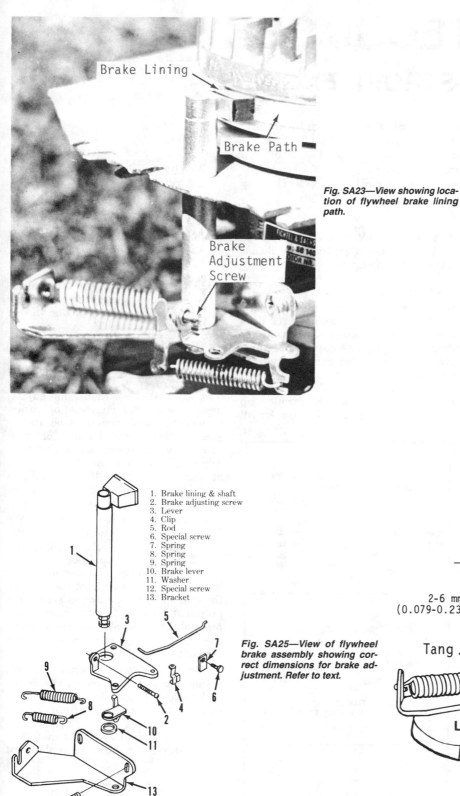

Fig. SA23—View showing location of flywheel brake lining path.

1. Brake lining & shaft
2. Brake adjusting screw
3. Lever
4. Clip
5. Rod
6. Special screw
7. Spring
8. Spring
9. Spring
10. Brake lever
11. Washer
12. Special screw
13. Bracket

Fig. SA25—View of flywheel brake assembly showing correct dimensions for brake adjustment. Refer to text.

Fig. SA24—Exploded view of flywheel brake component parts.

stallation. Lightly coat spring with oil and install cover plate. Knot rope end and pull rope tightly into eye of pulley. Wind rope around pulley 5¾ turns. Reverse removal procedure for remainder of reassembly.

FLYWHEEL BRAKE. To disassemble flywheel brake assembly (Fig. SA23), remove fuel tank and cooling shroud assembly. Disconnect springs (8 and 9 – Fig. SA24). Remove special screws (12) and remove bracket (13), washer (11), brake lever (10) and lever (3). Pull shaft and brake lining assembly (1) upward out of shaft bore in crankcase half.

To reassemble, insert shaft and brake lining assembly (1) into shaft bore in crankcase half. Install lever (3), brake lever (10), washer (11) and bracket (13) onto shaft (1). Loosely install special screws (12) through bracket (13) and into crankcase. Position brake lining so it will run on braking path of flywheel (Fig. SA23). Secure bracket in this position by tightening the two special screws (12).

To adjust flywheel brake, release engine control. Turn brake adjustment screw shown in Fig. SA23 or SA25 so there is 2-6 mm (0.079-0.236 in.) between adjustment screw and brake lever tang. Refer to Fig. SA25. If brake lining is worn to a point that 2 mm (0.079 in.) cannot be obtained, hook spring into upper hole (U) and turn adjustment screw counterclockwise until measurement is 6 mm (0.236 in.).

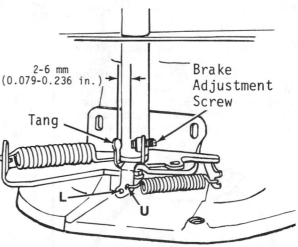

TECUMSEH
2-STROKE ENGINES

Model	Bore	Stroke	Displacement	Power Rating
AV600	2.09 in.	1.75 in.	6.00 cu.in.	3.8 hp
	(53 mm)	(44.5 mm)	(98 cc)	(2.8 kW)
TVS600	2.09 in.	1.75 in.	6.00 cu.in.	3.25 hp
	(53 mm)	(44.5 mm)	(98 cc)	(2.4 kW)

ENGINE IDENTIFICATION

All models are two-stroke, single-cylinder, air-cooled engines with a unit block type construction. Prefixes before engine type and serial number indicate the following information.

T-Tecumseh

A-Aluminum

V, VS-Vertical crankshaft

Engine prefix, type number and serial numbers are located as shown in Fig. TP2-1. Figs. TP2-2 and TP2-3 show number interpretations. Always furnish engine model, type and serial numbers when ordering parts or service material.

MAINTENANCE

LUBRICATION. Engines are lubricated by mixing a good quality engine oil designed for two-stroke, air-cooled engines with unleaded, regular grade gasoline. Oil must be rated SAE 30 or 40. Automotive or multiviscosity type oils are not recommended. Manufacturer states that gasoline containing methanol must not be used, and if gasohol is used, it must not contain more than 10 per cent ethanol. Recommended fuel:oil ratio is 24:1 for Model AV600 and 32:1 for Model TVS600. Use a separate container to mix oil and gasoline; do not mix directly in engine fuel tank.

SPARK PLUG. Spark plug should be removed, cleaned and adjusted periodically. Note that manufacturer does not recommend using a sand blaster to clean spark plugs as particles of abrasive left in the plug can damage the engine.

Tecumseh recommends a Champion RJ17LM spark plug. Electrode gap should be 0.030 inch (0.76 mm) for all models. Tighten spark plug to 216 in.-lbs. (24.4 N•m) torque.

CARBURETOR. Float type carburetor is used on rotary mower engines. Refer to Fig. TP2-4 for exploded view of carburetor.

Carburetor is equipped with an adjustable idle mixture screw and a fixed main fuel jet. Initial adjustment of idle fuel mixture screw is one turn open from a lightly seated position. Final adjustment is made with engine at operating temperature and running. Operate engine at idle speed and adjust idle mixture screw for smoothest engine idle. Adjust idle speed screw so engine idles at desired idle speed. If engine fails to accelerate smoothly, slight adjustment of fuel mixture screw may be necessary.

To disassemble carburetor, remove fuel bowl mounting nut (27—Fig. TP2-4) and fuel bowl (25). Remove float pin (23), float (24) and fuel inlet valve (21). Inlet valve seat (20) can be removed by inserting a small wire with a hook on the end through opening in seat, then pull seat from carburetor body. Compressed air can also be used to dislodge the inlet valve seat by directing air through the fuel inlet fitting.

Remove idle mixture screw (15). Use a small chisel or scratch awl to pierce and remove Welch plugs (14 and 18). Remove mounting screws from throttle plate (12) and choke plate (7), and withdraw throttle shaft and choke shaft. The carburetor body must be replaced if

Fig. TP2-1—View showing location of engine model, type and serial number. Refer also to Figs. TP2-2 and TP2-3.

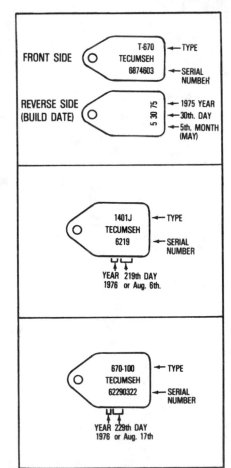

Fig. TP2-2—View showing identification tag from engine and interpretation of letters and numbers.

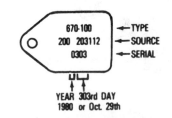

Fig. TP2-3—View of identification tag from replacement short block and interpretation of letters and numbers.

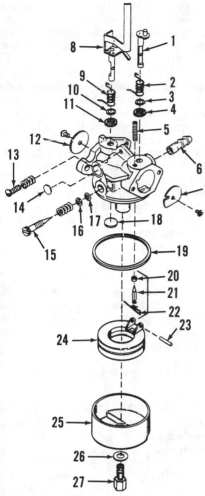

Fig. TP2-4—Exploded view of typical Tecumseh float type carburetor.

1. Choke shaft
2. Spring
3. Washer
4. Felt washer
5. Choke detent
6. Fule inlet
7. Choke plate
8. Throttle shaft
9. Spring
10. Washer
11. Felt washer
12. Throttle plate
13. Idle speed screw
14. Welch plug
15. Idle mixture screw
16. Washer
17. "O" ring
18. Welch plug
19. Gasket
20. Valve seat
21. Fuel inlet valve
22. Clip
23. Float shaft
24. Float
25. Float bowl
26. Gasket
27. Bowl retainer nut

there is excessive throttle or choke shaft play as bushings are not available.

Clean all metallic parts in suitable solvent. Blow out all passages with compressed air in the opposite direction of normal fuel flow. Do not use wires or drills to clean orifices or passages.

Install new Welch plug with the raised side facing up. Use a flat-end punch that is the same size as the plug to flatten the plug (Fig. TP2-5). Do not indent the plug. Install the fuel valve inlet seat with the flat side out and the grooved side towards the carburetor (Fig. TP2-6). Be sure that seat bottoms against shoulder in carburetor body.

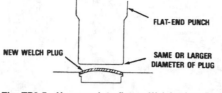

Fig. TP2-5—Use punch to flatten Welch plug. Do not indent the plug.

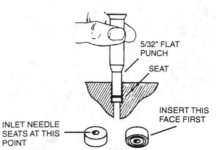

Fig. TP2-6—Fuel inlet valve seat must be installed in carburetor body with grooved side facing inward.

Choke plate should be installed with flat edge toward bottom of carburetor.

A gauge is available from Tecumseh (part No. 670253A) that can be used to determine the correct float height. With carburetor inverted, position gauge 670253A at a 90° angle to the carburetor bore and resting on the nozzle stanchion as shown in Fig. TP2-7. The toe of the float should not be higher than the first step on the gauge or lower than the second step. Bend the float tab to adjust the float height. If float gauge is not available, float height (H—Fig. TP2-8) can be set as follows: Invert carburetor and measure distance from float to surface of nozzle stanchion at a point opposite fuel inlet valve as shown in Fig. TP2-8. The float should be $3/16$ inch (5.0 mm) below surface of stanchion. Bend the float tab to adjust the float level.

Install the fuel bowl so the indented portion is on the same side as the fuel inlet.

GOVERNOR. An air vane type governor is attached to the carburetor throttle shaft on all models. The high speed (maximum) stop screw is located on the speed control lever as shown in

Fig. TP2-7—Tecumseh gauge 670253A is available for setting float level. Refer to text.

Fig. TP2-8—If float setting gauge is not available, measure float height as shown. Refer to text.

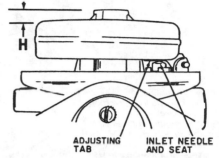

Fig. TP2-9. Engine speed must not exceed maximum speed specified by the equipment manufacturer.

IGNITION SYSTEM. Engines may be equipped with either a magneto type (breaker points) or a solid-state ignition system. Refer to the appropriate paragraph for model being serviced. Refer to FLYWHEEL paragraph in REPAIRS section when removing flywheel.

Breaker-Point Ignition System. Breaker-point gap at maximum opening should be set before adjusting the ignition timing. On some models, ignition timing is not adjustable.

Some models may be equipped with external coil and magnet laminations. Air gap (Fig. TP2-10) between external ignition coil laminations and flywheel magnet should be 0.005-0.008 inch (0.13-0.20 mm).

Ignition points and condenser are located under flywheel and flywheel must be removed for service. Refer to the following specifications for point gap and piston position before top dead center (BTDC) when breaker points just begin to open to correctly set ignition timing.

AV600 (type No. 641)

Point gap	0.018 in.
	(0.46 mm)
BTDC	0.100 in.
	(2.54 mm)

AV600 (type No. 643)

Point gap	0.020 in.
	(0.51 mm)
BTDC	0.087 in.
	(2.21 mm)

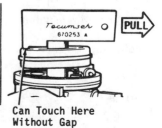

No Higher Than Here

Can Touch Here Without Gap

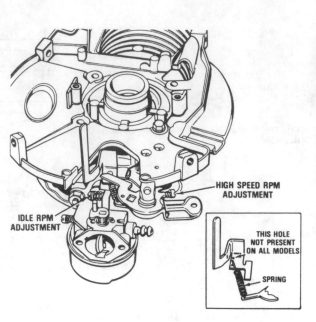

Fig. TP2-9—View of governor and carburetor linkage on vertical engine with variable engine speed control. Note location of idle speed and high speed adjusting screws.

HIGH SPEED RPM ADJUSTMENT

IDLE RPM ADJUSTMENT

THIS HOLE NOT PRESENT ON ALL MODELS

SPRING

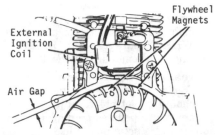

Fig. TP2-10—On engines with ignition coil mounted outside of flywheel, air gap between coil laminations and flywheel magnets should be set to 0.005-0.008 inch (0.13-0.20 mm).

External Ignition Coil

Air Gap

Flywheel Magnets

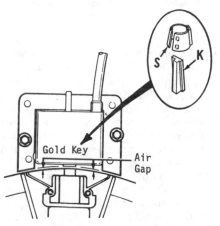

Fig. TP2-12—On solid-state ignition system, set coil lamination air gap at 0.0125 inch (0.32 mm) at locations shown. Ignition module will be marked (arrow) to indicate color of flywheel sleeve (S) or crankshaft key (K) that must be installed.

Gold Key

Air Gap

S

K

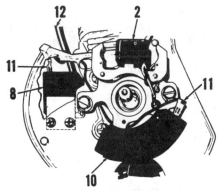

Fig. TP2-11—The solid-state ignition charging coil, triggering system and mounting plate (2 and 10) are available only as an assembly and cannot be serviced.

2. Charging coil
8. Pulse transformer
10. Trigger system
11. Low tension lead
12. High tension lead

AV600 (type No. 660-02 thru 660-38)

Point gap . . . . 0.020 in.
        (0.51 mm)
BTDC . . . . 0.070 in.
        (1.78 mm)

TVS600

Point gap . . . . 0.020 in.
        (0.51 mm)

BTDC . . . . *
*On models with external coil, timing is not adjustable. Set coil air gap to specified dimension.

Solid-State Ignition System. The Tecumseh solid-state ignition system does not use ignition points. The only moving part of the system is the rotating flywheel with the charging magnets. Early systems utilize individual components contained under the flywheel as shown in Fig. TP2-11, while later systems are modular with a one-piece ignition coil and ignition module externally mounted as shown in Fig. TP2-12. Note that module is square as opposed to a breaker point ignition coil which is round.

On early systems, the ignition charging coil, electronic triggering system and mounting plate are available only as an assembly. If necessary to renew this assembly, place the unit in position

on the engine. Start the retaining screws, turn the mounting plate counterclockwise as far as possible, then tighten retaining screws to 5-7 ft.-lbs. (7-10 N•m) torque.

The ignition coil/module on later models is a one-piece unit. The module is marked with "GOLD KEY" on the module and a gold colored crankshaft key and a gold colored flywheel sleeve must be used. See Fig. TP2-12. The correct air gap setting between the flywheel magnets and the laminations on ignition module is 0.0125 inch (0.32 mm). Use Tecumseh gauge 670297 or equivalent thickness plastic strip to set gap as shown in Fig. TP2-12. Tighten mounting screws to 30-40 in.-lbs. (3.4-4.5 N•m) torque.

CARBON. Muffler and exhaust ports should be cleaned after every 50 to 75 hours of operation. The cylinder head, piston and cylinder wall should be cleaned of carbon if excessive carbon buildup is noted.

REPAIRS

TIGHTENING TORQUES. Recommended tightening torque specifications are as follows:

Carburetor	60-75 in.-lbs. (6.8-8.5 N•m)
Connecting rod.	40-50 in.-lbs. (5-6 N•m)
Crankcase cover.	80-100 in.-lbs. (9.0-11.3 N•m)
Cylinder head	80-100 in.-lbs. (9.0-11.3 N•m)
Flywheel nut	22-27 ft.-lbs. (30-36 N•m)
Muffler	80-100 in.-lbs. (9.0-11.3 N•m)
Reed plate	35-45 in.-lbs. (4.0-5.0 N•m)
Spark plug	16-22 ft.-lbs. (22-29 N•m)

CRANKCASE PRESSURE TEST. An improperly sealed crankcase can cause the engine to be hard to start, run rough, have low power and overheat. If crankcase leakage is suspected, pressurize crankcase and use a soap and water solution to check gaskets, seals, carburetor pulse line and casting for leakage.

FLYWHEEL. Disengage flywheel brake as outlined in FLYWHEEL BRAKE section. If flywheel has tapped holes, use a suitable puller to remove flywheel. If no holes are present, screw a knock-off nut onto crankshaft as shown in Fig. TP2-13 so there is a small gap between nut and flywheel. Gently

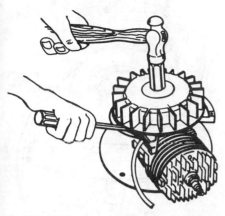

Fig. TP2-13—View showing use of a knock-off tool (nut) to separate flywheel from crankshaft end.

pry against bottom of flywheel while tapping sharply on nut. After installing flywheel, tighten flywheel nut to 22-27 ft.-lbs.(30-36 N•m) torque.

On engines with a ball bearing at flywheel end of crankshaft, using a knock-off nut may result in bearing and crankshaft moving toward pto end. This will reduce clearance between crankshaft and crankcase. Rap sharply on pto end of crankshaft with a rawhide mallet to reseat ball bearing.

Some engines are equipped with a flywheel sleeve similar to the sleeve shown in Fig. TP2-12. Gold colored sleeves are used with solid-state ignitions while grey colored sleeves are used with breaker-point ignitions. The sleeve must be discarded if it is sheared or damaged. Install sleeve so it is flush or just below inside surface of flywheel.

CYLINDER HEAD. To remove cylinder head, remove all interfering shrouds and brackets. Clean area around cylinder head to prevent entrance of foreign material. Unscrew cylinder head screws and remove cylinder head.

Clean combustion deposits from cylinder head taking care not to damage head gasket sealing area. A new head gasket should be installed when installing cylinder head. Tighten cylinder head retaining screws evenly to a torque of 80-100 in.-lbs. (9.0-11.3 N•m) torque.

DISASSEMBLY. Refer to Fig. TP2-14 or Fig. TP2-15 for exploded view of engine. When disassembling engine, note that piston and connecting rod must be removed before crankcase cover is removed. The crankshaft is removed with the crankcase cover. Unbolt and remove blower housing and fuel tank. Remove flywheel as previously outlined. Remove magneto (5) if so equipped. Remove carburetor (32) and

reed plate (30). Remove cylinder head (25). Remove connecting rod cap and push the rod and piston unit out through top of cylinder. Do not lose bearing rollers which will fall out when rod cap is loosened. To prevent damage to piston and rings, it may be necessary to remove the ridge from top of cylinder bore before removing piston and connecting rod assembly.

Unbolt and remove crankcase cover (8) with crankshaft from cylinder block. To separate crankshaft and crankcase cover, carefully heat bearing area so crankshaft and bearing can be separated from crankcase cover; do not use excessive heat. Remove crankshaft seals (6 and 28).

PISTON, PIN, RINGS AND CYLINDER. The piston and connecting rod can be removed after removing the cylinder head and end cover or reed valve. The piston pin rides in a roller bearing in the small end of the connecting rod. The piston pin can be extracted after removing the retaining clips and using a suitable piston pin puller or press.

Inspect piston for scuffing, scratches or excessive wear and renew as necessary. Standard piston skirt diameter is listed in following table:

Type Number	Diameter
660-11 thru	
660-38	2.0870-2.0880 in.
	(53.010-53.035 mm)

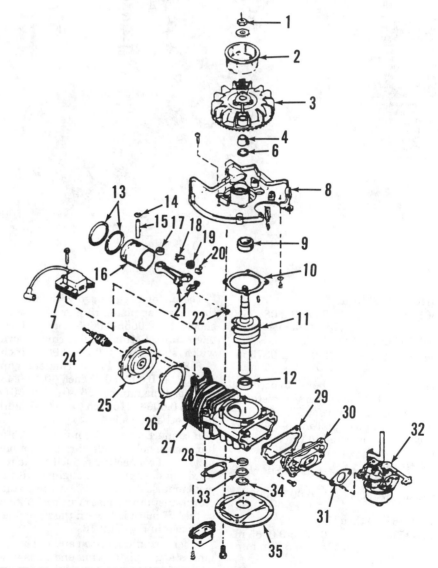

Fig. TP2-14—Exploded view of typical AV600 series engine.

1. Flywheel nut
2. Starter cup
3. Flywheel
4. Flywheel sleeve
5. Seal
6. Seal
7. Ignition module
8. End plate
9. Bearing
10. Gasket
11. Crankshaft
12. Bearing
13. Piston rings
14. Clip
15. Piston pin
16. Piston
17. Bearing
18. Liner
19. Roller bearings
20. Liner
21. Connecting rod & cap
22. Rod bolt
23. Head bolt
24. Spark plug
25. Cylinder head
26. Gasket
27. Cylinder
28. Seal
29. Gasket
30. Reed valve assy.
31. Gasket
32. Carburetor
33. Seal retainer
34. Snap ring
35. Adapter plate

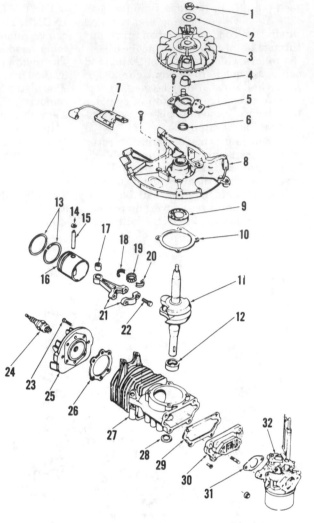

Fig. TP2-15—Exploded view of typical TVS600 series engine.

1. Flywheel nut
2. Washer
3. Flywheel
4. Flywheel sleeve
5. Magneto
6. Seal
7. Coil
8. Crankcase cover
9. Bearing (ball)
10. Gasket
11. Crankshaft
12. Bearing (roller)
13. Piston rings
14. Clip
15. Piston pin
16. Piston
17. Bearing
18. Liner
19. Roller bearings
20. Liner
21. Connecting rod
22. Rod bolt
23. Head bolt
24. Spark plug
25. Cylinder head
26. Head gasket
27. Cylinder
28. Seal
29. Gasket
30. Reed valve
31. Gasket
32. Carburetor

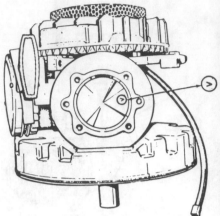

Fig. TP2-16—The "V" mark stamped on top of piston must be toward side shown. Lubrication hole in side of connecting rod must be toward top on all vertical shaft models.

type needle bearing that is pressed into connecting rod small end. A steel insert (liner) is used on inside of connecting rod and needle bearing rollers are used at the crankpin end. Connecting rod may contain 30 or 37 bearing rollers, depending on engine model. Standard crankpin journal diameter is either 0.8113-0.8118 inch (20.607-20.620 mm) for TVS600 models or 0.8442-0.8450 inch (21.443-21.463 mm) for AV600 models. Measure unworn portion of crankpin to determine standard diameter.

Inspect connecting rod, crankpin, bearing rollers and bearing liners for damage and excessive wear. Bearing rollers should be renewed only as a set. Renew bearing set if any roller is damaged. New bearing rollers are serviced in a strip and can be installed by wrapping the strip around crankpin. Old bearing rollers can be held in place using grease. After new needle rollers and connecting rod cap are installed, force lacquer thinner into needles to remove the beeswax or grease, then lubricate bearing with oil.

When installing rod on crankshaft, make certain match marks on connecting rod and cap are aligned (Fig. TP2-17). Ends of bearing liners must correctly engage when match marks on connecting rod and cap are aligned.

Tighten connecting rod cap retaining screws to 40-50 in.-lbs. (5-6 N•m) torque.

CRANKSHAFT AND CRANK-CASE. The crankshaft can be removed after the piston, connecting rod, flywheel and magneto end bearing plate are removed.

A ball type main bearing (9—Fig. TP2-14 or Fig. TP2-15) is used at flywheel end of crankshaft and a cartridge

660-40, 661-30 thru
661-45 . . . . 2.0880-2.0885 in.
(53.035-53.048 mm)
661-01 thru
661-29 . . . . 2.0865-2.0875 in.
(52.997-53.022 mm)

The cylinder can be bored to accept a 0.010 inch (0.25 mm) oversize piston if it is excessively worn, out-of-round or scored. Standard piston-to-cylinder bore clearance is listed in the following table:

Type Number	Clearance
660-11 thru	
660-38	0.005-0.007 in.
	(0.13-0.18 mm)
660-40, 661-30 thru	
661-45	0.0045-0.0065 in.
	(0.115-0.165 mm mm)
661-01 thru	
661-29	2.0865-2.0875 in.
	(52.997-53.022 mm)

The piston pin (15—Fig. TP2-14) is available only as an assembly with the piston. Piston pin diameter should be 0.4997-0.4999 inch (12.692-12.697 mm).

The piston is equipped with two piston rings. Top piston ring groove width should be 0.0655-0.0665 inch (1.664-1.689 mm). Bottom piston ring groove width should be 0.0645-0.0655 inch (1.638-1.664 mm). Piston ring end gap should be 0.007-0.017 inch (0.18-0.43 mm) for type number 661-01 thru 661-29 and 0.006-0.016 inch (0.15-0.41 mm) for all other models.

If connecting rod is equipped with a lubrication hole in side of rod, assemble piston and connecting rod with hole toward top of engine. On engines with a piston marked with a "V" on the piston crown, install the piston in the engine so the "V" mark is toward the right side as shown in Fig. TP2-16.

When installing piston and rod in engine, stagger piston ring end gaps and use a ring compressor. Make certain rings do not catch in recess at top of cylinder.

CONNECTING ROD. The engine is equipped with an aluminum connecting rod. The piston pin rides in a cartridge

Illustrations courtesy Tecumseh Products Co.

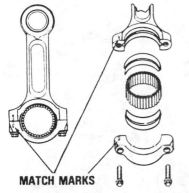

Fig. TP2-17—Match marks on connecting rod and cap must be aligned.

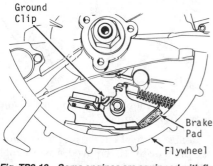

Fig. TP2-18—Some engines are equipped with flywheel band brake system.

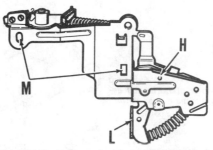

Fig. TP2-19—Push against lever (L) and insert a pin through holes (H) to hold brake pad away from flywheel.

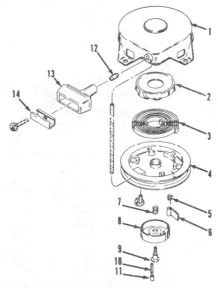

Fig. TP2-20—Exploded view of typical pawl type rewind starter with teardrop shaped housing (1) using retainer screw (9). Some starters may have three starter pawls (6).

1. Housing
2. Spring keeper
3. Rewind spring
4. Pulley
5. Spring
6. Pawl
7. Brake spring
8. Retainer
9. Screw
10. Centering pin
11. Nylon bushing
12. Rope coupler
13. Handle
14. Insert

type bearing (12) is used at pto end of crankshaft. It should be necessary to bump the crankshaft out of the bearing inner races. Heating the crankcase cover around the bearing area with a propane torch will make removal easier. Ball and roller bearing outer races should be a tight fit in bearing bores.

Before installing bearing on crankshaft, clean area on crankshaft where bearing locates and apply Loctite 609 in the grooves. On all models, bearings should be installed with printed face on race toward center of engine. Press bearing onto crankshaft using a sleeve that contacts inner race of bearing only. Heat the crankcase cover before installing ball bearing and crankshaft assembly.

Crankshaft end play for all models is zero. Install crankshaft seals so lip is toward inside of engine. It is recommended that the crankcase be pressure tested for leakage before proceeding with remainder of engine reassembly.

REED VALVES. Vertical crankshaft engines are equipped with a reed type inlet valve located in the crankcase end cover (30—Fig. TP2-14 and Fig. TP2-15). Reed petals should not stand out more than 0.010 inch (0.25 mm) from the reed plate and must not be bent, distorted or cracked. The reed plate must be smooth and flat. Reed petals

are available only as part of the crankcase end cover. Tighten end cover mounting screws to 35-45 in.-lbs. (4.0-5.0 N·m).

FLYWHEEL BRAKE. A flywheel brake is used on some engines that will stop the engine within three seconds when the equipment safety handle is released. The ignition circuit is grounded also when the brake is actuated. Refer to Fig. TP2-18.

The brake shown in Fig. TP2-18 contacts the inside of the flywheel. Before the flywheel can be removed, the brake must be disengaged from the flywheel. Push lever (L—Fig. TP2-19) toward spark plug so brake pad moves away from flywheel, then insert Tecumseh tool 670298 or a suitable pin in hole (H) to hold lever.

Inspect mechanism for excessive wear and damage. Minimum allowable thickness of brake pad at narrowest point is 0.060 inch (1.52 mm). Flywheel surface must be clean and undamaged. Install brake mechanism and push up on bracket so bracket mounting screws are at bottom of slotted holes (M) in bracket. Tighten mounting screws to 90 in.-lbs. (10.2 N·m) torque.

REWIND STARTER

Dog Type Starter

TEARDROP HOUSING. To disassemble starter (Fig. TP2-20), release tension of rewind spring by removing rope handle and allowing rope to wind slowly into starter. Remove retainer screw (9), retainer (8) and spring (7). Remove pawl (6) and spring (5). Remove pulley with spring. Wear appropriate safety eyewear and gloves before disengaging keeper (2) and rewind spring (3) from pulley as spring may uncoil uncontrolled.

To reassemble, reverse the disassembly procedure. Standard rope length is 69 inches (175 cm) and diameter is $^5/_{32}$ inch (4 mm). Spring (3) should be lightly

greased. Install the pawl (6) and spring (5) so the spring end forces the pawl toward the center of the pulley. Assemble starter but install rope last as follows: Turn pulley counterclockwise until tight, then allow to unwind so hole in pulley aligns with rope outlet as shown in Fig. TP2-21. Insert rope through starter housing and pulley hole, tie a knot in rope end, allow rope to wind onto pulley and install rope handle. Some models use centering pin (10—Fig. TP2-20) to align starter with starter cup. Place nylon bushing (11) on pin (10), then bottom pin in hole in retainer screw (9). Pin and bushing should index in end of crankshaft when installing starter on engine.

STYLIZED STARTER. The "stylized" starter is shown in Fig. TP2-22. To

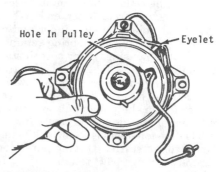

Fig. TP2-21—Insert rope through starter housing eyelet and hole in pulley, then tie knot in rope end.

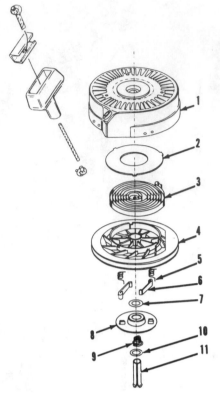

Fig. TP2-22—Exploded view of "stylized" rewind starter.

1. Starter housing	7. Plastic washers (2)
2. Cover	8. Pawl retainer
3. Rewind spring	9. Brake spring
4. Pulley	10. Metal washer
5. Springs (2)	11. Pin
6. Pawls (2)	

Fig. TP2-23—Exploded view of horizontal engagement gear starter.

1. Mounting bracket
2. Rope guide
3. Snap ring
4. Washer
5. Brake spring
6. Gear
7. Pulley
8. Insert
9. Handle
10. Bracket
11. Rope
12. Rewind spring
13. Cover
14. Spring anchor
15. Hub screw

disassemble starter, remove rope handle and allow rope to wind slowly into starter. Position a suitable sleeve support under pawl retainer (8) and using a 5/16 inch (8 mm) diameter punch, drive pin (11) free of starter. Remove brake spring (9), retainer (8), pawls (6) and springs (5). Wear appropriate safety eyewear and gloves before disengaging pulley from starter as spring may uncoil uncontrolled. Place shop towel around pulley and lift pulley out of housing; spring should remain with pulley.

Inspect components for damage and excessive wear. Reverse disassembly procedure to install components. Rewind spring coils wind in counterclockwise direction from outer end. When installing pulley, be sure inner end of rewind spring engages spring retainer adjacent to housing center post. Install the pawl (6—Fig. TP2-22) and spring (5) so the spring end forces the pawl toward the center of the pulley. Place the retainer (8) on the pulley hub so tabs on retainer are inside ends of pawls. Install pin (11) so top of pin is 1/8 inch (3.2 mm) below top of starter. Driving pin in too far may damage pawl retainer.

With starter assembled, except for rope, install rope as follows: Rotate pul-

ley counterclockwise until tight, then allow to unwind so hole in pulley aligns with rope outlet. Insert rope through starter housing and pulley hole, tie a knot in rope end, allow rope to wind onto pulley and install rope handle.

Side-Mounted Starter

HORIZONTAL ENGAGEMENT GEAR STARTER. When the rope handle is pulled, the starter gear moves horizontally to engage the gear teeth on the flywheel. An exploded view of the starter is shown in Fig. TP2-23. Most starters use a rope that is 61 inches (155 cm) long.

After installing starter assembly, clearance between teeth on gear (6) and teeth on flywheel should be checked when starter is operated. When teeth are fully engaged, there should be at least 1/16 inch (1.6 mm) clearance from top of gear tooth to base of opposite gear teeth. Remove spark plug wire, operate starter several times and check gear engagement. Insufficient gear tooth clearance could cause starter gear to hang up on flywheel gear when engine starts, which could damage starter.

To disassemble starter, proceed as follows: Detach rope from insert (8—Fig. TP2-23) and handle (9), then allow the rope to wind slowly onto the pulley to relieve spring tension. Unscrew screws securing spring cover (13) and carefully remove cover without disturbing rewind spring. Safety eyewear and gloves should be worn when working on or around the rewind spring. Remove rewind spring (12). Remove hub screw (15) and spring hub (14), then withdraw pulley and gear assembly. Remove snap

ring (3), washer (4), brake spring (5) and gear (6) from pulley.

Reassemble starter using the following procedure: If removed, install rope guide (2) on starter bracket so dimple on guide fits in depression on bracket. Install rope on pulley. Wrap rope around pulley in a counterclockwise direction when viewing pulley from rewind spring side of pulley. Place gear on pulley. Do not lubricate helix in gear or on pulley shaft. Install brake spring (5) in groove of gear (6). The bent end of brake spring should point away from gear. The brake spring should fit snugly in groove. Do not lubricate brake spring. Install washer (4) and snap ring (3) on pulley shaft. Lightly lubricate shaft on starter bracket then install pulley and gear assembly on bracket shaft. The closed end of brake spring (5) must fit around tab (A) on bracket. Install spring anchor (14) and screw (15). Tighten screw to 44-55 in.-lb. (5.0-6.2 N·m) torque. Install rewind spring. The spring coils should wind in a clockwise direction from outer end. A new spring is contained in a holder that allows spring installation by pushing spring from holder into spring cavity on pulley. Pass outer end of rope through rope bracket (10) and install rope handle and insert. Pull a portion of rope out past rope guide and wrap any excess rope around pulley, then turn pulley 2-2½ turns against spring tension to preload rewind spring. Check starter operation.

VERTICAL ENGAGEMENT GEAR STARTER. When the rope handle is pulled, the starter gear moves vertically to engage the gear teeth on

Illustrations courtesy Tecumseh Products Co.

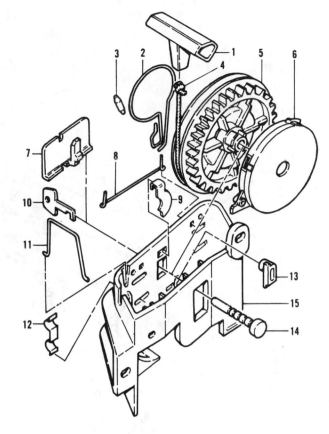

Fig. TP2-24—Exploded view of vertical engagement gear starter.

1. Handle
2. Brake spring
3. Staple
4. Rope
5. Rope pulley
6. Rewind spring & housing
7. Rope clip
8. Pawl spring
9. Pawl
10. Key (not all models)
11. Rope clip
12. Clip (not all models)
13. Lock pawl (not all models)
14. Pin
15. Mounting bracket

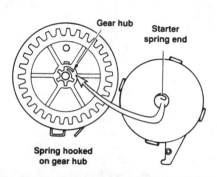

Fig. TP2-26—Housing rotation may be prevented by inserting a pin or rod through strut hole and into gear teeth.

Fig. TP2-27—If removed, place spring housing on rope pulley while being sure inner spring end engages anchor on pulley.

Fig. TP2-25—Drawing of vertical engagement gear starter. Note location of "V" notch.

the flywheel. An exploded view of the starter is shown in Fig. TP2-24.

To replace the starter rope, proceed as follows: If the starter bracket has a "V" notch (V—Fig. TP2-25), then the inner end of the rope is accessible and the rope can be replaced without disassembling the starter. Typical rope lengths are 65 inches (165 cm) and 98 inches (249 cm). If rope is unbroken, remove rope handle and let rope wind onto rope pulley. Note that inner end of rope was originally retained by a staple, while inner end on replacement ropes is inserted through a hole in pulley and knotted. Rotate pulley so that either the stapled rope end or knotted rope end is visible in the "V" notch. Pry out staple or untie knot and

pull out rope. Rotate pulley counterclockwise until rewind spring is tight, then allow pulley to turn clockwise until rope hole in pulley is visible in "V" notch. Route new rope through pulley hole and tie a knot in rope end. Pull the knot into pulley cavity so rope end does not protrude. Allow pulley to wind rope onto pulley. Attach rope handle to rope end.

To disassemble starter, proceed as follows: If rope is unbroken, remove rope handle and let rope wind onto rope pulley. Drive or press out pulley spindle (14—Fig. TP2-24) by placing starter over a deep-well socket and forcing spindle into socket. Turn spring housing (6) so strut aligns with legs on brake spring (2). Prevent housing rotation by inserting a pin or rod through strut hole and into gear teeth as shown in Fig. TP2-26. Remove pulley assembly from starter bracket.

CAUTION: Do not allow spring housing to separate from rope pulley until spring tension has been relieved.

Hold spring housing (6—Fig. TP2-24) against rope pulley so spring housing cannot rotate. Withdraw pin or rod in spring housing strut (Fig. TP2-26) and allow spring housing to rotate thereby relieving rewind spring tension. If necessary, separate spring housing from rope pulley. Do not attempt to remove

rewind spring from spring housing. The spring and housing are available only as a unit assembly.

If rope replacement is necessary, note that inner end of rope was originally retained by a staple, while inner end on replacement ropes is inserted through a hole in pulley and knotted. Pry out staple, if so equipped, to release rope. Route new rope through pulley hole and tie a knot in rope end. The knot must be positioned in pulley cavity so rope end does not protrude.

To assemble starter, proceed as follows: Do not lubricate any starter components. When viewed from gear side of rope pulley, wind rope onto pulley in a clockwise direction. Install brake spring (2—Fig. TP2-24) on rope pulley while being careful not to distort spring legs. If removed, place spring housing on rope pulley while being sure inner spring end engages anchor on pulley. See Fig. TP2-27. Rotate spring housing four turns counterclockwise, then align legs on brake spring with hole in strut. Prevent housing rotation by inserting a pin or rod through strut hole and into gear teeth. If so equipped, install clip (7—Fig. TP2-24), key (10) and pawl (9). Install rope pulley assembly in starter bracket while inserting brake spring legs into slots in starter bracket (Fig. TP2-28). Route outer rope end past rope guide and install rope handle. With-

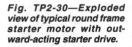

Fig. TP2-28—Install rope pulley assembly in starter bracket while inserting brake spring legs into slots in starter bracket.

Guide brake ends through slot

draw pin or rod in strut hole. The strut will rotate until it contacts starter bracket. Press or drive in a new pulley spindle (14—Fig. TP2-24).

ELECTRIC STARTER. While several electric starter motors have been used on Tecumseh engines, the motors are basically divided into those with a round frame or a square frame. Several variations of each type have been produced, but service is basically similar except as noted in following paragraphs.

Tecumseh does not provide test specifications for electric starter motors, so service is limited to replacing components that are known or suspected faulty.

CAUTION: The starter motor field magnets may be made of ceramic material. Do not clamp starter housing in a vise or hit housing as field magnets may be damaged.

Refer to Figs. TP2-29 and Fig. TP2-30 for exploded views of typical starter motors. Note the following when servicing electric starter motor: Prior to disassembly, mark drive plate, frame and end cap so they can be aligned during assembly. Some motors have alignment notches, in which case alignment marks are not necessary.

Minimum brush length is not specified. If brush wire bottoms against slot in brush holder or brush is less than half its original length, replace brush. Be sure brushes do not bind in holders.

Check strength of brush springs. The spring must force brush against commutator with sufficient pressure to ensure good contact.

Bushings in drive plate and end cap are not available separately, only as a

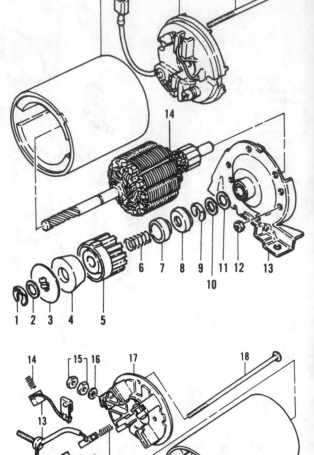

Fig. TP2-29—Exploded view of typical round frame starter motor with inward-acting starter drive.

1. "E" ring
2. Plastic washer
3. Drive hub
4. Rubber driver
5. Pinion gear
6. Spring
7. Plastic spring cup
8. Metal cup
9. "E" ring
10. Metal washer
11. Plastic washer
12. Nut
13. Drive plate
14. Armature
15. Frame
16. End cap assy.
17. Through-bolt

Fig. TP2-30—Exploded view of typical round frame starter motor with outward-acting starter drive.

1. Boot
2. Snap ring
3. Spring cup
4. Spring
5. Pinion gear
6. Nut
7. Drive hub
8. Drive plate
9. Armature
10. Washer
11. Washer
12. Frame
13. Brushes
14. Brush springs
15. Nuts
16. Washer
17. End cap
18. Through-bolt

unit assembly with drive plate or end cap.

Apply a light coat of grease to helix. All other parts should be assembled dry.

On some motors, a brush holding tool may be helpful to retain brushes and springs during assembly. If end cap has two brushes, a piece of manual rewind starter spring can be bent double and inserted between the brushes to hold brushes in position. Use care when installing end cap so commutator and brushes are not damaged.

Illustrations courtesy Tecumseh Products Co.

TECUMSEH
2-STROKE ENGINES

Model	Bore	Stroke	Displacement	Power Rating
TVS840, TVXL840	2.44 in.	1.81 in.	8.46 cu.in.	4.0 hp
	(62 mm)	(46 mm)	(138 cc)	(3.0 kW)

ENGINE IDENTIFICATION

All models are two-stroke, single-cylinder, air-cooled engines. Engine model and type numbers are stamped in blower housing as shown in Fig. TP3-1. Always furnish engine model and type numbers when ordering parts.

MAINTENANCE

LUBRICATION. The engine is lubricated by mixing regular unleaded gasoline with a good quality two-stroke, air-cooled engine oil rated SAE 30 or SAE 40 at a 50:1 ratio. Automotive or multiviscosity type oils are not recommended. Manufacturer states that gasoline containing methanol must not be used, and if gasohol is used, it must not contain more than 10 per cent ethanol. Use a separate container to mix oil and gasoline; do not mix directly in engine fuel tank.

AIR FILTER. The filter element may be made of foam or paper, or a combination of both foam and paper. The recommended maintenance interval depends on the type of filter element.

Foam type filter elements should be cleaned, inspected and re-oiled after every 25 hours of engine operation, or after three months, whichever occurs first. Clean the filter in soapy water

then squeeze the filter until dry (don't twist the filter). Inspect the filter for tears and holes or any other opening. Discard the filter if it cannot be cleaned satisfactorily or if the filter is torn or otherwise damaged. Pour clean engine oil into the filter, then squeeze the filter to remove the excess oil and distribute oil throughout the filter.

Paper type filter elements should be replaced annually or more frequently if the engine operates in a severe environment, such as extremely dusty conditions. A dirty filter element cannot be cleaned and must be discarded.

SPARK PLUG. Spark plug should be removed, cleaned and adjusted periodically. Note that manufacturer does not recommend using a sand blaster to clean spark plugs as particles of abrasive left in the plug can damage the engine.

Recommended spark plug for is either a Champion CJ8Y or RJ19LM, depending on application. Specified spark plug electrode gap is 0.030 inch (0.76 mm). Tighten spark plug to 16-20 ft.-lbs. (22-27 N m) torque.

CARBURETOR. All models are equipped with a Tecumseh Series VI float type carburetor. Carburetor is equipped with fixed high speed and low speed mixture jets.

To service the carburetor, note that fuel bowl retaining bolt (Fig. TP3-2) is manufactured with left-hand threads. Remove float bowl retaining bolt (18—Fig. TP3-3), float bowl (16), float hinge

pin (14), float fuel inlet needle and spring (12). Use a hooked wire to remove the fuel inlet needle seat. Remove primer bulb retaining ring (9) and primer bulb (8). Remove throttle plate (7), throttle shaft (1), spring (2) and dust seal (4). Remove Welch plug (10) from

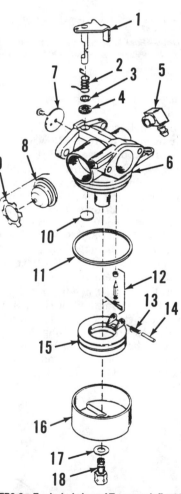

Fig. TP3-3—Exploded view of Tecumseh float type carburetor used on all models. Note that bowl nut (18) has left hand threads.

1. Throttle shaft	10.	Welch plug
2. Throttle spring	11.	Bowl gasket
3. Washer	12.	Fuel inlet needle & seat
4. Dust seal	13.	Spring
5. Fuel inlet elbow	14.	Pivot pin
6. Carburetor body	15.	Float
7. Throttle plate	16.	Float bowl
8. Primer bulb	17.	Seal washer
9. Retainer	18.	Bowl nut

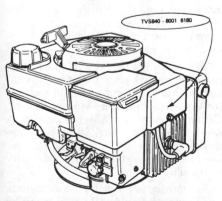

Fig. TP3-1—Engine model and type numbers are stamped on blower housing in location shown.

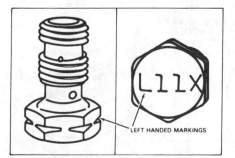

Fig. TP3-2—Float bowl retaining bolt marked as shown is manufactured with left-hand threads.

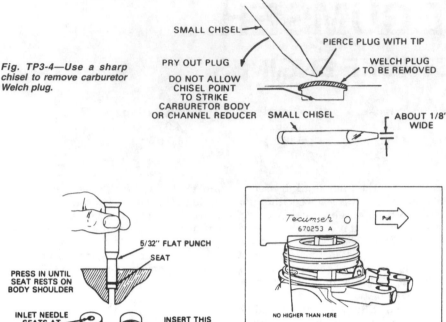

Fig. TP3-4—Use a sharp chisel to remove carburetor Welch plug.

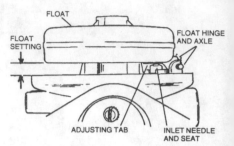

Fig. TP3-7B—Measure float setting between float and carburetor body.

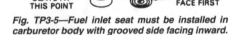

Fig. TP3-5—Fuel inlet seat must be installed in carburetor body with grooved side facing inward.

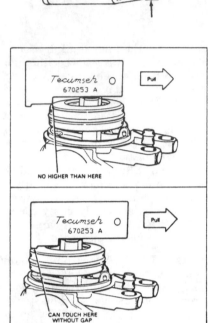

Fig. TP3-7A—Tecumseh go-no go gage 670253 should be used to set correct float height. Refer to text.

carburetor body using a sharp chisel (Fig. TP3-4).

Clean carburetor body and bowl nut in carburetor cleaner. Blow out passages with compressed air.

To reassemble carburetor, install the new fuel inlet needle seat with grooved side of seat facing down (Fig. TP3-5). Be sure that seat bottoms against shoulder in carburetor body. Install new Welch plug (10—Fig. TP3-3) with the raised side facing up. Use a flat-end punch that is the same size as the plug to flatten the plug. Do not indent the plug.

Install fuel inlet needle and clip (12) on float with long end of clip pointing toward air cleaner end of carburetor. When installing dampening spring on float, the short leg hooks onto carburetor body and the longer end points toward choke end (Fig. TP3-6).

Use Tecumseh float tool 670253A to set the correct float height (Fig. TP3-

7A). The gauge is a go-no go type. Pull the tool in a 90° direction to the hinge pin. The toe of the float, end opposite the hinge, must be under the first step and can touch the second step without a gap. Carefully bend the float tab holding the fuel inlet needle to obtain correct height.

If Tecumseh float setting tool is not available, invert carburetor and measure distance from carburetor body to float as shown in Fig. TP3—7B. Float setting height should be 11/64 inch (4.3

mm). Adjust float height by bending float tab. Use care when bending float tab so as not to apply pressure to fuel inlet needle which could damage needle and seat.

Install float bowl with flat area of bowl parallel to the float hinge pin. Install throttle shaft and shutter with a new dust seal (4—Fig. TP3-3). Make certain that scribe mark on throttle plate (7) is in twelve o'clock position and facing outward.

To install the primer bulb (8—Fig. TP3-3), place the retainer ring (9) around the bulb with retainer tabs pointing outward. Push the bulb and retainer into the carburetor using a ¾-inch deep well socket.

GOVERNOR. All models are equipped with a mechanical type governor located at pto end of crankshaft. All governor linkage positions should be marked prior to disassembly. To adjust governor, shut off engine and loosen governor lever clamp screw (Fig. TP3-8). Move governor lever to place the throttle at wide-open position, then turn slotted governor shaft clockwise as far as it will go without forcing it. Tighten holding screw to secure adjustment.

IGNITION SYSTEM. Standard ignition system on all models is a solid-state electronic system which does not have breaker points. There is no scheduled maintenance.

To test for spark, remove spark plug cable from spark plug. Insert metal conductor into cable end and hold conductor ⅛ inch (3 mm) from cylinder shroud. Crank engine and observe spark. A weak spark or no spark indicates a defective ignition coil. Also check for broken, loose or shorted wiring or a faulty spark plug.

Air gap between solid-state module and flywheel should be 0.0125 inch (0.32 mm).

Fig. TP3-6—Install fuel inlet needle spring as shown. Refer to text.

Illustrations courtesy Tecumseh Products Co.

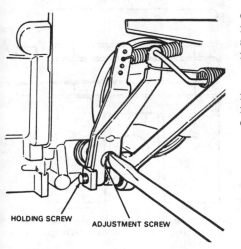

Fig. TP3-8—View of external governor linkage. Refer to text for adjustment procedure.

CARBON. Carbon and other combustion deposits should be cleaned from exhaust port and EGR tube after every 75-100 hours of normal operation. Before cleaning the ports, remove the muffler and position the piston at bottom dead center. Clean ports using a pointed 3/8-inch (9.5 mm) wooden dowel rod. Refer also to EGR tube in REPAIRS section for EGR tube cleaning or removal.

GENERAL MAINTENANCE. Periodically check and tighten all loose bolts, nuts or clips. Check for fuel leakage and repair as necessary. Clean dust, dirt, grease or any foreign material from cylinder head and cylinder block cooling fins after every 100 hours of operation or more frequently if needed. Inspect fins for damage and repair if necessary.

REPAIRS

TIGHTENING TORQUES. Recommended tightening torques are as follows:

Adapter-to-crankcase ... 13-18 ft.-lbs.
　　　　　　　　　　　　(18-24 N m)
Carburetor .... 120-150 in.-lbs.
　　　　　　　　　　　(13.6-16.9 N m)
Crankcase .... 10-17 ft.-lbs.
　　　　　　　　　　　　(13-23 N m)
Flywheel nut .... 30-33 ft.-lbs.
　　　　　　　　　　　　(41-45 N m)
Ignition coil .... 30-40 in.-lbs.
　　　　　　　　　　　　(3.4-4.5 N•m)
Muffler .... 100-120 in.-lbs.
　　　　　　　　　　　(11.3-13.5 N•m)
Spark plug .... 16-20 ft.-lbs.
　　　　　　　　　　　　(22-27 N m)
Blower housing ...... 90-120 in.-lbs.
　　　　　　　　　　　(10.2-13.5 N•m)

CRANKCASE PRESSURE TEST. An improperly sealed crankcase can cause the engine to be hard to start, run rough, have low power and overheat. If crankcase leakage is indicated, pressurize crankcase and use a soap and water solution to check gaskets, seals, carburetor pulse line and casting for leakage.

DISASSEMBLY. Refer to Fig. TP3-9 for an exploded view of engine. The cylinder is an integral part of one crankcase half (11).

To disassemble engine, drain all fuel and remove fuel tank. Remove air cleaner assembly, muffler and blower housing. Remove solid-state ignition module. Use strap wrench 670305 to hold flywheel, then remove flywheel retaining nut. Pull brake lever away from return spring as far as it will go and place an alignment pin through the

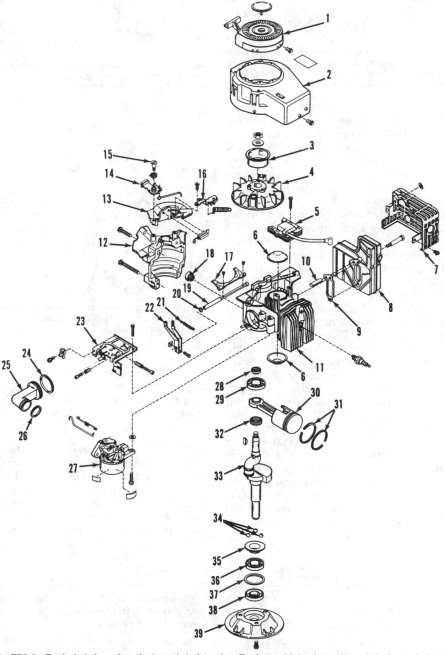

Fig. TP3-9—Exploded view of vertical crankshaft engine. Engines with horizontal crankshaft are similar, however, adapter (39) and EGR tube (10) are not used.

1. Rewind starter	11. Cylinder & crankcase half	21. Governor spring
2. Blower housing	12. Crankcase half	22. Governor lever
3. Starter cup	13. Brake mounting bracket	23. Governor linkage bracket
4. Flywheel	14. Flywheel brake	24. "O" ring
5. Ignition coil/module	15. Spring	25. Intake pipe
6. Port cover	16. Brake control lever	26. "O" ring
7. Heat shield	17. Governor arm	27. Carburetor
8. Muffler	18. Fuel filter	28. Seal
9. Gasket	19. Governor shaft	29. Ball bearing
10. EGR tube	20. Oil seal	30. Piston & rod assy.

31. Piston rings	
32. Bearing rollers (31)	
33. Crankshaft	
34. Governor balls (3)	
35. Slide ring	
36. Ball bearing	
37. Retainer	
38. Seal	
39. Adapter	

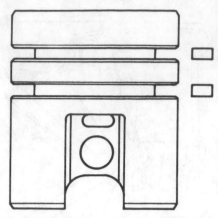

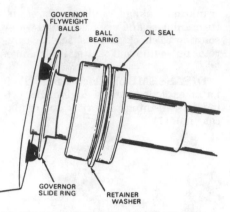

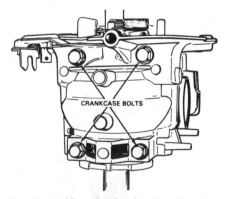

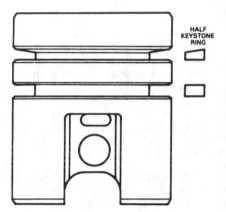

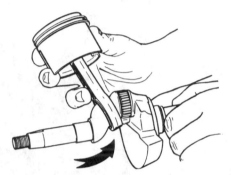

Fig. TP3-10—Disengage flywheel brake, on models so equipped, by extending brake lever as shown, then install an alignment pin through hole in lever to retain position.

Fig. TP3-12—Install governor flyweight balls, governor slide ring, ball bearing, retainer washer and oil seal onto flywheel side of crankshaft as shown.

Fig. TP3-14—View showing piston used on engines equipped with standard rectangular type piston rings.

lever hole so it catches on the shroud (Fig. TP3-10). This will hold the brake pad off the flywheel. Use flywheel puller, Tecumseh No. 670306, to remove the flywheel. DO NOT pry on flywheel or use a knockoff tool to remove flywheel. Remove the three screws retaining the speed control to the cylinder block. Mark all linkage connections and disconnect all governor and carburetor linkage. Remove the three screws from the pto mounting adapter. Lightly tap adapter to separate it from crankcase. Remove carburetor, then remove intake elbow and reed valve assembly. Remove brake assembly. Remove the four crankcase bolts (Fig. TP3-11) and separate crankcase half from cylinder and crankcase assembly. Carefully lift crankshaft and piston assembly from crankcase.

Slide oil seal, retainer washer, ball bearing and governor slide ring off crankshaft (Fig. TP3-12). Catch the governor flyweight balls as governor slide ring is removed. Remove the oil seal and ball bearing from flywheel end of crankshaft. Slide the piston and connecting rod off toward the flywheel end of crankshaft (Fig. TP3-13). The 31 needle bearings in connecting rod are loose and will fall out during connecting rod removal.

Fig. TP3-13—Piston and connecting rod assembly are installed by working connecting rod over crankshaft as shown.

Clean and inspect all parts. Refer to following sections for service of engine components. Refer to REASSEMBLY section to reassemble engine.

PISTON AND RINGS. Model TVS840 engines are equipped with standard rectangular rings (Fig. TP3-14) and either ring can be installed in either piston ring groove. Model TVXL840 engines are equipped with a piston ring set containing one half-keystone ring and one standard rectangular ring (Fig. TP3-15). The half-keystone ring and piston ring groove are beveled on one side and ring must be installed in the upper piston ring groove with beveled side of ring toward top of piston.

Standard piston diameter is 2.4320-2.4326 inches (61.772-61.788 mm). Piston ring groove width should be 0.0645-0.0655 inch (1.638-1.664 mm) for all rectangular type ring grooves. Side clearance of new ring (rectangular rings) in piston ring groove should be 0.002-0.004 inch (0.05-0.10 mm). Renew piston if ring side clearance is excessive. Specified piston ring end gap is 0.007-

Fig. TP3-15—View showing piston used on engines equipped with one half-keystone type ring and one rectangular ring. Note correct position of each ring.

0.017 inch (0.18-0.43 mm). Standard cylinder bore diameter is 2.437-2.438 inches (61.89-61.93 mm).

CRANKSHAFT AND CONNECTING ROD. Crankshaft main bearing journal diameter at pto end should be 0.9833-0.9838 inch (24.976-24.989 mm). Crankshaft main bearing journal diameter at flywheel end should be 0.7864-0.7869 inch (19.975-19.987 mm). Crankpin journal diameter should be 0.9710-0.9715 inch (24.663-24.676 mm). Crankshaft end play should be 0.0004-0.0244 inch (0.010-0.62 mm).

Connecting rod and piston assembly must be installed on crankshaft as shown in Fig. TP3-16.

REED VALVE. The reed plate is located on the intake elbow (Fig. TP3-17). If clearance between end of reed and intake elbow is 0.020 inch (0.5 mm) or more, intake elbow must be renewed.

Fig. TP3-11—View showing location of the four crankcase screws.

Illustrations courtesy Tecumseh Products Co.

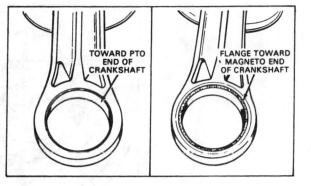

Fig. TP3-16—Connecting rod must be installed on crankshaft so flanged side of connecting rod is toward magneto end of crankshaft.

TOWARD PTO END OF CRANKSHAFT

FLANGE TOWARD MAGNETO END OF CRANKSHAFT

when cleaning combustion deposits from exhaust ports.

To remove the EGR tube, measure distance EGR tube protrudes from cylinder block, then clamp tube with locking pliers and rotate in a clockwise direction. This will collapse the tube and allow removal (Fig. TP3-19).

Install new tube with seam in tube facing 45 degrees to the exhaust port as shown in Fig. TP3-20 and to the same depth as old tube. Tecumseh tool 670318 is available to aid installation of EGR tube to correct depth.

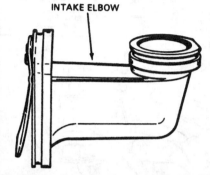

INTAKE ELBOW

Fig. TP3-17—Reed valve is an integral part of the intake elbow. Refer to text.

Fig. TP3-19—To remove the EGR tube, clamp locking pliers onto tube and rotate in a clockwise direction to collapse tube.

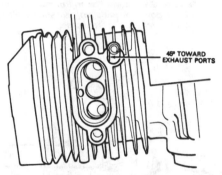

ANTI-PUDDLING METER HOLE SCREEN.
Engines built since 1986 have a screen pressed into cavity above the anti-puddling meter hole (Fig. TP3-18). The screen can be installed in engines built prior to 1987.

With crankshaft assembly removed, clean and inspect anti-puddling meter hole for obstructions. If meter hole screen becomes plugged with debris, pull screen from the hole using a wire

hook. Install new screen with brass ring side facing upward (Fig. TP3-18). Tap the screen into the hole using a punch until screen is seated securely in the hole.

EGR TUBE.
Models TVS840 and TVXL840 are equipped with an EGR (exhaust gas recirculation) tube located near the cylinder exhaust ports. A controlled amount of exhaust gas is drawn into the crankcase to aid movement of the air-fuel mixture to the combustion chamber. This tube should be cleaned

45° TOWARD EXHAUST PORTS

Fig. TP3-20—EGR tube must be installed with seal toward exhaust ports as shown.

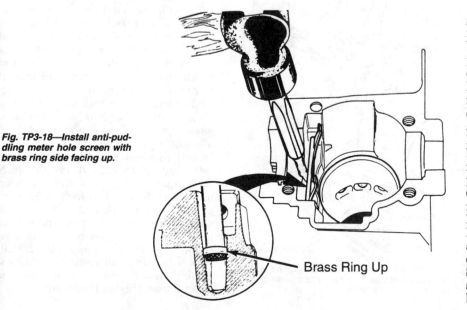

Fig. TP3-18—Install anti-puddling meter hole screen with brass ring side facing up.

Brass Ring Up

REASSEMBLY.
To reassemble engine, use heavy grease to retain connecting rod needle bearings (new bearings are retained on a strip) and position piston and connecting rod on crankshaft as shown in Fig. TP3-13. Make certain flanged side of connecting rod (Fig. TP3-16) is toward flywheel end of crankshaft, then work connecting rod and piston assembly onto crankshaft. Install the three governor flyweight balls into the crankshaft. Install governor slide ring onto crankshaft so flat portion of ring covers flyweight balls (Fig. TP3-12). Install ball bearing type main bearing, retainer washer and the large oil seal as shown in Fig. TP3-12. Install ball bearing type main bearing and smaller oil seal onto flywheel end of crankshaft as shown in Fig. TP3-21. Stagger ring end gaps and carefully install piston and connecting rod assembly into cylinder and crankcase

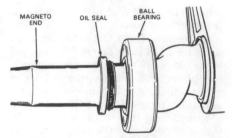

Fig. TP3-21—Install ball bearing and oil seal onto flywheel side of crankshaft as shown.

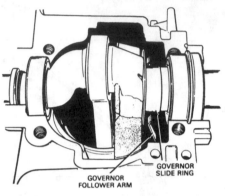

Fig. TP3-22—Governor follower arm must be on pto side of governor slide ring as shown after crankshaft installation in crankcase.

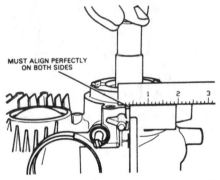

Fig. TP3-23—Crankcase halves must be perfectly aligned.

Fig. TP3-24—View showing assembled position of flywheel brake assembly on models so equipped.

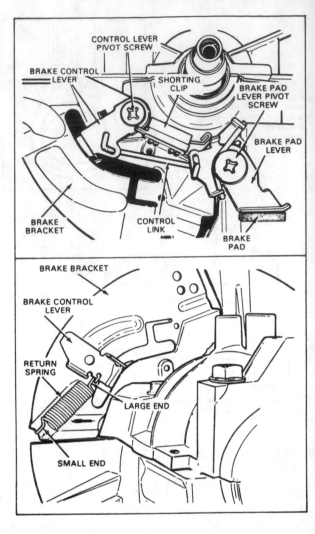

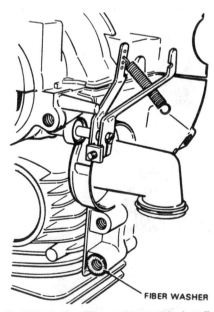

Fig. TP3-25—One fiber washer must be installed on each carburetor post prior to mounting carburetor on cylinder block.

assembly. Tapered edge at bottom of cylinder will compress piston rings. Position governor follower arm so it rides on the pto side of the governor slide ring as shown in Fig. TP3-22.

Apply a thin layer of Loctite 515 Gasket Sealant Eliminator on mating surfaces of crankcase halves before assembling. Crankcase halves must be aligned at pto end of crankcase as shown in Fig. TP3-23. Use a straightedge to make certain crankcase halves are aligned, then tighten the four crankcase screws to 10-17 ft.-lbs. (13-23 N m) torque. It is recommended that the crankcase be pressure tested for leakage before proceeding with remainder of engine reassembly.

Refer to Fig. TP3-24 and install flywheel brake assembly. Install new "O" rings on intake elbow and reed assembly prior to installation. Position one fiber washer on each carburetor post prior to mounting carburetor on cylinder block (Fig. TP3-25). Float bowl of carburetor must be facing pto side of engine. Install the pto adapter (39—Fig. TP3-9) and tighten retaining screws to 13-18 ft.-lbs. (18-24 N m) torque. Disengage flywheel brake and install an alignment pin as shown in Fig. TP3-10. Install flywheel and tighten flywheel retaining nut to 30-33 ft.-lbs. (41-45 N m) torque. Install solid-state ignition module with a 0.0125 inch (0.32 mm) gap between module and flywheel magnets. Tighten module retaining screws to 30-40 in.-lbs. (3.4-4.5 N m) torque. Remove brake alignment pin. Install blower housing and rewind starter assembly. Install gasket and muffler, air cleaner assembly and fuel tank.

Fig. TP3-26—Exploded view of rewind starter.

1. Starter housing
2. Cover
3. Rewind spring
4. Pulley
5. Springs (2)
6. Pawls (2)
7. Plastic washers (2)
8. Retainer
9. Brake spring
10. Metal washer
11. Pin

REWIND STARTER. To disassemble starter, remove rope handle and allow rope to wind slowly into starter. Position a suitable sleeve support (a ¾-inch deep socket) under retainer (8—Fig. TP3-26), then use a punch to drive pin (11) free of starter. Remove brake spring (9), retainer (8), pawls (6) and springs (5). Wear appropriate safety eyewear and gloves before disengaging pulley from starter as spring may uncoil uncontrolled. Place shop towel around pulley and lift pulley out of housing; spring should remain with pulley.

Inspect components for damage and excessive wear. Standard rope length is 98 inches (249 cm) and rope diameter is ⁹⁄₆₄ inch (3.5 mm).

Note the following when reassembling starter. Install starter pawls (6) so hook end of pawls face inward. Be sure that pawl springs (5) snap the pawls back to center of pulley. Retainer (8) must be installed so that tabs on retainer will force starter pawls to engage starter cup when rope is pulled. Rewind spring coils wind in clockwise direction from outer end. Be sure inner end of rewind spring engages spring retainer adjacent to housing center post. Use two new plastic washers (7). Install a new pin (11) so top of pin is ⅛ inch (3.2 mm) below top of starter. Driving pin in too far may damage retainer pawl. Wind rope around pulley in counterclockwise direction as viewed from retainer side of pulley.

Wind starter pulley counterclockwise four or five turns to preload the rewind spring. Thread rope through starter housing eyelet and tie a temporary knot in rope about 12 inches (30 cm) from outer end of rope. Attach handle to rope, then remove temporary knot and allow rope to wind into housing. Rope handle should be held snugly against starter housing.

TECUMSEH

4-STROKE ENGINES
(Except Vector & Overhead Valve Engines)

Model	Bore	Stroke	Displacement	Power Rating
LAV30, TVS75	2.500 in.	1.844 in.	9.05 cu.in.	3.0 hp
	(63.50 mm)	(46.84 mm)	(148 cc)	(2.25 kW)
LAV35, TVS90	2.500 in.	1.844 in	9.05 cu.in.	3.5 hp
	(63.50 mm)	(46.84 mm)	(148 cc)	(2.6 kW)
ECV100	2.625 in.	1.844 in.	9.98 cu.in.	3.5 hp
	(66.68 mm)	(46.84 mm)	(164 cc)	(2.6 kW)
ECV105, LAV40	2.625 in.	1.938 in.	10.49 cu.in.	4.0 hp
	(66.68 mm)	(49.23 mm)	(172 cc)	(3 kW)
ECV110	2.750 in.	1.938 in.	11.50 cu.in.	4.0 hp
	(69.85 mm)	(49.22 mm)	(189 cc)	(3.0 kW)
ECV120, TNT120	2.812 in.	1.938 in.	12.04 cu.in.	5.0 hp
	(71.43 mm)	(49.23 mm)	(197 cc)	(3.7 kW)
LAV50, TVS120	2.812 in.	1.938 in.	12.04 cu.in	5.0 hp
	(71.43 mm(	(49.23 mm)	(197 cc)	(3.7 kW)
V40 Std. Ignition	2.500 in.	2.250 in.	11.04 cu.in.	4.0 hp
	(63.50 mm)	(57.15 mm)	(181 cc)	(3 kW)
V40 Ext. Ignition	2.625 in.	1.938 in.	10.49 cu.in.	4.0 hp
	(66.68 mm)	(49.23 mm)	(172 cc)	(3 kW)
V50, TVM125	2.625 in.	2.250 in.	12.18 cu.in.	5.0 hp
	(66.68 mm)	(57.15 mm)	(229 cc)	(3.7 Kw)
V60, TVM140	2.625 in.	2.500 in.	13.53 cu.in.	6.0 hp
	(66.68 mm)	(63.50 mm)	(222 cc)	(4.5 kW)
TNT100, TVS100	2.625 in.	1.844 in.	9.98 cu.in.	4.0 hp
	(66.68 mm)	(46.84 mm)	(164 cc)	(3 kW)
TVS105, TVXL105	2.625 in.	1.938 in.	10.49 cu.in.	4.0 hp
	(66.68 mm)	(49.23 mm)	(172 cc)	(3.0 kW)
TVS115, TVXL115	2.812 in.	1.844 in.	11.45 cu.in.	4.5 hp
	(71.44 mm)	(46.84 mm)	(188 cc)	(3.3 kW)

ENGINE IDENTIFICATION

Engines must be identified by the complete model number, including the specification number in order to obtain correct repair parts. Engine identification numbers, including the model number, specification number and serial number, are located on the blower housing or on a tag attached to the engine. The numbers are stamped in an identification plate or directly in the blower housing metal as shown in Fig. T1.

The engine model number identifies the basic engine family. Refer to Fig. T2 for a breakdown and example of a typical Tecumseh engine model number.

The specification number specifies the parts configuration of the engine, as well as cosmetic details such as paint color and decals. The specification number also determines governor speed settings depending on the engine's application, i.e., lawn mower, tractor, pump, etc.

The serial number provides information concerning the manufacturing of the engine. Refer to Fig. T2 for a breakdown of a typical serial number.

Note that some engines are classified using the term "frame." Tecumseh classifies the basic engine structure according to the type of metal, either aluminum or cast iron, used to manufacture the engine crankcase and the metal in the cylinder bore. A small frame engine is made of aluminum with an aluminum cylinder bore. A medium frame engine is made of aluminum and has a cast iron liner in the cylinder bore. A heavy frame engine is made of cast iron with a cast iron cylinder bore.

It is important to transfer the blower housing or identification tag from the original engine to a replacement short block assembly so unit can be identified when servicing.

If selecting a replacement engine and model or type number of the old engine is not known, refer to chart in Fig. T3 and proceed as follows:

1. List the corresponding number which indicates the crankshaft position.

2. Determine the horsepower needed.

3. Determine the primary features needed. (Refer to the Tecumseh Engines Specification Book No. 692531 for specific engine variations.)

4. Refer to Fig. T2 for Tecumseh engine model number and serial number interpretation.

Note that new short blocks are identified by a tag marked SBH (Short Block Horizontal) or SBV (Short Block Vertical).

MAINTENANCE

LUBRICATION. Vertical crankshaft engines are equipped with a barrel and plunger type oil pump.

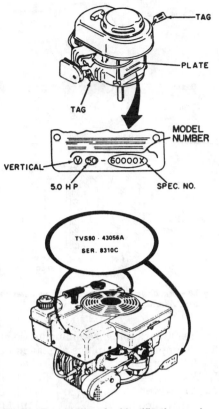

Fig. T1—Tecumseh engine identification numbers are stamped in blower housing or a plate attached to engine. Some engines have a decal listing the identification numbers.

V	Verrtical Crankshaft
LAV	Lightweight Aluminum Vertical Crankshaft
VM	Vertical Crankshaft Medium Frame
TVM	Tecumseh Vertical Crankshft (Medium Frame)
VH	Vertical Crankshaft Heavy Duty (Cast Iron)
TVS	Tecumseh Styled Vertical Crankshaft
TNT	Toro N'Tecumseh
ECV	Exclusive Craftsman Vertical Crankshaft
TVXL	Tecumseh Vertical Extra Life
H	Horizontal Crankshaft
HS	Horizontal Crankshaft Small Frame
HSSK	Horizontal Small Frame Snow King
HM	Horizontal Crankshaft Medium Frame
HMSK	Horizontal Medium Frame Snow King
HHM	Horizontal Crankshaft Heavy Duty (Cast Iron) Medium Frame
HH	Horizontal Crankshaft Heavy Duty (Cast Iron)
ECH	Exclusive Craftsman Horizontal Crankshaft
HSK	Horizontal Snow King

EXAMPLE

Engine model and specification numbers: TVS115-57010B, Serial No. 3105C

TVS	Tecumseh Vertical Styled
115	Indicates a 11.5 cubic inch displacement
57010B	Is the specification number used for properly identifying the parts of the engine

Engine serial number: 3105C

3	First digit is the year of manufacture (1993)
105	Indicates calendar day of that year (105th day or April 15, 1993)
C	Represents the line and shift on which the engine was built at the factory

Fig. T2—Table showing Tecumseh engine model number and serial number interpretation.

Oil level should be checked after every five hours of operation. Maintain oil level at lower edge of filler plug or at "FULL" mark on dipstick.

Engine oil should meet or exceed latest API service classification. Use SAE 30 or SAE 10W-30 motor oil for temperatures above 32° F (0° C). Use SAE 5W-30 or SAE 10W for temperatures below 32° F (0° C). Manufacturer explicitly states: DO NOT USE SAE 10W-40 motor oil.

Oil should be changed after the first two hours of engine operation (new or rebuilt engine) and after every 25 hours of operation thereafter. Drain the oil after engine has been operating and is still warm. Oil drain plug is located in the crankcase cover/oil pan and is accessible on underside of mower deck. Approximate crankcase capacities are as follows:

Engine Model	Capacity
LAV30-50	1.25 pt. (0.6 L)
V50-60,	1.7 pt. (0.8 L)
ECV100-120, TNT100-120	1.3 pt. (0.6 L)
TVM125, 140	1.7 pt. (0.8 L)
TVS75-120, TVXL105	1.25 pt. (0.6 L)

AIR FILTER. The filter element may be made of foam or paper, or a

TECUMSEH SERVICE NUMBER SYSTEM

(EXAMPLE) 8 0 4 1 0 1 A

1st DIGIT	2nd & 3rd DIGIT	4th DIGIT	5th & 6th DIGIT	7th DIGIT
CRANKSHAFT POSITION	HORSEPOWER OR 2 CYCLE	PRIMARY FEATURES	ENGINE VARIATION NUMBER	REVISION LETTER
8 - Vertical 9 - Horizontal	00 = 2 Cycle 02 = 3 H.P. 03 = 3.5 H.P. 04 = 4 H.P. 05 = 5 H.P. 06 = 6 H.P. 07 = 7 H.P. 08 = 8 H.P. 10 = 10 H.P. 12 = 12 H.P. 14 = 14 H.P. 16 = 16 H.P. 18 = 18 H.P.	1 = Rotary Mower 2 = Industrial 3 = Snow King 4 = Mini Bike 5 = Tractor 6 = Tiller 7 = Rider 8 = Rotary Mower	00 thru 99 00 thru 99 00 thru 99 00 thru 99 00 thru 99 00 thru 99 00 thru 99 00 thru 99	

Fig. T3—Reference chart used to select or identify Tecumseh replacement engines.

combination of both foam and paper. The recommended maintenance interval depends on the type of filter element.

Foam type filter elements should be cleaned, inspected and re-oiled after every 25 hours of engine operation, or after three months, whichever occurs first. Clean the filter in soapy water then squeeze the filter until dry (don't twist the filter). Inspect the filter for tears and holes or any other opening.

Illustrations courtesy Tecumseh Products Co.

Fig. T4—On some engines, crankcase breather is located in valve tappet cover (C).

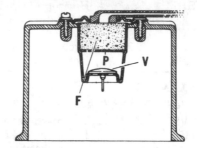

Fig. T6—View of top-mounted crankcase breather used on some engines with a vertical crankshaft.

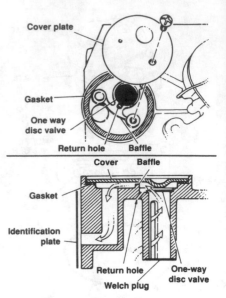

Fig. T8—Drawing of integral type breather used on some ECV series engines.

Fig. T5—Drain hole (D) must be down when installing valve tappet cover.

Fig. T7—Cross-section of top-mounted crankcase breather.

Discard the filter if it cannot be cleaned satisfactorily or if the filter is torn or otherwise damaged. Pour clean engine oil into the filter, then squeeze the filter to remove the excess oil and distribute oil throughout the filter.

Paper type filter elements should be replaced annually or more frequently if the engine operates in a severe environment, such as extremely dusty conditions. A dirty filter element cannot be cleaned and must be discarded.

CRANKCASE BREATHER. Three types of crankcase breather have been used: an integral breather, a top-mounted breather and a side-mounted breather.

Side-Mounted Crankcase Breather. This type of breather is located in the valve tappet cover (C—Fig. T4). A disc valve regulates pressure in the crankcase. Unscrew retaining screws to remove breather.

On some engines breather can be separated for access to internal filter element, while on other engines, breather is a unit assembly. On unit type breather, a removable filter element resides inside breather. A barb inside the housing holds element in place. Insert a smooth blade between the barb and filter element to remove element. Clean filter element in a suitable solvent.

Install either type breather so drain hole (D—Fig. T5) is down. Some units have two gaskets located between breather and engine. Install both gaskets if so equipped.

Top-Mounted Crankcase Breather. Some vertical crankshaft engines are equipped with crankcase breather (B—Fig. T6) mounted on top of crankcase. Remove flywheel for access to the crankcase breather. Unscrew the breather cover and lift out the breather assembly. Remove and clean filter element (F—Fig. T7) in a suitable solvent. Inspect check valve (V) for damage. Removal may damage the valve. Lubricate stem of new check valve to ease installation. Install baffle plate (P) above check valve.

Integral Crankcase Breather. An integral type breather is found on some ECV series engines. This type breather is mounted on top of the crankcase and functions using passages in the crankcase (Fig. T8). Gases are vented out the back of the crankcase, sometimes behind the identification plate.

Remove flywheel for access to crankcase breather. Check for blocked passages and a damaged valve. A replacement parts set is available.

SPARK PLUG. Spark plugs should be removed, cleaned and adjusted periodically. Note that manufacturer does not recommend using a sand blaster to clean spark plugs as particles of abrasive left in the plug can damage the

engine. Spark plug recommendations for Champion spark plugs are listed in the following chart.

LAV30-50, V40-60 . . . . RJ17LM
TVM125-140 . . . . RJ17LM
All Other Models RJ19LM

Specified spark plug electrode gap for all models is 0.030 inch (0.76 mm). Tighten spark plug to 15 ft.-lbs. (20 N·m) torque. If torque wrench is not available, install plug finger tight then use spark plug wrench to tighten plug additional 1/8-1/4 turn.

CARBURETOR. Float type carburetors are used on rotary mower engines. Series I carburetors (Fig. T9) may have adjustable idle and main mixture screws or may have an adjustable idle mixture screw and a fixed main jet. Dual System and Series VI carburetors (Fig. T10) are identified by the primer bulb located on the side of carburetor body. These carburetors have fixed idle and main jets and are not adjustable. Refer to appropriate paragraph for carburetor type being serviced.

Tecumseh Series I Carburetor. Initial adjustment of idle mixture screw (I—Fig. T9) from a lightly seated position is one turn open. Initial adjustment of main mixture screw (M), if used, is 1-1/2 turns open. Clockwise rotation leans mixture and counterclockwise rotation enriches mixture.

Final fuel mixture adjustment is made with engine at operating temperature and running. Operate engine at rated speed and adjust main fuel mixture screw (M) for smoothest engine operation. Operate engine at idle speed and adjust idle mixture screw (I) for smoothest engine idle. If engine does not accelerate smoothly or hesitates

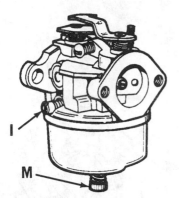

Fig. T9—Drawing of typical Tecumseh Series I float type carburetor. Some models are not equipped with adjustable main mixture screw (M).

Fig. T10—Drawing of Tecumseh Series VI float type carburetor. This carburetor is identified by the primer bulb (P) on side of carburetor and the absence of fuel mixture screws. Dual System carburetor is similar.

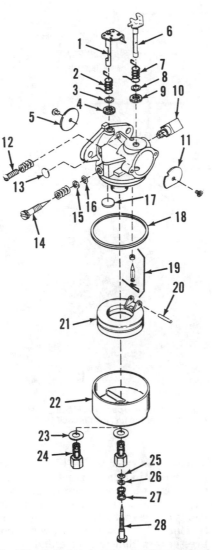

Fig. T11—Exploded view of typical Tecumseh adjustable float type carburetor. Some carburetors are equipped with fixed jet main nozzle (24) which is not adjustable.

1. Throttle shaft
2. Spring
3. Washer
4. Felt washer
5. Throttle plate
6. Choke shaft
7. Spring
8. Washer
9. Felt washer
10. Fuel inlet fitting
11. Choke plate
12. Idle speed screw
13. Welch plug
16. Idle mixture screw
15. Washer
16. "O" ring
17. Welch plug
18. Gasket
19. Fuel inlet valve needle & seat
20. Float pin
21. Float
22. Fuel bowl
23. Washer
24. Fuel bowl nut
25. "O" ring
26. Washer
27. Spring
28. High speed mixture screw

Fig. T12—Do not attempt removal of main nozzle (N).

when engaging load, turn adjusting screw counterclockwise ⅛ turn at a time until condition is corrected.

To disassemble carburetor, remove bowl nut (24—Fig. T11) and float bowl (22). Remove hinge pin (20), float (21) and fuel inlet needle (19). Remove idle mixture screw (14). To remove throttle and choke assemblies, remove screws retaining throttle plate (5) and choke plate (11) to shafts (1 and 6). Remove dust seals (4 and 9). Use a small chisel to pry out Welch plugs (13 and 17). Do not remove any brass or ball plugs.

The fuel inlet valve needle (19—Fig. T11) seats against a Viton seat which must be removed before cleaning. The seat can be removed by blowing compressed air in from the fuel inlet fitting or by using a hooked wire to pull seat from carburetor body. All neoprene or Viton rubber parts must be removed before carburetor is immersed in cleaning solvent.

Renew needle and seat if fuel delivery problems such as flooding or starvation are experienced. Check float for cracks, wear or evidence of leagage and renew as necessary. Do not attempt to reuse any expansion plugs. Install new plugs if any are removed for cleaning. Do not

attempt to remove main nozzle (N—Fig. T12) as it is pressed into position and movement will affect carburetor operation.

To reassemble carburetor, reverse the disassembly procedure while noting the following special instructions. The grooved face of fuel inlet needle valve seat should be in toward bottom of bore and the valve needle should seat on smooth side of the Viton seat (Fig. T13). Install the throttle plate (5—Fig. T11)

with the two stamped marks out and at 12 and 3 o'clock positions. The 12 o'clock line should be parallel with the throttle shaft and toward top of carburetor. Install choke plate (11) with flat side down toward bottom of carburetor. Fuel inlet fitting (10) is pressed into body on some models. Start fitting into body, then apply a light coat of Loctite sealant to shank and press fitting into position. Install the fuel inlet needle retaining clip on the float tab so the long end is toward the choke end of carburetor.

A gauge is available from Tecumseh (part No. 670253A) that can be used to determine the correct float height. With carburetor inverted, position gauge 670253A at a 90° angle to the carburetor bore and resting on the nozzle stanchion as shown in Fig. T14. The toe of the float should not be higher than the first step on the gauge or lower than the second step. Bend the float tab to adjust the float height. If float gauge is not available, float height (H—Fig. T15) can be set as follows: Invert carburetor and measure distance from float to surface of nozzle stanchion at a point opposite fuel inlet valve as shown in Fig. T15. The float should be ³⁄₁₆ inch (5.0 mm) below surface of stanchion. Bend the float tab to adjust the float level.

Install fuel bowl so indent (N—Fig. T16) on fuel bowl is under the fuel inlet fitting. Be sure to use correct parts when servicing the carburetor. Some fuel bowl gaskets are square section, while others are round. The bowl retainer nut (24—Fig. T11) contains a drilled passage for fuel to the high speed metering needle. The fuel bowl retaining nut may have one or two holes adjacent to the hex. If a replacement nut is required, the new nut must have the same number of holes as the original nut.

Dual System and Series VI Float Carburetors. Refer to Fig. T17 for an exploded view of typical carburetor. Dual System and Series VI carburetors

Fig. T13—Fuel inlet valve seat must be installed so grooved side is toward body and flat side is out as shown. Drive in until seat rests on body shoulder.

5/32" FLAT PUNCH

SEAT

INLET NEEDLE SEATS AT THIS POINT

INSERT THIS FACE FIRST

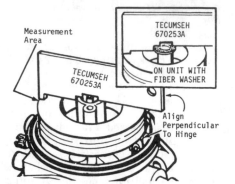

Measurement Area

TECUMSEH 670253A

TECUMSEH 670253A

ON UNIT WITH FIBER WASHER

Align Perpendicular To Hinge

Fig. T14—Float height can be set using Tecumseh float tool 670253A as shown.

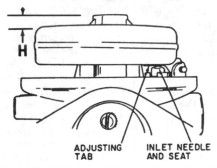

Fig. T16—Indented part of float bowl (N) should be located under the fuel inlet fitting (A).

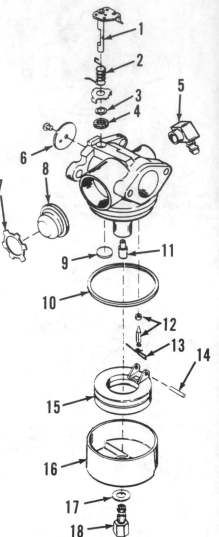

Fig. T17—Exploded view of Series VI carburetor. Dual System carburetor is similar.

1. Throttle shaft	10. Gasket
2. Spring	11. Fuel well spacer
3. Washer	12. Fuel inlet needle & seat
4. Felt washer	13. Clip
5. Fuel inlet fitting	14. Hinge pin
6. Throttle plate	15. Float
7. Retainer	16. Fuel bowl
8. Primer bulb	17. Washer
9. Welch plug	18. High speed bowl nut

Fig. T15—Float height (H) should be ³⁄₁₆ inch (5 mm).

seat can be removed by blowing compressed air in from the fuel inlet fitting or by using a hooked wire to pull seat from carburetor body. Clean carburetor using commercial carburetor cleaning solvent. Blow out passages with compressed air. Renew needle and seat if fuel delivery problems such as flooding or starvation are experienced. Check float for cracks, wear or evidence of leagage and renew as necessary.

Note the following special instructions when reassembling carburetor. The grooved face of fuel inlet needle valve seat should be in toward bottom of bore and the valve needle should seat on smooth side of the Viton seat (Fig. T13). Install the fuel inlet needle retaining clip on the float tab so the long end faces away from the throttle end of carburetor.

With carburetor inverted, measure float height (H—Fig. T15) at a point opposite the fuel inlet. The float height should be 0.162-0.215 inch (4.11-5.46 mm). Bend the float tab to adjust the float height.

A gauge is available from Tecumseh (Tecumseh part 670253A) that can be used to determine the correct float height. With carburetor inverted, position gauge 670253A at a 90° angle to the carburetor bore and resting on the nozzle stanchion as shown in Fig. T14. The toe of the float should not be higher than

are not equipped with fuel mixture screws. A priming bulb located on side of the carburetor is used instead of a choke plate for starting purposes. When primer bulb is depressed, air pressure from the bulb forces fuel through the main jet and up the nozzle, thereby enriching the air:fuel mixture for starting.

To disassemble, remove fuel bowl retaining nut (18) and withdraw fuel bowl (16). Push hinge pin (14) from carburetor body and remove float (15) and fuel inlet needle (12). Remove screw attaching throttle plate (6) to throttle shaft (1). Withdraw throttle shaft and remove washer (3) and dust seal (4). Pull primer bulb (8) from side of carburetor, then pry out retainer (7). Remove Welch plug (9).

The fuel inlet valve needle (12—Fig. T17) seats against a Viton seat which must be removed before cleaning. The

the first step on the gauge or lower than the second step. Bend the float tab to adjust the float height.

Install fuel bowl (16—Fig. T17) and bowl nut (18) with new gaskets (10 and 17). Flat area of bowl is located over fuel inlet valve and crease runs parallel to float pin. To install the primer bulb (8), start the bulb and retainer ring (7) into housing with retainer tabs facing outward. Push the bulb and retainer into the carburetor using a deep well socket.

SPEED CONTROL PANEL. Engines with a vertical crankshaft may be equipped with a speed control panel that is a separate component adjacent

Illustrations courtesy Tecumseh Products Co.

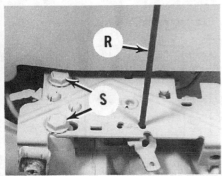

Fig. T18—View of speed control panel. Refer to text for adjustment.

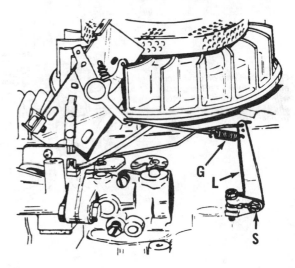

Fig. T20—View of typical governor mechanism on vertical crankshaft engines showing location of governor spring (G), governor lever (L) and adjusting screw (S).

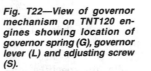

Fig. T19—Drawing of underside of speed control panel.

7. Control lever	16. Idle speed stop
10. Ignition stop switch	18. High speed stop screw

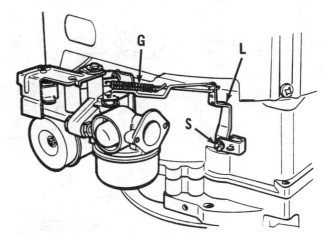

Fig. T21—View of governor mechanism on TNT100 vertical crankshaft engines showing location of governor spring (G), governor lever (L) and adjusting screw (S).

to the carburetor (Fig. T18). The idle speed screw (16—Fig. T19) and high speed stop screw (18) are located on the panel.

The position of the panel must be adjusted so the linkage is synchronized. To adjust panel position, loosen mounting screws (S—Fig. T18). Insert rod (R) through holes in panel, choke actuating lever and choke as shown, then retighten mounting screws. Check operation.

GOVERNOR. All engines are equipped with a mechanical (flyweight) type governor. To adjust the governor linkage, refer to Fig. T20 through Fig. T25 and loosen governor lever screw (S). Rotate governor shaft clamp counterclockwise as far as possible on vertical crankshaft engines. On all models, move the governor lever (L) until carburetor throttle shaft is in wide open position, then tighten governor lever clamp screw.

Binding or worn governor linkage will result in hunting or unsteady engine operation. An improperly adjusted carburetor will also cause a surging or hunting condition.

Refer to Figs. T20 through T25 for views of typical mechanical governor speed control linkage installations. Note location of springs and linkage connection points prior to disassembly so components can be reinstalled in their original location.

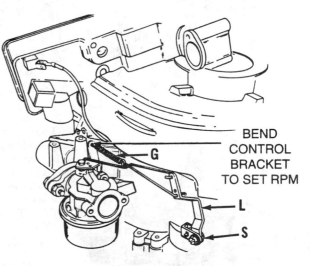

Fig. T22—View of governor mechanism on TNT120 engines showing location of governor spring (G), governor lever (L) and adjusting screw (S).

BEND CONTROL BRACKET TO SET RPM

IGNITION SYSTEM. A magneto ignition system with breaker points or capacitor-discharge ignition (CDI) may have been used according to model and application. Refer to appropriate paragraph for model being serviced.

Breaker-Point Ignition System. Breaker-point gap at maximum opening should be 0.020 inch (0.51 mm) for all models. Marks are usually located on stator and mounting post to facilitate timing (Fig. T26).

Illustrations courtesy Tecumseh Products Co.

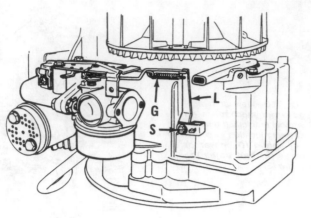

Fig. T23—View of governor mechanism on TVS engines with Dual System carburetor showing location of governor spring (G), governor lever (L) and adjusting screw (S).

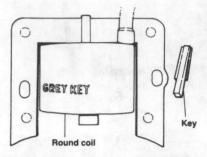

Fig. T27—Drawing of ignition coil and flywheel key used on engines equipped with a breaker-point ignition system and an external ignition coil. Coil is marked "GREY KEY" and key is colored grey.

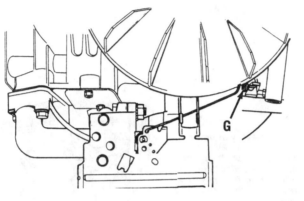

Fig. T24—View of governor mechanism on TVS115 engines with "snap in" speed control.

Some models may be equipped with the coil and laminations mounted outside the flywheel. Engines equipped with breaker-point ignition have the ignition points and condenser mounted under the flywheel, and the coil and laminations mounted outside the flywheel. This system is identified by the round shape of the coil (Fig. T27) and a stamping "Grey Key" in the coil to identify the correct flywheel key.

The correct air gap setting between the flywheel magnets and the coil laminations is 0.0125 inch (0.32 mm). Use Tecumseh gage 670297 or equivalent thickness plastic strip to set gap.

Solid-State Ignition System. The Tecumseh solid-state ignition system does not use ignition breaker points. The only moving part of the system is the rotating flywheel with the charging magnets. Engines with solid-state (CDI) ignition have all the ignition components sealed in a module and located outside the flywheel. There are no components under the flywheel except a spring clip to hold the flywheel key in position. This system is identified by the square shape module and a stamping "Gold Key" to identify the correct flywheel key. See Fig. T28.

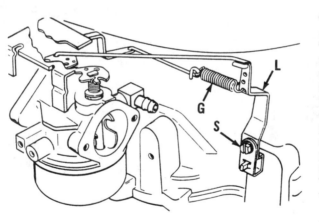

Fig. T25—View of governor mechanism on TVM engines without governor override.

The correct air gap setting between the flywheel magnets and the laminations on ignition module is 0.0125 inch (0.32 mm). Insert 0.0125 inch (0.32 mm) feeler gauge (such as Tecumseh gauge 670297) between the flywheel magnet and ignition module armature legs. Loosen armature retaining screws and push armature legs against feeler gauge, then tighten armature retaining screws.

FLYWHEEL BRAKE. A flywheel brake is used on some engines that will stop the engine within three seconds when the mower safety handle is released. The ignition circuit is grounded also when the brake is actuated. On electric start models, an interlock switch prevents energizing the starter motor if the brake is engaged.

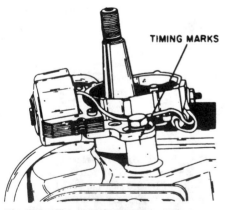

Fig. T26—View of ignition timing marks on engines with a breaker-point ignition system.

Ignition timing can be checked and adjusted to occur when piston is at specific location (BTDC) if marks are missing. Refer to the following specifications for recommended timing.

Model	Piston Position BTDC
LAV40, TVS105, ECV100, ECV105, ECV110, ECV120, TNT100, TNT120	0.035 in. (0.89 mm)
V40, LAV50, TVS120	0.050 in. (1.27 mm)
LAV30, LAV35, TVS75, TVS90	0.065 in. (1.65 mm)
V50, V60, TVM125, TVM140	0.080 in. (2.03 mm)

Illustrations courtesy Tecumseh Products Co.

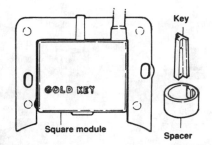

Fig. T28—Drawing of ignition coil, flywheel key and spacer used on some engines with a solid-state ignition system. Coil is marked "GOLD KEY" and key is colored gold.

Refer to FLYWHEEL BRAKE in REPAIRS section for adjustment and service.

VALVE ADJUSTMENT. To check valve clearance, remove muffler and carburetor. Remove valve tappet chamber cover/breather assembly. Rotate crankshaft to position piston at top dead center of compression stroke. Measure clearance between valve tappet and valve stem using a feeler gauge.

Specified clearance (engine cold) is 0.010 inch (0.25 mm) for intake and exhaust valves for Models TVM125 and TVM140. Valve tappet clearance for all other models is 0.008 inch (0.03 mm) for intake and exhaust valves. To reduce clearance, grind valve stem end as necessary to obtain specified clearance. If clearance is excessive, renew valve and/or tappet.

REPAIRS

TIGHTENING TORQUES. Recommended tightening torque specifications are as follows:

Carburetor to intake pipe. . . 68 in.-lbs.
(7.7 N•m)

Connecting rod:
TVM125, TVM140. . . . . . 170 in.-lb.
(19.2 N•m)
All other models . . . . 105 in.-lb.
(11.8 N•m)

Cylinder head . . . . 200 in.-lbs.
(22.6 N•m)

Flywheel:
TVM125, TVM140. . . . . . . 38 ft.-lbs.
(52 N•m)
All other models . . . . 35 ft.-lbs.
(48 N•m)

External ignition. . . . . 40 in.-lbs.
(4.5 N•m)

Intake pipe to cylinder . . . . . 90 in.-lbs.
(10.2 N•m)

Magneto stator . . . . 65 in.-lbs.
(7.3 N•m)

Oil pan . . . . 115 in.-lbs.
(13.0 N•m)

Spark plug . . . . 20 ft.-lbs.
(28 N•m)

Electric starter . . . . 65 in.-lbs.
(7.3 N•m)

FLYWHEEL. To remove flywheel, first disconnect and ground spark plug cable. Remove air cleaner assembly. Drain fuel from tank and remove tank. Remove screws retaining dipstick tube, if so equipped, and blower housing. Lift blower housing from engine. On models so equipped, disengage flywheel brake as outlined in FLYWHEEL BRAKE section. If flywheel has tapped holes, use a suitable puller to remove flywheel. If no holes are present, screw a knock-off nut onto crankshaft so there is a small gap between nut and flywheel. Gently pry against bottom of flywheel while tapping sharply on nut.

On engines originally equipped with a breaker-point ignition system and an external ignition coil, the ignition coil is round and stamped "GREY KEY" as shown in Fig. T27. The flywheel key is colored grey.

The ignition coil on some engines equipped with an electronic ignition (often used as a replacement for the external coil on the breaker-point ignition system) has a square shape and is stamped "GOLD KEY" as shown in Fig. T28. A gold colored flywheel key must be used with this ignition coil for proper ignition timing. A spacer must also be installed on the crankshaft.

Install a stepped flywheel key so the stepped end is toward the engine. Install a tapered flywheel key so the big end is toward the engine. If a spacer is used, install the spacer so the protrusion fits in the keyway and is toward the end of the crankshaft.

After installing flywheel, tighten flywheel nut to torque listed in TIGHTENING TORQUES table.

CYLINDER HEAD. To remove cylinder head (16—Fig. T29), remove all interfering shrouds and brackets. Clean area around cylinder head to prevent entrance of foreign material. Unscrew cylinder head screws and remove cylinder head.

Clean carbon from cylinder head being careful not to damage gasket mating surface. Use a straightedge to check cylinder head for distortion. If warped excessively, renew the cylinder head.

A new head gasket should be installed when installing cylinder head. Do not apply any type of sealer to the head gasket. Some cylinder head screws are equipped with flat washers, while some screws are equipped with a Belleville washer (B—Fig. T30) as well as a flat washer (W). The Belleville washer must be installed so the concave side is toward the screw threads.

Tighten the cylinder head screws on engines with eight cylinder head screws in the sequence shown in Fig. T31.

Tighten the cylinder head screws on engines with nine cylinder head screws in the sequence shown in Fig. T32. Tighten cylinder head retaining screws in 50 in.-lb. (5.6 N•m) increments to final torque of 200 in.-lbs. (22.6 N•m).

VALVE SYSTEM. To remove valves (18 and 19—Fig. T29), remove cylinder head as previously outlined. Remove muffler and carburetor. Remove valve tappet chamber cover/breather assembly. Use suitable valve spring compressor to compress valve spring, then rotate spring retainer (22) to allow valve stem to pass through opening in retainer. Release spring tension and remove valve and spring.

Clean carbon from valve face and stem. Inspect valves for burnt or warped valve head and stem and renew as necessary. Valve should be renewed if valve face margin is less than $\frac{1}{32}$ inch (0.8 mm) after grinding.

Valve face angle is 45 degrees and valve seat angle is 46 degrees for intake and exhaust. Valve seats are not renewable. If burned or pitted they can be refaced using grinding stone or valve seat cutter. Valve seat width should be 0.042-0.052 inch (1.07-1.32 mm) for Models TVM125 and TVM140; and 0.035-0.045 inch (0.89-1.14 mm) for all other models. Use a 60° cutter to narrow seat from bottom toward center and a 30° cutter to narrow seat from top toward center.

Valve stem guides are cast into cylinder block and are not renewable. If excessive clearance exists between valve stem and guide, guide should be reamed and a new valve with an oversize stem installed. After reaming valve guide oversize, recut the valve seats to align with the guides.

When reinstalling valves, renew valve stem seals (20—Fig. T29) if used. Note that some valve springs have dampening coils (coils that are located closer together than standard coils) at one end. Install springs with dampening coils positioned away from valve retainers (22). Adjust valve clearance as previously outlined.

CAMSHAFT. The camshaft (40—Fig. T29) and camshaft gear are an integral part which rides on journals at each end of camshaft. Camshaft on some models also has a compression release mechanism mounted on camshaft gear which lifts exhaust valve at low cranking rpm to reduce compression and aid starting.

Crankcase cover (44—Fig. T29) must be removed to gain access to camshaft. When removing camshaft, align timing marks (Fig. T33) on camshaft gear and crankshaft gear to relieve valve spring

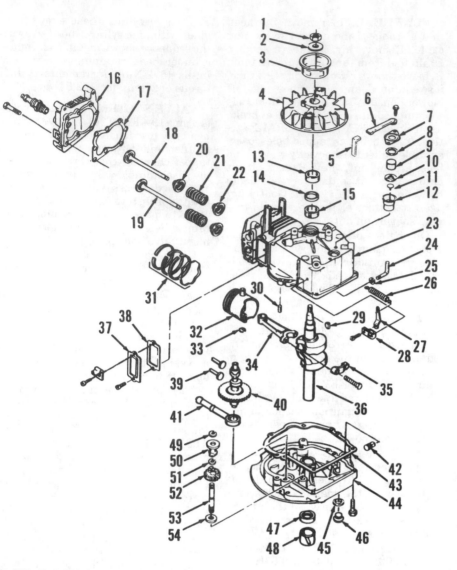

Fig. T31—Tighten cylinder head screws in sequence shown on engines equipped with eight cylinder head screws.

Fig. T32—Tighten cylinder head screws in sequence shown on engines equipped with nine cylinder head screws.

Fig. T29—Exploded view of typical engine with a vertical crankshaft.

1. Nut
2. Belleville washer
3. Starter cup
4. Flywheel
5. Elbow
6. Breather tube
7. Cover
8. Gasket
9. Filter
10. Baffle
11. Valve
12. Housing
13. Spacer
14. Oil seal

15. Bushing
16. Cylinder head
17. Gasket
18. Intake valve
19. Exhaust valve
20. Valve seal
21. Spring
22. Retainer
23. Crankcase
24. Governor shaft
25. Washer
26. Governor spring
27. Governor lever

28. Clamp
29. Key
30. Dowel pin
31. Piston rings
32. Piston
33. Retaining ring
34. Connecting rod
35. Rod cap
36. Crankshaft
37. Tappet cover
38. Gasket
39. Tappets
40. Camshaft

41. Oil pump
42. Drain plug
43. Gasket
44. Oil pan
45. Gasket
46. Drain plug
47. Bushing
48. Oil seal
49. Snap ring
50. Governor spool
51. Snap ring
52. Flyweight assy.
53. Governor shaft
54. Washer

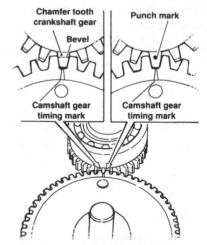

Fig. T33—Drawing showing timing marks on crankshaft and camshaft gears.

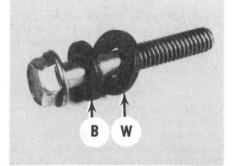

Fig. T30—If used, install Belleville washer (B) and flat washer (W) on cylinder head screw as shown.

pressure on camshaft lobes. On models with compression release, it is necessary to rotate crankshaft three teeth past the aligned position to allow compression release mechanism to clear the exhaust valve tappet. Mark the valve tappets (39—Fig. T29) prior to removal so they can be reinstalled in original positions.

Inspect camshaft lobes and journals for scoring, scuffing and excessive wear. It is recommended that valve tappets be renewed when renewing the camshaft. Spring on compression release mecha-

nism should snap weight against camshaft. Compression release mechanism and camshaft are serviced as an assembly only.

Camshaft rides directly in the aluminum bearing bore of crankcase and oil pan. Refer to following chart for standard bearing diameter:

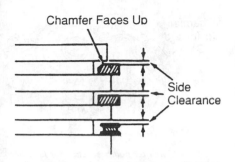

Fig. T34—To check piston ring side clearance, insert feeler gauge between ring and piston ring land. Renew piston if clearance is excessive.

Model	Camshaft Bearing Diameter
V40 std. ignition, V50, V60, TVM125, TVM140	0.6230-0.6235 in. (15.824-15.836 mm)
All other models	0.4975-0.4980 in. (12.636-12.649 mm)

All models are equipped with a barrel and plunger type oil pump that is operated by an eccentric on the camshaft. Refer to OIL PUMP paragraph for service procedures.

Lubricate camshaft and tappets with engine oil prior to reassembly. When installing camshaft, align crankshaft and camshaft timing marks as shown in Fig. T33. Note that timing tooth on crankshaft gear will be identified by either a punch mark or beveled tooth. Install oil pump so that chamfered side of oil pump drive collar is facing the camshaft gear.

PISTON, PIN AND RINGS. Piston and connecting rod assembly is removed from cylinder head end of engine. Remove cylinder head, crankcase cover and connecting rod cap. Before removing piston, remove any carbon or ring ridge from top of cylinder to prevent damage to piston and rings. Push connecting rod and piston out of cylinder.

Aluminum alloy pistons are equipped with two compression rings and one oil control ring. Piston ring end gap is 0.007-0.017 inch (0.18-0.43 mm) on models without external ignition and displacement of 12.04 cu. in. (197 cc) or less. If engine is equipped with a solid state external ignition, or displacement is 12.18 cu. in. (229 cc) or greater, piston

ring end gap should be 0.010-0.020 inch (0.25-0.50 mm).

Inspect piston skirt for scuffing, scoring or other damage. Refer to following table for specified piston skirt-to-cylinder clearances:

Model	Piston Clearance
LAV30, TVS75	0.0025-0.0043 in. (0.064-0.110 mm)
V40 (std. ignition)	0.0055-0.0070 in. (0.140-0.0.177 mm)
ECV110 (std. ignition)	0.0045-0.0060 in. (0.114-0.152 mm)
V50, V60, TVM125-140	0.0030-0.0048 in. (0.076-0.121 mm)
All other models	0.0040-0.0058 in. (0.101-0.147 mm)

Standard piston diameters, measured at piston skirt 90 degrees from piston pin bore, are listed in the following table (if engine has external ignition, check list for a different specification than engines not so equipped):

Model	Piston Diameter
LAV30, TVS75	2.3092-2.3100 in. (58.654-58.674 mm)
ECV100, ECV105, LAV40, TNT100, TVS100, TVS105 TVXL105	2.6202-2.6210 in. (66.553-66.573 mm)
V40	2.4945-2.4950 in. (63.360-63.373 mm)
V40 (ext. ignition)	2.6202-2.6210 in. (66.553-66.573 mm)
ECV110	2.7450-2.7455 in. (69.723-69.735 mm)
LAV35, TVS90	2.4952-2.4960 in. (63.378-63.398 mm)
TVM125, TVM140	2.6210-2.6215 in. (66.573-66.586 mm)
V50, V60	2.6210-2.6215 in. (66.573-66.586 mm)
TVM125(ext. ignition), TVM140(ext. ignition)	2.6212-2.6220 in. (66.578-66.599 mm)
ECV120, TNT120, LAV50, TVS120	2.8072-2.8080 in. (71.303-71.323 mm)

Clean carbon deposits from ring grooves being careful not to damage ring lands. To check grooves for wear, insert new ring in groove and measure side clearance (Fig. T34) with a feeler

gauge. Standard ring side clearance in ring grooves is listed in the following table. Renew piston and rings if clearance is excessive.

Model	Ring Side Clearance
ECV110, V50, V60, TVM125, TVM140 (std. ignition):	
Compression rings	0.002-0.004 in. (0.05-0.10 mm)
Oil control ring (max.)	0.004 in. (0.10 mm)
All other engines:	
Compression rings	0.002-0.005 in. (0.05-0.13 mm)
Oil control ring (max.)	0.004 in. (0.10 mm)

Some engine models have offset piston pins; for these models it is imperative that the connecting rod and piston be installed corerectly. The piston used in these engines will have either a number cast on inside of piston skirt (Fig. T35), an arrow stamped below piston pin bore (Fig. T35) or an arrow stamped on piston crown (Fig. T36). Position connecting rod in relation to marking on piston as indicated in Fig. T35 or Fig. T36. Piston pin should be a tight push fit in piston pin bore and connecting rod pin bore. Piston pin is retained by retainer clips at each end of piston pin bore.

Install top and second piston rings with beveled edge toward piston crown as shown in Fig. T34. Stagger ring end gaps equally around circumference of piston before installation. If the area adjacent to the valves has been machined (trenched), position the piston rings on the piston so the end gaps are staggered and none of the end gaps will coincide with the machined area. This will prevent a piston ring end from

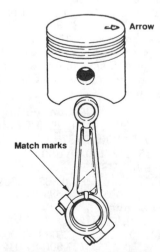

Fig. T36—If piston crown is marked with an arrow, assemble piston and rod as shown. Match marks on rod and cap must be aligned and facing outward when rod and piston are installed in cylinder block.

Fig. T35—On models with offset connecting rod, it is imperative that rod is positioned in relation to casting number on inside of piston skirt or to the arrow stamped below piston pin as shown.

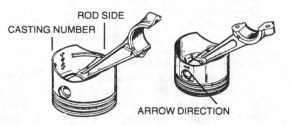

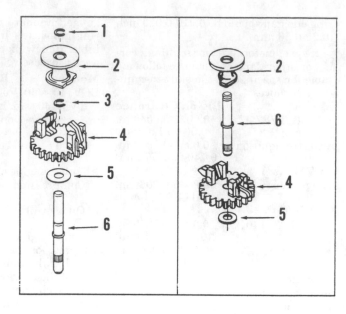

Fig. T37—Exploded view of two versions of mechanical governor used on vertical crankshaft engines. Later style governor (right view) does not use snap rings to secure governor spool.

1. Snap ring
2. Spool
3. Snap ring
4. Governor flyweight & gear
5. Thrust washer
6. Governor shaft

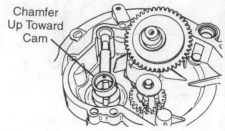

Fig. T38—Install oil pump so chamfer is toward camshaft.

Model	Shaft Height
TVM125, TVM140	$1\frac{19}{32}$ in. (40.48 mm)
All other models	$1\frac{21}{64}$ in. (34.92 mm)

OIL PUMP. Vertical crankshaft engines are equipped with a barrel and plunger type oil pump. The large end of the pump surrounds an eccentric on the camshaft which forces pump plunger to reciprocate when the camshaft rotates. Ball end of pump plunger fits in a recess in the oil pan. Remove crankcase cover/oil pan for access to the oil pump.

When installing the pump, note that chamfered side of drive collar (Fig. T38) should be toward camshaft gear. Oil pumps may be equipped with two chamfered sides, one chamfered side or with flat boss as shown. Be sure installation is correct.

CRANKSHAFT, MAIN BEARINGS AND SEALS. Always note oil seal depth and seal lip direction before removing oil seal from crankcase or cover. New seals must be pressed into seal bores to the same depth as old seals on all models.

Refer to CONNECTING ROD section for standard crankshaft crankpin journal diameters.

Crankshaft main bearing journals on some models ride directly in the aluminum alloy bores in the cylinder block and crankcase cover or oil pan. Other engines were originally equipped with renewable steel backed bronze bushings.

Standard main bearing bore diameters for main bearings are listed in the following table (if engine has external ignition, check list for a different specification than engines not so equipped):

Model	Main Bearing Inside Diameter
LAV30, TVS75, LAV35, ECV100, TVS90	0.8755-0.8760 in. (22.238-22.250 mm)
ECV100(external ignition), TVS75(external ignition), TVS90(external ignition), TNT100, TVS100:	

---

catching the machined surface during installation. When installing connecting rod and piston assembly, align the match marks (casting projections) on connecting rod and cap as shown in Fig. T36. Install piston and rod so match marks on connecting rod are toward power take-off (pto) end of crankshaft.

CONNECTING ROD. The aluminum alloy connecting rod rides directly on crankshaft crankpin.

Refer to the following table for standard crankpin journal diameter:

Model	Crankpin Diameter
LAV30, TVS75, ECV100, LAV35, TNT100, TVS90, TVS100, TVS115, TVXL115	0.8610-0.8615 in. (21.869-21.882 mm)
V40 (std. ignition), V50, V60, TVM125, TVM140	1.0615-1.0620 in. (26.962-26.974 mm)
All other engines	0.9995-1.0000 in. (25.387-25.400 mm)

Standard inside diameter for connecting rod big end is listed in the following table:

Model	Connecting Rod Big End Diameter
ECV100, LAV30, TVS75, LAV35, TNT100, TVS90, TVS100, TVS115, TVXL115	0.8620-0.8625 in. (21.894-21.907 mm)
V40 (std. ignition), V50, V60, TVM125, TVM140	1.0630-1.0635 in. (27.000-27.012 mm)
All other engines	1.0005-1.0010 in. (25.412-25.425 mm)

Connecting rod bearing-to-crankpin journal clearance should be 0.0005-0.0015 inch (0.013-0.038 mm) for all models.

Assemble connecting rod and piston as outlined in previous section. Tighten connecting rod screws to 170 in.-lb. (19.2 N•m) torque on TVM125 and TVM140 engines or to 105 in.-lb. (11.8 N•m) torque on all other models.

GOVERNOR. On most engines, the governor is retained on the shaft by snap ring (1—Fig. T37). To remove spool, detach upper snap ring. Detach lower snap ring (3) to remove flyweight assembly (4). A washer (5) is located under the flyweight assembly. On some engines, a spacer is located under washer.

On later small frame engines and replacement shafts, no snap rings are used on the governor shaft. The governor is held in place by a boss on the governor shaft. The flyweights and gear are available only as a unit assembly.

The governor shaft is pressed into the crankcase cover/oil pan and may be replaced if the mounting boss is not damaged or the hole is not enlarged. To remove the governor shaft, clamp the shaft in a vise and using a soft mallet, drive the crankcase cover or oil pan off the shaft. Do not attempt to twist governor shaft out of boss. Twisting will enlarge hole. Apply Loctite 271 (red) to shaft end. If shaft is retainerless design, position washer and governor gear assembly on shaft before installing shaft, then press in shaft until the governor gear has 0.010-0.020 inch (0.25-0.50 mm) axial play. If snap rings are used on the governor shaft, press shaft into oil pan until the height from top of shaft to oil pan boss is as specified in the following table:

Illustrations courtesy Tecumseh Products Co.

Crankcase side   1.0005-1.0010 in.
(25.413-25.425 mm)
Cover (flange)
side . . . . 0.8755-0.8760 in.
(22.238-22.250 mm)
TNT120, TVM125, TVM140,
TVS105, TVS115,
TVS120 . . . . . . 1.0005-1.0010 in.
(25.413-25.425 mm)

Standard diameters for crankshaft main bearing journals are shown in the following table (if engine has external ignition, check list for a different specification than engines not so equipped):

Model	Main Bearing Journal Diameter
LAV30, LAV35, TVS75, TVS90, ECV100	0.8735-0.8740 in. (22.187-22.200 mm)

ECV100(external ignition),
TVS75(external ignition),
TVS90(external ignition),
TNT100, TVS100:
Crankcase side   0.9985-0.9990 in.
(25.362-25.375 mm)
Oil pan side . . . 0.8735-0.8740 in.
(22.187-22.200 mm)
TNT120, TVM125,
TVM140, TVS105,
TVS115, TVS120. 0.9985-0.9990 in.
(25.362-25.375 mm)

Main bearing clearance should be 0.0015-0.0025 inch (0.038-0.064 mm). Crankshaft end play should be 0.005-0.027 inch (0.13-0.069 mm) for all models.

When installing crankshaft, align the crankshaft gear tooth that is beveled or has a punch mark (Fig. T33) with the mark on the camshaft gear.

CYLINDER AND CRANKCASE.
Cylinder and crankcase are an integral casting on all models. Cylinder should be honed and fitted to nearest oversize for which piston and ring set are available if cylinder is scored, tapered or out-of-round more than 0.005 inch (0.13 mm).

Standard cylinder bore diameters are listed in the following table (if engine has external ignition, check list for a different specification than engines not so equipped):

Model	Cylinder Bore Diameter
LAV30, TVS75	2.3125-2.3135 in. (58.738-58.763 mm)
LAV35, TVS90, V40 std. ign.	2.5000-2.5010 in. (63.500-63.525 mm)
V40 ext. ign.	2.625-2.626 in. (66.675-66.700 mm)
LAV40, ECV100, TNT100, TVM125, TVS100, TVM140, TVXL105, V50, V60	2.6250-2.6260 in. (66.675-66.700 mm)

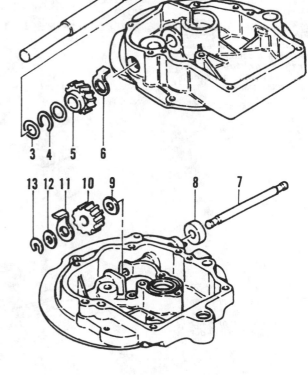

Fig. T39—Exploded views of 8.5:1 auxiliary pto drive systems that may be used.

1. Shaft
2. Seal
3. Washers (2)
4. Snap ring
5. Gear
6. Tang washer
7. Shaft
8. Seal
9. Thick washer
10. Gear
11. Tang washer
12. Washer
13. Snap ring

Model	
LAV50, TNT120, TVS120	2.8120-2.8130 in. (71.425-71.450 mm)

Refer to PISTON, PIN AND RINGS section for correct piston-to-cylinder block clearance. Note also that cylinder block used on Models TVM125 and TVM140 has been "trenched" to improve fuel flow and power.

REDUCED SPEED PTO SHAFT.
A slow speed (8.5:1) auxiliary pto shaft is used on some vertical shaft engines. Two designs have been used as shown in Fig. T39. A worm gear on the crankshaft turns the pto gear and pto shaft. Several different versions of this unit have been used.

The pto shaft is held in place by a snap ring (4 or 13). To disassemble the unit, remove oil pan from crankcase. Detach snap ring from the shaft and remove components from oil pan. When assembling unit, note that the tang of washer (6 or 11) is installed facing away from the gear. Seal (2 or 8) is installed with lip facing inward.

FLYWHEEL BRAKE.
A flywheel brake is used on some engines. Two configurations have been used. The brake shown in Fig. T40A contacts the bottom surface of the flywheel while the brake shown in Fig. T40B contacts the inside of the flywheel. Before the flywheel can

be removed for either type, the brake must be disengaged from the flywheel. On bottom surface type, unhook brake torsion spring (Fig. T40A). On inside surface type, push lever (L—Fig. T41) toward spark plug so brake pad moves away from flywheel, then insert Tecumseh tool 670298 or a suitable pin in hole (H) to hold lever.

Inspect mechanism for excessive wear and damage. Tighten mounting screws on bottom surface type brake to 60-70 in.-lbs. (6.8-7.9 N·m) torque. On inside surface type, minimum allowable thickness of brake pad at narrowest point is 0.060 inch (1.52 mm). Install brake mechanism and push up on bracket so bracket mounting screws are at bottom of slotted holes (M—Fig. 41) in bracket. Tighten mounting screws to 90 in.-lbs. (10.2 N·m) torque.

REWIND STARTER

The rewind starter may be mounted on the blower housing or attached to the side of the engine. Refer to appropriate following paragraphs for service.

STARTERS MOUNTED ON BLOWER HOUSING—TEARDROP HOUSING.
Note shape of starter housing in Fig. T42. The pulley may be secured with either a retainer screw or

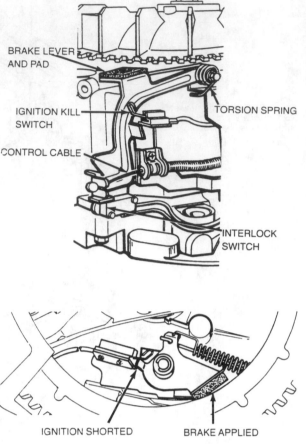

Fig. T40A—View of bottom-surface type flywheel brake showing location of brake spring, ignition cut-out switch and interlock switch for electric starter.

BRAKE LEVER AND PAD

IGNITION KILL SWITCH

CONTROL CABLE

TORSION SPRING

INTERLOCK SWITCH

Fig. T43—Spring end (E) should force pawl toward center of pulley.

Hole In Pulley   Eyelet

Fig. T44—Insert rope through starter housing eyelet and hole in pulley, then tie knot in rope end.

Fig. T40B—View of inner edge type flywheel brake showing location of brake pad and ignition cut-out switch.

IGNITION SHORTED   BRAKE APPLIED

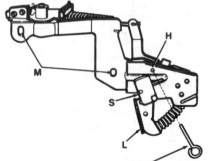

Fig. T41—On inner edge type brake, push against lever (L) and insert pin (P) through holes (H) to hold brake pad away from flywheel. Interlock switch (S) is used on engines with an electric starter.

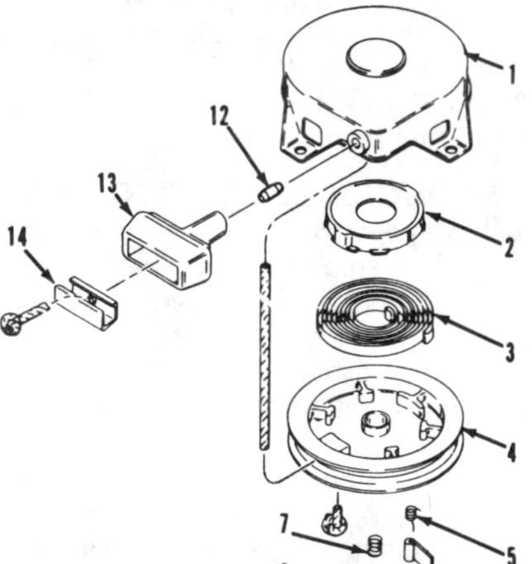

retainer pin. Most starters use a rope that is 54 inches (137 cm) long. Refer to following paragraphs for service.

To disassemble starter equipped with retainer screw (Fig. T42), release preload tension of rewind spring by removing rope handle and allowing rope to wind slowly into starter. Remove retainer screw (9), retainer (8) and spring (7). Remove pawl (6) and spring (5). Remove pulley with spring. Wear appropriate safety eyewear and gloves before disengaging keeper (2) and rewind

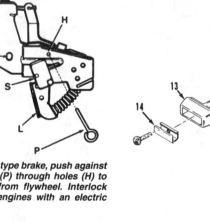

Fig. T42—Exploded view of typical pawl type rewind starter with teardrop shaped housing (1) using retainer screw (9). Some starters may have three starter pawls (6).

1. Housing
2. Spring keeper
3. Rewind spring
4. Pulley
5. Spring
6. Pawl
7. Brake spring
8. Retainer
9. Screw
10. Centering pin
11. Nylon bushing
12. Rope coupler
13. Handle
14. Insert

spring (3) from pulley as spring may uncoil uncontrolled.

To reassemble, reverse the disassembly procedure. Spring (3) should be lightly greased. Install the pawl and spring so the spring end (E—Fig. T43) forces the pawl toward the center of the pulley.

With starter assembled, except for rope, install rope as follows: Turn pulley counterclockwise until tight, then allow to unwind so hole in pulley aligns with rope outlet as shown in Fig. T44. Insert rope through starter housing and pulley hole, tie a knot in rope end and allow rope to wind onto pulley. Install rope handle. Some models use centering pin (10—Fig. T42) to align starter with starter cup. Place nylon bushing (11) on pin, then bottom the pin in hole in retainer screw. Pin and bushing should index in end of crankshaft when installing starter on engine.

To disassemble starter equipped with retainer pin (11—Fig. T45), release preload tension of rewind spring by removing rope handle and allowing rope to wind slowly into starter. Remove retainer pin (11) by supporting pulley and driving out pin using a ¼ inch (6 mm) diameter punch. Remove spring (7) and retainer (8). Remove pawl (6) and spring (5). Remove pulley with spring. Wear appropriate safety eyewear and gloves before disengaging keeper (2) and re-

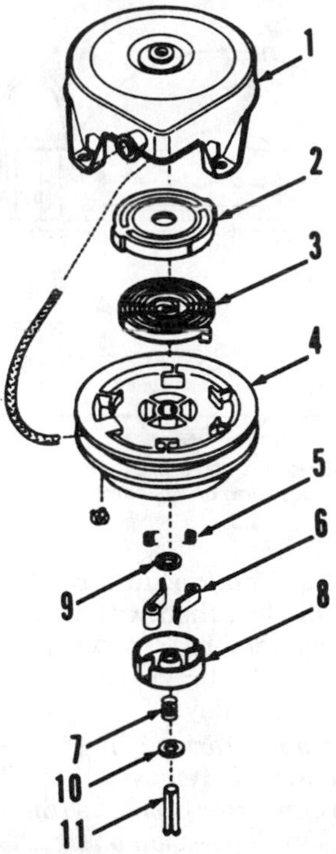

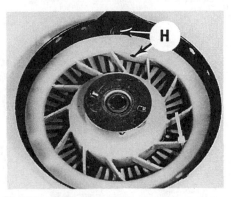

Fig. T48—Tabs (T) on retainer must fit inside pawls during assembly.

Fig. T49—Align holes (H) in pulley and starter housing then insert rope through holes.

Fig. T45—Exploded view of typical pawl type re-wind starter with teardrop shaped housing (1) using retainer pin (11).

1. Housing
2. Spring keeper
3. Rewind spring
4. Pulley
5. Spring
6. Pawl
7. Brake spring
8. Retainer
9. Washer
10. Washer
11. Pin

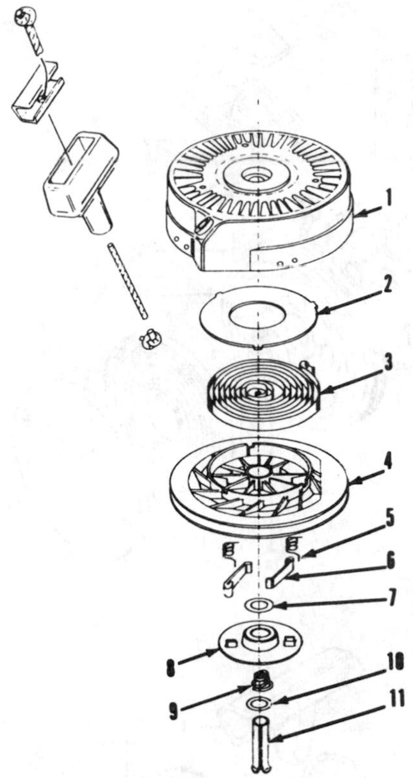

Fig. T46—Exploded view of "stylized" rewind starter.

1. Starter housing
2. Cover
3. Rewind spring
4. Pulley
5. Springs (2)
6. Pawls (2)
7. Plastic washers (2)
8. Pawl retainer
9. Brake spring
10. Metal washer
11. Pin

wind spring (3) from pulley as spring may uncoil uncontrolled.

To reassemble, reverse the disassembly procedure. Spring (3) should be lightly greased. Install the pawl and spring so the spring end (E—Fig. T43) forces the pawl toward the center of the pulley. Drive in retainer pin (11—Fig. T45) until seated against shoulder of housing.

With starter assembled, except for rope, install rope as follows: Rotate pulley counterclockwise until tight, then allow to unwind so hole in pulley aligns with rope outlet as shown in Fig. T44. Insert rope through starter housing and pulley hole, tie a knot in rope end and allow rope to wind onto pulley. Install rope handle.

STYLIZED STARTER. The "stylized" starter is shown in Fig. T46. Typical rope lengths are 69 inches (175 cm), 98 inches (249 cm) and 114 inches (290 cm).

To disassemble starter, remove rope handle and allow rope to wind slowly into starter. Position a suitable sleeve support under pawl retainer (8) and using a ⁵⁄₁₆ inch (8 mm) punch, drive pin (11) free of starter. Remove brake spring (9), retainer (8), pawls (6) and springs (5). Wear appropriate safety eyewear

Fig. T47—Spring end (E) should force pawl toward center of pulley.

and gloves before disengaging pulley from starter as spring may uncoil uncontrolled. Place shop towel around pulley and lift pulley out of housing; spring should remain with pulley.

Inspect components for damage and excessive wear. Reverse disassembly procedure to install components. Rewind spring coils wind in counterclockwise direction from outer end. When installing pulley, be sure inner end of rewind spring engages spring retainer adjacent to housing center post. Install

the pawl and spring so the spring end (E—Fig. T47) forces the pawl toward the center of the pulley. Place the retainer on the pulley hub so tabs (T—Fig. T48) are inside ends of pawls. Install pin (11—Fig. T46) so top of pin is ¹⁄₈ inch (3.2 mm) below top of starter. Driving pin in too far may damage retainer pawl.

With starter assembled, except for rope, install rope as follows: Rotate pulley counterclockwise until tight, then allow to unwind so hole (H—Fig. T49) in pulley aligns with rope outlet. Insert rope through starter housing and pulley hole, tie a knot in rope end and allow rope to wind onto pulley. Install rope handle.

VERTICAL-PULL REWIND STARTERS. Two types of vertical-pull starters have been used. The types are identified by the manner of gear engagement, either horizontal or vertical.

Horizontal Engagement Gear Starter. When the rope handle is pulled, the starter gear moves horizontally to engage the gear teeth on the flywheel. An exploded view of the starter is shown in Fig. T50. Most starters use a ⁵⁄₃₂ inch (4 mm) diameter rope that is 61 inches (155 cm) long.

After installing starter assembly, clearance between teeth on gear (6) and teeth on flywheel should be checked

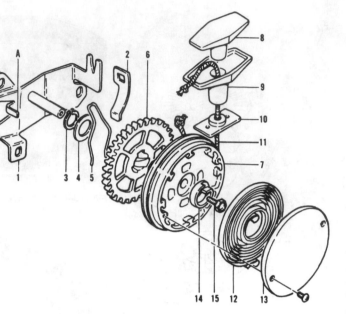

Fig. T50—Exploded view of horizontal engagement gear starter.

1. Mounting bracket
2. Rope guide
3. Snap ring
4. Washer
5. Brake spring
6. Gear
7. Pulley
8. Insert
9. Handle
10. Bracket
11. Rope
12. Rewind spring
13. Cover
14. Spring anchor
15. Hub screw

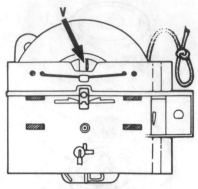

Fig. T52—Drawing of vertical engagement gear starter. Note location of "V" notch.

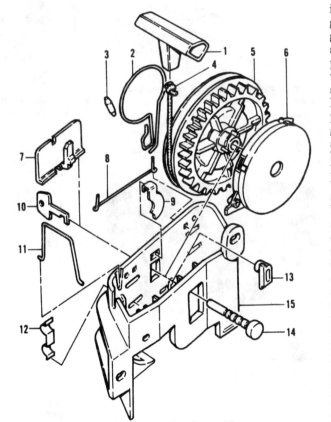

Fig. T51—Exploded view of vertical engagement gear starter.

1. Handle
2. Brake spring
3. Staple
4. Rope
5. Rope pulley
6. Rewind spring & housing
7. Rope clip
8. Pawl spring
9. Pawl
10. Key (not all models)
11. Rope clip
12. Clip (not all models)
13. Lock pawl (not all models)
14. Pin
15. Mounting bracket

when starter is operated. When teeth are fully engaged, there should be at least 1/16 inch (1.6 mm) clearance from top of gear tooth to base of opposite gear teeth. Remove spark plug wire, operate starter several times and check gear engagement. Insufficient gear tooth clearance could cause starter gear to hang up on flywheel gear when engine starts, which could damage starter.

To disassemble starter, proceed as follows: Detach rope from insert (8—Fig. T50) and handle (9), then allow the rope to wind slowly onto the pulley to relieve spring tension. Unscrew screws securing spring cover (13) and carefully remove cover without disturbing rewind spring (12). Safety eyewear and gloves should be worn when working on or around the rewind spring. Remove re-

wind spring. Remove hub screw (15) and spring hub (14), then withdraw pulley and gear assembly. Remove snap ring (3), washer (4), brake spring (5) and gear (6) from pulley.

Reassemble starter using the following procedure: If removed, install rope guide (2) on starter bracket so dimple on guide fits in depression on bracket. Install rope on pulley. Wrap rope around pulley in a counterclockwise direction when viewing pulley from rewind spring side of pulley. Place gear on pulley. Do not lubricate helix in gear or on pulley shaft. Install brake spring (5) in groove of gear (6). The bent end of brake spring should point away from gear. The brake spring should fit snugly in groove. Do not lubricate brake spring. Install washer (4) and snap ring (3) on pulley shaft. Lightly lubricate shaft on starter bracket then install pulley and gear assembly on bracket shaft. The closed end of brake spring (5) must fit around tab (A) on bracket. Install spring anchor (14) and screw (15). Tighten screw to 44-55 in.-lb. (5.08-6.21 N·m) torque. Install rewind spring. The spring coils should wind in a clockwise direction from outer end. A new spring is contained in a holder that allows spring installation by pushing spring from holder into spring cavity on pulley. Pass outer end of rope through rope bracket (10) and install rope handle and insert. Pull a portion of rope out past rope guide and wrap any excess rope around pulley, then turn pulley 2-2½ turns against spring tension to preload rewind spring. Check starter operation.

Vertical Engagement Gear Starter. When the rope handle is pulled, the starter gear moves vertically to engage the gear teeth on the flywheel. An exploded view of the starter is shown in Fig. T51.

To replace the starter rope, proceed as follows: If the starter bracket has a "V" notch (V—Fig. T52), then the inner end of the rope is accessible and the rope can

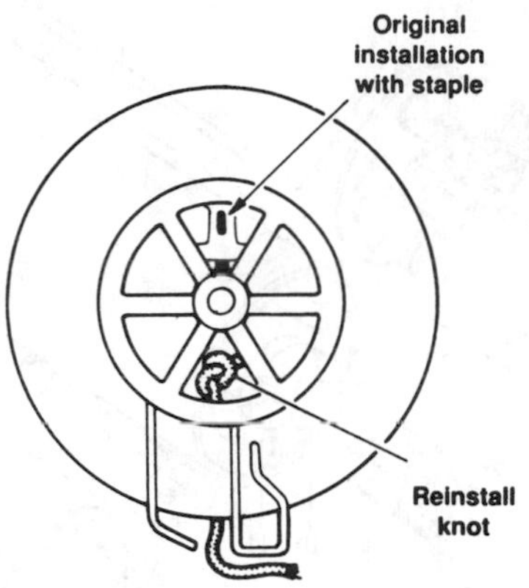

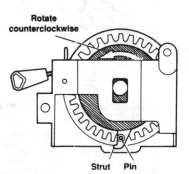

Fig. T53—Original rope was attached to pulley with a staple. Replacement rope must be secured with a knot.

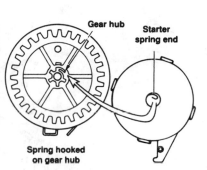

Fig. T55—If removed, place spring housing on rope pulley while being sure inner spring end engages anchor on pulley.

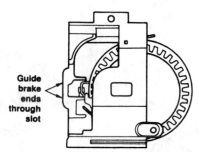

Fig. T57—Install rope pulley assembly in starter bracket while inserting brake spring legs into slots in starter bracket.

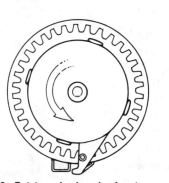

Fig. T54—Housing rotation may be prevented by inserting a pin or rod through strut hole and into gear teeth.

Fig. T56—Rotate spring housing four turns counterclockwise then align legs on brake spring with hole in strut.

be replaced without disassembling the starter. Typical rope lengths are 65 inches (165 cm) and 98 inches (249 cm). If rope is unbroken, remove rope handle and let rope wind onto rope pulley. Note in Fig. T53 that inner end of rope was originally retained by a staple, while inner end on replacement ropes is inserted through a hole in pulley and knotted. Rotate pulley so that either the stapled rope end or knotted rope end is visible (Fig. T52) in the "V" notch. Pry out staple or untie knot and pull out rope. Rotate pulley counterclockwise until rewind spring is tight, then allow pulley to turn clockwise until rope hole in pulley is visible in "V" notch. Route new rope through pulley hole and tie a knot in rope end. Pull the knot into pulley cavity so rope end does not protrude. Allow pulley to wind rope onto pulley. Attach rope handle to rope end.

To disassemble starter, proceed as follows: If rope is unbroken, remove rope handle and let rope wind onto rope pulley. Drive or press out pulley spindle (14—Fig. T51) by placing starter over a deep-well socket and forcing spindle into socket. Turn spring housing (6) so strut aligns with legs on brake spring (2). Prevent housing rotation by inserting a pin or rod through strut hole and

into gear teeth as shown in Fig. T54. Remove pulley assembly from starter bracket.

CAUTION: Do not allow spring housing to separate from rope pulley until any spring tension has been relieved.

Hold spring housing (6—Fig. T51) against rope pulley so spring housing cannot rotate. Withdraw pin or rod in spring housing strut (Fig. T54) and allow spring housing to rotate thereby relieving rewind spring tension. If necessary, separate spring housing from rope pulley. Do not attempt to remove rewind spring from spring housing. The spring and housing are available only as a unit assembly.

If rope replacement is necessary, note in Fig. T53 that inner end of rope was originally retained by a staple, while inner end on replacement ropes is inserted through a hole in pulley and knotted. Pry out staple, if so equipped, to release rope. Route new rope through pulley hole and tie a knot in rope end. The knot must be positioned in pulley cavity so rope end does not protrude.

To assemble starter, proceed as follows: Do not lubricate any starter components. When viewed from gear side of rope pulley, wind rope onto pulley in a clockwise direction. Install brake spring (2—Fig. T51) on rope pulley while being

careful not to distort spring legs. If removed, place spring housing on rope pulley while being sure inner spring end engages anchor on pulley. See Fig. T55. Rotate spring housing four turns counterclockwise (Fig. T56) then align legs on brake spring with hole in strut. Prevent housing rotation by inserting a pin or rod through strut hole and into gear teeth. If so equipped, install clip (7—Fig. T51), key (10) and pawl (9). Install rope pulley assembly in starter bracket while inserting brake spring legs into slots in starter bracket (Fig. T57). Route outer rope end past rope guide and install rope handle. Withdraw pin or rod in strut hole. The strut will rotate until it contacts starter bracket. Press or drive in a new pulley spindle (14—Fig. T51).

ELECTRIC STARTER. While several electric starter motors have been used on Tecumseh engines, the motors are basically divided into those with a round frame or a square frame. Several variations of each type have been produced, but service is basically similar except as noted in following paragraphs.

Tecumseh does not provide test specifications for electric starter motors, so service is limited to replacing components that are known or suspected faulty.

CAUTION: The starter motor field magnets may be made of ceramic material. Do not clamp starter housing in a vise or hit housing as field magnets may be damaged.

Refer to Figs. T58, T59 and T60 for exploded views of typical starter motors. Note that starter drive assemblies shown may be used on other types of motors. Some motors may be equipped with a covered drive (Fig. T61).

Note the following when servicing electric starter motor: Prior to disassembly, mark drive plate, frame and end cap so they can be aligned during assembly. Some motors have alignment notches and marks are not necessary.

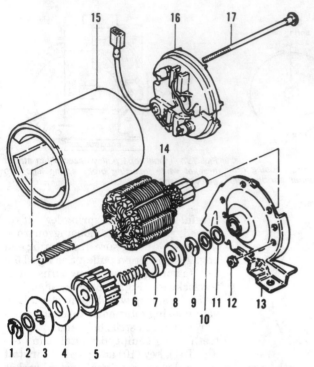

Fig. T58—Exploded view of round frame starter motor with inward-acting starter drive.

1. "E" ring
2. Plastic washer
3. Drive hub
4. Rubber driver
5. Pinion gear
6. Spring
7. Plastic spring cup
8. Metal cup
9. "E" ring
10. Metal washer
11. Plastic washer
12. Nut
13. Drive plate
14. Armature
15. Frame
16. End cap assy.
17. Through-bolt

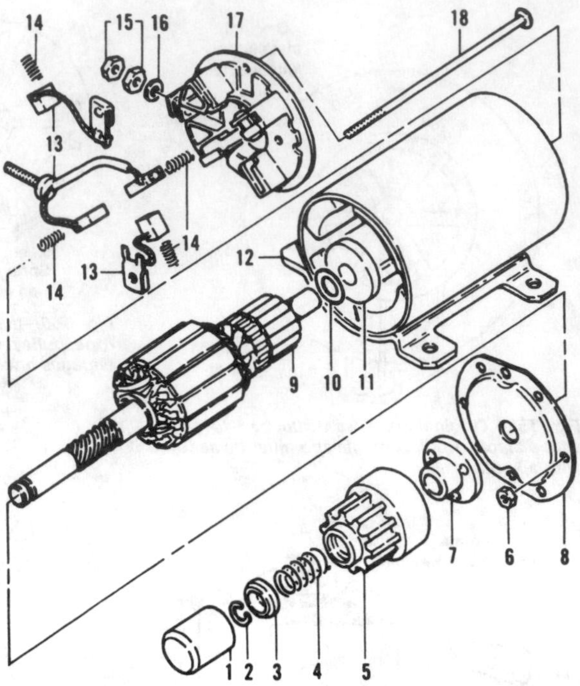

Fig. T59—Exploded view of round frame starter motor with outward-acting starter drive.

1. Boot
2. Retaining ring
3. Spring cup
4. Spring
5. Pinion gear
6. Nut
7. Drive hub
8. Drive plate
9. Armature
10. Washer
11. Washer
12. Frame
13. Brushes
14. Brush springs
15. Nuts
16. Washer
17. End cap
18. Through-bolt

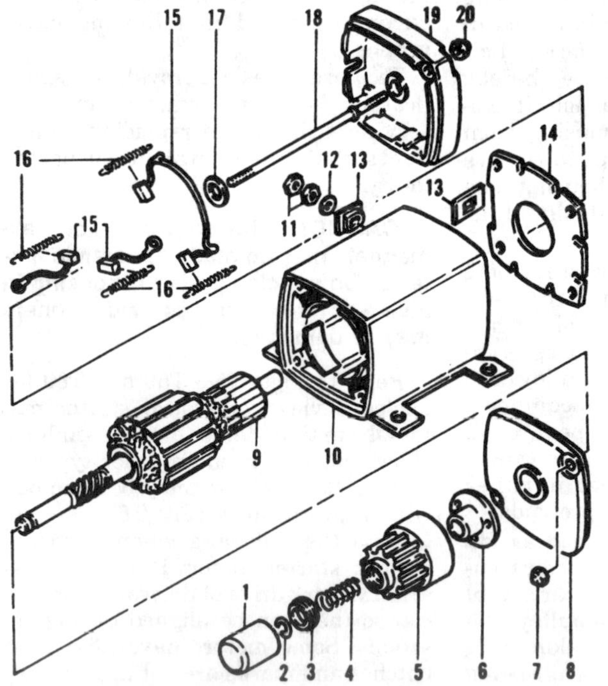

Fig. T60—Exploded view of square frame starter motor.

1. Boot
2. Snap ring
3. Spring cup
4. Spring
5. Pinion gear
6. Drive hub
7. Nut
8. Drive plate
9. Armature
10. Frame
11. Nuts
12. Washer
13. Grommet
14. Brush card
15. Brushes
16. Brush springs
17. Washer
18. Stud
19. End cap
20. Nut

Illustrations courtesy Tecumseh Products Co.

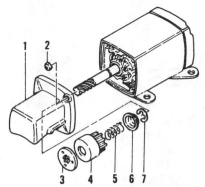

Fig. T61—Exploded view of covered starter drive used on square frame starter motor.

1. Drive cap
2. Nut
3. Drive hub
4. Pinion gear
5. Spring
6. Spring cup
7. "E" ring

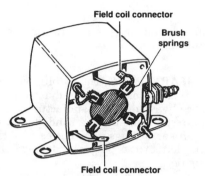

Field coil connector

Brush springs

Field coil connector

Fig. T62—Drawing of brush holder card and brush leads on square frame starter motor.

Minimum brush length is not specified. If brush wire bottoms against slot in brush holder or brush is less than half its original length, replace brush. Be sure brushes do not bind in holders. On some round frame motors, the brushes are available only as a unit assembly with end cap.

On square frame motors, brush leads connected to frame field coils must be cut so new brushes can be installed. The new brushes must be connected and soldered to field coil leads using rosin core solder. See Fig. T62.

Check strength of brush springs. The spring must force brush against commutator with sufficient pressure to ensure good contact.

On square frame motors, replace brush holder card (14—Fig. T60) if card is warped or otherwise damaged.

Bushings in drive plate and end cap are not available separately, only as a unit assembly with drive plate or end cap.

Apply a light coat of grease to helix. All other parts should be assembled dry.

On some motors, a brush holding tool may be helpful to retain brushes and springs during assembly. If end cap has two brushes, a piece of manual rewind starter spring can be modified to hold brushes as shown in Fig. T63. Use care

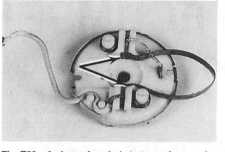

Fig. T63—A piece of rewind starter spring may be positioned as shown to hold brushes in place.

when installing end cap so commutator and brushes are not damaged.

Charging System

The engine may be equipped with an alternator to provide battery charging direct current. The alternator coils may be located under the flywheel, or on some models with an external ignition module, the alternator coils are attached to the legs of the ignition coil. Rectification is accomplished either with a regulator-rectifier unit, external or internal, or by an inline diode contained in the harness.

Refer to the following sections.

EXTERNAL IGNITION MODULE ALTERNATOR. Engines with an external ignition may have an alternator coil attached to the ignition module (Fig. T64). The alternator produces approximately 350 milliamperes for battery charging. To check alternator output, connect a DC voltmeter to the battery (battery must be in normal circuit) as shown in Fig. T65. Run the engine. Voltage should be higher when the engine is running or the alternator is defective.

INLINE DIODE SYSTEM. The inline diode system has a diode connected into alternator wire leading from engine. The system diagrammed in Fig. T66 provides direct current only. The system produces approximately 3 amps direct current for battery charging. The diode rectifies alternator alternating current into direct current and a 6 amp fuse provides overload protection. To check system, disconnect harness connector and using a DC voltmeter connect tester positive lead to red wire connector terminal and ground negative tester lead to engine. At 3600 rpm engine speed, voltmeter reading should be at least 11.5 volts. If engine speed is less, voltmeter reading will be less. If voltage reading is unsatisfactory, check alternator coils by taking an AC voltage reading. Connect one tester lead between diode and engine and ground

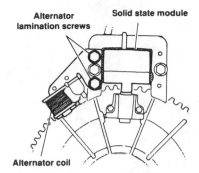

Alternator lamination screws — **Solid state module**

Alternator coil

Fig. T64—Drawing of external ignition module alternator.

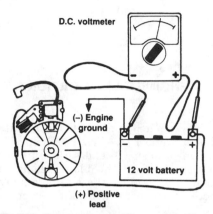

D.C. voltmeter

(−) Engine ground

(+) Positive lead

12 volt battery

Fig. T65—To test external ignition module alternator, refer to drawing and text.

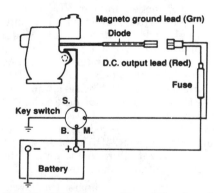

Magneto ground lead (Grn)

Diode

D.C. output lead (Red)

Fuse

S.
Key switch

B. **M.**

Battery

Fig. T66—Wiring diagram of 3 amp DC system with inline diode.

other tester lead to engine. At an engine speed of 3600 rpm, voltage reading should be 26 volts, otherwise alternator is defective. If engine cannot attain 3600 rpm, voltage reading will be less.

To replace an inline diode proceed as follows: Pull back wire sheathing so diode is accessible and cut diode wires. If using heat-shrink tubing, slide tubing over wires. Bend wire ends into hooks and connect new diode to wire ends. The diode must be installed so arrowhead on diode points toward output end of wire. Tightly squeeze wire ends together. Solder wire ends together using rosin core solder. If not using heat-shrink tubing, apply insulating tape.

Illustrations courtesy Tecumseh Products Co.

TECUMSEH

4-STROKE VECTOR ENGINES

Model	Bore	Stroke	Displacement	Rated Power
VLV40	2.797 in.	2.047 in.	12.6 cu.in.	4.0 hp
	(71 mm)	52 mm)	(206 cc)	(3.0 kW)
VLV50, VLXL50	2.797 in.	2.047 in.	12.6 cu.in.	5.0 hp
	(71 mm)	(52 mm)	(206 cc)	(3.7 kW)
VLV55, VLXL55	2.797 in.	2.047 in.	12.6 cu.in.	5.5 hp
	(71 mm)	(52 mm)	(206 cc)	(4.1 kW)
VLV60	2.797 in.	2.047 in.	12.6 cu.in.	6.0 hp
	(71 mm)	(52 mm)	206 cc)	(4.5 kW)

ENGINE IDENTIFICATION

Engine is identified by complete model number (A—Fig. T201), specification number (B) and serial number (C) stamped in the blower housing above the muffler. These numbers are necessary in order to obtain correct repair parts.

The model number specifies the engine design and horsepower rating. For instance, model number VLV50 indicates the engine is a Vector Lightweight Vertical with 5.0 horsepower. Model numbers with "XL" indicate the engine has a cast iron cylinder sleeve. The specification number is used when identifying engine parts. The serial number (1024D) is the production date code: 1 — year of manufacture (1991), 024 —last three digits of date code represent calendar day of year (24th day of January), D — represents shift and assembly line on which engine was produced.

It is important to transfer the blower housing from an original engine to a replacement short block assembly so the engine can be identified when servicing.

MAINTENANCE

LUBRICATION. All engines are equipped with a barrel and plunger type oil pump. Oil is forced through the camshaft into a passage on top of the crankcase and through holes to the upper main bearing and an oil spray hole.

Oil level should be checked after every five hours of operation. Maintain oil level at lower edge of filler plug or at "FULL" mark on dipstick.

Engine oil should meet or exceed latest API service classification. Use SAE 30 or SAE 10W-30 motor oil for temperatures above 32° F (0° C). Use SAE 5W-30 or SAE 10W for temperatures below 32° F (0° C). SAE 10W-40 motor oil should not be used.

Oil should be changed after the first two hours of engine operation (new or rebuilt engine) and after every 25 hours of operation thereafter. Oil drain plug is located in the oil pan and is accessible on underside of mower deck. Drain oil after engine has been operating and is still warm.

SPARK PLUG. Spark plug should be removed, cleaned and adjusted periodically. Note that manufacturer does not recommend using a sand blaster to clean spark plugs as particles of abrasive left in the plug can damage the engine.

Recommended spark plug is Champion RJ19LM or equivalent. Specified spark plug electrode gap for all models is 0.030 inch (0.76 mm). Tighten spark plug to 15 ft.-lbs. (20 N•m) torque. If torque wrench is not available, install plug finger tight then use spark plug wrench to tighten plug additional 1/8-1/4 turn.

AIR FILTER. The engine is equipped with a paper filter and a foam precleaner filter (Fig. T202). To service air filter, loosen screw securing filter cover (12) and swing cover down on hinge. Remove paper filter (11) and foam precleaner (6).

The foam filter should be cleaned, inspected and re-oiled after every 25 hours of engine operation, or after three months, whichever occurs first. Clean the filter in soapy water then squeeze the filter until dry (don't twist the filter). Inspect the filter for tears and holes or any other opening. Discard the filter if it cannot be cleaned satisfactorily or if the filter is torn or otherwise damaged. Pour clean engine oil into the filter, then squeeze the filter to remove the excess oil and distribute oil throughout the filter.

The paper filter should be replaced annually or more frequently if the engine operates in a severe environment, such as extremely dusty conditions. A

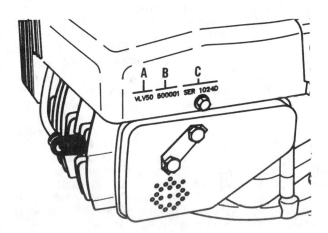

Fig. T201—Model number (A), specification number (B) and serial number (C) are stamped in blower housing above muffler.

Illustrations courtesy Tecumseh Products Co.

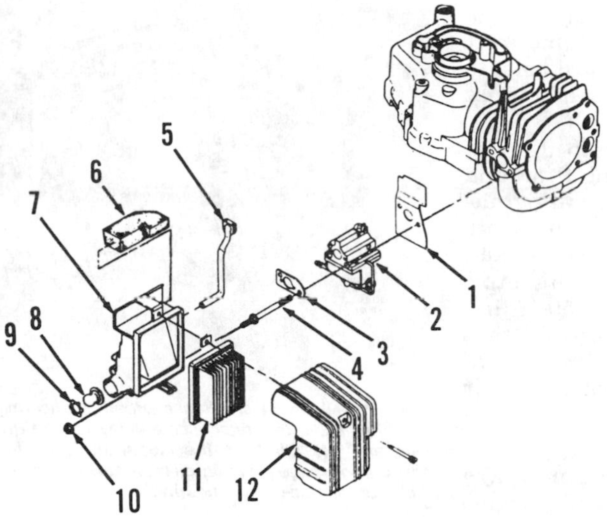

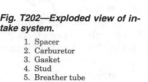

Fig. T202—Exploded view of intake system.

1. Spacer
2. Carburetor
3. Gasket
4. Stud
5. Breather tube
6. Precleaner element
7. Air cleaner box
8. Primer bulb
9. Retainer
10. Nut
11. Air filter element
12. Cover

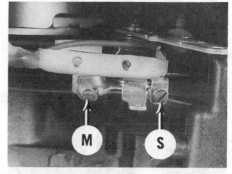

Fig. T205—View showing location of idle speed screw (S) and maximum governed speed screw (M).

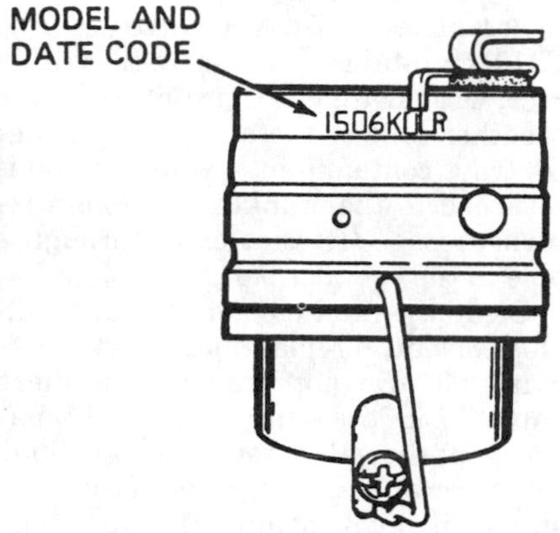

MODEL AND DATE CODE

Fig. T203—Carburetor model and date code number is stamped on carburetor body.

dirty filter cannot be cleaned and must be discarded.

Prior to installing filter, clean all dirt from around carburetor air inlet. Install paper filter with pleated side facing outward. Install precleaner filter and filter cover making certain that hinge engages slot in bottom of cover. Tighten cover screw.

CARBURETOR. A Tecumseh float type carburetor is used on all models. The carburetor is identified by a model number and date code stamped on carburetor body (Fig. T203). Use the engine and carburetor model numbers when obtaining parts.

Refer to Fig. T204 for an exploded view of the carburetor. The body is extruded aluminum while the plastic fuel bowl is secured by a bail wire (22). Some carburetors may be equipped with a removable main jet (18), however, only one size is available.

A primer bulb (8—Fig. T202) is located on the side of the air cleaner body. A tube connects the primer bulb to the

carburetor. Air pressurized by the primer bulb forces fuel up the carburetor nozzle into the carburetor bore for starting.

Fuel mixture is not adjustable. Engine idle speed is adjusted by turning idle speed screw (S—Fig. T205) which is accessible through a slot in the control panel. Engine idle speed should be adjusted to the idle speed specified by the equipment manufacturer, or if unavailable, adjust the idle speed so the engine idles smoothly (approximately 1500 rpm).

Because most major carburetor components are contained in the fuel bowl, most service can be performed by removing the fuel bowl without removing the carburetor body. Push the bail that secures the fuel bowl towards the engine to release the fuel bowl. To remove carburetor, first remove air cleaner cover (12—Fig. T202) and air cleaner box (7). Remove studs retaining carbu-

retor, withdraw carburetor from engine and disconnect throttle linkage.

When disassembling the carburetor, refer to Fig. T204 and note the following: Detach fuel bowl retaining bail by pushing towards throttle end of carburetor. Don't lose spring (15) under nozzle (13). Insert a screwdriver under float arm and carefully pry float pin free from posts in fuel bowl. A retaining ring (10) is located above the fuel inlet seat which should be extracted before removing the fuel inlet valve seat. Compressed air can be used to dislodge the inlet valve seat, but cover the fuel bowl so the seat will not be ejected uncontrolled. Some engines are equipped with a removable main jet (18). When removing Welch plug (6) be sure underlying metal is not damaged.

Clean carburetor with suitable carburetor cleaning solution. Blow out passages with compressed air. Inspect components for excessive wear and damage. Float height is not adjustable.

When assembling carburetor note the following: Install Welch plug (6) with concave side toward carburetor. Do

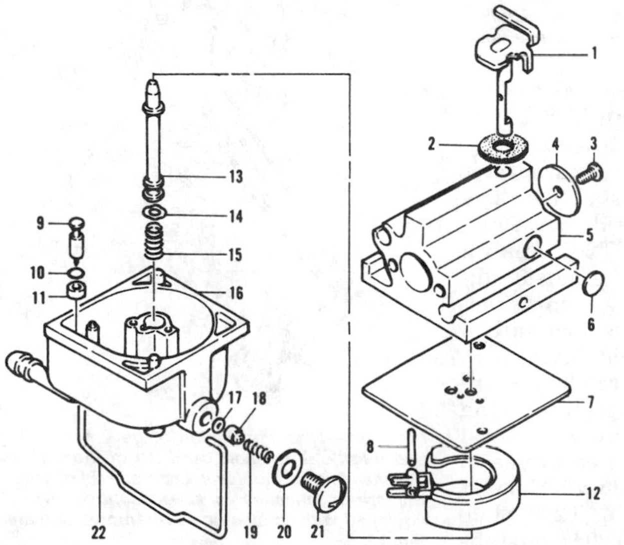

Fig. T204—Exploded view of carburetor. Main jet (18) is not used on all models.

1. Throttle shaft
2. Felt washer
3. Screw
4. Throttle plate
5. Body
6. Welch plug
7. Gasket
8. Float pin
9. Fuel valve
10. Retaining ring
11. Fuel inlet valve seat
12. Float
13. Nozzle
14. "O" ring
15. Spring
16. Fuel bowl
17. "O" ring
18. Main jet
19. Spring
20. Washer
21. Drain screw
22. Bail

Fig. T206—Install throttle plate so line is as shown.

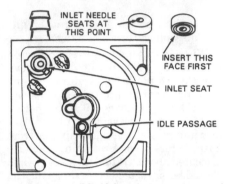

Fig. T207—Install fuel inlet valve seat so grooved side is down and ridged side is up as shown.

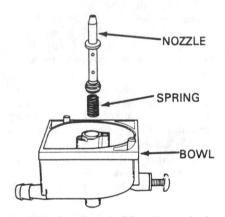

Fig. T208—Install nozzle (N) as shown. Apply a small amount of oil to "O" ring to ease insertion.

not indent plug; plug should be flat after installation. Install throttle plate so line is visible and toward top of carburetor as shown in Fig. T206. Install fuel valve inlet seat with grooved side down and ridge up as shown in Fig. T207. Apply a small amount of oil to the outside diameter of the seat to ease insertion. Push the seat in using a tool with a 5/32-inch diameter so seat bottoms in bore. Be careful not to scratch bore. Install and push down retaining ring against valve seat. Apply a small amount of oil to "O" ring on nozzle to ease insertion of the nozzle, which must be installed as shown in Fig. T208. Slide fuel inlet valve (9—Fig. T204) into tabs

on float (12) and insert float pin (8) into hinge on float. Position float and inlet valve in fuel bowl and snap float pin into tabs in fuel bowl. The float height is not adjustable.

To install the primer bulb (8—Fig. T202), place the retainer ring (9) around the bulb with retainer tabs pointing outward. Push the bulb and retainer into the carburetor using a deep well socket.

When reinstalling carburetor, tighten carburetor studs to 50-75 in.-lbs. (5.7-8.4 N•m). Make certain that breather tube (5—Fig. T202) is connected to breather compartment and air cleaner box.

GOVERNOR. All engines are equipped with a mechanical (flyweight) type governor. Maximum governed speed is adjusted by turning adjusting screw (M—Fig. T205) which is accessible through a slot in the control panel.

To adjust the governor linkage, refer to Fig. T209 and loosen governor lever screw (S). Rotate governor shaft clamp clockwise as far as possible. Move the governor lever until carburetor throttle shaft is in wide open position, then tighten governor lever clamp screw.

Binding or worn governor linkage will result in hunting or unsteady engine operation. An improperly adjusted carburetor will also cause a surging or hunting condition.

Note attachment of governor spring and throttle link to governor lever in Fig. T209. The throttle link end with the short bend should be attached to the governor lever.

CRANKCASE BREATHER. The crankcase breather is located under the

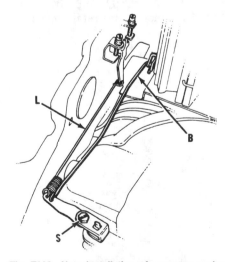

Fig. T209—Note installation of governor spring and throttle link. Short bend (B) of throttle link attaches to governor lever. Long end (L) of governor spring attaches to speed control lever. If equipped with an electric starter motor, see also Fig. T226.

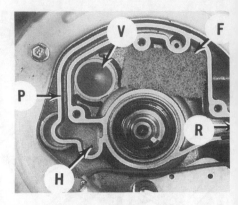

Fig. T210—View of crankcase breather showing breather valve (V), filter element (F) and return passage (R). Oil from the camshaft is routed through passage (P) to an oil mist hole and an oil hole for the upper main bearing.

flywheel beneath a cover on the top of the crankcase. Disc type valve (V—Fig. T210) maintains a vacuum in the crankcase. Crankcase gases are routed via a breather tube to the air cleaner. Filter (F) traps contaminants, while any oil is returned to the crankcase through return passage (R) that exits through a hole in the cylinder bore.

Clean the filter element (F) in a suitable solvent. A replacement parts set is available. Do not remove the check valve (V) unless faulty as removal may break off the valve stem, which will fall into the crankcase. The edge of the valve should fit snugly against the valve seat, which is pressed into the crankcase. Inspect the valve for cracks and other damage. Check for a blocked return passage. Lubricate stem of new check valve to ease installation.

Oil leaking around the cover may be due to the filter element trapped under outer edge of cover or a plugged lubrication hole (H).

IGNITION SYSTEM. Standard ignition system on all models is a solid-state electronic system which does not have breaker points. The only moving part of the system is the rotating flywheel with the charging magnets. There is no scheduled maintenance.

Air gap between solid-state module and flywheel should be 0.0125 inch (0.32 mm). Use Tecumseh gage 670297 or equivalent thickness plastic strip to set gap.

VALVE ADJUSTMENT. Clearance between valve tappet and valve stem (engine cold) is 0.008 inch (0.03 mm) for intake and exhaust valves. To check clearance, first remove spark plug and ground spark plug wire to cylinder block. Remove muffler (29—Fig. T211) and valve tappet chamber cover (28—

Illustrations courtesy Tecumseh Products Co.

Fig. T211). Rotate crankshaft so piston is at TDC on compression stroke (both valves closed). Use a feeler gauge to measure clearance between each tappet and valve stem end. Grind valve stem end as necessary to increase clearance. Cut valve seat deeper or renew valve and/or tappet to reduce clearance.

REPAIRS

TIGHTENING TORQUES. Recommended tightening torque specifications are as follows:

Carburetor studs ...... 50-75 in.-lbs.
(5.6-8.5 N•m)
Connecting rod........ 95-110 in.-lb.
(11-12 N•m)
Cylinder head........ 180-220 in.-lbs.
(20.3-24.8 N•m)
Flywheel.............. 33-36 ft.-lbs.
(45-50 N•m)
Oil pan .... 100-130 in.-lbs.
(11.3-14.7 N•m)

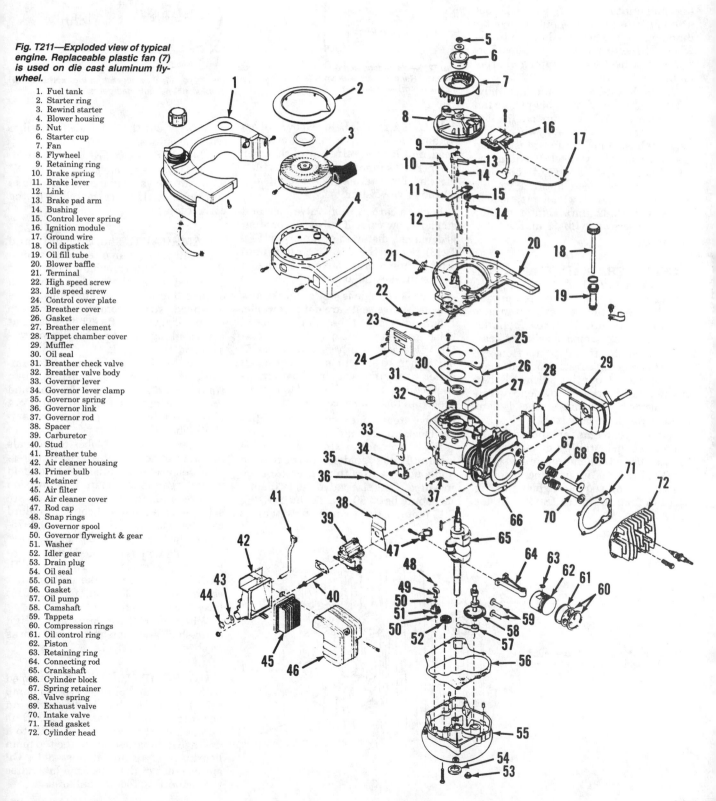

Fig. T211—Exploded view of typical engine. Replaceable plastic fan (7) is used on die cast aluminum flywheel.

1. Fuel tank
2. Starter ring
3. Rewind starter
4. Blower housing
5. Nut
6. Starter cup
7. Fan
8. Flywheel
9. Retaining ring
10. Brake spring
11. Brake lever
12. Link
13. Brake pad arm
14. Bushing
15. Control lever spring
16. Ignition module
17. Ground wire
18. Oil dipstick
19. Oil fill tube
20. Blower baffle
21. Terminal
22. High speed screw
23. Idle speed screw
24. Control cover plate
25. Breather cover
26. Gasket
27. Breather element
28. Tappet chamber cover
29. Muffler
30. Oil seal
31. Breather check valve
32. Breather valve body
33. Governor lever
34. Governor lever clamp
35. Governor spring
36. Governor link
37. Governor rod
38. Spacer
39. Carburetor
40. Stud
41. Breather tube
42. Air cleaner housing
43. Primer bulb
44. Retainer
45. Air filter
46. Air cleaner cover
47. Rod cap
48. Snap rings
49. Governor spool
50. Governor flyweight & gear
51. Washer
52. Idler gear
53. Drain plug
54. Oil seal
55. Oil pan
56. Gasket
57. Oil pump
58. Camshaft
59. Tappets
60. Compression rings
61. Oil control ring
62. Piston
63. Retaining ring
64. Connecting rod
65. Crankshaft
66. Cylinder block
67. Spring retainer
68. Valve spring
69. Exhaust valve
70. Intake valve
71. Head gasket
72. Cylinder head

Spark plug . . . . 180 in.-lbs.
(20.3 N·m)

FLYWHEEL. Before removing flywheel (8—Fig. T211), disengage flywheel brake as outlined in FLYWHEEL BRAKE section. Remove ignition module (16). Remove flywheel nut (5) and cup (6). Use a suitable flywheel puller or knockoff nut to remove flywheel. Do not attempt to use jaw type puller on outer diameter of flywheel as damage to flywheel will occur. Gently pry against bottom of flywheel while tapping sharply on nut.

Compress brake lever and install flywheel. Note that removable plastic fan (7) has a boss on the bottom that fits into a recess on top of the flywheel. The Tecumseh logo on the fan must be on magnet side of flywheel. Tighten flywheel nut to 33-36 ft.-lbs. (45-50 N·m). Set air gap between ignition module laminations and flywheel magnets to 0.0125 inch (0.32 mm). Tighten module mounting screws to 30-40 in.-lbs. (3.4-4.5 N·m).

CYLINDER HEAD. To remove cylinder head (72—Fig. T211), remove blower housing (4). Clean area around cylinder head to prevent entrance of foreign material. Unscrew cylinder head screws and remove cylinder head.

Clean combustion deposits from cylinder head being careful not to damage cylinder head mounting surface. Renew cylinder head if there is evidence of broken fins or if mounting surface is damaged or warped excessively.

A new head gasket should be installed when installing cylinder head. Tighten cylinder head retaining screws in 50 in-lb. (5.6 N·m) increments following tightening sequence shown in Fig. T212 to final torque of 180-220 in.-lbs. (20.3-24.8 N·m).

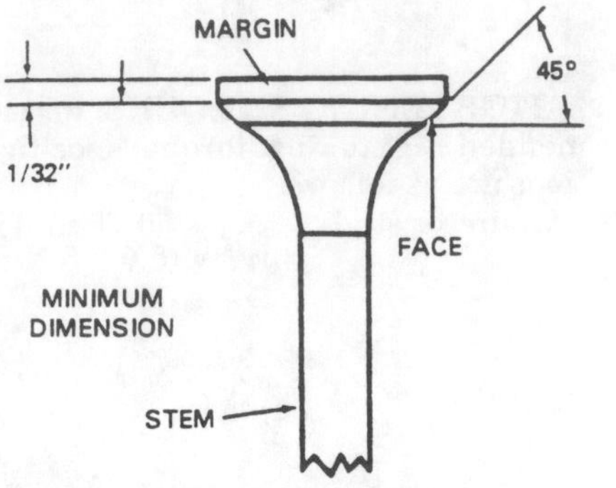

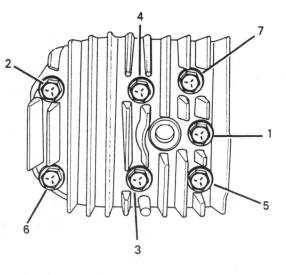

Fig. T212—Tighten cylinder head screws in sequence shown.

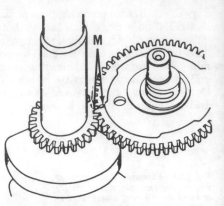

Fig. T214—View of aligned timing marks (M) on crankshaft and camshaft gears.

Fig. T213—Valve face angle is 45° for intake and exhaust. Renew valve if margin is less than 1/32 inch (0.8 mm) after grinding.

VALVE SYSTEM. To remove valves (69 and 70—Fig. T211), remove cylinder head, muffler and valve tappet chamber cover (28). Compress valve spring, then move spring retainer (67) so it will slip off end of valve stem.

Remove carbon from valve face and stem. Renew valve if valve face or stem is damaged, distorted or if margin (Fig. T213) is less than 1/32 inch (0.8 mm) after grinding face. Valve face angle is 45° for intake and exhaust.

Valve seat angle is 46° for intake and exhaust. Valve seats are not renewable. If burned or pitted they can be refaced using grinding stone or valve seat cutter. Valve seat width should be 0.035-0.045 inch (0.89-1.14 mm). Use a 60° cutter to narrow seat from bottom toward center and a 30° cutter to narrow seat from top toward center.

Valve stem guides are cast into cylinder block and are not renewable. If excessive clearance exists between valve stem and guide, guide should be reamed and a new valve with an oversize stem installed. Oversize valve guide diameter should be 0.2807-0.2817 inch (7.130-7.155 mm). After reaming valve guides

oversize, recut the valve seats to align with the guides.

Note that valves are not identical. Exhaust valve is marked "EX" or "X" while intake valve is marked "I". Make certain that they are installed in the correct location.

CAMSHAFT. The camshaft and camshaft gear are an integral part (58—Fig. T211). The camshaft journals at each end of camshaft ride in bores in cylinder block and oil pan. Camshaft is equipped with a compression release mechanism which lifts exhaust valve at low cranking rpm to reduce compression and aid starting.

Remove oil pan (55) for access to camshaft. When removing camshaft, align timing marks on camshaft gear and crankshaft gear as shown in Fig. T214 to relieve valve spring pressure on camshaft lobes.

Renew camshaft if lobes or journals are worn or scored. Spring on compression release mechanism should hold weight against camshaft. Compression release mechanism and camshaft are serviced as an assembly only. Standard camshaft journal diameter is 0.4975-0.4980 inch (12.637-12.649 mm).

The oil pump is operated by an eccentric on the camshaft. Refer to OIL PUMP paragraph. Make certain that chamfered side of oil pump (Fig. T215) faces the camshaft gear.

When installing camshaft, align crankshaft and camshaft timing marks as shown in Fig. T214.

OIL PUMP. The engine is equipped with a barrel and plunger type oil pump (57—Fig. T211) that is driven by an eccentric on the camshaft. Oil is pumped up through the camshaft to a passage in breather box to the top main bearing and to an oil mist hole. Oil sprayed out of the mist hole lubricates the connecting rod journal area.

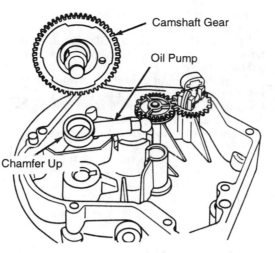

Fig. T215—Install oil pump so chamfered side is toward camshaft gear.

Camshaft Gear

Oil Pump

Chamfer Up

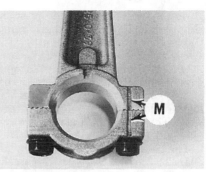

Fig. T218—Match marks (M) on connecting rod and rod cap must be aligned and toward pto end of crankshaft after installation.

Pump is available only as a unit assembly. When installing oil pump, make certain that chamfered side of drive collar (Fig. T215) is toward camshaft gear.

PISTON, PIN AND RINGS. Aluminum alloy piston is equipped with two compression rings and one oil control ring. To remove piston, remove cylinder head, oil pan and connecting rod cap. Before removing piston, remove any carbon or ring ridge from top of cylinder to prevent ring breakage. Piston and connecting rod assembly is removed from cylinder head end of engine.

If piston is removed from connecting rod, identify the valve side of piston. Install piston to connecting rod so that piston will be in same position when installed in engine. New piston can be installed on connecting rod in either direction.

Remove rings from piston and clean deposits from ring grooves and piston crown. Inspect piston skirt for scoring, scuffing or other damage and renew as necessary. Piston and rings are available in standard size and 0.010 inch (0.25 mm) and 0.020 inch (0.50 mm) oversizes for all engines. Oversize pistons are identified by the size imprinted on piston crown.

Standard piston diameter measured at piston skirt 90 degrees from piston pin bore is 2.7900-2.7910 inches (70.866-70.891 mm). Piston skirt-to-cylinder clearance is 0.004-0.006 inch (0.10-0.15 mm).

Piston ring end gap is 0.007-0.020 inch (0.18-0.50 mm). To check ring end gap (Fig. T216), use the piston to push ring squarely down into cylinder approximately 1 inch (25 mm). Use a feeler gauge to measure ring end gap.

To check piston ring grooves for wear, insert piston ring in ring groove and use a feeler gauge to measure clearance between piston ring land and top of ring

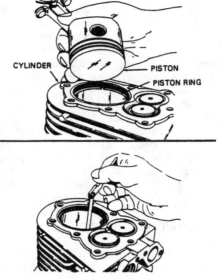

CYLINDER

PISTON

PISTON RING

Fig. T216—Measure piston ring end gap with a feeler gauge.

(Fig. T217). Standard ring side clearance in ring grooves is 0.002-0.005 inch (0.05-0.13 mm) for compression rings and 0.0005-0.0035 inch (0.013-0.089 mm) for oil ring. Renew piston if clearance exceeds specifications. Excessive side clearance can cause piston ring "flutter" resulting in a poor seal between ring and cylinder and possible ring breakage.

Piston pin is retained by retaining rings at each end of piston pin bore. Piston pin should be a tight push fit in

piston pin bore and connecting rod pin bore.

When installing rings on piston, take care that rings are not spread too wide or breakage will result. Install top and second piston rings with beveled edge toward piston crown (Fig. T217). Oil control ring may be installed either side up. When installing connecting rod and piston assembly, align the match marks on connecting rod and cap as shown in Fig. T218. Install piston so match marks on connecting rod face outward (toward power take-off end of crankshaft). Lubricate piston and cylinder with clean engine oil. Stagger ring end gaps equally around circumference of piston before installation.

CONNECTING ROD. The aluminum alloy connecting rod rides directly on crankshaft crankpin.

Crankpin diameter should be 1.0230-1.0235 inch (25.088-25.103 mm). Standard inside diameter for connecting rod big end should be 1.0240-1.0246 inch (25.088-25.103 mm). Connecting rod bearing-to-crankpin journal clearance should be 0.0005-0.0016 inch (0.013-0.041 mm) for all models.

Assemble connecting rod and piston as outlined in previous section. Be sure that match marks (M—Fig. T218) on connecting rod and cap are aligned and facing outward when installed in engine. Tighten connecting rod screws to 95-110 in.-lb. (11-12 N·m).

GOVERNOR. On early models, the governor is retained on the shaft by snap rings (48—Fig. T211). To remove

Fig. T217—Top and second compression rings must be installed with beveled inside edge toward piston crown. Measure ring side clearance with feeler gauge. Refer to text.

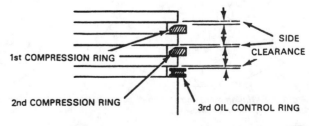

1st COMPRESSION RING

2nd COMPRESSION RING

3rd OIL CONTROL RING

SIDE CLEARANCE

governor spool (49), detach upper snap ring. Detach lower snap ring to remove flyweight and gear assembly (50). Washer (51) is located under the gear.

On later engines and replacement governor shafts, no snap rings are used on the governor shaft. The governor is held in place by a boss on the governor shaft. The flyweights and gear are available only as a unit assembly.

The governor gear is driven by idler gear (52) that meshes with the camshaft gear. The idler gear shaft is pressed into the oil pan and is not renewable.

The governor shaft is pressed into the oil pan and may be replaced if the mounting boss is not damaged or the hole is not enlarged. To remove the governor shaft, clamp the shaft in a vise and using a soft mallet, drive the oil pan off the shaft. Do not attempt to twist governor shaft out of boss. Twisting will enlarge hole. Apply Loctite 271 (red) to shaft end. When installing the retainerless design shaft, position washer and governor gear assembly on shaft before installing shaft, then press shaft into oil pan until the governor gear has 0.010-0.020 inch (0.25-0.50 mm) axial play.

CRANKSHAFT, MAIN BEARINGS AND SEALS. Always note oil seal depth and direction before removing oil seal from crankcase or cover. New seals must be pressed into seal bores to the same depth as old seal before removal on all models. Lubricate lip of new seal with grease prior to installing crankshaft.

The crankshaft gear is pressed on the crankshaft. The crankshaft gear timing mark should be in the 2:30 position relative to the crankpin (see Fig. T219), otherwise the gear has moved. In some instances the gear can be relocated sat-

isfactorily, but if not, the crankshaft must be replaced.

Refer to CONNECTING ROD section for standard crankshaft crankpin journal diameters.

Crankshaft main bearing journals ride directly in the aluminum alloy bores in the cylinder block and oil pan. Standard main bearing bore diameter for main bearings is 1.0257-1.0262 inch (26.053-26.066 mm).

Standard diameter for crankshaft main bearing journals is 1.0237-1.0242 inch (26.002-26.015 mm).

When installing crankshaft, align crankshaft and camshaft gear timing marks as shown in Fig. T214.

CYLINDER AND CRANKCASE. Cylinder and crankcase are an integral casting on all models. Models VLXL50 and VLXL55 are equipped with a cast iron sleeve in the cylinder bore. Oversize piston and rings are available for all engines. Cylinder should be honed and fitted to nearest oversize for which piston and ring set are available if cylinder is scored, tapered or out-of-round more than 0.005 inch (0.13 mm).

Standard cylinder bore diameter is 2.7950-2.7960 inch (70.993-71.018 mm). Note that some engines were manufactured with cylinders that are oversize. The piston is marked on the piston crown with the oversize value.

FLYWHEEL BRAKE. The engine is equipped with a flywheel brake that simultaneously stops the flywheel and grounds the ignition. The brake should stop the engine within three seconds when the operator releases the mower safety control and the speed control is in high speed position. Engine rotation is stopped by a pad type brake that contacts the inside of the flywheel when the operator's handle is released (Fig T220).

On engines with an electric starter, a switch mounted on the flywheel brake

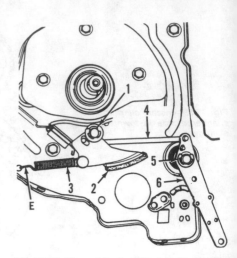

Fig. T221—View of flywheel brake with flywheel removed. Long hook end (E) of spring must attach to baffle plate.

1. "E" ring	4. Brake link
2. Brake pad arm	5. "E" ring
3. Brake spring	6. Brake lever

lever prevents starter engagement unless the flywheel brake is disengaged.

To hold the flywheel brake in the disengaged position, bend a piece of 3/32 inch (2.5 mm) metal rod so there is approximately one inch (25 mm) between the bends. Remove the left screw securing the speed control cover. Move the flywheel brake lever to the disengaged position and insert bent ends of the metal rod into the outer hole of the brake lever and the speed control cover screw hole. Tecumseh offers tool No. 36114 to hold the brake lever in the disengaged position.

To disassemble flywheel brake assembly, hold flywheel brake in disengaged position as previously outlined. Remove blower housing and flywheel. To remove brake pad (2—Fig. T221), remove pad arm "E" ring (1). Disconnect brake spring (3) and link (4) and withdraw pad arm. For reference during assembly, mark hole (H—Fig. T222) on bottom of baffle plate that holds brake lever spring end. If equipped with electric starter, mark and disconnect wires to starter switch on brake lever. Remove

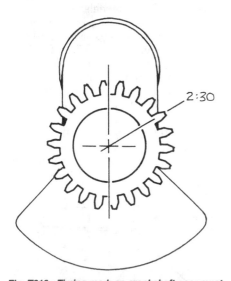

Fig. T219—Timing mark on crankshaft gear must be in 2:30 position as shown.

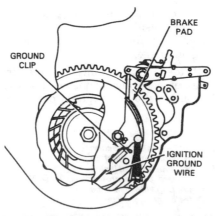

Fig. T220—The flywheel brake contacts the inside edge of flywheel.

Fig. T222—Flywheel brake lever spring end should be installed in original hole (H) in baffle plate.

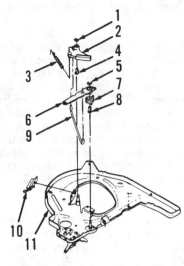

Fig. T223—Exploded view of flywheel brake.

1. "E" ring	
2. Brake arm	7. Spring
3. Brake spring	8. Bushing
4. Bushing	9. Link
5. "E" ring	10. Switch
6. Brake lever	11. Baffle plate

Fig. T225—Exploded view of electric starter motor.

1. "E" ring
2. Plastic washer
3. Drive hub
4. Rubber driver
5. Pinion gear
6. Spring
7. Plastic spring cup
8. Metal cup
9. "E" ring
10. Metal washer
11. Plastic washer
12. Locknuts
13. Nut
14. Drive plate
15. Armature
16. Frame
17. End cap & brush assy.
18. Through-bolt

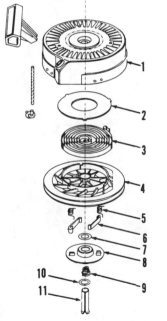

Fig. T224—Exploded view of rewind starter.

1. Starter housing	
2. Cover	7. Plastic washers (2)
3. Rewind spring	8. Retainer
4. Pulley	9. Brake spring
5. Springs (2)	10. Metal washer
6. Pawls (2)	11. Pin

"E" ring (5), disconnect control link (4) and withdraw brake lever (6).

Replace the brake pad and arm if the pad is damaged, contaminated by oil, or worn to a thickness less than 0.060 inch (1.52 mm).

Note the following when reassembling flywheel brake components. The brake pad arm and brake lever ride on renewable plastic bushings. Install bushings (4 and 8—Fig. T223) so flange is toward bottom of brake arm (2) or lever (6). Correct installation of brake link (9) is determined by number of bosses on link end. The end that attaches to brake pad arm has four bosses, while brake lever end has three bosses. The brake lever spring end must be inserted in original hole (H—Fig. T222) in baffle plate. Note that brake spring (3—Fig. T221) end with the short hook must be attached to brake arm (2) and long hook end (E) to baffle plate.

REWIND STARTER. An exploded view of starter is shown in Fig. T224. To disassemble starter, remove rope handle and allow rope to wind into starter. Position a suitable sleeve support under pawl retainer (8), then use a 5/16 inch (8 mm) punch to drive pin (11) out of starter. Remove brake spring (9), retainer (8), pawls (6) and springs (5). Wear appropriate safety eyewear and gloves before disengaging pulley from starter as spring may uncoil uncontrolled. Place shop towel around pulley and lift pulley out of housing; spring should remain with pulley.

Inspect components for damage and excessive wear. Rope length is 98 inches (249 cm) and rope diameter is 9/64 inch. Reverse disassembly procedure to install components. Rewind spring coils wind in clockwise direction from outer end. Wind rope around pulley in counterclockwise direction as viewed from retainer side of pulley. Be sure inner end of rewind spring engages spring retainer adjacent to housing center post. Use two plastic washers (7). Install a new pin (11) so top of pin is 1/8 inch (3.2 mm) below top of starter. Driving pin in too far may damage retainer pawl.

ELECTRIC STARTER. Tecumseh does not provide test specifications for electric starter motors, so service is limited to replacing components that are known or suspected faulty.

Refer to Fig. T225 for an exploded view of the starter motor. Disassembly and reassembly is evident after inspection of motor and referral to Fig. T225 Minimum brush length is not specified. Renew brushes if the brush wire bottoms against the slot in the brush holder. Brushes must not bind in the holders. Brushes are available only as a unit assembly with end cap. Bushings are not available separately; only as a

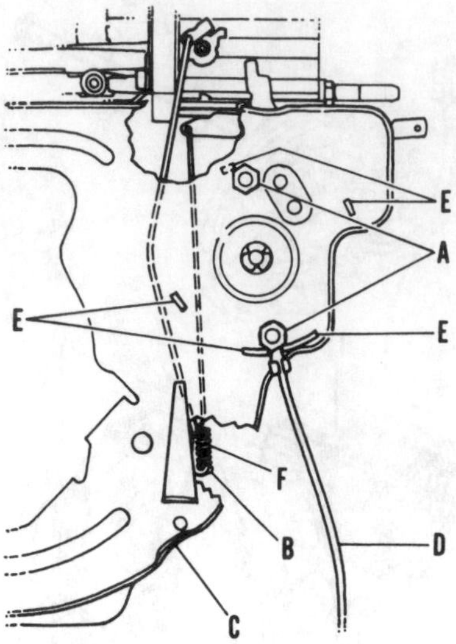

Fig. T226—Drawing showing installation of starter motor. Index tabs on motor fit in slots (T) in baffle plate. Governor spring (S) passes between index tabs on motor.

A. Starter nuts
B. Governor lever
C. Baffle plate

D. Ground wire
E. Slots
F. Governor spring

unit assembly with drive plate or end cap.

When installing starter motor, place ground wire on starter motor stud near governor lever (B—Fig. T226) before installing motor on baffle plate (C). The ground wire (D) fits between two adjacent index tabs on drive end plate of starter motor. The index tabs must fit into slots (E) on baffle plate. Note that governor spring (F) passes between tabs on starter motor. Tighten starter mounting nuts to 20-30 in.-lbs. (2.5-3.4 N•m)

A switch mounted on the flywheel brake lever prevents starter engagement unless the flywheel brake is disengaged.

TECUMSEH
4-STROKE OHV ENGINES

Model	Bore	Stroke	Displacement	Rated Power
OVRM40	2.5 in.	1.844 in.	9.05 cu.in.	4.0 hp
	(63.5 mm)	(46.8 mm)	(148.3 cc)	(3.0 kW)
OVRM50	2.625 in.	1.938 in.	10.49 cu.in.	5.0 hp
	(66.68 mm)	(49.23 mm)	(172 cc)	(3.7 kW)
OVRM55	2.625 in.	1.938 in.	10.49 cu.in.	5.5 hp
	(66.68 mm)	(49.23 mm)	(172 cc)	(4.1 kW)
OVRM60	2.625 in.	1.938 in.	12.00 cu.in.	6.0 hp
	(66.68 mm)	(49.23 mm)	(172 cc)	(4.5 kW)

ENGINE INFORMATION

All engines are air-cooled, four-stroke, single-cylinder engines. The engine has a vertical crankshaft and utilizes an overhead valve system.

Engine is identified by model number and specification number stamped in the blower housing (Fig. T301). These numbers are necessary in order to obtain correct repair parts.

The model number specifies the engine design and horsepower rating. For instance, model number OVRM55 indicates the engine is an overhead valve rotary mower model with 5.5 horsepower.

It is important to transfer the blower housing from an original engine to a replacement short block assembly so the engine can be identified when servicing.

MAINTENANCE

LUBRICATION. All engines are equipped with a barrel and plunger type oil pump that provides pressure lubrication to top main bearing and camshaft upper bearing.

Oil level should be checked after every five hours of operation. Maintain oil level at lower edge of filler plug or at "FULL" mark on dipstick.

Engine oil should meet or exceed latest API service classification. Use SAE 30 or SAE 10W-30 motor oil for temperatures above 32° F (0° C). Use SAE 5W-30 or SAE 10W for temperatures below 32° F (0° C). SAE 10W-40 motor oil should not be used.

Oil should be changed after the first two hours of engine operation (new or rebuilt engine) and after every 25 hours of operation thereafter. Oil drain plug is located in the oil pan and is accessible on underside of mower deck. Drain oil after engine has been operating and is still warm.

AIR FILTER. The filter element may be made of foam or paper, or a combination of both foam and paper. The recommended maintenance inter-

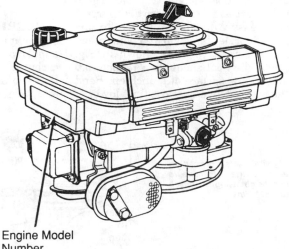

Fig. T301—Model and specification number are stamped in blower housing.

Engine Model
Number

val depends on the type of filter element.

Foam type filter elements should be cleaned, inspected and re-oiled after every 25 hours of engine operation, or after three months, whichever occurs first. Clean the filter in soapy water then squeeze the filter until dry (don't twist the filter). Inspect the filter for tears and holes or any other opening. Discard the filter if it cannot be cleaned satisfactorily or if the filter is torn or otherwise damaged. Pour clean engine oil into the filter, then squeeze the filter to remove the excess oil and distribute oil throughout the filter.

Paper type filter elements should be replaced annually or more frequently if the engine operates in a severe environment, such as extremely dusty conditions. A dirty filter element cannot be cleaned and must be discarded.

SPARK PLUG. Spark plug should be removed, cleaned and adjusted periodically. Note that manufacturer does not recommend using a sand blaster to clean spark plugs as particles of abrasive left in the plug can damage the engine. Renew spark plug if electrode is pitted or burned or if porcelain is cracked.

Recommended spark plug is a Champion RN4C or equivalent. Specified spark plug electrode gap is 0.030 inch (0.76 mm). Tighten spark plug to 20 ft.-lbs. (27 N•m). If a torque wrench is not available, finger tighten plug then use spark plug wrench to turn a used plug an additional 1/8-1/4 turn or a new plug an additional 1/2 turn.

CARBURETOR. A float type carburetor is used on all engines. No adjustments are possible. A primer bulb is located on the side of the carburetor for cold starting enrichment.

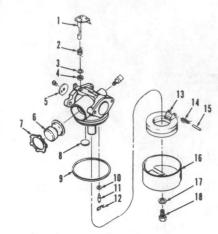

Fig. T302—Exploded view of carburetor.

1. Throttle shaft	10. Inlet valve seat
2. Spring	11. Fuel inlet valve
3. Washer	12. Clip
4. Seal	13. Float
5. Throttle plate	14. Dampener spring
6. Primer bulb	15. Pin
7. Retainer	16. Fuel bowl
8. Welch plug	17. Washer
9. "O" ring	18. Main jet/nut

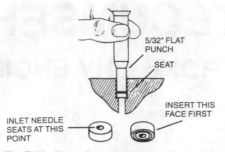

Fig. T303—Use a flat punch to install new inlet valve seat. Be sure that smooth side of seat faces outward and that bottoms in the bore.

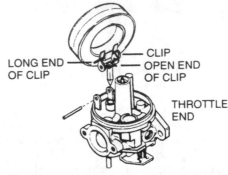

Fig. T304—Install inlet valve clip so long end points toward intake end of carburetor.

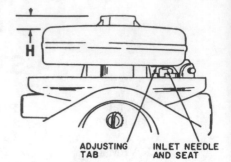

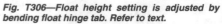

Fig. T306—Float height setting is adjusted by bending float hinge tab. Refer to text.

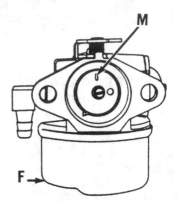

Fig. T307—Mark (M) on throttle plate must point up. Flat area (F) of fuel bowl must be positioned over fuel inlet valve and parallel with float hinge pin.

Refer to Fig. T302 for an exploded view of carburetor. To disassemble, remove fuel bowl retaining nut (18) and withdraw fuel bowl (16). Push hinge pin (15) from carburetor body and remove float (13) and fuel inlet needle (11). Remove screw attaching throttle plate (5) to throttle shaft (1). Withdraw throttle shaft and remove washer (3) and dust seal (4). To remove primer bulb (6), grasp bulb with pliers and roll bulb out of carburetor body. Pry primer bulb retainer away from carburetor body. Remove Welch plug (8).

The fuel inlet valve needle seats against a Viton seat (10) which must be removed before cleaning. The seat can be removed using a hooked wire to pull seat from carburetor body. Welch plug (8) must be removed to thoroughly clean fuel passages. Use a small sharp punch to pry Welch plug from body, using care not to damage metal beneath the plug. Clean carburetor body and fuel bowl using commercial carburetor cleaning solvent. Blow out passages with compressed air.

Renew needle and seat if fuel delivery problems such as flooding or starvation are experienced. Check float for cracks, wear or evidence of leagage and renew as necessary.

Note the following special instructions when reassembling carburetor. The grooved face of fuel inlet needle valve seat should be in toward bottom of bore and the valve needle should seat on smooth side of the Viton seat (Fig. T303). Be sure seat is installed squarely and bottomed in bore. Install Welch plug (8—Fig. T302) with concave side toward carburetor. Do not indent plug;

plug should be flat after installation. Install inlet valve clip as shown in Fig. T304 so long end of clip will point toward intake end of carburetor (away from throttle plate).

A gauge is available from Tecumseh (part No. 670253A) that can be used to determine the correct float height. With carburetor inverted, position gauge 670253A at a 90° angle to the carburetor bore and resting on the nozzle stanchion as shown in Fig. T305. The toe of the float should not be higher than the first step on the gauge or lower than the second step. Bend the float tab to adjust the float height. If float gauge is not available, float height (H—Fig. T306) can be set as follows: Invert carburetor and measure distance from float to surface of nozzle stanchion at a point opposite fuel inlet valve as shown in Fig. T306. The float should be 3/16 inch (5.0 mm) below surface of stanchion. Bend the float tab to adjust the float level.

Fig. T305—Use procedure described in text to measure float height using Tecumseh tool 670253A.

Install throttle plate so scribe mark points up as shown in Fig. T307; no light should be visible around throttle plate when closed. A new throttle plate retaining screw should be used. Install fuel bowl with new gasket. Flat area (F—Fig. T307) of bowl is located over fuel inlet valve and crease runs parallel to float pin. To install the primer bulb (6—Fig. T302), start the bulb and retainer ring (7) into housing with retainer tabs facing outward. Push the bulb and retainer into the carburetor using a deep well socket.

CARBURETOR CONTROL. The engine may be equipped with a control panel mounted on intake pipe above the carburetor or on the side of the engine that contains a high speed stop screw and an idle speed stop screw. Adjust

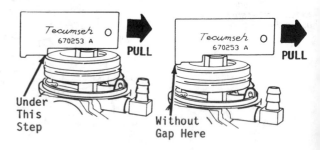

Illustrations courtesy Tecumseh Products Co.

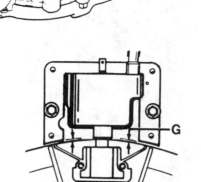

Fig. T308—Drawing of typical governor linkage. Refer to text for adjustment procedure.

PUSH LEVER TO WIDE OPEN THROTTLE

GOVERNOR CLAMP SCREW

screws as necessary to set engine speeds to equipment manufacturer's specifications.

GOVERNOR. The engine is equipped with a mechanical, flyweight type governor. To adjust governor linkage, proceed as follows: With engine stopped, loosen governor lever clamp screw (Fig. T308). Push governor lever so throttle plate is fully open and hold lever in place. Turn governor shaft clamp counterclockwise as far as possible, then tighten lever clamp screw.

If internal governor assembly must be serviced, refer to REPAIRS section.

CRANKCASE BREATHER. The engine is equipped with a crankcase breather that provides a vacuum for the crankcase. Vapor from the crankcase is evacuated to the intake manifold. A check valve in the breather vents positive pressure pulsations into the breather element. A tube directs crankcase gases to the air cleaner. The breather system must operate properly or excessive oil consumption may result.

The breather assembly is mounted in the top rear side of cylinder block. Periodically remove and clean the breather element.

IGNITION SYSTEM. A one-piece ignition coil/module is located adjacent to the outer periphery of the flywheel. Ignition timing is not adjustable. Set air gap between module leg laminations and flywheel by loosening mounting screws and positioning module to obtain an air gap of 0.0125 inch (0.32 mm). See Fig. T309. Tighten mounting screws to 30-40 in.-lbs. (3.4-4.5 N•m).

VALVE ADJUSTMENT. Clearance between rocker arm and valve stem is checked and adjusted with engine cold. Remove rocker arm cover. Rotate crankshaft so piston is at top dead center on compression stroke (both valves closed). Valve clearance should be 0.004 inch (0.10 mm) for intake and exhaust. To

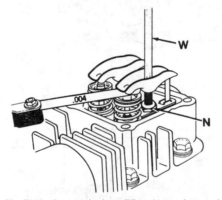

Fig. T309—Air gap (G) between coil legs and flywheel should be 0.0125 inch (0.32 mm).

Fig. T310—Loosen locknut (N) and turn pivot stud using Allen wrench (W) to adjust valve clearance. Specified clearance is 0.004 inch (0.10 mm) for intake and exhaust.

adjust clearance, loosen locknut (N—Fig. T310) and using an Allen wrench (W), turn rocker pivot stud to obtain desired clearance. Tighten lock nut to 65-85 in.-lbs. (7.3-9.6 N•m).

REPAIRS

TIGHTENING TORQUES. Recommended tightening torque specifications are as follows:

Connecting rod	105 in.-lbs. (12.0 N•m)
Oil pan	115 in.-lbs. (13.0 N•m)
Cylinder head	230 in.-lbs. (26.0 N•m)
Flywheel nut	35 ft.-lbs. (47 N•m)
Intake pipe	95 in.-lbs. (10.5 N•m)
Ignition module	45 in.-lbs. (5.0 N•m)
Rocker arm cover	40 in.-lbs. (4.5 N•m)
Rocker stud lock nut	75 in.-lbs. (8.5 N•m)
Spark plug	20 ft.-lbs. (27 N•m)

FLYWHEEL. Before flywheel can be removed, first remove fuel tank assembly, rewind starter and blower shroud. Disengage flywheel brake as outlined in FLYWHEEL BRAKE section. Remove flywheel retaining nut and starter cup. If flywheel has tapped holes, use a suitable puller to remove flywheel. If no holes are present, screw a knockoff nut onto crankshaft as shown in Fig. T311 so there is a small gap between nut and flywheel. Gently pry against bottom of flywheel while tapping sharply on nut. After installing flywheel, tighten flywheel nut to 33-36 ft.-lbs. (45-49 N•m).

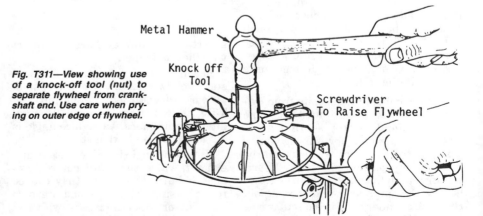

Fig. T311—View showing use of a knock-off tool (nut) to separate flywheel from crankshaft end. Use care when prying on outer edge of flywheel.

Metal Hammer

Knock Off Tool

Screwdriver To Raise Flywheel

Illustrations courtesy Tecumseh Products Co.

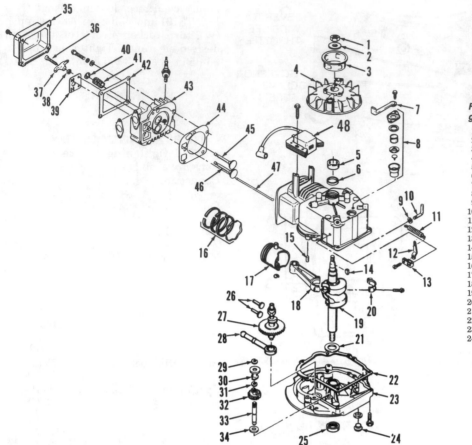

Fig. T312—Exploded view of Model OVRM50 engine. Other models are similar.

1.	Flywheel nut	25.	Oil seal
2.	Belleville washer	26.	Tappets
3.	Starter cup	27.	Camshaft
4.	Flywheel	28.	Oil pump
5.	Spacer	29.	Snap ring
6.	Oil seal	30.	Governor spool
7.	Breather tube	31.	Snap ring
8.	Crankcase breather assy.	32.	Governor gear
9.	Washer	33.	Shaft
10.	Governor shaft	34.	Washer
11.	Governor spring	35.	Rocker arm cover
12.	Governor lever	36.	Pivot stud
13.	Clamp	37.	Rocker arm
14.	Key	38.	Locknut
15.	Dowel pin	39.	Push rod guide plate
16.	Piston rings	40.	Valve spring retainer
17.	Piston	41.	Valve spring
18.	Connecting rod	42.	Gasket
19.	Crankshaft	43.	Cylinder head
20.	Connecting rod cap	44.	Head gasket
21.	Thrust washer	45.	Intake valve
22.	Gasket	46.	Exhaust valve
23.	Oil pan	47.	Push rod
24.	Drain plug	48.	Ignition coil/module

CYLINDER HEAD AND VALVE SYSTEM. Refer to Fig. T312 for an exploded view of cylinder head and valve system. To remove the cylinder head, first remove fuel tank, rewind starter and blower housing. Note governor and throttle linkage connecting points to aid in reassembly, then remove air cleaner, carburetor and intake manifold. Remove muffler and rocker arm cover. Loosen pivot stud lock nuts (38) and remove rocker arm studs (36), rocker arms (37) and guide plate (39); mark components so they can be returned to original location. Unscrew cylinder head bolts and remove cylinder head (43), head gasket (44) and push rods (47). To remove valves, compress valve spring and move spring retainer (40) so valve stem slides through large opening in the retainer.

Clean combustion deposits from cylinder head taking care not to damage cylinder head gasket sealing area. Check cylinder head for warpage using a straightedge. Slight warpage can be corrected by placing sheet of 400 grit wet/dry sandpaper on a flat surface. Lubricate the sandpaper with honing oil, then rub cylinder head in a circular pattern on the sandpaper until the entire

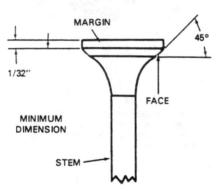

Fig. T313—Drawing of engine valve. Renew valve if margin is less than 1/32 inch (0.8 mm) after grinding face.

gasket area shows evidence of contact with the sandpaper.

Remove carbon from valve face and stem. Renew valve if valve face or stem is damaged, distorted or if margin (Fig. T313) is less than 1/32 inch (0.8 mm) after grinding face. Valve face angle is 45° for intake and exhaust.

Valve seat angle is 46° for intake and exhaust. Valve seats are not replaceable. If burned or pitted they can be refaced using grinding stone or valve seat cutter. Specified seat width is 0.035-0.045 inch (0.90-1.15 mm). Use a

60° cutter to narrow seat from bottom toward center and a 30° cutter to narrow seat from top toward center.

Valve guides are cast into cylinder head and are nonrenewable. If excessive clearance exists between valve stem and guide, guide must be reamed and a new valve with an oversize stem installed. Oversize valve guide diameter should be 0.2807-0.2817 inch (7.130-7.155 mm) for intake and 0.2787-2797 inch (7.078-7.106 mm) for exhaust to fit valve with 1/32 inch (0.8 mm) oversize stem. After reaming valve guides oversize, recut the valve seats to align with the guides.

Renew push rods if bent or if ends are worn or damaged. If excessive wear is evident, inspect rocker arms and valve lifters for wear also.

Renew valve springs if they are distorted or show signs of overheating. Valve spring free length should be minimum of 1.105 inch (28.07 mm).

Note the following when reinstalling cylinder head. If valve spring has dampening coils (Fig. T314), install spring with dampening coils toward cylinder head. Install push rod guide plate (39—Fig. T312) with tabs around push rod guide slots facing outward. Make cer-

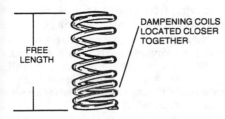

Fig. T314—Some valve springs are made with dampening coils which should be installed toward the cylinder head.

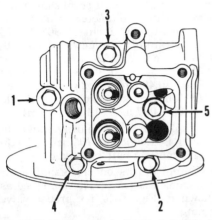

Fig. T315—Tighten cylinder head bolts in 60 in.-lb. (6.7 N•m) increments in sequence shown.

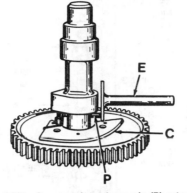

Fig. T316—Compression release pin (P) extends during starting to hold exhaust valve off its seat.

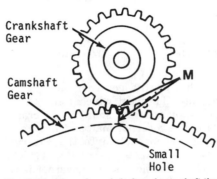

Fig. T317—View of crankshaft and camshaft timing marks (M). Marks must be aligned during assembly for proper valve timing.

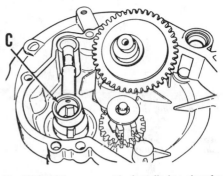

Fig. T318—Oil pump must be installed so chamfer (C) is toward camshaft.

tain that mating surfaces of cylinder block and head are clean. The metal head gasket must be renewed whenever cylinder head is removed. Do not apply sealer to cylinder head gasket; new gasket is precoated with a sealing substance. If coating is scratched or if gasket is bent, gasket should be discarded and another gasket installed. Leakage may occur if a damaged gasket is installed. Tighten cylinder head bolts in steps of 60 in.-lbs. (6.8 N•m) using sequence shown in Fig. T315 until final torque reading of 230 in.-lbs. (26.0 N•m) is obtained.

Install push rods (47—Fig. T312), locknuts (38), rocker arms (37) and pivot studs (36) in their originial locations. Rotate crankshaft until piston is at top dead center on compression stroke. Turn pivot stud until clearance between valve stem and rocker arm is 0.004 inch (0.10 mm) for intake and exhaust. Tighten locknut to 75 in.-lbs. (8.5 N•m) while holding pivot stud. Install rocker arm cover with new gasket and tighten screws to 40 in.-lbs. (4.5 N•m).

CAMSHAFT. Camshaft and camshaft gear are an integral casting which is equipped with a compression release mechanism. The compression release pin (P—Fig. T316) extends at cranking speed to hold the exhaust valve open

slightly thereby reducing compression pressure.

To remove camshaft, remove engine from mower deck. Remove rocker arm cover (35—Fig. T312) and disengage push rods (47) from rocker arms (37). Drain engine oil, then remove oil pan (23) and withdraw camshaft.

Specified camshaft bearing journal diameter is 0.4975-0.4980 inch (12.636-12.649 mm). Renew camshaft if lobes or journals are excessively worn or scored. Inspect compression release mechanism and check for proper operation. Compression release components and camshaft are available only as a unit assembly.

When installing camshaft, align crankshaft and camshaft timing marks shown in Fig. T317.

OIL PUMP. The engine is equipped with a barrel and plunger type oil pump located in the oil pan. The pump is driven by an eccentric on the camshaft. As the camshaft rotates, the eccentric moves the barrel back and forth on plunger. Oil is pumped up through a passage in the camshaft to lubricate the top main bearing and camshaft bearing. Oil is sprayed out under pressure through a mist hole located between top

of camshaft and crankshaft to lubricate piston, connecting rod and other rotating parts.

Pump is available only as a unit assembly. When installing oil pump, make certain that chamfered side of drive collar (Fig. T318) is toward camshaft gear.

PISTON, PIN, RINGS AND CONNECTING ROD. To remove piston and rod assembly, drain engine oil and remove engine from mower deck. Remove cylinder head as previously outlined. Clean pto end of crankshaft and remove any burrs or rust. Unscrew fasteners and remove oil pan. Remove camshaft. Remove carbon or ring ridge (if present) from top of cylinder before removing piston. Unscrew connecting rod screws and push piston and rod assembly out top of cylinder.

To separate piston from connecting rod, remove piston pin retaining ring and push piston pin from piston and connecting rod. Remove rings from piston and clean combustion deposits from ring grooves. Inspect all parts for wear or damage.

Insert new rings in piston ring grooves and measure side clearance (Fig. T319) between ring and ring land using a feeler gauge. Piston ring side clearance should be .002-0.005 inch (0.05-0.13 mm) for compression rings and 0.0005-0.0035 inch (0.013-0.089

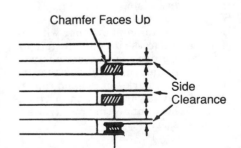

Fig. T319—Inside chamfer on top compression ring must face top of piston. Measure ring side clearance to determine ring groove wear.

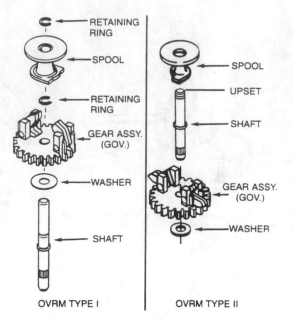

Fig. T320—Type I governor used retaining rings to secure components to governor shaft, while Type II unit uses a boss on shaft to retain gear and spool.

mm) for oil ring. Renew piston if side clearance is excessive.

Position piston rings squarely in cylinder bore and measure ring end gap using a feeler gauge. Specified piston ring end gap is 0.007-0.017 inch (0.18-0.43 mm). If ring end gap exceeds specifications, cylinder should be rebored for installation of oversize piston and rings.

Standard piston diameter measured at bottom of skirt 90 degrees from piston pin hole is 2.4950-2.4952 inches (63.373-63.378 mm) for Model OVRM40 and 2.6202-2.6210 inches (66.553-66.573 mm) for Models OVRM50 and OVRM55. Piston-to-cylinder clearance should be 0.0040-0.0058 inch (0.10-0.15 mm). Oversize pistons are available in sizes of 0.010 and 0.020 inch (0.25 and 0.50 mm).

The connecting rod rides directly on crankshaft. Connecting rod big end diameter is 0.8620-0.8625 inch (21.895-21.907 mm) for OVRM40 and 1.0005-1.0010 inch (25.413-25.425 mm) for OVRM50 and OVRM55.

When installing piston rings, be careful not to spread the rings too wide or breakage could result. Place top compression ring on piston so inside chamfer is toward piston crown (Fig. T319). Stagger ring end gaps around piston. Lubricate piston and cylinder with engine oil, compress rings and install piston and connecting rod assembly in cylinder. Install piston and connecting rod so match marks on rod and cap are aligned and toward pto end of crankshaft. Tighten connecting rod screws to 105 in.-lbs. (11.8 N•m).

GOVERNOR. The governor gear and flyweight assembly is located on the inside of the crankcase cover. The fly-

weights on the governor gear (T320) actuate the spool which contacts the governor arm and shaft in the crankcase. The governor shaft and arm transfer governor action to the external governor linkage.

On early models, the governor is retained on the shaft by a snap ring (left drawing—Fig. T320). To remove spool, detach upper snap ring. Detach lower snap ring to remove flyweight and gear assembly. Washer is located under the gear.

On later engines, no snap rings are used on the governor shaft (right drawing—Fig. T320). The governor is held in place by a boss on the governor shaft. The governor shaft must be removed to remove governor gear. The flyweights and gear are available only as a unit assembly.

The governor shaft is pressed into the oil pan and may be replaced if the mounting boss is not damaged or the hole is not enlarged. To remove the governor shaft, clamp the shaft in a vise and using a soft mallet, drive the oil pan off the shaft. Do not attempt to twist governor shaft out of boss. Twisting will enlarge hole.

To install new governor shaft, apply Loctite 271 (red) to shaft end. When installing the retainerless design governor shaft, position washer and governor gear assembly on shaft before installing shaft, then press shaft into oil pan boss until the governor gear has 0.010-0.020 inch (0.25-0.50 mm) axial play.

CRANKSHAFT, MAIN BEARINGS AND OIL SEALS. The crankshaft rides directly in aluminum alloy bores of crankcase. Make certain crankshaft is free of rust, scale or burrs before

removing from engine to prevent damage to crankshaft main bearings.

Note oil seal depth and direction before removing old seals (6 and 25—Fig. T312) from crankcase or cover. Install new seals to depth of old seals. Lubricate seal lip with engine oil before reinstalling crankshaft.

Inspect crankshaft bearing journals for wear, scoring or out of round condition. Check crankshaft for straightness. DO NOT attempt to straighten a bent crankshaft. Standard crankshaft main bearing journal diameter for both ends is 0.9985-0.9990 inch (25.362-25.375 mm). Crankpin diameter is 0.8610-0.8615 inch (21.869-21.882 mm) for OVRM40 and 0.9995-1.000 inch (25.387-25.400 mm) for OVRM50 and OVRM55. Crankshaft end play should be 0.005-0.027 inch (0.13-0.69 mm).

Crankcase main bearing inner diameter is 1.0005-1.0010 inch (25.413-25.425 mm) for both bearing bores.

Timing marks on crankshaft gear and camshaft gear must be aligned as shown in Fig. T317 for proper valve timing.

CYLINDER. Standard cylinder bore diameter is 2.500-2.501 inches (63.500-63.525 mm) for Model OVRM40 and 2.625-2.626 inches (66.675-66.700 mm) for Models OVRM50 and OVRM55. If cylinder bore wear or out-of-round exceeds 0.005 inch (0.13 mm), cylinder should be bored to the next oversize.

FLYWHEEL BRAKE. The engine is equipped with a flywheel brake that utilizes a pad which is forced against the inner surface of the flywheel (Fig. T321). The brake should stop the engine within three seconds when the operator releases mower safety control and the speed control is in high speed position. A ground clip kills the ignition when the brake is actuated. On models with electric start, a switch prevents starting when the brake pad contacts the flywheel.

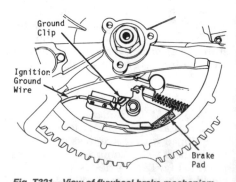

Fig. T321—View of flywheel brake mechanism.

Illustrations courtesy Tecumseh Products Co.

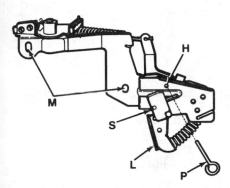

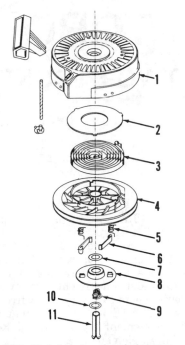

Fig. T322—Push against lever (L) and insert pin (P) through holes (H) to hold brake pad away from flywheel. Interlock switch (S) is used on engines with an electric starter.

The flywheel must be removed to service the brake pad. Before removing flywheel, push lever (L—Fig. T322) towards spark plug so brake pad moves away from flywheel. Insert Tecumseh tool 670298 or a suitable pin in hole (H) to hold lever. Inspect mechanism for damage and excessive wear. Minimum allowable thickness of brake pad at narrowest point is 0.060 inch (1.52 mm). Install brake mechanism and push up on bracket so bracket mounting screws are at bottom of slotted holes (M) in bracket. Tighten mounting screws to 90 in.-lbs. (10.2 N•m).

REWIND STARTER. To disassemble starter, unbolt and remove starter assembly from blower housing. Remove rope handle and allow rope to wind into starter. Remove plastic disc from center of starter housing and position a suitable sleeve support (a 1 inch deep well socket) under pawl retainer (8—Fig. T323). Using a ⁵⁄₁₆ inch diameter punch, drive pin (11) free of starter. Remove brake spring (9), retainer (8), pawls (6) and springs (5). Wear appropriate safety eyewear and gloves before disengaging pulley (4) from starter as spring

Fig. T323—Exploded view of rewind starter.

1. Starter housing
2. Cover
3. Rewind spring
4. Pulley
5. Springs (2)
6. Pawls (2)
7. Plastic washers (2)
8. Pawl retainer
9. Brake spring
10. Metal washer
11. Pin

may uncoil uncontrolled. Place shop towel around pulley and lift pulley out of housing; spring should remain with pulley.

Inspect components for damage and excessive wear. Rope length is 98 inches (249 cm) and rope diameter is ⁹⁄₆₄ inch (3.5 mm).

When reassembling, note the following: Rewind spring coils wind in clockwise direction from outer end. Replacement rewind spring (3) is contained in a holder. To install spring, align outside spring hook with notch in pulley. Carefully push spring out of holder into pulley cavity while guiding outside spring hook into deep notch in

pulley. Push spring cover (2) in until seated in pulley. Install starter pawls (6) so hook end of pawls face inward. Be sure that pawl springs (5) snap the pawls back to center of pulley. Retainer (8) must be installed so that tabs on retainer will force starter pawls to engage starter cup when rope is pulled. Be sure inner end of rewind spring engages spring retainer adjacent to housing center post. Use two new plastic washers (7). Install a new pin (11) so top of pin is ⅛ inch (3.2 mm) below top of starter. Driving pin in too far may damage pawl retainer. Wind rope around pulley in counterclockwise direction as viewed from retainer side of pulley.

Wind starter pulley counterclockwise four or five turns to preload the rewind spring. Thread rope through starter housing eyelet and tie a temporary knot in rope about 12 inches (30 cm) from outer end of rope. Attach handle to rope, then remove temporary knot and allow rope to wind into housing. Rope handle should be held snugly against starter housing.

ELECTRIC STARTER AND ALTERNATOR. Some engines may be equipped with an electric starter and an alternator for battery charging.

Use standard electric motor testing procedures to check starter. If brushes require replacement, entire end cap assembly (14—Fig. T324) must be renewed.

Alternator coil is attached to side of ignition module. Alternator is considered satisfactory if output exceeds battery voltage. To check charging system, connect voltmeter across battery teminals (Fig. T325) and read battery voltage with engine not running. Start engine and again observe voltmeter reading. System is satisfactory if there is an increase in voltage reading when engine is running. If there is no change in voltage, alternator is faulty and should be renewed.

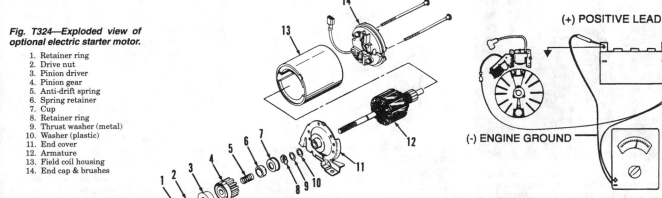

Fig. T324—Exploded view of optional electric starter motor.

1. Retainer ring
2. Drive nut
3. Pinion driver
4. Pinion gear
5. Anti-drift spring
6. Spring retainer
7. Cup
8. Retainer ring
9. Thrust washer (metal)
10. Washer (plastic)
11. End cover
12. Armature
13. Field coil housing
14. End cap & brushes

Fig. T325—Use a voltmeter to check alternator output. Refer to text.

Illustrations courtesy Tecumseh Products Co.

TORO
TWO-STROKE

Model Series 47PZ2, 47PD3, 47PE4, 47PF5	Bore	Stroke	Displacement	Rated Power
	58 mm (2.3 in.)	46 mm (1.8 in.)	121 cc (7.4 cu.in.)	2.6 kW (3.5 hp)

NOTE: Metric fasteners are used throughout engine.

ENGINE INFORMATION

The Toro (Suzuki) 47P engine model series is used on Toro walk-behind lawn mowers. The engine is an air-cooled, two-stroke, single-cylinder with a vertical crankshaft. The engine model number and serial number for all models except Model 47PF5 engines built before 1986 are stamped on blower housing behind the air cleaner (Fig. TO10). Model 47PF5 engines built for 1986 and after are stamped in the blower housing above the spark plug. Always furnish engine model and serial numbers when ordering parts.

MAINTENANCE

LUBRICATION. The engine is lubricated by mixing oil with unleaded gasoline (gasoline blended with alcohol is not recommended). A good quality oil designed for two-stroke engines must be used. Fuel:oil ratio should be 50:1.

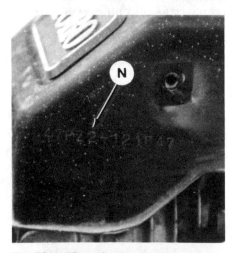

Fig. TO10—View showing location of engine model and serial numbers (N) on all models except Model 47PF5 built for 1986 and after. Model 47PF5 serial numbers are located just above spark plug on cooling shroud.

AIR CLEANER. Engine is equipped with a foam type air cleaner which should be removed and cleaned after every 50 hours of operation. Wash element in a mild detergent and water solution and squeeze out excess water. Allow element to air dry. Apply five teaspoons of SAE 30 oil to element and squeeze element to distribute oil. Reinstall filter element.

FUEL FILTER. A fuel filter is located in the fuel tank outlet. The filter is molded in the tank. If filter is damaged or cleaning will not remove dirt or debris, the fuel tank must be renewed. Some engines may be equipped with an inline fuel filter in the fuel hose.

SPARK PLUG. Spark plug should be removed, cleaned and adjusted periodically. Recommended spark plug is a NGK BPMR4A spark plug or equivalent. Electrode gap should be 0.8 mm (0.032 in.). Tighten spark plug to 9-14 N•m (80-124 in.-lbs.).

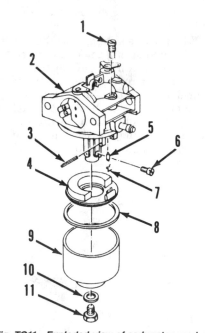

Fig. TO11—Exploded view of carburetor used on Model 47PZ2.

1. Pilot jet
2. Carburetor body
3. Float pin
4. Float
5. Fuel inlet valve
6. Main jet
7. Spring
8. Gasket
9. Float bowl
10. Gasket
11. Bolt

CARBURETOR. All models are equipped with a float type carburetor with a fixed main fuel jet (6—Fig. TO11 or Fig. TO12). Model 47PZ2 engines are equipped with carburetor shown in Fig. TO11. Standard main jet size is a #80, and a high altitude jet #77.5 is available. All other models are equipped with a Mikuni BV 18-15 carburetor shown in Fig. TO12. Standard main jet size is a #76.3, and a high altitude #72.5 main jet is available. Fuel mixture is not adjustable other than replacement of fixed jets.

To disassemble carburetor, refer to Fig. TO11 or Fig. TO12 and remove retaining nut (11) and float bowl (9). Remove float pin (3) by pushing against round end of pin towards the square end of pin. Remove float (4) and fuel inlet needle (5). Unscrew pilot jet (1) and main jet (6). Note that no other parts of carburetor are seviceable separately. Disassembly of throttle and choke plates is not recommended as the retaining screws are locked in place and the threads may be damaged during removal.

Metal parts should be cleaned in carburetor cleaner. Use compressed air to blow out all orifices and passageways. Do not use wires or drill bits to clean orifices as enlargement of the orifice could affect the calibration of the carburetor. Original equipment float for carburetors on 47PZ2 engines should be replaced with a new black float with a metal hinge during service. This float is alcohol resistant and adjustable.

To check float height, invert carburetor and measure float height as shown in Fig. TO13. Float height should be 17.5 mm ($^{11}/_{16}$ in.). Bend float tab to adjust float height. Reassembly of the carburetor is the reverse of disassembly procedure.

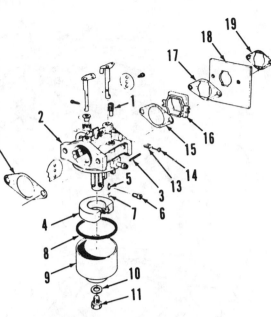

Fig. TO12—Exploded view of carburetor used on Models 47PD3, 47PE4 and 47PF5.

1. Pilot jet
2. Carburetor body
3. Float pin
4. Float
5. Fuel inlet valve
6. Main jet
7. Spring
8. Gasket
9. Fuel bowl
10. Gasket
11. Screw
12. Gasket
13. Spring
14. Idle speed screw
15. Gasket
16. Insulator
17. Gasket
18. Heat deflector
19. Gasket

nected in center hole (B) of bracket (8). Connecting spring in hole (A) increases engine speed by 150 rpm and connecting spring in hole (C) decreases engine speed by 150 rpm.

REPAIRS

TIGHTENING TORQUES. Recommended tightening torque specifications are as follows:

Adapter plate	11.3-15.8 N·m (100-140 in.-lbs.)
Blade cap screw	61-81 N·m (45-60 ft.-lbs.)
Crankcase	7.9-12.4 N·m (70-110 in.-lbs.)
Flywheel nut	40-48 N·m (29-36 ft.-lbs.)
Muffler	11.3-15.8 N·m) (100-140 in.-lbs.)
Spark plug	9.1-13.5 N·m (80-120 in.-lbs.)

IGNITION. Model 47PZ2 engine is equipped with a breaker point type ignition. Flywheel must be removed for access to breaker points. Breaker point gap should be 0.35 mm (0.014 in.). This

Fig. TO13—Float level should be 17.5 mm (¹¹/₁₆ in.).

17.5 mm (11/16 in.)

should allow points to begin opening at 22° BTDC (Fig. TO14).

All other models are equipped with solid-state ignition system. Ignition timing is fixed and not adjustable. Air gap between ignition module and flywheel is adjustable. Air gap between flywheel and module should be 0.38-50 mm (0.05-0.20 in.).

GOVERNOR. The mechanical flyweight governor is located inside engine crankcase. To adjust governor external linkage, first make certain all linkage is in good condition and tension spring (5—Fig. TO15) is not stretched or damaged. Spring (2) must pull governor lever (3) and throttle pivot (4) toward each other. With engine stopped, loosen clamp bolt (7) and move governor lever (3) to the right. Hold governor lever in this position and rotate governor shaft (6) in clockwise direction until it stops. Tighten clamp screw.

Correct engine speed is 3000 rpm and is obtained with tension spring (5) con-

CRANKCASE. The engine is equipped with a split crankcase design. The cylinder (2—Fig. TO16) is integral with a crankcase half. It is necessary to separate crankcase halves for access to internal engine components.

To disassemble crankcase, remove rewind starter, disconnect fuel line at carburetor and lift fuel tank from blower shroud. Remove muffler and heat shield. Remove air cleaner and housing, then remove blower shroud.

Compress mower control bar against handlebar to compress flywheel brake spring. Remove cap screw retaining ignition switch and brake assembly, disconnect switch and slowly release control bar to release flywheel brake spring. Disconnect brake control cable. Remove starter cup and flywheel (use Toro puller 41-7650 or equivalent). DO NOT pry on flywheel or strike end of crankshaft as damage may result. Remove blade, blade adapter and self-propelled components, if so equipped.

Fig. TO014--When timing pointer is aligned with middle mark as shown, timing is set at 22° BTDC. Refer to text.

Timing Marks

Pointer

Fig. TO15—Drawing of governor linkage.

1. Rod
2. Spring
3. Governor lever
4. Throttle lever
5. Governor spring
6. Governor shaft
7. Clamp bolt
8. Bracket
A. Upper hole
B. Middle hole (3000 rpm)
C. Lower hole

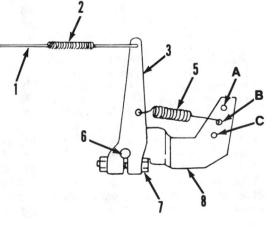

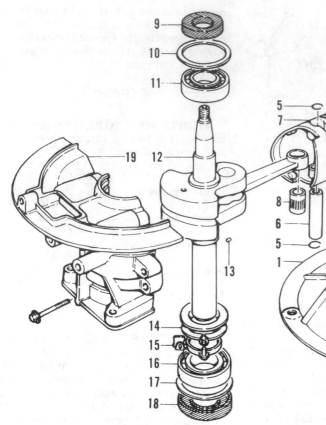

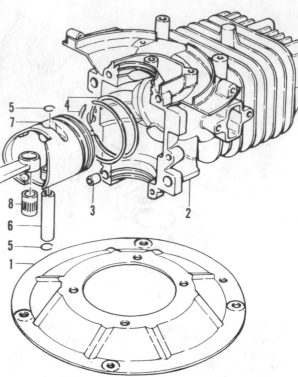

Fig. TO16—Exploded view of engine.

1. Adapter plate
2. Cylinder
3. Dowel pin
4. Piston rings
5. Retaining ring
6. Piston pin
7. Piston
8. Bearing
9. Oil seal
10. Locating ring
11. Bearing
12. Crankshaft assy.
13. Locating pin
14. Governor collar
15. Governor bracket
16. Bearing
17. Locating ring
18. Oil seal
19. Crankcase half

Fig. TO17—Crankcase cap screws are three different lengths on Model 47PZ2 engine.

Disconnect control linkage from engine. Remove engine mounting screws and lift engine from mower deck.

If equipped with breaker points, remove contact point cover and disconnect electrical wires. Remove ignition coil, points and condenser. Remove flywheel key, then slide timing cam off crankshaft and remove cam locating pin.

On all models, remove governor lever, control rod and springs, carburetor, spacer and gaskets. Remove engine adapter plate (1—Fig. TO16). Unscrew crankcase retaining screws (note location of different length screws). Carefully separate crankcase halves. Remove crankshaft and piston assembly. Remove seals (9 and 18), bearing locating rings (10 and 17) and bearings (11 and 16) from crankshaft ends. Slide governor assembly from crankshaft; use care not to lose locating pin (13) for governor flyweight collar (14). Remove retaining rings (5) from piston pin bores and remove piston pin (6) and piston (7) from connecting rod. DO NOT attempt to disassemble the three-piece crankshaft assembly (12) as crankshaft damage will occur. The crankshaft and connecting rod are serviced as an assembly.

When reassembling engine, note the following special instructions: Lubricate piston, connecting rod needle bear-

ings and crankshaft main bearings with two-cycle engine oil. Make certain that the piston ring end gaps are aligned with the locating studs in piston ring grooves before pushing the piston into the cylinder.

NOTE: Arrow on piston crown must face toward exhaust port side of cylinder.

Be sure that the locating pin (13—Fig. TO16) is in place in the crankshaft and that the governor collar (14) engages the pin. Apply small amount of #2 grease to lip of seals (9 and 18). Remove any burrs from either end of crankshaft, then install seals with lip facing into the

crankcase. Apply a thin coat of Loctite 515 sealant to crankcase mating surfaces before mating crankcase halves. Note that three different length screws are used to attach crankcase halves together on Model 47PZ2; see Fig. TO17 for screw location. Cap screws on all other models are all the same length. Tighten crankcase screws to 9-12 N·m (80-106 in.-lbs.). On Model 47PZ2, install ignition cam with locating pin, condenser, contact points and ignition coil. Rotate crankshaft until contact point cam follower is on high point of cam, and adjust point gap to 0.35 mm (0.014 in.). On all models, assemble gaskets, heat deflector, and carburetor in order shown in Fig. TO12. Assemble governor control lever, linkage and springs. Adjust gover-

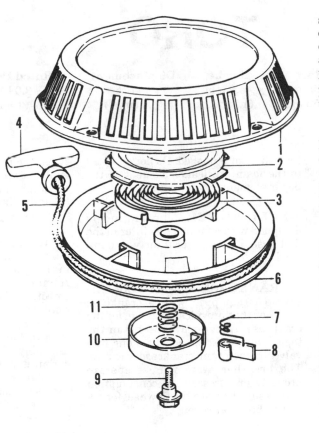

Fig. TO18—Exploded view of rewind starter.

1. Starter housing
2. Spring case
3. Rewind spring
4. Rope handle
5. Rope
6. Pulley
7. Pawl spring
8. Pawl
9. Center screw
10. Retainer
11. Spring

scored, excessively worn, out-of-round or otherwise damaged. Measure cylinder diameter at top of cylinder, just above intake port and just below third port at bottom. Specified cylinder diameter is 58.000-58.115 mm (2.2835-2.2880 in.).

CRANKSHAFT, MAIN BEARINGS AND SEALS. Crankshaft and connecting rod are serviced as a unit assembly. Crankshaft and connecting rod are not available separately. Refer to CRANKCASE section for disassembly procedure.

Crankshaft runout should be checked at a point 38.1 mm (1.5 in.) from each end of crankshaft. Standard runout is 0-0.05 mm (0-0.002 in.). Renew crankshaft if total indicated runout exceeds 0.20 mm (0.008 in.). Standard crankshaft end play is 0-0.94 mm (0-0.037 in.) and maximum allowable end play is 1.5 mm (0.060 in.). Standard crankshaft diameter at flywheel end is 19.993-20.00 mm (0.7871-0.7874 in.). Crankshaft diameter at pto end is 24.972-24.993 mm (0.9831-0.9840 in.).

REWIND STARTER. To remove rewind starter, unscrew four retaining screws and lift starter assembly off of blower housing.

To disassemble starter, remove rope handle and allow rope to wind slowly into starter housing. Remove center screw (9—Fig. TO18), then remove pawl retainer (10), spring (11), pawl (8) and spring (7). Wear appropriate safety eyewear and gloves when removing pulley from starter or when separating rewind spring (3) and spring case (2) from pulley.

When reassembling starter, install spring (7) and pawl (8) so the spring end forces the pawl toward the center of the pulley. Apply Loctite 242 to threads of center screw (9). Tighten screw to 8-11 N•m (71-97 in.-lbs.).

FLYWHEEL BRAKE. Some engines are equipped with a pad type flywheel brake. The brake should stop the engine within three seconds when the operator releases mower safety control and the speed control is in high speed position. Adjust cable as needed for proper operation.

nor linkage as previously outlined in MAINTENANCE section. Install flywheel and tighten mounting nut to 40-48 N•m (29-36 ft.-lbs.). Adjust air gap between flywheel magnets and ignition coil laminations to 0.5 mm (0.020 in.). Install engine on mower deck and reconnect control linkage. Tighten blade retaining screw to 61-81 N•m (45-60 ft.-lbs.). Install blower housing, fuel tank and rewind starter.

PISTON, PIN AND RING. The engine is equipped with a cam-ground aluminum piston and two piston rings. Disassemble engine as outlined in CRANKCASE section for access to piston. When removing and installing piston rings, be careful not to overstretch and distort the rings.

Standard piston ring end gap is 0.15-0.35 mm (0.006-0.014 in.) and maximum allowable end gap is 0.7 mm (0.027 in.). Specified piston ring side clearance in piston ring grooves is 0.03-0.15 mm (0.001-0.006 in.) measured at

bottom side of ring. Renew piston if side clearance is excessive.

Standard piston-to-cylinder clearance is 0.025-0.055 mm (0.0010-0.0022 in.). Piston-to-cylinder bore clearance should not exceed 0.1 mm (0.004 in.). Measure piston diameter at points perpendicular to piston pin and 2.5 mm (1 in.) from bottom of piston skirt. Measure cylinder diameter 110 mm (4.3 in.) from bottom of cylinder.

Specified piston pin diameter is 11.955-12.005 mm (0.4707-0.4726 in.).

The top piston ring has chrome plating on the outer diameter. Install piston rings with side marked "R" toward top of piston. Align the ring end gaps with the locating studs in piston ring grooves before installing piston in cylinder. Lubricate piston pin, rings and cylinder with two-cycle engine oil when reassembling. Arrow on piston crown must face toward exhaust port side of cylinder.

CYLINDER. Cylinder (2—Fig. TO16) is integral with upper crankcase half. Cylinder should be renewed if

TORO

Model Series	Bore	Stroke	Displacement	Rated Power
VM	64.0 mm	44.0 mm	141 cc	3.0 kW
	(2.52 in.)	(1.73 in.)	(8.6 cu.in.)	(4 hp)

NOTE: Metric fasteners are used throughout engine.

ENGINE INFORMATION

The Toro (Suzuki) VM engine model series is used on Toro walk-behind lawn mowers. The engine is an air-cooled, four-stroke, single-cylinder engine with a vertical crankshaft and an overhead valve system. Engine identification numbers are stamped in the blower housing.

MAINTENANCE

LUBRICATION. The engine is lubricated by oil supplied by a rotor type oil pump located in the bottom of the crankcase, as well as by a slinger driven by the camshaft gear.

Change oil after first two hours of operation and after every 25 hours of operation or at least once each operating season.

Engine oil level should be maintained at full mark on dipstick. Engine oil should meet or exceed latest API service classification. Manufacturer recommends SAE 30 or SAE 10W-30 oil.

Crankcase capacity is 0.55 L (18.6 fl. oz.). Fill engine with oil so oil level reaches, but does not exceed, full mark on dipstick.

AIR CLEANER. Engine may be equipped with a foam filter element or with a paper filter element and a foam precleaner element.

Foam filter elements should be cleaned after every 25 hours of operation. Paper filter elements should be cleaned or replaced after every 50 hours of operation. Service either type filter element more frequently if severe operating conditions are encountered.

Clean a foam filter in soapy water and squeeze until dry. Inspect filter for tears and holes or any other opening. Discard filter if it cannot be cleaned satisfactorily or if it is torn or otherwise damaged. Pour clean engine oil into the filter, then squeeze to remove excess oil and distribute oil throughout.

Clean a paper filter by tapping gently to dislodge accumulated dirt. Renew fil-ter if dirty or damaged. Do not apply oil to the foam precleaner element or the paper element.

FUEL FILTER. The engine is equipped with an inline fuel filter in the fuel hose. Renew filter if dirty or damaged.

CRANKCASE BREATHER. The engine is equipped with a crankcase breather that provides a vacuum for the crankcase. A reed valve located in the top of the crankcase acts as a one-way valve to maintain crankcase vacuum. The breather system must operate properly or excessive oil consumption may result. Remove the flywheel for access to breather cover.

SPARK PLUG. Recommended spark plug is NGK BPR6ES. Specified spark plug electrode gap is 0.8 mm (0.032 in.).

CARBURETOR. The engine is equipped with a Mikuni BV 18-13 float type carburetor. Refer to Fig. TO51 for exploded view of carburetor. Carburetor is equipped with a fixed idle mixture jet (7) and a fixed high speed jet (22).

Initial adjustment of idle pilot screw (10) should be one turn open from a lightly seated position. Make final carburetor adjustment with engine at normal operating temperature and running. Adjust pilot screw to obtain smoothest idle operation and acceleration.

To remove carburetor, drain fuel and remove fuel tank. Remove air cleaner assembly. Note the connecting points of carburetor control linkage and springs to insure correct reassembly, then disconnect choke rod and throttle rod and remove carburetor. To install carburetor, reverse the removal procedure. Note that a gasket should be installed on both sides of insulator block (9—Fig. TO51) and raised rib on air cleaner gasket (24) should be toward the air cleaner.

Remove float pin by pushing against round end of pin towards the square end of pin. Float is plastic and float level is not adjustable. Fuel inlet valve (21) is

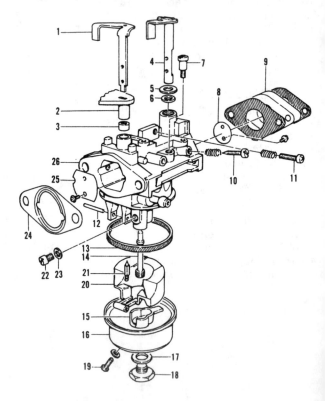

Fig. TO51—Exploded view of carburetor.

1. Choke shaft
2. Choke detent
3. Spacer
4. Throttle shaft
5. Washer
6. Dust seal
7. Idle pilot jet
8. Choke plate
9. Insulator block
10. Pilot screw
11. Idle speed screw
12. Float pin
13. Gasket
14. Nozzle
15. Spacer
16. Float bowl
17. Gasket
18. Screw
19. Drain screw
20. Float
21. Fuel inlet valve
22. Main jet
23. Spacer
24. Gasket
25. Throttle plate
26. Carburetor body

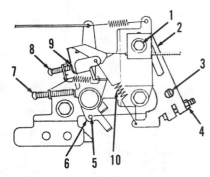

Fig. TO52—Drawing of governor and speed control linkage.

1. Screw
2. Governor lever
3. Governor shaft
4. Nut
5. Alignment hole
6. Speed control lever
7. Maximum speed screw
8. Stop screw
9. Tang
10. Governor spring

renewable but valve seat is not removable and body must be renewed if seat is damaged.

Metal parts should be cleaned in carburetor cleaner. Use compressed air to blow out all orifices and passageways. Do not use wires or drill bits to clean orifices as enlargement of the orifice could affect the calibration of the carburetor.

Apply Loctite 271 thread locking compound to threads of choke and throttle plate screws when assembling carburetor.

SPEED CONTROL CABLE. When the speed control is in the "FAST" position, holes (5—Fig. TO52) in speed control lever (6) and bracket should be aligned. Unscrew throttle cable clamp screw (1) and relocate cable to align holes, then retighten clamp screw.

GOVERNOR. All engines are equipped with a mechanical (flyweight) type governor. Maximum governed speed is adjusted by turning adjusting screw (7—Fig. TO52). With speed control in the "FAST" position so holes (5) in speed control lever (6) and bracket are aligned, rotate adjusting screw so engine runs at 3000 rpm. Rotate stop screw (8) so screw end is 0.00-0.05 mm (0.000-0.020 in.) from tang (9).

To adjust the governor linkage, refer to Fig. TO52 and loosen governor lever clamp nut (4). Rotate governor shaft (3) clockwise as far as possible. Move the governor lever until carburetor throttle shaft is in wide open position, then tighten governor lever clamp nut.

IGNITION. The engine is equipped with a breakerless ignition system. All components are located outside the flywheel. Armature air gap should be 0.38-0.50 mm (0.015-0.020 in.).

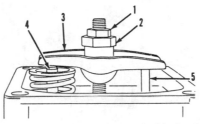

Fig. TO53—View of rocker arm and related parts.

1. Jam nut
2. Adjustment nut
3. Rocker arm
4. Valve stem clearance
5. Push rod

VALVE ADJUSTMENT. Specified clearance between rocker arm (3—Fig. TO53) and end of valve stem (4) is 0.025-0.13 mm (0.001-0.005 in.) for both valves. To adjust valve clearance, remove rocker arm cover. Rotate crankshaft so piston is at top dead center (TDC) on compression stroke. Insert a suitable thickness feeler gauge between rocker arm and end of valve stem. Loosen rocker arm jam nut (1) and turn adjusting nut (2) to obtain desired clearance (a slight drag should be felt when withdrawing the feeler gauge). Tighten jam nut and recheck clearance. Install rocker arm cover. Note that cutaway portion of cover mounting flange must be adjacent to spark plug.

REPAIRS

TIGHTENING TORQUES. Recommended tightening torque specifications are as follows:

Connecting rod . . . . 5.9-9.8 N•m
(54-118 in.-lbs.)
Cylinder head . . . . 17.6-27.4 N•m
(156-242 in.-lbs.)
Flywheel . . . . 55-63 N•m
(41-46 ft.-lbs.)
Oil pan. . . . . 3.9-6.8 N•m
(35-60 in.-lbs.)

CYLINDER HEAD. To remove the cylinder head, first remove fuel tank, air cleaner, blower housing, carburetor, speed control bracket, muffler, and rocker arm cover. Loosen jam nuts, and remove rocker arm pivots (4—Fig. TO54), rocker arms (5) and push rods (6); mark all parts so they can be returned to original location. Unscrew cylinder head screws and remove cylinder head (8).

Clean cylinder head thoroughly, then check for cracks, distortion or other damage. Cylinder head warpage should not exceed 0.030 mm (0.0012 in.).

Install cylinder head using a new head gasket. Tighten cylinder head screws adjacent to spark plug hole first, then tighten screws adjacent to push rod opening in a crossing pattern. Final

torque reading should be 17.6-27.4 N•m (156-242 in.-lbs.). Adjust valve clearance as outlined in VALVE ADJUSTMENT section. Install rocker arm cover with the cut out side of the cover toward the spark plug. Be sure that a flat washer is installed on each rocker cover retaining screw, and tighten screws to 4.1-6.7 N•m (36-60 in.-lbs.).

VALVE SYSTEM. To remove valves (11 and 12—Fig. TO54) from cylinder head, compress valve springs (3) by hand or with a suitable spring compressor tool and remove slotted retainers (2). The intake and exhaust valve springs and retainers are identical and interchangeable.

Valve face and seat angles are 45 degrees. Standard valve seat width is 0.90-1.10 mm (0.035-0.043 in.).

Standard valve stem diameter is 5.460-5.475 mm (0.2150-0.2156 in.) for intake valve and 5.440-5.455 mm (0.2142-0.2148 in.) for exhaust valve.

Standard valve guide inside diameter is 5.500-5.512 mm (0.2165-0.2170 in.) for both valves. Standard valve stem-to-guide clearance is 0.025-0.052 mm (0.0010-0.0020 in.) for intake and 0.045-0.072 mm (0.0018-0.0028 in.) for exhaust. Maximum valve stem-to-guide clearance is 0.080 mm (0.0032 in.) for intake valve and 0.100 mm (0.0039 in.) for exhaust valve. Oversize valve guides may be installed.

Valve guides (9—Fig. TO54) can be renewed using Toro valve guide driver 81-4880 or other suitable tool. Press or drive guide out towards rocker arm side of head. Use Toro reamer 81-4850 or other suitable reamer so valve guide bore diameter in head is 9.300-9.315 mm (0.3661-0.3667 in.). Press or drive guide in from rocker arm side of cylinder head so valve guide is 27.5 mm (1.08 in.) below head gasket surface of cylinder head. Ream guide with Toro reamer 81-4840 or other suitably sized reamer to obtain desired valve stem clearance. Valve guide finished inside diameter should be 5.500-5.512 mm (0.2165-0.2170 in.).

Valve spring free length should be 32.0-34.0 mm (1.26-1.34 in.). Minimum allowable valve spring length is 31.0 mm (1.22 in.).

R&R ENGINE. The following procedure applies to engines equipped with a blade brake clutch. The procedure for engines with a flywheel brake (zone start) is similar, although the blade brake components are absent.

To remove engine, disconnect and properly ground spark plug lead. Disconnect any electrical wires to engine. Remove blade mounting assembly and

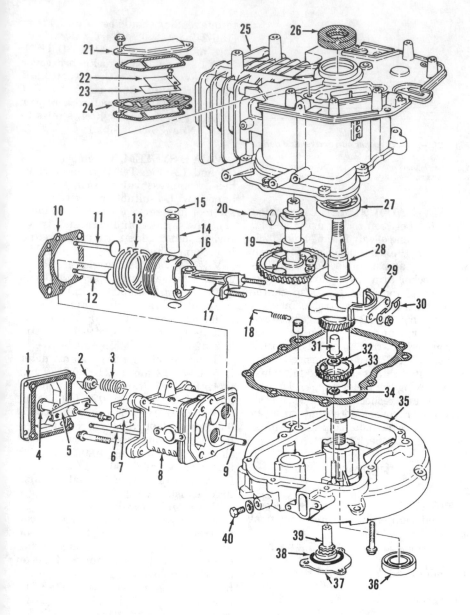

Fig. TO54—Exploded view of engine assembly.

1. Rocker cover
2. Valve retainer
3. Valve spring
4. Rocker arm pivot
5. Rocker arm
6. Push rod
7. Push rod guide
8. Cylinder head
9. Valve guide
10. Head gasket
11. Exhaust valve
12. Intake valve
13. Piston rings
14. Piston pin
15. Retaining ring
16. Piston
17. Connecting rod
18. Compression release spring
19. Camshaft
20. Tappet
21. Breather cover
22. Reed stop
23. Reed valve
24. Breather plate
25. Engine block
26. Oil seal
27. Ball bearing
28. Crankshaft
29. Rod cap
30. Lock plate
31. Thrust sleeve
32. Washer
33. Governor
34. Washer
35. Oil pan
36. Oil seal
37. Oil pump cover
38. "O" ring
39. Oil pump rotors
40. Oil drain plug

bottom cover. Unscrew crankshaft nut, push back belt idler, and remove bearing block, brake drum and flywheel plate. Separate transmission drive belt from drive pulley and remove drive pulley. If desired, drain engine oil. Unscrew engine mounting screws and remove engine while disconnecting throttle cable.

Reverse removal procedure to reinstall engine while noting the following: Pegs on drive pulley must be toward bottom of crankshaft. Note that center of flywheel is tapered to fit crankshaft. Install flywheel so pegs on drive pulley fit in slots in flywheel plate.

CAUTION: Drive pulley will be damaged if pegs on pulley do not fit properly in flywheel slots during assembly. Before tightening crankshaft nut, rotate flywheel slightly. If pegs are in slots, flywheel rotation will be stopped by pegs.

Stepped side of bearing block fits in center of brake drum. Note that flat side on head of blade mounting bolts must be toward center of brake drum. Tighten bearing block retaining nut to 79 N·m (58 ft.-lbs.). When tightening nut, be sure blade brake drive belt is not trapped between drum and flywheel. Tighten blade retaining nuts to 37 N·m (27 ft.-lbs.).

CAMSHAFT. To remove camshaft (19—Fig. TO54) proceed as follows: Remove engine as previously outlined. Drain oil from crankcase. Clean pto end of crankshaft and remove any burrs or rust. Remove rocker arm cover (1), rocker arms (5) and push rods (6); mark all parts so they can be returned to original position. Unscrew fasteners and remove oil pan (35). Rotate crankshaft so timing marks on crankshaft and camshaft gears are aligned (this

will position valve tappets out of the way). Withdraw camshaft and remove tappets (20). Mark the tappets so they can be installed in their original positions if reused.

Specified camshaft lobe height is 30.517-30.577 mm (1.2014-1.2038 in.). Renew camshaft and tappets if lobes are excessively worn or scored.

Reverse removal procedure to reassemble components. Lubricate tappets and camshaft with engine oil during assembly. Install camshaft while aligning timing marks on crankshaft and camshaft gears. Note that roll pin in end of camshaft must engage oil pump drive shaft in oil pan during assembly. Tighten oil pan screws to 3.9-6.8 N·m (35-60 in.-lbs.) in a crossing pattern. Do not force mating of oil pan with crankcase. Be sure thrust sleeve (31) on governor does not fall off during assembly. Reassemble remainder of components.

PISTON, PIN AND RINGS. To remove piston and rod assembly, remove engine as previously outlined. Remove cylinder head and camshaft as previously outlined. Unscrew connecting rod cap nuts and remove piston and rod.

Measure piston diameter at points perpendicular to piston pin and 14 mm (0.55 in.) from bottom of piston skirt. Specified piston diameter is 63.960-63.975 mm (2.5181-2.5187 in.) with a wear limit of 63.915 mm (2.5163 in.). Specified piston-to-cylinder bore clearance is 0.025-0.055 mm (0.0010-0.0022 in.) with a wear limit of 0.120 mm (0.0047 in.). Oversize pistons are not available.

Specified piston ring end gap for compression rings is 0.2-0.4 mm (0.008-0.016 in.) with a limit of 0.70 mm (0.028 in.). Piston ring groove width for compression rings should be 1.52-1.54 mm (0.060-0.061 in.) and ring thickness should be 1.47-1.49 mm (0.058-0.059 in.). Specified piston ring side clearance in groove is 0.03-0.07 mm (0.001-0.003 in.) with a limit of 0.10 mm (0.004 in.).

Specified piston pin diameter is 14.995-15.000 mm (0.5904-0.5906 in.). Specified piston pin bore diameter is 15.006-15.014 mm (0.5908-0.5911 in.).

Top compression ring is chrome plated. One side of piston ring is marked with the letter "N" to indicate correct installation position. Install the piston rings on piston so that "N" on side of ring is toward piston crown.

When assembling piston and connecting rod, note that arrow on piston crown and arrow on side of connecting rod must point in same direction. Lubricate piston rings and pin with engine oil, then install piston and rod assembly in engine with arrow on piston crown toward push rod side of engine. Install rod cap on connecting rod so match marks on rod and cap are aligned. Tighten connecting rod nuts to 5.9-9.8 N•m (54-118 in.-lbs.).

Install camshaft and cylinder head as previously outlined.

CONNECTING ROD. Connecting rod rides directly on crankshaft journal. Connecting rod and piston are removed as an assembly as outlined in previous section.

Specified clearance between piston pin and connecting rod small end is 0.006-0.019 mm (0.0002-0.0007 in.) with a maximum allowable clearance of 0.050 mm (0.0020 in.).

Specified clearance between crankpin journal and connecting rod bore is 0.015-0.035 mm (0.0006-0.0014 in.) with a maximum allowable clearance of 0.080 mm (0.0031 in.). Specified connecting rod big end diameter is 26.015-26.025 mm (1.0242-1.0246 in.).

Install connecting rod as outlined in previous section.

GOVERNOR. The internal centrifugal flyweight governor is mounted on the oil pan. The governor is driven by the camshaft gear.

To remove governor assembly (33—Fig. FO54), first separate oil pan (35) from crankcase. Use two screwdrivers to snap governor gear and flyweight assembly off governor stub shaft.

Install governor by pushing down on the stub shaft until it snaps onto the shaft locating groove. Be sure that thrust washers (32 and 34) are positioned on either side of governor. A small amount of grease may be used to hold the thrust washer (32) and sleeve (31) in place on stub shaft. When installing oil pan, it may be necessary to turn crankshaft slightly to mesh the camshaft gear teeth with the governor gear. Do not force the oil pan into place.

Refer to MAINTENANCE section for external governor linkage adjustment.

CRANKSHAFT, MAIN BEARINGS AND OIL SEALS. The crankshaft is supported at flywheel end by a ball bearing (27—Fig. TO54) located in the crankcase. The crankshaft may be removed after removing piston and connecting rod as previously outlined.

Specified main bearing journal diameter is 21.960-21.980 mm (0.8646-0.8654 in.) for flywheel end and 24.959-24.980 mm (0.9826-0.9835 in.) for pto end. Specified crankpin journal diameter is 25.99-26.00 mm (1.023-1.024 in.). Maximum allowable crankshaft runout is 0.05 mm (0.002 in.).

When installing crankshaft, make certain crankshaft and camshaft gear timing marks are aligned.

Inspect ball bearing and renew if rough, loose or damaged. Install oil seals (26 and 36) so lip is toward main bearing. Lubricate oil seals with engine oil prior to installing crankshaft. Be sure to align timing marks on crankshaft gear and camshaft gear.

CYLINDER. Renew cylinder if wear in bore exceeds 0.100 mm (0.0039 in.) or if out-of-round exceeds 0.030 mm (0.0012 in.).

OIL PUMP. A rotor type oil pump driven by the camshaft is located in the bottom of the oil pan.

Remove engine from equipment for access to oil pump cover (37—Fig. TO54). Remove cover and extract pump rotors (39). Mark rotors so they can be reinstalled in their original position. Renew any components which are damaged or excessively worn.

REWIND STARTER. Refer to Fig. TO55 for exploded view of rewind starter.

To disassemble starter, remove rope handle and allow rope to wind into starter. Unscrew retainer nut (14). Remove retainer (13), pawl guide (12), spring (11), spacer (10), washer (9), pawl (8) and pivot pin (7). Wear appropriate safety eyewear and gloves before disengaging pulley (6) from starter as spring

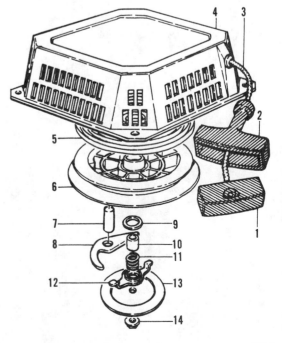

Fig. TO55—Exploded view of rewind starter.

1. Rope retainer
2. Rope handle
3. Rope
4. Starter housing
5. Rewind spring
6. Pulley
7. Pivot pin
8. Pawl
9. Washer
10. Spacer
11. Spring
12. Pawl guide
13. Retainer
14. Locknut

(5) may uncoil uncontrolled. Place shop towel around pulley and lift pulley out of housing; spring should remain with pulley.

Inspect components for damage and excessive wear. A new starter rope is $5/32$ inch (4 mm) in diameter and 70 inches (175 cm) long. A new rewind spring is provided with a retainer to hold it in the coiled position. When replacing the spring, first position it in the pulley, then remove the retainer. Note that rewind spring coils wind in counterclockwise direction from outer end. Install rope on pulley in a counterclockwise direction as viewed from engagement side of pulley. Be sure that pawl guide (12) is positioned as shown in Fig. TO55 when installing in pulley (6). Apply Loctite 242 to threads of retaining nut (14).

With starter assembled, pass rope through rope outlet and install rope handle. To apply spring tension to pulley, pull a loop of rope into notch in pulley and rotate pulley counterclockwise a couple of turns, then pull rope out of notch and allow rope to wind into starter housing. Rope handle should be snug against housing, if not, increase spring tension by rotating pulley another turn.

ELECTRIC STARTER. Some models may be equipped with an electric starter motor. Individual parts of starter drive assembly are available, however, motor unit is available only as a unit assembly. If starter malfunctions, inspect and test components of starter circuit before replacing starter motor.

ALTERNATOR. Some engines may be equipped with an alternator. To test alternator output, disconnect alternator lead and connect a voltmeter to alternator lead and engine ground. With engine running at 3000 rpm, alternator output should be 13.2 volts DC. Test rectifier if output is low or zero.

To check for a faulty rectifier diode, connect positive lead of an ohmmeter to alternator lead and negative ohmmeter lead to alternator stator. Ohmmeter should read infinity. With ohmmeter leads reversed, ohmmeter should indicate approximately 700 ohms.

Alternator and rectifier are available only as a unit assembly.

TORO

Model Series	Bore	Stroke	Displacement	Rated Power
GTS 150	2.56 in.	1.78 in.	9.2 cu.in.	5.5 hp
	(65.0 mm)	(45.2 mm)	(150 cc)	(4.1 kW)

ENGINE INFORMATION

The Toro GTS 150 engine model series is used on Toro walk-behind lawn mowers. The engine is an air-cooled, four-stroke, single-cylinder engine with a vertical crankshaft and an overhead valve system. Engine identification numbers are stamped in the rocker arm cover as shown in Fig. TO100.

MAINTENANCE

LUBRICATION. The engine is lubricated by oil supplied by a rotor type oil pump located in the bottom of the crankcase, as well as by a slinger driven by the camshaft gear.

Change oil after first two hours of operation and after every 25 hours of operation or at least once each operating season.

Engine oil level should be maintained at full mark on dipstick. Engine oil should meet or exceed latest API service classification. Manufacturer recommends SAE 30 or SAE 10W-30 oil.

Crankcase capacity is 25 fl. oz. (0.74 L). Fill engine with oil so oil level reaches, but does not exceed, full mark on dipstick.

AIR CLEANER. The air cleaner consists of a canister and the foam filter element it contains.

The filter element should be cleaned after every 25 hours of operation, or more frequently if severe operating conditions are encountered. Clean filter in soapy water and squeeze until dry. Inspect filter for tears and holes or any other opening. Discard filter if it cannot be cleaned satisfactorily or if it is torn or otherwise damaged. Pour clean engine oil into the filter, then squeeze to remove excess oil and distribute oil throughout.

FUEL FILTER. A fuel filter is located in the fuel tank. The filter is molded in the tank. If filter is damaged or cleaning will not remove dirt or debris, the fuel tank must be renewed.

CRANKCASE BREATHER. The crankcase breather is built into the tappet chamber cover (C—Fig. TO101). A fiber disc acts as a one-way valve. Clearance between fiber disc valve and breather body should not exceed 0.045

Fig. TO101—The crankcase breather is located in valve tappet cover (C).

inch (1.14 mm). If it is possible to insert a 0.045 inch (1.14 mm) wire gauge (W—Fig. TO102) between disc and breather body, renew breather assembly. Do not use excessive force when measuring gap. Disc should not stick or bind during operation. Renew if distorted or damaged. Inspect breather tube for leakage.

SPARK PLUG. Recommended spark plug is Champion RC12YC. Specified spark plug electrode gap is 0.030 inch (0.76 mm).

CARBURETOR. The engine is equipped with a Walbro LMS float type carburetor.

Adjustment. Initial setting of idle mixture screw (IM—Fig. TO103) is 1¼ turns out from a lightly seated position. Run engine until normal operating temperature is attained. Be sure choke is open. Run engine with speed control in slow position and adjust idle speed screw so engine speed is 1500 rpm. Turn idle mixture screw clockwise until engine begins to stumble and note screw position. Turn idle mixture screw counterclockwise until engine begins to stumble and note screw position. Turn the idle mixture screw clockwise to a position that is midway from clockwise (lean) and counterclockwise (rich) positions. With engine running at idle, rapidly move speed control to full throttle position. If engine stumbles or hesitates, slightly turn idle mixture screw

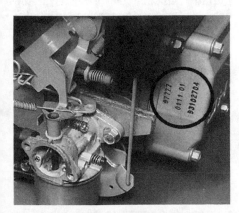

Fig. TO100—Engine identification numbers are stamped in rocker arm cover.

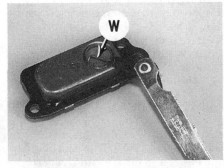

Fig. TO102—Clearance between fiber disc valve and crankcase breather housing must be less than 0.045 inch (1.15 mm). A spark plug wire gauge (W) may be used to check clearance as shown, but do not apply pressure against disc valve.

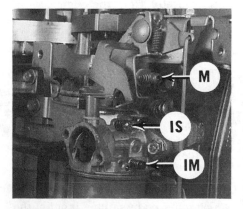

Fig. TO103—View showing location of idle mixture screw (IM), idle speed screw (IS) and maximum governed speed screw (M).

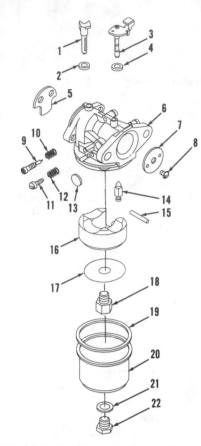

Fig. TO104—Exploded view of carburetor.

1. Choke shaft	12. Spring
2. Washer	13. Welch plug
3. Throttle shaft	14. Fuel inlet valve
4. Washer	15. Pin
5. Choke plate	16. Float
6. Body	17. Float stop plate
7. Throttle plate	18. Main jet
8. Screw	19. Gasket
9. Idle mixture screw	20. Fuel bowl
10. Spring	21. Gasket
11. Idle speed screw	22. Bowl screw

counterclockwise and repeat test. Recheck idle speed and, if necessary, readjust idle speed screw.

High speed mixture is controlled by a fixed main jet (18—Fig. TO104) that is not adjustable.

R&R And Overhaul. Before removing carburetor from the engine, carefully note the position of all control linkage and springs to insure correct reassembly. Remove air cleaner assembly from the carburetor. Remove fuel from tank and disconnect fuel line from carburetor. Disconnect choke spring. Remove two screws retaining carburetor, pull carburetor away from engine and disconnect governor link rod.

Disassembly of carburetor is evident after inspection and referral to Fig. TO104. Note that choke plate (5) is retained in a slot in choke shaft with a slight interference fit. The choke plate can be removed by pulling it out of the slot. The throttle plate (7) is retained with a screw. To remove the Welch plug

(13), pierce the plug with a small chisel or other sharp pointed tool, then pry out the plug, but do not damage underlying metal. The fuel inlet valve seat can be removed by inserting a hooked wire through opening in the seat and pulling the seat out of the carburetor body.

Metal parts may be cleaned in carburetor cleaner. Direct compressed air through orifices and passageways in the opposite direction of normal fuel flow. Do not use wires or drill bits to clean orifices as enlargement of the orifice could affect the calibration of the carburetor. Inspect carburetor and renew any damaged or excessively worn components. The body must be replaced if there is excessive throttle shaft or choke shaft play as bushings are not available.

Install Welch plug using a punch that is larger in diameter than the Welch plug. Be careful not to indent the plug; the plug should be flat after installation. After plug is installed, seal outside edge of plug with fingernail polish or other suitable sealant. Use a ⅛ inch (3 mm) diameter rod to install the fuel inlet valve seat. The groove on the seat must be down (towards carburetor bore). Push in the seat until it bottoms. Install the choke plate so the numbers are visible when the choke is closed. Install the throttle plate so the numbers are visible and towards the idle mixture screw when the throttle is closed. Apply Loctite 271 thread locking compound on throttle plate retaining screw. The float level is not adjustable. If the float is not approximately parallel with the body when the carburetor is inverted, then the float, fuel valve and/or valve seat must be replaced. Float stop plate (17) is secured by main jet (18).

To install carburetor, reverse the removal procedure. Make certain that the gasket is in place between the air cleaner housing and the carburetor and that the breather vent hose on the back of the air cleaner housing mates with the breather vent tube.

SPEED CONTROL CABLE. When the speed control is in the "FAST" position, holes (H—Fig. TO105) in throttle lever (L) and bracket should be aligned. Unscrew throttle cable clamp screw (S) and relocate cable to align holes, then tighten clamp screw.

GOVERNOR. To adjust governor linkage, loosen governor lever clamp nut (N—Fig. TO106). Move throttle lever (L—Fig. TO105) to fast position and insert a ⅛ inch rod into holes (H) in the lever and bracket. Rotate governor shaft (S—Fig. TO106) counterclockwise as far as possible, hold shaft and tighten clamp nut.

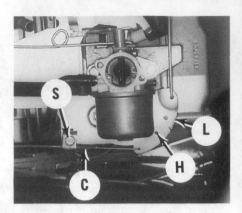

Fig. TO105—When speed control is in "FAST" position, holes (H) in throttle lever (L) and bracket should be aligned. Loosen clamp screw (S) to reposition cable housing (C).

Fig. TO106—View of governor lever (L), shaft (S) and clamp nut (N). Refer to text for adjustment.

Maximum governed speed is adjusted by turning screw (M—Fig. TO103). Maximum governed speed should be 3000 rpm.

IGNITION. The engine is equipped with a breakerless ignition system. All components are located outside the flywheel. Armature air gap should be 0.006-0.012 inch (0.15-0.30 mm).

VALVE ADJUSTMENT. Remove rocker arm cover. Remove spark plug. Rotate crankshaft so piston is at top dead center on compression stroke. Insert a suitable measuring device through spark plug hole, then rotate crankshaft clockwise as viewed at flywheel end so piston is ¼ inch (6.4 mm) below TDC to prevent interference by the compression release mechanism with the exhaust valve. Clearance between rocker arm (R—Fig. TO107) and valve stem cap (V) should be 0.005-0.007 inch (0.12-0.18 mm) for intake and exhaust. Check clearance using feeler gauges. Loosen lock screw (S) and turn rocker arm pivot nut (N) to obtain desired clearance. Hold pivot nut and tighten lock screw to 45 in.-lbs. (5.1 N•m) torque. Install rocker arm cover

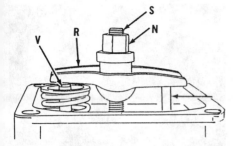

Fig. TO107—Loosen lock screw (S) and rotate adjusting nut (N) to adjust valve clearance. Clearance between rocker arm (R) and valve stem cap (V) should be 0.005-0.007 inch (0.12-0.18 mm) for intake and exhaust.

and tighten cover screws in a diagonal sequence to 45 in.-lbs. (5.1 N•m) torque.

NOTE: Pivot nut is 10 mm and lock screw is Torx design.

CYLINDER HEAD. The cylinder head should be removed periodically and cleaned of deposits.

REPAIRS

TIGHTENING TORQUES. Recommended tightening torque specifications are as follows:

Carburetor mounting
   screws . . . . 60 in.-lbs.
                              (6.8 N•m)
Connecting rod . . . . 100 in.-lbs.
                              (11.3 N•m)
Cylinder head . . . . 160 in.-lbs.
                              (18.1 N•m)
Flywheel nut . . . . 60 ft.-lbs.
                              (81.6 N•m)
Muffler . . . . 85 in.-lbs.
                              (9.6 N•m)
Oil pan . . . . 85 in.-lbs.
                              (9.6 N•m)
Rocker arm cover . . . . 45 in.-lbs.
                              (5.1 N•m)

Rocker arm studs . . . . 110 in.-lbs.
                              (12.4 N•m)
Spark plug . . . . 170 in.-lbs.
                              (19.2 N•m)

CYLINDER HEAD. To remove the cylinder head, first remove fuel tank, air cleaner, blower housing, carburetor, speed control bracket, muffler, and rocker arm cover. Loosen lock screws (10—Fig. TO108), and remove rocker arm pivot nuts (11), rocker arms (12) and push rods (15); mark all parts so they can be returned to original location. Unscrew cylinder head screws and remove cylinder head (16). Clean cylinder head thoroughly, then check for cracks, distortion or other damage.

When reinstalling cylinder head, do not apply sealer to cylinder head gasket. Be sure the cylinder head alignment pins are installed in cylinder block. Install the push rods making sure that they are in the valve tappets, then install the cylinder head over the push rods. Tighten cylinder head bolts in three steps following sequence of numbers embossed on cylinder head. Final torque reading should be 160 in.-lbs. (18.1 N•m).

VALVE SYSTEM. Valves are actuated by rocker arms mounted on studs threaded into the cylinder head. To remove valves from cylinder head, remove valve wear caps (3—Fig. TO108). Depress valve springs until slot in valve spring retainer (4) can be aligned with end of valve stem. Release spring pressure and remove retainer, spring and valve from cylinder head.

Valve face and seat angles are 45 degrees for intake and exhaust. Standard seat width is 0.060 inch (1.5 mm).

The cylinder head is equipped with renewable valve guides for both valves. Renew valve guide if inside diameter is 0.240 inch (6.10 mm) or more. Guides

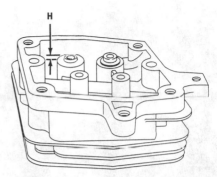

Fig. TO109—Install valve guide so top of guide protrudes (H) above boss 0.120-0.150 inch (3.05-3.81 mm).

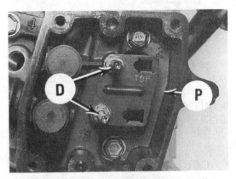

Fig. TO110—Install push rod guide plate (P) so "TOP" is toward flywheel side of head.

may be installed either way up. Top of guide should protrude 0.120-0.150 inch (3.05-3.81 mm) as shown in Fig. TO109.

Install push rod guide plate (P—Fig. TO110) so "TOP" mark is toward flywheel side of cylinder head. Rocker arm studs (D) are screwed into cylinder head. Hardening sealant should be applied to threads contacting cylinder head.

Install gasket (8—Fig. TO108) and valve seal (7) on intake valve. Do not lubricate wear caps (3).

R&R ENGINE. The following procedure applies to engines equipped with a blade brake clutch. The procedure for engines with a flywheel brake (zone start) is similar, although the blade brake components are absent.

To remove engine, disconnect and properly ground spark plug lead. Disconnect any electrical wires to engine. Remove blade mounting assembly and bottom cover (C—Fig. TO111). Unscrew nut (N—Fig. TO112), push back belt idler (I), and remove bearing block (B), brake drum (D) and flywheel (F). Separate transmission drive belt from drive pulley (P—Fig. TO113) and remove drive pulley. If desired, drain engine oil. Unscrew engine mounting screws and remove engine while disconnecting throttle cable.

Fig. TO108—Exploded view
of cylinder head assembly.

   1. Rocker cover
   2. Gasket
   3. Valve cap
   4. Valve retainer
   5. Valve spring
   6. Exhaust valve
   7. Valve seal
   8. Gasket
   9. Intake valve
   10. Lock screw
   11. Adjusting nut
   12. Rocker arm
   13. Stud
   14. Push rod guide
   15. Push rod
   16. Cylinder head
   17. Head gasket

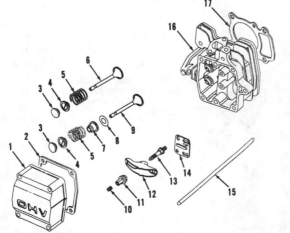

Fig. TO111—Remove cover (C) to access to mower drive components.

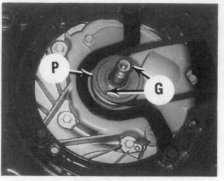

Fig. TO113—Pegs (G) on drive pulley (P) must engage slots (S—Fig. TO114) in flywheel.

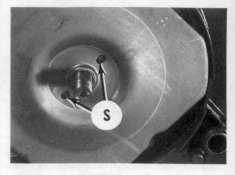

Fig. TO114—Be sure pegs (G--Fig. TO113) on drive pulley engage slots (S) in flywheel.

Reverse removal procedure to reinstall engine while noting the following: Pegs (G—Fig. TO113) on drive pulley must be toward bottom of crankshaft. Note that center of flywheel is tapered to fit crankshaft. Install flywheel so pegs on drive pulley fit in slots (S—Fig. TO114) on flywheel.

CAUTION: Drive pulley will be damaged if pegs on pulley do not fit properly in flywheel slots during assembly. Before tightening bearing block nut, rotate flywheel slightly. If pegs are in slots, flywheel rotation will be stopped by pegs.

Stepped side of bearing block (B—Fig. TO112) fits in center of brake drum. Note that flat side on head of blade mounting bolts must be toward center of brake drum. Tighten bearing block retaining nut to 58 ft.-lbs. (79 N•m). When tightening nut, be sure blade brake drive belt is not trapped between drum and flywheel. Tighten blade retaining nuts to 27 ft.-lbs. (37 N•m).

CAMSHAFT. To remove camshaft (26—Fig. TO115) proceed as follows: Re-

move engine as previously outlined. Drain engine oil. Clean pto end of crankshaft and remove any burrs or rust. Remove rocker arm cover, rocker arms and push rods; mark all parts so they can be returned to original position. Unscrew fasteners and remove oil pan. Remove governor assembly (G—Fig. TO116). Rotate crankshaft so timing marks (M—Fig. TO117) on crankshaft and camshaft gears are aligned (this will position valve tappets out of way). Withdraw camshaft and remove tappets. Mark the tappets so they can be reinstalled in their original position.

Renew camshaft if either camshaft bearing journal diameter is 0.615 inch (15.62 mm) or less. Renew camshaft if lobes are excessively worn or scored.

Lubricate valve tappets with engine oil prior to installation. Lubricate camshaft with engine oil, then install camshaft while aligning timing marks (M—Fig. TO117) on crankshaft and camshaft gears. Install governor assembly on camshaft. Make certain that the governor plunger is positioned against the governor shaft arm and that the flyweights move freely. Note that roll pin (P) in end of camshaft must engage oil pump drive shaft in oil pan during assembly. Install oil pan and apply non-

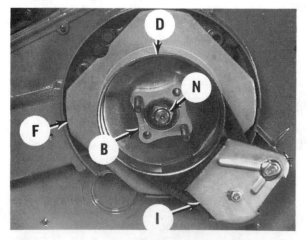

Fig. TO112—View of bearing block (B), brake drum (D), brake idler (I), flywheel (F) and retaining nut (N).

hardening sealant such as Permatex #2 to screw (4—Fig. TO118). Tighten cover screws to 85 in.-lbs. (9.6 N•m) in sequence shown in Fig. TO118. Do not force mating of oil pan with crankcase. Reassemble remainder of components.

PISTON, PIN AND RINGS. To remove piston and rod assembly, remove engine as previously outlined. Remove cylinder head and camshaft as previously outlined. Unscrew connecting rod screws and remove piston and rod.

Maximum allowable piston ring end gap is 0.030 inch (0.76 mm) for compression rings and 0.060 inch (1.52 mm) for oil ring rails. Renew piston if ring side clearance exceeds 0.005 inch (0.12 mm) with a new piston ring installed in groove. Oversize as well as standard size piston and rings are available.

Piston pin is a slip fit in piston and rod. Renew piston if piston pin bore diameter is 0.552 inch (14.02 mm) or greater. Renew piston pin if diameter is 0.551 inch (14.00 mm) or less.

Top piston ring may be installed with either side up. Second piston ring must be installed with notch (S—Fig. TO119) toward piston skirt.

When assembling piston and rod, note that arrow on piston crown and "MAG" on connecting rod must be on same side. See Fig. TO120. Install piston and rod assembly in engine with arrow on piston crown toward flywheel as shown in Fig. TO121. Install rod cap so arrow on cap (R—Fig. TO122) points in same direction as arrow (A) on rod. Tighten rod screws to 100 in.-lbs. (11.3 N•m).

Install camshaft and cylinder head as previously outlined.

CONNECTING ROD. The connecting rod rides directly on crankpin. Connecting rod and piston are removed as an assembly as outlined in previous section.

Connecting rod reject size for crankpin hole is 1.127 inch (28.63 mm). Re-

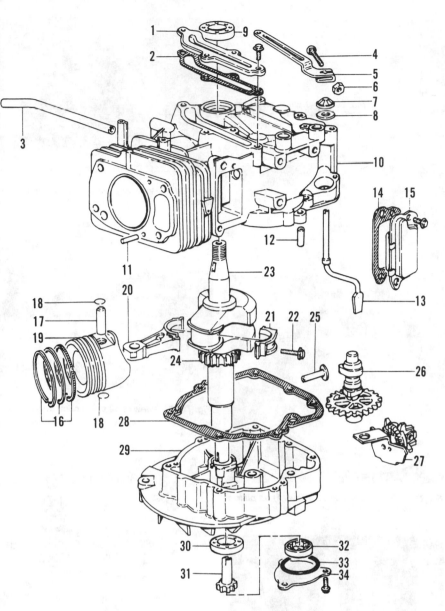

Fig. TO115—Exploded view of engine.

1. Cover		26. Camshaft
2. Gasket	10. Crankcase	27. Governor
3. Breather tube	11. Dowel pin	28. Gasket
4. Clamp bolt	12. Dowel pin	29. Oil pan
5. Governor lever	13. Governor shaft	30. Oil seal
6. Nut	14. Gasket	31. Oil pump inner rotor
7. Push nut	15. Tappet cover	32. Outer rotor
8. Washer	16. Piston rings	33. "O" ring
9. Oil seal	17. Piston pin	34. Cover
	18. Retaining ring	
	19. Piston	
	20. Connecting rod	
	21. Rod cap	
	22. Screw	
	23. Crankshaft	
	24. Gear	
	25. Tappet	

Fig. TO116—The governor assembly (G) is mounted on end of camshaft.

Fig. TO117—Install camshaft so timing marks (M) on camshaft and crankshaft gears are aligned. Pin (P) in camshaft end must engage slot in oil pump drive shaft when installing crankcase cover.

nal 0.873 inch (22.17 mm); crankpin 1.122 inch (28.50 mm). A connecting rod with 0.020 inch (0.51 mm) undersize big end diameter is available to accommodate a worn crankpin.

The crankcase main bearing bore rejection size is 0.878 inch (22.30 mm). The oil pan main bearing bore rejection size is 1.065 inch (27.05 mm).

Install oil seals so lip is toward inside of crankcase.

Tighten oil pan screws to 85 in.-lbs. (9.6 N·m) in sequence shown in Fig. TO118.

CYLINDER. If cylinder bore wear is 0.003 inch (0.76 mm) or more, or out-of-round is 0.0015 inch (0.038 mm) or greater, cylinder must be rebored to next oversize.

Standard cylinder bore diameter is 2.5615-2.5625 inch (65.06-65.09 mm).

OIL PUMP. A rotor type oil pump (Fig. TO124) driven by the camshaft is located in the bottom of the oil pan.

Remove engine from equipment for access to oil pump cover (C—Fig. TO118). Remove cover and extract pump rotors (31 and 32—Fig. TO115 or TO124). Mark rotors so they can be reinstalled in their original position. Re-

new connecting rod if piston pin bore diameter is 0.5525 inch (14.03 mm) or greater. A connecting rod with 0.020 inch (0.51 mm) undersize big end diameter is available to accommodate a worn crankpin (machining instructions are included with new rod).

GOVERNOR. The engine is equipped with a mechanical governor (Fig. TO123) that is driven by the camshaft gear as shown in Fig. TO116. The flyweight assembly is mounted on end of camshaft along with oil slinger. The oil slinger and flyweight assembly are only available as a unit assembly. Inspect flyweight assembly for broken components. When installing governor, make certain that the governor plunger is positioned against the governor shaft arm and that the flyweights move freely.

CRANKSHAFT AND MAIN BEARINGS. The crankshaft rides directly in the crankcase and oil pan bearing bores. Rejection sizes for crankshaft are: pto-end bearing journal 1.060 inch (26.92 mm); flywheel-end bearing jour-

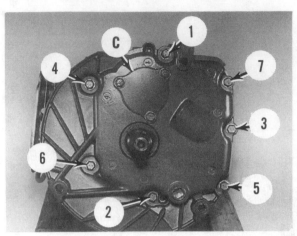

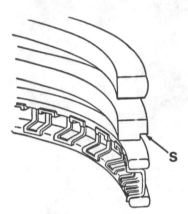

Fig. TO118—Tighten oil pan retaining screws in sequence shown. Apply sealant to screw (4).

Fig. TO123—View of governor and oil slinger assembly.

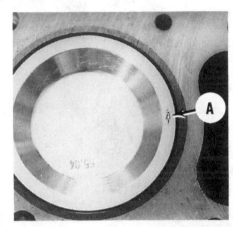

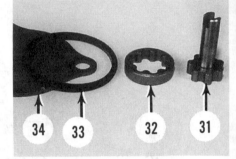

Fig. TO119—Install second compression piston ring so notch (S) is toward piston skirt.

Fig. TO121—Install piston so arrow (A) on piston crown points toward flywheel side of engine.

Fig. TO124—View of oil pump components.

31. Oil pump inner rotor
32. Outer rotor
33. "O" ring
34. Cover

Fig. TO120—Assemble piston and rod so arrow (A) on piston crown and "MAG" on side of rod are positioned as shown.

Fig. TO122—Install rod cap so arrow on cap (R) points in same direction as arrow (A) on rod.

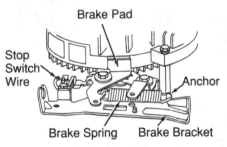

Fig. TO125—A flywheel brake is used on some engines.

new any components which are damaged or excessively worn.

FLYWHEEL BRAKE. Some engines are equipped with a pad type flywheel brake. The brake should stop the engine within three seconds when the operator releases mower safety control and the speed control is in high speed position.

To service flywheel brake, remove fuel tank, dipstick and oil fill tube, blower housing and rewind starter. Disconnect brake spring (Fig. TO125). Dis-

connect stop switch wire. Remove two retaining screws from brake pad arm and brake bracket.

The brake pad is available only as part of the bracket assembly. Minimum allowable brake pad thickness is 0.090 inch (2.3 mm). When installing brake assembly, tighten retaining screws to 35 in.-lbs. (4.0 N•m) torque.

REWIND STARTER. Refer to Fig. TO126 for exploded view of rewind starter.

To disassemble starter, remove rope handle and allow rope to wind slowly into starter. Remove plastic sleeve (11) and centering pin (10), then unscrew retainer screw (9). Remove retainer (8), brake spring (7), pawls (6) and springs (5). Wear appropriate safety eyewear and gloves before disengaging pulley from starter as spring may uncoil uncontrolled. Place shop towel around pulley and lift pulley out of housing; spring should remain with pulley.

Inspect components for damage and excessive wear. Reverse disassembly procedure to install components. Rewind spring coils wind in counterclockwise direction from outer end. When installing pulley, be sure inner end of rewind spring engages spring retainer adjacent to housing center post. Install

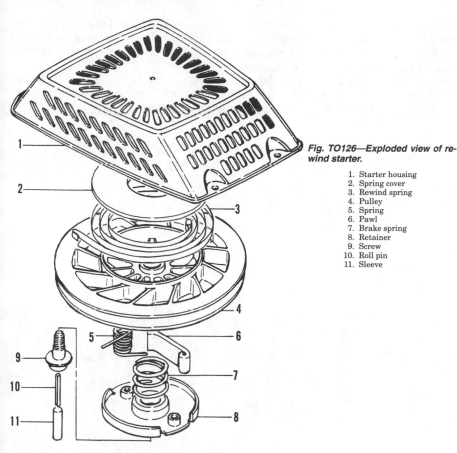

Fig. TO126—Exploded view of re-wind starter.

1. Starter housing
2. Spring cover
3. Rewind spring
4. Pulley
5. Spring
6. Pawl
7. Brake spring
8. Retainer
9. Screw
10. Roll pin
11. Sleeve

the pawl and spring so the spring end (E—Fig. TO127) forces the pawl toward the center of the pulley. Place the retainer on the pulley hub so bosses (B—Fig. TO128) are inside ends of pawls.

With starter assembled, except for rope, install rope as follows: Rotate pulley counterclockwise until tight, then allow to unwind so hole in pulley aligns with rope outlet. Insert rope through starter housing and pulley hole, tie a knot in rope end, allow rope to wind onto pulley and install rope handle.

Install centering pin (10—Fig. TO126) and sleeve (11) in retainer screw. Insert centering pin (10) in retainer screw until bottomed, then install sleeve (11) on pin.

ELECTRIC STARTER MOTOR.
Refer to Fig. TO129 for an exploded view of 12-volt electric starter motor used on some models. Do not run starter for more than five seconds when testing. Starter pinion and helix must move without binding. Do not apply oil to helix (2) or nylon gear (3). Renew brushes if length is $5/64$ inch (2.0 mm) or less.

When assembling starter, note location of washers as shown in Fig. TO129. Be sure notches in end cap, frame and end bracket are aligned. Apply approxi-

Fig. TO127—Spring end (E) should force pawl toward center of pulley.

Fig. TO128—Bosses (B) on retainer must fit inside pawls during assembly.

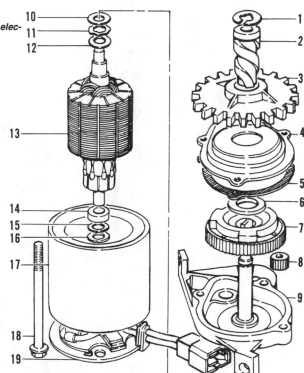

Fig. TO129—Exploded view of electric starter motor.

1. "E" ring
2. Helix
3. Nylon gear
4. Cover
5. Gasket
6. Felt
7. Clutch gear
8. Pinion gear
9. Drive end bracket
10. Plastic washer
11. Spring washer
12. Metal washer
13. Armature
14. Spacer
15. Metal washer
16. Plastic washer
17. Frame
18. Through-bolt
19. Brush end cap

mately ¾ ounce of gear lubricant under clutch (7). Tap end cap (19) to seat bearings.

ALTERNATOR. Engines equipped with an electric starter motor are equipped with an alternator adjacent to the flywheel to charge the battery.

To test alternator output, disconnect black stator lead at white connector. Connect red lead of a DC ammeter to stator lead and black ammeter lead to engine. With engine running, alternator output should be at least 0.5 amps DC at 2800 rpm. If alternator output is zero or low and stator air gap is correct, replace stator.

The air gap between the stator and the flywheel magnets should be 0.010 inch (0.25 mm).

SELF-PROPELLED DRIVE SYSTEMS

ARIENS DISC DRIVE

MAINTENANCE. Drive wheel assemblies are sealed and require no regular maintenance. Periodically check condition of drive belt, drive disc, driven disc, pulleys and control cable.

DRIVE ADJUSTMENT. Position mower cutting height control levers in middle positions. Adjust cable nuts (N—Fig. AR1) to provide a slight amount of slack. Place speed control lever in "SLOW" position. Loosen adjustment screws (S). Hold lever (L) against mower deck and adjust drive assembly to provide 1/32 to 1/16 inch (0.8-1.6 mm) clearance between drive wheel (D) and driven wheel (W). Tighten adjustment screws (S).

DRIVE BELT. To renew drive belt (DB—Fig. AR1), drain fuel from fuel tank and oil from engine crankcase. Disconnect spark plug lead and properly ground lead. Remove battery, as equipped. Set right rear cutting height adjustment lever on notch forward of left rear cutting height adjustment lever to obtain clearance between drive disc (D) and driven disc (W). Place speed control in "SLOW" position. Tip mower onto left side, disconnect idler spring and push idler pulley (I—Fig. AR1) to

one side. Carefully work drive belt (DB) from drive wheel (D) and through mower deck opening under engine. Remove blade and work belt from engine pulley and shaft.

Reverse removal procedure for reinstallation. Make certain idler spring is connected and cutting height adjustment levers are set back in equal positions. Refill crankcase with specified oil and fill fuel tank. Connect spark plug.

DRIVE GEARS AND DRIVE ASSEMBLY. To disassemble drive gears and remove drive assembly, drain fuel tank and engine crankcase. Disconnect and properly ground spark plug lead. Block rear of mower up so drive wheels are off the ground. Remove snap ring and washer retaining left rear wheel to axle and remove wheel. Remove snap ring (SR—Fig. AR1) and gear cover (GC) retaining screws and remove gear cover. Slide differential assembly from axle and remove idler gear by sliding it from idler shaft. Use care not to lose needles from needle bearing pressed into center of idler gear. Support pinion gear and drive roll pin retaining pinion gear on hex shaft out and remove pinion gear.

Remove compression spring at front of drive mount. Remove the two screws securing clutch collar to drive mount and arm and remove clutch collar. Remove cotter pin, washer and shift link.

To remove drive mount for bearing renewal, remove snap ring from behind

axle spline on left side of mower and remove axle bearing. Remove cotter pin retaining left side of trailing shield on bracket. Remove washer and pivot shield end to one side. spread snap ring at right side of axle and pull right wheel and axle out right side of mower. Drive assembly may now be disassembled and bearing or driven disc renewed. Use Ariens bearing drive tool 000026, bearing puller and press to remove bearing. Use Ariens bearing driver 000058 to reinstall bearing.

DRIVE DISC. To renew drive disc, remove drive belt as previously outlined. Remove nut, lock washer and flat washer at top center of drive disc and allow carriage bolt to drop out of disc. Remove the four bolts retaining bearing retainer to drive disc and remove retainer and bearing spindle. Press out the two ball bearings and shim washer from drive disc using Ariens bearing driver 000026. Use Ariens bearing driver 000046 to reinstall bearing.

CHAIN DRIVE SYSTEM

MAINTENANCE. Periodically check all nuts and bolts, bushings and pivots for tightness and smooth operation. Use light oil at pivots and bushings.

To adjust chain tension, mark position of left and right drive brackets. Loosen nuts retaining bracket at chain side and move bracket until all slack has just been removed from chain. Tighten nuts. Measure distance bracket was moved (distance from mark just made to bracket's new position). Loosen opposite drive bracket retaining nuts and move bracket exact distance measured at chain side drive bracket. Tighten nuts. Unequally adjusted brackets may cause mower to drift to right or left from a straight line.

CAUTION: With drive rollers fully engaged, chain must be able to be easily moved side-to-side on drive sprockets. Excessive chain tension will cause rapid chain and sprocket wear as well as damage to auxiliary pto shaft and bushings in engine crankcase.

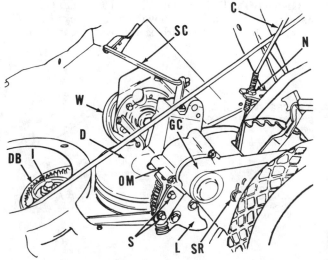

Fig. AR1—View of Ariens disc drive assembly. Engine was removed for clarity only. Service may be performed with engine installed.

 C. Cable
 D. Drive disc
 DB. Drive belt
 DM. Drive mount
 GC. Gear cover
 I. Idler pulley
 L. Lever
 N. Cable adjustment nuts
 S. Adjustment screws
 SC. Speed control rod
 SR. Snap ring
 W. Driven disc

CHAIN DRIVE MECHANISM. A variety of chain drive mechanisms which derive power from a sprocket on auxiliary drive shaft on the engine have been used. Fig. CD1 represents an exploded view typical of most models. Service and disassembly is obvious after inspection and reference to Fig. CD1.

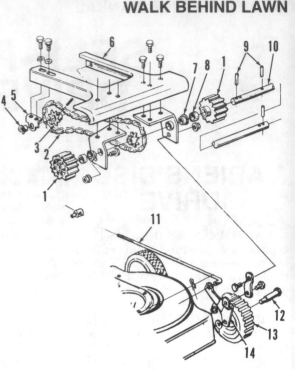

Fig. CD1—Exploded view of typical chain drive mechanism used by a variety of mower manufacturers.

1. Drive roller
2. Chain
3. Drive sprocker
4. Bushing
5. Bracket
6. Shield
7. Bushing
8. Spacer
9. Roll pins
10. Drive shaft
11. Control rod
12. Shoulder bolt
13. Wheel & tire
14. Pivot bracket

CRAFTSMAN GEARBOX

Single Speed Models

MAINTENANCE. Bolt (B—Fig. CR1) should be removed yearly and a good quality lithium base grease pumped into gearbox to assure adequate gear and bearing lubrication. Light oil should be applied to wheel axles at 25-hour intervals.

DRIVE ADJUSTMENT. Drive control cable should be adjusted so that gearbox fully engages and disengages. Loosen cable clamp (C) and adjust cable housing to obtain correct shift lever (S) movement. Tighten cable clamp.

DRIVE BELT. To renew drive belt (D), remove shield to expose gearbox. Disconnect and properly ground spark plug lead. Remove mower blade. Remove left and right wheel hub caps, retaining pins, washers, snap rings, drive gears, dust covers and wheels. Remove the two screws on each side which retain wheel height adjuster plats. Re-

Fig. CR2—View of Craftsman gearbox (G) showing location of drive shaft (D), pulley (P), snap ring (S), cable bracket (C) and bolt (B).

move cable clamp and disconnect drive cable at shift lever. Drive belt may now be removed. Gearbox may be removed if necessary.

GEARBOX. Refer to DRIVE BELT paragraph for gearbox removal procedure. To disassemble gearbox, remove

snap ring (S—Fig. CR2) from input shaft and remove pulley (P) and snap ring located just below pulley. Remove the four screws retaining gearbox halves and remove cable bracket (C). Separate gearbox halves.

Remove worm drive gear (6—Fig. CR3) and shift fork retaining pin (5). Remove shift fork (4) and lift drive shaft (1) and gear assembly from gearbox half. Remove steel pin from input shaft (7) and push input shaft out of gearbox half. Use care not to lose thrust washer between steel pin and gearbox.

To disassemble drive shaft and gear assembly, remove seal (2—Fig. CR4), bushing (3) and snap ring (4). Remove sliding clutch ring (5) and key (6). Remove driven gear (7), bushing (3) and seal (2).

Inspect all parts for wear and damage. Gear surfaces should be flat and dogs on sliding clutch ring and driven gear should be in good condition to pre-

Fig. CR1—View of gearbox used on Craftsman self-propelled walk behind lawn mowers.

B. Bolt
C. Cable clamp
D. Drive belt
G. Gearbox
H. Cable housing
S. Shift lever

Fig. CR3—View of Craftsman gearbox showing components assembled correctly.

1. Drive shaft
2. Seal
3. Bushing
4. Shift fork
5. Shift fork pin
6. Worm gear
7. Input shaft
8. Sliding clutch ring
9. Driven gear

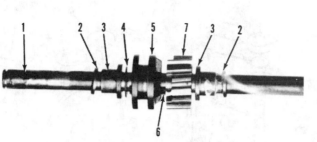

Fig. CR4—View of drive shaft and components removed from gearbox.

1. Drive shaft
2. Seal
3. Bushing
4. Snap ring
5. Sliding clutch ring
6. Key
7. Driven gear

DRIVE BELT REPLACEMENT. Disconnect spark plug cable and ground cable against engine block. Tip mower on its side with carburetor facing up. Remove skirt from rear of mower deck. Unhook belt tension spring (19—Fig. CR5). Remove belt (20) from transmission pulley (14). Pull belt forward off engine pulley and slip belt over the blade. Install new belt in reverse of removal procedure.

REAR WHEELS AND PINION. The rear wheels are driven by pinion

Fig. CR5—Partially exploded view of Sears-Craftsman three speed self drive system.

1. Hub cap
2. Nut
3. Rear wheel
4. Bushing
5. Washer
6. Dust cover
7. Height adjuster
8. Washer
9. "E" ring
10. Pinion
11. Drive pin
12. Drive control head
13. Drive control bar
14. Pulley
15. Gearbox bracket
16. Clutch lever
17. Gearbox assy.
18. Pin
19. Belt tension spring
20. Drive belt

vent jumping out of gear. Reassemble by reversing disassembly procedure. Pack housing with a good quality lithium base grease prior to joining gearbox halves.

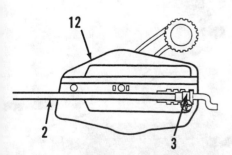

Fig. CR6—To adjust clutch control cable, remove drive control head (12) and reposition clutch cable (2) in control head slots (3).

Three Speed Models

MAINTENANCE. The gearbox is a sealed unit and is packed with grease at the factory. If unit is serviced, refill with good quality lithium base grease.

The wheel drive pinions should be cleaned periodically and lubricated with a spray lubricant or dry powdered graphite lubricant.

DRIVE ADJUSTMENT. The drive should engage when drive control bar (13—Fig. CR5) is squeezed against the handlebar and it should disengage when control bar is released. To adjust, remove drive control head (12) from handle and reposition clutch cable in next slot down from upper end of control head (Fig. CR6).

gears (10—Fig. CR5) that are not interchangeable from side to side. To remove, pry hub cap (1) off wheel and remove retaining nut (2). Withdraw rear wheel (3), bushing (4) and washer (5). Pry "E" ring (9) off axle shaft and remove pinion (10) and drive pin (11).

To reinstall, reverse the removal procedure while noting the following special instructions. Note that pinions are stamped with an "L" for left pinion or "R" for right pinion. The drive will not operate if pinions are installed incorrectly. Lubricate pinions with spray lubricant or dry graphite type lubricant.

GEARBOX. To remove gearbox, remove rear wheels and pinions as outlined above. Disconnect belt tension

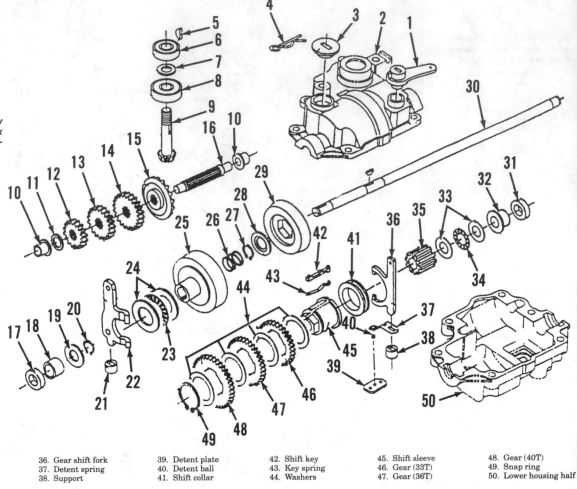

Fig. CR7—Exploded view of three speed gearbox used on some Sears-Craftsman mowers.

1. Shift arm
2. Upper housing half
3. Clutch arm support
4. Pin
5. Key
6. Bearing
7. Washer
8. Bearing
9. Bevel pinion
10. Bushings
11. Washer
12. Gear (12T)
13. Gear (16T)
14. Gear (19T)
15. Bevel ring gear
16. Countershaft
17. Seal
18. Bushing
19. Washer
20. Snap ring
21. Support
22. Clutch shift fork
23. Thrust bearing
24. Thrust washers
25. Sliding clutch half
26. Spring
27. Snap ring
28. Washer
29. Clutch cone
30. Output shaft
31. Seal
32. Bushing
33. Thrust washers
34. Thrust bearing
35. Key support

36. Gear shift fork
37. Detent spring
38. Support

39. Detent plate
40. Detent ball
41. Shift collar

42. Shift key
43. Key spring
44. Washers

45. Shift sleeve
46. Gear (33T)
47. Gear (36T)

48. Gear (40T)
49. Snap ring
50. Lower housing half

spring (19—Fig. CR5), clutch cable and shift cable. Unbolt and remove wheel adjuster assemblies (7) and withdraw gearbox (17) from mower deck.

To disassemble, remove pulley (14), gearbox bracket (15), clutch lever (16) and shift lever. Remove screws from gearbox and separate upper housing half (2—Fig. CR7) from lower housing (50). Lift the output shaft (30) with gears and shift components and countershaft (16) with gears from lower housing.

Separate components from shafts and thoroughly clean. Inspect for wear or damage and renew as needed.

When reassembling, refer to Fig. CR7 for proper placement of components. Note that locating tab of each bushing (10 and 32) must be positioned in bore of lower case. Pinion shaft bearing (6) must be installed with sealed side facing away from bevel gear. Lubricate parts with grease while assembling. Pack lower housing with grease before assembling housing halves. Do not fill the gearcase completely. Clean the mating surface of the housings, then apply sealer to the mating surfaces before fastening upper housing to lower housing.

FOOTE GEARBOXES

Foote gearboxes are used on a variety of self-propelled walk-behind lawn mowers from several different mower manufacturers. Fig. F1 shows an external view of a Foote gearbox and shows serial number location (S). Fig. F2 shows an exploded view of a Foote 2820 series gearbox. Foote 2840 series gearboxes are similar.

Fig. F1—Foote gearbox serial numbers (S) are stamped into gearbox upper housing. Parts indicated are L—Shift lever, I—Input shaft and C—Cap screw.

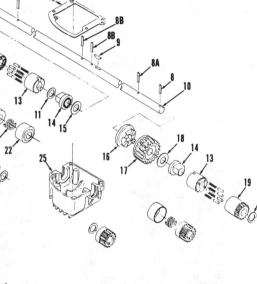

Fig. F2—Exploded view of Foote 2820 series gearbox. Foote 2840 series is similar.

1. Bolts
2. Upper housing
3. Snap ring
4. Washer (0.015, 0.020, 0.030 in.)
5. Key
6. Input shaft
7. Gasket
8. Roll pin
8A. Roll pin
8B. Roll pin
9. Key
10. Drive shaft
11. Washer
12. Ratchet gear (some models)
13. Ratchet assy.
14. Bushing
15. Washer
16. Sliding clutch gear
17. Driven gear
18. Washer
19. Ratchet gear (some models)
20. Ratchet gear (some models)
21. Spring (some models)
22. Dust cover
23. Ratchet gear (some models)
24. Washer
25. Lower housing

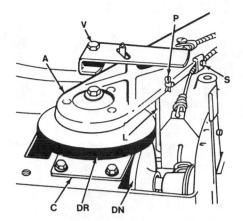

Fig. J1—View of front-wheel drive system used on Jacobsen mowers.

A. Drive support arm		L. Clutch link
C. Gearbox cover		P. Pin
DN. Driven wheel		S. Clamp screw
DR. Drive wheel		V. Pivot pin

MAINTENANCE. Foote gearboxes are a sealed unit and are packed with grease at the factory. Periodically check drive belt condition and make certain all bolts are tight.

DRIVE ADJUSTMENT. Drive control cable or linkage must be adjusted so gearbox shift lever (L—Fig. F1) fully disengages gearbox when mower control is in disengaged position.

GEARBOX. To disassemble gearbox, remove snap ring, pulley and lower snap ring from input shaft (6—Fig. F2). Remove cap screw (C—Fig. F1), flat washer and shift lever (L). Remove the four cap screws from gearbox and carefully lift off upper housing (2—Fig. F2). Input shaft (6) may be removed from upper housing after removing key (5) and snap ring (3). Remove gasket (7). Carefully lift drive shaft (10) and gear assembly from lower housing (25). Remove roll pins (8B) and slide thrust washer (11), bushing (14), washer (15) and sliding clutch ring (16) from drive shaft. Remove key (9), driven gear (17), washer (18) and bushing (14). The plastic shift assembly is riveted to the upper case and cannot be disassembled.

Reassemble by reversing disassembly procedure. Pack lower housing with a good quality multipurpose grease before installing upper housing.

HOMELITE/ JACOBSEN

Front-Wheel Drive Models

LUBRICATION. The gearbox should not require lubrication unless leakage has occurred. To check lubricant level or add lubricant, remove cover over drive assembly. Detach cotter pin (P—Fig. J1) and disengage clutch link (L) from support arm (A). Remove pivot pin (V) and move support arm (A) so there is access to gearbox cover (C). Remove cover (C). Grease should be just below or level with drive shaft. Fill with SAE 250EP gear grease as needed. After assembly, adjust cable as outlined in following paragraph. When reinstalling drive cover, be sure shortest screw is in rear hole and longest screw is in front hole.

CABLE ADJUSTMENT. Be sure cable is in good condition and operates freely. Remove cover over drive assembly and determine that drive support arm (A—Fig. J1) is tight. With drive control in neutral position there must be a gap between the drive wheel (DR) and driven wheel (DN) not to exceed 1/2 inch (3.1 mm). To adjust gap, move speed control to "FAST" position. Loosen cable

clamp screw (S) and pull cable housing so there is 1/16 inch (1.5 mm) gap between drive and driven wheels. Tighten cable clamp screw and recheck gap. When reinstalling drive cover, be sure shortest screw is in rear hole and longest screw is in front hole.

DRIVE BELT. To remove and replace drive belt proceed as follows. Properly ground spark plug wire. Remove drive belt cover. Remove blade. Unscrew flange nut (F—Fig. J2) and remove spacer (R) between idler pulleys (I). Install new belt using diagram shown in Fig. J3. Tighten blade retaining screw to 55-65 ft.-lbs. (75-88 N•m). When reinstalling drive cover, be sure shortest screw is in rear hole and longest screw is in front hole.

DRIVE MECHANISM. A gear and shaft assembly is located in the front of the mower deck. A belt-driven disc system drives the gears and shaft.

The drive disc rides on a hub that is supported in a bearing located in the support arm (A—Fig. J1). Unscrew re-

Fig. J2—Flange nut (F) and spacer (R) between idler pulleys (I) must be removed to remove drive belt.

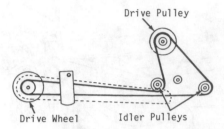

Fig. J3—Diagram of belt routing on Jacobsen front-wheel drive mowers.

taining bolt to remove disc and hub. Drill out rivets and remove bearing cover for access to bearing.

To disassemble gear assembly, remove cover over drive assembly. Detach cotter pin (P—Fig. J1) and disengage link (L) from support arm (A). Remove pivot pin (V) and move support arm (A) so there is access to gearbox cover (C). Remove cover (C). Remove wheels, pinions and pawls. Detach snap ring (16—Fig. J4) and remove wheel support (26). Drive out roll pin (4) and disassemble shaft and gears.

Inspect components for damage and excessive wear. Reassemble unit by reversing disassembly procedure. Install shims (2 and 9) as needed to remove excessive end play. Fill gearbox to level of drive shaft with SAE 250EP gear

grease. Adjust control cable as previously outlined.

Rear-Wheel Drive Models

LUBRICATION. Early models with steel gears are lubricated by removing the gearbox cover and packing gearbox with 40 cc of #2 automotive wheel bearing grease. On models prior to 1983 with a gear type clutch and a nylon worm gear, fill to bottom of oil fill plug (approximately 30 cc) with SAE 140 gear lubricant. On models after 1982, fill with type "F" automatic transmission fluid to level of oil fill hole (approximately 40 cc).

Some early models are equipped with an oil hole in the top of the drive cover. Every month or after every 40 hours of operation inject a few drops of SAE 30 oil to lubricate pulley shaft.

CABLE ADJUSTMENT. Models Prior to 1983. The tension spring attached to the cable should stretch approximately 1/8 inch (3.2 mm) when the drive control lever is in fully engaged position. Roll mower back and forth to be sure drive is engaged. The gearbox should not emit a clicking sound when rolling mower. The cable is adjusted too tight if clicking is heard. To adjust cable, loosen cable clamp on deck and reposi-

tion cable housing. Recheck adjustment.

Models After 1982. If drive cable is equipped with a clevis at lower end, adjust clevis so drive engages and disengages properly. If there is no clevis present at lower end of cable, loosen cable housing clamp and reposition clamp to remove any slack. If drive does not disengage, then cable is too tight and cable must be repositioned in clamp.

DRIVE BELT. Models Prior to 1978. To remove drive belt, disconnect and properly ground spark plug wire. Remove drive cover. Unscrew drive pulley screw (pulley is spring-loaded so hold spring retainer while removing screw) and remove upper pulley half. Remove blade, slide drive pulley down and pull belt out through bottom of deck. Install belt by reversing removal procedure. Be sure drive pulley key is installed.

Models After 1977. To remove drive belt disconnect and properly ground spark plug wire. Remove drive cover, tilt gearbox forward and detach belt from gearbox pulley. Pull belt down through bottom of deck and away from blade. Reinstall belt by reversing removal procedure. On some models the drive pulley has two grooves to adjust mower travel speed; installing belt in small diameter pulley will provide slow travel speed.

GEARBOX. Three variations of a similar gearbox design have been used. Refer to Figs. J5, J6 and J7 for exploded views of gearbox. Note that component parts for early model gearboxes may not be available; renewal of gearbox assembly will be necessary if components are excessively worn or damaged.

Note position of all shims and washers during disassembly. Note that wheel drive pinions are designed for use at right or left end of drive shaft and are not interchangeable. The worm shaft bearing on later models (Figs. J6 and J7) is retained in the gearbox by Loctite retaining compound. Carefully heat housing in bearing area using a propane torch to loosen Loctite, then pull up drive pulley to withdraw worm shaft and bearing assembly from gearbox. (Don not use excess heat as bearing and seals will be damaged.) If drive pulley must be removed from worm shaft on later models, press shaft out of pulley so roll pin is sheared.

Inspect components for damage and excessive wear. When installing bearing on worm shaft, apply Loctite bearing retaining fluid to inner diameter. Apply Loctite bearing retaining compound to outer diameter of bearing when installing worm shaft assembly into gearbox.

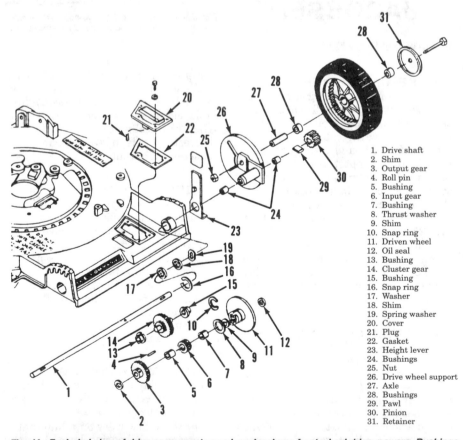

1. Drive shaft
2. Shim
3. Output gear
4. Roll pin
5. Bushing
6. Input gear
7. Bushing
8. Thrust washer
9. Shim
10. Snap ring
11. Driven wheel
12. Oil seal
13. Bushing
14. Cluster gear
15. Bushing
16. Snap ring
17. Washer
18. Shim
19. Spring washer
20. Cover
21. Plug
22. Gasket
23. Height lever
24. Bushings
25. Nut
26. Drive wheel support
27. Axle
28. Bushings
29. Pawl
30. Pinion
31. Retainer

Fig. J4—Exploded view of drive components used on Jacobsen front-wheel drive mowers. Bushings and oil seals in mower housing are not shown.

Fig. J5—Exploded view of gearbox used on early Jacobsen rear-wheel drive mowers.

1. Retainer
2. Spring
3. Pulley halves
5. Snap ring
6. Bearing
7. Key
8. Worm shaft
9. Washer
10. Bearing
11. Selector lever
12. Snap ring
13. Washer
14. Oil seal
15. Bushing
16. Gearbox
17. Selector fork
18. Drive shaft
20. Bearing
21. Worm gear
22. Bushing
23. Washer
24. Snap ring
25. Spring
26. Coupler
27. Gasket
28. Washer
29. Cover
30. Bushing
31. Oil seal

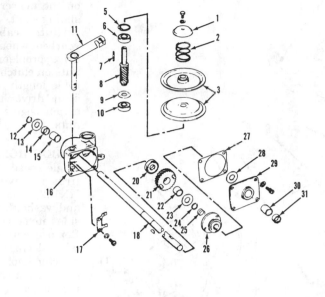

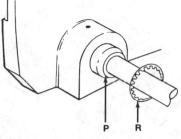

Fig. J8—On early models, install toothed retainer ring (R) on pivot shaft (P) so teeth point away from pivot shaft.

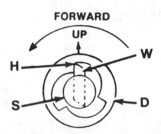

Fig. J9—On later models using drive pawls (W) inside the drive pinions (D), install pawl and pinion as shown with high edge (H) on pawl toward front of mower.

Fill gearbox with lubricant as outlined in LUBRICATION section. Tighten gearbox cover screws to 60-80 in.-lbs.. (6.8-9.0 N•m).

On early models the wheel pivot shaft is secured by a toothed, "push-on" retainer which is installed so teeth point away from wheel as shown in Fig. J8.

The wheel drive pinions on early models are secured by a roll pin. On later models the pinions are coupled to the drive shaft by a pawl. The pawl must be installed as shown in Fig. J9.

Fig. J6—Exploded view of gearbox used on later Jacobsen rear-wheel drive mowers prior to 1983.

1. Selector lever
2. Snap ring
3. "O" ring
4. Seal
5. Cover
7. Bushings
8. Pin
9. Selector fork
10. Coupler
11. Spring
12. Worm gear
14. Drive shaft
16. Gearbox
17. Seal
18. Pulley
19. Roll pin
20. Bearing
21. Worm shaft

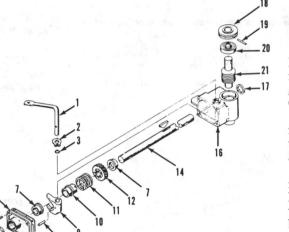

HONDA

SINGLE AND TWO-SPEED GEARBOX

MAINTENANCE. Both the single and the two-speed gearboxes contain 130 cc (1/4 pint) of SAE 90 hypoid gear oil. Gearboxes are sealed and no general maintenance is required. If leakage is apparent, correct leak, clean and refill gearbox.

CLUTCH. Forward mower motion is controlled by the engagement of a clutch dog on the bevel gear (5—Fig. HN100 or Fig. HN101). Low and high speeds on two-speed gearbox are controlled by moving the shift sliding shaft (31—Fig. HN101) and shifter (11) to engage one of the two drive gears (12 and 13) with the countershaft (7). A gear change lever

Fig. J7—Exploded view of typical gearbox used on Homelite/Jacobsen rear-wheel drive mowers after 1982.

1. Selector lever
2. Snap ring
3. "O" ring
4. Seal
5. Cover
6. Gasket
7. Bushing
8. Pin
9. Selector fork
10. Coupler
11. Friction cone
12. Worm gear
13. Thrust washers
14. Thrust bearing
15. Plug
16. Gearbox
17. Drive shaft
19. Pulley
20. Roll pin
21. Bearing
22. Washer
23. Spacer
24. Worm
25. Vent
26. Input shaft
27. Roll pin
28. Bearing

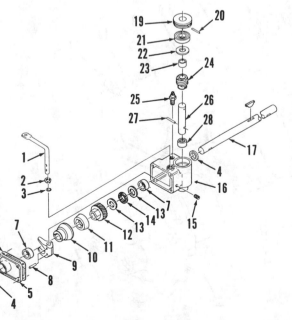

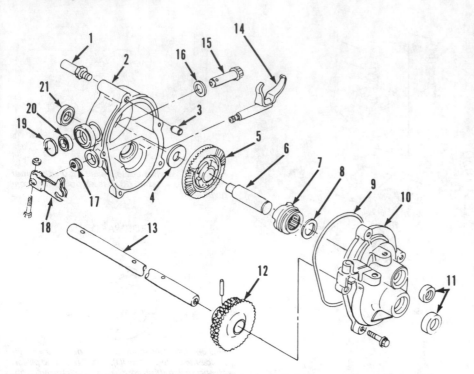

Fig. HN100—Exploded view of single-speed Honda gearbox used on some self-propelled models.

1. Guide stud
2. Case half
3. Dowel pin
4. Thrust washer
5. Bevel gear
6. Countershaft
7. Driven clutch gear
8. Thrust washer
9. Sealing ring
10. Case half
11. Oil seal
12. Axle gear
13. Axle
14. Clutch shift fork
15. Pinion gear
16. Thrust washer
17. Oil seal
18. Clutch shift lever
19. Pin retaining spring
20. Oil seal
21. Oil seal

on the mower deck actuates the shift sliding shaft.

Clutch cable should be adjusted yearly or whenever there is an apparent drive problem. To adjust, loosen jam nuts on clutch control cable and adjust cable length to provide 5-10 mm ($\frac{3}{16}$-$\frac{3}{8}$ in.) drive clutch lever free play before clutch begins to engage. Tighten jam nuts.

GEARBOX. To remove either the single-speed or the two-speed gearbox, first remove rear wheels (8—Fig. HN102), washer (6), ratchet (5), pin (4) and washer (3). Note that left and right side ratchets must not be interchanged. Remove cutting height control spring (9) and cross-shaft (11). Remove gear selector knob (two-speed models). Disconnect clutch cable at gearbox. Slide rubber dust cover from pto coupler, remove spring and pin from coupler. Withdraw gearbox from mower.

When reinstalling gearbox, note that washer (3—Fig. HN102) is installed with cupped side toward wheel. Adjust clutch control as previously outlined.

SINGLE-SPEED GEARBOX. Refer to Fig. HN100 for exploded view of single-speed gearbox. To disassemble,

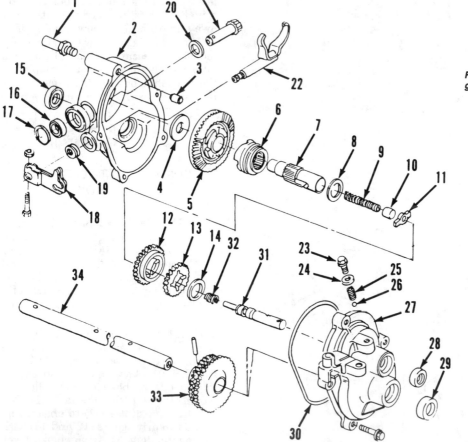

Fig. HN101—Exploded view of two-speed Honda gearbox used on some self-propelled models.

1. Guide stud
2. Case half
3. Dowel pin
4. Thrust washer
5. Bevel gear
6. Driven clutch gear
7. Countershaft
8. Thrust washer
9. Spring
10. Spring retainer
11. Shifter
12. High gear
13. Low gear
14. Thrust washer
15. Oil seal
16. Oil seal
17. Pin retaining spring
18. Clutch shift lever
19. Oil seal
20. Thrust washer
21. Pinion gear
22. Clutch shift fork
23. Bolt
24. Washer
25. Spring
26. Detent ball
27. Case half
28. Oil seal
29. Oil seal
30. Sealing ring
31. Shift sliding shaft
32. Shift spring
33. Axle gear
34. Axle

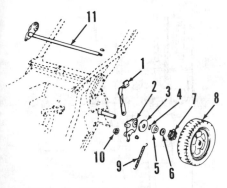

Fig. HN102—Exploded view of rear wheel and axle assembly on Honda self-propelled mowers.

1. Height adjustment
   lever
2. Adjustment arm
3. Cupped washer
4. Pin
5. Ratchet

6. Washer
7. Ratchet outer ring
8. Tire
9. Spring
10. Bushing
11. Cross-shaft

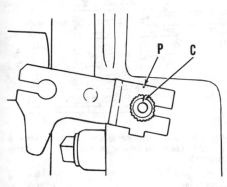

Fig. HN103—When installing clutch fork shift lever, punch mark (P) on shift lever must be aligned with chisel mark (C) on clutch fork shaft end.

remove cap screws attaching gearbox case halves and separate the case halves. Drain gear oil into suitable container. Remove axle (13) and axle gear (12). Remove countershaft (6) and clutch dog (7). Withdraw pinion gear (15) from inside case and remove bevel gear (5). Loosen clamp bolt and separate shift lever (18) from shift fork (14). Drive oil seals from case halves.

Inspect clutch dog and bevel gear for wear and renew as needed. Renew all oil seals. When reassembling, be sure that lip (open side) of all oil seals faces inward. Use care when installing shafts through oil seals to avoid damaging seal lip. When installing clutch shift fork and shift lever, note that punch mark (P—Fig. HN103) must be aligned with chisel mark (C) on end of clutch fork shaft. Make certain that thrust washers (4, 8 and 16—Fig. HN100) are installed in correct location. Fill gearbox case with 130 cc (¼ pint) SAE 90 gear oil. Assemble case halves with new "O" ring (9). After assembly check for smooth operation of pinion gear and shift lever.

TWO-SPEED GEARBOX. Refer to Fig. HN101 for exploded view of two-speed gearbox. To disassemble, remove cap screws attaching gearbox case halves and separate the case halves. Drain gear oil into suitable container. Remove axle (34) and axle gears (33). Remove shift slider (31), gears (12 and 13), countershaft (7) and clutch dog (6). Rotate shifter (11) 90 degrees to disengage it from the countershaft. Withdraw pinion gear (21) from inside case and remove bevel gear (5). Loosen clamp bolt and remove shift lever (18) and shift fork (22). Drive oil seals from case halves.

Inspect clutch dog and gear teeth for wear or damage and renew as necessary. Renew all oil seals. When reassembling, be sure that lip (open side) of all oil seals faces inward. Use care when installing shafts through oil seals to avoid damaging seal lip. When installing clutch fork shift lever, note that punch mark (P—Fig. HN103) must be aligned with chisel mark (C) on end of clutch fork shaft. Make certain that thrust washers (4, 8 14 and 20—Fig. HN101) are installed in correct location. Note that shift spring (9), spring retainer (10) and shifter (11) are installed inside bore of countershaft (7). Install shifter (11) and rotate 90 degrees to lock in position. Refill gearbox case with 130 cc (¼ pint) SAE 90 gear oil. Assemble case halves with new "O" ring (30). After assembly check for smooth operation of pinion gear (21), clutch shift lever and shift sliding shaft.

THREE-SPEED GEARBOX

MAINTENANCE. Oil capacity of gearbox is 200 cc (0.4 pint). Recommended oil is SAE 90 hypoid gear oil. The gearbox is sealed. If leakage is apparent, correct leak and refill gearbox.

CLUTCH. Forward mower motion is controlled by the engagement of clutch dogs on the bevel gear and clutch dogs on the driven clutch gear inside the gearbox. Clutch control is controlled at the handlebar via control cable connected to the gearbox.

To adjust clutch cable, loosen lock nuts on control cable and adjust cable length to provide 10-15 mm (⅜-⁹⁄₁₆ inch) free play at top of operating bar before clutch engages. Tighten lock nuts.

SHIFT CONTROL CABLE. When the gearbox is in second gear the handlebar control lever should align with "2" on the gear indicator panel. If not, loosen lock nuts on cable and turn

nuts until control lever is correctly positioned. Tighten lock nuts.

GEARBOX. To remove gearbox, loosen lock nuts on clutch cable and shift cable at handlebar end of cables. Remove rear wheels (8—Fig. HN102), washer (6), ratchet (5), pin (4) and washer (3). Note that left and right side ratchets are not interchangeable. Detach height control spring (9) and crossshaft (11). Remove deck cover. Disengage clip from pto coupler pin, remove pin and disconnect pto coupler from gearbox input shaft. Remove gearbox from mower. Detach clutch and shift cables and arms from gearbox while noting alignment marks on arms and shaft ends.

To disassemble, remove retaining screws from transmission case and separate case halves (Fig. HN104). Remove shift detent assembly (42 through 46). Withdraw countershaft (16) with drive gears and clutch dog (14). Remove bevel gear (12), bevel pinion shaft (9) and clutch fork (6). Separate output gears and washers (23 through 28) and shift components (30 through 35) from axle shaft (22). Unbolt and remove seal retainer (38 and 39) and shift fork (41) from case.

Inspect components for wear or damage and renew as necessary. It is recommended that all oil seals and "O" rings be renewed when reassembling.

To reassemble gearbox, assemble shift boss (30—Fig. HN104) springs (31), drive keys (32) and shift collar (33), then insert key holder (34) in shift collar. Position detent ball (46) in second (center) notch of shift shaft (41). Tighten shift detent screw (42) to 10 N•m (88 in.-lbs.). Assemble drive and output gears in order shown in Fig. HN104. Make certain that thrust washers are located correctly. Fill case half with 200 cc (0.4 pint) of SAE 90 hypoid gear oil before mating cases. Be sure that clutch fork (6) engages groove in clutch dog (14). Check for smooth operation after assembly.

Before installing gearbox, install clutch and shift arms so punch marks on arm and shaft are aligned. When properly installed, the bottom face of the bottom lock nut of the shift cable should be flush with or within 1 mm (0.040 inch) of the bottom thread of shift cable. Tighten lock nuts to 18 N•m (13 ft.-lbs.). If pto shaft was disconnected at spline coupling, connect engine coupler and transmission coupler so pin at transmission end and pin at engine end are aligned.

After gearbox installation, install remainder of drive components. Install washers (3—Fig. HN102) with cupped

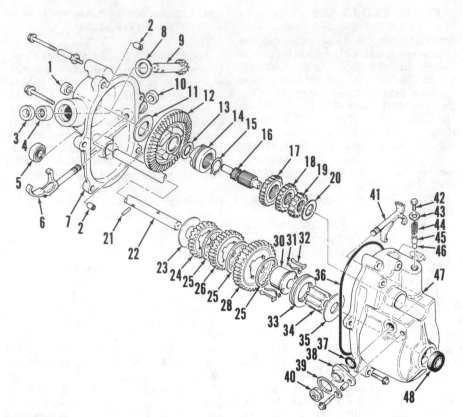

Fig. HN104—Exploded view of typical three-speed gearbox used on some Honda self-propelled mowers.

1. Seal plug
2. Dowel pin
3. Oil seal
4. Bearing
5. Oil seal
6. Clutch fork
7. Cover
8. Washer
9. Pinion shaft
10. Oil seal
11. Thrust washer
12. Bevel gear
13. Washer
14. Clutch dog
15. Snap ring
16. Countershaft
17. 3rd drive gear (20T)

18. 2nd drive gear (18T)
19. 1at drive gear (14T)
20. Thrust washer
21. Shift boss pin
22. Axle shaft
23. Washer
24. 3rd output gear (27T)
25. Washers
26. 2nd output gear (29T)
28. 1st output gear (33T)
30. Shift boss
31. Key spring
32. Drive key

33. Shift collar
34. Key holder
35. Thrust washer
36. "O" ring
37. "O" ring
38. Seal holder
39. Retainer
40. Oil seal
41. Shift fork
42. Screw
43. Seal washer
44. Spring
45. Ball retainer
46. Detent ball
47. Case
48. Oil seal

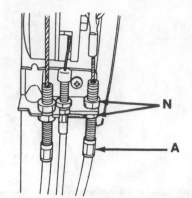

Fig. HN105—Drawing of mower control cables typical of many Honda mowers. To adjust cable, loosen locknuts (N) and turn cable adjuster (A).

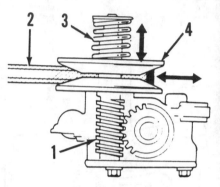

Fig. HN106—On Honda Model HR21 mowers, a variable speed pulley (4) drives gearbox worm gear (1).

1. Worm gear
2. Drive belt
3. Tension spring
4. Driven pulley

side toward mower deck. Adjust clutch and shift cables as previously outlined.

THREE-SPEED VARIABLE PULLEY DRIVE

Models HR21 and HR21-5

MAINTENANCE. Gearbox oil capacity is 50 cc (0.1 pint). Recommended oil is SAE 90 hypoid gear oil. The gearbox is sealed. If leakage is apparent, correct leak and refill gearbox with recommended lubricant.

Model HRA21

MAINTENANCE. Gearbox oil capacity is 80 cc (0.16 pint). Recommended oil is SAE 90 hypoid gear oil. The gearbox is sealed. If leakage is ap-

parent, correct leak and refill gearbox with recommended lubricant.

All Models

CLUTCH. Forward mower motion is controlled by the engagement of clutch dogs on the worm drive gear and the sliding shift collar inside the gearbox. The clutch is controlled at the handlebar via a control cable connected to the gear box.

To adjust clutch cable, stop engine and release drive control handle. Measure free play at outer tip of drive control handle. Lever free play should be 5-10 mm ($^3/_{16}$-$^3/_8$ in.) for Model HR21, 7-12 mm ($^5/_{16}$-$^1/_2$ in.) for Model HRA21 or 15-20 mm ($^5/_8$-$^3/_4$ in.) for Model HR21-5. To adjust, loosen locknut (N—Fig. HN105) on clutch cable and turn cable adjuster (A) to shorten or lengthen cable

as necessary. Tighten locknut and check clutch operation.

Model HR21

DRIVE BELT AND VARIABLE SPEED PULLEY. The driven pulley (4—Fig. HN106) features a spring-loaded moveable sheave that creates a variable diameter for the drive belt. Depending on position of shift lever, the belt tension arm increases or decreases drive belt tension. With shift lever in third speed position, belt tension is increased to the maximum. Belt tension forces pulley halves to spread apart and compress the pulley spring, allowing the drive belt (2) to be pulled to inside (smallest) diameter of the driven pulley resulting in maximum speed. With shift lever in first speed, belt tension is reduced which allows pulley spring (3) to slide the pulley halves together, forcing belt to the outside (largest) diameter of pulley. Mower speed is reduced to slowest speed with pulley and belt in this position.

The traction drive belt (2—Fig. HN107) can be renewed without removing the mower blade. Stop engine and

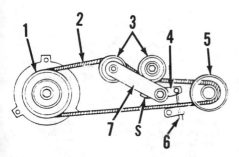

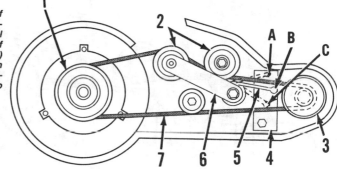

Fig. HN107—Drawing of Honda Model HR21 variable speed drive system.

1. Engine pulley
2. Drive belt
3. Idler pulleys
4. Shift arm
5. Driven pulley
6. Shift cable
7. Tension arm

Fig. HN109—Drawing of variable speed drive system used on Honda Model HR21-5. The position of belt tension spring (5) must be changed to match speed setting of driven pulley (Fig. HN108). Refer to text.

1. Engine pulley
2. Idler pulleys
3. Driven pulley
4. Spring hook plate
5. Belt tension spring
6. Tension arm
7. Drive belt

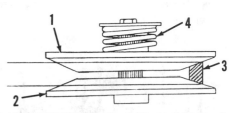

Fig. HN110—Drawing of variable speed driven pulley used on Honda Model HRA21 mowers. Refer to text for operating principles.

remove spark plug cable. Remove belt cover from mower deck. Remove belt from tension arm rollers (3), driven pulley (5) and drive pulley (1). Work the belt over the blade and remove from mower.

Install new belt, routing it around the tension arm rollers as shown in Fig. HN107. Adjust shift cable as follows: Loosen shift cable locknut and screw the cable adjusting bolt fully in. Move shift lever to third speed position. Push in on drive belt so belt is pulled to the inside (smallest) diameter of driven pulley. Turn cable adjusting bolt out so shift arm stop (S) contacts the tension arm, then turn adjusting bolt out an additional 4 turns. Tighten locknut.

Model HR21-5

DRIVE BELT AND VARIABLE SPEED PULLEY. The self-propelled drive features a variable diameter driven pulley (HN108) that can be set to any one of three speed settings. The mower is set at the factory in the intermediate (second speed) setting as shown in Fig. HN108. To change speed setting, remove belt cover from top of mower. Remove cap screw retaining driven pulley halves and reposition spacers (A and B—Fig. HN108) on the pulley. Positioning both spacers on top of pulley results in largest diameter pul-

ley setting and slowest (first) speed. Positioning one spacer between pulley halves and one spacer on top as shown in Fig. HN108 gives intermediate (second) speed setting. Positioning both spacers between pulley halves results in smallest pulley diameter and fastest (third) speed setting.

The belt tension arm (6—Fig. HN109) is spring-loaded. Drive belt tension must be adjusted when changing driven pulley speed setting. In first speed setting, tension arm spring (5) should be hooked in hole (A—Fig. HN109) of spring hook plate (4). Hook spring in middle hole (B) for second speed setting and in hole (C) of hook plate for third speed setting.

The traction drive belt (7—Fig. HN109) can be renewed without removing the mower blade. Stop engine and remove spark plug cable. Remove belt cover from mower deck. Remove belt from tension arm rollers (2), driven pulley (3) and drive pulley (1). Work the belt over the blade and remove from mower. Install new belt, routing it around the tension arm rollers as shown in Fig. HN109. Adjust clutch cable as previously outlined.

Model HRA21

DRIVE BELT AND VARIABLE SPEED PULLEY. The self-propelled drive features a variable diameter driven pulley (Fig. HN110) that can be set to any one of three speed settings. Fig. HN110 illustrates the spring-loaded pulley halves (1 and 2) with belt (3) in the intermediate (second speed) position. The speed settings are determined by the amount of tension that is placed on the drive belt. The belt tension setting is changed by repositioning the transmission and driven pulley closer to or farther away from the drive pulley. When belt tension is at maximum setting, belt tension forces pulley halves to spread apart and compress the pulley spring. The drive belt (3—Fig. HN110) is pulled to inside (smallest)

diameter of the driven pulley resulting in maximum (third) speed. When belt tension is at minimum setting, belt tension is reduced which allows pulley spring to slide the pulley halves together, forcing belt to the outside (largest) diameter of pulley. Mower speed is reduced to slowest (first) speed with pulley and belt in this position.

To change speed setting, remove belt cover and grasp drive belt (2—Fig. HN111). Pull up on the belt and work it into bottom of driven pulley (6). Pull out lock pin (4) and reposition the pin to one of three holes in the speed change arm (5). Moving pin to hole (A) closest to front end of speed change arm results in greatest belt tension setting and provides maximum speed. Moving pin to intermediate hole (B) or rear hole (C) in speed change arm, decreases belt tension and provides intermediate and low speed settings.

The traction drive belt (2—Fig. HN111) can be renewed without removing the mower blade. Stop engine and remove spark plug cable. Remove belt cover from mower deck. Remove lock pin (4) from speed change arm (5). Move the transmission to remove tension on belt, then work belt off driven pulley (6), drive pulley (1) and idler (7). It may be necessary to remove idler pulley belt keeper to provide clearance for removal of belt from idler. Work the belt over the blade and remove from mower. Install new belt.

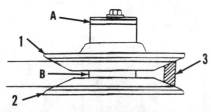

Fig. HN108—Drawing of three-speed driven pulley used on Honda Model HR21-5 mowers. Speed settings are determined by position of spacers (A) and (B).

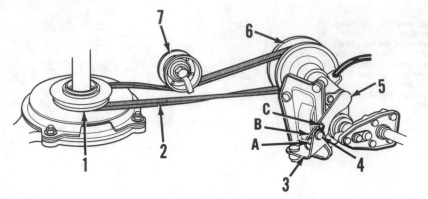

Fig. HN111—Drawing of three-speed drive system used on Honda Model HR21-5. Speed setting is changed by repositioning pin (4) in one of the three holes (A, B and C) in speed change arm (5).

1. Engine pulley
2. Drive belt
3. Bracket
4. Pin
5. Speed change arm
6. Driven pulley
7. Idler

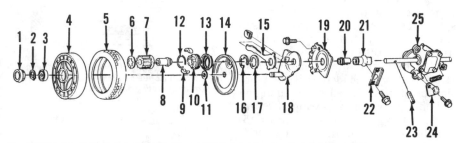

Fig. HN112—Exploded view of Honda Model HR21 rear wheel and pinion assembly.

1. Hub cap	8. Bushing	14. Dust cover	20. Bushing
2. Snap ring	9. Pawl	15. Height adjusting lever	21. Shaft boss
3. Bearing	10. One-way clutch	16. "E" ring	22. Mounting plate
4. Wheel	11. Thrust washer	17. Thrust washer	23. Pin
5. Tire	12. Retaining ring	18. Lever holder	24. Spring holder
6. Push nut	13. Pinion gear cap	19. Adjuster plate	25. Gearbox assy.
7. Pinion gear			

Model HR21

REAR WHEELS AND PINION. To remove rear wheels and drive pinion, remove hub cap (1—Fig. HN112), snap ring (2) and wheel assembly (3, 4 and 5).

Pry push nut (6) off axle shaft and withdraw pinion gear (7), bushing (8), pawls (9), ratchet (10), gear cap (13) and wheel cover (14). Inspect all parts for wear or damage and renew as necessary. When reassembling, lubricate pinion gear cap

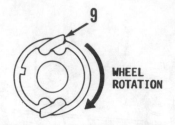

Fig. HN113—Pawls (9) must be installed in one-way clutch so pawl points in direction of forward wheel travel.

(13) with multipurpose grease. Note that pawls (9) must be installed so they point in direction of forward wheel rotation as shown in Fig. HN113.

Model HR21-5

REAR WHEELS AND PINION. To remove rear wheels and drive pinion, remove hub cap (1—Fig. HN114), retaining bolt (2) and wheel (3). Unscrew pinion gear retaining bolt (4) and withdraw pinion gear and one-way clutch assembly (6). Compress adjusting lever (12) and thrust washer (11), then disengage "E" ring (10) from shaft. Remove retaining screws and separate height adjusting arm (15) from wheel cover (9). Inspect all parts for wear or damage and renew as necessary.

Model HRA21

REAR WHEELS. To remove rear wheel assembly, unscrew wheel retaining bolt (1—Fig. HN115). Separate dust cover (7) from clutch holder (6), then withdraw wheel (3) and one-way clutch as a unit. Remove clutch holder mounting bolts (3) and separate clutch holder

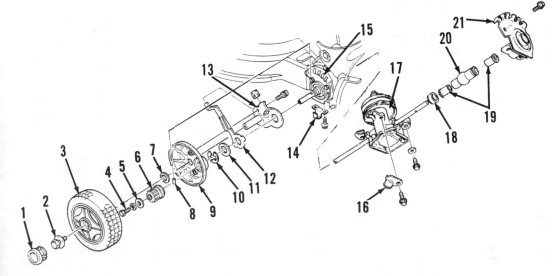

Fig. HN114—Exploded view of rear wheel and drive pinion assembly used on Honda Model HR21-5 mowers.

1. Hub cap
2. Retaining bolt
3. Wheel
4. Bolt
5. Thrust washer
6. Pinion gear
7. Thrust washer
8. Pin
9. Dust cover
10. "E" ring
11. Washer
12. Height adjusting lever
13. Adjusting arm
14. Axle mounting bracket
15. Adjusting plate, L.H.
16. Spring holder
17. Gearbox assy.
18. Dust seal
19. Bushings
20. Bushing boss
21. Adjusting plate, R.H.

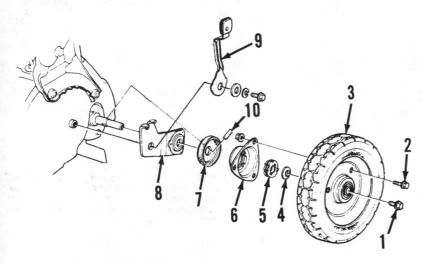

Fig. HN115—Exploded view of rear wheel and drive pinion used on Honda Model HRA21 mowers.

1. Retaining bolt	6. Clutch holder
2. Bolt	7. Dust cover
3. Wheel	8. Adjuster arm
4. Thrust washer	9. Adjuster lever
5. One-way clutch	10. Pin

(6), one-way clutch pawl (5) and thrust washer (4) from wheel. Inspect clutch pawl and gear teeth in wheel for wear or damage. When reassembling, make certain that clutch pawl is installed so pawl teeth point in direction of forward wheel travel and that drive pin (10) engages slot in pawl.

Models HR21 and HR21-5

GEARBOX. To remove gearbox (25—Fig. HN112) from Model HR21, first disconnect spark plug cable to prevent accidental starting. Remove drive belt cover and disengage drive belt from gearbox pulley. Tip mower on its right side to prevent oil from entering crankcase ventilation chamber. Remove rear wheels as outlined previously. Remove cap screws attaching wheel height adjuster plates (19) and axle retaining plates (22) to mower deck. Disconnect drive clutch cable from gearbox and remove gearbox assembly. Remove "E" ring (16—Fig. HN112) and withdraw height adjuster components, bushing (20) and bushing holder (21) from axle shaft.

To remove gearbox (17—Fig. HN114) from Model HR21-5, first disconnect spark plug cable to prevent accidental starting. Remove drive belt cover and disengage drive belt from gearbox pulley. Tip mower on its right side to prevent oil from entering crankcase ventilation chamber. Remove rear wheels as outlined previously. Remove cap screws attaching height adjusting plates (15 and 21) to mower deck. Disconnect drive clutch cable and remove gearbox assembly from mower. When reinstalling gearbox, pack multipurpose grease in the cavity in bushing holder (20) between axle bushings (19) and in grooves inside the dust seal (18).

To disassemble gearbox on all models, remove gearbox cover (1—Fig. HN116) and drain oil from housing. Loosen clamp bolt and remove clutch arm (13). Drive split pin (5) out of axle shaft (10); note that a pocket is provided in bottom of the gearbox housing to provide clearance for pin removal. Withdraw axle shaft from gearbox. Remove thrust washers (3), gear (8), clutch dog (7), shift fork (6) and spline shaft (4). Pry oil seals (9 and 12) from gearbox.

On Model HR21, disassemble driven pulley as follows: Use an open end wrench on flat surface of worm (15—Fig. HN116) to prevent worm shaft from turning, then remove pulley retaining bolt (25) and spring retainer (24). Withdraw tension spring (23) and pulley halves (21).

On Model HR21-5, disassemble driven pulley as follows: Secure pulley flange in vise to secure worm shaft (15—Fig. HN116), then remove retaining bolt (25). Withdraw pulley halves (21) and spacers (22). Note that position of spacers (22) on pulley halves determines speed setting.

On all models, pry out oil seal (19) and remove snap ring (18). Pull worm (15) and bearing (16) out of housing.

Inspect all parts for wear or damage and renew as necessary. Reassemble using new oil seals and seal rings. Make certain that all thrust washers are positioned correctly. Refill housing with 50 cc (0.1 pt.) of SAE 90 hypoid gear oil.

Model HRA21

GEARBOX. To remove gearbox, first disconnect spark plug cable to prevent accidental starting. Remove drive belt cover and disengage drive belt from gearbox pulley. Tip mower on its right side to prevent oil from entering crankcase ventilation chamber. Remove rear wheels and one-way clutch as previously outlined. Drive the roll pin (10—Fig. HN115) out of axle shaft and remove dust cover (7), height adjuster lever (9) and bracket (8). Disconnect drive clutch cable from gearbox. Disconnect speed change arm from anchor bracket. Unbolt gearbox mounting bracket and withdraw gearbox and reduction gear case as an assembly from mower deck.

To disassemble, unbolt and remove gearbox cover (1—Fig. HN117) and drain oil from case. Unscrew driven pulley retaining bolt and remove spring retainer (11), spring (12) and pulley halves (13). Drive split pin (8) out of spline shaft (7), then separate reduction gear case (26) from gearbox. Remove thrust washers (3), worm wheel (4), shifter (6) and spline shaft (7). Loosen clutch arm clamp bolt, remove shift arm (22) and withdraw clutch shift fork (5). Pry out oil seal (14). Remove snap ring (15) and pull worm (19) with bearing (18) from gear case.

Remove cap screws retaining reduction gear case halves (28 and 42—Fig. HN118) and separate case halves. Remove axle shaft (27), reduction gear shaft (33) and idler gear (40) from gear case.

Inspect all parts for wear or damage and renew as necessary. To reassemble, reverse the disassembly procedure. Pack inside of reduction gear case with multipurpose grease. Fill gearbox with 80 cc (1.6 pt.) SAE 90 hypoid gear oil.

HYDROSTATIC TRANSAXLE

OPERATION. The hydrostatic transaxle provides infinitely variable selection of forward speed from stopped to full speed. The transaxle utilizes a variable displacement hydraulic pump that is driven by a pto drive shaft from the

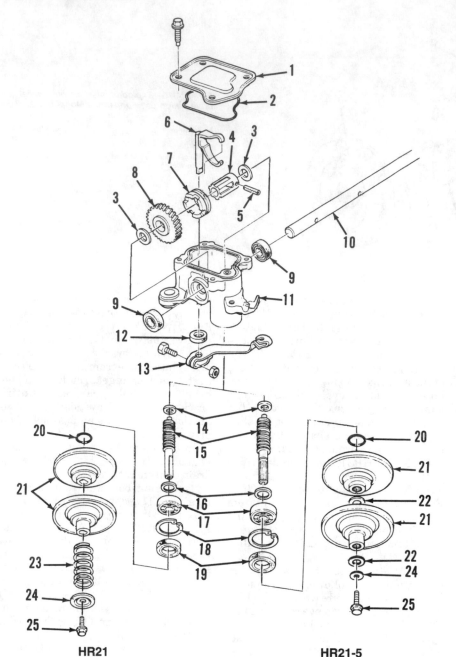

Fig. HN116—Exploded view of gearbox used on Honda Models HR21 and HR21-5. Spring-loaded variable pulley shown in left side view is for Model HR21; right side view is for Model HR21-5. Refer to text for operating principles.

1. Cover
2. "O" ring
3. Thrust washers
4. Spline shaft
5. Pin
6. Shift fork
7. Clutch dog
8. Gear
9. Oil seals
10. Axle shaft
11. Gear case
12. Oil seal
13. Shift arm
14. Thrust washer
15. Worm
16. Thrust washer
17. Bearing
18. Snap ring
19. Oil seal
20. "O" ring
21. Pulley
22. Spacers
23. Spring
24. Washer
25. Retaining bolt

HR21

HR21-5

engine. Pressurized oil is directed from the pump to a hydraulic motor that is connected to the axle through a set of gears. Both pump and motor are a multiple-piston type that uses a swashplate to vary the stroke of the pump pistons. A manually actuated control lever on the side of the transaxle controls swashplate position which determines pump output, thereby setting mower speed. Pump and motor assemblies are constructed to close tolerances and clean oil is a requirement to obtain a long service life.

LUBRICATION. Fluid level should be checked after every 300 hours of operation. To check fluid level, remove access panel, clean area around filler cap, unscrew filler cap and read level on dip-

stick. Note that filler cap must be fully screwed into transaxle for an accurate fluid level to be indicated on dipstick. Check fluid level when transaxle is at ambient temperature. Fill as needed with Honda hydrostatic transaxle fluid.

NOTE: Due to close tolerances present in the hydrostatic transaxle, particular care must be taken to prevent debris or other contaminants from entering transaxle.

Transaxle fluid should be changed after every 1000 hours of operation. To drain fluid, remove transaxle, remove filler cap and pour out fluid through opening. Refill with Honda hydrostatic transaxle oil. Fluid capacity is 350 cc

(0.37 quarts). Gradual filling may be required to allow entry of all oil. Refer to BLEEDING paragraph before operating lawn mower.

BLEEDING. The bleeding procedure requires two steps, one with the transaxle off the mower and other step with the transaxle installed. With the transaxle removed, hold the speed control lever on the side of the transaxle in its full speed position. This can be done either with a wire, or some models are equipped with a bracket in which a suitable screw can be inserted to bear against the lever. Unscrew bleed screw on back of transaxle (screw is equipped with an "O" ring that should be discarded). Rotate transaxle input shaft 5-10 turns clockwise and axle shaft 2-3

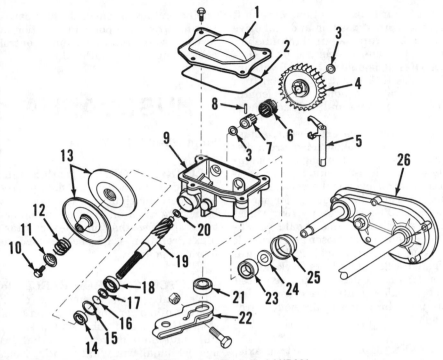

Fig. HN117—Exploded view of gearbox used on Honda Model HRA21 mower.

1. Cover
2. "O" ring
3. Thrust washers
4. Gear
5. Shift fork
6. Shift dog
7. Spline shaft
8. Pin
9. Gear case
10. Retaining bolt
11. Spring retainer
12. Spring
13. Pulley
14. Oil seal
15. Snap ring
16. "O" ring
17. Washer
18. Bearing
19. Worm
20. Thrust washer
21. Oil seal
22. Clutch arm
23. Oil seal
24. Washer
25. Dust cover
26. Reduction gear case

turns in direction of forward wheel rotation. Rotate shafts until air bubbles are absent from bleed screw hole. Do not turn shafts in opposite direction as air may enter oil. Install bleed screw with a new "O" ring and tighten to 13 N•m (115 in.-lbs.). Remove wire or screw holding speed control lever and recheck oil level. Install transaxle on mower.

The second bleeding step requires operating the mower with the engine running (area must be well-ventilated). Clutch cable must be properly adjusted. Position the mower so the front wheels are against a wall or other immovable object. Surface under rear wheels should be smooth and wet so wheels can spin without damaging wheel tread. Run engine at full throttle with transaxle shift lever in full speed position. Run mower with wheels spinning at full speed for 25 seconds, then shift to neutral for 5 seconds. Repeat cycle five more times. Recheck oil level.

CONTROL CABLE. Two devices determine mower speed. A control cable (C—Fig. HN119) moves the speed control lever on the transaxle. The handlebar shift lever determines mower speed by setting the distance the control cable can be pulled. The drive clutch bar removes control cable free play when en-

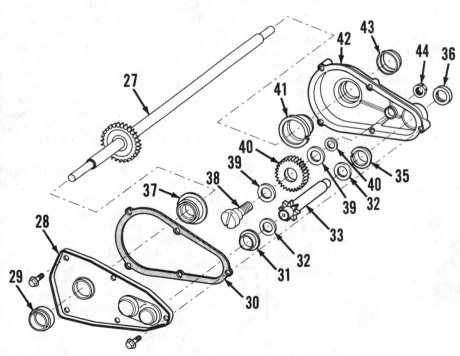

Fig. HN118—Exploded view of reduction gear case assembly used on Honda Model HRA21 mower.

27. Axle shaft
28. Gear case half
29. Dust seal
30. Gasket
31. Seal
32. Thrust washer
33. Reduction gear shaft
35. Bushing
36. Oil seal
37. Bushing
38. Idler gear shaft
39. Thrust washers
40. Idler gear
41. Bushing
42. Gear case half
43. Dust seal
44. Nut

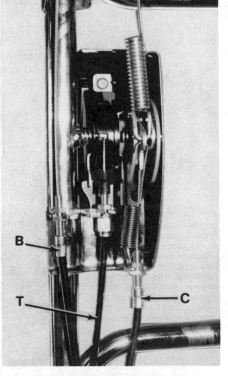

Fig. HN119—View of control cables on Honda mower showing blade brake cable (B), drive cable (C) and throttle cable (T).

Fig. HN120—View of hydrostatic transaxle used on some Honda self-propelled mowers. Drive shaft coupler pin is located under pin clip (P). Mark (M) on hydrostatic housing should be aligned with notch on control lever (L) when handlebar speed control lever is in slow speed position and drive clutch lever is moved all the way forward against handlebar.

gaged so mower moves at speed set by shift lever. Releasing the drive clutch bar allows the transaxle to return to neutral.

Two methods may be used to adjust control cable. Remove access panel and determine if an index mark (M—Fig. HN120) is present on transaxle pump case. If mark is present, static adjustment is possible. If mark is absent, mower speed must be measured.

If transaxle mark is present, adjust control cable as follows: Check position of control cable retaining straps shown in Fig. HN121; reposition straps if necessary. Move rear deck height adjusters

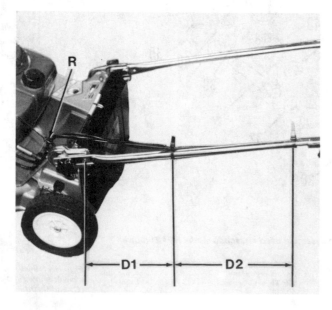

Fig. HN121—The first cable retaining strap (R) should be located just after point where outer protective rubber sleeve stops on drive control cable. Distance (D1) from handlebar retaining screw to second strap is 75 mm (3 inches) and distance (D2) from second strap to third strap is 280 mm (11 inches).

to maximum height position. Move shift lever to slowest position and pull drive clutch bar fully against handlebar. Notch on transaxle control lever (L—Fig. HN120) should be aligned with index mark (M). If not, loosen and turn nuts on cable to adjust cable length. Tighten lock nuts and recheck adjustment.

If transaxle mark is absent, adjust control cable as follow: Measure a distance of 30 feet. Run engine at minimum throttle and run mower with speed control lever at slowest speed setting. Measure time required for mower to travel 30 feet with no rear wheel slippage. Elapsed time should be 9.6-12.4 seconds. If not, loosen and turn lock nuts on cable to adjust cable length. Tighten lock nuts and recheck adjustment. An index mark should be placed on transaxle for future reference using the procedure in the previous paragraph.

TRANSAXLE. To remove transaxle, remove wheels and axle components. Note that left and right side ratchets are not interchangeable. Remove access cover from rear of mower. Displace pin clip (P—Fig. HN120), remove coupler pin and disconnect pto coupler from gearbox input shaft. Detach control cable. Remove transaxle.

At time of publication, the hydrostatic transaxle was available only as a unit assembly. Manufacturer does not recommend overhaul except by manufacturer.

Note the following when reinstalling transaxle: If pto shaft was disconnected at spline coupling, connect engine coupler and transaxle coupler so pin (P—Fig. HN120) at transaxle end and pin at

engine end are aligned. Be sure pawls in wheel ratchets point in direction of forward wheel rotation. Adjust control cable as previously outlined.

HUSQVARNA

Front Wheel Drive Models

LUBRICATION. The gearbox is lubricated at the factory and does not require periodic changing. If service has been performed on gearbox, manufacturer specifies that only Texaco Starplex Premium 1 grease be used to lubricate gearbox.

CLUTCH CONTROL CABLE. To adjust control cable, remove drive cover at front of mower and loosen jam nuts (Fig. HU101) and cable clamp screw. Pull and hold drive control handle against handlebar. While rotating front wheels, move shift arm to engaged position (against spring tension). Pull cable sleeve as shown in Fig. HU101; do not pull control cable. Tighten clamp screw until sleeve is snug, then tighten jam nuts. Check operation.

DRIVE BELT. Mower drive belt (Fig. HU102) can be replaced without removing mower blade. Remove drive cover at front of mower. Push down on gearbox and work the belt off driven pulley. Tip mower on its right side so fuel tank is up. Loosen belt snubber retaining bolt and move snubber away from the belt. Remove belt from engine pulley and slip belt over the blade.

Install new belt in reverse order of removal. Position belt snubber so there is approximately $1/32$ inch (0.8 mm) clearance between snubber and belt.

FRONT WHEELS AND DRIVE PINIONS. To remove front wheels and drive pinions, pry hub cap (1—Fig. HU103) from wheel. Remove hairpin cotter (2) and withdraw wheel (5) with bushing (4) from wheel adjuster. Pry "E" ring (6) off drive shaft and remove drive pinion (7) and dust cover (8).

Install drive pinions and wheels in reverse order of removal. Do not apply any lubricant on pinion and wheel.

GEARBOX. To remove gearbox, remove drive cover from front of mower. Push down on gearbox and work the drive belt off gearbox pulley. Disconnect clutch cable (15—Fig. HU103) and clutch spring (16) from gearbox shift arm. Remove belt tension spring (11).

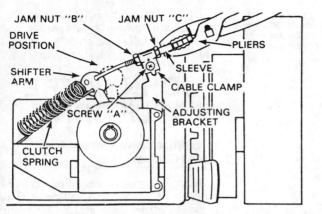

Fig. HU101—Drawing of drive control cable. Adjust cable as outlined in text.

Fig. HU102—Mower drive belt can be replaced without removing mower blade. Refer to text.

Remove front wheels (5), drive pinions (7), Woodruff keys (17) and dust covers (8). Unbolt and remove wheel adjuster (9) and gearbox (12) from mower deck.

To disassemble gearbox, remove snap ring (14—Fig. HU103), pulley (13) and Woodruff key from input shaft. Remove screws securing gearbox halves (4 and 21—Fig. HU104). Drive out pin (3) and separate case halves. Remove input shaft (17) and drive shaft (14) from case. Separate components from the shafts as needed.

Thoroughly clean all parts and inspect for wear or damage. Renew as necessary. When reassembling, be sure that all thrust washers are installed correctly. Manufacturer specifies that

only Texaco Starplex Premium 1 grease, Part No. 750355, be used to lubricate gearbox. Apply thin bead of Loctite 515 Gasket Eliminator to mating surface of case halves to reseal gearbox.

Rear Wheel Drive Models

REAR WHEELS AND DRIVE PINIONS. To remove wheels and drive pinions, pry hub caps (1—Fig. HU105) from wheels. Remove hairpin cotter (2), washer (3) wheel (4) and washer (5). Pry "E" ring (7) off drive shaft and remove drive pinion (8) and drive pawl (9).

Inspect drive pawl, pinion and wheel for wear or damage and renew as necessary. Drive pawls must slide freely in

drive shaft. Pawls may be lubricated with spray type lubricant such as WD-40.

When reassembling, note that drive pawls must be positioned as shown in Fig. HU106. Pinion gears (8—Fig. HU105) are not interchangeable. Pinion gear stamped with letter "L" must be installed on left side and gear stamped with letter "R" must be installed on right side. If pawls or gears are installed incorrectly, drive system will not operate.

DRIVE BELT. To replace drive belt (1—Fig. HU107), remove drive cover from rear of mower. Remove rear wheels, drive pinion gears and drive

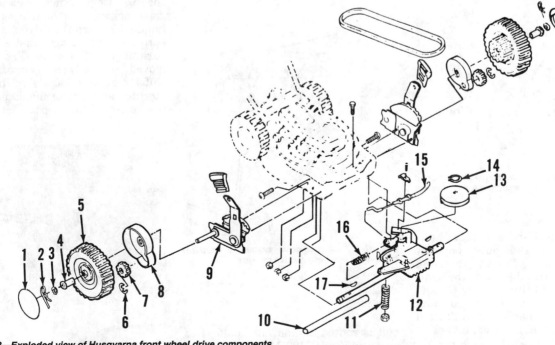

Fig. HU103—Exploded view of Husqvarna front wheel drive components.

1. Hub cap	4. Bushing	7. Pinion gear	10. Drive shaft cover	13. Driven pulley	16. Spring
2. Hairpin cotter	5. Wheel	8. Dust shield	11. Spring	14. Retaining ring	17. Woodruff key
3. Washer	6. "E" ring	9. Wheel adjuster	12. Gearbox	15. Clutch control cable	

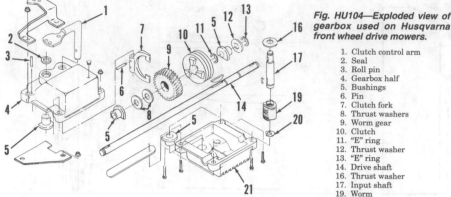

1. Clutch control arm
2. Seal
3. Roll pin
4. Gearbox half
5. Bushings
6. Pin
7. Clutch fork
8. Thrust washers
9. Worm gear
10. Clutch
11. "E" ring
12. Thrust washer
13. "E" ring
14. Drive shaft
16. Thrust washer
17. Input shaft
19. Worm
20. "E" ring
21. Gearbox half

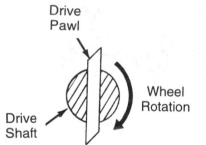

Fig. HU105—Exploded view of wheel and drive pinion used on Husqvarna rear wheel drive mowers.

1. Hub cap
2. Hairpin cotter
3. Washer
4. Wheel
5. Washer
6. Dust shield
7. "E" ring
8. Pinion gear
9. Drive pawl

must be installed as shown in Fig. HU106 and pinion gear marked "L" must be installed be on left side and gear marked "R" is on right side.

JOHN DEERE SELF-DRIVE

Rear Wheel Drive Two and Five Speed Gearbox

John Deere self propelled mowers may be equipped with self-drive that provides either two or five different speeds. The self-drive clutch is engaged by moving the lever located on the left side of the gearbox; gear selection is controlled by the lever located at the right side of the gearbox. The gear selector and clutch engagement levers are both moved by controls mounted on the handlebar via attaching cables. Refer to the following for service.

MAINTENANCE. Lubricate the drive wheels after 50 hours of operation by injecting grease through the grease fittings provided. Lubricate the linkage as needed to provide smooth operation. The gearbox is lubricated and sealed at the factory. The gearbox should not require additional lubrication.

ADJUSTMENT. Adjust the clutch control and shift cables as described in the appropriate following paragraphs.

Clutch Control Cable. To check clutch cable adjustment, first remove the cover from the mower deck. Pull the drive engagement handle against the handlebar. Turn the drive wheels to be sure they are engaged and check to be sure the clutch arm (A—Fig. JD1) has moved to the fully engaged position. The clutch control linkage is spring loaded, but the hand control should permit full movement of the gearbox lever. Make

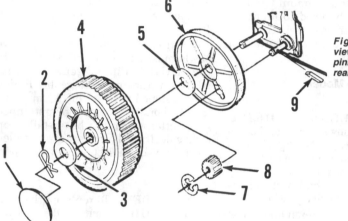

Fig. HU106—Drive pawl must be installed in drive shaft so pawl points in direction of forward wheel travel.

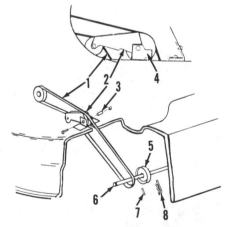

Fig. HU107—A belt drive system is used on Husqvarna front wheel drive mowers.

1. Drive belt
2. Idler assy.
3. Bushing
4. Mounting bracket
5. Driven pulley
6. Drive shaft
7. Roll pin
8. Hairpin cotter

pawls as outlined above. Remove hairpin cotter (8) and slide pulley on shaft to expose roll pin (7). Drive the pin from the drive shaft (6), then slide the shaft to the right until drive pulley (5) and belt is free of shaft. Remove bolt and bushing (3) from idler assembly (2), and withdraw idler and belt from mower.

To install new belt, reverse the removal procedure while noting the following special instructions. Be sure that

belt is routed around idler pulleys as shown in Fig. HU107. Make certain that idler pivot bracket (2) moves freely after retaining bolt is tightened. Drive pawls

Fig. JD1—Clutch lever, linkage and cable is shown for models with zone starting.

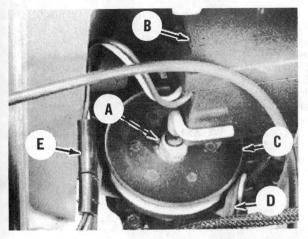

Fig. JD2—View of gearbox drive pulley typical of models with blade brake clutch. Electric starting battery is shown at (B).

A. Lock nut
B. Battery
C. Drive pulley
D. Drive belt
E. Connector

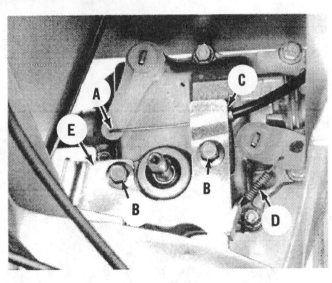

Fig. JD3—View of gearbox shift controls typical of models with blade brake clutch.

A. Shift arm
B. Bolts
C. Shift cable
D. Clutch spring
E. Belt guide bracket

remove the cutting blade, then unbolt and remove the belt guides. Unscrew the nut (C—Fig. JD1) and remove the pulley from the gearbox input shaft. Withdraw the belt from around the crankshaft.

Note the following when installing the drive belt: Tighten the drive pulley retaining self locking nut to 25 ft.-lb. (34 N·m) and the blade retaining fasteners to 35 ft.-lb. (47 N·m) torque. Be sure all belt guards are properly located and that belt does not rub. Be sure that any wiring or cables are away from the belt.

DRIVE WHEELS AND PINIONS. Each of the two drive wheels is equipped with a ratchet type clutch that allows the gearbox output shaft and pinion to drive the wheel, permitting the two wheels to turn at different speeds to facilitate turning the mower. The clutches also allow the wheels to turn freely when the drive is not engaged. Each drive wheel (4—Fig. JD4) can be removed after removing the shoulder bolt (2) from the center.

The drive pinions (12) are retained at the ends of the gearbox output shaft by snap rings (10). A spring-loaded key (21) will be free when the drive pinion is removed. The spring (20) should also be removed. The drive pinions are marked "L" or "R" indicating left or right side and should not be interchanged. Note the location of the washer (11) and snap rings (10 and 13).

sure that operating the control engages and disengages the clutch. Turn the cable adjusting nuts (B) as required, then tighten the nuts to maintain the setting.

Shift Cable. To check the adjustment of the shift cable, first remove the cover from the mower deck.

On models with zone starting, loosen the shift cable clamp. Move the handlebar mounted control lever to the fastest speed position. Relocate the cable housing in the clamp so the gearbox lever is moved to the fastest speed, then tighten the retaining clamp. Be careful not to bend the cable or bracket. Move the handlebar mounted shift control to the first speed position and make sure the lever on the gearbox moves to engage the slowest speed. Be sure that all gears can be engaged, then reinstall the cover.

On models with blade brake clutch, remove the pulley retaining nut (A—Fig. JD2), then lift the pulley from the gearbox input shaft. It will be necessary to remove the battery (B) from models with electric start. Move the handlebar mounted control lever to the fastest speed position and check to see if the gearbox lever (A—Fig. JD3) is in the

fastest speed position. If necessary, loosen the bolts (B) attaching the cable clamp, relocate the cable housing (C) so the gearbox lever is moved to the fastest speed, then tighten the retaining clamp. Move the handlebar mounted shift control to the first speed position and make sure the lever on the gearbox moves to engage the slowest speed. Be sure that all gears can be engaged, then reinstall the drive pulley and belt. Install the battery on electric starting models.

DRIVE BELT REPLACEMENT. It is necessary to remove the engine from models equipped with blade brake clutch to remove the belt. Refer to the Blade Brake Clutch section for removal of the belt from models so equipped.

NOTE: Be sure the spark plug lead is detached and properly grounded before working under the mower. Always be careful while working around the sharpened blade.

On models with zone starting, the belt can be removed as follows. Unbolt and remove the belt covers. Unbolt and

GEARBOX REMOVAL. To remove the gearbox, remove the drive belt from the pulley as outlined in DRIVE BELT REPLACEMENT paragraphs. Remove the rear wheels and drive pinions as described above. Disconnect the shift cable and clutch control cable from the transmission control levers. Remove retaining screws from height adjustment plates, slide the height adjustment plates from the mower housing and remove the transmission.

Reverse the removal procedure to install the gearbox. Adjust the control cables as described above when assembling.

OVERHAUL GEARBOX. Remove the screws attaching the housing halves, then separate the housings. Refer to Fig. JD5 or JD6 which shows typical two and five speed units. The shafts can be lifted from the housing.

Refer to Fig. JD5 or JD6 when assembling components of the output shaft and the countershaft. Coat transmission parts with grease when assembling. Install new gears, bushings or bearings as necessary before finishing the assembly.

On five-speed transaxle, install gears on axle shaft (17—Fig. JD6) with tooth bevel facing flange end of shift collar (22). Install gears on countershaft (44) with tooth bevel facing ring gear (43). Install shift collar (15) on key carrier (21) so that thicker flange of collar is on same side as long end of keys (9). Install washer (20) with recessed side facing shift collar (32).

On all transaxles, note that locating tab on bushings (15 and 32—Fig. JD5 or 19 and 35—Fig. JD6) must be positioned in bores of lower housing half (38 or 45). Pinion shaft bearing (5) must be installed with seal side facing away from bevel gear. Pack additional grease around the gears in the gearbox before installing the lower housing half. Add about 70 g (2.5 oz.) of John Deere Non-Clay High-Temperature (or equivalent) grease to the gearcase before assem-

bling the housing halves. Do not fill the gearcase completely. Clean the mating surface of the housings, then apply sealer to the mating surfaces. Assemble upper housing half to lower housing half and tighten screws attaching housing halves to 87 in.-lb. (9.8 N•m) torque.

On all models, refer to the DRIVE WHEELS paragraphs in this section when assembling the axle bearings and drive gears on the output shaft.

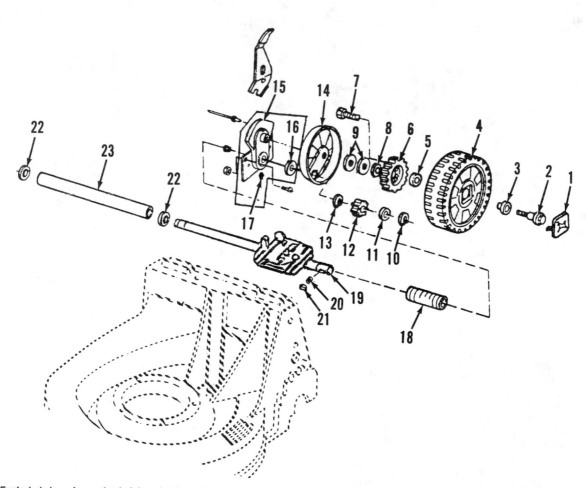

Fig. JD4—Exploded view of one wheel pinion clutch and height adjuster. The unit shown is typical.

1. Cover	5. Ball bearing	9. Washers	13. Snap ring	17. Grease fitting
2. Shoulder bolt	6. Driven gear	10. Snap ring	14. Dust cover	18. Tube	21. Key
3. Bushing	7. Screw	11. Washer	15. Height adjuster	19. Gearbox assy.	22. Thrust washers
4. Wheel	8. Washer	12. Pinion	16. Needle bearing	20. Spring	23. Tube

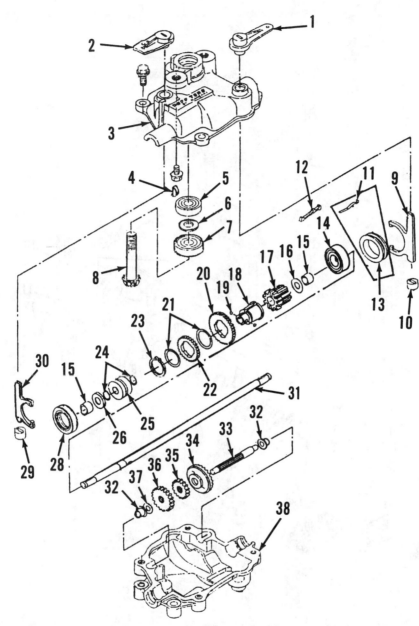

Fig. JD5—Exploded view of the two speed gearbox used on some John Deere mowers.

1. Shift lever
2. Clutch lever
3. Housing half
4. Pulley drive key
5. Bearing
6. Washer
7. Bearing
8. Bevel pinion
9. Gear shift fork
10. Support
11. Spring
12. Shift key
13. Shift collar
14. Seal
15. Bushings
16. Washer
17. Key carrier
18. Gear shift collar
19. Balls
20. First speed gear
21. Washers
22. Second speed gear
23. Snap ring
24. Retaining rings
25. Clutch shift collar
26. Washer
28. Seal
29. Retainer
30. Clutch shift fork
31. Axle shaft
32. Bushings
33. Countershaft
34. Bevel ring gear
35. Second speed gear
36. First speed gear
37. Washer
38. Lower housing half

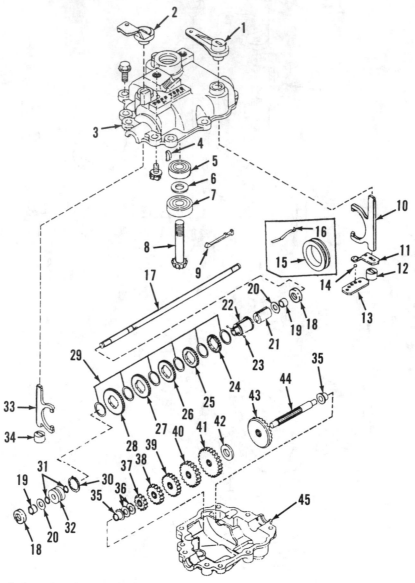

Fig. JD6—Exploded view of the five speed gearbox used on some John Deere mowers.

1. Shift lever	9. Shift key		38. Second gear
2. Clutch lever	10. Gear shift fork	17. Axle shaft	24. Fifth speed gear	31. Rings	39. Third gear
3. Housing half	11. Detent spring arm	18. Seal	25. Fourth speed gear	32. Shift collar	40. Fourth gear
4. Pulley drive key	12. Retainer	19. Bushing	26. Third speed gear	33. Clutch shift fork	41. Fifth gear
5. Bearing	13. Detent plate	20. Washer	27. Second speed gear	34. Retainer	42. Washer
6. Washer	14. Detent ball	21. Shift key carrier	28. First speed gear	35. Bushing	43. Bevel gear
7. Bearing	15. Shift collar	22. Shift collar	29. Washers	36. Washers	44. Countershaft
8. Bevel pinion	16. Shift key spring	23. Balls	30. Snap ring	37. First gear	45. Lower housing half

JOHN DEERE

Front Wheel Drive Single-Speed Gearbox

LUBRICATION. Gearbox is lubricated at the factory with John Deere Transmission Lubricant and does not require periodic changing. If lubrication is required, use John Deere Transmission Lubricant or an equivalent SAE 90 gear lubricant.

CLUTCH CONTROL CABLE. A V-belt transmits power from the engine to gearbox driven pulley. A worm gear inside the gearbox transmits power from input shaft to axle shaft through a sliding dog clutch. The clutch lever on the mower handle is connected by a cable to the dog clutch. A pinion gear on each end of axle shaft drives each front wheel.

To adjust clutch control cable, remove belt guard from front of mower. Loosen clutch cable retaining clamp and place clutch control lever in disengaged position. Move shift arm (21—Fig. JD10) rearward as far as possible. While holding cable in this position, tighten cable clamp screw.

DRIVE BELT. To renew drive belt, disconnect and properly ground spark plug cable. Remove mower blade. Remove belt cover from front of mower. Slip belt off gearbox pulley. Guide belt down through hole in mower deck and remove belt from engine shaft.

Install new belt by reversing the removal procedure. Mowers with serial number 175,001 and later have a spring that applies tension to the belt and no adjustment is required. On early models (prior to S.N. 175,001), an adjusting screw is provided at front corner of gearbox for belt tension adjusting purposes. To check belt tension on early models, squeeze belt together at a point midway between the pulleys with moderate finger pressure. There should be a clearance of no less than 1 inch (25 mm) between inner sides of belt. Loosen adjusting screw lock nut and turn adjusting screw clockwise to increase belt tension (decrease clearance between inner sides of belt).

GEARBOX AND DRIVE PINIONS. To remove gearbox and drive pinions, disconnect and properly ground spark plug cable. Remove belt guard from front of mower deck. Disconnect clutch cable from gearbox shift arm. Slip the drive belt off gearbox pulley. Pry hub caps (1—Fig. JD10) from front wheels. Remove wheel mounting bolts (2) and the wheels (3). Remove lock nut (4) from both ends of axle shaft. Unscrew pinion gear (5) and remove dust cover (7), pivot arm (9) and end cap (13) from axle ends. Remove gearbox and axle assembly from mower deck.

To disassemble gearbox, use a suitable puller to remove pulley (26—Fig. JD10) from worm shaft, taking care not to deform pulley flange. Drive two spring pins (31) out of gearbox cover (25). Remove cover mounting screws and separate cover with worm shaft from gearbox lower housing. Remove retaining screw (24), shift arm (21), dust cover (20) and latch (19). Pull spring pin (23) from shift rod (28) through hole in cover and remove shift rod and spring (29). Drive spring pin (35) out of sleeve (36), then withdraw axle shaft (32) from gearbox. Remove worm gear (38), clutch jaw (37), sleeve (36) and thrust washer (39).

Thoroughly clean all components and check for wear or damage. Bushings (33—Fig. JD10) and seals (14) can be renewed if excessively worn. Press new seal into gearbox housing with lip of seal facing inward. Outer face of seal should be flush with outside of housing. Apply light coat of multipurpose grease to seal lip.

Install thrust washer (39—Fig. JD10), worm gear (38), clutch jaw (37), sleeve (36) and axle shaft (32) in lower housing. Drive spring pin (35) into sleeve and axle until flush with outer surface of sleeve. Fill lower housing approximately 2/3 full with John Deere Transmission Lubricant or an equivalent SAE 90 gear lubricant. Assemble shift rod (28) and spring (29) in top cover, then install spring pin (23) through hole in cover and drive pin into shift rod. Install shift fork (34), worm shaft (17) and bearing (18) in cover. Be sure that shift fork engages groove in clutch jaw (37). Install cover with new gasket and drive spring pins (31) into cover. Tighten cover mounting screws evenly to 60-70 in.-lbs. (6.8-7.9 N·m) torque. Install latch (19), dust cover (20) and shift arm (21). Install tolerance ring (27) in pulley (26), then press pulley onto worm shaft.

To reinstall gearbox, reverse the removal procedure while noting the following special instructions: Tighten pinion gears (5—Fig. JD10) and lock nuts (4) to 25-29 ft.-lbs. (34-39 N·m) torque. Tighten wheel mounting bolts (2) to 25-29 ft.-lbs. (34-39 N·m) torque.

Rear Wheel Drive Single-Speed Gearbox (Models Prior to Serial Number 155,001)

CLUTCH CONTROL CABLE. A worm gear on engine camshaft drives the transmission pinion drive shaft (37—JD11). The pinion gear shaft

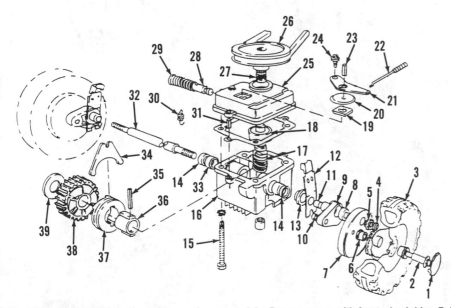

Fig. JD10—Exploded view of gearbox used on some John Deere mowers with front wheel drive. Belt tension spring (30) is used on late models.

1. Hub cap	11. Bushing	21. Shift arm	31. Pin
2. Wheel bolt	12. Adjuster lever	22. Clutch control cable	32. Axle shaft
3. Wheel	13. End cap	23. Pin	33. Bushing
4. Locknut	14. Oil seal	24. Screw	34. Shift fork
5. Pinion gear	15. Screw	25. Cover	35. Pin
6. Bushing	16. Gear case	26. Pulley	36. Sleeve
7. Dust cover	17. Worm	27. Tolerance ring	37. Clutch jaw
8. Bearing	18. Bearing	28. Shift rod	38. Worm gear
9. Pivot arm	19. Latch	29. Spring	39. Thrust washer
10. Locknut	20. Dust cover	30. Belt tension spring	

drives the bevel gear (36) inside the gearbox. A spring-loaded clutch assembly controls the engagement and disengagement of drive shaft gear (21) and axle gear (12).

To adjust clutch control cable, loosen clutch cable jam nut and turn cable adjusting sleeve (early models) or adjusting nut (later models) until there is approximately 1/16 inch (1.6 mm) clearance between clutch control lever stop and mower handle.

GEARBOX. To remove gearbox, first drain fuel and disconnect spark plug cable. Remove drive shaft cover. Drive pin (42—Fig. JD11) out of drive shaft coupling (41) and separate coupling halves. Remove knob from wheel adjuster lever (5). Remove cap screw attaching clutch cable bracket to mower deck. Disconnect clutch control cable

from clutch arm (15). Remove "E" ring (1), washers (2), wheels and drive pawls (7). Note that left and right wheels are not interchangeable. Identify wheels so they can be installed correctly. Remove screws attaching rear axle frame (9) to mower deck. Remove screws attaching gearbox to mower deck and remove rear axle and gearbox as an assembly.

Unbolt and remove clutch arm (15—Fig. JD11) and spring (16). Drive pin (10) out of gear (12), then slide axle shaft (8) out of gear and rear axle frame (9). Remove screws from gearbox and separate gearbox halves. Remove pinion gear shaft (37). Drive spiral pins out of drive shaft (33), then slide drive shaft out of clutch assembly and bevel gear.

NOTE: If disassembly of clutch is necessary, scribe a mark on bearing and collar (26) before pressing bearing

out of clutch. This ensures that holes for spiral pin in bearing and collar will be aligned when reassembling.

Press bearing out of clutch and separate gear (21—Fig. JD11), cam (22), hub (23) spring (24) and collar (26). Inspect all parts for wear or damage and renew as necessary. When reassembling gearbox, note the following: Install drive shaft (33) so end with one hole is on right (wheel adjuster lever) side of rear axle frame. Slide bevel gear (36) on drive shaft so gear hub is towards left side (facing away from wheel adjuster lever). Align scribe marks (made prior to disassembly) on clutch bearing and collar, then press bearing through clutch assembly. Slide drive shaft through clutch bracket (18) and clutch assembly. Pack gearbox lower half with John Deere Multi-Purpose Lubricant or

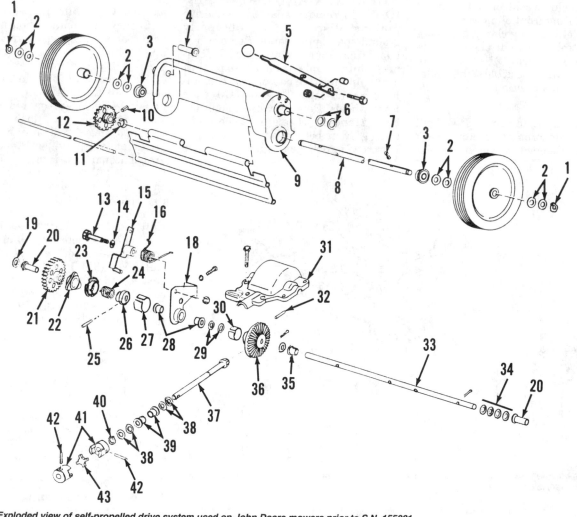

Fig. JD11—Exploded view of self-propelled drive system used on John Deere mowers prior to S.N. 155001.

1. Snap ring	8. Axle shaft	15. Clutch arm	23. Clutch hub	30. Collar	37. Bevel pinion shaft
2. Washers	9. Rear axle frame	16. Spring	24. Spring	31. Gearbox half	38. Washers
3. Bearing	10. Pin	18. Clutch bracket	25. Pin	32. Pin	39. Bushings
4. Bushing	11. Collar	19. Washer	26. Sleeve	33. Drive shaft	40. Snap ring
5. Wheel adjuster lever	12. Axle gear	20. Bushing	27. Collar	34. Washers	41. Coupling
6. Washer	13. Bolt	21. Gear	28. Bushing	35. Bushing	42. Pin
7. Pawl	14. Wave washer	22. Cam	29. Washers	36. Bevel gear	43. Spider

Illustration for Fig. JD11 reproduced by permission of Deere & Company, Copyright Deere & Company.

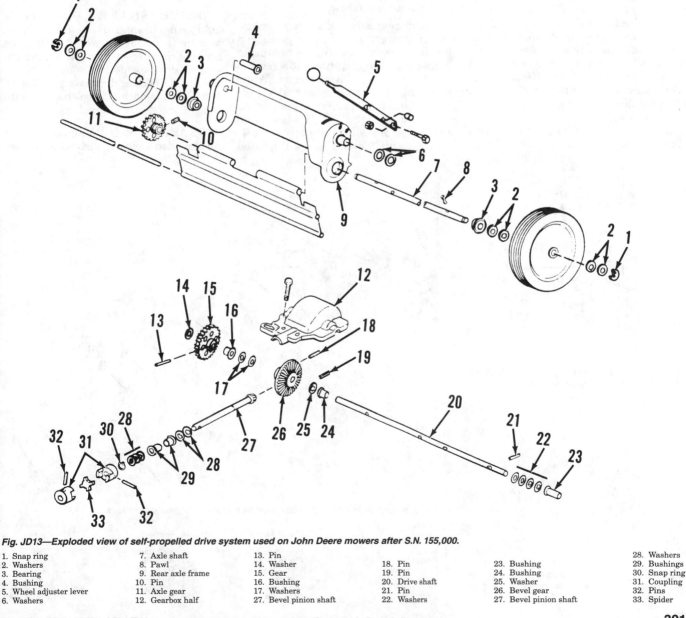

Fig. JD12—Drawing showing correct installation of drive pawl (P).

an equivalent multi-purpose grease, then install bevel pinion shaft (37) in gearbox lower half. Assemble gearbox halves on drive shaft and tighten gear-

box screws to 110-120 in.-lbs. (12.2-13.5 N•m) torque. Make certain that pinion gear shaft turns freely. Assemble axle shaft (8) and gear (12) in rear axle frame. Install clutch arm (15) and spring (16), hook short leg of spring on arm and other leg on clutch bracket. Be sure that clutch arm is centered on clutch cam (22) and that clutch arm stud engages one of the notches in clutch hub (23).

Mount rear axle and gearbox assembly to mower deck. Smear grease on inside of rear axle frame mounting brackets and tighten bracket screws to 120 in.-lbs. (13.5 N•m) torque. When installing rear wheels, note that wheels are not interchangeable. Install pawls as shown in Fig. JD12. If wheels and

pawls are installed properly, wheels should rotate forward freely. If rotated backwards, wheel should lock on the pawl and rotate axle shaft backwards. Adjust clutch control linkage as previously outlined.

Rear Wheel Drive Single-Speed Gearbox (Models After Serial Number 155,000)

CLUTCH CONTROL CABLE. The mower drive system utilizes a worm and clutch assembly on engine camshaft. When clutch control lever is moved to drive position, the worm engages with worm gear, driving the transmission pinion shaft (27—JD13). The pinion gear shaft drives the bevel gear (26) inside the gearbox which turns the drive

Fig. JD13—Exploded view of self-propelled drive system used on John Deere mowers after S.N. 155,000.

1. Snap ring	7. Axle shaft	13. Pin	23. Bushing	28. Washers
2. Washers	8. Pawl	14. Washer	18. Pin	24. Bushing	29. Bushings
3. Bearing	9. Rear axle frame	15. Gear	19. Pin	25. Washer	30. Snap ring
4. Bushing	10. Pin	16. Bushing	20. Drive shaft	26. Bevel gear	31. Coupling
5. Wheel adjuster lever	11. Axle gear	17. Washers	21. Pin	27. Bevel pinion shaft	32. Pins
6. Washers	12. Gearbox half	27. Bevel pinion shaft	22. Washers		33. Spider

shaft (20). The drive shaft gear (15) turns axle shaft gear (11) which turns the rear wheels.

To adjust clutch control cable, remove cable retaining clip from mower deck. Loosen clutch cable upper adjusting nut and turn lower adjusting nut to remove all slack from cable (moving threaded part of cable down toward mower deck decreases slack). Pull clutch control lever up against mower handle and check that clutch arm contacts rear boss on engine oil pan. Release clutch control lever and check that clutch arm contacts front boss on oil pan. Turn cable adjusting nuts as necessary to obtain correct clutch operation.

GEARBOX. To remove gearbox, first drain fuel and disconnect spark plug cable. Remove drive shaft cover. Drive pin (32—Fig. JD13) out of drive shaft coupling (31) and separate coupling halves. Remove knob from wheel adjuster lever. Remove "E" ring (1), washers (2), wheels and drive pawls (8). Note that left and right wheels are not interchangeable. Identify wheels so they can be installed correctly. Remove screws attaching rear axle frame (9) to mower deck. Remove screws attaching gearbox to mower deck and remove rear axle and gearbox as an assembly.

Drive pin (10) out of gear (11), then slide axle shaft (7) out of gear and rear axle frame (9). Remove screws from gearbox and separate gearbox halves. Remove pinion gear shaft (27). Drive spiral pins out of drive shaft (20), then slide drive shaft out of rear axle frame.

Inspect all parts for wear or damage and renew as necessary. When reassembling gearbox, note the following: Install drive shaft (20—Fig. JD13) so end with one hole is on right (wheel adjuster lever) side of rear axle frame. Slide bevel gear (26) on drive shaft so gear hub is towards left side (facing away from wheel adjuster lever). Pack gearbox lower half with John Deere Multi-Purpose Lubricant or an equivalent multi-purpose grease, then install bevel pinion shaft (27) in gearbox lower half. Assemble gearbox halves on drive shaft and tighten gearbox screws to 110-120 in.-lbs. (12.2-13.5 N•m) torque. Make certain that pinion gear shaft turns freely. Assemble axle shaft (7) and gear (11) in rear axle frame.

Mount rear axle and gearbox assembly to mower deck. Smear grease on inside of rear axle frame mounting brackets and tighten bracket screws to 120 in.-lbs. (13.5 N•m) torque. When installing rear wheels, note that wheels are not interchangeable. Install pawls as shown in Fig. JD12. If wheels and pawls are installed properly, wheels should rotate forward freely. If rotated backwards, wheel should lock on the pawl and rotate axle shaft backwards.

KUBOTA

LUBRICATION. Unless leakage occurs, the gearbox should not require refilling. Gearbox capacity is 0.1 liter (0.1 quart). Recommended lubricant is heavy duty 80W or 90W gear oil.

CONTROL CABLE. Measure total travel of drive clutch handle at top of handle from rest to contact with handlebar. Measure free play of clutch handle and subtract from total travel. Desired specification is 80-83 mm (3.15-3.27 inches). To adjust cable, loosen lock nuts (N—Fig. KU301) and reposition cable adjuster (A). Tighten lock nuts. Check operation and be sure clutch operates properly.

DRIVE SHAFT. On models equipped with a gearbox, a drive shaft transmits power between the engine and gearbox. To remove either the engine or gearbox, detach snap ring (1 or 5—Fig. KU302) and remove pin (2 or 4). When reassembling drive shaft, be sure pins (2 and 4) are aligned.

GEARBOX. Refer to Fig. KU303 for an exploded view of gearbox. To remove

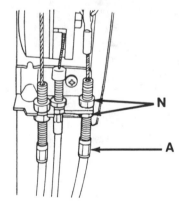

Fig. KU301—Loosen nuts (N) and reposition adjuster (A) to adjust drive control cable.

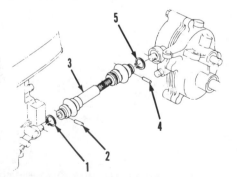

Fig. KU302—View of drive shaft (3) assembly. Detach snap ring (1 or 5) for access to pin (2 or 4). Pins (2 and 4) must be aligned.

Fig. KU303—Exploded view of gearbox used on Kubota self-propelled mowers.

1. Oil seal	10. Thrust washer	18. Shift dog	27. Gearbox half
2. Oil seal	11. Ball	19. Washer	28. Oil seal
3. Gearbox half	12. Bevel gear	20. Shift shaft	29. Oil seal
4. Shift arm	13. Clutch sleeve	21. Bushings	30. Plug
5. Dowel pin	14. Thrust washer	22. Washers	31. Gasket
6. Thrust washer	15. Bushing	23. Pin	32. Screw
7. Pinion gear	16. Countershaft	24. Driven gear	33. Gasket
8. "O" ring	17. Drive gear	25. Axle	34. Spring
9. Clutch fork		26.	35. Detent ball

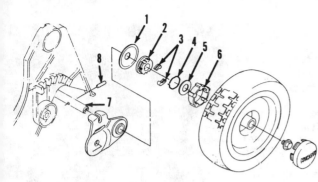

Fig. KU304—Exploded view of rear wheel ratchet assembly. Ratchet (2) is designed for either right or left wheel location and is not interchangeable.

1. Washer
2. Ratchet
3. Pawls
4. Retainer
5. Washer
6. Driver
7. Axle shaft
8. Pin

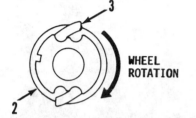

Fig. KU305—Pawls (3) must be installed on ratchet (2) so pawl points in direction of forward wheel travel.

gearbox, detach control cable and drive shaft. Remove rear wheels and gearbox assembly. Detach shields and shift lever. Unscrew plug (30) and drain oil. Remove shift detent ball components (32, 33, 34 and 35). Mark shift arm (4) so it can be returned to its original position. Remove screws retaining gearbox halves and separate halves so gears remain in right half (3). Disassemble remainder of components being careful not to lose clutch balls (11). Note the following specifications:

Shaft diameter of pinion (7) is 0.978-9.987 mm (0.3929-0.3932 inch). Bore diameter in gearbox half (3) is 10.000-10.015 mm (0.3937-0.3943 inch). Shaft clearance should be 0.013-0.037 mm (0.0005-0.0015 inch) with an allowable limit of 0.1 mm (0.004 inch).

Countershaft (16) outside diameter is 14.973-14.984 mm (0.5895-0.5899 inch). Bevel gear (12) inside diameter is 15.000-15.018 mm (0.5906-0.5913 inch). Shaft clearance should be 0.016-0.045 mm (0.0006-0.0018 inch) with an allowable limit of 0.07 mm (0.0028 inch).

Clutch sleeve (13) inside diameter is 21.55-21.65 mm (0.848-0.852 inch). Bevel gear (12) outside diameter is 21.40-21.47 mm (0.8425-0.8453 inch). Shaft clearance should be 0.08-0.25 mm (0.003-0.010 inch) with an allowable limit of 0.4 mm (0.016 inch).

Shift rod (20) diameter is 9.78-9.87 mm (0.385-0.389 inch). Countershaft (16) inside diameter is 10.05-10.10 mm (0.396-0.398 inch). Shaft clearance should be 0.18-0.32 mm (0.007-0.013 inch) with an allowable clearance of 0.4 mm (0.016 inch).

Bushing (21) inside diameter is 15.000-15.068 mm (0.5906-0.5932 inch). Axle (25) diameter is 14.957-15.000 mm (0.5889-0.5906 inch). Axle clearance should be 0.000-0.111 mm (0.0000-0.0044 inch) with an allowable limit of 0.20 mm (0.008 inch).

Bushing (15) inside diameter is 12.000-12.068 mm (0.4724-0.4751 inch). Countershaft (16) diameter is 11.989-12.000 mm (0.4720-0.4724 inch). Shaft clearance should be 0.000-0.079 mm (0.0000-0.0031 inch) with an allowable limit of 0.20 mm (0.008 inch).

When reassembling gearbox, apply a bead of Loctite 515 Gasket Eliminator (no gasket is used) to face of gearbox half. Adjust control cable after installation.

REAR WHEELS. Wheel ratchet assemblies shown in Fig. KU304 are not interchangeable from side to side. Be sure drive pin (8) in axle (7) engages slot in back of ratchet (2). Install pawls (3) so they point in direction of forward wheel rotation as shown in Fig. KU305.

LAWN-BOY SELF-DRIVE

Series C, D & F Mowers

Self propelled series "C", "D" and "F" Lawn-Boy mowers may be equipped with one of several different self-drive systems: LOWER BELT DRIVE MODELS, UPPER BELT DRIVE MODELS or one of two different GEARBOX DRIVE MODELS. Refer to the appropriate following paragraphs for service to the system used. Some adjustments and service may be the same for the different models.

LOWER BELT DRIVE MODELS

MAINTENANCE. At 25-hour intervals, release the spring clips and remove the drive assembly cover. Light oil should be applied to the idler belt pulley bearing (4—Fig. LB99), driven pulley bearing (5) and clutch linkage (3). A good quality axle bearing grease should be applied to drive gears (2). Lubricate the drive shaft needle bearings (1) as outlined in DRIVE SHAFT NEEDLE BEARING section. Grease fitting on sub-base (Fig. LB103) should be given 4 pumps from a grease gun.

CONTROL ROD ADJUSTMENT. Loosen the clamp screw on the control rod and position handle in "out-of-drive" position. With handle in this position, adjust control rod length to obtain 3/16 inch (5 mm) space between the drive collar roller and the tire as shown in Fig. LB100.

NOTE: Whenever wheel height or handle position is changed, the clutch control rod and lever must be readjusted.

If 3/16 inch (5 mm) space cannot be obtained, remove the right rear wheel, loosen shoulder bolt and adjust axle as necessary.

DRIVE ROLLERS. Drive rollers must be installed as shown in Fig. LB100. "V" cuts on roller point to tire to preserve their self-cleaning feature.

DRIVE SHAFT NEEDLE BEARINGS. Drive shaft needle bearings should be lubricated at 25-hour intervals. To lubricate, remove screw (I—Fig. LB101) and pack the cavity with a good quality axle grease. Install and tighten the screw (I). Repeat the procedure until grease is forced from the bearing at (G). Repeat the procedure for the bearing on the opposite side.

DRIVE BELT. To install a new drive belt, remove the blade, drive assembly cover and the drive roller for the wheel on the right side. Pull the drive shaft to

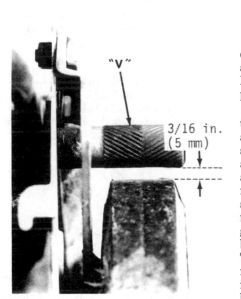

Fig. LB99—View showing maintenance point locations on self-propelled mowers with lower belt drive.

1. Drive shaft needle bearings
2. Gears
3. Clutch linkage
4. Idler pulley
5. Driven pulley bearing
6. Variable speed control

Fig. LB100—A ³⁄₁₆ inch (5 mm) space must be maintained between tire and drive rollers when mower drive control is in "neutral". "V" cuts on drive roller point to tire when correctly installed.

Fig. LB101—To lubricate the drive shaft needle bearings, screw (I) must be removed. Refer to text for correct procedure. Grease should be squeezed from bearings at (G).

Assemble models with variable speed drive as follows. Clean the drive pulley and coat the fixed pulley journal with Lubriplate. Install the sliding pulley portion onto the fixed pulley.

On all models, install the pulley on the crankshaft and clean the sub-base and the crankcase mating surfaces. Install the drive belt on the drive pulley, align the sub-base with the crankcase and install the sub-base. Tighten the retaining screws evenly. Lubricate the sub-base needle bearing at the grease fitting (Fig. LB103). Reinstall the engine, drive belt and the sub-base assembly. Install belt on the driven pulley. The idler pulley alignment can be corrected by placing a pipe over the end of idler pulley stud and bending the pulley bracket (Fig. LB104) slightly. The belt must ride in the center of all pulleys. Pull the drive shaft to the right and install the drive roller. Install drive assembly cover and the blade.

the left and remove the belt from the driven pulley. Remove the engine, belt and sub-base (Fig. LB102) as an assembly. Separate the sub-base from the engine, then remove the belt.

Inspect drive pulley (3—Fig. LB102) and bearing (12). On models with variable speed, improper drive pulley and belt alignment, needle bearing failure or sticking drive pulley can cause damage to the drive pulley. If a new needle bearing (12) is installed, make certain that hole in bearing outer race is aligned with the grease hole and fitting in the base.

DRIVEN PULLEY. Two adjustments are required to ensure proper mesh of the drive gears. A clearance of 0.018-0.019 inch (0.46-0.48 mm) must be maintained between the bottom of the horizontal drive shaft and the face of the bevel gear above the horizontal driven pulley. To adjust the clearance, install or remove shims from under the pulley to raise or lower the gear. Shims are available in a variety of thicknesses.

Adjust the mesh position of the bevel gears as follows. Loosen set screw on left (viewed from operator's position) drive

roller so the roller is loose on the horizontal shaft, then move the shaft to the right as far as possible and hold it in this position. Insert a 0.010 inch (0.25 mm) feeler gauge between the nylon bushing assembly and inner side of the right-side roller. Adjust the roller snug against the blade of the feeler gauge and tighten the set screw. Make sure the set screw is centered over the flat spot on the shaft before tightening. Bring the left-side drive roller snug against the bearing, and tighten the set screw. Gear clearance is now set to provide required backlash.

UPPER BELT DRIVE MODELS

MAINTENANCE. At 25 hour intervals, the clutch linkage and drive shaft needle bearings should be lubricated

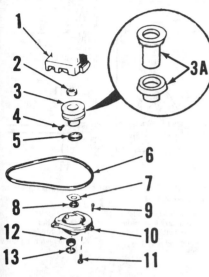

Fig. LB102—Exploded view of lower engine pulley and belt assembly on lower belt drive models.

1. Crankcase	7. Washer
2. Seal	8. Felt seal
3. Drive pulley	9. Sub-base to muffler
3A. Drive pulley	plate screws
(variable speed	10. Sub-base
models)	11. Sub-base to
4. Set screw	crankcase screws
5. Retainer	12. Needle bearing
6. Belt	13. Seal

with light oil. Refer to the DRIVE SHAFT NEEDLE BEARINGS section for lubricating these bearings.

CONTROL ROD ADJUSTMENT. Place handle in "out-of-drive" position. Loosen jam nuts on control rod and adjust the turnbuckle until there is $3/16$ inch (5 mm) space between drive rollers and tires as shown in Fig. LB100. Tighten jam nuts against the turnbuckle when adjustment is complete.

NOTE: Whenever wheel height or handle position is changed, clutch control rod and lever must be adjusted.

DRIVE ROLLERS. Proper drive roller engagement is obtained by loosening the top nut and bolt on the right side of link (B—Fig. LB101) and moving the drive shaft in or out until rollers are equal distance from tires. Tighten the nut and bolt when adjustment is complete.

Drive rollers must be installed as shown in Fig. LB100. The "V" cuts on roller point to tire to preserve their self cleaning feature.

DRIVE SHAFT NEEDLE BEARINGS. Drive shaft needle bearings should be lubricated at 25-hour intervals. To lubricate, remove the screw (I—Fig. LB101) and pack cavity with a good quality axle grease. Install and tighten

the screw to force grease into the bearing. Repeat the procedure until grease appears at bearing (G). Lubricate the bearing on opposite side using a similar procedure.

DRIVE BELT. To renew drive belt, remove cover (10—Fig. LB106), drive roller (20—Fig. LB107), washer (16) and sleeve (15) from left side. Withdraw belt from opening in handle bracket where sleeve (15) was installed.

Due to changes in design of roller bracket (2—Fig. LB106) there are two belt alignment procedures. Refer to Fig. LB108 to determine the style of bracket on the unit being serviced.

To correctly align the drive belt with the early style (Fig. LB108) bracket, position a straightedge against edge of driven pulley as shown at (W—Fig. LB109). Locate the driven pulley (12) on drive shaft (14) so straightedge is aligned with inside of pulley (9S) as shown at (X). Distance between straightedge and belt at point where belt just enters movable pulley (9M) should be $15/32$ inch (12 mm) as shown at (A). If clearance (A) is incorrect, move pulley (12) either way as necessary. Minimum clearance between belt and fuel tank (B) should be $3/32$ inch (2 mm) when mower is in drive position. If belt is too close to tank, loosen mounting bracket and move tank.

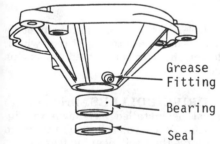

Fig. LB103—The sub-base of some models has a grease fitting installed to lubricate the bearing.

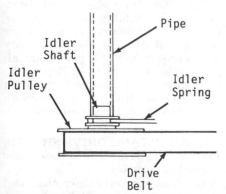

Fig. LB104—The belt must be centered in all of the pulleys. The idler shaft may be bent slightly using a pipe over the idler shaft if necessary.

Fig. LB106—Exploded view typical of self propelled drive for models with D-series engine and upper belt drive. Refer to Fig. LB107 for view of mower base and remainder of drive.

1. Drive pulley
2. Idler bracket
3. Spring retainer bracket
4. Lever
5. Spring
6. Shim
7. Grommet
8. Lockwasher
9. Idler pulleys
10. Belt cover

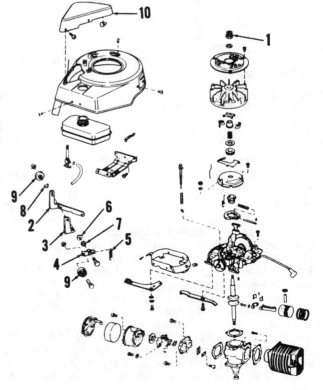

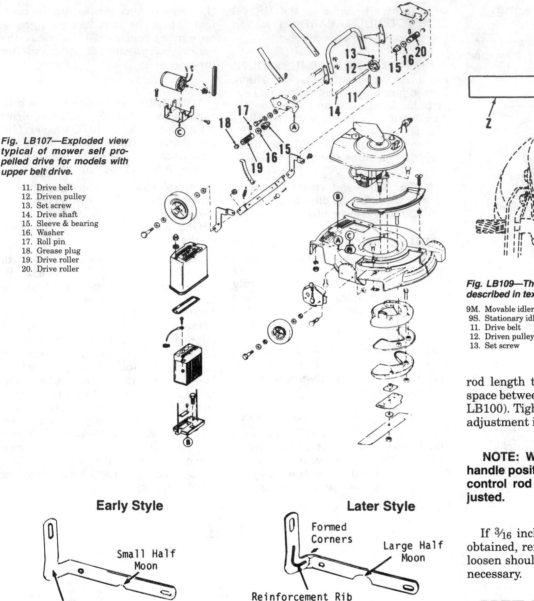

Fig. LB107—Exploded view typical of mower self propelled drive for models with upper belt drive.

11. Drive belt
12. Driven pulley
13. Set screw
14. Drive shaft
15. Sleeve & bearing
16. Washer
17. Roll pin
18. Grease plug
19. Drive roller
20. Drive roller

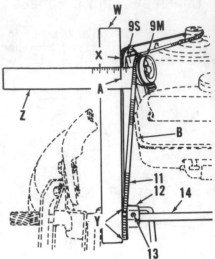

Fig. LB109—The drive belt should be aligned as described in text.

9M. Movable idler pulley
9S. Stationary idler pulley
11. Drive belt
12. Driven pulley
13. Set screw
14. Drive shaft
W. Straightedge
X. Inside edge of pulley
Z. Ruler

rod length to obtain ³⁄₁₆ inch (5 mm) space between drive roller and tire (Fig. LB100). Tighten the clamp screw when adjustment is complete.

NOTE: Whenever wheel height or handle position is changed, the clutch control rod and lever must be readjusted.

If ³⁄₁₆ inch (5 mm) space cannot be obtained, remove the right rear wheel, loosen shoulder bolt and adjust axle as necessary.

DRIVE ROLLERS. Drive rollers must be installed as shown in Fig. LB100. "V" cuts on roller point to tire to preserve their self-cleaning feature.

UPPER DRIVE SHAFT NEEDLE BEARINGS. Drive shaft needle bearings should be lubricated at 25-hour intervals. To lubricate, remove screw (I—Fig. LB101) and pack the cavity with a good quality axle grease. Install and tighten the screw (I). Repeat the procedure until grease is forced from the bearing at (G). Repeat the procedure for the bearing on the opposite side.

GEARBOX AND DRIVE SHAFTS. Refer to Fig. LB110 for an exploded view of gearbox assembly.

To adjust the lower drive shaft end play, measure between the drive roller (54) and washer (56) for ¹⁄₁₆ inch (1.6 mm) end play at each end. If play ex-

Early Style

Small Half Moon

No Reinforcement Rib

Later Style

Formed Corners

Large Half Moon

Reinforcement Rib

Fig. LB108—Comparison views of early and later style idler brackets used on self-propelled models with upper belt drive. Refer to text for details

If the later style bracket (Fig. LB108) is used, procedure steps are as before except the dimension (A—Fig. LB109) should be ⅛ inch (3 mm).

It may not be possible to adjust drive belt correctly due to excessive play in the drive shaft (14—Fig. LB109). If this is the condition, especially in 1968-1969 models, remove wave washers fitted to the shoulder bolt which holds bearing carrier bracket to the handle bracket, then substitute plain washers as necessary to limit the play to 0.012-0.015 inch (0.30-0.38 mm). If this change does not correct looseness, install the later type shoulder bolt (part number 606672).

GEARBOX DRIVE MODELS
(With External Clutch)

Refer to Fig. LB110 when servicing these models.

MAINTENANCE. Lubricate the drive wheels and clutch linkage at 25-hour intervals. Make certain all bushings are tight and linkage is in good condition.

CLUTCH ADJUSTMENT. Loosen clamp screw on control rod and position handle in "out-of-drive" position. With handle in this position, adjust control

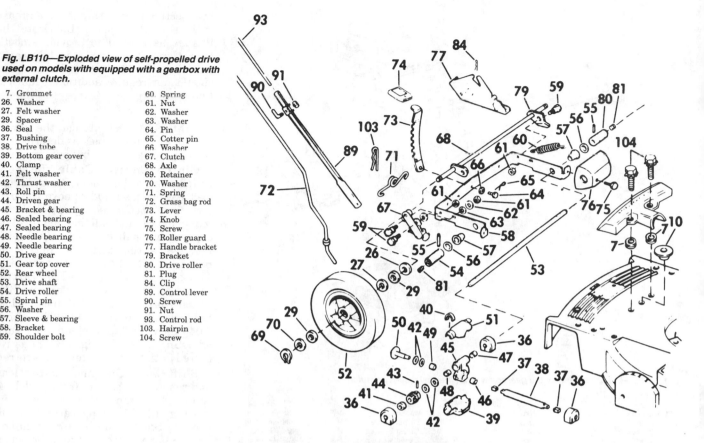

Fig. LB110—Exploded view of self-propelled drive used on models with equipped with a gearbox with external clutch.

7. Grommet	60. Spring
26. Washer	61. Nut
27. Felt washer	62. Washer
29. Spacer	63. Washer
36. Seal	64. Pin
37. Bushing	65. Cotter pin
38. Drive tube	66. Washer
39. Bottom gear cover	67. Clutch
40. Clamp	68. Axle
41. Felt washer	69. Retainer
42. Thrust washer	70. Washer
43. Roll pin	71. Spring
44. Driven gear	72. Grass bag rod
45. Bracket & bearing	73. Lever
46. Sealed bearing	74. Knob
47. Sealed bearing	75. Screw
48. Needle bearing	76. Roller guard
49. Needle bearing	77. Handle bracket
50. Drive gear	79. Bracket
51. Gear top cover	80. Drive roller
52. Rear wheel	81. Plug
53. Drive shaft	84. Clip
54. Drive roller	89. Control lever
55. Spiral pin	90. Screw
56. Washer	91. Nut
57. Sleeve & bearing	93. Control rod
58. Bracket	103. Hairpin
59. Shoulder bolt	104. Screw

ceeds ¹⁄₁₆ inch (1.6 mm), add an additional washer (56) on the right side.

End play of drive shaft tube (38) should be 0.035-0.135 inch (0.89-3.43 mm). If end play of the tube is 0.136-0.235 inch (3.45-5.97 mm), add one "O" ring (part number 303067) between nylon bushing (37) and square end of driven shaft (50). If the measurement exceeds 0.236 inch (6 mm), add an "O" ring at each end of the drive tube. If nylon bushings (37) are worn enough that the tube is loose in rotation, install new bushings.

If the bronze driven gear is to be separated from the worm gear of the engine crankshaft, it must be marked for reinstallation exactly as removed. If not, a new gear must be installed. If bevel gear set in gearbox is worn or damaged, renew both gears. Needle bearings (46, 47, 48 and 49) can be renewed individually. These bearings must pressed from their bores in bracket.

GEARBOX DRIVE MODELS
(With Internal Clutch)

Some models are equipped with a single-speed gearbox with an internal disc-type clutch. The gearbox can be identified by the vertical input shaft. Refer to Figs. LB111 and LB112.

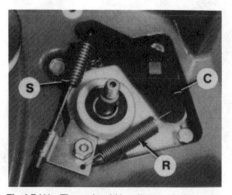

Fig. LB111—There should be slight end play at the end of spring (S) with the clutch arm (C) fully rotated clockwise.

MAINTENANCE. The gearbox is lubricated by injecting Lawn-Boy "A" grease (or suitable equivalent) into the gearbox through the grease fitting located in the bottom of the gearbox. Unless the gearbox is losing lubricant, inject grease as needed after 50 hours of operation. Do not overfill the gearbox as seals may be damaged. An indication of overfilling is upward movement of the clutch shaft arm.

CLUTCH CABLE. To check clutch cable adjustment, rotate clutch arm (C—Fig. LB111) clockwise until stopped. There should be a slight amount of end play at the end of cable spring (S). Turn the adjusting nuts at handlebar end of cable to obtain the desired end play. Check operation of the clutch after adjusting.

DRIVE BELT AND PULLEY. The engine must be removed to remove or install the drive belt. Drive belt tension is correct if finger pressure will deflect belt ³⁄₈ inch (9.5 mm) at the midway point on the long side of belt. Reposition the idler pulley to adjust belt tension. The gearbox drive pulley is assembled at the factory with four shim washers between the pulley halves. This provides fastest mower ground speed. If desired, mower ground speed may be reduced by removing shims(s) from between the pulley halves and placing the shims(s) on top of the pulley. Slowest mower speed is obtained with none of the shims between the pulley halves.

GEARBOX. To remove the gearbox, remove the engine, drive belt, clutch control cable, control arm and drive pulley. Remove the rear wheels and drive pinions. Note that a spring loaded key will be loose when the drive pinion is removed. Unfasten and remove gearbox.

Refer to Fig. LB112 for an exploded view of the gearbox assembly. Input shaft (23) and worm gear (13) are available only as a set. The clutch pack con-

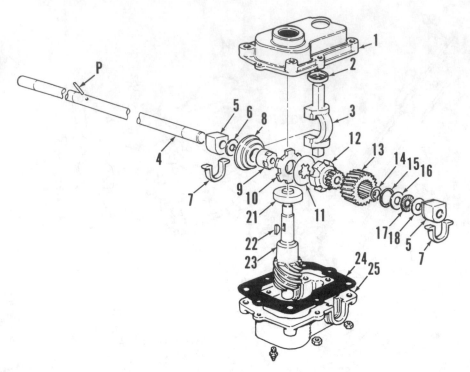

Fig. LB112—Exploded view of the gearbox with an internal disc-type clutch.

1. Upper gearbox half	7. Packing	13. Worm gear
2. Oil seal	8. Clutch collar	14. Snap ring
3. Clutch fork	9. Driven sleeve	15. Washer
4. Drive shaft	10. Drive discs (7)	16. Thrust washer (thick)
5. Bushings	11. Driven discs (6)	17. Thrust bearing
6. Washer	12. Driver	18. Thrust washer (thin)

21. Bearing
22. Key
23. Input shaft
24. Gasket
25. Gearbox half

sists of seven drive discs (10) and six driven discs (11). Drive discs are identified by external lugs while driven discs have internal splines. Clutch disc pack should be renewed as a set.

When assembling disc pack, install a drive disc first and last. Be sure that pin (P) engages notch in clutch sleeve (9). Assemble worm gear (13), snap ring (14), spacer washer (15), thick thrust washer (16), thrust bearing (17), thin thrust washer (18), shift collar (8), thrust washer (6) and bearings (5) onto shaft. Position shift fork (3) in shift collar groove, push the bearings together and place assembly in lower gearbox half. Fill lower gearbox half with Lawn-Boy "A" (or equivalent) grease. Install input shaft (23) and gearbox top half (1). Tighten gearbox screws in two steps to 35-45 in.-lbs. (4-5 N•m) using a crossing pattern. Rotate shafts and check for binding.

Check operation of wheel drive pinions. With the clutch engaged, it should be possible to push mower forward, but wheels should lock if pushed backward. If not, turn the pinion end for end.

LAWN-BOY SELF-DRIVE

Series M Mowers

Self propelled series "M" Lawn-Boy mowers may be equipped with self-drive that is serviced as follows.

MAINTENANCE. Lubricate the drive wheels after 50 hours of operation

by injecting grease through the grease fittings in the wheels. Lubricate the linkage as needed to provide smooth operation. The gearbox is lubricated and sealed at the factory. The gearbox should not require additional lubrication.

ADJUSTMENT. Adjust the clutch control and shift cables as described in the appropriate following paragraphs.

Clutch Control Cable. To check clutch cable adjustment, first disconnect battery lead and remove the battery from models so equipped. Raise rear of mower and pull the self propelled engagement bail to the engaged position against the handle bar. Rotate the rear wheels backward until they lock. The coils of spring (R—Fig. LB113) should just begin to separate after the clutch arm (A—Fig. LB114) has reached full travel. Clutch arm should be within 0.040 inch (1.02 mm) of stop (T). Turn adjusting nuts (N—Fig. LB113) as required until the spring tension is corret.

Shift Cable. Disconnect battery lead and remove the battery from models so equipped. Loosen cable retaining screw (S—Fig. LB115) being careful not to bend the bracket. Move the gear shift on handle bar so second gear is selected. Move the gearbox shift lever (L) to the middle detent position, which is second gear. Tighten the cable retaining screw.

DRIVE BELT REPLACEMENT. Be sure the spark plug lead is detached and properly grounded before working under the mower. On electric start models, remove the battery. On other models, remove the rear access plate. On models equipped with a blade brake clutch, remove the blade brake clutch. On other models, remove the belt guard located above the blade. On all models, unscrew the metric nut (M—Fig. LB113) and remove the pulley from the gearbox.

Fig. LB113—Adjust the clutch cable by turning adjusting nuts (N) as described in the text.

Fig. LB114—When the self-propelled bail is pulled against the handlebar, there should be a gap (G) of 0.040 inch (1.02 mm) between the clutch arm (A) and stop (T).

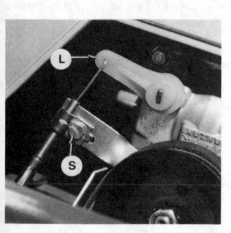

Fig. LB115—Adjust the shift control cable by loosening screw (S), moving the cable in the clamp, then tightening the screw. Position of the lever (L) must be synchronized with the handle bar control lever.

Note the following when installing the drive belt: Apply Loctite to the gearbox pulley nut and tighten the nut to 21 ft.-lb. (28 N•m) torque. On electric start models, apply Loctite to the screws attaching the belt guard located above the blade, then tighten the screws to 155 in.-lb. (17.5 N•m) torque. On models with blade brake, apply Loctite to the mounting screws, center the plate on the crankshaft and tighten the screws to 155 in.-lb. (17.5 N•m) torque. Be sure all belt guards are properly located and that belt does not rub. Be sure that any wiring or cables are away from the belt.

GEARBOX, AXLE AND PINIONS. The gearbox and output shaft is available as a service part from Lawn-Boy only as a unit assembly. The drive pinions are retained at the ends of the output shaft by snap rings. A spring-loaded key will be free when the drive pinion is removed. The drive pinions are marked "L" and "R" and should not be interchanged. Note the location of the washers and snap rings in Fig. LB116.

To remove the gearbox, remove the drive belt and pulley as outlined in DRIVE BELT REPLACEMENT paragraphs. Remove the rear wheels and drive pinions as described. Disconnect the shift cable and clutch control cable spring from the transmission control levers. Remove retaining screws from height adjustment plates, slide the height adjustment plates from the mower housing and remove the transmission.

Reverse the removal procedure to install the gearbox. Adjust the control cables as described when assembling.

LAWN-BOY SELF-DRIVE

Silver Series Mowers

Lawn-Boy Silver series (10201 and 10301—SN No. 4900001 & up) self propelled mowers are equipped with a single speed gearbox. The self-drive is engaged by tipping the gearbox to tighten the drive belt.

MAINTENANCE. Lubricate the drive wheels after 25 hours of operation or at least once each season by injecting grease through the fittings (Fig. LB117). Lubricate the control cables as needed to provide smooth operation. The gearbox is lubricated and sealed at the factory. The gearbox should not require additional lubrication.

Every 25 hours of operation or once each season, remove the attaching screw and slide the belt drive cover to the rear until it can be lifted away from the mower deck. See Fig. LB118. Clean any grass or other debris from the pulley and gearbox area.

ADJUSTMENT. Adjust the traction control cables as follows. Loosen the nut (A—Fig. LB119), hold the traction control bar 1-1 ½ inch (25-38 mm) from the handlebar (B), then pull the cable housing (C) down to remove all slack from the cable. Tighten the clamp nut (A) to hold the cable housing in position.

DRIVE BELT REPLACEMENT. Be sure the spark plug lead is detached and properly grounded before working under the mower. Unbolt and remove the blade and the belt covers. Unbolt the belt guide from the gearbox. Remove the belt from the gearbox pulley, then withdraw the belt from around the crankshaft. It may be necessary to loosen the traction cable adjustment before removing the drive belt. Install the belt by reversing the removal procedure, then adjust the traction control cable as described in the preceding paragraph. Be sure all belt guards are properly located and that belt does not rub.

DRIVE WHEELS AND PINIONS. Each of the two drive wheels is equipped with a ratchet type clutch that allows the gearbox output shaft and pinion to drive the wheel, permitting the two wheels to turn at different speeds to facilitate turning the mower. The clutches also allow the wheels to turn freely when the drive is not engaged. Refer to Fig. LB120.

Fig. LB116—Exploded view of output shaft pinion components.

1. Snap ring (thin)
2. Pinion
3. Washer (thin)
4. Snap ring (thick)
5. Washer (thick)
6. Key
7. Spring
8. Output shaft

Fig. LB117—The mower drive should be lubricated at fittings located on the drive wheel housings. The mower shown is typical.

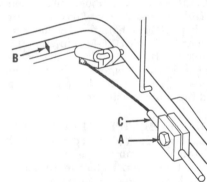

Fig. LB118—The traction drive belt is covered, but may trap some grass and other debris.

Fig. LB119—The traction control cable can be adjusted by moving the cable housing (C) in its clamp (A). Refer to text.

To reassemble, lubricate the output shaft (1), bushing (3) and bearing (6) with #2 lithium-based grease. Slide the pivot arm/bearing assembly onto the output shaft. Install thrust washer (7) with its external tabs engaging the notches in the pivot arm. Install tab washer (8) with the tab properly engaging the notch in the output shaft. Install the clip (9) with the tab engaging the notch in the output shaft. Install the friction ring (10) with the flat side out, toward the clutch washer, then install the clutch washer (11). Position the key (12) in the output shaft groove and slide the ratchet pawl against the clutch washer. The key and ratchet pawl are different for the left and right sides of the mower. The key should fit in the groove with the top of the key flat and the straight part of the ratchet pawl should be perpendicular to the shaft. The clutch washer has two notches for the ratchet pawl, but the ratchet pawl will only fit correctly in one. The other is used for the opposite side. Before continuing, rotate the clutch washer (11) slightly and see if the ratchet pawl moves properly. The pawl should tip the key up to engage the drive gear, then lower to allow freewheeling. Install the drive gear (13) and tab washer (14). The gear can be installed either way, but the tab on the washer should properly engage the groove in the output shaft. Install the spring (15) and retainer clip (16). Make sure the tab on the clip properly engages the groove in the output shaft. Grease the assembly through fitting (5). The original fitting is pressed into the pivot arm, but if damaged or lost, a screw-in fitting may be installed.

put shaft (1). The height adjustment arm should be attached to the pivot arm with a screw. The bushing and needle bearing should remain in the bore of the pivot arm. If it is necessary to install new bushings, press the new part into its bore until flush. Clean all parts thoroughly, then inspect each part for wear or damage.

Each drive wheel can be removed after removing the shoulder bolt from the center. The nut should remain in the pocket of the pivot arm. Remove the retaining clip (16) and spring (15). Notice that clip (16) is not a standard E-ring, but the center tab extends into the groove in the output shaft. Withdraw the tab washer (14) and gear (13), then remove the drive key (12). Remove the clutch washer (11) and the friction ring (10). Damage to the friction ring (10) or the clutch washer (11) will prevent proper operation. Remove the retaining clip (9), which is like clip (16). Remove the internal tab washer (8) and the external tab washer (7). Pull the pivot arm/bearing assembly (4) from the out-

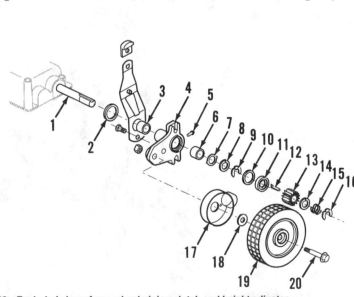

Fig. LB120—Exploded view of one wheel pinion clutch and height adjuster.

1. Gearbox output shaft	6. Bearing	11. Clutch washer	16. Special retaining clip
2. Spacer	7. Washer (external tabs)	12. Wheel pinion key	17. Cover
3. Bushing	8. Thrust washer (internal tab)	13. Wheel pinion	18. Stepped washer
4. Housing/pivot arm	9. Special retaining clip	14. Thrush washer (internal tab)	19. Wheel
5. Grease fitting	10. Friction ring	15. Spring	20. Shoulder bolt

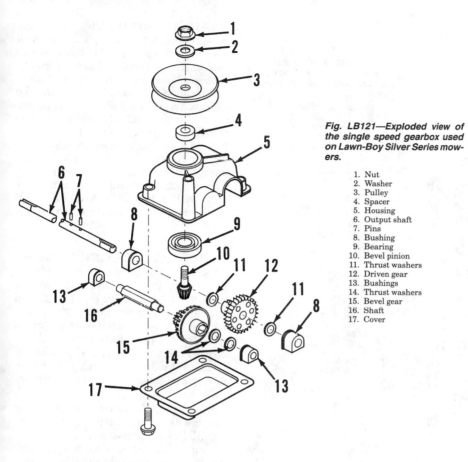

Fig. LB121—Exploded view of the single speed gearbox used on Lawn-Boy Silver Series mowers.

1. Nut
2. Washer
3. Pulley
4. Spacer
5. Housing
6. Output shaft
7. Pins
8. Bushing
9. Bearing
10. Bevel pinion
11. Thrust washers
12. Driven gear
13. Bushings
14. Thrust washers
15. Bevel gear
16. Shaft
17. Cover

gearbox to tighten the drive belt. The gearbox provides three gear ratios that drive the mower at different speeds.

MAINTENANCE. Lubricate the drive wheels after 25 hours of operation or at least one each season by injecting grease through the fittings (Fig. LB117). Lubricate the control cables as needed to provide smooth operation. The gearbox is lubricated and sealed at the factory. The gearbox should not require additional lubrication.

Every 25 hours of operation or once each season, remove the attaching screw and slide the belt drive cover to the rear until it can be lifted away from the mower deck. See Fig. LB118. Clean any grass or other debris from the pulley and gearbox area.

ADJUSTMENT. Adjust the traction control cables as follows. Loosen the nut (A—Fig. LB118), hold the traction control bar 1-1 ½ inch (25-38 mm) from the handlebar (B), then pull the cable housing (C) down to remove all slack from the cable. Tighten the clamp nut (A) to hold the cable housing in position.

DRIVE BELT REPLACEMENT. Be sure the spark plug lead is detached and properly grounded before working under the mower. Unbolt and remove the blade and the belt covers. Unbolt the belt guide from the gearbox. Remove the belt from the gearbox pulley, then withdraw the belt from around the crankshaft. It may be necessary to loosen the traction cable adjustment before removing the drive belt. Install the belt by reversing the removal procedure, then adjust the traction control cable as described in the preceding paragraph. Be sure all belt guards are properly located and that belt does not rub.

DRIVE WHEELS AND PINIONS. Each of the two drive wheels is equipped with a ratchet type clutch that allows the gearbox output shaft and pinion to drive the wheel, permitting the two wheels to turn at different speeds to facilitate turning the mower. The clutches also allow the wheels to turn freely when the drive is not engaged. Refer to Fig. LB120.

Each drive wheel can be removed after removing the shoulder bolt from the center. The nut should remain in the pocket of the pivot arm. Remove the retaining clip (16) and spring (15). Notice that clip (16) is not a standard E-ring, but the center tab extends into the groove in the output shaft. Withdraw the tab washer (14) and gear (13), then remove the drive key (12). Remove the clutch washer (11) and the friction ring (10). Damage to the friction ring (10) or the clutch washer (11) will prevent

The gear should rotate freely one direction, but not the other.

When installing the wheel, use the original number and thickness of spacer washers on the shoulder bolt to provide correct spacing. Wheel covers, used on some models, should be installed before the wheels. The wheel shoulder bolt (20) tightens into a nylon self-locking nut located in a pocket of the pivot arm. It may be necessary to press the nut toward the shoulder bolt while starting the bolt. Tighten the shoulder bolt securely.

R&R GEARBOX. The drive axle passes through the gearbox and a wheel drive pinion is attached to each end. To remove the gearbox and axle assembly, remove the drive belt covers. Unbolt and remove the belt guide from the gearbox and lift the belt from the pulley. Remove both DRIVE WHEELS AND PINIONS as described in this section, then remove the screws attaching the height adjuster plates to each side of the mower deck. Reinstall the gearbox by reversing the removal procedure. Refer to the DRIVE WHEELS AND PINIONS paragraphs in this section when installing.

OVERHAUL GEARBOX. Refer to Fig. LB121. The gearbox can be disassembled after unbolting and removing

the lower cover. Lift the shafts (6 and 16) and their related gears and bushings from the housing to clean and inspect. Notice that two thrust washers (14) are installed behind the bevel gear (15). Failure of the bearing (9) will result in damage to the teeth of the bevel gears (10 and 15).

When assembling, lubricate all parts with #2 lithium-based grease. Two thrust washers (14) should be located behind the bevel gear (15). Check the backlash between the bevel gears before installing the cover (17). Install new gears, bushings or bearing as necessary before finishing the assembly. Pack additional grease around the gears in the gearbox before installing the cover. Do not fill the gear case completely.

LAWN-BOY SELF-DRIVE

Gold Series Mowers

Lawn-Boy Gold series (10515 and 10520—SN No. 3900001 & up and 10516 and 10521—SN No. 4900001 & up) self propelled mowers are equipped with a three speed gearbox. The self-drive clutch is engaged by tipping the

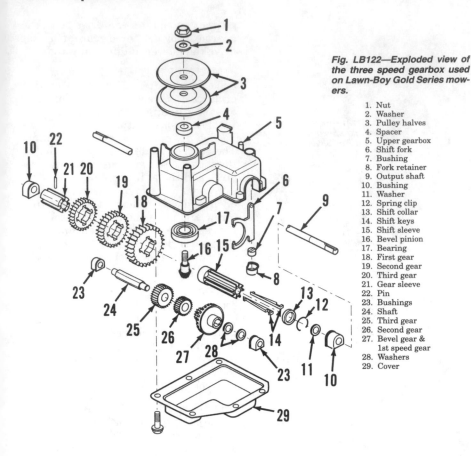

Fig. LB122—Exploded view of the three speed gearbox used on Lawn-Boy Gold Series mowers.

1. Nut
2. Washer
3. Pulley halves
4. Spacer
5. Upper gearbox
6. Shift fork
7. Bushing
8. Fork retainer
9. Output shaft
10. Bushing
11. Washer
12. Spring clip
13. Shift collar
14. Shift keys
15. Shift sleeve
16. Bevel pinion
17. Bearing
18. First gear
19. Second gear
20. Third gear
21. Gear sleeve
22. Pin
23. Bushings
24. Shaft
25. Third gear
26. Second gear
27. Bevel gear & 1st speed gear
28. Washers
29. Cover

R&R GEARBOX. The drive axle passes through the gearbox and a wheel drive pinion is attached to each end. To remove the gearbox and axle assembly, remove the drive belt covers. Unbolt and remove the belt guide from the gearbox and lift the belt from the pulley. Remove both DRIVE WHEELS AND PINIONS as described in this section, then remove the screws attaching the height adjuster plates to each side of the mower deck. Reinstall the gearbox by reversing the removal procedure. Refer to the DRIVE WHEELS AND PINIONS paragraphs in this section when installing.

OVERHAUL GEARBOX. Remove the screws attaching the cover or housing halves, then remove the cover or separate the housings. Fig. LB122 and LB123 show a typical unit. The shafts with gears can be lifted from the housing. Flats are provided on the bevel pinion gear of some models as shown in Fig. LB124 to facilitate holding it while removing and installing the pulley retaining nut.

Refer to Fig. LB125 when assembling components of the output shaft and to Fig. LB126 when assembling the countershaft. Coat transmission parts with grease when assembling. Two thrust washers (28—Fig. LB126) should be located behind the bevel gear (27). Check the backlash between the bevel gears (16 and 27) before installing the cover. Install new gears, bushings or bearing as necessary before finishing the assembly. Pack additional grease around the gears in the gearbox before installing the cover. Add about 177 cc (6 oz.) of #2 lithium-based grease to the gear case before installing the cover. Do not fill the gear case completely.

On all models, refer to the DRIVE WHEELS paragraphs in this section when assembling the axle bearings and drive gears on the output shaft.

proper operation. Remove the retaining clip (9), which is like clip (16). remove the internal tab washer (8) and the external tab washer (7). Pull the pivot arm/bearing assembly (4) from the output shaft (1). The bushing and needle bearing should remain in the bore of the pivot arm. If it is necessary to renew bushings, press the new part into its bore until flush. Clean all parts thoroughly, then inspect each part for wear or damage.

To reassemble, lubricate the output shaft (1), bushing (3) and bearing (6) with #2 lithium-based grease. Slide the pivot arm/bearing assembly onto the output shaft. Install thrust washer (7) with its external tabs engaging the notches in the pivot arm. Install tab washer (8) with the tab properly engaging the notch in the output shaft. Install the clip (9) with the tab engaging the notch in the output shaft. Install the friction ring (10) with the flat side out, toward the clutch washer, then install the clutch washer (11). Position the key (12) in the output shaft groove and slide the ratchet pawl against the clutch washer. The key and ratchet pawl are different for the left and right sides of the mower. The key should fit in the groove with the top of the key flat and the straight part of the ratchet pawl should be perpendicular to the shaft.

The clutch washer has two notches for the ratchet pawl, but the ratchet pawl will only fit correctly in one. The other is used for the opposite side. Before continuing, rotate the clutch washer (11) slightly and see if the ratchet pawl moves properly. The pawl should tip the key up to engage the drive gear, then lower to allow freewheeling. Install the drive gear (13) and tab washer (14). The gear can be installed either way, but the tab on the washer should properly engage the groove in the output shaft. Install the spring (15) and retainer clip (16). Make sure the tab on the clip properly engages the groove in the output shaft. Grease the assembly through fitting (5). The original fitting is pressed into the pivot arm, but if damaged or lost, a screw-in fitting may be installed. The gear should rotate freely one direction, but not the other.

When installing the wheel, use the original number and thickness of spacer washers on the shoulder bolt to provide correct spacing. Wheel covers, used on some models, should be installed before the wheels. The wheel shoulder bolt tightens into a nylon self-locking nut located in a pocket of the pivot arm. It may be necessary to press the nut toward the shoulder bolt while starting the bolt. Tighten the shoulder bolt securely.

Fig. LB123—View of a three speed gearbox with the lower cover removed showing the internal components.

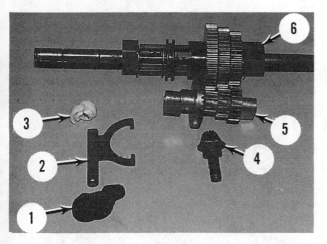

Fig. LB124—View of the shafts and gears removed from a typical three speed gearbox.

1. Shift lever
2. Shift fork
3. Retainer
4. Input pinion
5. Drive (cluster) gear assembly
6. Output shaft, shifter & gears

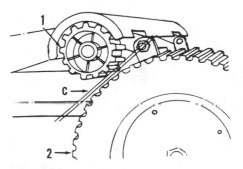

Fig. M1—Drive pinions (1) should be approximately 1/8 inch (3 mm) from drive wheels when clutch is disengaged.

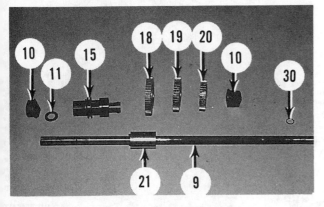

Fig. LB125—The output shaft of a typical three speed gearbox.

9. Output shaft
10. Bushing
11. Thrust washer
15. Sliding clutch (shift) assembly
18. Slow (1st) gear
19. Second gear
20. Fast (3rd) gear
21. Sliding clutch hub
30. O-ring

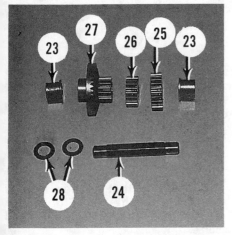

Fig. LB126—The drive gear assembly components typical of three speed models.

23. Bushing
24. Shaft
25. Fast (3rd) gear
26. Second gear
27. Bevel/small (1st) gear
28. Thrust washers (2 used)

MTD

There are several drive systems for self-propelled MTD mowers: Front or rear wheel/pinion chain drive, front wheel pinion V-belt drive, front wheel internal V-belt drive, rear wheel internal drive, rear wheel transmission (single-speed) drive and multispeed rear wheel transmission drive.

The drive systems covered in this section also apply to some Cub Cadet and Yard-Man mowers.

Wheel/Pinion Chain Drive

DRIVE CLUTCH CONTROL. The drive system utilizes a chain drive from engine pto to the pinion drive shaft. The drive shaft turns whenever the engine is running. Squeezing drive control handle causes the pinions to contact and drive the wheels. Releasing the control handle raises the pinions away from the wheel and stops the wheels from driving.

There should be approximately 1/8 inch (3 mm) clearance (C—Fig. M1) between the drive pinions (1) and wheels (2) when the drive is disengaged (control handle released). If clearance is less than 1/8 inch (3 mm), unhook clutch cable from the control handle and move it to the next higher hole provided in the control handle.

DRIVE CHAIN. On mowers built prior to 1990, drive chain tension and alignment must be manually adjusted. Mowers built in 1990 and later are equipped with an automatic chain tensioner and no adjustment is required.

To adjust chain on early models, loosen bolt on each of the pivot brackets (16 and 19—Fig. M2). Pull on the pinion cover plate (13) to obtain proper chain tension. Chain should have a small amount of slack; do not overtighten. The clearance between pinion and wheel should be equal on both sides. If not, reposition pinion cover plate until clearance is equal, then tighten pivot bracket bolts.

Front Wheel Pinion V-Belt Drive.

DRIVE CLUTCH CONTROL. The drive system utilizes a V-belt drive from engine pto to the external pinion drive shaft (Fig. M3). A belt idler is used as the clutch. Squeezing drive control handle moves the idler to increase belt tension and engage drive mechanism. Releasing drive control handle allows the V-belt to go slack and drive is disengaged. The drive pinions do not lift out of engagement with the wheels.

Depending on the clutch cable design, drive belt tension can be adjusted as follows: On early models, remove plastic cap from beneath drive control lever housing and reposition clutch cable to next adjustment position (Fig. M4). On some later models, an adjustable cable bracket (Fig. M5) is provided to allow cable to be repositioned. Cable adjustment holes are also provided in the drive control lever (3—Fig. M5). Move cable to one of the upper holes to increase belt tension. On 1990 and later models, an cable adjusting wheel is located in the clutch control housing (Fig. M6).

Front Wheel Ratchet Drive

DRIVE CLUTCH CONTROL. The drive system utilizes a V-belt drive from engine pto to front axle/jackshaft (Fig. M7). The jackshaft has internal pinions (21) that mate with internal teeth on the drive wheels (23). The belt idler pulleys

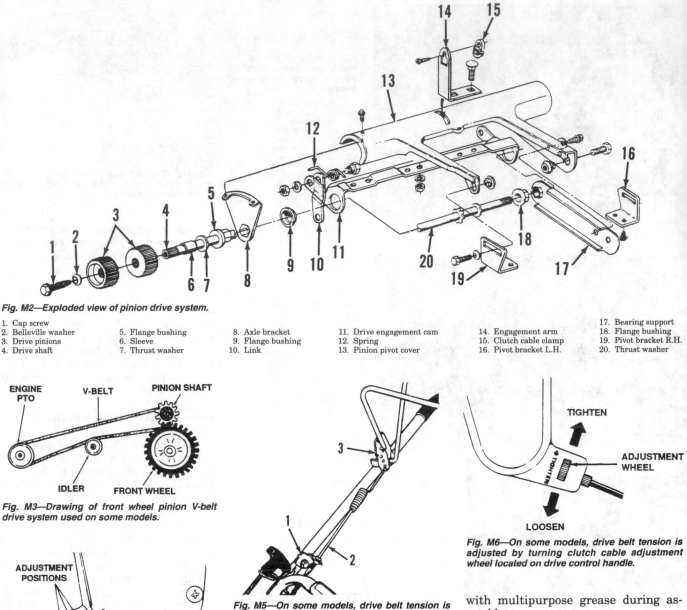

Fig. M2—Exploded view of pinion drive system.

1. Cap screw
2. Belleville washer
3. Drive pinions
4. Drive shaft
5. Flange bushing
6. Sleeve
7. Thrust washer
8. Axle bracket
9. Flange bushing
10. Link
11. Drive engagement cam
12. Spring
13. Pinion pivot cover
14. Engagement arm
15. Clutch cable clamp
16. Pivot bracket L.H.
17. Bearing support
18. Flange bushing
19. Pivot bracket R.H.
20. Thrust washer

Fig. M3—Drawing of front wheel pinion V-belt drive system used on some models.

Fig. M4—On some models, drive belt tension is adjusted by moving clutch cable to different adjustment position in clutch control housing.

Fig. M5—On some models, drive belt tension is adjusted by moving clutch cable to different adjustment hole in drive control lever.

Fig. M6—On some models, drive belt tension is adjusted by turning clutch cable adjustment wheel located on drive control handle.

(2 and 3) serve as the drive clutch. Squeezing drive control lever pivots the idler pulley bracket (1) which tightens the belt and engages the drive system.

To adjust drive clutch control, shut off engine and remove belt cover (8). Squeeze drive control handle against upper handle (drive engaged) and measure length of idler spring (5). Spring length should be approximately 2 inches (50 mm). To adjust, loosen screw attaching cable bracket to upper handle and move bracket up or down as necessary to obtain desired spring length.

R&R DRIVE BELT. To replace drive belt (9—Fig. M7), first disconnect and ground spark plug cable. Remove belt cover (8) and disconnect clutch control cable (7) from idler bracket (4). Remove shoulder bolt and flanged idler (2) from idler bracket. Remove hub cap from left wheel, remove hairpin clip from end of axle shaft (12) and withdraw wheel. Pry "E" ring (22) off axle and remove pinion gear (21) and thrust washer (20). Drive roll pin out of axle and remove dust cover (19). Unbolt and remove wheel height adjuster plate (15) and lever (17). Work V-belt off the pulleys and slip belt over end of axle/jackshaft.

To install new belt, reverse the belt removal procedure. Lubricate axle/jackshaft and needle bearing in idler pulley

with multipurpose grease during assembly.

NOTE: When installing idler pulley, make certain that cupped side of Belleville washer (6—Fig. M7) is against the idler bracket or pulley will seize.

When installing height adjuster assembly, be sure to align extruded hole in adjuster plate with hole in mower deck as shown in Fig. M8. Adjust drive clutch cable as previously outlined.

Rear Wheel Internal Drive

DRIVE CLUTCH CONTROL. The rear wheel internal drive system features a V-belt from engine pto to a jackshaft with an idler pulley used as a clutch (Fig. M9). Final drive from jackshaft to axle shaft is via a chain.

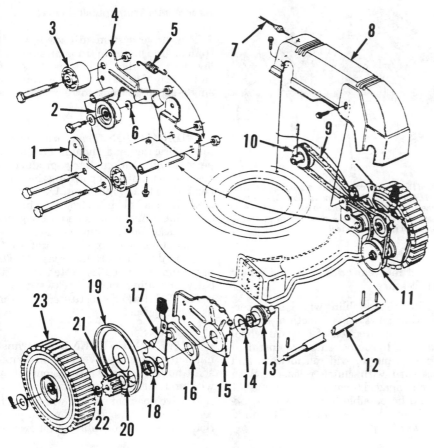

Fig. M7—Partially exploded view of internal V-belt front wheel drive system used on some models.

1. Idler pivot bracket
2. Flanged idler
3. Flat idlers
4. Idler bracket
5. Spring
6. Belleville washer
7. Clutch cable
8. Belt cover
9. Drive belt
10. Engine pulley
11. Wheel drive pulley
12. Front axle & jackshaft
13. Bearing
14. Belleville washer
15. Height adjuster plate
16. Adjuster pivot plate
17. Adjuster lever
18. Snap ring & washer
19. Dust cover
20. Thrust washer
21. Drive pinion
22. "E" ring
23. Front wheel

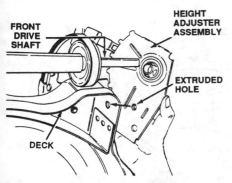

Fig. M8—When reassembling front wheel drive axle, be sure that extruded hole in height adjuster plate aligns with hole in mower deck.

When drive clutch control is squeezed, rear wheel should drive forward. Releasing clutch control should stop rear wheels from driving. If drive does not self-propel when clutch lever is squeezed, remove plastic cap from beneath drive control housing and move plastic fitting on clutch control cable to next adjustment position on the left (Fig. M4).

Note that the engine pto pulley and idler pulley are available in different diameters to provide additional belt adjustment.

BELT AND CHAIN DRIVE. There is no adjustment for the drive chain (10—Fig. M9). If chain comes off sprocket, it is either worn or sprockets are worn or bent. Disconnect master link to remove chain.

To renew drive belt, remove screws attaching belt cover (3—Fig. M9) to mower deck. Disconnect clutch cable (2) and spring (5) from idler bracket (4). Disconnect chain master link and remove drive chain (10) from sprocket. Unbolt pivot bracket (18) from pulley shaft (25). Work belt (24) off the pulleys, slip belt over end of pulley shaft and remove from mower deck.

To install new belt, reverse the removal procedure. Adjust clutch control cable as previously outlined.

To disassemble drive, remove rear wheels. Unbolt and remove pivot brackets (18—Fig. M9), flange bushings (13) and spacers (12). Remove axle with sprocket (9) from mower. Drive spring pin out of spacer (20) and withdraw flange bushings (8) and driven pulley (21) from pulley shaft (25).

Inspect all parts and renew as necessary. When reassembling, note that no lubricant is required with plastic flange bushings (8 and 13).

REAR WHEELS. The rear wheels are equipped with a ratchet assembly shown in either Fig. M10 or Fig. M11.

1. Engine pto shaft
2. Clutch cable
3. Belt cover
4. Idler arm
5. Spring
6. Spacer
7. Thrust washer
8. Flange bushing
9. Rear axle
10. Chain
11. Washer
12. Spacer
13. Flange bushing
14. Height adjuster lever
15. Washer
16. Nut
17. Belleville washer
18. Pivot bracket
19. Thrust washer
20. Spacer
21. Pulley & sprocket assy.
22. Idler pulley
23. Engine pulley
24. Drive belt
25. Pulley shaft

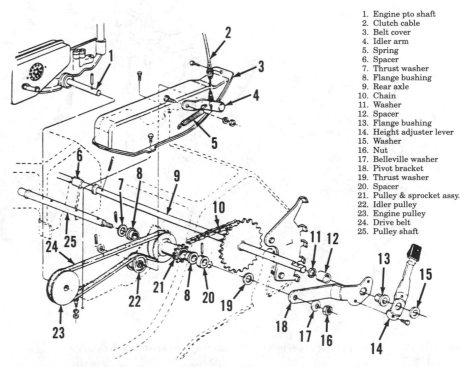

Fig. M9—Exploded view of rear wheel ratchet drive system used on some models.

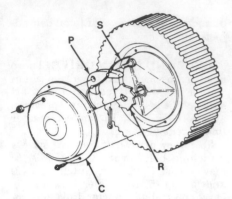

Fig. M10—Some rear wheels are equipped with pawl (P), nylon spring (S) and ratchet (R) mounted in hub cap (C). A right-side wheel is shown. Reverse direction of pawl and ratchet on left-side wheel.

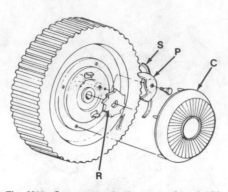

Fig. M11—Some rear wheels are equipped with pawl (P), nylon spring (S) and ratchet (R) mounted to the wheel rather than in hub cap (C). A left-side wheel is shown. Reverse direction of pawl and ratchet on right-side wheel.

Note that some pawls are attached to the hub cab (Fig. M10) and some pawls are attached to the wheel (Fig. M11). When disassembling rear wheel, note position of ratchet (R), pawl (P) and nylon spring (S) for correct reassembling.

To remove wheels remove screws attaching hub cap (C) to wheel and remove hub cap. Remove cotter pin from end of axle and slide wheel and ratchet off axle shaft. Inspect pawl and teeth of ratchet for wear or damage and renew as necessary.

When reassembling wheel, make certain that pawl (P) and teeth of ratchet (R) face in direction of forward wheel rotation. If components are installed correctly, mower will roll forward and backward with clutch released. With clutch engaged (engine not running), it should be possible to push mower forward, but wheels will lock if pulled backward.

Rear Wheel Transmission Drive

This drive system utilizes a V-belt from engine pulley to transmission pulley with an idler pulley used as the clutch (Fig. M12). Final drive from the single-speed gearbox to rear axle is a chain.

LUBRICATION. The gearbox is factory lubricated and should not require periodic lubrication. Early production gearboxes required separating the gearbox halves to add lubricant. Later gearboxes have a hole in gearbox top half to allow lubricant to be added after gearbox is assembled. Manufacturer recommends filling gearbox with 2 ounces (60 mL) of Alvania EPROO grease (MTD part number 737-0168). Note that difficulty in pulling mower backward may result if a thicker substitute grease is used in gearbox.

DRIVE ADJUSTMENT. The transmission is driven by a V-belt from crankshaft pulley to the transmission pulley with an idler pulley used as a clutch.

If drive does not engage when clutch control lever is moved to engaged position, adjust control cable as follows: If

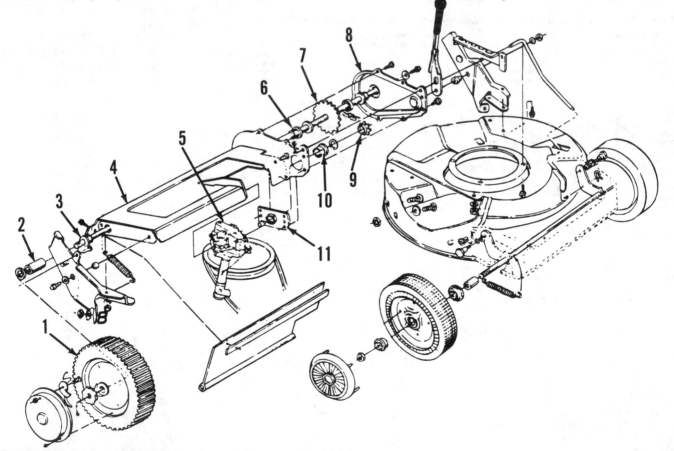

Fig. M12—Exploded view of rear wheel transmission drive system used on some models.

1. Wheel	3. Bearing	5. Gearbox	7. Sprocket	9. Sprocket
2. Sleeve	4. Axle assy.	6. Bearing	8. Chain cover	10. Bearing
				11. Bearing retainer

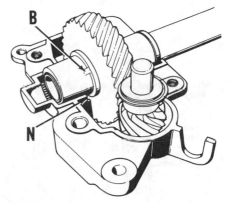

Fig. M14—Rib (B) on bushings must index with notch (N) in gearbox half.

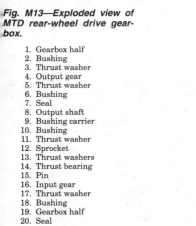

Fig. M13—Exploded view of MTD rear-wheel drive gearbox.

1. Gearbox half
2. Bushing
3. Thrust washer
4. Output gear
5. Thrust washer
6. Bushing
7. Seal
8. Output shaft
9. Bushing carrier
10. Bushing
11. Thrust washer
12. Sprocket
13. Thrust washers
14. Thrust bearing
15. Pin
16. Input gear
17. Thrust washer
18. Bushing
19. Gearbox half
20. Seal
21. Input shaft
22. Hex washer
23. Pulley
24. Belleville washer
25. Nut
26. Clutch idler pulley
27. Idler bracket
28. Shoulder spacer
29. Clutch control cable

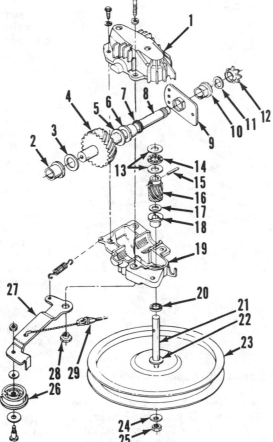

drive control lever is equipped with a cable adjusting wheel (Fig. M6), turn the adjusting wheel to increase idler pulley tension on drive belt. If drive control lever does not have an adjusting wheel, remove plastic cap from beneath the drive clutch control lever housing. Move the plastic fitting on end of cable to next adjustment position on the left (Fig. M4). If drive does not disengage, adjust control cable to move idler pulley away from drive belt when clutch control is in disengaged position.

DRIVE BELT. To renew drive belt, disconnect and properly ground spark plug lead. Drain fuel tank or place a piece of plastic wrap beneath fuel tank cap to prevent fuel leakage.

Remove three bolts on left side of grass catcher panel to loosen panel. Remove two bolts retaining transmission belt guard, lift up grass catcher panel and remove belt guard. Tip mower on its side and remove inside belt guard. Unbolt and remove blade and adapter with pulley from crankshaft. Loosen idler pulley bolt to make it easier to slip belt between pulley and belt guard. Remove belt from idler pulley and transmission pulley.

To install new belt, push idler pulley up out of the way and slide new belt in from the rear and place it around transmission pulley. Slide belt in place between idler pulley and idler belt guard. Tighten idler bolt. Position belt on crankshaft pulley, then install pulley and blade assembly on crankshaft. Install inside belt guard and transmission belt guard. Make sure that there is at least ⅛ inch (3 mm) clearance between belt and transmission belt guard. Adjust drive control cable as necessary.

GEARBOX. To remove gearbox, first remove drive belt as outlined in previous paragraph. Disconnect drive chain and drive control cable. Unbolt and remove transmission from rear axle housing.

Refer to Fig. M13 for an exploded view of a typical gearbox assembly. To disassemble gearbox, unscrew pulley nut (25) and remove pulley (23).

NOTE: Nut (25) on early models has right-hand threads while nut on later models has left-hand threads. Attempt to determine thread direction before unscrewing nut.

Unscrew three screws securing gearbox halves and separate two halves. Lift output shaft assembly out of gearbox half and remove bearing (2) and thrust washer (3) from end of shaft. Drive output shaft (8) out of sprocket (12), then slide thrust washers (11), bearing (10), bearing retainer (9), seal (7), bearing (6) and thrust washer (5) off the shaft. Output gear (4) is pressed on output shaft and removal is not recommended unless renewal is necessary. On early models, drive out roll pin (15) to separate input gear (16) from input shaft (21). On later models, input shaft and gear are serviced as one assembly. Pry seal (20) from gearbox half. Bushings in gearbox can be removed by cutting threads into bushing using a ⁷⁄₁₆ inch (11 mm) tap. Thread the tap into bushing, then pull upward on tap to remove bushing.

NOTE: If unit being serviced is equipped with pulley shaft (21) having right-hand threads and pulley nut (25) has loosened during operation, it is recommended that newer style shaft and nut with left-hand threads be installed.

Reassemble gearbox by reversing disassembly procedure while noting the following: Inspect hex on drive pulley (23), special hex washer (22) and input shaft (21) for wear or damage and renew as necessary. Install seals (7 and 20) so lip is toward gear. If reusing sprocket (12), be sure to align serrations on shaft with sprocket serrations. A new sprocket must be pressed or driven onto output shaft until it is seated against end of shaft serrations. Install output shaft assembly in gearbox lower half making certain that rib (B—Fig. M14) on bearings indexes with locating notch (N) in gearbox half.

Fill gearbox with 2 ounces (60 mL) of Alvania EPROO grease. Apply gasket

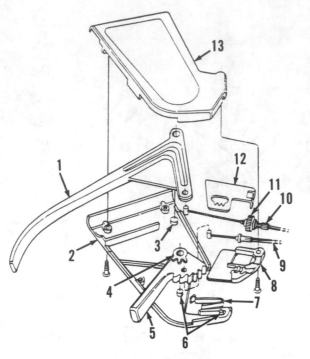

Fig. M15—Exploded view of six-speed clutch control.

1. Drive control lever
2. Housing bottom cover
3. Plastic pin
4. Three-tooth rack insert
5. Six-speed shift lever
6. Plastic pins
7. Shift lever spring
8. Cable mounting cap
9. Shift cable
10. Clutch cable
11. Adjuster wheel
12. Six-speed rack bracket
13. Housing upper cover

in closer to the crankshaft and speed of the lawn mower decreases. Moving pulley halves closer together forces the belt outward to the larger diameter section of the pulley and speed of lawn mower increases. The drive clutch control cable (10) controls idler belt tension to engage and disengage mower drive.

Adjustment of drive clutch cable may be needed if mower does not self-propel when clutch control lever is squeezed against upper handle, or if drive belt is slipping (mower speed decreases while engine maintains same speed). Turn the cable adjustment wheel (11—Fig. M15) located on underside of clutch control housing to tighten the drive belt.

Be sure that mower drive returns to neutral when drive control lever is released. Turn adjusting wheel in opposite direction to loosen drive belt tension if necessary.

SIX-SPEED SHIFT CABLE. Periodic adjustment of shift cable may be needed to compensate for cable stretch and wear. If all six speeds cannot be obtained, adjust cable as follows: Loosen nut (2—Fig. M16) that secures the cable bracket (3). Move shift lever to 6th speed. Move drive belt away from drive pulley to make certain that pulley halves are not being held apart by the belt. Pull rearward on cable bracket and tighten bracket retaining nut. Start engine and recheck mower speeds.

To disassemble, remove cover cap (8—Fig. M15). Remove screws attaching bottom half of control cover (2) to upper half (13) and separate the control cover. Remove clutch control cable (10) and six-speed shift cable (9). Remove clutch control lever (1), shift lever spring (7), shift lever (5) and six-speed cable bracket (12).

Inspect all parts for wear or damage and renew as necessary. When reassembling, align the teeth on three-tooth rack gear (4) with slots in six-speed cable bracket (12). Make certain that three-tooth rack is seated fully into six-speed cable bracket and shift cable is

maker sealant such as Loctite 280 to mating surface of upper half. Assemble the two gearbox halves and tighten retaining bolt and screws evenly in a cross pattern. Be sure that idler bracket (27—Fig. M13) and shoulder spacer (28) are positioned correctly. Rotate the input shaft after assembly and check for binding. Install drive pulley so small diameter is nearer gearbox. Tighten pulley retaining nut to 120-160 in.-lbs. (13.6-18.0 N·m).

REAR WHEELS. The rear wheels are equipped with a ratchet assembly shown in either Fig. M10 of Fig. M11. Note that some pawls are attached to the hub cab (Fig. M10) and some pawls are attached to the wheel (Fig. M11). When disassembling rear wheel, note position of ratchet (R), pawl (P) and nylon spring (S) for correct reassembling.

To remove wheels remove screws attaching hub cap (C) to wheel and remove hub cap. Remove cotter pin from end of axle and slide wheel and ratchet off axle shaft. Inspect pawl and teeth of ratchet for wear or damage and renew as necessary.

When reassembling wheel, make certain that pawl (P) and teeth of ratchet (R) face in direction of forward wheel rotation. If components are installed correctly, mower will roll forward and backward with clutch released. With clutch engaged (engine not running), it should be possible to push mower forward, but wheels will lock if pulled backward.

Multispeed (Six Speed) Drive

The multispeed drive system utilizes a split drive pulley mounted on engine crankshaft. Up or down movement of the pulley upper half varies the working diameter of the pulley which results in variable speed ratios.

The single-speed gearbox, rear axle and rear wheels used on multispeed models are the same as those used on rear wheel transmission drive single-speed models covered in previous paragraphs.

DRIVE CLUTCH CONTROL. The multispeed drive system utilizes a split drive pulley mounted on engine crankshaft. The six-speed shift lever (5—Fig. M15) controls up and down movement of upper half of the engine pulley, providing variable pulley diameters which results in six different drive speeds. As pulley halves separate, drive belt moves

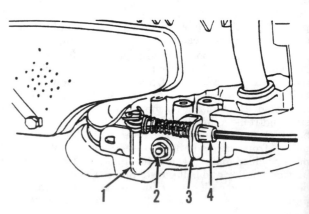

Fig. M16—Drawing showing six-speed cable adjustment point. Refer to text.

1. Shift rod
2. Nut
3. Cable adjusting bracket
4. Six-speed shift cable

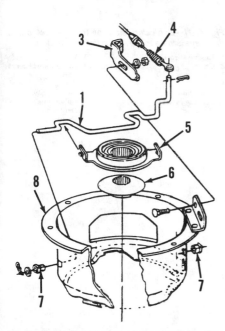

Fig. M17—Exploded view of six-speed housing. Up and down movement of pulley upper half (5) is controlled by shift rod (1) to provide six speed ratios.

1. Shift rod
3. Cable bracket
4. Six-speed shift cable
5. Pulley upper half
6. Pulley lower half
7. Flanged bushings
8. Six-speed housing

located in first notch toward the handle of six-speed shift lever (5). Be sure that shift lever spring (7) is installed behind pin (6) in lower housing and that shift lever moves freely through all six speed positions.

SIX-SPEED HOUSING. To disassemble six-speed housing, first disconnect spark plug cable and properly ground it against frame. Disconnect shift control cable (3—Fig. M17) from

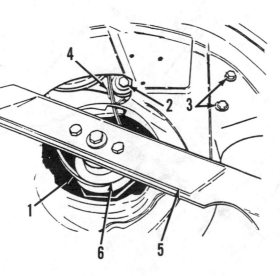

Fig. M18—On six-speed models, loosen idler bolt (2) and remove blade (5) to replace drive belt (1).

1. Belt
2. Idler bolt
3. Inside belt guard screws
4. Idler belt guide
5. Mower blade

shift rod (1). Unbolt and remove mower blade, blade adapter and lower pulley half (6). Remove engine mounting bolts and separate engine from cable mounting bracket (8). Lift movable pulley half (5) off shift rod (1). Remove hairpin cotter from shift rod withdraw shift rod from cable mounting bracket. Remove flanged bushings (7) from mounting bracket.

Inspect all parts for wear or damage and renew as necessary. When reassembling, lubricate splines of engine shaft and movable pulley half with dry graphite lubricant. Adjust shift control cable as outlined previously.

DRIVE BELT REPLACEMENT. Disconnect spark plug cable and ground it against frame. Remove grass bag, discharge chute and grass catcher panel. Remove transmission belt cover from rear of mower deck. Tip mower on its side and remove center bolt attaching blade to crankshaft. Remove blade (5—Fig. M18), blade adapter and bottom pulley half (6). Remove two screws (3) securing inside belt guard and remove the guard. Loosen idler pulley bolt (2) to make it easier to remove the belt (1) from between idler and idler belt guard (4). Slip the belt off idler pulley and transmission pulley.

To install new belt, push idler pulley up out of the way and slide belt in from rear of deck. Position belt around transmission pulley, then release idler pulley so it falls down into position. Slide belt between idler belt guard and idler pulley, then tighten idler pulley bolt (2—Fig. M18). Place belt between pulley halves on crankshaft and reinstall blade holder and blade. Install inside belt guard and outside transmission belt cover.

MURRAY

Front Wheel Chain Drive

CLUTCH CABLE ADJUSTMENT. The wheel drive pinions rotate whenever the engine is running. Clutch cable should be adjusted so that there is approximately 1/8 inch (3 mm) clearance between pinions (5—Fig. MU1) and front wheels (16) when drive control lever is released (neutral position). When drive control lever is squeezed against upper handle, drive pinions must engage and drive the front wheels. To adjust clutch cable, turn jam nuts located at the cable mounting bracket on mower handle to lengthen or shorten cable as necessary.

Rear Wheel V-Belt Drive

CLUTCH CABLE ADJUSTMENT. The belt idler (20—Fig. MU2) serves as the clutch for the V-belt drive system. Clutch cable should be adjusted so that mower drive is disengaged when drive control lever is released. Drive should engage when drive control lever is squeezed against upper handle. To adjust clutch cable, turn adjusting nuts (18) at the cable bracket (17) to lengthen or shorten cable as necessary.

DRIVE BELT REPLACEMENT To replace drive belt (2—Fig. MU2), first disconnect spark plug wire and ground it properly. Unbolt and remove belt cover (3). Remove upper and lower belt guides (11 and 12) and slip drive belt off engine pulley. Remove nut securing rear wheel (4) and remove wheel. Remove retaining ring (6) and withdraw washer (7) and pinion gear (9) from axle shaft (26). Remove dust cover (8), height adjuster lever (13) and adjuster bracket (14). Disconnect clutch cable (16) and spring (21) from idler arm (19). Remove shoulder bolt (28) attaching idler arm (19) to axle bracket (24). Remove idler pulley (20) from idler arm and slip belt off end of axle shaft.

To install new belt, reverse the removal procedure. Adjust clutch cable as outlined previously.

Rear Wheel Drive Models With Gearbox

LUBRICATION. The gearbox is lubricated with type "F" automatic transmission fluid. Fill gearbox to level of oil fill hole.

CABLE ADJUSTMENT. To adjust drive control cable, loosen cable housing clamp and reposition clamp to remove any slack. If drive does not disengage,

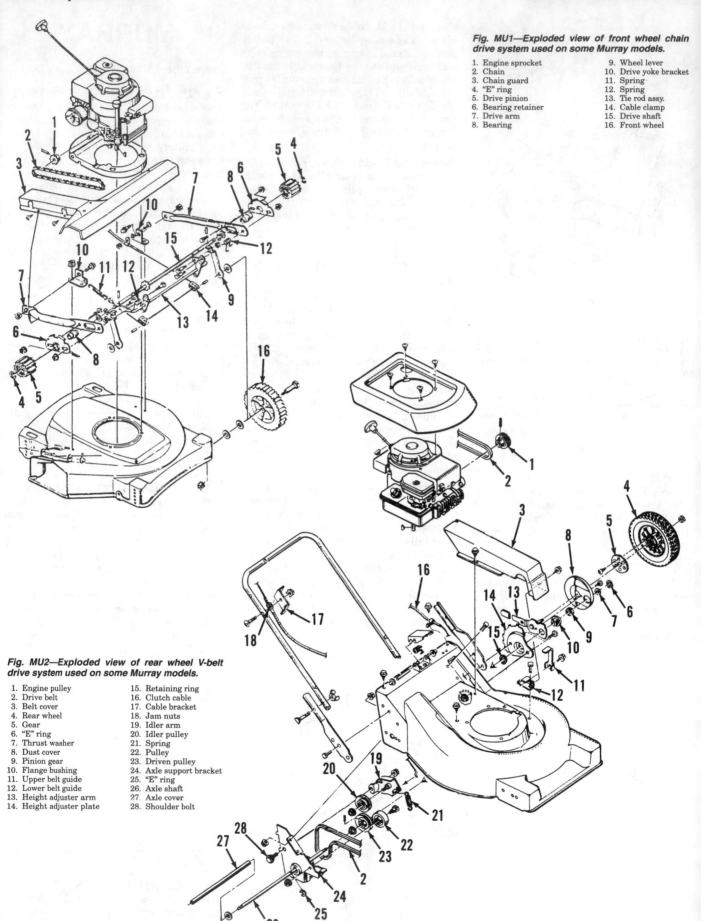

Fig. MU1—Exploded view of front wheel chain drive system used on some Murray models.

1. Engine sprocket
2. Chain
3. Chain guard
4. "E" ring
5. Drive pinion
6. Bearing retainer
7. Drive arm
8. Bearing
9. Wheel lever
10. Drive yoke bracket
11. Spring
12. Spring
13. Tie rod assy.
14. Cable clamp
15. Drive shaft
16. Front wheel

Fig. MU2—Exploded view of rear wheel V-belt drive system used on some Murray models.

1. Engine pulley
2. Drive belt
3. Belt cover
4. Rear wheel
5. Gear
6. "E" ring
7. Thrust washer
8. Dust cover
9. Pinion gear
10. Flange bushing
11. Upper belt guide
12. Lower belt guide
13. Height adjuster arm
14. Height adjuster plate
15. Retaining ring
16. Clutch cable
17. Cable bracket
18. Jam nuts
19. Idler arm
20. Idler pulley
21. Spring
22. Pulley
23. Driven pulley
24. Axle support bracket
25. "E" ring
26. Axle shaft
27. Axle cover
28. Shoulder bolt

Fig. MU3—Exploded view of gearbox used on some Murray rear wheel drive mowers.

1. Selector lever
2. Snap ring
3. "O" ring
4. Seal
5. Cover
6. Gasket
7. Bushings
8. Pin
9. Shift fork
10. Clutch coupler
11. Friction cone
12. Worm gear
13. Thrust washers
14. Thrust bearings
15. Plug
16. Gearbox
17. Drive shaft
19. Pulley
20. Roll pin
21. Bearing
22. Washer
23. Spacer
24. Worm
25. Vent
26. Input shaft
27. Roll pin
28. Bearing

of pull rod. To reduce clearance, turn outer spring clockwise; to increase clearance, turn outer spring counterclockwise.

DRIVEN DISC ADJUSTMENT. Disconnect and properly ground spark plug cable. Place ground speed control lever into "HIGH SPEED" position. If driven disc is properly adjusted, it will be 1/8-1/4 inch (3.6 mm) from outer edge of drive disc. Nut on connector may be loosened and disc correctly positioned as necessary. Connect spark plug led.

ENGINE BELT. Disconnect and properly ground spark plug lead and remove mower blade. Cut and remove old belt. Disconnect wheel drive spring from driven disc and move disc assembly to one side. Install belt below drive disc pulley but do not place it in pulley groove. Insert belt through deck opening and place belt in groove of engine pulley. Work belt onto drive disc pulley. Install blade and tighten cap screw to 15-30 ft.-lbs. (20-40 N·m). Reconnect wheel drive spring and spark plug lead.

Bottom edge of engine pulley should be 1 1/2 inch (38 mm) from end of crankshaft to ensure correct belt alignment. Loosen set screw to reposition pulley as necessary.

CLUTCH BELT. To renew clutch belt, remove clip from transfer rod and disconnect rod from speed control lever. Disconnect drive spring from driven disc and remove driven disc from hex shaft. Note location of old belt before removing. Install new belt over hex shaft and around hex shaft pulley. Twist belt sideways and pull it upward between the differential bracket and input pulley on gearbox. Make certain belt is above hex shaft pulley belt guide and install driven disc assembly and wheel drive spring. Connect transfer rod to speed control lever.

then cable is too tight and cable must be repositioned in clamp.

DRIVE BELT. To remove drive belt, disconnect and properly ground spark plug wire. Remove drive cover, tilt gearbox forward and detach belt from gearbox pulley. Pull belt down through bottom of deck and away from blade. Reinstall belt by reversing removal procedure.

GEARBOX. Refer to Fig. MU3 for an exploded view of gearbox. Note position of all shims and washers during disassembly. Note that wheel drive pinions are designed for use at right or left end of drive shaft and are not interchangeable. To disassemble, unbolt and remove cover (5). Drive pins (8) out of shift fork (9) and withdraw shift lever (1) and fork. Remove clutch components (10 and 11), worm gear (12), thrust bearing (13 and 14) and drive shaft (17). The worm shaft bearing (28) is retained in the gearbox by Loctite. Heat housing in bearing area using a propane torch and pull up drive pulley (19) to withdraw input shaft (26) and bearing assembly from gearbox (do not use excess heat as bearing and seals will be damaged). If drive pulley must be removed from worm shaft, press shaft out of pulley so roll pin (20) is sheared. Drive pin (27) from the input shaft to remove worm gear (24).

Inspect components for damage and excessive wear. When installing bearing on worm shaft, apply Loctite 609 bearing retaining compound to inner diameter. Apply Loctite 609 bearing retaining compound to outer diameter of bearing when installing worm shaft assembly into gearbox. Install new oil seals (4) in

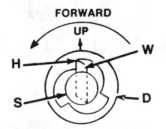

FORWARD

UP

H **W**

S **D**

Fig. MU4—On Murray rear wheel drive mower, install drive pawl (W) inside drive pinion (D) as shown with high edge (H) on pawl toward front of mower.

housing and cover. Reassemble gearbox by reversing disassembly procedure. Fill gearbox with lubricant as outlined in LUBRICATION section. tighten gearbox cover screws to 60-80 in.-lbs. (6.8-9.0 N·m).

The wheel drive pinions are coupled to the drive shaft by a pawl. The pawl must be installed as shown in Fig. MU4.

SNAPPER DISC DRIVE

MAINTENANCE. Remove gearbox check plug (6—Fig. S10) at 25-hour intervals to make certain grease is visible on input gear. If grease is not visible, add a new small amount of Snapper 00 grease. Amount added must not exceed 2 oz. (59 mL). Reinstall plug (6). Lightly oil height adjusting levers, wheel axles and shift lever.

CLUTCH ADJUSTMENT. With clutch handle released, there should be 1/16-1/8 inch (2-3 mm) clearance between clutch spring hook and inside eye

GEARBOX. To remove gearbox, remove cap screw retaining differential link bracket and remove belt from input pulley. Remove rear wheels and the wheel arm assembly from left side. Remove rear guard and slide gearbox/axle assembly left until axle clears differential link. Remove gearbox from mower.

Refer to Fig. S10 for exploded view of gearbox. Remove gearbox housing retaining screws and separate gearbox halves. Allow grease to drain into a suitable container. Remove input shaft and bearing assembly from housing. On models with two-piece cast bull gear, place in vise and drive roll pins out of gear halves. Separate gear halves. On late gearbox, remove the four cap screws and disassemble bull gear. Continue disassembly as necessary by referring to Fig. S10.

321

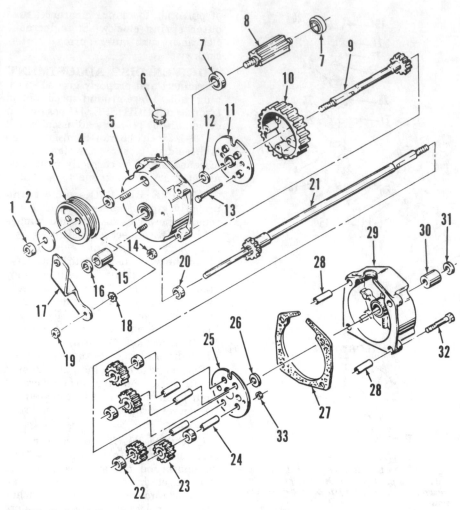

Fig. TO18—External view of Toro single speed gearbox used on some self-propelled Toro lawn mowers.

C. Shift lever
D. Drive shaft
G. Gearbox housings
I. Input shaft

L. Pulley
P. Oil level plug
S. Clutch fork spring

Fig. TO19—Fittings shown should be lubricated every 25 hours of operation.

Fig. S10—Exploded view of gearbox used on some Snapper self-propelled mowers with disc drive.

1. Nut	9. Short axle	17. Bracket	25. Plate
2. Washer	10. Bull gear	18. Washer	26. Thrust washer
3. Pulley	11. Plate	19. Locknut	27. Gasket
4. Seal	12. Thrust washer	20. Spacer	28. Roll pins
5. Housing	13. Cap screws	21. Long axle	29. Housing
6. Plug	14. Nut	22. Pinion spacers	30. Bearing
7. Bearings	15. Bearing	23. Pinion gears	31. Seal
8. Input shaft	16. Seal	24. Pinion shafts	32. Cap screws

Reassemble by reversing disassembly procedure. Tighten gearbox housing cap screws to 17 ft.-lbs. (23 N•m). Lubricate gearbox by installing 4 oz. (118 mL) of 00 Snapper grease through plug (6).

TORO GEARBOX

Self propelled Toro lawn mowers may be equipped with a gear box that provides only one speed or three different speeds. The rear wheel drive of all models is engaged by tipping the gearbox to tighten the drive belt. Some adjustments and service may be the same for different models.

LUBRICATION. Early gear boxes are lubricated by oil and the gearbox should always be filled to the lower edge of the hole for plug (P—Fig. TO18). Remove the plug and check oil level every 25 hours of operation or once each season. Add SAE 90 gear oil if necessary.

Later gearboxes are packed with 6 oz. (177 cc) of #2 lithium-based grease at assembly and additional lubrication should not be necessary.

On all models, lubricate all bushings and pivot points with oil. The necessary frequency of lubricating these points will depend upon operating conditions. If the mower operates in wet conditions or is washed frequently, lubricate before putting the mower away each day to prevent rust buildup. Grease fittings are located at the drive shaft bushings (Fig. TO19). The fittings should be lubricated with #2 lithium-based grease after each 25 hours of operation. Two pumps is usually a sufficient amount of grease, but be sure not to over grease.

SHIFT CONTROLS. The gear selection controls allow the single speed gear box to be shifted into either drive or neutral (nondriving) position. On models with three speeds, the controls allow shifting into neutral or any of the three drive positions.

The cable is attached to the control panel lever by pinching a tab to hold the cable. Bend the tab slightly to allow the cable to be removed from the upper end. At the lower end, a clamp attaches the cable housing to the gearbox housing. It may be easier to remove cotter pin attaching the shift lever, then removing the shift lever before detaching the housing from the clamp bracket. Withdraw the cable and housing if renewal is required.

When reinstalling, make sure the cable and housing are routed correctly without interference with other components. Attach the upper end of the cable to the control and bend the tabs to retain the cable. Attach the lower end of the shift lever and position the cable housing in the clamp. Move

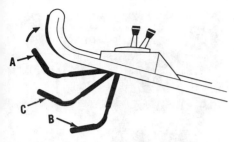

Fig. TO20—On self-propelled Toro models, the traction drive should engage when the control bar is the proper distance from the handle.

A. At rest position
B. "Cocking" position
C. Engaged position

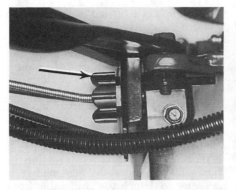

Fig. TO21B—Traction drive control cable adjuster used on later models.

Fig. TO23—View of the blade brake and clutch used on some models. Refer to Fig. TO22 for another similar type.

1. Nut
2. Blade belt
3. Blade brake & clutch idler assy.

Drain oil and gasoline from the engine and tank. Remove belt covers from the topside of the mower deck, then tip the mower on its side. Unbolt and remove the blade, then unbolt and remove the cover from the underside of the mower. Remove the large nut (1—Fig. TO22 or TO23), then remove the spacer (4—Fig. TO24) and brake drum (5). Lift the blade drive belt (2—Fig. TO22 or TO23) from around the crankshaft, pull the brake and clutch idler (3) back, then lift the drive plate (6—Fig. TO24) from the crankshaft. Remove the belt guard from around the gearbox pulley. Slide the traction drive pulley (Fig. TO25) on the crankshaft until clear of belt guard (G), then slip belt off the pulleys and remove it from the mower. The drive pulley is located by a Woodruff key, but should slide on the crankshaft.

When assembling, install the traction drive belt around the gearbox pulley, then around the crankshaft and crankshaft pulley. Install the belt guard around the gearbox pulley. Make sure the two drive protrusions (P—Fig. TO25) on the crankshaft pulley are in good condition. Install the drive plate (6—Fig. TO24) with the holes over the two protrusions (Fig. TO25). Position the blade drive belt over the crankshaft. Install the special drive screws through

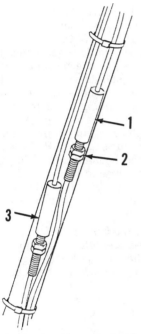

Fig. TO21A—Traction drive control cable adjuster used on early models.

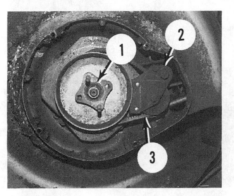

Fig. TO22—View of one type of mower with lower cover removed. Refer to Fig. TO23 for another type.

1. Nut
2. Blade belt
3. Blade brake & clutch idler assy.

the hand control and make sure the transmission shifts properly.

TRACTION CLUTCH CONTROL. Moving the control bar (Fig. TO20) closer to the handle should cause the traction drive to engage. Drive should be engaged when the bar is 38 mm (1 ½ in.) from the handle. Moving the control bar pulls the control cable to tip the traction drive gear box which tightens the drive belt.

Adjust the cable by turning the cable adjuster as required. On some models, the adjuster is located in the middle of the cable (Fig. TO21A); on other models, the cable adjuster is located at the mower deck (Fig. TO21B). Turning the adjuster will either lengthen or shorten the cable housing. Lengthening the cable housing will increase clearance between the control bar and the handle. Shortening the cable housing will reduce the distance between the control bar and the handle when the drive is

engaged. Tighten adjusting lock nuts when adjustment is correct. It may not be possible to adjust the cable sufficiently if the drive belt is worn or broken.

On models so equipped, a damaged control box (located at the handle bar) may make proper operation and adjustment difficult or impossible. Refer to the BLADE BRAKE CLUTCH section for trouble shooting the combined control box, which is located at the upper end of the handle bar.

R&R DRIVE BELT. The traction drive belt is located above the blade and blade brake clutch mechanism next to the engine. Remove the belt as follows.

Fig. TO24—When the clutch is disengaged and the blade is stopped by the brake, the crankshaft can turn inside the bearing located in spacer (4). The belt is located between the brake drum (5) and drive plate (6).

Fig. TO25—The traction drive pulley is located on the crankshaft as shown. The projections (P) on pulley engage the two holes in the drive plate (6—Fig. TO24).

Fig. TO26—On some models, the drive axle and gearbox is retained in the mower deck by attaching plates and four screws.

drive pinion is attached to each end. To remove the gearbox and axle assembly, remove the drive belt covers. Unbolt and remove the belt guide from the gearbox and lift the belt from the pulley. On some models, the drive axle is attached to the mower deck with the four screws (Fig. TO26). On other models, the wheel drive gears and axle bearing housings must be removed to remove the drive axle. Refer to the DRIVE WHEELS paragraphs in this section for removal and service. On most models, it is easier to detach the shift cable from the gearbox after the axle is separated from the mower deck.

Fig. TO30—View of a three speed gearbox with the lower cover removed showing the internal components.

shaft (I). Drive the two locating pins (P—Fig. TO28) from the upper gearbox housing. Remove the screws attaching the upper and lower housings together and separate the housing halves. The gearbox should contain oil that will drain as the housings are separated. Move the sliding clutch (4—Fig. TO29) away from the driven gear (5), then drive the roll pin (3) from the hub (1) and output shaft (2). Pull the shaft (2) from the housing, hub, sliding clutch, driven gear and thrust washer (6). Remove snap rings from the input shaft and remove the worm gear and input shaft assembly.

Coat the mating surfaces of housings with sealer before assembling. Make sure the shift fork (S—Fig. TO28) engages the groove in the sliding clutch (4—Fig. TO29). Fill the housing with SAE 90 gear oil to the level of the hole for plug (P—Fig. TO27).

On models with a three speed gearbox, remove the screws attaching the cover or housing halves, then remove the cover or separate the housings. Fig. TO30 shows a typical unit. The shafts

the brake drum and spacer, then install the drum and spacer over the crankshaft. Install and tighten the retaining nut (1—Fig. TO22 or TO23). Make sure the heads of the special blade retaining screws are not wedged between the drum and drive plate. Check the blade brake and clutch for proper operation and adjustment as described in the appropriate section. Check the traction drive for proper operation and adjustment as described in this section. Reinstall covers and blade to complete assembly.

R&R GEARBOX. The drive axle passes through the gearbox and a wheel

OVERHAUL GEARBOX. Several different gearboxes have been used providing a single drive speed or three different drive speeds. Service to the units may be similar, even though obvious differences may be noted.

Remove the wheel drives from the ends of the axle as described in the DRIVE WHEELS paragraphs in this section if they are not yet removed.

On single speed models, remove the pulley (L—Fig. TO27) from the input

Fig. TO27—View of a single speed gearbox used on some Toro models.

C. Clutch lever
D. Drive shaft
G. Gearbox housings
I. Input shaft
L. Pulley
P. Plug
S. Clutch fork spring

Fig. TO28—View of the single speed gearbox with upper (H) and lower (J) housings separated. Drive the pins (P) from the upper housing before separating.

H. Upper housing
I. Input shaft
J. Lower housing
P. Pin
S. Clutch fork spring

Fig. TO29—View of drive shaft components of single speed gearbox showing their relative position.

1. Sliding clutch hub
2. Drive shaft
3. Roll pin
4. Sliding clutch
5. Driven gear
6. Thrust washer

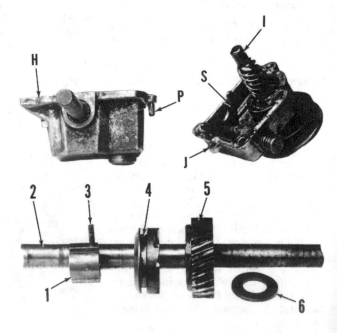

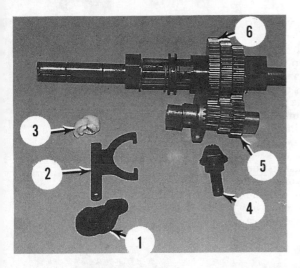

Fig. TO31—View of the shafts and gears removed from a typical three speed gearbox.

1. Shift lever
2. Shift fork
3. Lower bushing
4. Input pinion
5. Drive (cluster) gear assembly
6. Output shaft/shift/gears

wheels to turn freely when the drive is not engaged. Refer to Fig. TO34.

Each drive wheel can be removed after removing the shoulder bolt from the center. The nut should remain in the pocket of the pivot arm. Remove the retaining clip (16) and spring (15). Notice that clip (16) is not a standard E-ring, but the center tab extends into the groove in the output shaft. Withdraw the tab washer (14) and gear (13), then remove the drive key (12). Remove the clutch washer (11) and the friction ring (10). Damage to the friction ring (10) or the clutch washer (11) will prevent proper operation. Remove the retaining clip (9), which is like clip (16). remove the internal tab washer (8) and the external tab washer (7). Pull the pivot arm/bearing assembly (4) from the output shaft (1). The height adjustment arm should be attached to the pivot arm with a screw. The bushing and needle bearing should remain in the bore of the pivot arm.

If it is necessary to install a new bearing or bushing, press the new part into its bore until flush. O-ring (2) is located in a groove about 2 ¼ inches (5.7 mm) from the end of the output shaft (1). Clean all parts thoroughly, then inspect each part for wear or damage.

To reassemble, install O-ring (2) in its groove, then lubricate the output shaft (1), bushing (3) and bearing (6) with #2 lithium based grease. Slide the pivot arm/bearing assembly onto the output shaft. Install thrust washer (7) with its external tabs engaging the notches in the pivot arm. Install tab washer (8) with the tab properly engaging the notch in the output shaft. Install the clip (9) with the tab engaging the notch in the output shaft. Install the friction ring (10) with the flat side out, toward the clutch washer, then install the clutch washer (11).

Position the key (12) in the output shaft groove and slide the ratchet pawl against the clutch washer. The key and ratchet pawl are different for the left

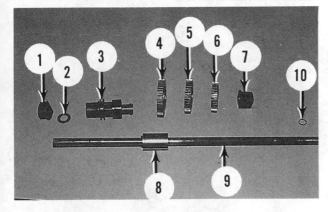

Fig. TO32—The output shaft of a typical three speed gearbox.

1. Bushing
2. Thrust washer
3. Sliding clutch (shift) assembly
4. Slow (1st) gear
5. Second gear
6. Fast (3rd) gear
7. Bushing
8. Sliding clutch hub
9. Output shaft
10. O-ring

tershaft. Coat transmission parts with grease when assembling and fill with 177 cc (6 oz.) of #2 lithium-based grease.

On all models, refer to the DRIVE WHEELS paragraphs in this section when assembling the axle bearings and drive gears on the output shaft.

DRIVE WHEELS. Each of the two drive wheels is equipped with a ratchet type clutch that allows the gearbox output shaft and pinion to drive the wheel, and also permits the two wheels to turn at different speeds to facilitate turning the mower. The clutches also allow the

Fig. TO33—The drive gear assembly components typical of three speed models.

1. Bushing
2. Bevel/small (1st) gear
3. Second gear
4. Fast (3rd) gear
5. Bushing
6. Thrust washers (2 used)
7. Shaft

with gears can be lifted from the housing. Flats are provided on the bevel pinion gear of some models as shown in Fig. TO31 to facilitate holding it while removing and installing the pulley retaining nut.

Refer to Fig. TO32 when assembling components of the output shaft and to Fig. TO33 when assembling the coun-

Fig. TO34—Exploded view of one wheel pinion clutch and height adjuster.

1. Gearbox output shaft
2. O-ring
3. Bushing
4. Housing/pivot arm
5. Grease fitting
6. Bearing
7. Washer (external tabs)
8. Thrust washer (internal tab)
9. Special retaining clip
10. Friction ring
11. Clutch washer
12. Wheel pinion key
13. Wheel pinion
14. Thrust washer (internal tab)
15. Spring
16. Special retaining clip

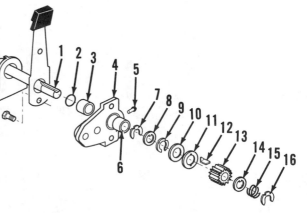

and right sides of the mower. The key should fit in the groove with the top of the key flat, and the straight part of the ratchet pawl should be perpendicular to the shaft. The clutch washer has two notches for the ratchet pawl, but the ratchet pawl will only fit correctly in one. The other is used for the opposite side. Before continuing, rotate the clutch washer (11) slightly and see if the ratchet pawl moves properly. The pawl should tip the key up to engage the drive gear, then lower to allow freewheeling. Install the drive gear (13) and tab washer (14). The gear can be installed either way, but the tab on the washer

should properly engage the groove in the output shaft.

Install the spring (15) and retainer clip (16). Make sure the tab on the clip properly engages the groove in the output shaft. Grease the assembly through fitting (5). The original fitting is pressed into the pivot arm, but if damaged or lost, a screw-in fitting may be installed. The gear should rotate freely one direction, but not the other.

When installing the wheel, use the original number and thickness of spacer washers on the shoulder bolt to provide correct spacing. Wheel covers, used on some models, should be installed before

the wheels. The wheel shoulder bolt tightens into a nylon self-locking nut located in a pocket of the pivot arm. It may be necessary to press the arm toward the shoulder bolt while starting the bolt. Tighten the shoulder bolt securely.

YARD-MAN

Refer to MTD section for service procedures covering self-propelled drive systems.

BLADE BRAKE CLUTCHES

OPERATION

Blade clutches, blade brake clutches and flywheel engine brakes are safety features designed to stop blade rotation.

Blade clutches allow the operator to stop blade rotation without stopping mower engine. Clutches are usually some form of centrifugal clutch which rely on slow engine speed to stop blade rotation. While a blade clutch stops engine power from turning the mower blade, it does not have a positive stopping feature and blade may freewheel.

Blade brake clutches are designed to allow the operator to stop blade rotation quickly without stopping the engine. A control handle or bail in conjunction with a control cable is used to control the engagement and disengagement of mower blade. Blade should stop within three seconds after control handle is placed in disengaged position to meet government safety standards and offer maximum operator protection. Blade brake clutch should be checked periodically for correct engagement and disengagement of mower blade.

CAUTION: When checking blade brake clutch operation, use extreme caution. Mower blade may be turning when you assume it has stopped.

Flywheel engine brakes are incorporated with an engine safety switch which grounds the ignition to stop engine power while the flywheel brake stops engine rotation within three seconds. Refer to appropriate engine section for flywheel brake service.

CAUTION: Before and while working on blade brake clutch, use a vacuum to remove lining dust in unit. Avoid inhaling dust.

ARIENS

ARIENS COMPANY
655 West Ryan St.
Brillion, WI 54110

Shown in Fig. AR10 is an exploded view of blade brake clutch used on some Ariens lawn mowers. Parts are renewable as separate components except the sealed bearing located in blade brake clutch leaf spring (12). No special tools are required for servicing, but good mechanical skills should be exercised dur-

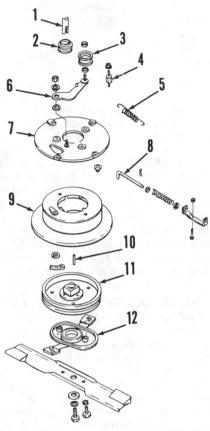

Fig. AR10—Exploded view of blade brake clutch used on some Ariens walking lawn mowers.

1. Engine crankshaft
2. Pulley
3. Idler pulley
4. Hex stud
5. Spring
6. Idler bracket
7. Ramp
8. Control rod
9. Brake actuator
10. Key
11. Blade brake flywheel
12. Leaf spring & bearing

ing servicing to ensure safe and correct operation.

Control cable bracket should be adjusted so engine is stopped and blade clutch actuated when control ball is moved 3/8 to 5/8 inch (10-16 mm) from handle bar.

COMET

COMET INDUSTRIES
358 Northwest F Street
Richmond, Indiana 47374

Shown in Fig. C1 is an exploded view of a Comet blade brake clutch. Parts are renewable as three separate subassemblies; flywheel, rotor or clutch and bowl and brake band. Sealed bearing in clutch assembly is renewable only with

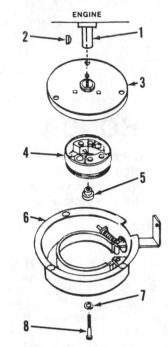

Fig. C1—Exploded view of a Comet blade brake clutch.

1. Crankshaft
2. Woodruff key
3. Flywheel
4. Clutch assy.
5. Clutch washer
6. Bowl & brake band assy.
7. Flat washer
8. Cap screw

clutch assembly. No special tools are required for servicing, but good mechanical skills should be exercised during servicing to ensure safe and correct operation.

NOTE: Cap screws with thread length longer than one inch (25.4 mm) should not be used to attach mower blade to clutch assembly.

Check actuating lever for correct travel length and control cable for correct initial adjustment as shown in Fig. C2. There should be 1-1/4 inch (32 mm) travel in actuating lever when control handle is moved from brake ON to brake OFF position. If lever does not travel the full length, then check lever for freedom of movement, correct control cable adjustment and tension of control spring. Correct initial adjustment of control cable in spring is 1/4 to 3/8 inch (6-10 mm) free movement with control handle placed in brake applied position.

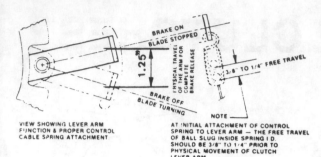

VIEW SHOWING LEVER ARM
FUNCTION & PROPER CONTROL
CABLE SPRING ATTACHMENT.

Fig. C2—View showing travel length of actuating lever and correct initial adjustment of control cable in spring.

HONDA

AMERICAN HONDA
MOTOR CO., INC.
4475 River Green Parkway
Duluth, Georgia 30136

Model HR17

BLADE BRAKE CLUTCH LINK-AGE. The blade brake clutch is operated by a cable attached to the Roto-Stop control lever (Fig. HN200). To disassemble, remove bolt attaching Roto-Stop lever (5) to control handle. Disconnect upper end of cable (6) from stop lever. Remove hinge pin (4) and ratchet return spring (2). Remove lock lever (3) and ratchet push rod (1).

When reassembling, hook big end of return spring (2) to stop lever (5) and other end to ratchet push rod (1). Adjust brake/clutch cable as follows: With engine stopped and control handle released, measure free travel (F—Fig. HN200) of Roto-Stop lever (5) at outer end of lever. Free travel should be 5-10 mm ($\frac{3}{16}$ -$\frac{3}{8}$ in.). To adjust, loosen cable locknut and turn adjusting bolt (6) to decrease or increase lever free travel. After adjusting, start engine and make sure that blade engages when Roto-Stop lever is squeezed against handle and stops when Roto-Stop lever is released.

BLADE BRAKE CLUTCH. An exploded view of Honda blade brake clutch is shown in Fig. HN201. Parts are renewable separately. No special tools are required for servicing. To remove blade brake clutch, first disconnect spark plug cable to prevent accidental starting. Remove retaining bolt (14) and withdraw blade (13) and blade holder (11), clutch spring (10), driven plate (8) and drive disc (7). Disconnect brake spring (1) and remove brake link (2). Remove three bolts retaining brake disc (6) and withdraw disc, ball carrier (5) and ball ramp plate (4).

Inspect rubber dampers on brake plate (6) for cracks or other damage and renew as necessary. Inspect brake disc and drive disc for wear. Minimum thickness of drive disc clutch lining is 4.7 mm (0.19 in.) and minimum thickness of brake disc lining is 4.1 mm (0.16 in.). Both disks should be renewed as a set if either is worn beyond minimum dimension. Renew clutch spring (10) if free length is less than 34 mm (1.34 in.). Maximum free length of brake return spring (1) is 107 mm (4.21 in.).

When reassembling, install ball carrier plate (5) so balls face the blade. Do not use any lubricant on the balls. Install brake disc (6) with rubber dampers facing ball ramp plate. Position ball ramp plate and brake disc so that notch in ball ramp plate and raised area on blade side of brake disc is aligned with brake link plate (2). Hook long end of brake spring (1) through hole in link plate, then use a screwdriver to hook short end of spring around anchor collar. Install drive plate (7), driven plate (8), clutch spring (10) and blade holder (11). Tighten center mounting bolt (14) and blade mounting nuts to 30-35 N•m (22-25 ft.-lbs.).

Models HR21, HR21-5 and HRA21

BLADE BRAKE CLUTCH LINK-AGE. The blade brake clutch is operated by a cable attached to the Roto-Stop lever on mower upper handle. With engine stopped and ball ramp plate arm (2—Fig. HN202) in contact with cable anchor bracket (1), measure free travel (F) at the Roto-Stop lever tip. There should be 5-10 mm ($\frac{3}{16}$-$\frac{3}{8}$ in.)

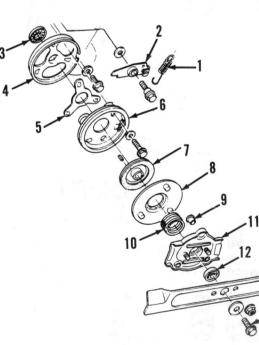

Fig. HN200—Drawing of Honda Roto-Stop blade brake/clutch linkage for Model HR17. Roto-Stop lever free play (F) should be 5-10 mm ($\frac{3}{16}$-$\frac{3}{8}$ in.) measured at tip of lever.

1. Push rod
2. Return spring
3. Lock lever
4. Hinge pin
5. Roto-Stop lever
6. Cable adjusting bolt

Fig. HN201—Exploded view of Honda blade brake/clutch assembly for Model HR17.

1. Brake return spring
2. Brake link plate
3. Ball bearing
4. Ball ramp plate
5. Ball retainer
6. Brake disc
7. Drive disc
8. Driven disc
9. Bushing
10. Clutch spring
11. Blade holder plate
12. Ball bearing
13. Blade
14. Bolt

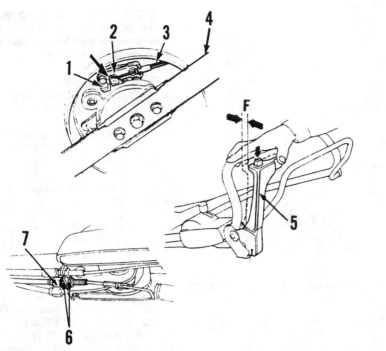

Fig. HN202—Drawing of blade brake linkage typical of Honda HR21, HR21-5 and HRA21 mowers. Roto-Stop lever should have 5-10 mm (⁵⁄₁₆-³⁄₈ in.) free play (F) measured at tip of lever.

1. Cable stop
2. Ball ramp plate arm
3. Cable
4. Blade
5. Roto-Stop lever
6. Locknuts
7. Cable adjuster

free travel. To adjust, loosen locknut (6) on Roto-Stop cable and turn cable adjusting bolt (7) to increase or decrease free travel. Tighten locknut after adjustment is completed, then start engine and make sure that blade engages when Roto-Stop lever is squeezed against handle and stops when Roto-Stop lever is released.

BLADE BRAKE CLUTCH. An exploded view of the blade clutch and blade brake assemblies is shown in Fig.

HN203 and Fig. HN204. No special tools are required for servicing.

NOTE: When servicing the blade brake clutch, tip mower on its right side to prevent oil from entering crankcase ventilation chamber.

To remove clutch assembly, first disconnect spark plug cable to prevent accidental starting. Unbolt and remove blade (2—Fig. HN203) and blade holder (4). Remove center retaining screw (3)

and withdraw clutch components (5 through 13). Unscrew special bolts (7) and separate driven disc (10), clutch disc (12) and drive pulley (13).

To remove blade brake, disconnect brake return spring (23—Fig. HN204). Note that some models use two brake return springs. Disconnect brake cable (26) from ball ramp plate arm. Remove brake mounting screws (14) and withdraw brake disc (17), ball retainer (18) and brake ramp plate (19).

Inspect parts for wear or damage and renew as necessary. Minimum thickness of clutch disc lining and brake shoe lining is 0.5 mm (0.020 in.). Renew clutch spring if free length is less than 34.5 mm (1.36 in.). Renew brake return spring if free length exceeds 81 mm (3.2 in.). Inspect brake rubbers (16—Fig. HN204) for cracks or other damage. Rubbers can be driven out of brake disc using a pin punch through the two small holes in brake disc. Ball bearings must turn freely and not have any excess play.

When reassembling, be sure that thrust washer (21—Fig. HN204) is installed before installing ball ramp plate (19). Attach brake cable (26) to ball ramp plate before installing the brake disc (17). Do not apply any lubricant to brake balls or ramps. Be sure washer (15) is installed as shown, otherwise brake rubbers will twist and be damaged when brake shoe mounting bolts (14) are tightened. Tighten special bolts (7—Fig. HN203) retaining clutch components to 20-30 N·m (15-22 ft.-lb.). Tighten clutch mounting bolt (3) to 40-50 N·m (29-36 ft.-lb.). Tighten blade mounting bolts to 20-30 N·m (15-22 ft.-lb.).

Models HR194 and HRA214

BLADE BRAKE CLUTCH LINKAGE. The blade brake clutch is operated by a cable attached to the Roto-Stop lever on mower upper handle. With engine stopped and ball ramp plate arm (2—Fig. HN202) in contact with cable anchor bracket (1), there should be 5-10 mm (³⁄₁₆-³⁄₈ in.) free travel (F) at the Roto-Stop lever tip. To adjust, loosen locknut (6) on Roto-Stop cable and turn cable adjusting bolt (7) to increase or decrease free travel. Tighten locknut after adjustment is completed, then start engine and make sure that blade engages when Roto-Stop lever is squeezed against handle and stops when Roto-Stop lever is released.

BLADE BRAKE CLUTCH. An exploded view of the blade clutch and blade brake assemblies is shown in Fig. HN205. No special tools are required for servicing.

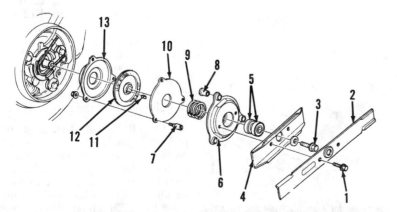

Fig. HN203—Exploded view of blade clutch typical of Honda HR21, HR21-5 and HRA21 mowers.

1. Bolt
2. Blade
3. Bolt
4. Blade holder
5. Ball bearings
6. Blade holder plate
7. Special bolt
8. Bushing
9. Clutch spring
10. Driven plate
11. Woodruff key
12. Drive plate
13. Drive pulley

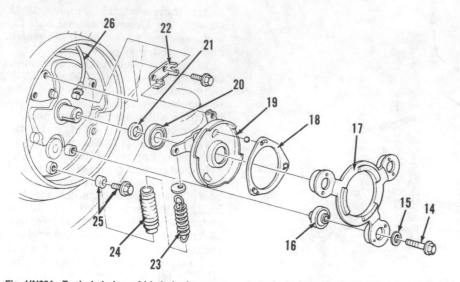

Fig. HN204—Exploded view of blade brake components typical of Honda HR21, HR21-5 and HRA21 mowers. Two brake return springs (23) are used on some models.

14. Bolt
15. Washer
16. Rubber bushing
17. Brake disc
18. Ball retainer
19. Ball ramp plate
20. Ball bearing
21. Thrust washer
22. Cable anchor plate
23. Brake return spring
24. Boot
25. Spacer
26. Cable

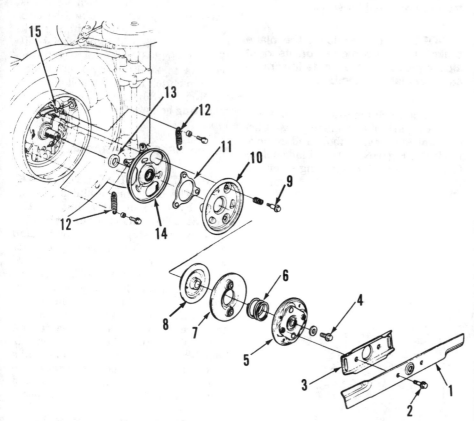

Fig. HN205—Exploded view of blade brake and clutch components for Honda HR194 and HRA214 mowers.

1. Blade
2. Bolt
3. Blade holder
4. Bolt
5. Blade holder plate
6. Clutch spring
7. Driven disc
8. Drive disc
9. Special bolt
10. Brake disc
11. Ball retainer
12. Brake return springs
13. Thrust washer
14. Ball ramp plate
15. Cable

NOTE: When servicing the blade brake clutch, tip mower on its right side to prevent oil from entering crankcase ventilation chamber.

To remove clutch assembly, first disconnect spark plug cable to prevent accidental starting. Unbolt and remove blade (1—Fig. HN205) and blade holder (3). Remove center retaining screw (4) and withdraw blade holder plate (5), spring (6), driven disc (7) and drive disc (8).

To remove blade brake, disconnect brake return springs (12—Fig. HN205). Disconnect brake cable (15) from ball ramp plate arm. Remove brake mounting screws (9) and withdraw brake disc (10), ball retainer (11) and brake ramp plate (14).

Inspect parts for wear or damage and renew as necessary. Renew driven disc if thickness of clutch lining and/or brake lining is less than 4.6 mm (0.18 in.). Renew clutch spring if free length is less than 40 mm (1.57 in.). Renew brake return spring if free length exceeds 58.5 mm (2.30 in.). Ball bearings must turn freely and not have any excess play.

When reassembling, be sure that thrust washer (13—Fig. HN205) is installed before installing ball ramp plate (14). Attach brake cable (15) to ball ramp plate before installing the brake disc (10). Do not apply any lubricant to brake balls or ramps. Tighten clutch mounting bolt (3) to 40-50 N•m (29-36 ft.-lb.). Tighten blade mounting bolts to 50-60 N•m (36-43 ft.-lb.).

KUBOTA

KUBOTA
550 W. Artesia Blvd.
Compton, California 90220

Refer to Fig. KU201 for a partial cross-sectional drawing of the blade brake clutch used on some Kubota mowers. The friction surfaces are engaged and disengaged as a result of balls (4) operating in their ramps. Actuating lever (1) is spring-loaded in the disengaged position. The control cable is pulled to engage the friction surfaces thereby rotating the mower blade.

CONTROL CABLE. Measure free play of blade control handle at top of handle. There should be 14-22 mm (9/16 to 7/8 inch) free play. Total amount of handle travel from rest to contact with handlebar should be 165-175 mm (6 to 6-7/8 inch). To adjust cable, loosen lock nuts (N—Fig. KU202) and reposition cable adjuster (A). Tighten lock nuts.

With spark plug wire properly grounded, tip mower on its side so muf-

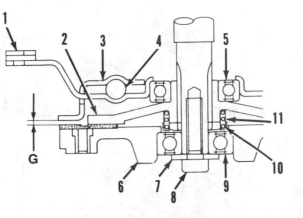

Fig. KU201—Partial cross-sectional view of Kubota blade brake assembly.

1. Actuator lever & plate
2. Drive flange
3. Brake flange
4. Ball
5. Bearing
6. Blade carrier
7. Washer
8. Flange screw
9. Bearing
10. Spring cup
11. Spring

operating arm (Fig. LB300 or LB301). Remove the socket head screw from the end of the crankshaft. Protect the end of the crankshaft (with tool part number 611592 or equivalent), then use a suitable puller to pull the brake and clutch assembly (1—Fig. LB302) from the crankshaft. The remaining parts can be removed if necessary, but service parts may not be available except as a complete blade brake clutch assembly. Bearing in the operating arm and cam assembly (5) may be stuck on the crankshaft, making removal difficult. Lining (L—Fig. LB303) on clutch and brake

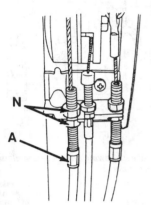

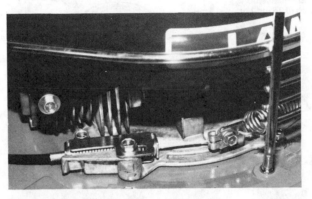

Fig. LB300—View of blade clutch control typical of the type used on some series "F" Lawn-Boy mowers.

Fig. KU202—Loosen nuts (N) and reposition adjuster (A) to adjust cable free play.

fler is up. Push and hold blade control handle against handlebar. Check gap (G—Fig. KU201) between brake flange (3) and blade carrier (6). If gap is less than 1.0 mm (0.039 inch), adjust control cable by repositioning cable adjuster (A—Fig. KU202).

OVERHAUL. After removing blade and fan, unscrew retaining screw in end of crankshaft to remove blade brake assembly. The blade carrier (6—Fig. KU201) must be renewed if lining depth is less than 0.5 mm (0.020 inch). Check all components for damage and excessive wear. Apply molybdenum disulfide to crankshaft splines before assembly.

LAWN-BOY

**LAWN-BOY, INC.
P. O. Box 152
Plymouth, Wisconsin 53073**

Some Lawn-Boy mowers are equipped with blade brake clutches with a spring-operated disc used to provide blade clutching and braking. Clutch is operated by a cable attached to a control handle. Adjust the cable by loosening the mounting bracket cap screws and sliding the bracket in slots until the proper engagement and disen-

Fig. LB301—View of blade brake clutch control typical of some "M" series Lawn-Boy mowers.

gagement is obtained. See Fig. LB300 or LB301.

To remove the unit, first detach and ground the spark plug cable to prevent accidental starting, then unbolt and remove the blade. Detach the control cable, clamp and spring from the

unit should be at least 0.030 inch (0.76 mm) thick.

NOTE: The ramps of the blade brake clutch are opposite for "F" and "M" series mowers. The operating cable is on the opposite side of the engine, so the clutch arm moves in the opposite direction.

When reassembling, install the ball assembly, and brake plate (B—Fig. LB304) with the balls and ball rams aligned. Apply Loctite thread locking compound to the threads, then install shoulder bolts (W) and springs (S). Tighten the shoulder bolts to 135 in.-lb. (15.3 N·m) torque. Install the flanged washer under the socket head screw so the small side is next to the screw head and large side is toward clutch and brake assembly. Tighten the socket head screw to 27 ft.-lb. (36.7 N·m) torque.

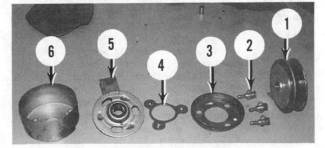

Fig. LB302—View of blade brake clutch components typical of the type used on some Lawn-Boy models.

1. Blade carrier assy.
2. Shoulder screws & springs
3. Brake pad
4. Ball assy.
5. Actuator & bearing assy.
6. Cover

Fig. LB303—Renew blade brake clutch assembly if thickness of lining (L) is 0.030 inch (0.76 mm) or less.

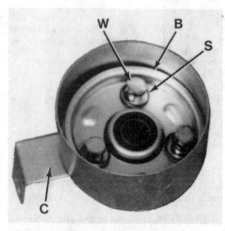

Fig. LB304—Spring (S) must be installed with small end next to head of screw (W). Brake plate (B) can be installed correctly in only one position.

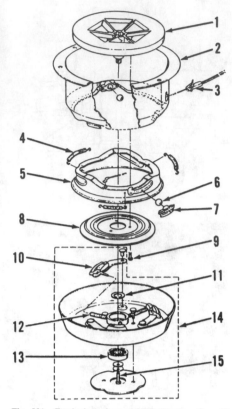

Fig. M1—Exploded view of MTD "Action Guard" blade brake clutch.

1. Fan adaptor
2. Clutch housing
3. Clutch control cable
4. Extension spring
5. Brake cup cone
6. Steel ball
7. Ball block
8. Clutching cone
9. Self-tapping screw
10. Brake pad assy.
11. Flat washer
12. Compression spring
13. Ball bearing
14. Brake/clutch housing assy.
15. Cap screw

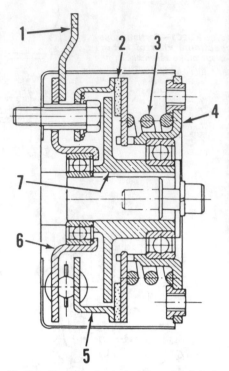

Fig. O1—View showing typical Ogura blade brake clutch assembly.

1. Actuating lever
2. Friction disc
3. Clutch spring
4. Blade carrier
5. Brake plate
6. Actuator cam
7. Clutch disc & flywheel

OGURA

KANEMATSU-GOSHO INC.
P.O. Box 392
S. Plainfield, New Jersey 07080

Fig. O1 shows an Ogura blade brake clutch, typical of all models. To engage blade, lever (1) is moved by control cable to engaged position. Lever causes actuator cam (6) to move brake plate (5) axially in relation to engine crankshaft. Clutch spring (3) pushes friction disc (2) against clutch disc (7) which is pinned to engine crankshaft. Clutch disc (7), friction disc (2), blade carrier (4) and blade now rotate at engine speed.

To stop blade, control handle is released permitting return spring to pull lever (1) to released position. The actuator cam (6) reverses rotation, pushing brake plate (5) against friction disc (2). This separates friction disc and clutch disc, thus stopping power flow to blade.

There is no adjustment for wear; clutch is completely self-adjusting. If lever operation is correct, but clutch brake fails to operate properly, disassembly and repair or renewal of faulty component is required.

Unit is serviceable as separate components or as sub-assemblies. No special tools are required for servicing, but good mechanical skills should be exercised during servicing to ensure safe and correct operation.

MTD

MTD PRODUCTS, INC.
P. O. Box 36900
Cleveland, Ohio 44136

Figure M1 shown an exploded view of a typical MTD blade brake clutch. On models with a belt-driven blade, a pulley is attached to bottom of brake/clutch housing. Unit is serviceable as separate components, with the exception of the brake pads (10). Brake pads (Fig. M2) are renewable only with brake/clutch housing assembly (14—Fig. M1). Operation of clutch assembly is controlled by cable (3). Periodically inspect cable to be sure it is not frayed or damaged.

No special tools are required for servicing. When servicing blade clutch, always disconnect spark plug wire and ground it against engine block. Drain fuel tank and engine crankcase if mower is tipped on its side.

If clutch has a pulley attached to bottom of brake/clutch housing, it will be necessary to lock engine flywheel so re-

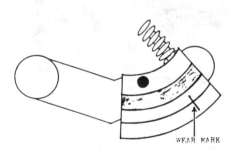

Fig. M2—Brake pads must be renewed if wear marks are not visible. Pads are only serviced with brake/clutch housing assembly.

taining screw (15) can be unscrewed. On other models, an access slot located in clutch housing (2) where control cable enters is provided to prevent crankshaft rotation so retaining screw (15) can be unscrewed. Insert a straight blade screwdriver through slot, then using the proper size wrench turn cap screw until screwdriver blade catches in groove of clutch. Screwdriver blade will prevent clutch from turning while loosening screw (15).

TORO

THE TORO COMPANY
811 Lyndale Ave. South
Minneapolis, MN 55420

Some Toro lawn mowers are equipped with a blade clutch and brake (Fig. TO201 or Fig. TO202). The brake is released and the blade is engaged by following this sequence.

1. The normal at rest position of the control bar is indicated by A—Fig. TO203.

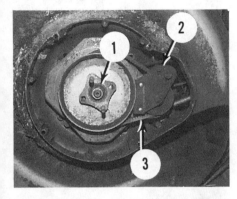

Fig. TO201—View of one type of blade brake clutch used on some Toro models. The clutch spring is located as shown in Fig. TO205.

Fig. TO202—View of one type of blade brake clutch used on some Toro models. The clutch spring is located as shown in Fig. TO204.

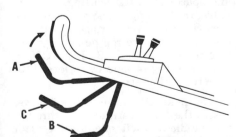

Fig. TO203—The blade brake should release and the blade clutch should engage when the control bar is the proper distance from the handle.

A. At rest position
B. "Cocking" position
C. Engaged position

2. "Cock" the system by pushing the control bar down as shown at position B—Fig. TO203.

3. Pull the control bar nearer the handle (position C—Fig. TO203). As the control bar is pulled nearer the handle, the blade is engaged.

4. On self-propelled models, movement of the control bar near the handle engages or disengages the traction drive belt to propel the mower.

TESTING. The blade brake and clutch should be checked for proper operation at the beginning of each season or when proper operation is questioned.

Check for operation as follows: Start the engine and push the control bar to its lowest position to latch the control mechanism and begin operation. Lift the control bar to the normal blade engaged position. When the control bar is about 2 inches (50 mm) from the handle the grass bag should be inflated, indicating the blade is engaged. Release the control bar and observe operation. An audible bang should be heard and the grass bag should immediately (within 3 seconds) deflate (indicating the blade brake is engaged and the blade is not turning).

Locate the engagement point as follows: If the engine is not running, start the engine and push the control bar to its lowest position to latch the control mechanism and begin operation. Lift the control bar slowly until the blade **just begins spinning.** The grass bag will inflate, indicating the blade is engaging, and the control bar should be approximately 5 inches (125 mm) from the handle.

If the blade will not engage, if the brake does not stop the blade quickly or if the blade begins to engage too close or too far from the handlebar, adjust the cable. Other problems such as worn, rusted, bent or otherwise damaged components can also prevent proper operation. If adjusting the control cable does

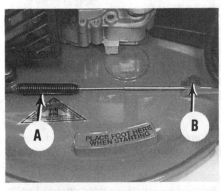

Fig. TO204—View of the clutch spring used with the engagement mechanism shown in Fig. TO202.

not correct operation, locate and repair the damaged parts.

CABLE ADJUSTMENT. The control cable must be properly adjusted for the brake to engage and release properly and for the clutch to engage at the proper time.

If the bellcrank and spring are as shown in Fig. TO204, the spring (A) should be relaxed when the control bar is released; however, the control cable should not have excessive play. Adjust cable if necessary. Loosen the clamp screw (B), move the cable housing as necessary, then tighten the clamp screw.

If the bellcrank assembly is located at the rear of the deck as shown in Fig. TO205, remove the screws attaching the cover and lift the cover from the mower deck. With the engine stopped, push the control bar down to cock the mechanism, then pull the control bar up against the handlebar and check the length of the spring. The compressed length of spring (A—Fig. TO206) should be 1-1 ¼ inches (25-32 mm). If spring length is incorrect, loosen cable locknut

Fig. TO205—View of the clutch spring used with the engagement mechanism shown in Fig. TO201.

Fig. TO206—Measure the length of the clutch spring (A) as shown when the clutch is engaged. Adjustment is accomplished by turning the cable adjuster (B).

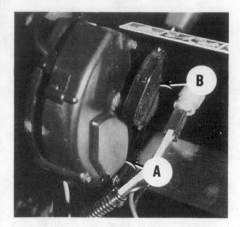

Fig. TO207—The control box (A) is located on the handle as shown and the throttle control (B) is installed in the control panel.

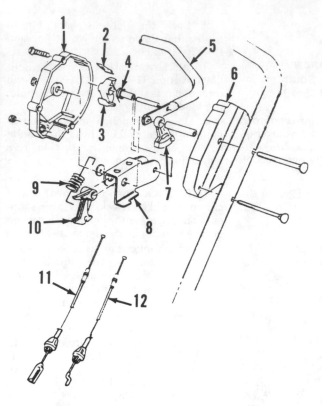

Fig. TO208—Exploded view of the control box.

1. Cover
2. Leaf spring
3. Control hook
4. Torsion spring
5. Control bar
6. Control housing
7. Traction cable lever
8. Rocker arm
9. Buckling spring
10. BBC cable lever
11. Blade brake/clutch cable
12. Traction cable

and turn cable adjuster (B) to obtain specified spring length. Recheck operation and spring length after changing the cable adjustment.

CONTROL BOX. Engagement of the traction drive, blade drive and blade brake are all controlled by the control bar at the upper end of the handle bar. The control box provides emergency engagement of the blade brake and disengagement of the blade and traction drives. For normal operation, the controls must be "cocked" by pushing the control bar down as shown at position B—Fig. TO203, before pulling the bar up to the drive positions. Damage or malfunction of the control box (A—Fig. TO207) may make proper operation and adjustment difficult or impossible.

Trouble Shooting and Disassembly. It is important to disassemble the control box as little as necessary to determine the cause of the problem. Only the right side of the control box housing should be removed when trouble shooting. If an extra cover is available, part of the right side should be cut-away and installed in place of the original cover to hold the parts together when observing its operation.

Remove the throttle control (B—Fig. TO207) from the control panel as follows. Bend the locking tab away from the underside of the control panel, then push the throttle control down to remove it from the control panel. It may be necessary to use a soft mallet to bump the throttle control from the panel.

Remove the three flanged head screws that attach the two halves of the control box together.

Tape across the heads of the carriage bolts which pass through the control box and the handlebar to prevent them from falling out. Remove the two self-locking

nuts attaching the control box to the handle bar, then carefully remove the right side half of the control box.

NOTE: Be careful not to allow internal parts to fall from the cover. If a cut-away right side cover is available, install the cover to help hold the parts in place.

Operate the control bar as described in the preceding TESTING paragraphs and observe the operation of the components inside the control box.

CAUTION: Wear eye protection and gloves to reduce the danger of parts flying from the control box. Danger is greatest if a cut-away right side cover is not used, but broken or otherwise damaged parts can be propelled by the spring action.

NOTE: If a cut-away right side cover is not used, the cable ends and the buckling spring will not be held in place. It will be necessary to hold these parts in place by hand while operating the controls.

Remove parts from the left side housing as follows. Detach the buckling spring (9—Fig. TO208) and the washer from the rocker arm (8) and remove the spring. Detach the upper (blade brake cable) from the cable lever (10) and lift

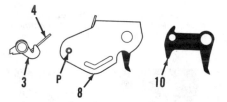

Fig. TO209—The control hook (3) and spring (4) are installed in the rocker arm (8) as shown. The control hook latches the cable lever (10).

the cable (11) from the left housing (6). Remove the rocker arm assembly, including the control hook and the cable lever. See Fig. TO209. Detach the traction cable (12—Fig. TO208) from the traction lever (7) and lift the cable from the left housing. Remove tape used to retain the upper carriage bolt in the left housing and withdraw the bolt from the left housing. Lift the traction cable lever and spacer from the housing. The left half of the housing can be removed after removing the lower carriage bolt. If necessary, remove the roll pin, then separate the control hook (3—Fig. TO209), torsion spring (4) and cable lever (10) from the rocker arm (8).

Assemble the control box as follows. Insert the lower carriage bolt through the handle and left side of the control box. Attach the end of the traction control cable to the traction lever. Install the traction lever, traction cable and control bar in the left housing, then slide the upper carriage bolt through all

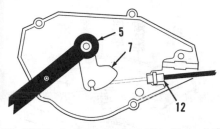

Fig. TO210—Assemble the control bar (5), traction lever (7) and traction cable (12) as shown. Refer to text when assembling the control box.

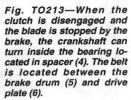

Fig. TO213—When the clutch is disengaged and the blade is stopped by the brake, the crankshaft can turn inside the bearing located in spacer (4). The belt is located between the brake drum (5) and drive plate (6).

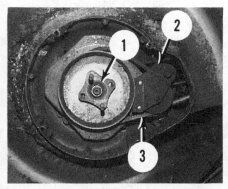

Fig. TO211—View of one type of mower with lower cover removed. Refer to Fig. TO212 for another type.

Fig. TO214—The blade brake clutch shown in Fig. TO211 with the brake drum removed.

Fig. TO212—View of the blade brake and clutch used on some models. Refer to Fig. TO211 for another similar type.

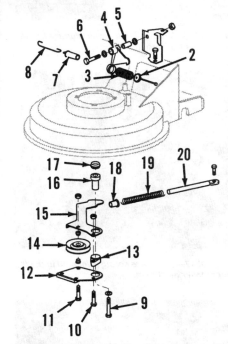

Fig. TO215—The blade brake clutch shown in Fig. TO211 includes the linkage shown.

2. Spring retainer
3. Clutch spring
4. Bellcrank
5. Pivot bearing
6. Bolt
7. Control pin
8. Link
9. Pivot screw
10. Bolt
11. Idler pulley bolt
12. Brake plate
13. Brake plate hub
14. Idler pulley
15. Brake plate lever
16. Bushing
17. Seal
18. Spring guide
19. Brake spring
20. Spring rod

of the components as shown in Fig. TO210. Apply tape over the heads of the carriage bolts to hold them in place during the remainder of the assembly. Install the sleeve onto the upper carriage bolt making sure it passes through the control bar, traction lever and the left side of the control box housing.

Assemble the control hook and torsion spring in the rocker arm, then install the roll pin (P) as shown in Fig. TO209. Be sure the roll pin is flush with the side of the rocker arm. Insert the blade brake clutch cable lever into the rocker arm assembly, making sure the control hook engages the cable lever. Slide the rocker arm assembly over the upper carriage bolt and sleeve. Be sure

the sleeve passes through the cable lever. The roll pin must also pass through the hole in the control bar. Release the control hook from the cable lever, then attach the blade brake clutch cable to the cable lever. Install the buckling spring as shown in Fig. TO208 with the white nylon washer on the "J" shaped end. Assemble the leaf spring(12) in the right side housing and hold the spring in place with the pin. Make sure ends of the cable housings are properly assembled, then install the right side of the housing against the left side. Install the two self-locking nuts and tighten securely. Install the three flanged head screws that attach the sides of the control box together and tighten the screws securely. Reinstall the throttle control in the control panel and fix in position with the tab. Adjust the blade brake control cable as described in this section. On self-propelled models, refer to the SELF-PROPELLED DRIVE SYSTEMS section and adjust the traction drive cable.

BLADE BRAKE. The blade brake is engaged by pressing the brake shoe against the brake drum as shown in Fig. TO211 or TO212. Brake pressure is exerted by a spring and failure to stop the blade may be caused by a broken spring or linkage that is stuck or broken. The two types of drive are serviced differently.

Drain gasoline and oil from the engine and tank, then tip the mower on its side. Unbolt and remove the blade, then

unbolt and remove the cover from the underside of the mower. Remove the large nut (1—Fig. TO211 or Fig. TO212), then remove the spacer (4—Fig. TO213) and brake drum (5). Check to make sure the idler pulley turns freely and that the brake shoe is not worn into the metal backing.

On models shown in Fig. TO211, remove the bolt (A—Fig. TO214) and the idler bolt (B). Spring (C) is the spring that engages the blade brake. Also check the condition of the linkage (Fig. TO215).

On models shown in Fig. TO212, remove the muffler. Loosen the cable clamp (B—Fig. TO204), then remove the pivot bolt from the bellcrank. Detach link (A—Fig. TO216), then remove the screw (B). Remove the upper lever

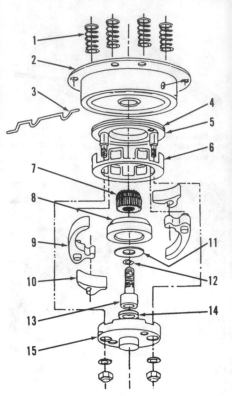

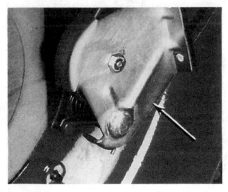

Fig. TO216—View of blade brake control linkage used on some Toro mowers.

Fig. TO219—The blade brake clutch operating assembly pivots on bearings located in the mower deck.

Fig. TO217—The brake spring is located under the upper lever as shown.

Fig. TO218—The blade brake clutch assembly can be pulled from the deck after removing the upper lever.

Fig. W1—Exploded view of typical Worthington blade brake clutch.

1. Spring
2. Housing
3. Brake lever
4. Brake disc assy.
5. Brake shoe
6. Spring pressure ring
7. Clutch cone insert
8. Clutch cone
9. Articulated flyweight
10. Flyweight toe
11. Friction clutch washer
12. Lockwasher
13. Socket head screw
14. Bushing
15. Cone housing

pivot shaft bearings (Fig. TO219) if they are damaged. Install new idler pulley if the bearings are not free.

Assemble by reversing the disassembly procedure. Install the clutch belt over the crankshaft. Install the special drive screws through the brake drum and spacer, then install the drum and spacer over the crankshaft. Install and tighten the retaining nut (Fig. TO211 or TO212). Make sure the heads of the special blade retaining screws are not wedged between the drum and drive plate. Check the blade brake and clutch for proper operation and adjustment as described in this section. Check the traction drive for proper operation and adjustment as described in the appropriate section. Reinstall covers and blade to complete assembly.

WORTHINGTON

**WORTHINGTON INDUSTRIES
MOWSAFE PRODUCTS
6500 Huntley Road
Worthington, Ohio 43085**

Shown in Fig. W1 is an exploded view of a typical blade clutch. Blade clutch uses two-piece articulated (jointed) flyweights. The jointed design allows clutch to be engaged when engine is running at low rpm.

The engagement of clutch is dependent upon blade speed, not engine speed. When the blade is cutting under heavy loads, the clutch will release as the blade rpm slows down below an effective cutting speed. This prevents engine lugging and the need of restarting the engine when heavy cutting would otherwise stall the engine.

No special tools are required for servicing clutches, but good mechanical skills should be exercised during servicing to ensure safe and correct operation.

No adjustment within blade clutch is provided. If lever operation is correct, but clutch fails to operate properly, disassembly and repair or renewal is serviceable as separate components.

and brake spring (Fig. TO217). Pull the clutch and brake assembly (Fig. TO218) down, from the mower deck. Install new

STORAGE

A proper storage procedure can extend the life of an engine by preventing damage when the engine is not used. Exact procedures for storing depend on the type of equipment, length of storage, time of year stored and storage location.

To obtain satisfactory results, storage must be coordinated with a regular maintenance program. The following outline lists procedures applicable for extended storage of most small engines.

ENTERING INTO STORAGE

Drain old oil from engine crankcase, gearboxes, chain cases, etc., while oil is warm. Refill with new approved oil specified by engine manufacturer.

Clean and dry all exterior surfaces. Remove all accumulated dirt and repair any damaged surface. Paint exposed surfaces to prevent rust.

Clean all cooling air passages and straighten, repair or renew any part which would interfere with normal air flow. Remove shrouds and deflectors, then inspect and clean all cooling air passages.

Lubricate all moving parts requiring lubrication with approved oil or grease.

Inspect for worn or broken parts. Make necessary adjustments and repair all damage. Tighten all loose hardware.

Fuel should be either drained or treated with an approved stabilizer. All fuel should be drained from tank, filters, lines, pumps and carburetor unless specifically discouraged by manufacturer. Do not add fuel stabilizer to any fuel containing alcohol. Fuel containing alcohol will separate if permitted to sit for long period of time and internal parts may be extensively damaged by corrosion. Some manufacturers recommend coating inside of tank with a small amount of oil to deter rusting in tank. Filter should be serviced initially and water traps should be serviced regularly while in storage.

Loosen all drive belts and remove pressure from friction drive components. Inspect and note condition of drive belts. If condition is questionable, a new belt should be installed when removing equipment from storage.

Install new filter elements. Some filters can be cleaned and serviced, but most should be installed new at this time.

Pour a small amount (usually 1 tablespoon) of oil into cylinder of engine through spark plug hole. Crank engine with starter about 12 revolutions to distribute oil, then install spark plug and reconnect spark plug wire.

Install protective caps at ends of all disconnected lines. Seal openings of exhaust, air intake, engine dipstick and crankcase breather tube.

Remove battery and store in a cool, dry place. Do not permit battery to freeze and maintain fully charged, checking approximately every 30 days.

Store the mower in a dry, protected place. If necessary to store outside, cover mower to prevent entrance of water, but don't seal tightly. Sealing may cause condensation and accelerate rusting.

REMOVING FROM STORAGE

Check for obvious damage to covering and equipment. Remove any blocks used during storage.

Charge battery, then install in equipment making sure that battery is properly retained. Clean battery cables and battery posts, then attach cables to battery terminals.

Remove covers from exhaust, air intake, engine dipstick and crankcase breather tube. Remove any protective caps from lines disconnected during disassembly. Be sure ends are clean, then reconnect lines. Check all filters. Install new filters, or clean and service existing filters as required.

Adjust all drive belts and friction drive components to correct tension as recommended by the manufacturer. New belts should be installed if condition is questionalbe.

Fill fuel tank with correct type of fuel. Check for leaks. Gaskets may dry up or carburetor needle valve may stick during storage. Repair any problems before attempting to start.

Drain water traps and check condition of fuel filters.

Check for worn or broken parts and repair before returning to service.

Lubricate all surfaces normally lubricated with oil or grease. Check cooling passages for restrictions such as insect, bird or animal nests. Check oil in all compartments such as engine crankcase, gearboxes, chain cases, etc., for proper level. Evidence of too much oil may indicate water settled below oil.

Drain oil if contamination is suspected or if time of storage exceeds recommended time change interval. Fill to proper level with correct type of oil.

NOTES

NOTES

NOTES

NOTES

NOTES

NOTES

NOTES